Documents of American Constitutional and Legal History

Documents of American Constitutional and Legal History

VOLUME II: FROM THE AGE OF INDUSTRIALIZATION TO THE PRESENT

Second Edition

MELVIN I. UROFSKY
Virginia Commonwealth University

PAUL FINKELMAN
University of Tulsa College of Law

New York   Oxford
OXFORD UNIVERSITY PRESS
2002

Oxford University Press

Oxford   New York
Athens   Auckland   Bangkok   Bogotá   Buenos Aires   Calcutta
Cape Town   Chennai   Dar es Salaam   Delhi   Florence   Hong Kong   Istanbul
Karachi   Kuala Lumpur   Madrid   Melbourne   Mexico City   Mumbai
Nairobi   Paris   São Paulo   Shanghai   Singapore   Taipei   Tokyo   Toronto   Warsaw

and associated companies in
Berlin   Ibadan

Copyright © 2002 by Oxford University Press, Inc.

Published by Oxford University Press, Inc.
198 Madison Avenue, New York, New York 10016
http://www.oup-usa.org

Oxford is a registered trademark of Oxford University Press

Library of Congress Cataloging-in-Publication Data

Documents of American constitutional and legal history / edited by Melvin I. Urofsky,
Paul Finkelman. — 2nd ed.
    p. cm.
    Includes bibliographical references and index.
    Contents: v. 1. From the founding through the age of industrialization —
    ISBN 0-19-512870-2 (pbk. : alk. paper) v. 2. From the age of industrialization to the present—
    ISBN 0-19-512872-9 (pbk. : alk. paper)
        1. Law—United States—History—Sources. 2. Constitutional history—United
    States—Sources. I. Urofsky, Melvin I. II. Finkelman, Paul, 1949–

KF350 .D633 2002
342.73′029—dc21
                                                            2001021142

Printing number: 9 8 7 6 5 4 3 2 1

Printed in the United States of America
on acid-free paper

For our children

Abby
Isaac
Philip and Melissa
Robert and Leslie

Contents

꩜

Preface

⚘

AT ONE TIME little could be found in books on constitutional history other than Supreme Court decisions. If an important constitutional issue did not appear in one of the Court's cases, then essentially there would be no trace of it in the materials. We now understand that often important constitutional decisions take place outside the Marble Palace, and this second edition of *Documents,* like the first, has a fair sprinkling of these other records—founding documents of the colonial era, state law and court decisions, presidential proclamations, articles of impeachment and occasional private writings as well. Like *A March of Liberty,* for which this collection is a companion, we have tried to take as broad a view of constitutional and legal history as possible.

Given the broad nature of the subject, we could have easily doubled or even trebled the size of these volumes, and no doubt teachers using this set will at one point or another say "Why isn't that statute—or case—or proclamation in here?" The short answer is that it probably ought to be, but the economics of publishing make it impossible to put together a collection that included everything and still make it affordable to the student. So we have tried to include a sampling from as many different areas and topics as we can, leaving it to the individual user to fill in with supplemental materials when and if necessary.

We have been guided by our own sense of what is important, and our own understanding of the type of materials we think need to be included. Just as in *A March of Liberty* we tried to be as inclusive as possible within the boundaries of space provided to us, so we have tried to create a reader that addresses the same broad concerns.

Documents of American Constitutional and Legal History

In 1869, Louisiana chartered the Crescent City Live-Stock Landing and Slaughter-House Company, and gave it a twenty-five-year monopoly in an area comprising three parishes with a population of two hundred thousand, including the city of New Orleans. Butchers not included in the monopoly, many of them identified with the Confederate rebellion, argued that they had been deprived of the important "right" to ply their trade, and they challenged the statute under the Thirteenth and Fourteenth amendments. (The plaintiffs were, in fact, not completely deprived of their livelihood, but only inconvenienced; they could continue to butcher animals, but only at the facilities of the company, which was owned by Republican allies.)

The suit raised for the first time in the Supreme Court the issue of substantive due process; that is, whether the Due Process Clause of the Fourteenth Amendment protected certain nonarticulated property rights from state interference. Although there had been some prewar references to such rights, the Court by a five-to-four majority ruled that the Civil War amendments had no other purpose than to protect the rights of the former slaves. That four justices dissented from this conclusion and supported the idea of substantive due process led corporate attorneys to keep bringing the question back to the Court, which finally gave formal approval to the doctrine in 1897 (Document 142).

One should note that the plaintiffs, former Confederates, were represented in the Supreme Court by John Campbell, who had resigned his seat to become a Confederate judge.

See Edward S. Corwin, "The Supreme Court and the Fourteenth Amendment," 7 *Michigan Law Review* 643 (1909); Loren Beth, "The Slaughterhouse Cases," 23 *Louisiana Law Review* (1963); William Nelson, *The Fourteenth Amendment* (1988); and William Wiecek, *The Lost World of Classical Legal Thought* (1998).

———

Justice Miller delivered the opinion of the Court:

The regulation of the place and manner of conducting the slaughtering of animals is among the most necessary and frequent exercises of the police power. The 1869 law is aptly framed to remove from the more densely populated part of the city, the noxious slaughter-houses; and large and offensive collections of animals necessarily incident to them, and to locate them where the convenience, health, and comfort of the people

Source: 16 Wallace 36 (1873).

require they shall be located. And it must be conceded that the means adopted by the act for this purpose are appropriate, are stringent, and effectual. But it is said that in creating a corporation for this purpose, and conferring upon it exclusive privileges—privileges which it is said constitute a monopoly—the legislature has exceeded its power. . . .

The most cursory glance at [the three post-Civil War Amendments] discloses a unity of purpose, when taken in connection with the history of the times, which cannot fail to have an important bearing on any question of doubt concerning their true meaning. . . . Fortunately that history is fresh within the memory of us all, and its leading features, as they bear upon the matter before us, free from doubt.

. . . The overshadowing and efficient cause [of the war] was African slavery. In that struggle slavery, as a legalized social relation, perished. It perished as a necessity of the bitterness and force of the conflict. . . . But the war being over, those who had succeeded in re-establishing the authority of the Federal government were not content to permit this great act of emancipation to rest on the actual results of the contest or the proclamation of the Executive, both of which might have been questioned in after times, and they determined to place this main and most valuable result in the Constitution of the restored Union as one of its fundamental articles. Hence the [13th Amendment].

To withdraw the mind from the contemplation of this grand yet simple declaration of the personal freedom of all the human race within the jurisdiction of this government—a declaration designed to establish the freedom of four millions of slaves—and with a microscopic search endeavor to find in it a reference to servitudes, which may have been attached to property in certain localities, requires an effort, to say the least of it. That a personal servitude was meant is proved by the use of the word "involuntary," which can only apply to human beings. [The] word servitude is of larger meaning than slavery, as the latter is popularly understood in this country, and the obvious purpose was to forbid all shades and conditions of African slavery. . . .

. . . Notwithstanding the formal recognition by those [southern] States of the abolition of slavery, the condition of the slave race would, without further protection of the Federal government, be almost as bad as it was before. Among the first acts of legislation adopted by several of the States were laws which imposed upon the colored race onerous disabilities and burdens, and curtailed their rights in the pursuit of life, liberty, and property to such an extent that their freedom was of little value, while they had lost the protection which they had received from their former owners from motives both of interest and humanity. They were in some States forbidden to appear in the towns in any other character than menial servants. They were required to reside on and cultivate the soil without the right to purchase or own it. They were excluded from many occupations of gain, and were not permitted to give testimony in the courts in any case where a white man was a party. It was said that their lives were at the mercy of bad men, either because the laws for their protection were insufficient or were not enforced.

These circumstances, whatever of falsehood or misconception may have been mingled with their presentation, forced upon the statesmen who had conducted the Federal government in safety through the crisis of the rebellion, and who supposed that by the thirteenth article of amendment they had secured the result of their labors, the conviction that something more was necessary in the way of constitutional protection to the unfortunate race who had suffered so much. They accordingly [proposed the 14th Amendment].

A few years' experience satisfied the thoughtful men who had been the authors of the other two amendments that, notwithstanding the restraints of those articles on the States, and the laws passed under the additional powers granted to Congress, these were inadequate for the protection of life, liberty, and property, without which freedom to the slave was no boon. They were in all those States denied the right of suffrage. The laws were administered by the white man alone. It was urged that a race of men distinctively marked as was the negro, living in the midst of another and dominant race, could never be fully secured in their person and the property without the right of suffrage. Hence [the 15th Amendment].

We repeat, then, in the light of this recapitulation of events, almost too recent to be called history, but which are familiar to us all; and on the most casual examination of the language of these amendments, no one can fail to be impressed with the one pervading purpose found in them all, lying at the foundation of each, and without which none of them would have been even suggested; we mean the freedom of the slave race, the security and firm establishment of that freedom, and the protection of the newly-made freeman and citizen from the oppressions of those who had formerly exercised unlimited dominion over him. . . .

We do not say that no one else but the negro can share in this protection. Both the language and spirit of these articles are to have their fair and just weight in any question of construction. Undoubtedly while negro slavery alone was in the mind of the Congress which proposed the thirteenth article, it forbids any other kind of slavery, now or hereafter. . . .

Up to the adoption of the recent amendments, no claim or pretence was set up that those rights depended on the Federal government for their existence or protection, beyond the very few express limitations which the Federal Constitution imposed upon the States—such, for instance, as the prohibition against ex post facto laws, bills of attainder, and laws impairing the obligation of contracts. But with the exception of these and a few other restrictions, the entire domain of the privileges and immunities of citizens of the States, as above defined, lay within the constitutional and legislative power of the States, and without that of the Federal government. Was it the purpose of the fourteenth amendment, by the simple declaration that no State should make or enforce any law which shall abridge the privileges and immunities of *citizens of the United States,* to transfer the security and protection of all the civil rights which we have mentioned, from the States to the Federal government? And where it is declared that Congress shall have the power to enforce that article, was it intended to bring within the power of Congress the entire domain of civil rights heretofore belonging exclusively to the States?

All this and more must follow, if the proposition of the plaintiffs in error be sound. For not only are these rights subject to the control of Congress whenever in its discretion any of them are supposed to be abridged by State legislation, but that body may also pass laws in advance, limiting and restricting the exercise of legislative power by the States, in their most ordinary and usual functions, as in its judgment it may think proper on all such subjects. And still further, such a construction followed by a reversal of the judgments of the Supreme Court of Louisiana in these cases, would constitute this court a perpetual censor upon all legislation of the States, on the civil rights of their own citizens, with authority to nullify such as it did not approve as consistent with those rights, as they existed at the time of the adoption of this amendment. The argument we admit is not always the most conclusive which is drawn from the consequences urged against the adoption of a particular construction of an instrument. But when, as in the case before us, these consequences are so serious, so far-reaching and pervading, so great a departure from the structure and spirit of our institutions; when the effect is to fetter and degrade the State governments by subjecting them to the control of Congress, in the exercise of powers heretofore universally conceded to them of the most ordinary and fundamental character; when in fact it radically changes the whole theory of the relations of the State and Federal governments to each other and of both these governments to the people; the argument has a force that is irresistible, in the absence of language which expresses such a purpose too clearly to admit of doubt. We are convinced that no such results were intended by the Congress which proposed these amendments, nor by the legislatures of the States which ratified them. . . .

Unquestionably [the civil war] added largely to the number of those who believe in the necessity of a strong National government. But, however pervading this sentiment, and however it may have contributed to the adoption of the amendments we have been considering, we do not see in those amendments any purpose to destroy the main features of the general system. Under the pressure of all the excited feeling growing out of the war, our statesmen have still believed that the existence of the States with powers for domestic and local government, including the regulation of civil rights—the rights of person and of property—was essential to the perfect working of our complex form of government, though they have thought proper to impose additional limitations on the States, and to confer additional power on that of the Nation.

But whatever fluctuations may be seen in the history of public opinion on this subject during the period of our national existence; we think it will be found that this court, so far as its functions required, has always held with a steady and an even hand the balance between State and Federal power, and we trust that such may continue to be the history of its relation to the subject.

Affirmed.

Justice Field, joined by Chief Justice Chase and Justices Swayne and Bradley, dissented:

Upon the theory on which the exclusive privileges granted by the act in question are sustained, there is no monopoly, in the most odious form, which may not be upheld. The question presented is, therefore, one of the gravest importance, not merely to the parties here, but to the whole country. It is nothing less than the question whether the recent amendments to the Federal Constitution protect the citizens of the United States against the deprivation of their common rights by State legislation. In my judgment the fourteenth amendment does afford such protection. . . .

The amendment does not attempt to confer any new privileges or immunities upon citizens, or to enumerate or define those already existing. It assumes that there are such privileges and immunities which belong of right to citizens as such, and ordains that they shall not be abridged by State legislation. If this inhibition has no reference to privileges and immunities of this character, but only refers, as held by [the majority], to such privileges and immunities as were before its adoption specifically designated in the Constitution or necessarily implied as belonging to citizens of the United States, it was a vain and idle enactment, which accomplished nothing, and most unnecessarily excited Congress and the people on its passage. With privileges and immunities thus designated or implied no State could ever have interfered by its laws, and no new constitutional provision was required to inhibit such interference. The supremacy of the Constitution and the laws of the United States always controlled any State legislation of that character. But if the amendment refers to the natural and inalienable rights which belong to all citizens, the inhibition has a profound significance. . . .

The terms, privileges and immunities, are not new in the amendment; they were in the Constitution before the amendment was adopted. . . . The privileges and immunities designated are those *which of right belong to the citizens of all free governments.* Clearly among these must be placed the right to pursue a lawful employment in a lawful manner, without other restraint that such as equally affects all persons. . . .

What [Art. IV, § 2] did for the protection of the citizens of one State against hostile and discriminating legislation of other States, the fourteenth amendment does for the protection of every citizen of the United States against hostile and discriminating legislation against him in favor of others, whether they reside in the same or in different States. If under the fourth article of the Constitution equality of privileges and immunities is secured between citizens of different States, under the fourteenth amendment the same equality is secured between citizens of the United States. . . .

This equality of rights, with exemption from all disparaging and partial enactments, in the lawful pursuits of life, throughout the whole country, is the distinguishing privilege of citizens of the United States. To them, everywhere, all pursuits, all professions, all avocations are open without other restrictions than such as are imposed equally upon all others of the same age, sex, and condition. The State may prescribe such regulations for every pursuit and calling of life as will promote the public health, secure the good order and advance the general prosperity of society, but when once prescribed, the pursuit or calling must be free to be followed by every citizen who is within the conditions designated, and will conform to the regulations. This is the fundamental idea upon which our institutions rest, and unless adhered to in the legislation of the country our government will be a republic only in name. The fourteenth amendment, in my judgment, makes it essential to the validity of the legislation of every State that this equality of right should be respected. It is to me a matter of profound regret that the validity [of the Louisiana law] is recognized by a majority of this court, for by it the right of free labor, one of the most sacred and imprescriptible rights of man, is violated. Grants of exclusive privileges are opposed to the whole theory of free government, and it requires no aid from any bill of rights to render them void. That only is a free government, in the American sense of the term, under which the inalienable right of every citizen to pursue his happiness is unrestrained, except by just, equal, and impartial laws.

128   *Bradwell v. Illinois (1873)*

Women had begun agitating for greater legal rights during the Jacksonian era (Document 89), and when Oberlin College in Ohio opened its doors in 1835, they began to enjoy some limited opportunities in higher education. But for the most part, nineteenth-century society saw the proper roles and place for women as wives and mothers at home. The idea of women joining the learned professions horrified many people, and as late as 1905, the eminent psychologist G. Stanley Hall explained that professionalization meant specialization, which was alien to the female brain.

Nonetheless, some women began knocking on the doors of the professions and found nearly all these doors—whether to the ministry, medicine, or law—not only closed, but barred. The bar associations organized in the latter nineteenth century not only raised professional standards but also kept out "undesirables." Here and there one could find a woman attorney; one was admitted to the Iowa bar in 1869. That same year, Illinois denied admission to Myra Bradwell, a lawyer's wife and suffragist. The Illinois Supreme Court declared that the "hot strife of the bar, in the presence of the public," would destroy femininity. As the following case shows, the nation's highest court held similar views, and it would not be until Illinois changed its laws that Bradwell gained admission to the bar, in 1890. By 1910, about 1,500 women practiced law in this country; in 1920, the number was still small, with women constituting only 3 percent of American lawyers.

See Jane M. Friedman, *America's First Woman Lawyer: The Biography of Myra Bradwell* (1993); Sheila M. Rothman, *Women's Proper Place* (1978); Barbara Harris, *Beyond Her Sphere: Women and the Professions in American History* (1978); Virginia G. Drachman, *Sisters in Law* (1998); and Jill Norgren, "Before It Was Merely Difficult: Belva Lockwood's Life in Law and Politics, 23 *Journal of Supreme Court History* 16 (1999).

Justice Miller delivered the opinion of the Court:

The record in this case is not very perfect, but it may be fairly taken that the plaintiff asserted her right to a license on the grounds, among others, that she was a citizen of the United States, and that having been a citizen of Vermont at one time, she was, in the State of Illinois, entitled to any right granted to citizens of the latter State. . . .

As regards the provision of the Constitution that citizens of each State shall be entitled to all the privileges and immunities of citizens in the several States, the plaintiff in her affidavit has stated very clearly a case to which it is inapplicable.

Source: 16 Wallace 130 (1873)

The protection designed by that clause, as has been repeatedly held, has no application to a citizen of the State whose laws are complained of. If the plaintiff was a citizen of the State of Illinois, that provision of the Constitution gave her no protection against its courts or its legislation.

The plaintiff seems to have seen this difficulty, and attempts to avoid it by stating that she was born in Vermont.

While she remained in Vermont that circumstance made her a citizen of that State. But she states, at the same time, that she is a citizen of the United States, and that she is now, and has been for many years past, a resident of Chicago, in the State of Illinois. . . .

. . . The plaintiff states nothing to take her case out of the definition of citizenship of a State as defined by the first section of the fourteenth amendment.

In regard to that amendment counsel for the plaintiff in this court truly says that there are certain privileges and immunities which belong to a citizen of the United States as such; otherwise it would be nonsense for the fourteenth amendment to prohibit a State from abridging them, and he proceeds to argue that admission to the bar of a State of a person who possesses the requisite learning and character is one of those which a State may not deny.

In this latter proposition we are not able to concur with counsel. We agree with him that there are privileges and immunities belonging to citizens of the United States, in that relation and character, and that it is these and these alone which a State is forbidden to abridge. But the right to admission to practice in the courts of a State is not one of them. This right in no sense depends on citizenship of the United States. It has not, as far as we know, ever been made in any State, or in any case, to depend on citizenship at all. Certainly many prominent and distinguished lawyers have been admitted to practice, both in the State and Federal courts, who were not citizens of the United States or of any State. But, on whatever basis this right may be placed, so far as it can have any relation to citizenship at all, it would seem that, as to the courts of a State, it would relate to citizenship of the State, and as to Federal courts, it would relate to citizenship of the United States.

The opinion just delivered in the *Slaughter-House Cases* renders elaborate argument in the present case unnecessary; for, unless we are wholly and radically mistaken in the principles on which those cases are decided, the right to control and regulate the granting of license to practice law in the courts of a State is one of those powers which are not transferred for its protection to the Federal government, and its exercise is in no manner governed or controlled by citizenship of the United States in the party seeking such license.

It is unnecessary to repeat the argument on which the judgment in those cases is founded. It is sufficient to say they are conclusive of the present case.

Judgment Affirmed.

Justice Bradley, concurring:

I concur in the judgment of the court in this case, by which the judgment of the Supreme Court of Illinois is affirmed, but not for the reasons specified in the opinion just read. . . .

. . . The civil law, as well as nature herself, has always recognized a wide difference in the respective spheres and destinies of man and woman. Man is, or should be, woman's protector and defender. The natural and proper timidity and delicacy which belongs to the female sex evidently unfits it for many of the occupations of civil life. The constitution of the family organization, which is founded in the divine ordinance, as well as in the nature of things, indicates the domestic sphere as that which properly belongs to the domain and functions of womanhood. The harmony, not to say identity, of interests and views which belong, or should belong, to the family institution is repugnant to the idea of a woman adopting a distinct and independent career from that of her husband. So firmly fixed was this sentiment in the founders of the common law that it became a maxim of that system of jurisprudence that a woman had no legal existence separate from her husband, who was regarded as her head and representative in the social state; and, notwithstanding some recent modifications of this civil status, many of the special rules of law flowing from and dependent upon this cardinal principle still exist in full force in most States. One of these is, that a married woman is incapable, without her husband's consent, of making contracts which shall be binding on her or him. This very incapacity was one circumstance which the Supreme Court of Illinois deemed important in rendering a married woman incompetent fully to perform the duties and trusts that belong to the office of an attorney and counsellor.

It is true that many women are unmarried and not affected by any of the duties, complications, and incapacities arising out of the married state, but these are exceptions to the general rule. The paramount destiny and mission of woman are to fulfil the noble and benign offices of wife and mother. This is the law of the Creator. And the rules of civil society must be adapted to the general constitution of things, and cannot be based upon exceptional cases.

The humane movements of modern society, which have for their object the multiplication of avenues for woman's advancement, and of occupations adapted to her condition and sex, have my heartiest concurrence. But I am not prepared to say that it is one of her fundamental rights and privileges to be admitted into every office and position, including those which require highly special qualifications and demanding special responsibilities. In the nature of things it is not every citizen of every age, sex, and condition that is qualified for every calling and position. It is the prerogative of the legislator to prescribe regulations founded on nature, reason, and experience for the due admission of qualified persons to professions and callings demanding special skill and confidence. This fairly belongs to the police power of the State; and, in my opinion, in view of the peculiar characteristics, destiny, and mission of woman, it is within the province of the legislature to ordain what offices, positions, and callings shall be filled and discharged by men, and shall receive the benefit of those energies and responsibilities, and that decision and firmness which are presumed to predominate in the sterner sex.

For these reasons I think that the laws of Illinois now complained of are not obnoxious to the charge of abridging any of the privileges and immunities of citizens of the United States.

Mr. Justice SWAYNE and Mr. Justice FIELD concurred in the foregoing opinion of Mr. Justice BRADLEY.

The Chief Justice dissented from the judgment of the court, and from all the opinions.

129   *Minor v. Happersett (1875)*

Common law had seen younger women as adjuncts of their fathers, and married woman subsumed under their husbands' legal identities. There had been agitation for separate legal status ever since revolutionary times, and women began making some progress toward having separate legal rights in the Jacksonian era, especially with the passage of married women's property acts. But the suffrage movement, which began with the Seneca Falls Declaration (see Document 89), had failed to develop widespread support and had in large measure been swept up in the antislavery movement. With the passage of the Fourteenth Amendment, suffragists tried to secure a legal ruling that voting was an adjunct of citizenship, and as citizens, women were entitled to the vote. (Women's rights activists opposed the Fifteenth Amendment because it gave black men but not white women the vote.) This argument failed in the courts as well. Although a few states allowed women to vote after the turn of the century, women did not get the vote at the national level until the passage of the Nineteenth Amendment in 1920.

See Candace L. Bredbenner, *A Nationality of Her Own: Women, Marriage, and the Law of Citizenship* (1998); Rogers M. Smith, *Civic Ideals: Conflicting Visions of Citizenship in U.S. History* (1997); and Ellen C. Du Bois, "Outgrowing the Compact of the Fathers," 74 *Journal of American History* 836 (1987).

Chief Justice Morrison R. Waite delivered the opinion of the Court:

The question is presented in this case, whether, since the adoption of the fourteenth amendment, a woman, who is a citizen of the United States and of the State of Missouri, is a voter in that State, notwithstanding the provision of the constitution and laws of the State, which confine the right of suffrage to men alone. . . .

There is no doubt that women may be citizens. They are persons, and by the fourteenth amendment "all persons born or naturalized in the United States and subject to the jurisdiction thereof" are expressly declared to be "citizens of the United States and of the State wherein they reside." But, in our opinion, it did not need this amendment to give them that position. Before its adoption the Constitution of the United States did not in terms prescribe who should be citizens of the United States or of the several States, yet there were necessarily such citizens without such provision. There cannot be a nation without a people. The very idea of a political community, such as a nation is, implies an association of persons for the promotion of their general welfare. Each one of the per-

---

Source: 21 Wallace 162 (1875)

sons associated becomes a member of the nation formed by the association. He owes it allegiance and is entitled to its protection. Allegiance and protection are, in this connection, reciprocal obligations. The one is a compensation for the other; allegiance for protection and protection for allegiance.

Sex has never been made one of the elements of citizenship in the United States. In this respect men have never had an advantage over women. The same laws precisely apply to both. The fourteenth amendment did not affect the citizenship of women any more than it did of men. In this particular, therefore, the rights of Mrs. Minor do not depend upon the amendment. She has always been a citizen from her birth, and entitled to all the privileges and immunities of citizenship. The amendment prohibited the State, of which she is a citizen, from abridging any of her privileges and immunities as a citizen of the United States; but it did not confer citizenship on her. That she had before its adoption.

If the right of suffrage is one of the necessary privileges of a citizen of the United States, then the constitution and laws of Missouri confining it to men are in violation of the Constitution of the United States, as amended, and consequently void. The direct question is, therefore, presented whether all citizens are necessarily voters.

The Constitution does not define the privileges and immunities of citizens. For that definition we must look elsewhere. In this case we need not determine what they are, but only whether suffrage is necessarily one of them. . . .

The amendment did not add to the privileges and immunities of a citizen. It simply furnished an additional guaranty for the protection of such as he already had. No new voters were necessarily made by it. Indirectly it may have had that effect, because it may have increased the number of citizens entitled to suffrage under the constitution and laws of the States, but it operates for this purpose, if at all, through the States and the State laws, and not directly upon the citizen.

It is clear, therefore, we think, that the Constitution has not added the right of suffrage to the privileges and immunities of citizenship as they existed at the time it was adopted. This makes it proper to inquire whether suffrage was coextensive with the citizenship of the States at the time of its adoption. If it was, then it may with force be argued that suffrage was one of the rights which belonged to citizenship, and in the enjoyment of which every citizen must be protected. But if it was not, the contrary may with propriety be assumed. . . .

In respect to suffrage in the several States it cannot for a moment be doubted that if it had been intended to make all citizens of the United States voters, the framers of the Constitution would not have left it to implication. So important a change in the condition of citizenship as it actually existed, if intended, would have been expressly declared. . . .

After the adoption of the fourteenth amendment, it was deemed necessary to adopt a fifteenth, as follows: "The right of citizens of the United States to vote shall not be denied or abridged by the United States, or by any State, on account of race, color, or previous condition of servitude." The fourteenth amendment had already provided that no State should make or enforce any law which should abridge the privileges or immunities of citizens of the United States. If suffrage was one of these privileges or immunities, why amend the Constitution to prevent its being denied on account of race, &c? Nothing is more evident than that the greater must include the less, and if all were already protected why go through with the form of amending the Constitution to protect a part? . . .

It is true that the United States guarantees to every State a republican form of government. . . . The guaranty is of a republican form of government. No particular government is designated as republican, neither is the exact form to be guaranteed, in any manner especially designated. . . .

All the citizens of the States were not invested with the right of suffrage. In all, save perhaps New Jersey, this right was only bestowed upon men and not upon all of them. Under these circumstances it is certainly now too late to contend that a government is not republican, within the meaning of this guaranty in the Constitution, because women are not made voters.

The same may be said of the other provisions just quoted. Women were excluded from suffrage in nearly all the States by the express provision of their constitutions and laws. If that had been equivalent to a bill of attainder, certainly its abrogation would not have been left to implication. Nothing less than express language would have been employed to effect so radical a change. So also of the amendment which declares that no person shall be deprived of life, liberty, or property without due process of law, adopted as it was as early as 1791. If suffrage was intended to be included within its obligations, language better adapted to express that intent would most certainly have been employed. The right of suffrage, when granted, will be protected. He who has it can only be deprived of it by due process of law, but in order to claim protection he must first show that he has the right. . . .

Certainly, if the courts can consider any question settled, this is one. For nearly ninety years the people have acted upon the idea that the Constitution, when it conferred citizenship, did not necessarily confer the right of suffrage. If uniform practice long continued can settle the construction of so important an instrument as the Constitution of the United States confessedly is, most certainly it has been done here. Our province is to decide what the law is, not to declare what it should be.

We have given this case the careful consideration its importance demands. If the law is wrong, it ought to be changed; but the power for that is not with us. The arguments addressed to us bearing upon such a view of the subject may perhaps be sufficient to induce those having the power, to make the alteration, but they ought not to be permitted to influence our judgment in determining the present rights of the parties now litigating before us. No argument as to woman's need of suffrage can be considered. We can only act upon her rights as they exist. It is not for us to look at the hardship of withholding. Our duty is at an end if we find it is within the power of a State to withhold.

Being unanimously of the opinion that the Constitution of the United States does not confer the right of suffrage upon any one, and that the constitutions and laws of the several States which commit that important trust to men alone are not necessarily void, we *affirm the judgment.*

130

Commonwealth v. Hamilton Manufacturing Co. (1876)

This is the earliest case dealing with the question of whether the state, under its police powers, could regulate the hours of labor for women workers. Although employers raised questions of freedom of contract, the Massachusetts Supreme Court found no barrier to the state's actions, and in fact took as axiomatic that the police power could be exercised in this manner. Although the court declared reference to precedents to be "unnecessary," one suspects that the judges lacked appropriate prior decisions and decided the case on an intuitive rather than an analytical basis. *Hamilton Manufacturing* would be cited in nearly all cases involving protective legislation regulating hours of labor, working conditions, and wages, but it would be another thirty years before its basic assumption would be accepted (Document 147).

See Judith Baer, *The Chains of Protection: Judicial Response to Women's Labor Legislation* (1978); Alice Kessler-Harris, *Out to Work: The History of Wage-Earning Women in the United States* (1982); and Elizabeth Brandeis, "Labor Legislation," in J. Commons et al., 3 *History of Labor in the United States* (1935).

Justice Lord:
The defendant contends that the St. of 1874, *c.* 221, under which the complaint in this case is made, is unconstitutional and void. The provision, which it is alleged is without authority under the Constitution, is, that "no minor under the age of eighteen years, and no woman over that age, shall be employed in laboring by any person, firm or corporation in any manufacturing establishment in this Commonwealth more than ten hours in any one day," except in certain cases, and that "in no case shall the hours of labor exceed sixty per week."

The learned counsel for the defendant in his argument did not refer to any particular clause of the Constitution to which this provision is repugnant. His general proposition was, that the defendant's act of incorporation, . . . is a contract with the Commonwealth, and that this act impairs that contract. The contract, it is claimed, is an implied one; that is, an act of incorporation to manufacture cotton and woollen goods by necessary implication confers upon the corporation the legal capacity to contract for all the labor needful for this work. If this is conceded to the fullest extent, it is only a contract with the corporation that it may contract for all lawful labor. There is no contract implied

Source: 120 Mass. 385 (1876).

that such labor as was then forbidden by law might be employed by the defendant; or that the General Court would not perform its constitutional duty of making such wholesome laws thereafter as the public welfare should demand. The law, therefore, violates no contract with the defendant; and the only other question is, whether it is in violation of any right reserved under the Constitution to the individual citizen. Upon this question, there seems to be no room for debate. It does not forbid any person, firm or corporation from employing as many persons or as much labor as such person, firm or corporation may desire; not does it forbid any person to work as many hours a day or a week as he chooses. It merely provides that in an employment, which the Legislature has evidently deemed to some extent dangerous to health, no person shall be engaged in labor more than ten hours a day or sixty hours a week. There can be no doubt that such legislation may be maintained either as a health or police regulation, if it were necessary to resort to either of those sources for power. This principle has been so frequently recognized in this Commonwealth that reference to the decisions is unnecessary.

It is also said that the law violates the right of Mary Shirley to labor in accordance with her own judgment as to the number of hours she shall work. The obvious and conclusive reply to this is, that the law does not limit her right to labor as many hours per day or per week as she may desire; it does not in terms forbid her laboring in any particular business or occupation as many hours per day or per week, as she may desire; it merely prohibits her being employed continuously in the same service more than a certain number of hours per day or week, which is so clearly within the power of the Legislature, that it becomes unnecessary to inquire whether it is a matter of grievance of which this defendant has the right to complain.

Judgment affirmed.

131   *Munn v. Illinois (1877)*

Farmers faced a number of economic hardships following the Civil War and blamed many of their difficulties on the allegedly unfair and exorbitant rates charged by railroads. Actually, relatively little of the agricultural depression was due to rate gouging; even if the railroads and the grain elevators they controlled had charged far lower rates, the situation in national and international grain markets would have caused American farmers a great deal of distress. But the railroads were visible culprits, and organized political protest led five midwestern states to enact "Granger laws," which established maximum rate schedules for railroads and grain warehouses. Common law had long held that government could regulate the rates charged by common carriers and certain other types of businesses serving the public, such as inns. In this particular case, an Illinois law fixed rates for grain elevators in cities of 100,000 or more people. The only city in the state that size was Chicago, and the legislature was attempting to control the monopoly that nine elevator companies had established in the Midwest's largest rail terminus. The owners attacked the law and denounced any and all state meddling in business affairs as a violation of the Due Process Clause of the Fourteenth Amendment.

The Court's opinion avoided the due process argument, and Chief Justice Waite relied on common law precedent. In ruling that states could regulate businesses "affected with a public interest," he declared that companies operating in such fields would have to accept regulation as a condition of business. But Waite went beyond this issue, and while explicitly denying the due process argument, conceded that a state might go too far in its regulations and violate the Fourteenth Amendment. With this wedge, corporate attorneys redoubled their effort to get the Court to accept the notion of substantive due process.

See George. H. Miller, *Railroads and the Granger Laws* (1973); Charles Fairman, "The So-Called Granger Cases, Lord Hale, and Justice Bradley," 5 *Stanford Law Review* 557 (1953); Gabriel Kolko, *Railroads and Regulation, 1877–1916* (1965); Harry N. Scheiber, "The Road to *Munn:* Eminent Domain and the Concept of Public Purpose in the State Courts," 5 *Perspectives* 329 (1917); and Albro Martin, *Enterprise Denied: Origins of the Decline of American Railroads* (1971).

———

Chief Justice Waite delivered the opinion of the Court:

The question to be determined in this case is whether the general assembly of Illinois can, under the limitations upon the legislative power of the States imposed by the Constitution of the United States, fix by law the maximum of charges for the storage of grain in warehouses at Chicago and other places in the State having not less than one hundred thousand inhabitants, "in which grain is stored in bulk, and in which the grain of different owners is mixed together, or in which grain is stored in such a manner that the identity of different lots or parcels cannot be accurately preserved."

It is claimed that such a law is repugnant—

1. To that part of sect. 8, art. 1, of the Constitution of the United States which confers upon Congress the power "to regulate commerce with foreign nations and among the several States;"

2. To that part of sect. 9 of the same article which provides that "no preference shall be given by any regulation of commerce or revenue to the ports of one State over those of another;" and

3. To that part of amendment 14 which ordains that no State shall "deprive any person of life, liberty, or property, without due process of law, nor deny to any person within its jurisdiction the equal protection of the laws."

———

Source: 94 U.S. 113 (1877)

We will consider the last of these objections first. . . .

The Constitution contains no definition of the word "deprive," as used in the Fourteenth Amendment. To determine its signification, therefore, it is necessary to ascertain the effect which usage has given it, when employed in the same or a like connection.

While this provision of the amendment is new in the Constitution of the United States, as a limitation upon the powers of the States, it is old as a principle of civilized government. It is found in Magna Charta, and, in substance if not in form, in nearly or quite all the constitutions that have been from time to time adopted by the several States of the Union. By the Fifth Amendment, it was introduced into the Constitution of the United States as a limitation upon the powers of the national government, and by the Fourteenth, as a guaranty against any encroachment upon an acknowledged right of citizenship by the legislature of the States. . . .

When one becomes a member of society, he necessarily parts with some rights or privileges which, as an individual not affected by his relations to others, he might retain. "A body politic," as aptly defined in the preamble of the Constitution of Massachusetts, "is a social compact by which the whole people covenants with each citizen, and each citizen with the whole people, that all shall be governed by certain laws for the common good." This . . . authorize[s] the establishment of laws requiring each citizen to so conduct himself, and so use his own property, as not unnecessarily to injure another. . . . From this source come the police powers. . . . Under these powers the government regulates the conduct of its citizens one towards another, and the manner in which each shall use his own property, when such regulation becomes necessary for the public good. In their exercise it has been customary in England from time immemorial, and in this country from its first colonization, to regulate ferries, common carriers, hackmen, bakers, millers, wharfingers, innkeepers, &c., and in so doing to fix a maximum of charge to be made for services rendered, accommodations furnished, and articles sold. To this day, statutes are to be found in many of the States upon some or all these subjects; and we think it has never yet been successfully contended that such legislation came within any of the constitutional prohibitions against interference with private property. . . .

From this it is apparent that, down to the time of the adoption of the Fourteenth Amendment, it was not supposed that statutes regulating the use, or even the price of the use, of private property necessarily deprived an owner of his property without due process of law. Under some circumstances they may, but not under all. The amendment does not change the law in this particular: it simply prevents the States from doing that which will operate as such a deprivation.

This brings us to inquire as to the principles upon which this power of regulation rests, in order that we may determine what is within and what without its operative effect. Looking, then, to the common law, from whence came the right which the Constitution protects, we find that when private property is "affected with a public interest, it ceases to be *juris privati* only." This was said by Lord Chief Justice Hale more than two hundred years ago. . . . Property does become clothed with a public interest when used in a manner to make it of public consequence, and affect the community at large. When, therefore, one devotes his property to a use in which the public has an interest, he, in effect, grants to the public an interest in that use, and must submit to be controlled by the public for the common good, to the extent of the interest he has thus created. He may withdraw his grant by discontinuing the use; but, so long as he maintains the use, he must submit to the control. . . .

But we need not go further. Enough has already been said to show that, when private property is devoted to a public use, it is subject to public regulation. It remains only to ascertain whether the warehouses of these plaintiffs in error, and the business which is carried on there, come within the operation of this principle. . . .

In this connection it must also be borne in mind that, although in 1874 there were in Chicago fourteen warehouses adapted to this particular business, and owned by about thirty persons, nine business firms controlled them. . . . Thus it is apparent that all the elevating facilities through which these vast productions "of seven or eight great States of the West" must pass on the way "to four or five of the States on the seashore" may be a "virtual" monopoly.

Under such circumstances it is difficult to see why, if the common carrier, or the miller, or the ferryman, or the innkeeper, or the wharfinger, or the baker, or the cartman, or the hackney-coachman, pursues a public employment and exercises "a sort of public office," these plaintiffs in error do not. They stand, to use again the language of their counsel, in the very "gateway of commerce," and take toll from all who pass. Their business most certainly "tends to a common charge, and is become a thing of public interest and use." . . .

For our purposes we must assume that, if a state of facts could exist that would justify such legislation, it actually did exist when the statute now under consideration was passed. For us the question is one of power, not of expediency. If no state of circumstances could exist to justify such a statute, then we may declare this one void, because . . . in excess of the legislative power of the State. But if it could, we must presume it did. Of the propriety of legislative interference within the scope of legislative power, the legislature is the exclusive judge. . . .

It matters not in this case that these plaintiffs in error had built their warehouses and established their business before the regulations complained of were adopted. What they did was from the beginning subject to the power of the body politic to require them to conform to such regulations as might be established by the proper authorities for the common good. They entered upon their business and provided themselves with the means to carry it on subject to this condition. If they did not wish to submit themselves to such interference, they should not have clothed the public with an interest in their concerns. The same principle applies to them that does to the proprietor of a hackney-carriage, and as to him it has never been supposed that he was exempt from regulating statutes or ordinances because he had purchased his horses and carriage and established his business before the statute or the ordinance was adopted.

It is insisted, however, that the owner of property is entitled to a reasonable compensation for its use, even though it be clothed with a public interest, and that what is reasonable is a judicial and not a legislative question.

As has already been shown, the practice has been otherwise. In countries where the common law prevails, it has been customary from time immemorial for the legislature to declare what shall be a reasonable compensation under such circumstances, or, perhaps more properly speaking, to fix a maximum beyond which any charge made would be unreasonable. Undoubtedly, in mere private contracts, relating to matters in which the public has no interest, what is reasonable must be ascertained judicially. But this is because the legislature has no control over such a contract. So, too, in matters which do affect the public interest, and as to which legislative control may be exercised, . . . the courts must determine what is reasonable. The controlling fact is the power to regulate at all. If that exists, the right to establish the maximum of charge, as one of the means of regulation, is implied. . . .

We know that this is a power which may be abused; but that is no argument against its existence. For protection against abuses by legislatures the people must resort to the polls, not to the courts. . . .

Mr. Justice Field and Mr. Justice Strong dissented.

---

132   *Civil Rights Cases (1883)*

In the Civil Rights Act of 1875, the last of the great Reconstruction acts, Republicans in Congress tried to secure and protect by law civil equality for the freedmen. Among its provisions the statute prohibited racial discrimination in access to public accommodations, made violation of the law a misdemeanor, and entitled aggrieved persons to recover 8500 from offenders for each violation. The entire bill rested on Section 5 of the Fourteenth Amendment, which gave Congress power to enforce the amendment's other provisions. Although there is no question that in the debates over the Fourteenth Amendment its sponsors intended just this type of legislation, the Supreme Court denied that Section 5 gave Congress any affirmative power. All Congress could do, according to the Court, was respond to discriminatory measures taken by the states, an anticipation of the later "state action" doctrine; Congress itself could not set independent rules. The decision vitiated the power of the Fourteenth Amendment in the area of civil rights for several generations and made it possible for the states to sanction a variety of discriminatory measures (Document 140).

See J. David Hoeveler, Jr., "Reconstruction and the Federal Courts: The Civil Rights Act of 1875,"31 *Hisorian* 604 (1969); John A. Scott, "Justice Bradley's Evolving Concept of the Fourteenth Amendment," 25 *Rutgers Law Review* 552 (1971); Jonathan Lurie, "Mr. Justice Bradley: A Reassessment," 16 *Seton Hall Law Review* 343 (1986); and C. Vann Woodward, *The Strange Career of Jim Crow* (1966, rev. ed.).

Justice Bradley delivered the opinion of the Court:

Has Congress constitutional power to make such a law? Of course, no one will contend that the power to pass it was contained in the Constitution before the adoption of the last three amendments. The power is sought, first, in the 14th Amendment. It is State action of a particular character that is prohibited. . . . Individual invasion of individual rights is not the subject-matter of the amendment. It nullifies and makes void all State legislation, and State action of every kind, which impairs the privileges and immunities of citizens of the United States, or which injures them in life, liberty or property without due process of law, or which denies to any of them the equal protection of the laws. The last section of the amendment invests Congress with power to enforce it by appropriate legislation. To enforce what? To enforce the prohibition. To adopt appropriate legislation for correcting the effects of such prohibited State laws and State acts, and thus to render them effectually null, void, and innocuous. This is the legislative power conferred upon Congress, and this is the whole of it. It does not invest Congress with power to legislate upon subjects which are within the domain of State legislation; but to provide modes of relief against State legislation, or State action, of the kind referred to. It does not authorize Congress to create a code of municipal law for the regulation of private rights; but to provide modes of redress against the operation of State laws, and the action of State officers executive or judicial, when these are subversive of the fundamental rights specified in the amendment. And so in the present case, until some State law has been passed, or some State action through its officers or agents has been taken, adverse to the rights of citizens sought to be protected by the 14th Amendment, no legislation of the United States under said amendment, nor any proceeding under such legislation, can be called into activity: for the prohibitions of the amendment are against State laws and acts done under State authority. . . .

An inspection of the law shows that it proceeds *ex directo* to declare that certain acts committed by individuals shall be deemed offences, and shall be prosecuted and punished by proceedings in the courts of the United States. It does not profess to be corrective of any constitutional wrong committed by the States; it applies equally to cases arising in States which have the justest laws respecting the personal rights of citizens, and whose authorities are ever ready to enforce such laws, as to those which arise in States that may have violated the prohibition of the amendment. In other words, it steps into the domain of local jurisprudence, and lays down rules for the conduct of individuals in society towards each other, and imposes sanctions for the enforcement of those rules, without referring in any manner to any supposed action of the State or its authorities.

Civil rights, such as are guaranteed by the Constitution against State aggression, cannot be impaired by the wrongful acts of individuals, unsupported by State authority in the shape of laws, customs, or judicial or executive proceedings. The wrongful act of an individual, unsupported by any such authority, is simply a private wrong, or a crime of that individual. . . . The abrogation and denial of rights, for which the States alone were or could be responsible, was the great seminal and fundamental wrong which was intended to be remedied. And the remedy to be provided must necessarily be predicated upon that wrong. Of course, these remarks do not apply to those cases in which Congress is clothed with direct and plenary powers of legislation over the whole subject as in the regulation of commerce. It is clear that the law in question cannot be sustained by any grant of legislative power made to Congress by the 14th Amendment. This is not corrective legislation; it is primary and direct. . . .

But the power of Congress to adopt direct and primary, as distinguished from corrective legislation on the subject in hand, is sought, in the second place, from the Thirteenth Amendment. Such legislation may be primary and direct in its character; for the amendment is not a mere prohibition of State laws establishing or upholding slavery, but an absolute declaration that slavery or involuntary servitude shall not exist in any part of the United States. It is assumed, that the power vested in Congress to enforce the article by appropriate legislation, clothes Congress with power to pass all laws necessary and proper for abolishing all badges and incidents of slavery in the United States: and upon this assumption it is claimed, that this is sufficient authority for enacting this law; the argument being, that the denial of such equal accommodations and privileges is, in itself, a subjection to a species of servitude within the meaning of the amendment. Conceding the major proposition to be true, that Congress has a right to enact all necessary and proper laws for the obliteration and prevention of slavery with all its badges and incidents, is the minor proposition also true? Can the act of a mere individual, the owner of the inn, the public conveyance or place of amusement, refusing the accommodation, be justly regarded as imposing any badge of slavery or servitude upon the applicant, or only as inflicting an ordinary civil injury, properly cognizable by the laws of the State, and presumably subject to redress by those laws until the contrary appears: We are forced to the conclusion that such an act of refusal has nothing to do with slavery or involuntary servitude, and that if it is violative of any right of the party, his redress is to be sought under the laws of the State; or if those laws are adverse to his rights and do not protect him, his remedy will be found in the corrective legislation which Congress has adopted, or may adopt, for counteracting the effect of State laws, or State action, prohibited by the 14th Amendment. It would be running the slavery argument into the ground to make it apply to every act of discrimination which a person may see fit to make as to the guests he will entertain, or as to the people he will take into his coach or cab or car, or admit to his concert or theatre, or deal with in other matters of intercourse or business. Innkeepers and public carriers, by the laws of all the States, so far as we are aware, are bound, to the extent of their facilities, to furnish proper accommodation to all unobjectionable persons who in good faith apply for them. If the laws themselves make any unjust discrimination, amenable to the prohibitions of the 14th Amendment, Congress has full power to afford a remedy under that amendment and in accordance with it. When a man has emerged from slavery, and by the aid of beneficent legislation has shaken off the inseparable concomitants of that state, there must be some stage in the progress of his elevation when he takes the rank of a mere citizen, and ceases to be the special favorite of the laws. . . .

Justice Harlan, dissenting:

The opinion in these cases proceeds, it seems to me, upon grounds entirely too narrow and artificial. I cannot resist the conclusion that the substance and spirit of the recent amendments of the Constitution have been sacrificed by a subtle and ingenious verbal criticism. Was it the purpose . . . simply to destroy the institution . . . and then remit the race, theretofore held in bondage, to the several States for such protection, in their civil rights, necessarily growing out of freedom, as those States, in their discretion, might choose to provide? That there are burdens and disabilities which constitute badges of slavery and servitude, and that the power to enforce by appropriate legislation the Thirteenth Amendment may be exerted by legislation of a direct and primary character, for the eradication, not simply of the institution, but of its badges and incidents, are propositions which ought to be deemed indisputable. I do not contend that the Thirteenth Amendment invests Congress with authority, by legislation, to define and regulate the entire body of the civil rights which citizens enjoy, or may enjoy, in the several States. But I hold that since slavery was the moving or principal cause of the adoption of that amendment, and since that institution rested wholly upon the inferiority, as a race, of those held in bondage, their freedom necessarily involved immunity from, and protection against, all discrimination against them, because of their race, in respect of such civil rights as belong to freemen of other races. Congress, therefore, under its express power to enforce that amendment, may enact laws to protect that people against the deprivation, *because of their race,* of any civil rights granted to other freemen in the same State; and such legislation may be of a direct and primary character operating upon States, their officers and agents, and, also, upon, at least, such individuals and corporations as exercise public functions and wield power and authority under the State. . . .

But what was secured to colored citizens of the United States—as between them and their respective States—by the national grant to them of State citizenship? With what rights, privileges, or immunities did this grant invest them? There is one, if there be no other—exemption from race discrimination in respect of any civil right belonging to citizens of the white race in the same State. It is fundamental in American citizenship that, in respect of such rights, there shall be no discrimination by the State, or its officers, or by individuals or corporations exercising public functions or authority.

But if it were conceded that the power of Congress could not be brought into activity until the rights specified in the act of 1875 had been abridged or denied by some State law or State action, I maintain that the decision of the court is erroneous. In every material sense applicable to the practical enforcement of the 14th Amendment, railroad corporations, keepers of inns, and managers of places of public amusement are agents or instrumentalities of the State, because they are charged with duties to the public, and are amenable, in respect of their duties and functions, to governmental regulation. It seems to me a denial, by these instrumentalities of the State, to the citizen, because of his race, of that equality of civil rights secured to him by law, is a denial by the State, within the meaning of the 14th Amendment. I agree that if one citizen chooses not to hold social intercourse with another, he is not and cannot be made amenable to the law; no legal right of a citizen is violated by the refusal of others to maintain merely social relations with him, even upon grounds of race. The rights which Congress, by the act of 1875, endeavored to secure and protect are legal, not social rights.

133   *Yick Wo v. Hopkins (1886)*

In this case, the Court found the type of state-sanctioned discrimination specifically prohibited by the Fourteenth Amendment. A San Francisco ordinance prohibited operating a laundry located in a wooden building without the consent of the Board of Supervisors; laundries in brick or stone buildings needed no comparable approval. By itself, the law seemed a valid exercise of the police power, since the wooden buildings were vulnerable to fire. At the time, over 95 percent of the 320 laundries in San Francisco were located in wooden buildings, and of these, two-thirds had Chinese owners. The Board of Supervisors granted permits to operate laundries in wooden buildings to all but one of the non-Chinese owners, but none to any of the 200 Chinese applicants. Yick Wo, a Chinese alien who had operated a laundry in the city for many years, was refused a permit and, when he continued to operate his laundry, was convicted under the ordinance. The Court reversed the conviction, not because the ordinance was discriminatory on its face, but because it had been administered in a discriminatory fashion. *Yick Wo* is the first instance of the Court inferring existence of discrimination from data about a law's application, a technique that would be used again in the 1960s.

See Hyung-chan Kim, *A Legal History of Asian Americans, 1790–1990* (1994); Stuart C. Miller, *The Unwelcome Immigrant: The American Image of the Chinese, 1785–1882* (1969); and Lucy E. Salyer, *Laws Harsh as Tigers: Chinese Immigrants and the Shaping of Modern Immigration Law* (1995).

———

Justice Matthews delivered the opinion of the court:

In the case of the petitioner, brought here by writ of error to the Supreme Court of California, our jurisdiction is limited to the question, whether the plaintiff in error has been denied a right in violation of the Constitution, laws, or treaties of the United States. . . .

We are consequently constrained, at the outset, to differ from the Supreme Court of California upon the real meaning of the ordinances in question. That court considered these ordinances as vesting in the board of supervisors a not unusual discretion in granting or withholding their assent to the use of wooden buildings as laundries, to be exercised in reference to the circumstances of each case, with a view to the protection of the public against the dangers of fire. We are not able to concur in that interpretation of the power conferred upon the supervisors. There is nothing in the ordinances which points

Source: 118 U.S. 356 (1886)

to such a regulation of the business of keeping and conducting laundries. They seem intended to confer, and actually do confer, not a discretion to be exercised upon a consideration of the circumstances of each case, but a naked and arbitrary power to give or withhold consent, not only as to places, but as to persons. So that, if an applicant for such consent, being in every way a competent and qualified person, and having complied with every reasonable condition demanded by any public interest, should, failing to obtain the requisite consent of the supervisors to the prosecution of his business, apply for redress by the judicial process of *mandamus,* to require the supervisors to consider and act upon his case, it would be a sufficient answer for them to say that the law had conferred upon them authority to withhold their assent, without reason and without responsibility. The power given to them is not confided to their discretion in the legal sense of that term, but is granted to their mere will. It is purely arbitrary, and acknowledges neither guidance nor restraint. . . .

The ordinance drawn in question in the present case . . . does not prescribe a rule and conditions for the regulation of the use of property for laundry purposes, to which all similarly situated may conform. It allows without restriction the use for such purposes of buildings of brick or stone; but, as to wooden buildings, constituting nearly all those in previous use, it divides the owners or occupiers into two classes, not having respect to their personal character and qualifications for the business, nor the situation and nature and adaptation of the buildings themselves, but merely by an arbitrary line, on one side of which are those who are permitted to pursue their industry by the mere will and consent of the supervisors, and on the other those from whom that consent is withheld, at their mere will and pleasure. And both classes are alike only in this, that they are tenants at will, under the supervisors, of their means of living. The ordinance, therefore, also differs from the not unusual case, where discretion is lodged by law in public officers or bodies to grant or withhold licenses to keep taverns, or places for the sale of spirituous liquors, and the like, when one of the conditions is that the applicant shall be a fit person for the exercise of the privilege, because in such cases the fact of fitness is submitted to the judgment of the officer, and calls for the exercise of a discretion of a judicial nature.

The rights of the petitioners, as affected by the proceedings of which they complain, are not less, because they are aliens and subjects of the Emperor of China. . . .

The Fourteenth Amendment to the Constitution is not confined to the protection of citizens. It says: "Nor shall any State deprive any person of life, liberty, or property without due process of law; nor deny to any person within its jurisdiction the equal protection of the laws." These provisions are universal in their application, to all persons within the territorial jurisdiction, without regard to any differences of race, of color, or of nationality; and the equal protection of the laws is a pledge of the protection of equal laws. It is accordingly enacted by § 1977 of the Revised Statutes, that "all persons within the jurisdiction of the United States shall have the same right in every State and Territory to make and enforce contracts, to sue, be parties, give evidence, and to the full and equal benefit of all laws and proceedings for the security of persons and property as is enjoyed by white citizens and shall be subject to like punishment, pains, penalties, taxes, licenses, and exactions of every kind, and to no other." The questions we have to consider and decide in these cases, therefore, are to be treated as involving the rights of every citizen of the United States equally with those of the strangers and aliens who now invoke the jurisdiction of the court.

It is contended on the part of the petitioners, that the ordinances for violations of which they are severally sentenced to imprisonment, are void on their face, as being within the prohibitions of the Fourteenth Amendment; and, in the alternative, if not so, that they are void by reason of their administration, operating unequally, so as to punish in the present petitioners what is permitted to others as lawful, without any distinction of circumstances—an unjust and illegal discrimination, it is claimed, which, though not made expressly by the ordinances is made possible by them. . . .

. . . In the present cases we are not obliged to reason from the probable to the actual, and pass upon the validity of the ordinances complained of, as tried merely by the opportunities which their terms afford, of unequal and unjust discrimination in their administration. For the cases present the ordinances in actual operation, and the facts shown establish an administration directed so exclusively against a particular class of persons as to warrant and require the conclusion, that, whatever may have been the intent of the ordinances as adopted, they are applied by the public authorities charged with their administration, and thus representing the State itself, with a mind so unequal and oppressive as to amount to a practical denial by the State of that equal protection of the laws which is secured to the petitioners, as to all other persons, by the broad and benign provisions of the Fourteenth Amendment to the Constitution of the United States. Though the law itself be fair on its face and impartial in appearance, yet, if it is applied and administered by public authority with an evil eye and an unequal hand, so as practically to make unjust and illegal discriminations between persons in similar circumstances, material to their rights, the denial of equal justice is still within the prohibition of the Constitution. . . .

The present cases, as shown by the facts disclosed in the record, are within this class. It appears that both petitioners have complied with every requisite, deemed by the law or by the public officers charged with its administration, necessary for the protection of neighboring property from fire, or as a precaution against injury to the public health. No reason whatever, except the will of the supervisors, is assigned why they should not be permitted to carry on, in the accustomed manner, their harmless and useful occupation, on which they depend for a livelihood. And while this consent of the supervisors is withheld from them and from two hundred others who have also petitioned, all of whom happen to be Chinese subjects, eighty others, not Chinese subjects, are permitted to carry on the same business under similar conditions. The fact of this discrimination is admitted. No reason for it is shown, and the conclusion cannot be resisted, that no reason for it exists except hostility to the race and nationality to which the petitioners belong, and which in the eye of the law is not justified. The discrimination is, therefore, illegal, and the public administration which enforces it is a denial of the equal protection of the laws and a violation of the Fourteenth Amendment of the Constitution. The imprisonment of the petitioners is, therefore, illegal, and they must be discharged.

134

Wabash, St. Louis & Pacific Ry. Co. v. Illinois (1886)

On one of the Granger cases, the Court upheld state regulation of railroads—even if this involved interstate operations—in the absence of federal legislation in this area. The Court had ample precedent for this ruling, since in several pre-war cases, state laws affecting interstate commerce had been sustained on similar grounds (see Document 95). By the mid-1880s, differing state regulations and the varying impact they had on interstate operations led some railroad officials to suggest a uniform national regulatory scheme. The railroads also renewed their attacks on state regulation, seeking to have the Court reverse its approval of state regulation of interstate activities in the absence of federal action.

In this case, the railroad challenged an Illinois statute prohibiting long haul–short haul discrimination, complaining specifically that it cost more to ship goods to New York from Gilman, Illinois, than from Peoria, although Gilman was eighty-six miles closer to New York. Most of the route, however, lay outside Illinois borders and obviously involved interstate commerce. By ruling that states could not regulate interstate commerce, the Court invalidated most state schemes, since nearly all railroad routes ran in two or more states. The decision spurred Congress to establish the first regulatory agency, the Interstate Commerce Commission.

See Gabriel Kolko, *Railroads and Regulation, 1877–1916* (1965); George Miller, *Railroads and the Granger Laws* (1973); J. J. Hellman, *Competition and Railroad Price Discrimination* (1973); and Richard C. Cortner, *The Iron Horse and the Constitution: The Railroads and the Transformation of the Fourteenth Amendment* (1993).

––––––––

Justice Miller delivered the opinion of the Court:

The question of the right of the State to regulate the rate of fares and tolls on railroads, and how far that right was affected by the commerce clause of the Constitution of the United States, was presented to the court in [the Granger] cases. And it must be admitted that, in a general way, the court treated the cases then before it as belonging to that class of regulations of commerce which, like pilotage, bridging navigable rivers, and many others, could be acted upon by the States in the absence of any legislation by Congress on the same subject. . . .

Source: 118 U.S. 557 (1886)

The great question to be decided, and which was decided, and which was argued in all those cases, was the right of the State within which a railroad company did business to regulate or limit the amount of any of these traffic charges. . . .

It cannot be too strongly insisted upon that the right of continuous transportation from one end of the country to the other is essential in modern times to that freedom of commerce from the restraints which the State might choose to impose upon it, that the commerce clause was intended to secure. This clause, giving to Congress the power to regulate commerce among the States and with foreign nations, as this court has said before, was among the most important of the subjects which prompted the formation of the Constitution. . . . And it would be a very feeble and almost useless provision, but poorly adapted to secure the entire freedom of commerce among the States which was deemed essential to a more perfect union by the framers of the Constitution, if, at every stage of the transportation of goods and chattels through the country, the State within whose limits a part of this transportation must be done could impose regulations concerning the price, compensation, or taxation, or any other restrictive regulation interfering with and seriously embarrassing this commerce.

The argument on this subject can never be better stated than it is by Chief Justice Marshall in *Gibbons* v. *Ogden*. . . . He there demonstrates that commerce among the States, like commerce with foreign nations, is necessarily a commerce which crosses State lines, and extends into the States, and the power of Congress to regulate it exists wherever that commerce is found. . . .

We must, therefore, hold that it is not, and never has been, the deliberate opinion of a majority of this court that a statute of a State which attempts to regulate the fares and charges by railroad companies within its limits, for a transportation which constitutes a part of commerce among the States, is a valid law.

Let us see precisely what is the degree of interference with transportation of property or persons from one State to another which this statute proposes. A citizen of New York has goods which he desires to have transported by the railroad companies from that city to the interior of the State of Illinois. A continuous line of rail over which a car loaded with these goods can be carried, and is carried habitually, connects the place of shipment with the place of delivery. He undertakes to make a contract with a person engaged in the carrying business at the end of this route from whence the goods are to start, and he is told by the carrier,

> "I am free to make a fair and reasonable contract for this carriage to the line of the State of Illinois, but when the car which carries these goods is to cross the line of that State, pursuing at the same time this continuous tract, I am met by a law of Illinois which forbids me to make a free contract concerning this transportation within that State, and subjects me to certain rules by which I am to be governed as to the charges which the same railroad company in Illinois may make, or has made, with reference to other persons and other places of delivery."

So that while that carrier might be willing to carry these goods from the city of New York to the city of Peoria at the rate of fifteen cents per hundred pounds, he is not permitted to do so because the Illinois railroad company has already charged at the rate of twenty-five cents per hundred pounds for carriage to Gilman, in Illinois, which is eighty-six miles shorter than the distance to Peoria.

So, also, in the present case, the owner of corn, the principal product of the country, desiring to transport it from Peoria, in Illinois, to New York, finds a railroad company willing to do this at the rate of fifteen cents per hundred pounds for a car-load, but is compelled to pay at the rate of twenty-five cents per hundred pounds, because the railroad company has received from a person residing at Gilman twenty-five cents per hundred pounds for the transportation of a car-load of the same class of freight over the same line of road from Gilman to New York. This is the result of the statute of Illinois, in its endeavor to prevent unjust discrimination, as construed by the Supreme Court of that State. The effect of it is, that whatever may be the rate of transportation per mile charged by the railroad company from Gilman to Sheldon, a distance of twenty-three miles, in which the loading and the unloading of the freight is the largest expense incurred by the railroad company, the same rate per mile must be charged from Peoria to the city of New York.

The obvious injustice of such a rule as this, which railroad companies are by heavy penalties compelled to conform to, in regard to commerce among the States, when applied to transportation which includes Illinois in a long line of carriage through several States, shows the value of the constitutional provision which confides the power of regulating interstate commerce to the Congress of the United States, whose enlarged view of the interests of all the States, and of the railroads concerned, better fits it to establish just and equitable rules.

Of the justice or propriety of the principle which lies at the foundation of the Illinois statute it is not the province of this court to speak. . . . But when it is attempted to apply to transportation through an entire series of States a principle of this kind, and each one of the States shall attempt to establish its own rates of transportation, its own methods to prevent discrimination in rates, or to permit it, the deleterious influence upon the freedom of commerce among the States and upon the transit of goods through those States cannot be overestimated. That this species of regulations is one which must be, if established at all, of a general and national character, and cannot be safely and wisely remitted to local rules and local regulations, we think is clear from what has already been said. And if it be a regulation of commerce, as we think we have demonstrated it is, and as the Illinois court concedes it to be, it must be of that national character, and the regulation can only appropriately exist by general rules and principles, which demand that it should be done by Congress of the United States under the commerce clause of the Constitution.

---

135   *The Police Power (1886)*

CHRISTOPHER J. TIEDEMAN

The development of substantive due process and freedom of contract received great impetus from a handful of influential law writers who erected the intellectual scaffolding for these ideas, upon which judges would build the doctrines. One of the most influential was Thomas M. Cooley, whose *Treatise on Constitutional Limitations,* first published in 1868, served as a handbook for state court judges for decades. The most conservative of the law writers was Christopher J. Tiedeman, a professor of law at the University of Missouri who wrote treatises on many subjects, but whose fame derives primarily form his very narrow interpretation of the police power. The role of government, he declared, consisted of no more "than to provide for the public order and personal security by the prevention and punishment of crimes and trespassers." As he candidly admitted, he had set out to write this work to prove that the police powers could not be employed to interfere with the marketplace, and far more than Cooley, he denounced any type of governmental regulations. The following excerpts show Tiedeman's broad concept of personal liberty and narrow view of governmental power.

See Charles E. Jacobs, *Law Writers and the Courts* . . . (1954); and Allan Jones, "Thomas M. Cooley and Laissez-Faire Constitutionalism: A Reappraisal," 52 *Journal of American History* 751 (1967).

---

1. Police Power—Defined and Explained

The private rights of the individual, apart from a few statutory rights, which when compared with the whole body of private rights are insignificant in number, do not rest upon the mandate of municipal law as a source. They belong to man in a state of nature; they are natural rights, rights recognized and existing in the law of reason. But the individual, in a state of nature, finds in the enjoyment of his own rights that he transgresses the rights of others. Nature wars upon nature, when subjected to no spiritual or moral restraint. The object of government is to impose that degree of restraint upon human actions, which is necessary to the uniform and reasonable conservation and enjoyment of private rights. Government and municipal law protect and develop, rather than create, private rights. The conservation of private rights is attained by the imposition of a wholesome restraint upon their exercise, such a restraint as will prevent the infliction of injury upon others in the enjoyment of them; it involves a provision of means for enforcing the legal maxim, which enunciates the fundamental rule of both the human and the natural law, *sic utere tuo, ut alienum non lældas* [use your own property in such a way as not to injure another's]. The power of the government to impose this restraint is called POLICE POWER. By this "general police power of the State, persons and property are subjected to all kinds of restraints and burdens, in order to secure the general comfort, health and prosperity of the State; of the perfect right in the legislature to do which no question ever was or upon acknowledged general principles ever can be made, so far as natural persons are concerned." Blackstone defines the police power to be "the due regulation and

---

Source: A Treatise on the Limitation of Police Power in the United States §§ 1, 30 (1886)

domestic order of the kingdom, whereby the inhabitants of a State, like members of a well-governed family, are bound to conform their general behavior to the rules of propriety, good neighborhood and good manners, and to be decent, industrious and inoffensive in their respective stations." . . . The continental jurists include, under the term *Police Power,* not only those restraints upon private rights which are imposed for the general welfare of all, but also all the governmental institutions, which are established with public funds for the better promotion of the public good, and the alleviation of private want and suffering. Thus they would include the power of the government to expend the public moneys in the construction and repair of roads, the establishment of hospitals and asylums and colleges, in short, the power to supplement the results of individual activity with what individual activity can not accomplish. "The governmental provision for the public security and welfare in its daily necessities, that provision which establishes the needful and necessary, and therefore appears as a bidding and forbidding power of the State, is the scope and character of the police." But in the present connection, as may be gathered from the American definitions heretofore given, the term must be confined to the imposition of restraints and burdens upon persons and property. The power of the government to embark in enterprises of public charity and benefit can only be limited by the restrictions upon the power of taxation, and to that extent alone can these subjects in American law be said to fall within the police power of the State.

It is to be observed, therefore, that the police power of the government, as understood in the constitutional law of the United States, is simply the power of the government to establish provisions for the enforcement of the common as well as civil-law maxim, *sic utere tuo, ut alienum non lœdas.* . . . Any law which goes beyond that principle, which undertakes to abolish rights, the exercise of which does not involve an infringement of the rights of others, or to limit the exercise of rights beyond what is necessary to provide for the public welfare and the general security, cannot be included in the police power of the government. It is a governmental usurpation, and violates the principles of abstract justice, as they have been developed under our republican institutions. . . .

30. Personal Liberty—How Guaranteed

It is altogether needless in this connection to indulge in a panegyric upon the blessings of guaranteed personal liberty. The love of liberty, of freedom from irksome and unlawful restraints, is implanted in every human breast. In the American Declaration of Independence, and in the bills of rights of almost every State constitution, we find that personal liberty is expressly guaranteed to all men equally. But notwithstanding the existence of these fundamental and constitutional guaranties of personal liberty, the astounding anomaly of the slavery of an entire race in more than one-third of the States of the American Union, during three-fourths of a century of national existence, gave the lie to their own constitutional declarations, that "*all* men are endowed by their Creator, with certain alienable rights, among which are the right to life, liberty, and the pursuit of happiness." But, happily, this contradiction is now a thing of the past, and in accordance with the provisions of the thirteenth amendment to the constitution of the United States, it is now the fundamental and practically unchangeable law of the land, that "neither slavery nor involuntary servitude, except as a punishment for crime whereof the party shall have been duly convicted, shall exist within the United States, or any place subject to their jurisdiction.

But to a practical understanding of the effect of these constitutional guaranties, a clear idea of what personal liberty consists is necessary. It is not to be confounded with a license to do what one pleases. Liberty, according to Montesquieu, consists "only in the power of doing what we ought to will, and in not being constrained to do what we ought not to will." No man has a right to make such a use of his liberty as to commit an injury to the rights of others. His liberty is controlled by the oft quoted maxim, *sic utere tuo, ut alienum non lædas*. Indeed liberty is that amount of personal freedom, which is consistent with a strict obedience to this rule. . . . While liberty does not consist in a paucity of laws, still it is only consistent with a limitation of the restrictive laws to those which exercise a wholesome restraint. "That man is free who is protected from injury," and his protection involves necessarily the restraint of other individuals from the commission of the injury. In the proper balancing of the contending interests of individuals, personal liberty is secured and developed; any further restraint is unwholesome and subversive of liberty. As Herbert Spencer has expressed it, "every man may claim the fullest liberty to exercise his faculties compatible with the possession of like liberty by every other man."

The constitutional guaranties are generally unqualified, and a strict construction of them would prohibit all limitations upon liberty, if any other meaning but the limited one here presented were given to the word. But these guaranties are to be liberally construed, so that the object of them may be fully attained. They do not prohibit the exercise of police power in restraint of licentious trespass upon the rights of others, but the restrictive measures must be kept within these limits. "Powers, which can be justified only on this specific ground (that they are police regulations), and which would otherwise be clearly prohibited by the constitution, can be such only as are so clearly necessary to the safety, comfort and well-being of society, or so imperatively required by the public necessity, as to lead to the rational and satisfactory conclusion that the framers of the constitution could not, as men of ordinary prudence and foresight have intended, to prohibit their exercise in the particular case, notwithstanding the language of the prohibition would otherwise include it."

The restrictions upon personal liberty, permissible under these constitutional limitations, are either of a public or private nature. In consequence of the mental and physical disabilities of certain classes, in the law of domestic relations, their liberty is more or less subjected to restraint, the motive being their own benefit. These restraints are of a private nature, imposed under the law by private persons who stand in domestic relation to those whose liberty is restrained. . . . In this connection we are only concerned with those restraints which are of a public nature, *i.e.,* those which are imposed by government. They may be subdivided under the following heading: 1. The police control of the criminal classes. 2. The police control of dangerous classes, other than by criminal prosecutions. 3. The regulation of domicile and citizenship. 4. Police control of morality and religion. 5. Police regulation of the freedom of speech and of the press. 6. Police regulation of trades and professions.

136

United States v. E.C. Knight Co. (1895)

Another aspect of late nineteenth-century industrialization that upset many Americans was the growth of large corporations that used their enormous economic resources and power to monopolize markets. In the Sherman Antitrust Act of 1890, Congress prohibited "every contract, combination . . . or conspiracy, in restraint of trade or commerce." Although the statute embodied traditional common law prescriptions against restraint of trade, most congressmen knew that in the highly charged business atmosphere of the late nineteenth century, all successful firms restricted trade to some extent. The exceedingly vague wording did not make clear whether Congress intended to attack all combinations or only unreasonable ones. Constitutional questions also arose over the reach of the Commerce Clause to manufacturing enterprises, which many people viewed as primarily local in nature.

In the first case brought under the Sherman Act, the government sought dissolution of the American Sugar Refining Company, through which a handful of firms controlled over 90 percent of the nation's sugar refining capacity. Although the decision is often attacked as evidence of the Court's blindness to modern industrial reality, some scholars have suggested that Chief Justice Fuller was trying to get the states—which chartered the companies—to take a more active role in policing their conduct. Whatever Fuller's intent may have been, the practical effect of the decision was to nullify enforcement of the Sherman Act for a decade until the courts adopted a more commonsense approach to the problems (see Documents 144 and 149).

See William Letwin, *Law and Economic Policy in America: The Evolution of the Sherman Antitrust Act* (1965); Charles McCurdy, "The *Knight* Sugar Decision of 1895 and the Modernization of American Corporate Law, 1869–1903," 53 *Business History Review* 304 (1979); Richard A. Epstein, "The Proper Scope of the Commerce Power," 73 *Virginia Law Review* 1432 (1987); Tony A. Freyer, "Economic Liberty, Antitrust and the Constitution, 1880–1925," in Paul & Dickman, eds., *Liberty, Property and Government* (1989); and James May "Antitrust in the Formative Era," 50 *Ohio State Law Journal* 257 (1989).

———

Chief Justice Fuller delivered the opinion of the Court:

The fundamental question is, whether conceding that the existence of a monopoly in manufacture is established by the evidence, that monopoly can be directly suppressed under the act of Congress in the mode attempted by this bill.

Source: 156 U.S. 1 (1895)

It cannot be denied that the power of a State to protect the lives, health, and property of its citizens, and to preserve good order and the public morals, "the power to govern men and things within the limits of its dominion," is a power originally and always belonging to the States, not surrendered by them to the general government, nor directly restrained by the Constitution of the United States, and essentially exclusive. The relief of the citizens of each State from the burden of monopoly and the evils resulting from the restraint of trade among such citizens was left with the States to deal with, and this court has recognized their possession of that power even to the extent of holding that an employment or business carried on by private individuals, when it becomes a matter of such public interest and importance as to create a common charge or burden upon the citizen; in other words, when it becomes a practical monopoly, to which the citizen is compelled to resort and by means of which a tribute can be exacted from the community, is subject to regulation by state legislative power. On the other hand, the power of Congress to regulate commerce among the several States is also exclusive. The Constitution does not provide that interstate commerce shall be free, but, by the grant of this exclusive power to regulate it, it was left free except as Congress might impose restraints. Therefore it has been determined that the failure of Congress to exercise this exclusive power in any case is an expression of its will that the subject shall be free from restrictions or impositions upon it by the several States, and if a law passed by a State in the exercise of its acknowledged powers comes into conflict with that will, the Congress and the State cannot occupy the position of equal opposing sovereignties, because the Constitution declares its supremacy and that of the laws passed in pursuance thereof; and that which is not supreme must yield to that which is supreme. . . . That which belongs to commerce is within the jurisdiction of the United States, but that which does not belong to commerce is within the jurisdiction of the police power of the State. . . .

The argument is that the power to control the manufacture of refined sugar is a monopoly over a necessary of life, to the enjoyment of which by a large part of the population of the United States interstate commerce is indispensable, and that, therefore, the general government in the exercise of the power to regulate commerce may repress such monopoly directly and set aside the instruments which have created it. But this argument cannot be confined to necessaries of life merely, and must include all articles of general consumption. Doubtless the power to control the manufacture of a given thing involves in a certain sense the control of its disposition, but this is a secondary and not the primary sense; and although the exercise of that power may result in bringing the operation of commerce into play, it does not control it, and affects it only incidentally and indirectly. Commerce succeeds to manufacture, and is not a part of it. The power to regulate commerce is the power to prescribe the rule by which commerce shall be governed, and is a power independent of the power to suppress monopoly. But it may operate in repression of monopoly whenever that comes within the rules by which commerce is governed or whenever the transaction is itself a monopoly of commerce.

It is vital that the independence of the commercial power and of the police power, and the delimitation between them, however sometimes perplexing, should always be recognized and observed, for while the one furnishes the strongest bond of union, the other is essential to the preservation of the autonomy of the States as required by our dual form of government; and acknowledged evils, however grave and urgent they may appear to be, had better be borne, than the risk be run, in the effort to suppress them, of more serious consequences by resort to expedients of even doubtful constitutionality. . . .

Again, all the authorities agree that in order to vitiate a contract or combination it is not essential that its result should be a complete monopoly: it is sufficient if it really tends to that end and to deprive the public of the advantages which flow from free competition. Slight reflection will show that if the national power extends to all contracts and combinations in manufacture, agriculture, mining, and other productive industries, whose ultimate result may affect external commerce, comparatively little of business operations and affairs would be left for state control.

It was in the light of well-settled principles that the act of July 2, 1890, was framed. Congress did not attempt thereby to assert the power to deal with monopoly directly as such; or to limit and restrict the rights of corporations created by the States or the citizens of the States in the acquisition, control, or disposition of property; or to regulate or prescribe the price or prices at which such property or the products thereof should be sold; or to make criminal the acts of persons in the acquisition and control of property which the States of their residence or creation sanctioned or permitted. Aside from the provisions applicable where Congress might exercise municipal power, what the law struck at was combinations, contracts, and conspiracies to monopolize trade and commerce among the several States or with foreign nations; but the contracts and acts of the defendants related exclusively to the acquisition of the Philadelphia refineries and the business of sugar refining in Pennsylvania, and bore no direct relation to commerce between the States or with foreign nations. . . .

Justice Harlan, dissenting:

While the opinion of the court in this case does not declare the act of 1890 to be unconstitutional, it defeats the main object for which it was passed. For it is, in effect, held that the statute would be unconstitutional if interpreted as embracing such unlawful restraints upon the purchasing of goods in one State to be carried to another State as necessarily arise from the *existence* of combinations formed for the purpose and with the effect, not only of monopolizing the ownership of all such goods in every part of the country, but of controlling the prices for them in all the States. This view of the scope of the act leaves the public, so far as national power is concerned, entirely at the mercy of combinations which arbitrarily control the prices of articles purchased to be transported from one State to another State. I cannot assent to that view. In my judgment, the general government is not placed by the Constitution in such a condition of helplessness that it must fold its arms and remain inactive while capital combines, under the name of a corporation, to destroy competition, not in one State only, but throughout the entire country, in the buying and selling of articles—especially the necessaries of life—that go into commerce among the States. The doctrine of the autonomy of the States cannot properly be invoked to justify a denial of power in the national government to meet such an emergency, involving as it does that freedom of commercial intercourse among the States which the Constitution sought to attain.

137 *In re Debs (1895)*

In 1894, the American Railway Union struck the Pullman Company in protest over a 20 percent wage cut. In addition to the direct strike by Pullman employees against the company, other members of the Railway Unions refused to handle Pullman cars in operation on the various railroads. The strike paralyzed rail transportation out of Chicago, and the federal government sought an injunction against the strike because it was obstructing the U.S. mail, which was shipped by rail. The federal district court issued an extremely broad injunction against the strikers and the union leaders, which union president Eugene V. Debs and three of his associates refused to obey. At the resulting contempt trial, union attorneys, including Clarence Darrow, protested that the original injunction had exceeded judicial authority, to which the trial judge responded that the defendants had violated the Sherman Act by conspiring to restrain trade.

Although the Sherman Act said nothing specific about labor unions, in the legislative debate it is clear that Congress did not intend to exempt either farm or labor groups from the law. In sharp contrast to the *Knight* decision, the Court here proclaimed a broad interpretation of national power, and for the next three decades one finds this dichotomy in Court decisions—a broad view of commerce to allow government to restrict union activities, and a narrow view to defeat governmental efforts to regulate business.

See A. Lindsey, *The Pullman Strike* (1942); Ray Ginger, *The Bending Cross: A Biography of Eugene V. Debs* (1969); Christopher L. Tomlins, *The State and the Unions* (1985); William E. Forbath, *Law and the Shaping of the American Labor Movement* (1991); and Daniel R. Ernst, *Lawyers Against Labor* (1995).

———

Justice Brewer delivered the opinion of the Court:

Under the power vested in Congress to establish post offices and post roads, Congress has, by a mass of legislation, established the great post office system of the country, with all its detail of organization, its machinery for the transaction of business, defining what shall be carried and what not, and the prices of carriage, and also prescribing penalties for all offences against it.

Obviously these powers given to the national government over interstate commerce and in respect to the transportation of the mails were not dormant and unused. Congress had taken hold of these two matters, and by various and specific acts had assumed and

Source: 158 U.S. 564 (1895)

exercised the powers given to it, and was in the full discharge of its duty to regulate inter-state commerce and carry the mails. The validity of such exercise and the exclusiveness of its control had been again and again presented to this court for consideration. . . .

As, under the Constitution, power over interstate commerce and the transportation of the mails is vested in the national government, and Congress by virtue of such grant has assumed actual and direct control, it follows that the national government may prevent any unlawful and forcible interference therewith. But how shall this be accomplished? Doubtless, it is within the competency of Congress to prescribe by legislation that any interference with these matters shall be offences against the United States, and prosecuted and punished by indictment in the proper courts. But is that the only remedy? Have the vast interests of the nation in interstate commerce, and in the transportation of the mails, no other protection than lies in the possible punishment of those who interfere with it? To ask the question is to answer it. . . .

The entire strength of the nation may be used to enforce in any part of the land the full and free exercise of all national powers and the security of all rights entrusted by the Constitution to its care. The strong arm of the national government may be put forth to brush away all obstructions to the freedom of interstate commerce or the transportation of the mails. If the emergency arises, the army of the Nation, and all its militia, are at the service of the Nation to compel obedience to its laws.

But passing to the second question, is there no other alternative than the use of force on the part of the executive authorities whenever obstructions arise to the freedom of interstate commerce or the transportation of the mails? Is the army the only instrument by which rights of the public can be enforced and the peace of the nation preserved? Grant that any public nuisance may be forcibly abated either at the instance of the authorities, or by any individual suffering private damage therefrom, the existence of this right of forcible abatement is not inconsistent with nor does it destroy the right of appeal in an orderly way to the courts for a judicial determination, and an exercise of their powers by writ of injunction and otherwise to accomplish the same result. . . .

Neither can it be doubted that the government has such an interest in the subject-matter as enables it to appear as party plaintiff in this suit. It is said that equity only interferes for the protection of property, and that the government has no property interest. A sufficient reply is that the United States have a property in the mails, the protection of which was one of the purposes of this bill. . . .

. . . Every government, entrusted, by the very terms of its being, with powers and duties to be exercised and discharged for the general welfare, has a right to apply to its own courts for any proper assistance in the exercise of the one and the discharge of the other, and it is no sufficient answer to its appeal to one of those courts that it has no pecuniary interest in the matter. The obligations which it is under to promote the interest of all, and to prevent the wrongdoing of one resulting in injury to the general welfare, is often of itself sufficient to give it a standing in court. This proposition in some of its relations has heretofore received the sanction of this court. . . .

Again, it is objected that it is outside of the jurisdiction of a court of equity to enjoin the commission of crimes. This, as a general proposition, is unquestioned. A chancellor has no criminal jurisdiction. Something more than the threatened commission of an offense against the laws of the land is necessary to call into exercise the injunctive powers of the court. There must be some interferences, actual or threatened, with property or rights of a pecuniary nature, but when such interferences appear the jurisdiction of a court of equity arises, and is not destroyed by the fact that they are accompanied by or are themselves violations of the criminal law. . . .

We enter into no examination of the [Sherman] act . . . upon which the Circuit Court relied mainly to sustain its jurisdiction. It must not be understood from this that we dissent from the conclusions of that court in reference to the scope of the act, but simply that we prefer to rest our judgment on the broader ground which has been discussed in this opinion, believing it of importance that the principles underlying it should be fully stated and affirmed.

---

138 *Pollock v. Farmers' Loan and Trust Co. (1895)*

The Interstate Commerce and Sherman acts marked two efforts by the federal government to regulate big business; the income tax represents a third. The Constitution prohibited direct taxes, but there had long been a debate over exactly what that phrase meant. Congress had imposed an income tax during the Civil War, and the Court had upheld it in *Springer* v. *United States* (1880). In the 1890s, political pressure rose to reduce the tariff and to shift the government's reliance on tariff income to revenue from a tax on personal and corporate incomes. Such a tax would not only yield considerable income, but also serve as a control on big business. The Democrats and Populists managed to tack on an income tax rider to the Wilson-Gorman Tariff of 1894, providing for a 2 percent tax on all individual and corporate incomes, and a $4,000 exemption for individuals.

From an economic viewpoint, the tax represented a logical step in establishing more reliable revenue for the government, but business spokesmen protested against this manifestation of "socialism, communism and devilism." A prestigious legal team led by Joseph Choate and George Edmunds attacked the tax, which came before the Court in two cases, both by the same title.

In the first case, Chief Justice Fuller dismissed all the precedents supporting an income tax as "a century of error." The Court invalidated the tax on income from rental property as a direct but unapportioned tax on land and also struck down the tax on income from state and municipal bonds, as an infringement on the power of a state to borrow money. The Court divided four to four on three other issues, and when the Court splits, it normally leaves the lower court decision intact. But the justices felt so strongly about these issues that when Justice Howell Jackson, who had been ill during the first case, returned to the bench, the Court reheard these questions—whether a tax on income from personal property constituted a direct tax, whether the invalidity of any one section voided the entire bill, and whether if any part of the tax could be considered indirect it still failed for want of uniformity. Although Howell voted to support the tax, one of the previous supporters now joined the chief justice to give him a majority to strike down the entire act. The decision incited enormous criticism of the Court, and agitation led to the enactment of the Sixteenth Amendment. Even before the amendment was enacted, the Court backed off from its extreme antitax stance and upheld taxes that were barely distinguishable from income taxes.

See Sidney Ratner, *Taxation and Democracy in America* (1967); Gerald Eggert, "Richard Olney and the Income Tax Cases," 48 *Mississippi Valley Historical Review* 24 (1961); and Robert Stanley, *Dimensions of Law in the Service of Order: Origins of the Federal Income Tax, 1861–1913* (1993).

————

Chief Justice Fuller delivered the opinion of the Court:
The Constitution divided Federal taxation into two great classes, the class of direct taxes, and the class of duties, imports, and excises; and prescribed two rules which qualified the grant of power as to each class.

The power to lay direct taxes apportioned among the several States in proportion to their representation in the popular branch of Congress, a representation based on population as ascertained by the census, was plenary and absolute; but to lay direct taxes without apportionment was forbidden. The power to lay duties, imposts, and excises was subject to the qualification that the imposition must be uniform throughout the United States.

Our previous decision was confined to the consideration of the validity of the tax on the income from real estate, and on the income from municipal bonds. . . .

We are now permitted to broaden the field of inquiry, and to determine to which of the two great classes a tax upon a person's entire income, whether derived from rents, or products, or otherwise, of real estate, or from bonds, stocks, or other forms of personal property, belongs; and we are unable to conclude that the enforced subtraction from the yield of all the owner's real or personal property, in the manner prescribed, is so different from a tax upon the property itself, that it is not a direct, but an indirect tax, in the meaning of the Constitution. . . .

Whatever the speculative views of political economists or revenue reformers may be, can it be properly held that the Constitution, taken in its plain and obvious sense, and with due regard to the circumstances attending the formation of the government, authorizes a general unapportioned tax on the products of the farm and the rents of real estate, although imposed merely because of ownership and with no possible means of escape from payment, as belonging to a totally different class from that which includes the property from whence the income proceeds?

————

Source: 158 U.S. 601 (1895)

There can be but one answer, unless the constitutional restriction is to be treated as utterly illusory and futile, and the object of its framers defeated. We find it impossible to hold that a fundamental requisition, deemed so important as to be enforced by two provisions, one affirmative and one negative, can be refined away by forced distinctions between that which gives value to property, and the property itself.

Nor can we perceive any ground why the same reasoning does not apply to capital in personalty held for the purpose of income or ordinarily yielding income, and to the income therefrom. All the real estate of the country, and all its invested personal property, are open to the direct operation of the taxing power if an appointment be made according to the Constitution. The Constitution does not say that no direct tax shall be laid by apportionment on any other property than land; on the contrary, it forbids all unapportioned direct taxes; and we know of no warrant for excepting personal property from the exercise of the power, or any reason why an apportioned direct tax cannot be laid and assessed. . . .

. . . Cannot Congress, if the necessity exist of raising thirty, forty, or any other number of million dollars for the support of the government, in addition to the revenue from duties, imposts, and excises, apportion the quota of each State upon the basis of the census, and thus advise it of the payment which must be made, and proceed to assess that amount on all the real and personal property and the income of all persons in the State, and collect the same if the State does not in the meantime assume and pay its quota and collect the amount according to its own system and in its own way? Cannot Congress do this, as respects either or all these subjects of taxation, and deal with each in such manner as might be deemed expedient . . . ? Inconveniences might possibly attend the levy of an income tax, notwithstanding the listing of receipts, when adjusted, furnishes its own valuation; but that it is apportionable is hardly denied, although it is asserted that it would operate so unequally as to be undesirable. . . .

We are not here concerned with the question whether an income tax be or be not desirable, nor whether such a tax would enable the government to diminish taxes on consumption and duties on imports, and to enter upon what may be believed to be a reform of its fiscal and commercial system. Questions of that character belong to the controversies of political parties, and cannot be settled by judicial decision. In these cases our province is to determine whether this income tax on the revenue from property does or does not belong to the class of direct taxes. If it does, it is, being unapportioned, in violation of the Constitution, and we must so declare.

Differences have often occurred in this court—differences exist now—but there has never been a time in its history when there has been a difference of opinion as to its duty to announce its deliberate conclusions unaffected by considerations not pertaining to the case in hand. . . .

Our conclusions may, therefore, be summed up as follows:

First. We adhere to the opinion already announced, that, taxes on real estate being indisputably direct taxes, taxes on the rents or income of real estate are equally direct taxes.

Second. We are of opinion that taxes on personal property, or on the income of personal property, are likewise direct taxes.

Third. The tax imposed by sections twenty-seven to thirty-seven, inclusive, of the act of 1894, so far as it falls on the income of real estate and of personal property, being a direct tax within the meaning of the Constitution, and, therefore, unconstitutional and void because not apportioned according to representation, all those sections, constituting one entire scheme of taxation, are necessarily invalid. . . .

Justice Harlan dissenting:

In my judgment—to say nothing of the disregard of the former adjudications of this court, and of the settled practice of the government—this decision may well excite the gravest apprehensions. It strikes at the very foundations of national authority, in that it denies to the general government a power which is, or may become, vital to the very existence and preservation of the Union in a national emergency, such as that of war with a great commercial nation, during which the collection of all duties upon imports will cease or be materially diminished. It tends to reestablish that condition of helplessness in which Congress found itself during the period of the Articles of Confederation, when it was without authority by laws operating directly upon individuals, to lay and collect, through its own agents, taxes sufficient to pay the debts and defray the expenses of government, but was dependent, in all such matters, upon the good will of the States, and their promptness in meeting requisitions made upon them by Congress. . . .

I cannot assent to an interpretation of the Constitution that impairs and cripples the just powers of the National Government in the essential matter of taxation, and at the same time discriminates against the greater part of the people of our country.

The practical effect of the decision to-day is to give to certain kinds of property a position of favoritism and advantage inconsistent with the fundamental principles of our social organization, and to invest them with power and influence that may be perilous to that portion of the American people upon whom rests the larger part of the burdens of the government, and who ought not to be subjected to the dominion of aggregated wealth any more than the property of the country should be at the mercy of the lawless.

139   *Ritchie v. People (1895)*

By the early 1890s, reformers had begun to push protective legislation as a means of ameliorating some of the harsher aspects of industrial life, and the popular press began to expose the terrible conditions in factories and sweatshops. With public attention focused on industrial conditions, reformers called for legislation to limit the working hours of women. An 1893 Illinois law prohibiting the employment of women in factories or workshops for more than eight hours a day or forty-eight hours a week is typical of the early laws on the subject.

One should note that nearly all of the early protective statutes were state legislation, and thus challenges to them arose in the state courts, which would judge them both on state and federal constitutional grounds. Very often the state constitutions explicitly permitted such laws, and liberal courts upheld the laws on state grounds. Conservative courts, on the other hand, would strike them down using the Due Process Clause of the Fourteenth Amendment. Under the rules of the United States Supreme Court at that time, state court decisions nullifying statutes on either state or federal grounds were not reviewable. If statutes were upheld at the state level, however, the opponents could appeal on federal grounds to the Supreme Court. This made state courts in the Progressive Era the primary battlegrounds for arguing the constitutionality of the many laws passed in response to industrial conditions.

In striking down this law as an unconstitutional infringement of liberty of contract, the Illinois Supreme Court provided a strategic model for other courts opposed to protective legislation. The court would concede the existence of the police power, but then subject it to tests of directness and reasonability, which, of course, the statute failed. *Ritchie* elicited an enormous chorus of public protest from labor and reform groups, but the Illinois tribunal refused to reverse its position until after the Supreme Court decision in *Muller* v. *Oregon* (Document 147).

See Judith A. Baer, *The Chains of Protection: The Judicial Response to Women's Labor Legislation* (1978); Melvin I. Urofsky, "State Courts and Protective Legislation," 72 *Journal of American History* 63 (1985); and Susan Lehrer, *Origins of Protective Legislation for Women* (1987).

————

Justice Magruder:

It is contended by counsel for plaintiff in error that that section is unconstitutional as imposing unwarranted restrictions upon the right to contract. On the other hand, it is claimed by counsel for the people that the section is a sanitary provision, and justifiable as an exercise of the police power of the state. Does the provision in question restrict the right to contract? The words, "no female shall be employed," import action on the part of two persons. There must be a person who does the act of employing and a person who consents to the act of being employed. . . . The prohibition of the statute is therefore twofold: First, that no manufacturer or proprietor of a factory or workshop shall employ any female therein more than eight hours in one day; and, second, that no female shall consent to be so employed. It thus prohibits employer and employé from uniting their minds or agreeing upon any longer service during one day than eight hours. . . . Section 5 does limit and restrict the right of the manufacturer and his employé to contract with each other in reference to the hours of labor.

Is the restriction thus imposed an infringement upon the constitutional rights of the manufacturer and the employé? Section 2 of article 2 of the constitution of Illinois pro-

Source: 155 Ill. 98 (1895)

vides that "no person shall be deprived of life, liberty or property, without due process of law." . . . The privilege of contracting is both a liberty and property right. . . . Liberty includes the right to acquire property, and that means and includes the right to make and enforce contracts. . . . The right to use, buy, and sell property and contract in respect thereto is protected by the constitution. Labor is property, and the laborer has the same right to sell his labor, and to contract with reference thereto, as has any other property owner. In this country the legislature has no power to prevent persons who are sui juris from making their own contracts, nor can it interfere with the freedom of contract between the workman and the employer. The right to labor or employ labor, and make contracts in respect thereto upon such terms as may be agreed upon between the parties, is included in the constitutional guaranty above quoted. . . .

We are not unmindful that the right to contract may be subject to limitations growing out of the duties which the individual owes to society, to the public, or the government. These limitations are sometimes imposed by the obligation to so use one's own as not to injure another, by the character of property as affected with a public interest or devoted to a public use, by the demands of public policy or the necessity of protecting the public from fraud or injury, by the want of capacity, by the needs of the necessitous borrower as against the demands of the extortionate lender. But the power of the legislature to thus limit the right to contract must rest upon some reasonable basis, and cannot be arbitrarily exercised. It has been said that such power is based in every case on some condition, and not on the absolute right to control. Where legislative enactments, which operate upon classes of individuals only, have been held to be valid, it has been where the classification was reasonable, and not arbitrary. . . .

Applying these principles to the consideration of section 5, we are led irresistibly to the conclusion that it is an unconstitutional and void enactment. . . .

. . . This enactment is a purely arbitrary restriction upon the fundamental rights of the citizen to control his or her own time and faculties. It substitutes the judgment of the legislature for the judgment of the employer and employé in a matter about which they are competent to agree with each other. It assumes to dictate to what extent the capacity to labor may be exercised by the employé, and takes away the right of private judgment as to the amount and duration of the labor to be put forth in a specified period. Where the legislature thus undertakes to impose an unreasonable and unnecessary burden upon any one citizen or class of citizens it transcends the authority intrusted to it by the constitution, even though it imposes the same burden upon all other citizens or classes of citizens. General laws may be as tyrannical as partial laws. . . .

But it is claimed on behalf of defendant in error that this section can be sustained as on exercise of the police power of the state. The police power of the state is that power which enables it to promote the health, comfort, safety, and welfare of society. It is very broad and farreaching, but is not without its limitations. Legislative acts passed in pursuance of it must not be in conflict with the constitution, and must have some relation to the ends sought to be accomplished; that is to say, to the comfort, welfare, or safety of society. Where the ostensible object of an enactment is to secure the public comfort, welfare, or safety, it must appear to be adapted to that end. It cannot invade the rights of persons and property under the guise of a mere police regulation, when it is not such in fact; and where such an act takes away the property of a citizen or interferes with his personal liberty, it is the province of the courts to determine whether it is really an appropriate measure for the promotion of the comfort, safety, and welfare of society. . . . There is nothing in the title of the act of 1893 to indicate that it is a sanitary measure. The first three sections contain provisions for keeping workshops in a cleanly state, and for inspection to ascertain whether they are so kept. But there is nothing in the nature of the employment contemplated by the act which is in itself unhealthy or unlawful or injurious to the public morals or welfare. . . . It is not the nature of the things done, but the sex of the persons doing them, which is made the basis of the claim that the act is a measure for the promotion of the public health. It is sought to sustain the act as an exercise of the police power upon the alleged ground that it is designed to protect woman on account of her sex and physique. It will not be denied that woman is entitled to the same rights, under the constitution, to make contracts with reference to her labor, as are secured thereby to men. . . . It has been held that a woman is both a "citizen" and a "person" within the meaning of [the Fourteenth Amendment]. . . . As a "citizen," woman has the right to acquire and possess property of every kind. As a "person," she has the right to claim the benefit of the constitutional provision that she shall not be deprived of life, liberty, or property without due process of law. Involved in these rights thus guarantied to her is the right to make and enforce contracts. The law accords to her, as to every other citizen, the right to gain a livelihood by intelligence, honesty, and industry in the arts, the sciences, the professions, or other vocations. Before the law, her right to a choice of vocations cannot be said to be denied or abridged on account of sex. . . . As a general thing, it is the province of the legislature to determine what regulations are necessary to protect the public health and secure the public safety and welfare. But, inasmuch as sex is no bar, under the constitution and law, to the endowment of woman with the fundamental and inalienable rights of liberty and property, which include the right to make her own contracts, the mere fact of sex will not justify the legislature in putting forth the police power of the state for the purpose of limiting her exercise of those rights, unless the courts are able to see that there is some fair, just, and reasonable connection between such limitation and the public health, safety, or welfare proposed to be secured by it.

---

140   *Plessy v. Ferguson (1896)*

Although the *Civil Rights Cases* left Congress the power to respond to state-sponsored discrimination, by the 1880s, little interest remained among Northern whites in safeguarding Negro rights. The South, recognizing that it could now deal with race relations without federal interference, began to establish a complex social, legal, and economic system designed to keep blacks in an inferior status. The Court helped this process along in *Hall* v. *DeCuir* (1878), ruling that a state could not prohibit segregation on common carriers, and a dozen years later approved a Mississippi statute requiring segregation in intrastate carriers.

In the best-known of these segregation cases, the majority ruled that distinctions based on race were not unconstitutional, and the Fourteenth Amendment had never been intended to bring about absolute equality. Plessy, a person of mixed blood, was refused a seat in a railroad car reserved for whites, under a Louisiana law requiring racial segregation in public transportation. He sued the state under the Equal Protection Clause of the Fourteenth Amendment, claiming that mandatory segregation was by definition discriminatory. The majority opinion of Justice Brown is notable for its casual indifference to racial discrimination and its obvious bias against the black race. Compare Justice Harlan's eloquent dissent to the majority ruling in *Brown v. Board of Education* (Document 199).

See C. Vann Woodward, *The Strange Career of Jim Crow* (rev. ed., 1966); Pauli Murray, *State Laws on Race and Color* (1952); Joel Williamson, *The Crucible of Race: Black-White Relations in the American South Since Emancipation* (1984); and Charles A. Lofgren, *The Plessy Case* (1987).

———

Justice Brown delivered the opinion of the Court:

This case turns upon the constitutionality of an act of the General Assembly of the State of Louisiana, passed in 1890, providing for separate railway carriages for the white and colored races. . . .

The constitutionality of this act is attacked upon the ground that it conflicts both with the Thirteenth Amendment of the Constitution, abolishing slavery, and the Fourteenth Amendment, which prohibits certain restrictive legislation on the part of the States.

1. That it does not conflict with the Thirteenth Amendment, which abolished slavery and involuntary servitude, except as a punishment for crime, is too clear for argument. . . .

. . . The proper construction of the 14th amendment was first called to the attention of this court in the *Slaughter-house cases,* . . . which involved, however, not a question of race, but one of exclusive privileges. The case did not call for any expression of opinion as to the exact rights it was intended to secure to the colored race, but it was said generally that its main purpose was to establish the citizenship of the negro; to give definitions of citizenship of the United States and of the States, and to protect from the hostile legislation of the States the privileges and immunities of citizens of the United States, as distinguished from those of citizens of the States.

The object of the amendment was undoubtedly to enforce the absolute equality of the two races before the law, but in the nature of things it could not have been intended to abolish distinctions based upon color, or to enforce social, as distinguished from political equality, or a commingling of the two races upon terms unsatisfactory to either.

———

Source: 163 U.S. 537 (1896)

Laws permitting, and even requiring, their separation in places where they are liable to be brought into contact do not necessarily imply the inferiority of either race to the other, and have been generally, if not universally, recognized as within the competency of the state legislatures in the exercise of their police power. The most common instance of this is connected with the establishment of separate schools for white and colored children, which has been held to be a valid exercise of the legislative power even by courts of States where the political rights of the colored race have been longest and most earnestly enforced. . . .

So far, then, as a conflict with the Fourteenth Amendment is concerned, the case reduces itself to the question whether the statute of Louisiana is a reasonable regulation, and with respect to this there must necessarily be a large discretion on the part of the legislature. In determining the question of reasonableness it is at liberty to act with reference to the established usages, customs and traditions of the people, and with a view to the promotion of their comfort, and the preservation of the public peace and good order. Gauged by this standard, we cannot say that a law which authorizes or even requires the separation of the two races in public conveyances is unreasonable, or more obnoxious to the Fourteenth Amendment than the acts of Congress requiring separate schools for colored children in the District of Columbia, the constitutionality of which does not seem to have been questioned, or the corresponding acts of state legislatures.

We consider the underlying fallacy of the plaintiff's argument to consist in the assumption that the enforced separation of the two races stamps the colored race with a badge of inferiority. If this be so, it is not by reason of anything found in the act, but solely because the colored race chooses to put that construction upon it. The argument necessarily assumes that if, as has been more than once the case, and is not unlikely to be so again, the colored race should become the dominant power in the state legislature, and should enact a law in precisely similar terms, it would thereby relegate the white race to an inferior position. We imagine that the white race, at least, would not acquiesce in this assumption. The argument also assumes that social prejudices may be overcome by legislation, and that equal rights cannot be secured to the negro except by an enforced commingling of the two races. We cannot accept this proposition. If the two races are to meet upon terms of social equality, it must be the result of natural affinities, a mutual appreciation of each other's merits and a voluntary consent of individuals. . . . Legislation is powerless to eradicate racial instincts or to abolish distinctions based upon physical differences, and the attempt to do so can only result in accentuating the difficulties of the present situation. If the civil and political rights of both races be equal one cannot be inferior to the other civilly or politically. If one race be inferior to the other socially, the Constitution of the United States cannot put them upon the same plane. . . .

Justice Harlan, dissenting:

While there may be in Louisiana persons of different races who are not citizens of the United States, the words in the act, "white and colored races," necessarily include all citizens of the United States of both races residing in that State. So that we have before us a state enactment that compels, under penalties, the separation of the two races in railroad passenger coaches, and makes it a crime for a citizen of either race to enter a coach that has been assigned to citizens of the other race. . . .

In respect of civil rights, common to all citizens, the Constitution of the United States does not, I think, permit any public authority to know the race of those entitled to be protected in the enjoyment of such rights. Every true man has pride of race, and under appropriate circumstances when the rights of others, his equals before the law, are not to be affected, it is his privilege to express such pride and to take such action based upon it as to him seems proper. But I deny that any legislative body or judicial tribunal may have regard to the race of citizens when the civil rights of those citizens are involved. Indeed, such legislation, as that here in question, is inconsistent not only with that equality of rights which pertains to citizenship, National and State, but with the personal liberty enjoyed by every one within the United States. . . .

The white race deems itself to be the dominant race in this country. And so it is, in prestige, in achievements, in education, in wealth and in power. So, I doubt not, it will continue to be for all time, if it remains true to its great heritage and holds fast to the principles of constitutional liberty. But in view of the Constitution, in the eye of the law, there is in this country no superior, dominant, ruling class of citizens. There is no caste here. Our Constitution is color-blind, and neither knows nor tolerates classes among citizens. In respect of civil rights, all citizens are equal before the law. The humblest is the peer of the most powerful. The law regards man as man, and takes no account of his surroundings or of his color when his civil rights as guaranteed by the supreme law of the land are involved. It is, therefore, to be regretted that this high tribunal, the final expositor of the fundamental law of the land, has reached the conclusion that it is competent for a State to regulate the enjoyment by citizens of their civil rights solely upon the basis of race.

In my opinion, the judgment this day rendered will, in time, prove to be quite as pernicious as the decision made by this tribunal in the *Dred Scott case*. . . . The present decision, it may well be apprehended, will not only stimulate aggressions, more or less brutal and irritating, upon the admitted rights of colored citizens, but will encourage the belief that it is possible, by means of state enactments, to defeat the beneficent purposes which the people of the United States had in view when they adopted the recent amendments of the Constitution, by one of which the blacks of this country were made citizens of the United States and of the States in which they respectively reside, and whose privileges and immunities, as citizens, the States are forbidden to abridge. Sixty millions of whites are in no danger from the presence here of eight millions of blacks. The destinies of the two races, in this country, are indissolubly linked together, and the interests of both require that the common government of all shall not permit the seeds of race hate to be planted under the sanction of law. What can more certainly arouse race hate, what more certainly create and perpetuate a feeling of distrust between these races, than state enactments, which, in fact, proceed on the ground that colored citizens are so inferior and degraded that they cannot be allowed to sit in public coaches occupied by white citizens? That, as all will admit, is the real meaning of such legislation as was enacted in Louisiana. . . .

If evils will result from the commingling of the two races upon public highways established for the benefit of all, they will be infinitely less than those that will surely come from state legislation regulating the enjoyment of civil rights upon the basis of race. We boast of the freedom enjoyed by our people above all other peoples. But it is difficult to reconcile that boast with a state of the law which, practically, puts the brand of servitude and degradation upon a large class of our fellow-citizens, our equals before the law. . . .

I am of opinion that the statute of Louisiana is inconsistent with the personal liberty of citizens, white and black, in that State, and hostile to both the spirit and letter of the Constitution of the United States. If laws of like character should be enacted in the several States of the Union, the effect would be in the highest degree mischievous. Slavery, as an institution tolerated by law would, it is true, have disappeared from our country, but there would remain a power in the States, by sinister legislation, to interfere with the full enjoyment of the blessings of freedom; to regulate civil rights, common to all citizens upon the basis of race; and to place in a condition of legal inferiority a large body of American citizens, now constituting a part of the political community called the People of the United States, for whom, and by whom through representatives, our government is administered.

141 *People's Party Platform (1896)*

Farmers as a group did not share in the general prosperity of the latter nineteenth century, and beginning in the 1870s, attempted in a number of ways to mount an effective political campaign to rectify the corruption of government and economic power they attributed to big business and railroads. The most successful of these agrarian revolts was the People's party, which, after the 1892 presidential campaign, appeared to have the strength to become a potent force in American politics.

The People's party platform of that year is notable for several reasons. First, it summed up two decades of resentment by the farmers against a system that they believed ignored their needs and exploited them mercilessly. Several of their complaints were directed against the structure and operation of government, including what they believed to be the unfair actions of the courts against labor. The demand for an income tax, of course, was a direct response to the Pollock case. One should also note how many of these proposals, such as the direct election of senators, moved into the mainstream of American reform and were adopted over the next generation.

See John D. Hicks, *The Populist Revolt* (1931); Richard Hofstadter, *The Age of Reform* (1955); and Lawrence Goodwyn, *The Populist Movement* (1978).

———

The People's Party, assembled in National Convention, reaffirms its allegiance to the principles declared by the founders of the Republic, and also to the fundamental principles of just government as enunciated in the platform of the party in 1892.

Source: Johnson and Porter, eds., *National Party Platforms, 1840–1972* 104 (1973)

We recognize that through the connivance of the present and preceding Administrations the country has reached a crisis in its National life, as predicted in our declaration four years ago, and that prompt and patriotic action is the supreme duty of the hour.

We realize that, while we have political independence, our financial and industrial independence is yet to be attained by restoring to our country the Constitutional control and exercise of the functions necessary to a people's government, which functions have been basely surrendered by our public servants to corporate monopolies. The influence of European moneychangers has been more potent in shaping legislation than the voice of the American people. Executive power and patronage have been used to corrupt our legislatures and defeat the will of the people, and plutocracy has thereby been enthroned upon the ruins of democracy. To restore the Government intended by the fathers, and for the welfare and prosperity of this and future generations, we demand the establishment of an economic and financial system which shall make us masters of our own affairs and independent of European control, by the adoption of the following declaration of principles:

The Finances

1. We demand a National money, safe and sound, issued by the General Government only, without the intervention of banks of issue, to be a full legal tender for all debts, public and private; a just, equitable, and efficient means of distribution, direct to the people, and through the lawful disbursements of the Government.

2. We demand the free and unrestricted coinage of silver and gold at the present legal ratio of 16 to 1, without waiting for the consent of foreign nations.

3. We demand that the volume of circulating medium be speedily increased to an amount sufficient to meet the demand of the business and population, and to restore the just level of prices of labor and production.

4. We denounce the sale of bonds and the increase of the public interest-bearing debt made by the present Administration as unnecessary and without authority of law, and demand that no more bonds be issued, except by specific act of Congress.

5. We demand such legislation as will prevent the demonetization of the lawful money of the United States by private contract.

6. We demand that the Government, in payment of its obligation, shall use its option as to the kind of lawful money in which they are to be paid, and we denounce the present and preceding Administrations for surrendering this option to the holders of Government obligations.

7. We demand a graduated income tax, to the end that aggregated wealth shall bear its just proportion of taxation, and we regard the recent decision of the Supreme Court relative to the income-tax law as a misinterpretation of the Constitution and an invasion of the rightful powers of Congress over the subject of taxation.

8. We demand that postal savings-banks be established by the Government for the safe deposit of the savings of the people and to facilitate exchange.

Railroads and Telegraphs

1. Transportation being a means of exchange and a public necessity, the Government should own and operate the railroads in the interest of the people and on a non-partisan basis, to the end that all may be accorded the same treatment in transportation, and that the tyranny and political power now exercised by the great railroad corporations, which result in the impairment, if not the destruction of the political rights and personal liberties of the citizens, may be destroyed. Such ownership is to be accomplished gradually, in a manner consistent with sound public policy.

2. The interest of the United States in the public highways built with public moneys, and the proceeds of grants of land to the Pacific railroads, should never be alienated, mortgaged, or sold, but guarded and protected for the general welfare, as provided by the laws organizing such railroads. The foreclosure of existing liens of the United States on these roads should at once follow default in the payment thereof by the debtor companies; and at the foreclosure sales of said roads the Government shall purchase the same, if it becomes necessary to protect its interests therein, or if they can be purchased at a reasonable price; and the Government shall operate said railroads as public highways for the benefit of the whole people, and not in the interest of the few, under suitable provisions for protection of life and property, giving to all transportation interests equal privileges and equal rates for fares and freight.

3. We denounce the present infamous schemes for refunding these debts, and demand that the laws now applicable thereto be executed and administered according to their intent and spirit.

4. The telegraph, like the Post Office system, being a necessity for the transmission of news, should be owned and operated by the Government in the interest of the people.

The Public Lands

1. True policy demands that the National and State legislation shall be such as will ultimately enable every prudent and industrious citizen to secure a home, and therefore the land should not be monopolized for speculative purposes. All lands now held by railroads and other corporations in excess of their actual needs should by lawful means be reclaimed by the Government and held for actual settlers only, and private land monopoly, as well as alien ownership, should be prohibited.

2. We condemn the land grant frauds by which the Pacific railroad companies have, through the connivance of the Interior Department, robbed multitudes of *bona-fide* settlers of their homes and miners of their claims, and we demand legislation by Congress which will enforce the exemption of mineral land from such grants after as well before the patent.

3. We demand that *bona-fide* settlers on all public lands be granted free homes, as provided in the National Homestead Law, and that no exception be made in the case of Indian reservations when opened for settlement, and that all lands not now patented come under this demand.

The Referendum

We favor a system of direct legislation through the initiative and referendum, under proper Constitutional safeguards.

Direct Election of President and Senators by the People

We demand the election of President, Vice-President, and United States Senators by a direct vote of the people. . . .

The Territories

We favor home rule in the Territories and the District of Columbia, and the early admission of the Territories as States.

Public Salaries

All public salaries should be made to correspond to the price of labor and its products.

Employment to Be Furnished by Government

In times of great industrial depression, idle labor should be employed on public works as far as practicable.

Arbitrary Judicial Action

The arbitrary course of the courts in assuming to imprison citizens for indirect contempt and ruling by injunction should be prevented by proper legislation.

Pensions

We favor just pensions for our disabled Union soldiers.

A Fair Ballot

Believing that the elective franchise and an untrammeled ballot are essential to a government of, for, and by the people, the People's party condemns the wholesale system of disfranchisement adopted in some States as unrepublican and undemocratic, and we declare it to be the duty of the several State legislatures to take such action as will secure a full, free and fair ballot and an honest count.

The Financial Question "The Pressing Issue"

While the foregoing propositions constitute the platform upon which our party stands, and for the vindication of which its organization will be main tained, we recognize that the great and pressing issue of the pending campaign, upon which the present election will turn, is the financial question, and upon this great and specific issue between the parties we cordially invite the aid and co-operation of all organizations and citizens agreeing with us upon this vital question.

---

142   *Allgeyer v. Louisiana (1897)*

The triumph of substantive due process came in a case involving a state law that banned insurance sales by companies not licensed by the state to do business in Louisiana. The Allgeyer Company (a Louisiana firm) had notified a New York marine insurance company (not licensed in Louisiana) that it would be shipping certain goods; this letter met the notice requirement of the policy Allgeyer had with the company. For this Allgeyer was convicted of violating the Louisiana statute for doing business with an unlicensed company, and he sued on the basis that the law infringed his right to do business with whom he pleased.

Justice Rufus Peckham, who had gained fame as an ultraconservative judge in New York before his appointment to the high court in 1895, had long before been converted to the idea of substantive due process, and in this case merged that notion with the equally potent notion of freedom of contract to strike down the state law. While the results might be interpreted as the Court thwarting local provincialism in order to protect national commerce, in fact with this ruling, the conservatives now had an extremely effective weapon to use against the tide of Progressive reform that would soon beset them.

See Edward Keynes, *Liberty, Property and Privacy* (1996); James W. Ely, Jr., *The Guardian of Every Other Right* (2nd ed., 1998); and Edward S. Corwin, *Liberty Against Government* (1948).

———

Justice Peckham delivered the opinion of the Court:

In this case the only act which it is claimed was a violation of the statute in question consisted in sending the letter through the mail notifying the company of the property to be covered by the policy already delivered. We have then a contract which it is conceded was made outside and beyond the limits of the jurisdiction of the State of Louisiana, being made and to be performed within the State of New York, where the premiums were to be paid and losses, if any, adjusted. . . .

It is natural that the state court should have remarked that there is in this "statute an apparent interference with the liberty of defendants in restricting their rights to place insurance on property of their own whenever and in what company they desired." Such interference is not only apparent, but it is real, and we do not think that it is justified for the purpose of upholding what the State says is its policy with regard to foreign insurance companies which had not complied with the laws of the State for doing business within its limits. In this case the company did no business within the State, and the contracts were not therein made.

The Supreme Court of Louisiana says that the act of writing within that State, the letter of notification, was an act therein done to effect an insurance on property then in the State, in a marine insurance company which had not complied with its laws, and such act was, therefore, prohibited by the statute. As so construed we think the statute is a violation of the Fourteenth Amendment of the Federal Constitution, in that it deprives the defendants of their liberty without due process of law. The statute which forbids such act does not become due process of law, because it is inconsistent with the provisions of the Constitution of the Union. The liberty mentioned in that amendment means not only the right of the citizen to be free from the mere physical restraint of his person, as by incarceration, but the term is deemed to embrace the right of the citizen to be free in the enjoyment of all his faculties; to be free to use them in all lawful ways; to live and work where he will; to earn his livelihood by any lawful calling; to pursue any livelihood or a vocation, and for that purpose to enter into all contracts which may be proper, necessary and essential to his carrying out to a successful conclusion the purposes above mentioned. . . .

Has not a citizen of a State, under the provisions of the Federal Constitution above mentioned, a right to contract outside of the State for insurance on his property—a right of which state legislation cannot deprive him? . . . When we speak of the liberty to contract for insurance or to do an act to effectuate such a contract already existing, we refer to and have in mind the facts of this case, where the contract was made outside the State, and as such was a valid and proper contract. The act done within the limits of the State

Source: 165 U.S. 578 (1897)

under the circumstances of this case and for the purpose therein mentioned, we hold a proper act, one which the defendants were at liberty to perform and which the state legislature had no right to prevent, at least with reference to the Federal Constitution. To deprive the citizen of such a right as herein described without due process of law is illegal. Such a statute as this in question is not due process of law, because it prohibits an act which under the Federal Constitution the defendants had a right to perform. This does not interfere in any way with the acknowledged right of the State to enact such legislation in the legitimate exercise of its police or other powers as to it may seem proper. In the exercise of such right, however, care must be taken not to infringe upon those other rights of the citizen which are protected by the Federal Constitution.

143   *Holden v. Hardy (1898)*

While *Allgeyer* (Document 142) and *Lochner* (Document 146) epitomized the conservative, pro-property views of the Supreme Court at this time, the justices did in fact recognize that changing industrial and economic conditions had to be taken into account in assessing the states' use of their police powers. In Utah, the state constitution required the legislature to "pass laws to provide for the health and safety of the employees in factories, smelters and mines." The state high court had upheld the provision and resulting hours laws as a legitimate exercise of the police power, and the smelter owner appealed to the Supreme Court on Fourteenth Amendment grounds.

Not only did the Supreme Court uphold the state court decision by a seven-to-two vote, but Justice Brown's opinion is unusual in its recognition of the disparities existing between employer and employee and his ruling that discretion over how to deal with that disparity lay in the legislative process. Holden became the model for numerous state and federal court decisions upholding protective legislation.

See John Semonche, *Charting the Future* (1978); Melvin I. Urofsky, "Myth and Reality: The Supreme Court and Protective Legislation," *Yearbook of the Supreme Court Historical Society* 53 (1983); T. M. Marshall, "The Miners' Law of Colorado," 25 *American Historical Review* 426 (1920); and William J. Novak, *The People's Welfare* (1996).

———

Justice Brown delivered the opinion of the Court:
This case involves the constitutionality of an act of the legislature of Utah, of March

Source: 169 U.S. 366 (1898)

30, 1896, c. 72, entitled "An act regulating the hours of employment in underground mines and in smelters and ore reduction works." . . .

The validity of the statute in question is, however, challenged upon the ground of an alleged violation of the Fourteenth Amendment to the Constitution of the United States, in that it abridges the privileges or immunities of citizens of the United States; deprives both the employer and the laborer of his property without due process of law, and denies to them the equal protection of the laws. As the three questions of abridging their immunities, depriving them of their property, and denying them the protection of the laws, are so connected that the authorities upon each are, to a greater or less extent, pertinent to the others, they may properly be considered together.

Prior to the adoption of the Fourteenth Amendment there was a similar provision against deprivation of life, liberty or property without due process of law incorporated in the Fifth Amendment; but as the first eight amendments to the Constitution were obligatory only upon Congress, the decisions of this court under this amendment have but a partial application to the Fourteenth Amendment, which operates only upon the action of the several States. The Fourteenth Amendment, which was finally adopted July 28, 1868, largely expanded the power of the Federal courts and Congress, and for the first time authorized the former to declare invalid all laws and judicial decisions of the States abridging the rights of citizens or denying them the benefit of due process of law. . . .

An examination of . . . cases under the Fourteenth Amendment will demonstrate that, in passing upon the validity of state legislation under that amendment, this court has not failed to recognize the fact that the law is, to a certain extent, a progressive science; that in some of the States methods of procedure, which at the time the Constitution was adopted were deemed essential to the protection and safety of the people, or to the liberty of the citizen, have been found to be no longer necessary; that restrictions which had formerly been laid upon the conduct of individuals, or of classes of individuals, had proved detrimental to their interests; while, upon the other hand, certain other classes of persons, particularly those engaged in dangerous or unhealthful employments, have been found to be in need of additional protection. . . .

Of course, it is impossible to forecast the character or extent of these changes, but in view of the fact that from the day Magna Charta was signed to the present moment, amendments to the structure of the law have been made with increasing frequency, it is impossible to suppose that they will not continue, and the law be forced to adapt itself to new conditions of society, and, particularly, to the new relations between employers and employés, as they arise. . . .

This court has never attempted to define with precision the words "due process of law," nor is it necessary to do so in this case. It is sufficient to say that there are certain immutable principles of justice which inhere in the very idea of free government which no member of the Union may disregard, as that no man shall be condemned in his person or property without due notice and an opportunity of being heard in his defence. . . .

As the possession of property, of which a person cannot be deprived, doubtless implies that such property may be acquired, it is safe to say that a state law which undertakes to deprive any class of persons of the general power to acquire property would also be obnoxious to the same provision. Indeed, we may go a step further, and say that, as property can only be legally acquired as between living persons by contract, a general prohibition against entering into contracts with respect to property, or having as their object the acquisition of property, would be equally invalid. . . .

This right of contract, however, is itself subject to certain limitations which the State may lawfully impose in the exercise of its police powers. While this power is inherent in all governments, it has doubtless been greatly expanded in its application during the past century, owing to an enormous increase in the number of occupations which are dangerous, or so far detrimental to the health of employés as to demand special precautions for their well-being and protection, or the safety of adjacent property. While this court has held, notably in the cases *Davidson* v. *New Orleans,* . . . and *Yick Wo* v. *Hopkins,* . . . that the police power cannot be put forward as an excuse for oppressive and unjust legislation, it may be lawfully resorted to for the purpose of preserving the public health, safety or morals, or the abatement of public nuisances, and a large discretion "is necessarily vested in the legislature to determine not only what the interests of the public require, but what measures are necessary for the protection of such interests." . . .

While the business of mining coal and manufacturing iron began in Pennsylvania as early as 1716, and in Virginia, North Carolina and Massachusetts even earlier than this, both mining and manufacturing were carried on in such a limited way and by such primitive methods that no special laws were considered necessary, prior to the adoption of the Constitution, for the protection of the operatives; but, in the vast proportions which these industries have since assumed, it has been found that they can no longer be carried on with due regard to the safety and health of those engaged in them, without special protection against the dangers necessarily incident to these employments. In consequence of this, laws have been enacted in most of the States designed to meet these exigencies and to secure the safety of persons peculiarly exposed to these dangers. Within this general category are ordinances providing for fire escapes for hotels, theatres, factories and other large buildings, a municipal inspection of boilers, and applicances designed to secure passengers upon railways and steamboats against the dangers necessarily incident to these methods of transportation. In States where manufacturing is carried on to a large extent, provision is made for the protection of dangerous machinery against accidental contact, for the cleanliness and ventilation of working rooms, for the guarding of well holes, stairways, elevator shafts and for the employment of sanitary appliances. In others, where mining is the principal industry, special provision is made for the shoring up of dangerous walls, for ventilation shafts, bore holes, escapement shafts, means of signalling the surface, for the supply of fresh air and the elimination, as far as possible, of dangerous gases, for safe means of hoisting and lowering cages, for a limitation upon the number of persons permitted to enter a cage, that cages shall be covered, and that there shall be fences and gates around the top of shafts, besides other similar precautions. . . .

But if it be within the power of a legislature to adopt such means for the protection of the lives of its citizens, it is difficult to see why precautions may not also be adopted for the protection of their health and morals. It is as much for the interest of the State that the public health should be preserved as that life should be made secure. . . .

Upon the principles above stated, we think the act in question may be sustained as a valid exercise of the police power of the State. The enactment does not profess to limit the hours of all workmen, but merely those who are employed in underground mines, or in the smelting, reduction or refining of ores or metals. These employments, when too long pursued, the legislature has judged to be detrimental to the health of the employés, and, so long as there are reasonable grounds for believing that this is so, its decision upon this subject cannot be reviewed by the Federal courts. . . .

We are of opinion that the act in question was a valid exercise of the police power of the State, and the judgments of the Supreme Court of Utah are, therefore,

Affirmed.

Mr. Justice Brewer and Mr. Justice Peckham dissented.

---

144   Northern Securities Co. v. United States (1904)

The obviously cramped reasoning of the *Knight* case (Document 136) flew in the face of reason, and the Court began its retreat from that reasoning in *Addystone Pipe & Steel Co. v. United States* in 1899. There it upheld an extremely well-reasoned opinion by Circuit Court Judge William Howard Taft that carefully detailed the connection between commerce and manufacturing in a suit against pipe manufacturers who had divided into the market. Although the McKinley administration had essentially considered the Sherman Act a dead letter after *Knight,* the new president, Theodore Roosevelt, decided that *Addystone* might have pumped some vitality back into the law, and his Justice Department launched a series of prosecutions.

Their chief case was against the Northern Securities Company, a railroad combination recently created by the James J. Hill, J. P. Morgan, and Edward H. Harriman interests, and capitalized at $400 million. The open purpose of the merger had been to eliminate competition and to integrate the railroad properties of the Northwest. Justice Harlan's opinion for the five-to-four majority took a far more expansive view of interstate commerce than did *Knight,* but his literalist interpretation of the statute seemed to put almost any business cooperation in danger of prosecution. The dissent by newly appointed Justice Oliver Wendell Holmes, Jr., with its call for a commonsense reading of the law, pointed the way to the rule of reason (Document 149).

See Balthasar H. Meyer, *A History of the Northern Securities Case* (1906); Hans Thorelli, *The Federal Anti-Trust Policy* (1955); Robert H. Bork, *The Antitrust Paradox* (1978); Tony A. Freyer, *Regulating Big Business: Antitrust in Great Britain and America* (1992); and R. W. Appel, Jr., "The Case of the Monopolistic Railroadmen," in John A. Garraty, ed., *Quarrels That Have Shaped the Constitution* (1975).

Justice Harlan delivered the opinion of the Court:

The Government charges that if the combination was held not to be in violation of the act of Congress, then all efforts of the National Government to preserve to the people the benefits of free competition among carriers engaged in interstate commerce will be wholly unavailing, and all transcontinental lines, indeed the entire railway systems of the country, may be absorbed, merged and consolidated, thus placing the public at the absolute mercy of the holding corporation. . . .

In our judgment, the evidence fully sustains the material allegations of the bill, and shows a violation of the act of Congress, in so far as it declares illegal every combination or conspiracy in restraint of commerce among the several States and with foreign nations, and forbids attempts to monopolize such commerce or any part of it. . . .

Is the act to be construed as forbidding every combination or conspiracy in restraint of trade or commerce among the States or with foreign nations? Or, does it embrace only such restraints as are unreasonable in their nature? Is the motive with which a forbidden combination or conspiracy was formed at all material when it appears that the necessary tendency of the particular combination or conspiracy in question is to restrict or suppress free competition between competing railroads engaged in commerce among the States? Does the act of Congress prescribe, as a *rule* for *interstate* or *international* commerce, that the operation of the natural laws of competition between those engaged in *such* commerce shall not be restricted or interfered with by any contract, combination or conspiracy? . . .

. . . Certain propositions are plainly deducible and embrace the present case. Those propositions are:

That although the act of Congress known as the Anti-Trust Act has no reference to the mere manufacture or production of articles or commodities within the limits of the several States, it does embrace and declare to be illegal every contract, combination or conspiracy, in whatever form, of whatever nature, and whoever may be parties to it, which directly or necessarily operates *in restraint* of trade or commerce *among the several States or with foreign nations;*

That the act is not limited to restraints of interstate and international trade or commerce that are unreasonable in their nature, but embraces *all* direct *restraints* imposed by any combination, conspiracy or monopoly upon such trade or commerce;

That railroad carriers engaged in interstate or international trade or commerce are embraced by the act;

That combinations even among *private* manufacturers or dealers whereby *interstate or international commerce* is restrained are equally embraced by the act;

That Congress has the power to establish *rules* by which *interstate and international* commerce shall be governed, and, by the Anti-Trust Act, has prescribed the rule of free competition among those engaged in such commerce;

That *every* combination or conspiracy which would extinguish competition between otherwise competing railroads engaged in *interstate trade or commerce,* and which would *in that way* restrain *such* trade or commerce, is made illegal by the act;

That the natural effect of competition is to increase commerce, and an agreement whose direct effect is to prevent this play of competition restrains instead of promotes trade and commerce;

Source: 193 U.S. 197 (1904)

That to vitiate a combination, such as the act of Congress condemns, it need not be shown that the combination, in fact, results or will result in a total suppression of trade or in a complete monopoly, but it is only essential to show that by its necessary operation it tends to restrain interstate or international trade or commerce or tends to create a monopoly in such trade or commerce and to deprive the public of the advantages that flow from free competition;

That the constitutional guarantee of liberty of contract does not prevent Congress from prescribing the rule of free competition for those engaged in *interstate and international* commerce; and,

That under its power to regulate commerce among the several States and with foreign nations, Congress had authority to enact the statute in question. . . .

The means employed in respect of the combinations forbidden by the Anti-Trust Act, and which Congress deemed germane to the end to be accomplished, was to prescribe as *a rule* for *interstate and international* commerce (not for domestic commerce), that it should not be vexed by combinations, conspiracies or monopolies which restrain commerce by destroying or restricting competition. . . . Now, can this court say that such a rule is prohibited by the Constitution or is not one that Congress could appropriately prescribe when exerting its power under the commerce clause of the Constitution? Whether the free operation of the normal laws of competition is a wise and wholesome rule for trade and commerce is an economic question which this court need not consider or determine. Undoubtedly, there are those who think that the general business interests and prosperity of the country will be best promoted if the rule of competition is not applied. But there are others who believe that such a rule is more necessary in these days of enormous wealth than it ever was in any former period of our history. Be all this as it may, Congress has, in effect, recognized the rule of free competition by declaring illegal every combination or conspiracy in restraint of interstate and international commerce. . . .

Many suggestions were made in argument based upon the thought that the Anti-Trust Act would in the end prove to be mischievous in its consequences. Disaster to business and wide-spread financial ruin, it has been intimated, will follow the execution of its provisions. Such predictions were made in all the cases heretofore arising under that act. But they have not been verified. It is the history of monopolies in this country and in England that predictions of ruin are habitually made by them when it is attempted, by legislation, to restrain their operations and to protect the public against their exactions. In this, as in former cases, they seek shelter behind the reserved rights of the States and even behind the constitutional guarantee of liberty of contract. But this court has heretofore adjudged that the act of Congress did not touch the rights of the States, and that liberty of contract did not involve a right to deprive the public of the advantages of free competition in trade and commerce. Liberty of contract does not imply liberty in a corporation or individuals to defy the national will, when legally expressed. Nor does the enforcement of a legal enactment of Congress infringe, in any proper sense, the general inherent right of every one to acquire and hold property. That right, like all other rights, must be exercised in subordination to the law. . . .

Guided by these long-established rules of construction, it is manifest that if the Anti-Trust Act is held not to embrace a case such as is now before us, the plain intention of the legislative branch of the Government will be defeated. If Congress has not, by the words used in the act, described this and like cases, it would, we apprehend, be impossible to find words that would describe them.

145   *McCray v. United States (1904)*

The Supreme Court had explicitly recognized the existence of a state police power in *Holden,* and in *Champion v. Ames* (1903), it intimated that a federal counterpart existed. While the Constitution did not specifically mention police powers, if such authority resided in the nature of sovereignty, then the federal government had as much claim to enact police measures as did the states. The Court faced the matter directly after Congress passed a measure taxing colored oleomargarine at a higher rate than noncolored. The bill had the obvious purpose not of raising revenue but of destroying any competition between coloured oleo and butter. For a six-to-three majority, Justice White read a very broad authority into the federal government's express power to levy taxes. This case, as well as the expansive interpretations given to the commerce power in *Northern Securities* (Document 144), *Hipolite Egg Co. v. United States* (1911), and *Hoke* v. *United States* (1913), seemed to validate progressive views on the power of the government. (See, however, Document 155.)

See John Semonche, *Charting the Future* (1978); William J. Novak, *The People's Welfare* (1996); and Ernst Freund, *The Police Power* (1904).

———

Justice White delivered the opinion of the Court:

2d. *Did Congress in passing the acts which are assailed, exert a power not conferred by the Constitution? . . .*

The summary which follows embodies the propositions contained in the assignments of error, and the substance of the elaborate argument by which those assignments are deemed to be sustained. Not denying the general power of Congress to impose excise taxes, and conceding that the acts in question, on their face, purport to levy taxes of that character, the propositions are these:

(a) That the power of internal taxation which the Constitution confers on Congress is given to that body for the purpose of raising revenue, and that the tax on artificially colored oleomargarine is void because it is of such an onerous character as to make it manifest that the purpose of Congress in levying it was not to raise revenue but to suppress the manufacture of the taxed article.

(b) The power to regulate the manufacture and sale of oleomargarine being solely reserved to the several States, it follows that the acts in question, enacted by Congress for the purpose of suppressing the manufacture and sale of oleomargarine, when artifi-

Source: 195 U.S. 27 (1904)

cially colored, are void, because usurping the reserved power of the States, and therefore exerting an authority not delegated to Congress by the Constitution. . . .

(d) As the tax levied by the acts which are assailed discriminates against oleomargarine artificially colored, and in favor of butter so colored, and creates an unwarranted and unreasonable distinction between the oleomargarine which is artificially colored and that which is not, and as the necessary operation and effect of the tax is to suppress the manufacture of artificially colored oleomargarine, and to aid the butter industry, therefore the acts are void. And with this proposition in mind it is insisted that wherever the judiciary is called upon to determine whether a power which Congress has exerted is within the authority conferred by the Constitution, the duty is to test the validity of the act, not merely by its face, or to use the words of the argument, "by the label placed upon it by Congress," but by the necessary scope and effect of the assailed enactment.

(e) Admitting that the power to tax as delegated to Congress by the Constitution as originally adopted was subject to no limitation except as expressed in that instrument, the amendments to the Constitution, it is urged, have imposed limitations on the taxing power not expressed in the original Constitution. Under this assumption it is insisted that the acts in question are void, because the burdens which they impose are repugnant to both the Fifth and Tenth Amendments. To the Fifth Amendment, because the amount of the tax is so out of proportion to the value of the property taxed as to destroy that property, and thus amount to a taking thereof without due process of law. To the Tenth Amendment, because the necessary operation and effect of the acts is to destroy the oleomargarine industry and thus exert a power not delegated to Congress, but reserved to the several States.

(f) Although, as a general rule, it be true that the power of Congress to tax, conferred by the Constitution, is unlimited, except as otherwise expressed in that instrument, and conceding, for the sake of the argument, that there is no express limitation either in the original Constitution or in the amendments thereto, by which the acts may be decided to be unconstitutional, nevertheless, it is urged, that, as the burdens which the acts impose are so onerous and so unjust as to be confiscatory, the acts are void, because they amount to a violation of those fundamental rights which it is the duty of every free government to protect. . . .

Whilst, as a result of our written constitution, it is axiomatic that the judicial department of the government is charged with the solemn duty of enforcing the Constitution, and therefore in cases properly presented, of determining whether a given manifestation of authority has exceeded the power conferred by that instrument, no instance is afforded from the foundation of the government where an act, which was within a power conferred, was declared to be repugnant to the Constitution, because it appeared to the judicial mind that the particular exertion of constitutional power was either unwise or unjust. To announce such a principle would amount to declaring that in our constitutional system the judiciary was not only charged with the duty of upholding the Constitution but also with the responsibility of correcting every possible abuse arising from the exercise by the other departments of their conceded authority. So to hold would be to overthrow the entire distinction between the legislative, judicial and executive departments of the government, upon which our system is founded, and would be a mere act of judicial usurpation.

It is, however, argued if a lawful power may be exerted for an unlawful purpose, and thus by abusing the power it may be made to accomplish a result not intended by the

Constitution, all limitations of power must disappear, and the grave function lodged in the judiciary, to confine all the departments within the authority conferred by the Constitution, will be of no avail. This, when reduced to its last analysis, comes to this, that, because a particular department of the government may exert its lawful powers with the object or motive of reaching an end not justified, therefore it becomes the duty of the judiciary to restrain the exercise of a lawful power wherever it seems to the judicial mind that such lawful power has been abused. But this reduces itself to the contention that, under our constitutional system, the abuse by one department of the government of its lawful powers is to be corrected by the abuse of its powers by another department.

The proposition, if sustained, would destroy all distinction between the powers of the respective departments of the government, would put an end to that confidence and respect for each other which it was the purpose of the Constitution to uphold, and would thus be full of danger to the permanence of our institutions. . . .

It is, of course, true, as suggested, that if there be no authority in the judiciary to restrain a lawful exercise of power by another department of the government, where a wrong motive or purpose has impelled to the exertion of the power, that abuses of a power conferred may be temporarily effectual. The remedy for this, however, lies, not in the abuse by the judicial authority of its functions, but in the people, upon whom, after all, under our institutions, reliance must be placed for the correction of abuses committed in the exercise of a lawful power. . . .

The decisions of this court from the beginning lend no support whatever to the assumption that the judiciary may restrain the exercise of lawful power on the assumption that a wrongful purpose or motive has caused the power to be exerted. As we have previously said, from the beginning no case can be found announcing such a doctrine, and on the contrary the doctrine of a number of cases is inconsistent with its existence. . . .

Lastly we come to consider the argument that, even though as a general rule a tax of the nature of the one in question would be within the power of Congress, in this case the tax should be held not to be within such power, because of its effect. This is based on the contention that, as the tax is so large as to destroy the business of manufacturing oleomargarine artificially colored, to look like butter, it thus deprives the manufacturers of that article of their freedom to engage in a lawful pursuit, and hence, irrespective of the distribution of powers made by the Constitution, the taxing laws are void, because they violate those fundamental rights which it is the duty of every free government to safeguard, and which, therefore, should be held to be embraced by implied though none the less potential guaranties, or in any event to be within the protection of the due process clause of the Fifth Amendment.

Let us concede, for the sake of argument only, the premise of fact upon which the proposition is based. Moreover, concede for the sake of argument only, that even although a particular exertion of power by Congress was not restrained by any express limitation of the Constitution, if by the perverted exercise of such power so great an abuse was manifested as to destroy fundamental rights which no free government could consistently violate, that it would be the duty of the judiciary to hold such acts to be void upon the assumption that the Constitution by necessary implication forbade them.

Such concession, however, is not controlling in this case. This follows when the nature of oleomargarine, artificially colored to look like butter, is recalled. As we have said, it has been conclusively settled by this court that the tendency of that article to deceive the public into buying it for butter is such that the States may, in the exertion of their police powers, without violating the due process clause of the Fourteenth Amendment, absolutely prohibit the manufacture of the article. It hence results, that even although it be true that the effect of the tax in question is to repress the manufacture of artificially colored oleomargarine, it cannot be said that such repression destroys rights which no free government could destroy, and, therefore, no ground exists to sustain the proposition that the judiciary may invoke an implied prohibition, upon the theory that to do so is essential to save such rights from destruction. And the same considerations dispose of the contention based upon the due process clause of the Fifth Amendment. That provision, as we have previously said, does not withdraw or expressly limit the grant of power to tax conferred upon Congress by the Constitution. From this it follows, as we have also previously declared, that the judiciary is without authority to avoid an act of Congress exerting the taxing power, even in a case where to the judicial mind it seems that Congress had in putting such power in motion abused its lawful authority by levying a tax which was unwise or oppressive, or the result of the enforcement of which might be to indirectly affect subjects not within the powers delegated to Congress. . . .

The Chief Justice, Mr. Justice Brown and Mr. Justice Peckham dissent.

---

146   *Lochner v. New York (1905)*

A New York statute prohibited the employment of workers in bakeries more than ten hours a day and sixty hours a week, and three New York courts had upheld the law as a valid exercise of the police power. In light of previous high court decisions on hours regulations (Document 143), few people expected that the justices would strike the law down. But the concept of substantive due process reached its apogee in this case, which has been condemned ever since by critics as unwarranted judicial activism. Recent scholarship suggests, however, that there might be more to the case than conservative opposition to regulation per se. Many bakers were women, and in this case Lochner was a baker, not an employer, suing in order to make more money. There is evidence that the law was less an exercise of police power than an effort to force bakeries to accept union standards. Note also the Court's reliance on the freedom of contract idea, as well as substantive due process. In addition, there have been defenders of the Court's reasoning in this case, however estranged it may have been from public sentiment. The dissent by Holmes quickly won the applause of reformers and also became the classic statement of judicial restraint.

See Charles W. McCurdy, "The Roots of Liberty of Contract Reconsidered" *Yearbook of the Supreme Court Historical Society* 20 (1984); Sidney Tarrow, "Lochner Versus New York: A Political Analysis," 5 *Labor History* 277 (1964); Paul Kens, *Judicial Power and Reform Politics* (1990); and Howard Gillman, *The Constitution Besieged* (1993).

———

Justice Peckham delivered the opinion of the Court:

The statute necessarily interferes with the right of contract between the employer and employés. The general right to make a contract in relation to his business is part of the liberty of the individual protected by the 14th Amendment. . . . The right to purchase or to sell labor is part of the liberty protected by this amendment, unless there are circumstances which exclude the right. There are, however, . . . powers relating to the safety, health, morals and general welfare of the public. When the state . . . in the assumed exercise of its police powers, has passed an act which seriously limits the right to labor or the right of contract in regard to their means of livelihood between persons who are sui juris (both employer and employé), it becomes of great importance to determine which shall prevail—the right of the individual to labor for such time as he may choose, or the right of the State to prevent the individual from laboring beyond a certain time prescribed by the State. . . .

It must, of course, be conceded that there is a limit to the valid exercise of the police power. Otherwise the 14th Amendment would have no efficacy and the legislatures of the States would have unbounded power, and it would be enough to say that any piece of legislation was enacted to conserve the morals, the health or the safety of the people. The claim of the police power would be a mere pretext. In every case that comes before this court, therefore, where legislation of this character is concerned, the question necessarily arises: Is this a fair, reasonable and appropriate exercise of the police power of the State, or is it an unreasonable, unnecessary and arbitrary interference with the right of the individual to his personal liberty or to enter into those contracts in relation to labor which may seem to him appropriate or necessary for the support of himself and his family? Of course the liberty of contract relating to labor includes both parties to it. The one has as much right to purchase as the other to sell labor. This is not a question of substituting the judgment of the court for that of the legislature. If the act be within the power of the State it is valid, although the judgment of the court might be totally opposed to the enactment of such a law. But the question would still remain: Is it within the police power of the State? and that question must be answered by the court.

The question whether this act is valid as a labor law, pure and simple, may be dismissed in a few words. There is no reasonable ground for interfering with the liberty of person or the right of free contract, by determining the hours of labor, in the occupation of a baker. There is no contention that bakers as a class are not equal in intelligence and capacity to men in other trades or manual occupations, or that they are not able to assert their rights and care for themselves without the protecting arm of the State, interfering

Source: 198 U.S. 4 (1905)

with their independence of judgment and of action. They are in no sense wards of the State. Viewed in the light of a purely labor law, with no reference whatever to the question of health, we think that a law like the one before us involves neither the safety, the morals nor the welfare of the public, and that the interest of the public is not in the slightest degree affected by such an act. The law must be upheld, if at all, as a law pertaining to the health of the individual engaged in the occupation of a baker. . . . Clean and wholesome bread does not depend upon whether the baker works but ten hours per day or only sixty hours a week. The limitation of the hours of labor does not come within the police power on that ground. The mere assertion that the subject relates though but in a remote degree to the public health does not necessarily render the enactment valid. The act must have a more direct relation, as a means to an end, and the end itself must be appropriate and legitimate, before an act can be held to be valid which interferes with the general right of an individual to be free in his person and in his power to contract in relation to his own labor. . . .

We think the limit of the police power has been reached and passed in this case. There is, in our judgment, no reasonable foundation for holding this to be necessary or appropriate as a health law to safeguard the public health or the health of the individuals who are following the trade of a baker. If this statute be valid, there would seem to be no length to which legislation of this nature might not go. . . .

. . . Not only the hours of employés, but the hours of employers, could be regulated, and doctors, lawyers, scientists, all professional men, as well as athletes and artisans, could be forbidden to fatigue their brains and bodies by prolonged hours of exercise, lest the fighting strength of the State be impaired. We mention these extreme cases because the contention is extreme. We do not believe in the soundness of the views which uphold this law. On the contrary, we think that such a law as this, although passed in the assumed exercise of the police power, and as relating to the public health, or the health of the employés named, is not within that power, and is invalid. The act is not, within any fair meaning of the term, a health law, but is an illegal interference with the rights of individuals, both employers and employés, to make contracts regarding labor upon such terms as they may think best, or which they may agree upon with the other parties to such contracts. . . .

. . . It seems to us that the real object and purpose were simply to regulate the hours of labor between the master and his employés (all being men, sui juris), in a private business, not dangerous in any degree to morals or in any real and substantial degree, to the health of the employés. Under such circumstances the freedom of master and employé to contract with each other in relation to their employment cannot be prohibited or interfered with, without violating the Federal Constitution.

Reversed.

Justice Holmes, dissenting:

This case is decided upon an economic theory which a large part of the country does not entertain. If it were a question whether I agreed with that theory, I should desire to study it further and long before making up my mind. But I do not conceive that to be my duty, because I strongly believe that my agreement or disagreement has nothing to do with the right of a majority to embody their opinions in law. It is settled by various decisions of this court that state constitutions and state laws may regulate life in many ways which we as legislators might think as injudicious or if you like as tyrannical as this, and which equally with this interfere with the liberty to contract. Sunday laws and usury laws are ancient examples. A more modern one is the prohibition of lotteries. The liberty of the citizen to do as he likes so long as he does not interfere with the liberty of others to do the same, which has been a shibboleth for some well-known writers, is interfered with by school laws, by the Post Office, by every state or municipal institution which takes his money for purposes thought desirable, whether he likes it or not. The 14th Amendment does not enact Mr. Herbert Spencer's Social Statics. The other day we sustained the Massachusetts vaccination law. Jacobson v. Massachusetts, 197 U.S. 11. United States and state statutes and decisions cutting down the liberty to contract by way of combination are familiar to this court. The decision sustaining an eight hour law for miners is still recent. Some of these laws embody convictions or prejudices which judges are likely to share. Some may not. But a constitution is not intended to embody a particular economic theory, whether of paternalism and the organic relation of the citizen to the State or of laissez faire. It is made for people of fundamentally differing views, and the accident of our finding certain opinions natural and familiar or novel and even shocking ought not to conclude our judgment upon the question whether statutes embodying them conflict with the Constitution of the United States.

General propositions do not decide concrete cases. The decision will depend on a judgment or intuition more subtle than any articulate major premise. But I think that the proposition just stated, if it is accepted, will carry us far toward the end. Every opinion tends to become a law. I think that the word liberty in the 14th Amendment is perverted when it is held to prevent the natural outcome of a dominant opinion, unless it can be said that a rational and fair man necessarily would admit that the statute proposed would infringe fundamental principles as they have been understood by the traditions of our people and our law. It does not need research to show that no such sweeping condemnation can be passed upon the statute before us. A reasonable man might think it a proper measure on the score of health. Men whom I certainly could not pronounce unreasonable would uphold it as a first instalment of a general regulation of the hours of work. Whether in the latter aspect it would be open to the charge of inequality I think it unnecessary to discuss.

[Justice Harlan also dissented, joined by Justices White and Day.]

---

147   *Muller v. Oregon (1908)*

Justice Harlan had also dissented in *Lochner,* and he suggested that if a valid reason could be found to justify the regulation of hours, it might withstand judicial scrutiny. Moreover, even the very conservative Peckham had conceded that there could be some limits on freedom to contract, but "no limit . . . ought to go beyond necessity." When an Oregon statute establishing a ten-hour working day for women came under attack, the National Consumers' League asked Louis D. Brandeis of Boston of defend it. He picked up on Harlan's suggestion and submitted a highly unusual brief. After only a few pages of legal precedents, he filled almost one hundred pages with sociological, economic, and physiological data to support the legislature's decision to establish maximum hours of women. Justice Brewer's opinion not only acknowledged the brief, a highly unusual step, but conceded that women were different from men; the decision took care, however, not to overrule *Lochner*, although many people assumed that it did. In recent years, feminist writers have attacked *Muller* and similar cases for locking women into an inferior legal position and preventing their achieving legal equality with men. At the time, however, nearly every important women's organization supported maximum hours laws for women.

See Louis D. Brandeis and Josephine Goldmark, *Women in Industry* (1908); Alpheus T. Mason, "The Case of the Overworked Laundress," in John Garraty, ed., *Quarrels That Have Shaped the Constitution* (1975); Judith Baer, *The Chains of Protection* (1978); Vivien Hart, *Bound by the Constitution: Women, Workers, and the Minimum Wage* (1994); and Nancy Erickson, "*Muller v. Oregon* Reconsidered: The Origins of a Sex-Based Doctrine of Liberty of Contract," 30 *Labor History* 228 (1989).

―――――

Justice Brewer delivered the opinion of the Court:

We held in *Lochner v. New York* [1905] that a law providing that no laborer shall be required or permitted to work in a bakery more than sixty hours in a week or ten hours in a day was not as to men a legitimate exercise of the police power of the State, but an unreasonable, unnecessary and arbitrary interference with the right and liberty of the individual to contract in relation to his labor, and as such was in conflict with, and void under, the Federal Constitution. That decision is invoked by plaintiff in error decisive of the question before us. But this assumes that the difference between the sexes does not justify a different rule respecting a restriction of the hours of labor.

In patent cases counsel are apt to open the argument with a discussion of the state of the art. It may not be amiss, in the present case, before examining the constitutional question, to notice the course of legislation as well as expressions of opinion from other than judicial sources. In the brief filed by Mr. Louis D. Brandeis, for the defendant in error, is a very copious collection of all these matters. . . .

The legislation and opinions referred to . . . may not be, technically speaking, authorities, and in them is little or no discussion of the constitutional question presented to us for determination, yet they are significant of a widespread belief that woman's physical structure, and the functions she performs in consequence thereof, justify spe-

―――――

Source: 208 U.S. 412 (1908)

cial legislation restricting or qualifying the conditions under which she should be permitted to toil. Constitutional questions, it is true, are not settled by even a consensus of present public opinion, for it is the peculiar value of a written constitution that it places in unchanging form limitations upon legislative action, and thus gives a permanence and stability to popular government which otherwise would be lacking. At the same time, when a question of fact is debated and debatable, and the extent to which a special constitutional limitation goes is affected by the truth in respect to that fact, a widespread and long continued belief concerning it is worthy of consideration. We take judicial cognizance of all matters of general knowledge.

It is undoubtedly true, as more than once declared by this court, that the general right to contract in relation to one's business is part of the liberty of the individual, protected by the Fourteenth Amendment to the Federal Constitution; yet it is equally well settled that this liberty is not absolute and extending to all contracts, and that a State may, without conflicting with the provisions of the Fourteenth Amendment, restrict in many respects the individual's power of contract. . . .

That woman's physical structure and the performance of maternal functions place her at a disadvantage in the struggle for subsistence is obvious. This is especially true when the burdens of motherhood are upon her. Even when they are not, by abundant testimony of the medical fraternity continuance for a long time on her feet at work, repeating this from day to day, tends to injurious effects upon the body, and as healthy mothers are essential to vigorous offspring, the physical well-being of woman becomes an object of public interest and care in order to preserve the strength and vigor of the race. . . .

. . . The two sexes differ in structure of body, in the functions to be performed by each, in the amount of physical strength, in the capacity for long-continued labor, particularly when done standing, the influence of vigorous health upon the future well-being of the race, the self-reliance which enables one to assert full rights, and in the capacity to maintain the struggle for subsistence. This difference justifies a difference in legislation and upholds that which is designed to compensate for some of the burdens which rest upon her. . . .

For these reasons, and without questioning in any respect the decision in *Lochner v. New York,* we are of the opinion that it cannot be adjudged that the act in question is in conflict with the Federal Constitution, so far as it respects the work of a female in a laundry.

148

Interstate Commerce Commission v. Illinois Central Railroad (1910)

In a series of cases in the 1890s, the Supreme Court stripped away nearly all of the powers Congress had intended for the Interstate Commerce Commission. In *Cinc., N.O. & Tex. Pac. Ry. Co. v. ICC* (1896), the Court denied that the Interstate Commerce Act gave the commission power to fix rates, and the following year, in another case involving the same parties, the Court read a narrow and limited meaning into the ICC's rate authority, saying that the commission could only investigate rates and declare them unreasonable. In 1897, in *ICC v. Ala. Midland Ry. Co.,* the Court cut back the commission's investigatory powers and left the agency nearly useless as a tool of effective regulation.

The problems that the ICC had been created to combat, however, grew worse, and in the Elkins Act of 1903 and the Hepburn Act of 1906, Congress strengthened the ICC at the same time that it limited judicial review of the agency. Eventually the Court accepted the necessity for administrative agencies with some quasijudicial powers. In 1907, it declared it would accept the ICC's findings of facts as conclusive; in the following case, it agreed to allow the ICC the policy-making power that Congress had intended the commission to have.

See Gabriel Kolko, *Railroads and Regulation, 1877–1916* (1965); Ari Hoogenboom and Olive Hoogenboom, *A History of the Interstate Commerce Commission* (1976); the relevant chapters in Stephen Skowronek, ed., *Building a New American State* (1982); and Richard C. Cortner, *The Iron Horse and the Constitution* (1993).

Justice White delivered the opinion of the Court:

In determining whether an order of the commission shall be suspended or set aside, we must consider, *a,* all relevant questions of constitutional power or right; *b,* all pertinent questions as to whether the administrative order is within the scope of the delegated authority under which it purports to have been made; and, *c,* a proposition which we state independently, although in its essence it may be contained in the previous one, viz., whether, even although the order be in form within the delegated power, nevertheless it must be treated as not embraced therein, because the exertion of authority which is questioned has been manifested in such an unreasonable manner as to cause it, in truth, to be within the elementary rule that the substance, and not the shadow, determines the valid-

Source: 215 U.S. 452 (1910)

ity of the exercise of the power. . . . Plain as it is that the powers just stated are of the essence of judicial authority, and which, therefore, may not be curtailed, and whose discharge may not be by us in a proper case avoided, it is equally plain that such perennial powers lend no support whatever to the proposition that we may, under the guise of exerting judicial power, usurp merely administrative functions by setting aside a lawful administrative order upon our conception as to whether the administrative power has been wisely exercised.

Power to make the order and not the mere expediency or wisdom of having made it is the question. . . .

We think the issues for decision will be best disposed of by at once considering the contentions advanced by the railroad company to establish that there was a want of power in the commission to make that portion of the order which the court below enjoined. The contentions on this subject are. . . .

First. That the act to regulate commerce has not delegated to the commission authority to regulate the distribution of company fuel cars in times of car shortage as a means of prohibiting unjust preference or undue discrimination. . . .

The deduction from the proposition is, as the movement of coal under the conditions stated is not commerce, it is therefore not within the authority delegated to the commission by the act of Congress, as all such acts have relation to the regulation of commerce, and do not, therefore, embrace that which is not commerce. It is to be observed, in passing, that if the proposition be well founded, it not only challenges the authority of the commission, but extends much further, and in effect denies the power of Congress to confer authority upon the commission over the subject. . . .

When the erroneous assumption upon which proposition must rest is considered, its unsoundness is readily demonstrable. That assumption is this, that commerce in the constitutional sense only embraces shipment in a technical sense, and does not, therefore, extend to carriers engaged in interstate commerce, certainly in so far as so engaged, and the instrumentalities by which such commerce is carried on, a doctrine the unsoundness of which has been apparent ever since the decision in *Gibbons v. Ogden*. . . . It may not be doubted that the equipment of a railroad company engaged in interstate commerce, included in which are its coal cars, are instruments of such commerce. From this it necessarily follows that such cars are embraced within the governmental power of regulation which extends, in time of car shortage, to compelling a just and equal distribution and the prevention of an unjust and discriminatory one.

The corporation as a carrier engaged in interstate commerce being then, as to its interstate commerce business, subject to the control exerted by the act to regulate commerce, and the instrumentalities employed for the purpose of such commerce, being likewise so subject to control, we are brought to consider the remaining proposition, which is,

Second. That even if power has been delegated to the commission by the act to regulate commerce, the order whose continued enforcement was enjoined by the court below was beyond the authority delegated by the statute.

In view of the facts found by the commission as to preferences and discriminations resulting from the failure to count the company fuel cars in the daily distribution in times of car shortage, and in further view of the far-reaching preferences and discriminations alleged in the answer of the commission in this case, and which must be taken as true as the cause was submitted on bill and answer, it is beyond controversy that the subject with which the order dealt was within the sweeping provisions of § 3 of the act to regulate commerce prohibiting preferences and discriminations. . . .

Mr. Justice Brewer dissented.

149
Standard Oil Co. of New Jersey v. United States (1911)

In his dissent in the *Northern Securities* case (Document 144), Oliver Wendell Holmes had warned that a rigid statutory application of the Sherman Act would lead to business confusion and economic distress, and instead he called for a commonsense interpretation by which the law would operate only against "unreasonable" combinations or restraints. Holmes's suggestion gave the Court the answer it needed in order in avoid, on the one hand, the overly narrow view of commerce it had adopted in *Knight* (Document 136) and, on the other, the broad view in *Northern Securities* tied to a literalist reading of the statute.

Holmes had continued the process of educating the Court, begun in his *Northern Securities* dissent, in his majority opinion in *Swift & Co. v. United States* (1905), when he convinced his brethren of the close connection between commerce in livestock and the butchering business itself, using the analogy of the stockyards as "throats of commerce." Once the Court conceded that a situation existed in which commerce and manufacturing were closely intertwined, it could then determine if a monopoly existed in which the Sherman Act applied.

In *Standard Oil,* a number of these threads came together. The Court adopted the "rule of reason" that Holmes had enunciated in *Northern Securities* and that Theodore Roosevelt had been popularizing in his distinction between "good" and "bad" trusts. After finding that Standard Oil had used questionable and unlawful methods to monopolize the oil industry, the Court ordered the dissolution of the holding company, which left the shareholders of the holding company in ownership of the thirty-four successor companies. Since Standard Oil had been organized along regional lines, the decree, according to some critics, broke up a national monopoly into a series of regional monopolies under common ownership and control. The stock of the company actually rose following the decree.

In his concurrence, Justice Harlan objected to adopting the rule of reason, saying that such a policy-making step should be left to Congress. The legislature had been quite clear, and the courts would now have the power to decide which monopolies were "good" and which "bad," a task they were unsuited to do. Harlan's fears were well founded; within a short time, businesses complained they had no idea of what the law meant or how it would be enforced.

See Hans J. Thorelli, *The Federal Anti-trust Policy* (1955); Simon N. Whitney, *Antitrust Policies—American Experience in Twenty Industries* (1958); Bruce Bringhurst, *Antitrust and the Oil Monopoly* (1979); and James May, "Antitrust in the Formative Era," 50 *Ohio State Law Journal* 257 (1989).

———

Chief Justice White delivered the opinion of the Court:

The debates show that doubt as to whether there was a common law of the United States which governed the subject in the absence of legislation was among the influences leading to the passage of the Act. They conclusively show, however, that the main cause which led to the legislation was the thought that it was required by the economic condition of the times, that is, the vast accumulation of wealth in the hands of corporations and individuals, the enormous development of corporate organization, the facility for combination which such organizations afforded, the fact that the facility was being used, and that combinations known as trusts were being multiplied, and the widespread impression that their power had been and would be exerted to oppress individuals and injure the public generally. . . .

There can be no doubt that the sole subject with which the first section deals is restraint of trade as therein contemplated, and that the attempt to monopolize and monopolization is the subject with which the second section is concerned. It is certain that those terms, at least in their rudimentary meaning, took their origin in the common law, and were also familiar in the law of this country prior to and at the time of the adoption of the act in question. . . .

Without going into detail and but very briefly surveying the whole field, it may be with accuracy said that the dread of enhancement of prices and of other wrongs which it was thought would flow from the undue limitation on competitive conditions caused by contracts or other acts of individuals or corporations, led, as a matter of public policy, to the prohibition or treating as illegal all contracts or acts which were unreasonably restrictive of competitive conditions, either from the nature or character of the contract or act or where the surrounding circumstances were such as to justify the conclusion that they had not been entered into or performed with the legitimate purpose of reasonably forwarding personal interest and developing trade, but on the contrary were of such a character as to give rise to the inference or presumption that they had been entered into or done with the intent to do wrong to the general public and to limit the right of individuals, thus restraining the free flow of commerce and tending to bring about the evils, such as enhancement of prices, which were considered to be against public policy. . . .

———

Source: 221 U.S. 1 (1911)

In view of the common law and the law in this country as to restraint of trade, which we have reviewed, and the illuminating effect which that history must have under the rule to which we have referred, we think it results:

a. That the context manifests that the statute was drawn in the light of the existing practical conception of the law of restraint of trade, because it groups as within that class, not only contracts which were in restraint of trade in the subjective sense, but all contracts or acts which theoretically were attempts to monopolize, yet which in practice had come to be considered as in restraint of trade in a broad sense.

b. That in view of the many new forms of contracts and combinations which were being evolved from existing economic conditions, it was deemed essential by an all-embracing enumeration to make sure that no form of contract or combination by which an undue restraint of interstate or foreign commerce was brought about could save such restraint from condemnation. The statute under this view evidenced the intent not to restrain the right to make and enforce contracts, whether resulting from combination or otherwise, which did not unduly restrain interstate or foreign commerce, but to protect that commerce from being restrained by methods, whether old or new, which would constitute an interference that is an undue restraint.

c. And as the contracts or acts embraced in the provision were not expressly defined, since the enumeration addressed itself simply to classes of acts, those classes being broad enough to embrace every conceivable contract or combination which could be made concerning trade or commerce or the subjects of such commerce, and thus caused any act done by any of the enumerated methods anywhere in the whole field of human activity to be illegal if in restraint of trade, it inevitably follows that the provision necessarily called for the exercise of judgment which required that some standard should be resorted to for the purpose of determining whether the prohibitions contained in the statute had or had not in any given case been violated. Thus not specifying but indubitably contemplating and requiring a standard, it follows that it was intended that the standard of reason which had been applied at the common law and in this country in dealing with subjects of the character embraced by the statute, was intended to be the measure used for the purpose of determining whether in a given case a particular act had or had not brought about the wrong against which the statute provided. . . .

Undoubtedly, the words "to monopolize" and "monopolize" as used in the section reach every act bringing about the prohibited results. The ambiguity, if any, is involved in determining what is intended by monopolize. But this ambiguity is readily dispelled in the light of the previous history of the law of restraint of trade to which we have referred and the indication which it gives of the practical evolution by which monopoly and the acts which produce the same result as monopoly, that is, an undue restraint of the course of trade, all came to be spoken of as, and to be indeed synonymous with, restraint of trade. In other words, having by the first section forbidden all means of monopolizing trade, that is, unduly restraining it by means of every contract, combination, etc., the second section seeks, if possible, to make the prohibitions of the act all the more complete and perfect by embracing all attempts to reach the end prohibited by the first section, that is, restraints of trade, by any attempt to monopolize, or monopolization thereof, even although the acts by which such results are attempted to be brought about or are brought about be not embraced within the general enumeration of the first section. And, of course, when the second section is thus harmonized with and made as it was intended to be the complement of the first, it becomes obvious that the criteria to be resorted to in any given case for the purpose of ascertaining whether violations of the section have been committed, is the rule of reason guided by the established law and by the plain duty to enforce the prohibitions of the act and thus the public policy which its restrictions were obviously enacted to subserve.

150   *Weeks v. United States (1914)*

The Fourth Amendment to the Constitution provides that "the right of the people to be secure in their persons, houses, papers, and effects, against unreasonable searches and seizures, shall not be violated, and no warrants shall issue, but upon probable cause." During the nineteenth century, there had been little litigation of this rule, probably because of the very limited police functions of the federal government. These increased in the twentieth century, however, and in this instance a federal marshal had seized papers without a warrant. In its decision, the Court set forth for the first time the so-called exclusionary rule, which prohibited the use of evidence seized illegally. Then and now, defenders of the rule argue that it is the only effective means to ensure obedience to the Fourth Amendment; critics, however, say that it allows criminals to go free on a technicality.

See Ernest W. Machen, *The Law of Search and Seizure* (1950); Lane V. Sunderland, "The Exclusionary Rule: A Requirement of Constitutional Principle," 69 *Journal of Criminal Law* 141 (1978); and M. A. Quintana, "The Erosion of the Fourth Amendment Exclusionary Rule," 17 *Howard Law Review* 805 (1973).

———

Justice Day delivered the opinion of the Court:
The defendant was arrested by a police officer, so far as the record shows, without warrant, at the Union Station in Kansas City, Missouri, where he was employed by an express company. Other police officers had gone to the house of the defendant and being told by a neighbor where the key was kept, found it and entered the house. They searched the defendant's room and took possession of various papers and articles found there, which were afterwards turned over to the United States Marshal. Later in the same day police officers returned with the Marshal, who thought he might find additional evi-

Source: 232 U.S. 383 (1914)

dence, and, being admitted by someone in the house, probably a boarder, in response to a rap, the Marshal searched the defendant's room and carried away certain letters and envelopes found in the drawer of a chiffonier. Neither the marshal nor the police officers had a search warrant. . . .

. . . Upon the introduction of such papers during the trial, the defendant objected on the ground that the papers had been obtained without a search warrant and by breaking open his home, in violation of the Fourth and Fifth Amendments to the Constitution of the United States, which objection was overruled by the court. Among the papers retained and put in evidence were a number of lottery tickets and statements with reference to the lottery, taken at the first visit of the police to the defendant's room, and a number of letters written to the defendant in respect to the lottery, taken by the Marshal upon his search of defendant's room. . . .

. . . The defendant contends that such appropriation of his private correspondence was in violation of rights secured to him by the Fourth and Fifth Amendments to the Constitution of the United States. We shall deal with the Fourth Amendment, which provides:

"The right of the people to be secure in their persons, houses, papers, and effects, against unreasonable searches and seizures, shall not be violated, and no warrants shall issue, but upon probable cause, supported by oath or affirmation and particularly describing the place to be searched, and the persons or things to be seized." . . .

. . . [This amendment] . . . took its origin in the determination of the framers of the Amendments to the Federal Constitution to provide for that instrument a Bill of Rights, securing to the American people, among other things, those safeguards which had grown up in England to protect the people from unreasonable searches and seizures, such as were permitted under the general warrants issued under authority of the Government by which there had been invasions of the home and privacy of the citizens and the seizure of their private papers in support of charges, real or imaginary, made against them. Such practices had also received sanction under warrants and seizures under the so-called writs of assistance, issued in the American colonies. . . . Resistance to these practices had established the principle which was enacted into the fundamental law in the Fourth Amendment, that a man's house was his castle and not to be invaded by any general authority to search and seize his goods and papers. Judge Cooley, in his Constitutional Limitations, pp. 425, 426, in treating of this feature of our Constitution, said: "The maxim that 'every man's house is his castle,' is made a part of our constitutional law in the clauses prohibiting unreasonable searches and seizures, and has always been looked upon as of high value to the citizen." . . .

The effect of the Fourth Amendment is to put the courts of the United States and Federal officials, in the exercise of their power and authority, under limitations and restraints as to the exercise of such power and authority, and to forever secure the people, their persons, houses, papers and effects against all unreasonable searches and seizures under the guise of law. This protection reaches all alike, whether accused of crime or not, and the duty of giving to it force and effect is obligatory upon all entrusted under our Federal system with the enforcement of the laws. The tendency of those who execute the criminal laws of the country to obtain conviction by means of unlawful seizures and enforced confessions, the latter often obtained after subjecting accused persons to unwarranted practices destructive of rights secured by the Federal Constitution, should find no sanction in the judgments of the courts which are charged at all times with the support of the Constitution and to which people of all conditions have a right to appeal for the maintenance of such fundamental rights. . . .

The case in the aspect in which we are dealing with it involves the right of the court in a criminal prosecution to retain for the purposes of evidence the letters and correspondence of the accused, seized in his house in his absence and without his authority, by a United States Marshal holding no warrant for his arrest and none for the search of his premises. The accused, without awaiting his trial, made timely application to the court for an order for the return of these letters, as well as other property. This application was denied, the letters retained and put in evidence, after a further application at the beginning of the trial, both applications asserting the rights of the accused under the Fourth and Fifth Amendments to the Constitution. If letters and private documents can thus be seized and held and used in evidence against a citizen accused of an offense, the protection of the Fourth Amendment declaring his right to be secure against such searches and seizures is of no value, and, so far as those thus placed are concerned, might as well be stricken from the Constitution. The efforts of the courts and their officials to bring the guilty to punishment, praiseworthy as they are, are not to be aided by the sacrifice of those great principles established by years of endeavor and suffering which have resulted in their embodiment in the fundamental law of the land. The United States Marshal could only have invaded the house of the accused when armed with a warrant issued as required by the Constitution, upon sworn information and describing with reasonable particularity the thing for which the search was to be made. Instead, he acted without sanction of law, doubtless prompted by the desire to bring further proof to the aid of the Government, and under color of his office undertook to make a seizure of private papers in direct violation of the constitutional prohibition against such action. Under such circumstances, without sworn information and particular description, not even an order of court would have justified such procedure, much less was it within the authority of the United States Marshal to thus invade the house and privacy of the accused. . . . To sanction such proceedings would be to affirm by judicial decision a manifest neglect if not an open defiance of the prohibitions of the Constitution, intended for the protection of the people against such unauthorized action. . . .

We therefore reach the conclusion that the letters in question were taken from the house of the accused by an official of the United States acting under color of his office in direct violation of the constitutional rights of the defendant; that having made a seasonable application for their return, which was heard and passed upon by the court, there was involved in the order refusing the application a denial of the constitutional rights of the accused, and that the court should have restored these letters to the accused. In holding them and permitting their use upon the trial, we think prejudicial error was committed. As to the papers and property seized by the policemen, it does not appear that they acted under any claim of Federal authority such as would make the Amendment applicable to such unauthorized seizures. The record shows that what they did by way of arrest and search and seizure was done before the finding of the indictment in the Federal court, under what supposed right or authority does not appear. What remedies the defendant may have against them we need not inquire, as the Fourth Amendment is not directed to individual misconduct of such officials. Its limitations reach the Federal Government and its agencies. . . .

It results that the judgment of the court below must be reversed, and the case remanded for further proceedings in accordance with this opinion.

---

151 *The Living Law (1916)*

LOUIS D. BRANDEIS

Brandeis's success in *Muller* led reformers to attempt similar approaches in defending other forms of protective legislation, and by the time this article was written, a majority of both state and federal courts had taken a more positive view of such laws. This speech, given just a few weeks before Woodrow Wilson appointed Brandeis to the Court, is really more a looking back than an indictment of the current situation. Nonetheless, many historians and reformers have taken it as the embodiment of the reform complaint against courts. The speech would be quoted often, in its own time and for the next twenty years, by reformers seeking to have the courts respond to current economic and social conditions rather than to a sterile legal logic.

See Gerald Fetner, *Contours of Legal Reform in Twentieth Century America* (1980); Philippa Strum, *Brandeis: Beyond Progressivism* (1993); and Stephen W. Baskerville, *Of Laws and Limitations* (1994).

———

The history of the United States, since the adoption of the Constitution, covers less than 128 years. Yet in that short period the American ideal of government has been greatly modified. At first our ideal was expressed as, "A government of laws and not of men." Then it became, "A government of the people, by the people, and for the people." Now it is, "Democracy and social justice."

In the last half century our democracy has deepened. Coincidently there has been a shifting of our longing from legal justice to social justice, and—it must be admitted—also a waning respect for law. Is there any causal connection between the shifting of our longing from legal justice to social justice and waning respect for law? If so, was that result unavoidable?

Many different causes contributed to this waning respect for law. Some related specifically to the lawyer, some to the courts and some to the substantive law itself. The

Source: 10 *Illinois Law Review* 461 (1916).

lessening of the lawyer's influence in the community came first. James Bryce called attention to this as a fact of great significance already a generation ago. Later criticism of the efficiency of our judicial machinery became widespread. Finally, the law as administered was challenged—a challenge which expressed itself vehemently a few years ago in the demand for recall of judges and of judicial decisions. . . .

In periods of rapid transformation, challenge of existing law, instead of being sporadic, becomes general. Such was the case in Athens, twenty-four centuries ago, when Euripides burst out in flaming words against "the trammelings of law which are not of the right." Such was the case also in Germany during the Reformation, when Ulrich Zäsius declared that, "All sciences have put off their dirty clothes; only jurisprudence remains in its rags."

And after the French Revolution, another period of rapid transformation, another poet-sage, Goethe, imbued with the modern scientific spirit, added to his protest a clear diagnosis of the disease:

> Customs and laws, in every place,
> Like a disease, an heirloom dread,
> Still trace their curse from race to race,
> And furtively abroad they spread.
> To nonsense, reason's self they turn;
> Beneficence becomes a pest;
> Woe unto thee, thou art a grandson born!
> As for the law, born with us, unexpressed
> That law, alas, none careth to discern.

Is not Goethe's diagnosis equally applicable to the twentieth-century challenge of the law in the United States? Has not the recent dissatisfaction with our law as administered been due, in large measure, to the fact that it had not kept pace with the rapid development of our political, economic, and social ideals? In other words, is not the challenge of legal justice due to its failure to conform to contemporary conceptions of social justice?

Since the adoption of the Federal Constitution, and notably within the last fifty years, we have passed through an economic and social revolution which affected the life of the people more fundamentally than any political revolution known to history. Widespread substitution of machinery for hand labor (thus multiplying hundred-fold man's productivity), and the annihilation of space through steam and electricity, have wrought changes in the conditions of life which are in many respects greater than those which had occurred in civilized countries during thousands of years preceding. The end was put to legalized human slavery—an institution which had existed since the dawn of history. But of vastly greater influence upon the lives of the great majority of all civilized peoples was the possibility which invention and discovery created of emancipating women and of liberating men called free from the excessive toil theretofore required to securing food, clothing, and shelter. Yet while invention and discovery created the possibility of releasing men and women from the thraldom of drudgery, there actually came with the introduction of the factory system and the development of the business corporation, new dangers to liberty. Large publicly owned corporations replaced small privately owned concerns. Ownership of the instruments of production passed from the workman to the employer. Individual personal relations between the proprietor and his help ceased. The individual contract of service lost its character, because of the inequality in position between employer and employee. The group relation of employee to employer, with collective bargaining, became common; for it was essential to the workers' protection.

Political as well as economic and social science noted these revolutionary changes. But legal science—the unwritten or judge-made laws as distinguished from legislation—was largely deaf and blind to them. Courts continued to ignore newly arisen social needs. They applied complacently eighteenth-century conceptions of the liberty of the individual and of the sacredness of private property. Early nineteenth-century scientific half-truths like "The survival of the fittest," which, translated into practice, meant "The devil take the hindmost," were erected by judicial sanction into a moral law. Where statutes giving expression to the new social spirit were clearly constitutional, judges, imbued with the relentless spirit of individualism, often construed them away. Where any doubt as to the constitutionality of such statutes could find lodgment, courts all too frequently declared the acts void. Also in other countries the strain upon the law has been great during the last generation; because there also the period has been one of rapid transformation; and the law has everywhere a tendency to lag behind the facts of life. But in America the strain became dangerous; because constitutional limitations were invoked to stop the natural vent of legislation. In the course of relatively few years hundreds of statutes which embodied attempts (often very crude) to adjust legal rights to the demands of social justice were nullified by the courts, on the grounds that the statutes violated the constitutional guaranties of liberty or property. Small wonder that there arose a clamor for the recall of judges and of judicial decisions and that demand was made for amendment of the constitutions and even for their complete abolition. . . .

The challenge of existing law does not, however, come only from the working classes. Criticism of the law is widespread among business men. The tone of their criticism is more courteous than that of the working classes; and the specific objections raised by business men are different. Business men do not demand recall of judges or of judicial decisions. Business men do not ordinarily seek constitutional amendments. They are more apt to desire repeal of statutes than enactment. But both business men and working-men insist that courts lack understanding of contemporary industrial conditions. Both insist that the law is not "up to date." Both insist that the lack of familiarity with the facts of business life results in erroneous decisions. . . . Both business men and working-men have given further evidence of their distrust of the courts and of lawyers by their efforts to establish non-legal tribunals or commissions to exercise functions which are judicial (even where not legal) in their nature, and by their insistence that the commissions shall be manned with business and working-men instead of lawyers. And business men have been active in devising other means of escape from the domain of the courts, as is evidenced by the widespread tendency to arbitrate controversies through committees of business organizations.

The remedy so sought is not adequate, and may prove a mischievous one. What we need is not to displace the courts, but to make them efficient instruments of justice; not to displace the lawyer, but to fit him for his official or judicial task. And, indeed, the task of fitting the lawyer and the judge to perform adequately the functions of harmonizing law with life is a task far easier of accomplishment than that of endowing men, who lack legal training, with the necessary qualifications.

The training of the practicing lawyer is that best adapted to develop men not only for the exercise of strictly judicial functions, but also for the exercise of administrative functions, quasi-judicial in character. It breeds a certain virile, compelling quality, which tends to make the possessor proof against the influence of either fear or favor. It is this quality to which the prevailing high standard of honesty among our judges is due. And it is certainly a noteworthy fact that in spite of the abundant criticism of our judicial system, the suggestion of dishonesty is rare; and instances of established dishonesty are extremely few. . . .

The last fifty years have wrought a great change in professional life. Industrial development and the consequent growth of cities have led to a high degree of specialization—specialization not only in the nature and class of questions dealt with, but also specialization in the character of clientage. The term "corporation lawyer" is significant in this connection. The growing intensity of professional life tended also to discourage participation in public affairs, and thus the broadening of view which comes from political life was lost. The deepening of knowledge in certain subjects was purchased at the cost of vast areas of ignorance and grave danger of resultant distortion of judgment. . . .

Charles R. Crane told me once the story of two men whose lives he should have cared most to have lived. One was Bogigish, a native of the ancient city of Ragusa off the coast of Dalmatia—a deep student of law, who after gaining some distinction at the University of Vienna, and in France, became professor at the University of Odessa. When Montenegro was admitted to the family of nations, its prince concluded that, like other civilized countries, it must have a code of law. Bogigish's fame had reached Montenegro—for Ragusa is but a few miles distant. So the prince begged the Tsar of Russia to have the learned jurist prepare a code for Montenegro. The Tsar granted the request; and Bogigish undertook the task. But instead of utilizing his great knowledge of laws to draft a code, he proceeded to Montenegro, and for two years literally made his home with the people—studying everywhere their customs, their practices, their needs, their beliefs, their points of view. Then he embodied in law the life which the Montenegrins lived. They respected that law, because it expressed the will of the people.

152

McPherson v. Buick Motor Co. (1916)

Until 1916, product liability law required privity, that is, direct contract, between the maker of the item and the consumer. This law made sense in preindustrial times, when small manufacturers sold their hand-made goods directly to the ultimate consumer; it made far less sense in the industrial age, when large factories turned out thousands of machine-made products that were then sold through one or more middlemen before winding up in the hands of the user.

Much of Benjamin Nathan Cardozo's reputation as the finest common law judge of his time rests on this case, in which he deliberately misstated the holding in prior cases in order to abandon the privity rule and introduce modern product liability law.

After *McPherson,* one jurisdiction after another abandoned the privity rule in cases involving physical injuries caused by defective products. Today every jurisdiction in the country accepts the *McPherson* rule, with Mississippi being the last state to sign on, in 1966. The decision totally transformed product liability law and is considered by most scholars to be one of the genuine landmark decisions in American law.

See Richard A. Posner, *Cardozo: A Study in Reputation* (1990); and David W. Peck, "McPherson and His Buick," in *Decision at Law* (1961), ch. 2.

————

Judge Cardozo for the Court:

The defendant is a manufacturer of automobiles. It sold an automobile to a retail dealer. The retail dealer resold to the plaintiff. While the plaintiff was in the car, it suddenly collapsed. He was thrown out and injured. One of the wheels was made of defective wood, and its spokes crumbled into fragments. The wheel was not made by the defendant; it was bought from another manufacturer. There is evidence, however, that its defects could have been discovered by reasonable inspection, and that inspection was omitted. There is no claim that the defendant knew of the defect and willfully concealed it. The charge is one, not of fraud, but of negligence. The question to be determined is whether the defendant owed a duty of care and vigilance to any one but the immediate purchaser.

The foundations of this branch of the law, at least in this state, were laid in *Thomas v. Winchester* (6 N.Y. 397). A poison was falsely labeled. The sale was made to a druggist, who in turn sold to a customer. The customer recovered damages from the seller who affixed the label. "The defendant's negligence," it was said, "put human life in imminent danger." A poison falsely labeled is likely to injure any one who gets it. Because the danger is to be foreseen, there is a duty to avoid the injury. Cases were cited by way of illustration in which manufacturers were not subject to any duty irrespective of contract. The distinction was said to be that their conduct, though negligent, was not likely to result in injury to any one except the purchaser. We are not required to say whether the chance of injury was always as remote as the distinction assumes. Some of the illustrations might be rejected to-day. The *principle* of the distinction is for present purposes the important thing.

Thomas v. Winchester became quickly a landmark of the law. In the application of its principle there may at times have been uncertainty or even error. There has never in this state been doubt or disavowal of the principle itself. The chief cases are well known,

————

Source: 217 N.Y. 382 (1916).

yet to recall some of them will be helpful. *Loop v. Litchfield* (42 N. Y. 351) is the earliest. It was the case of a defect in a small balance wheel used on a circular saw. The manufacturer pointed out the defect to the buyer, who wished a cheap article and was ready to assume the risk. The risk can hardly have been an imminent one, for the wheel lasted five years before it broke. In the meanwhile the buyer had made a lease of the machinery. It was held that the manufacturer was not answerable to the lessee. *Loop v. Litchfield* was followed in *Losee v. Clute,* the case of the explosion of a steam boiler. That decision has been criticised; but it must be confined to its special facts. It was put upon the ground that the risk of injury was too remote. The buyer in that case had not only accepted the boiler, but had tested it. The manufacturer knew that his own test was not the final one. The finality of the test has a bearing on the measure of diligence owing to persons other than the purchaser.

These early cases suggest a narrow construction of the rule. Later cases, however, evince a more liberal spirit. First in importance is *Devlin v. Smith.* The defendant, a contractor, built a scaffold for a painter. The painter's servants were injured. The contractor was held liable. He knew that the scaffold, if improperly constructed, was a most dangerous trap. He knew that it was to be used by the workmen. He was building it for that very purpose. Building it for their use, he owed them a duty, irrespective of his contract with their master, to build it with care.

From *Devlin v. Smith* we pass over intermediate cases and turn to the latest case in this court in which *Thomas v. Winchester* was followed. That case is *Statler v. Ray Mfg. Co.* The defendant manufactured a large coffee urn. It was installed in a restaurant. When heated, the urn exploded and injured the plaintiff. We held that the manufacturer was liable. We said that the urn "was of such a character inherently that, when applied to the purposes for which it was designed, it was liable to become a source of great danger to many people if not carefully and properly constructed."

It may be that *Devlin v. Smith* and *Statler v. Ray Mfg. Co.* have extended the rule of *Thomas v. Winchester.* If so, this court is committed to the extension. The defendant argues that things imminently dangerous to life are poisons, explosives, deadly weapons—things whose normal function it is to injure or destroy. But whatever the rule in *Thomas v. Winchester* may once have been, it has no longer that restricted meaning. A scaffold is not inherently a destructive instrument. It becomes destructive only if imperfectly constructed. A large coffee urn may have within itself, if negligently made, the potency of danger, yet no one thinks of it as an implement whose normal function is destruction. What is true of the coffee urn is equally true of bottles of aerated water. We have maintained only cases in this court. But the rule has received a like extension in our courts of intermediate appeal. . . .

We hold, then, that the principle of *Thomas v. Winchester* is not limited to poisons, explosives, and things of like nature, to things which in their normal operation are implements of destruction. If the nature of a thing is such that it is reasonably certain to place life and limb in peril when negligently made, it is then a thing of danger. Its nature gives warning of the consequences to be expected. If to the element of danger there is added knowledge that the thing will be used by persons other than the purchaser, and used without new tests, then, irrespective of contract, the manufacturer of this thing of danger is under a duty to make it carefully. That is as far as we are required to go for the decision of this case. There must be knowledge of a danger, not merely possible, but probable. It is possible to use almost anything in a way that will make it dangerous if defective. That is not enough to charge the manufacturer with a duty independent of his contract. Whether a given thing is dangerous may be sometimes a question for the court and sometimes a question for the jury. There must also be knowledge that in the usual course of events the danger will be shared by others than the buyer. Such knowledge may often be inferred from the nature of the transaction. But it is possible that even knowledge of the danger and of the use will not always be enough. The proximity or remoteness of the relation is a factor to be considered. We are dealing now with the liability of the manufacturer of the finished product, who puts it on the market to be used without inspection by his customers. If he is negligent, where danger is to be foreseen, a liability will follow. We are not required at this time to say that it is legitimate to go back of the manufacturer of the finished product and hold the manufacturers of the component parts. To make their negligence a cause of imminent danger, an independent cause must often intervene; the manufacturer of the finished product must also fail in his duty of inspection. It may be that in those circumstances the negligence of the earlier members of the series is too remote to constitute, as to the ultimate user, an actionable wrong. We leave that question open. We shall have to deal with it when it arises. The difficulty which it suggests is not present in this case. There is here no break in the chain of cause and effect. In such circumstances, the presence of a known danger, attendant upon a known use, makes vigilance a duty. We have put aside the notion that the duty to safeguard life and limb, when the consequences of negligence may be foreseen, grows out of contract and nothing else. We have put the source of the obligation where it ought to be. We have put its source in the law.

From this survey of the decisions, there thus emerges a definition of the duty of a manufacturer which enables us to measure this defendant's liability. Beyond all question, the nature of an automobile gives warning of probable danger if its construction is defective. This automobile was designed to go fifty miles an hour. Unless its wheels were sound and strong, injury was almost certain. It was as much a thing of danger as a defective engine for a railroad. The defendant knew the danger. It knew also that the car would be used by persons other than the buyer. This was apparent from its size; there were seats for three persons. It was apparent also from the fact that the buyer was a dealer in cars, who bought to resell. The maker of this car supplied it for the use of purchasers from the dealer just as plainly as the contractor in Devlin v. Smith supplied the scaffold for use by the servants of the owner. The dealer was indeed the one person of whom it might be said with some approach to certainty that by him the car would not be used. Yet the defendant would have us say that he was the one person whom it was under a legal duty to protect. The law does not lead us to so inconsequent a conclusion. Precedents drawn from the days of travel by stage coach do not fit the conditions of travel today. The principle that the danger must be imminent does not change, but the things subject to the principle do change. They are whatever the needs of life in a developing civilization require them to be.

In reaching this conclusion, we do not ignore the decisions to the contrary in other jurisdictions. . . . Some of them, at first sight inconsistent with our conclusion, may be reconciled upon the ground that the negligence was too remote, and that another cause had intervened. But even when they cannot be reconciled, the difference is rather in the application of the principle than in the principle itself. Judge Sanborn says, for example, that the contractor who builds a bridge, or the manufacturer who builds a car, cannot ordinarily foresee injury to other persons than the owner as the probable result. We take a different view. We think that injury to others is to be foreseen not merely as a possible, but as an almost inevitable result. . . .

In this view of the defendant's liability there is nothing inconsistent with the theory of liability on which the case was tried. It is true that the court told the jury that "an automobile is not an inherently dangerous vehicle." The meaning, however, is made plain by the context. The meaning is that danger is not to be expected when the vehicle is well constructed. The court left it to the jury to say whether the defendant ought to have foreseen that the car, if negligently constructed, would become "imminently dangerous." Subtle distinctions are drawn by the defendant between things inherently dangerous and things imminently dangerous, but the case does not turn upon these verbal niceties. If danger was to be expected as reasonably certain, there was a duty of vigilance, and this whether you call the danger inherent or imminent. In varying forms that thought was put before the jury. We do not say that the court would not have been justified in ruling as a matter of law that the car was a dangerous thing. If there was any error, it was none of which the defendant can complain.

We think the defendant was not absolved from a duty of inspection because it bought the wheels from a reputable manufacturer. It was not merely a dealer in automobiles. It was a manufacturer of automobiles. It was responsible for the finished product. It was not at liberty to put the finished product on the market without subjecting the component parts to ordinary and simple tests. Under the charge of the trial judge nothing more was required of it. The obligation to inspect must vary with the nature of the thing to be inspected. The more probable the danger, the greater the need of caution. . . . The judgment should be affirmed with costs.

---

153   *Lever Food Control Act (1917)*

During the Civil War, the Lincoln administration had exercised relatively little direct control over private economic activities, and that little had been done without explicit statutory authority. At the start of the First World War, the Wilson administration, reflecting the president's antipathy to big government, had tried to deal with mounting difficulties in production and supply on the basis of prewar procedures, which proved totally unsuited to the magnitude of problems generated by a modern, total war.

In 1916, well before American entry into the conflict, Congress had passed the National Defense Act, establishing a Council of National Defense, as well as numerous advisory bodies to help government agencies plan for defense needs. After the United States entered the war, the administration recognized that the advisory apparatus by itself would be insufficient. In December 1917, the president, relying upon his war powers as commander-in-chief, issued a proclamation taking control of the railroads. But the administration also sought statutory authority to exercise a hitherto unimagined degree of government control over the economy. The Lever Food Control Act of 1917 gave the president power to establish an agency to buy or sell food, offer guarantees to farmers, fix exchange prices, set retail prices, and in general organize the agricultural sector of the nation to eliminate waste and increase food production.

Probably no other wartime measure produced so many prosecutions, primarily for violation of Section Four, which made it unlawful to charge or conspire "to exact excessive prices for any necessaries." The vagueness of the statute led to conflicting interpretations in various federal courts, but the Supreme Court refused to take any case on appeal while hostilities lasted. After the war, in *United States v. Cohen Grocery Store* (1921), the Supreme Court did find Section Four unconstitutional on the grounds that it had failed to provide "an ascertainable standard of guilt" adequate to allow people to know when and if they violated the law. By then, of course, the war was over and the Lever Act had had its desired effect. The Court also did not deny that Congress had the power to enact such legislation; if it did so in future wars, however, it would have to draft the statute with greater care.

See Maxcy R. Dickson, *The Food Front in World War I* (1944); Daniel M. Smith, *The Great Departure: The United States in World War I* (1965); and David M. Kennedy, *Over Here: The First World War and American Society* (1980).

CHAP. 53. An Act To provide further for the national security and defense by encouraging the production, conserving the supply, and controlling the distribution of food products and fuel.

Be it enacted by the Senate and House of Representatives of the United States of America in Congress assembled, That by reason of the existence of a state of war, it is essential to the national security and defense, for the successful prosecution of the war, and for the support and maintenance of the Army and Navy, to assure an adequate supply and equitable distribution, and to facilitate the movement, of foods, feeds, fuel including fuel oil and natural gas, and fertilizer and fertilizer ingredients, tools, utensils, implements, machinery, and equipment required for the actual production of foods, feeds, and fuel, hereafter in this Act called necessaries; to prevent, locally or generally, scarcity, monopolization, hoarding, injurious speculation, manipulations, and private controls, affecting such supply, distribution, and movement; and to establish and maintain governmental control of such necessaries during the war. For such purposes the instrumentalities, means, methods, powers, authorities, duties, obligations, and prohibi-

Source: 40 *Statutes at Large* 276 (1917)

tions hereinafter set forth are created, established, conferred, and prescribed. The President is authorized to make such regulations and to issue such orders as are essential effectively to carry out the provisions of this Act. . . .

SEC. 4. That it is hereby made unlawful for any person willfully to destroy any necessaries for the purpose of enhancing the price or restricting the supply thereof; knowingly to commit waste or willfully to permit preventable deterioration of any necessaries in or in connection with their production, manufacture, or distribution; to hoard, as defined in section six of this Act, any necessaries; to monopolize or attempt to monopolize, either locally or generally, any necessaries; to engage in any discriminatory and unfair, or any deceptive or wasteful practice or device, or to make any unjust or unreasonable rate or charge, in handling or dealing in or with any necessaries; to conspire, combine, agree, or arrange with any other person, (a) to limit the facilities for transporting, producing, harvesting, manufacturing, supplying, storing, or dealing in any necessaries; (b) to restrict the supply of any necessaries; (c) to restrict distribution of any necessaries; (d) to prevent, limit, or lessen the manufacture or production of any necessaries in order to enhance the price thereof, or (e) to exact excessive prices for any necessaries; or to aid or abet the doing of any act made unlawful by this section. . . .

SEC. 14. That whenever the President shall find that an emergency exists requiring stimulation of the production of wheat and that it is essential that the producers of wheat, produced within the United States, shall have the benefits of the guaranty provided for in this section, he is authorized, from time to time, seasonably and as far in advance of seeding time as practicable, to determine and fix and to give public notice of what, under specified conditions, is a reasonable guaranteed price for wheat, in order to assure such producers a reasonable profit. The President shall thereupon fix such guaranteed price for each of the official grain standards for wheat as established under the United States grain standards Act, approved August eleventh, nineteen hundred and sixteen. The President shall from time to time establish and promulgate such regulations as he shall deem wise in connection with such guaranteed prices, and in particular governing conditions of delivery and payment, and differences in price for the several standard grades in the principal primary markets of the United States, adopting number one northern spring or its equivalent at the principal interior primary markets as the basis. Thereupon, the Government of the United States hereby guarantees every producer of wheat produced within the United States, that, upon compliance by him with the regulations prescribed, he shall receive for any wheat produced in reliance upon this guarantee within the period, not exceeding eighteen months, prescribed in the notice, a price not less than the guaranteed price therefore as fixed pursuant to this section. . . . For the purpose of making any guaranteed price effective under this section, or whenever he deems it essential in order to protect the Government of the United States against material enhancement of its liabilities arising out of any guaranty under this section, the President is authorized also, in his discretion, to purchase any wheat for which a guaranteed price shall be fixed under this section, and to hold, transport, or store it, or to sell, dispose of, and deliver the same to any citizen of the United States or to any Government engaged in war with any country with which the Government of the United States is or may be at war or to use the same as supplies for any department or agency of the Government of the United States. . . .

SEC. 15. That from and after thirty days from the date of the approval of this Act no foods, fruits, food materials, or feeds shall be used in the production of distilled spirits for beverage purposes. . . . Nor shall there be imported into the United States any distilled spirits. Whenever the President shall find that limitation, regulation, or prohibition of the use of foods, fruits, food materials, or feeds in the production of malt or vinous liquors for beverage purposes, or that reduction of the alcoholic content of any such malt or vinous liquor, is essential, in order to assure an adequate and continuous supply of food, or that the national security and defense will be subserved thereby, he is authorized, from time to time, to prescribe and give public notice of the extent of the limitation, regulation, prohibition, or reduction so necessitated. Whenever such notice shall have been given and shall remain unrevoked no person shall, after a reasonable time prescribed in such notice, use any foods, fruits, food materials, or feeds in the production of malt or vinous liquors, or import any such liquors except under license issued by the President and in compliance with rules and regulations determined by him governing the production and importation of such liquors and the alcoholic content thereof. . . .

SEC. 16. That the President is authorized and directed to commandeer any or all distilled spirits in bond or in stock at the date of the approval of this Act for redistillation, in so far as such redistillation may be necessary to meet the requirements of the Government in the manufacture of munitions and other military and hospital supplies, or in so far as such redistillation would dispense with the necessity of utilizing products and materials suitable for foods and feeds in the future manufacture of distilled spirits for the purposes herein enumerated. The President shall determine and pay a just compensation for the distilled spirits so commandeered. . . .

SEC. 24. That the provisions of this Act shall cease to be in effect when the existing state of war between the United States and Germany shall have terminated, and the fact and date of such termination shall be ascertained and proclaimed by the President.

---

154   *Masses Publishing Co. v. Patten (1917)*

The Wilson administration secured passage of several laws that attempted to silence nearly all criticism of the war. These included the Espionage Act (1917), the Trading with the Enemy Act (1917), the Sedition Act (1918), and the Alien Act (1918). The first test of these laws, involving a provision of the Trading with the Enemy Act that gave the postmaster-general power to ban certain materials from the mail, arose in the federal district court in New York before Judge Learned Hand, who showed a great deal of solicitude for speech. Civil libertarians have favorably contrasted Hand's test of whether the speech would actually incite specific action to Holmes's later and better-known "clear and present danger" standard (Document 157), which invited enormous subjective evaluation by the judges. Hand's ruling was reversed on appeal to the Circuit Court, which upheld broad discretionary powers given to the postmaster-general, and Hand later wrote that this opinion "seemed to meet with practically no professional approval whatsoever." By that he meant approval from other judges, for within the law schools it received wide approbation (see Document 156).

See Paul Murphy, *World War I and the Origins of Civil Liberties in the United States* (1979); Harry N. Scheiber, *The Wilson Administration and Civil Liberties, 1917–1921* (1960); David M. Rabban, *Free Speech in Its Forgotten Years* (1997); Gerald Gunther, *Learned Hand* (1994); and the classic Zechariah Chafee, Jr., *Free Speech in the United States* (1920; rev. ed., 1941).

———

District Judge Learned Hand delivered the opinion of the Court:

In this case there is no dispute of fact which the plaintiff can successfully challenge except the meaning of the words and pictures in the magazine. As to these the query must be: What is the extreme latitude of the interpretation which must be placed upon them, and whether that extremity certainly falls outside any of the provisions of the act of June 15, 1917. Unless this be true, the decision of the postmaster must stand. It will be necessary, first, to interpret the law, and, next, the words and pictures. No question arises touching the war powers of Congress. Here is presented solely the question of how far Congress after much discussion has up to the present time seen fit to exercise a power which may extend to measures not yet even considered, but necessary to the existence of the state as such. . . .

Coming to the act itself, I turn directly to section 3 of title 1, which the plaintiff is said to violate. That section contains three provisions. The first is, in substance, that no one shall make any false statements with intent to interfere with the operation or success of the military or naval forces of the United States or to promote the success of its enemies. The defendant says that the cartoons and text of the magazine, constituting, as they certainly do, a virulent attack upon the war, may interfere with the success of the military forces of the United States. That such utterances may have the effect so ascribed to them is unhappily true. Dissension within a country is a high source of comfort and assistance to its enemies. . . .

All this, however, is beside the question whether such an attack is a willfully false statement. That phrase properly includes only a statement of fact which the utterer knows to be false, and it cannot be maintained that any of these statements are of fact, or that the plaintiff believes them to be false. They are all within the range of opinion and of criticism; they are all certainly believed to be true by the utterer. As such they fall

Source: 244 Fed. 535 (S.D.N.Y., 1917)

within the scope of that right to criticise either by temperate reasoning, or by immoderate and indecent invective, which is normally the privilege of the individual in countries dependent upon the free expression of opinion as the ultimate source of authority. The argument may be trivial in substance, and violent and perverse in manner, but so long as it is confined to abuse of existing policies or laws, it is impossible to class it as a false statement of facts of the kind here in question. To modify this provision, so clearly intended to prevent the spreading of false rumors which may embarrass the military, into the prohibition of any kind of propaganda, honest or vicious, is to disregard the meaning of the language, established by legal construction and common use, and to raise it into a means of suppressing intemperate and inflammatory public discussion, which was surely not its purpose.

The next phrase relied upon is that which forbids any one from willfully causing insubordination, disloyalty, mutiny, or refusal of duty in the military or naval forces of the United States. The defendant's position is that to arouse discontent and disaffection among the people with the prosecution of the war and with the draft tends to promote a mutinous and insubordinate temper among the troops. This, too, is true; men who become satisfied that they are engaged in an enterprise dictated by the unconscionable selfishness of the rich, and effectuated by a tyrannous disregard for the will of those who must suffer and die, will be more prone to insubordination than those who have faith in the cause and acquiesce in the means. Yet to interpret the word "cause" so broadly would, as before, involve necessarily as a consequence the suppression of all hostile criticism, and of all opinion except what encouraged and supported the existing policies, or which fell within the range of temperate argument. It would contradict the normal assumption of democratic government that the suppression of hostile criticism does not turn upon the justice of its substance or the decency and propriety of its temper. Assuming that the power to repress such opinion may rest in Congress in the throes of a struggle for the very existence of the state, its exercise is so contrary to the use and wont of our people that only the clearest expression of such a power justifies the conclusion that it was intended.

The defendant's position, therefore, in so far as it involves the suppression of the free utterance of abuse and criticism of the existing law, or of the policies of the war, is not, in my judgment, supported by the language of the statute. Yet there has always been a recognized limit to such expressions, incident indeed to the existence of any compulsive power of the state itself. One may not counsel or advise others to violate the law as it stands. Words are not only the keys of persuasion, but the triggers of action, and those which have no purport but to counsel the violation of law cannot by any latitude of interpretation be a part of that public opinion which is the final source of government in a democratic state. The defendant asserts not only that the magazine indirectly through its propaganda leads to a disintegration of loyalty and a disobedience of law, but that in addition it counsels and advises resistance to existing law, especially to the draft. . . . To counsel or advise a man to an act is to urge upon him either that it is his interest or his duty to do it. While, of course, this may be accomplished as well by indirection as expressly, since words carry the meaning that they impart, the definition is exhaustive, I think, and I shall use it. Political agitation, by the passions it arouses or the convictions it engenders, may in fact stimulate men to the violation of law. Detestation of existing policies is easily transformed into forcible resistance of the authority which puts them in execution, and it would be folly to disregard the casual relation between the two. Yet to assimilate agitation, legitimate as such, with direct incitement to violent resistance, is to disregard the tolerance of all methods of political agitation which in normal times is a safeguard of free government. The distinction is not a scholastic subterfuge, but a hard-bought acquisition in the fight for freedom, and the purpose to disregard it must be evident when the power exists. If one stops short of urging upon others that it is their duty or their interest to resist the law, it seems to me one should not be held to have attempted to cause its violation. If that be not the test, I can see no escape from the conclusion that under this section every political agitation which can be shown to be apt to create a seditious temper is illegal. I am confident that by such language Congress had no such revolutionary purpose in view.

It seems to me, however, quite plain that none of the language and none of the cartoons in this paper can be thought directly to counsel or advise insubordination or mutiny, without a violation of their meaning quite beyond any tolerable understanding. I come, therefore, to the third phrase of the section, which forbids any one from willfully obstructing the recruiting or enlistment service of the United States. I am not prepared to assent to the plaintiff's position that this only refers to acts other than words, nor that the act thus defined must be shown to have been successful. One may obstruct without preventing, and the mere obstruction is an injury to the service; for it throws impediments in its way. Here again, however, since the question is of the expression of opinion, I construe the sentence, so far as it restrains public utterance, as I have construed the other two, and as therefore limited to the direct advocacy of resistance to the recruiting and enlistment service. If so, the inquiry is narrowed to the question whether any of the challenged matter may be said to advocate resistance to the draft, taking the meaning of the words with the utmost latitude which they can bear.

As to the cartoons it seems to me quite clear that they do not fall within such a test. Certainly the nearest is that entitled "Conscription," and the most that can be said of that is that it may breed such animosity to the draft as will promote resistance and strengthen the determination of those disposed to be recalcitrant. There is no intimation that, however hateful the draft may be, one is in duty bound to resist it, certainly none that such resistance is to one's interest. . . .

The text offers more embarrassment. The poem to Emma Goldman and Alexander Berkman, at most, goes no further than to say that they are martyrs in the cause of love among nations. Such a sentiment holds them up to admiration, and hence their conduct to possible emulation. The paragraphs upon conscientious objectors are of the same kind. It is plain enough that the paper has the fullest sympathy for these people, that it admires their courage, and that it presumptively approves their conduct. . . . These passages, it must be remembered, occur in a magazine which attacks with the utmost violence the draft and the war. That such comments have a tendency to arouse emulation in others is clear enough but that they counsel others to follow these examples is not so plain. Literally at least they do not, and while, as I have said, the words are to be taken, not literally, but according to their full import, the literal meaning is the starting point for interpretation. One may admire and approve the course of a hero without feeling any duty to follow him. There is not the least implied intimation in these words that others are under a duty to follow. The most that can be said is that, if others do follow, they will get the same admiration and the same approval. Now, there is surely an appreciable distance between esteem and emulation; and unless there is here some advocacy of such emulation, I cannot see how the passages can be said to fall within [the law].

The question before me is quite the same as what would arise upon a motion to dismiss an indictment at the close of the proof: Could any reason able man say, not that the indirect result of the language might be to arouse a seditious disposition, for that would not be enough, but that the language directly advocated resistance to the draft? I cannot think that upon such language any verdict would stand.

---

155   *Hammer v. Dagenhart (1918)*

Because not all states adopted stringent child labor laws, reformers called for a federal statute to ensure minimal standards nationwide, and they secured such a measure in the Child Labor Act of 1916. Congress relied on its commerce power to exclude goods made by children from interstate commerce, a power that the Court had seemingly ratified in previous cases involving lottery tickets, impure food and drugs, and even sexual conduct. It came as an enormous shock, therefore, when the Court struck down the law by a five-to-four vote, and Justice Day revived the old *Knight* distinction between commerce and manufacturing (Document 136). Reaction to the decision proved overwhelmingly negative, and the case soon assumed a position second only to *Lochner* (Document 146) as an odious example of the Court striking down laws that its conservative majority did not approve.

In response to public support of a child labor law, Congress passed a second measure, this time relying on the taxing power, which the Court had always interpreted as conveying a very broad and plenary power (Document 145). Nonetheless, in *Bailey v. Drexel Furniture Co.* (1922), the Court by an eight-to-one vote invalidated the law because Congress had tried to use the taxing power unlawfully, as a criminal penalty. Because the Court thus prevented Congress from using either the commerce or the taxing powers to deal with child labor, national legislation on this subject was doomed until the New Deal era. The Court finally reversed itself in 1941 (Document 188).

See Walter I. Trattner, *Crusade for the Children* (1970); Stephen B. Wood, *Constitutional Politics in the Progressive Era: Child Labor and the Law* (1958); Henry W. Biklé, "The Commerce Power and *Hammer* v. *Dagenhart,*" 67 *University of Pennsylvania Law Review* 21 (1919); and Thomas Reed Powell, "Child Labor, Congress and the Constitution," 1 *North Carolina Law Review* 61 (1922).

Justice Day delivered the opinion of the Court:

Is it within the authority of Congress in regulating commerce among the states to prohibit the transportation in interstate commerce of manufactured goods, the product of a factory in which, within thirty days prior to their removal therefrom, children under the age of fourteen have been employed, or children between the ages of fourteen and sixteen years have been employed or permitted to work more than eight hours in any day, or more than six days in any week, or after the hour of 7 o'clock P.M., or before the hour of 6 o'clock A.M.? . . .

The commerce power is one to control the means by which commerce is carried on, which is directly the contrary of the assumed right to forbid commerce from moving and thus destroying it as to particular commodities. But it is insisted that adjudged cases in this court establish the doctrine that the power to regulate given to Congress incidentally includes the authority to prohibit the movement of ordinary commodities. The cases demonstrate the contrary. They rest upon the character of the particular subjects dealt with and the fact that the scope of governmental authority, state or national, possessed over them is such that the authority to prohibit is as to them but the exertion of the power to regulate. . . .

[Justice Day here reviewed those cases involving the commerce power, especially those such as the *Lottery* case in which Congress had excluded certain items from interstate commerce.]

In each of these instances the use of interstate transportation was necessary to the accomplishment of harmful results. In other words, although the power over interstate transportation was to regulate, that could only be accomplished by prohibiting the use of the facilities of interstate commerce to effect the evil intended.

This element is wanting in the present case. The thing intended to be accomplished by this statute is the denial of the facilities of interstate commerce to those manufacturers in the States who employ children within the prohibited ages. The act in its effect does not regulate transportation among the states, but aims to standardize the ages at which children may be employed in mining and manufacturing within the states. The goods shipped are of themselves harmless. The act permits them to be freely shipped after thirty days from the time of their removal from the factory. When offered for shipment, and before transportation begins, the labor of their production is over, and the mere fact that they were intended for interstate commerce transportation does not make their production subject to federal control under the commerce power. . . .

Over interstate transportation, or its incidents, the regulatory power of Congress is ample, but the production of articles, intended for interstate commerce, is a matter of local regulation. If it were otherwise, all manufacture intended for interstate shipment would be brought under federal control to the practical exclusion of the authority of the States, a result certainly not contemplated by the framers of the Constitution when they vested in Congress the authority to regulate commerce among the States. . . .

It is further contended that the authority of Congress may be exerted to control interstate commerce in the shipment of child-made goods because of the effect of the circu-

Source: 247 U.S. 21 (1918)

lation of such goods in other States where the evil of this class of labor has been recognized by local legislation, and the right to thus employ child labor has been more rigorously restrained than in the State of production. In other words, that the unfair competition, thus engendered, may be controlled by closing the channels of interstate commerce to manufacturers in those States where the local laws do not meet what Congress deems to be the more just standard of other States.

There is no power vested in Congress to require the States to exercise their police power so as to prevent possible unfair competition. Many causes may cooperate to give one State, by reason of local laws or conditions, an economic advantage over others. The Commerce Clause was not intended to give to Congress a general authority to equalize such conditions. In some of the States laws have been passed fixing minimum wages for women, in others the local law regulates the hours of labor of women in various employments. Business done in such States may be at an economic disadvantage when compared with States which have no such regulations; surely, this fact does not give Congress the power to deny transportation in interstate commerce to those who carry on business where the hours of labor and the rate of compensation for women have not been fixed by a standard in use in other States and approved by Congress. . . .

That there should be limitations upon the right to employ children in mines and factories in the interest of their own and the public welfare, all will admit. It may be desirable that such laws be uniform, but our Federal Government is one of enumerated powers. . . . The maintenance of the authority of the States over matters purely local is as essential to the preservation of our institutions as is the conservation of the supremacy of the federal power in all matters entrusted to the Nation by the Federal Constitution. . . .

. . . The act in a two-fold sense is repugnant to the Constitution. It not only transcends the authority delegated to Congress over commerce but also exerts a power as to a purely local matter to which the federal authority does not extend. The far reaching result of upholding the act cannot be more plainly indicated than by pointing out that if Congress can thus regulate matters entrusted to local authority by prohibition of the movement of commodities in interstate commerce, all freedom of commerce will be at an end, and the power of the States over local matters may be eliminated, and thus our system of government be practically destroyed. . . .

Affirmed.

Justice Holmes, dissenting, with whom Justices McKenna, Brandeis, and Clarke concurred:

The objection urged against the power is that the States have exclusive control over their methods of production and that Congress cannot meddle with them, and taking the proposition in the sense of direct intermeddling I agree to it and suppose that no one denies it. But if an act is within the powers specifically conferred upon Congress, it seems to me that it is not made any less constitutional because of the indirect effects that it may have, however, obvious it may be that it will have those effects, and that we are not at liberty upon such grounds to hold it void.

The first step in my argument is to make plain what no one is likely to dispute—that the statute in question is within the power expressly given to Congress if considered only as to its immediate effects and that if invalid it is so only upon some collateral ground.

The statute confines itself to prohibiting the carriage of certain goods in interstate or foreign commerce. Congress is given power to regulate such commerce in unqualified terms. It would not be argued today that the power to regulate does not include the power to prohibit. Regulation means the prohibition of something, and when interstate commerce is the matter to be regulated I cannot doubt that the regulation may prohibit any part of such commerce that Congress sees fit to forbid. . . .

The question then is narrowed to whether the exercise of its otherwise constitutional power by Congress can be pronounced unconstitutional because of its possible reaction upon the conduct of the States in a matter upon which I have admitted that they are free from direct control. I should have thought that the most conspicuous decisions of this Court had made it clear that the power to regulate commerce and other constitutional powers could not be cut down or qualified by the fact that it might interfere with the carrying out of the domestic policy of any State.

The manufacture of oleomargarine is as much a matter of state regulation as the manufacture of cotton cloth. Congress levied a tax upon the compound when colored so as to resemble butter that was so great as obviously to prohibit the manufacture and sale. In a very elaborate discussion the present Chief Justice excluded any inquiry into the purpose of an act which apart from that purpose was within the power of Congress. McCray v. United States. . . . The Sherman Act has been made an instrument for the breaking up of combinations in restraint of trade and monopolies, using the power to regulate commerce as a foothold, but not proceeding because that commerce was the end actually in mind. The objection that the control of the States over production was interfered with was urged again and again but always in vain. . . .

The notion that prohibition is any less prohibition when applied to things now thought evil I do not understand. But if there is any matter upon which civilized countries have agreed—far more unanimously than they have with regard to intoxicants and some other matters over which this country is now emotionally aroused—it is the evil of premature and excessive child labor. I should have thought that if we were to introduce our own moral conceptions where in my opinion they do not belong, this was preëminently a case for upholding the exercise of all its powers by the United States. But I had thought that the propriety of the exercise of a power admitted to exist in some cases was for the consideration of Congress alone and that this Court always had disavowed the right to intrude its judgment upon questions of policy or morals. It is not for this Court to pronounce when prohibition is necessary to regulation if it ever may be necessary—to say that it is permissible as against strong drink but not as against the product of ruined lives.

The act does not meddle with anything belonging to the States. They may regulate their internal affairs and their domestic commerce as they like. But when they seek to send their products across the state line they are no longer within their rights. If there were no Constitution and no Congress their power to cross the line would depend upon their neighbors. Under the Constitution such commerce belongs not to the States but to Congress to regulate. It may carry out its views of public policy whatever indirect effect they may have upon the activities of the States. Instead of being encountered by a prohibitive tariff at their boundaries the State encounters the public policy of the United States which it is for Congress to express. The public policy of the United States is shaped with a view to the benefit of the nation as a whole. If, as has been the case within the memory of men still living, a State should take a different view of the propriety of sustaining a lottery from that which generally prevails, I cannot believe that the fact would require a different decision from that reached in Champion v. Ames. Yet in that case it would be said with quite as much force as in this that Congress was attempting to intermeddle with the State's domestic affairs. The national welfare as understood by Congress may require a different attitude within its sphere from that of some self-seeking State. It seems to me entirely constitutional for Congress to enforce its under-standing by all the means at its command.

156   *Freedom of Speech (1918)*

ZECHARIAH CHAFEE, JR.

As the administration's prosecution of radicals and dissenters increased, so too did criticism of the government's policies. The war to make the world safe for democracy had triggered the worst invasion of civil liberties at home since the Alien and Sedition Acts of 1798 (see Document 41) as Congress and state leg-islatures passed a variety of laws designed to silence dissent. Legal scholars, worried about the clear dangers they saw in these sedition laws, began to write about the value of free speech in a democracy and of the need to protect even that speech with which a majority disagreed. No one did more in this area than Harvard law professor Zechariah Chafee, Jr., whose article and subsequent book entitled *Free Speech in the United States* became the starting point for all future civil liberties jurisprudence.

See Zechariah Chafee, Jr., *Free Speech in the United States* (1920; rev. ed., 1941); David M. Rabban, *Free Speech in Its Forgotten Years* (1997); Jerald S. Auerbach, "The Patri-cian as Libertarian: Zechariah Chafee, Jr., and Freedom of Speech," 42 *New England Quarterly* 511 (1969); and Donald L. Smith, *Zechariah Chafee, Jr.: Defender of Liberty and Law* (1988).

———

On June 15th, 1917, Congress passed the original Espionage Act. Title I, Section 3, estab-lished three new offences: (1) false statements or reports interfering with military or naval operations or promoting the success of our enemies; (2) causing or attempting to cause insubordination, disloyalty, mutiny, or refusal of duty in the military and naval forces; (3)

Source: 17 *The New Republic* 66 (16 November 1918)

obstruction of enlistment and recruiting. On June 16th, 1918, Congress amended this section adding the offences set forth at the head of this article among others. Already over seventy prosecutions under the act for mere speaking, writing, or printing have come to trial or been otherwise heard in court. Convictions have followed in at least fourteen cases, some involving many defendants. . . . This widespread governmental action against the discussion of public questions deserves careful examination, for whether justified or not it is an important aspect of the war and our permanent national policy.

The First Amendment to the Federal Constitution guarantees "freedom of speech and of the press," but some judges have limited this to freedom from interference *before* publication, and would therefore hold the Espionage Act constitutional because it only imposes punishment *after* publication. By this view the government is prohibited from heading off objectionable discussion through a censorship or the use of injunctions, but is in no way restricted from prosecuting and punishing severely any utterance it chooses to consider criminal, however harmless in itself, when once it is spoken or written. This definition of liberty of the press originated with Blackstone, and ought to be knocked on the head once for all. In some respects it goes altogether too far. It would not allow the government to suspend a newspaper which habitually furnishes military information to the enemy, or censor indecent moving pictures before exhibition. Such film censorship has been held by the United States Supreme Court (1915) not to infringe freedom of speech—a clear repudiation of Blackstone's definition. And under the Espionage Act itself, a Federal judge enjoined production of The Spirit of '76, a film depicting the Wyoming Massacre and Paul Revere's Ride, because it tended "to make us a little bit slack in our loyalty to Great Britain in this great emergency."

On the other hand, the government which holds twenty years in prison before a speaker and calls him free to talk resembles the Bolshevik peasant described by Galsworthy, who would not let a street meeting silence an unpopular orator. "Brothers, you know that our country is now a country of free speech. We must listen to this man, we must let him say anything he will. But, brothers, when he's finished, we'll bash his head in!" Severe punishment for sedition will check political discussion as effectively as a censorship. The men who drafted the First Amendment knew this well. The censorship had been abolished in England a century before, but they had seen seventy English prosecutions for libel since 1760 with fifty convictions under rules of law which made conviction easy. Those rules had been detested in this country ever since they were repudiated by jury and populace in the famous trial of Peter Zenger, the New York printer, the account of which went through fourteen editions before 1791. Since Blackstone's definition was really just a statement of the objectionable English law of seditious publications, it throws no light on the meaning of the free speech clauses in our Federal and State Constitutions. Those clauses were written by men to whom Wilkes and Junius were household words, who intended to make prosecutions for seditious utterances impossible in this country. This is shown plainly by events soon after the First Amendment. When Congress enacted the Sedition Law of 1798, punishing "writings against the government of the United States and the President," Jefferson treated it as unconstitutional, while Hamilton a few years later defended a Federalist editor from prosecution in the name of the liberty of the press. Thus we have testimony from the leaders of both parties. . . .

Therefore, the First Amendment fixes limits upon the power of Congress to make speech criminal and punishable, and if the Espionage Act exceeds those limits it is unconstitutional. Still, judicial decisions and common sense put some utterances outside the protection of free speech clauses, and it may be that the offences specified in the Act can be punished as much as rank indecency, contempt of court, or incitement to assassination. Where shall we draw the line? It is useless to make a distinction between liberty and license, since "license" is too often liberty to the speaker and what happens to be anathema to the judge. Nor can we brush aside free speech by saying it is war-time and the Constitution gives Congress express power to raise armies. The First Amendment was drafted by men who had just been through a war. If it is to mean anything, it must restrict powers which are expressly granted to Congress, since Congress has no other powers, and it must apply to those activities of government which are most apt to interfere with free discussion, namely, the postal service and the conduct of war.

The true meaning of freedom of speech seems to be this. One of the most important purposes of society and government is the discovery and spread of truth on subjects of general concern. This is possible only through absolutely unlimited discussion, for, as Bagehot points out, once force is thrown into the argument, it becomes a matter of chance whether it is thrown on the false side or the true, and truth loses all its natural advantage in the contest. Nevertheless, there are other purposes of government, such as order, the training of the young, protection against external aggression. Unlimited discussion sometimes interferes with these purposes, which must then be balanced against freedom of speech, but freedom of speech ought to weigh very heavily in the scale. The First Amendment gives binding force to this principle of political wisdom.

In war-time, therefore, speech should be free, unless it is clearly liable to cause direct and dangerous interference with the conduct of the war. The original Espionage Act, under which most of the prosecutions have taken place, satisfies this test, for the three offences specified relate closely to military operations. Many Federal judges, for example, Judge Augustus Hand in the first Eastman trial, have construed it not to prohibit the expression of opposition to the war and the Conscription Act, even though this may indirectly discourage recruiting. Judge Learned Hand in the Masses suit states the proper attitude toward free speech in war.

"Political agitation, by the passions it arouses, may in fact stimulate men to the violation of law. . . . Yet to assimilate agitation, legitimate as such, with direct incitement to violent resistance, is to disregard the tolerance of all methods of political agitation, which in normal times is a safeguard of free government. The distinction is not a scholastic subterfuge, but a hard-bought acquisition in the fight for freedom."

Other judges, however, have interpreted the 1917 Act so broadly as to make practically all opposition to the war criminal, since it may conceivably come to the ears of soldiers and recruits. Still more extreme is the charge of Judge Van Valkenburgh in the trial of Rose Pastor Stokes. He told the jury that her letter to the Kansas City Star, "I am for the people, while the government is for the profiteers," might interfere with the operation of the military forces, because it might dampen the spirits of the Star subscribers, which included the wives, sisters, and sweethearts of soldiers, and "our armies in the field can succeed only so far as they are supported by the folks at home." On the accusation of causing disloyalty in the military and naval forces, he included in the forces "all able-bodied male citizens between the ages of 18 and 45 years." The right of criticism means "criticism friendly to the war." Mrs. Stokes was sentenced to prison for ten years. Such law suppresses free speech for all opponents of a war, but allows militant newspapers and politicians to block by unbounded abuse the efforts of the President to end a war by a just settlement.

Congress reached the same result by the 1918 Amendment to the Act, making it criminal to "oppose the cause of the United States" in any war.

The Espionage Act is not limited to this war. The pacifists and Socialists are wrong now, but they may be right next time. Balance military necessity in such a case against the harm of suppressing truth by a ten-year term. The government can argue better than Mrs. Stokes, and at its back are public opinion, press, police, the army, to prevent her words from causing unlawful acts. On the other hand, while national welfare doubtless demands that this just war be pushed to victory, it also demands that an unjust war be stopped. The only way to find out whether a war is unjust is to let people say so.

The 1918 clauses punishing attacks on the Constitution and our form of government raise still stronger objections. They have nothing to do with war. They may be used during some petty foreign squabble to arrest and imprison, here in this country, an excitable advocate of the Susan B. Anthony Amendment or the substitution of Soviets for Congress. If there was one thing which the First Amendment was meant by our ancestors to protect, it was criticism of the existing form of government, the kind of criticism which George III's judges punished. Even if the Act permits temperate discussion, which is doubtful, it still abridges free speech, for the greater the need of change, the greater the likelihood that agitators will lose their temper over the present situation.

Consequently, the whole extract from the Espionage Act preceding this article and charges like that in the Stokes case probably violate the First Amendment. . . .

. . . Just as Lord Ellenborough could see no motive for Leigh Hunt's attack on flogging in the army except the desire to cause a mutiny, so our judges are sometimes overready to infer a similar criminal intent from talk of profiteering or Wall Street. Just as Lord Kenyon, while trying a man who happened to sympathize with the French Revolution went out of his way to emphasize its massacres, so the judge in the Stokes trial called the Russian Revolution "the greatest betrayal of the cause of democracy the world has ever seen." Fox's words are not out of place now, that revolutions elsewhere were not owing to the freedom of popular opinions, but to the reverse. In one respect the parallelism does not hold. The maximum sentence imposed in the English trials was four years. We have sent four men to prison for twenty years.

A friend of Lovejoy, the Abolitionist printer killed in the Alton Riots, said at the time that we are more especially called upon to maintain the principles of free discussion in case of unpopular sentiments or persons, as in no other case will any effort to maintain them be needed. We have made a mistake under the pressure of a great crisis. We should admit it frankly before intolerance becomes a habit in our law, repeal this entire section of the Espionage Act, and leave our political prisoners as well situated as Liebknecht.

157

Schenck v. United States (1919)

The Supreme Court's first attempt to define constitutionally protected expression came in a series of cases growing out of prosecutions under the 1918 Sedition Act. In the first of these cases, Justice Holmes articulated the "clear and present danger" doctrine that would be a baseline in speech cases for the next generation. Despite criticism of the test as too amenable to judicial prejudice, Holmes actually rejected a far more restrictive and, at the time, more widely supported standard, the "bad tendency test," which would have punished "any tendency in speech to produce bad acts, no matter how remote." Within a few weeks, Holmes expanded upon the clear and present danger test in two other cases, *Debs v. United States* and *Frohwerk v. United States;* in all three cases he spoke for a unanimous bench in sustaining the convictions.

See Paul Murphy, *World War I and the Origin of Civil Liberties in the United States* (1979); Zechariah Chafee, Jr., *Free Speech in the United States* (1920; rev. ed., 1941); and F. E. Strong, "Fifty Years of Clear and Present Danger: From Schenck to Brandenberg—and Beyond," 1969 *Supreme Court Review* 41 (1969).

———

Justice Holmes delivered the opinion of the Court:

This is an indictment in three counts. The first charges a conspiracy to violate the Espionage Act of June 15, 1917, by causing and attempting to cause insubordination, &c., in the military and naval forces of the United States, and to obstruct the recruiting and enlistment service of the United States, when the United States was at war with the German Empire, to-wit, that the defendants wilfully conspired to have printed and circulated to men who had been called and accepted for military service a document alleged to be calculated to cause such insubordination and obstruction. . . .

The document in question upon its first printed side recited the first section of the Thirteenth Amendment, said that the idea embodied in it was violated by the Conscription Act and that a conscript is little better than a convict. In impassioned language it intimated that conscription was despotism in its worst form and a monstrous wrong against humanity in the interest of Wall Street's chosen few. It said "Do not submit to intimidation," but in form at least confined itself to peaceful measures such as a petition for the repeal of the act. The other and later printed side of the sheet was headed "Assert Your Rights." It stated reasons for alleging that any one violated the Constitution when he refused to recognize "your right to assert your opposition to the draft," and went on "If you do not assert and support your rights, you are helping to deny or disparage rights

Source: 249 U.S. 47 (1919)

which it is the solemn duty of all citizens and residents of the United States to retain." It described the arguments on the other side as coming from cunning politicians and a mercenary capitalist press, and even silent consent to the conscription law as helping to support an infamous conspiracy. It denied the power to send our citizens away to foreign shores to shoot up the people of other lands, and added that words could not express the condemnation such cold-blooded ruthlessness deserves, &c., &c., winding up "You must do your share to maintain, support and uphold the rights of the people of this country." Of course the document would not have been sent unless it had been intended to have some effect, and we do not see what effect it could be expected to have upon persons subject to the draft except to influence them to obstruct the carrying of it out. The defendants do not deny that the jury might find against them on this point.

But it is said, suppose that that was the tendency of this circular, it is protected by the First Amendment to the Constitution. Two of the strongest expressions are said to be quoted respectively from well-known public men. It well may be that the prohibition of laws abridging the freedom of speech is not confined to previous restraints, although to prevent them may have been the main purpose. . . . We admit that in many places and in ordinary times the defendants in saying all that was said in the circular would have been within their constitutional rights. But the character of every act depends upon the circumstances in which it is done. The most stringent protection of free speech would not protect a man in falsely shouting fire in a theatre and causing a panic. The question in every case is whether the words used are used in such circumstances and are of such a nature as to create a clear and present danger that they will bring about the substantive evils that Congress has a right to prevent. It is a question of proximity and degree. When a nation is at war many things that might be said in time of peace are such a hindrance to its effort that their utterance will not be endured so long as men fight, and that no Court could regard them as protected by any constitutional right. It seems to be admitted that if an actual obstruction of the recruiting service were proved, liability for words that produced that effect might be enforced. The statute of 1917 in § 4 punishes conspiracies to obstruct as well as actual obstruction. If the act (speaking, or circulating a paper), its tendency and the intent with which it is done are the same, we perceive no ground for saying that success alone warrants making the act a crime. . . . Indeed that case might be said to dispose of the present contention if the precedent covers all *media concludendi*. But as the right to free speech was not referred to specially, we have thought fit to add a few words. . . .

Judgments affirmed.

158   *Senate Round Robin (1919)*

Ever since Washington's day, there has been a latent conflict between Congress and the executive over control of foreign policy. Presidents usually claim that the Constitution delegates nearly all responsibility for foreign affairs into their hands; the legislature in turn insists that it too has a significant role to play. At least before the First World War the issue never reached crisis proportions because, for the most part, foreign policy matters played a relatively insignificant role in American political life.

During the war, President Woodrow Wilson insisted that he had full power over foreign affairs, and at least while the fighting continued, Congress preferred to leave conduct of the war and related foreign matters in his hands. But after the war, Wilson made a fateful mistake when, in going to the Versailles Peace Conference, he neither consulted Congress nor took any member of the Senate with him; Wilson could not, however, avoid submitting the treaty negotiated at Paris to the Senate. Shortly after the outlines of the peace proposal became known, and especially the nature of the League of Nations Covenant, thirty-seven senators, more than enough to block treaty ratification, issued what in effect amounted to a constitutional as well as political challenge to Wilson's alleged control over foreign affairs, by announcing they would oppose the treaty.

See John C. Vinson, *Referendum for Isolation* (1961); Ralph Stone, *The Irreconcilables* (1970); William C. Widenor, *Henry Cabot Lodge and the Search for an American Foreign Policy* (1980); and Daniel S. Stid, *The President as Statesman: Woodrow Wilson and the Constitution* (1998).

———

Whereas, under the Constitution it is a function of the Senate to advise and consent to, or dissent from the ratification of any treaty of the United States, and no such treaty can become operative without the consent of the Senate expressed by the affirmative vote of two-thirds of the Senators present, and,

Whereas, Owing to the victory of the arms of the United States and of the nations with whom it is associated, a Peace Conference was convened and is now in session in Paris for the purpose of settling the terms of peace, and,

Whereas, A committee of the conference has proposed a constitution for a League of Nations, and the proposal is now before the Peace Conference for its consideration:

Source: New York Times, March 4, 1919

Now, therefore, be it resolved, by the Senate of the United States in the discharge of its constitutional duty of advice in regard to treaties, that it is the sense of the Senate that, while it is the sincere desire that the nations of the world should unite to promote peace and general disarmament, the Constitution of the League of Nations in the form now proposed should not be accepted by the United States.

And be it resolved further, that it is the sense of the Senate that the negotiations on the part of the United States should immediately be directed to the utmost expedition of the urgent business of negotiating peace terms with Germany satisfactory to the United States and to the nations with whom the United States is associated in the war against the German Government, and the proposal for a League of Nations to insure the permanent peace of the world should then be taken up for careful and serious consideration.

159   *Abrams v. United States (1919)*

Holmes's three speech decisions (Document 157) were met with sharp criticism in the academic community. Professor Ernst Freund of Chicago, for example, argued that "tolerance of adverse opinion is not a matter of generosity but of political prudence." Holmes, who had always enjoyed the respect of legal scholars, did not understand their objections, and he agreed to meet with Zechariah Chafee, Jr. The Harvard professor convinced him that free speech served important national purposes, and the country would suffer more from restrictions on that speech than from alleged and vague dangers posed by unpopular doctrines. Early in the next term, Chafee's arguments bore fruit.

Abrams had been convicted of distributing pamphlets in Yiddish criticizing the Wilson administration for sending troops to Russia, although he did not necessarily oppose war against Russia. Seven members of the Court, speaking through Justice Clarke, sustained the conviction under the clear and present danger test. Holmes's dissent, joined in by Brandeis, is recognized as the starting point in modern judicial concern for free expression.

See items cited for Documents 154 and 156, as well as Fred D. Ragan, "Justice Oliver Wendell Holmes, Jr., Zechariah Chafee, Jr., and the Clear and Present Danger Test for Free Speech: The First Year, 1919," 58 *Journal of American History* 24 (1971); and Richard Polenburg, *Fighting Faiths: The Abrams Case, the Supreme Court, and Free Speech* (1987).

———

Justice Holmes dissenting:

This indictment is founded wholly upon the publication of two leaflets which I shall

Source: 250 U.S. 616, 624 (1919)

describe in a moment. The first count charges a conspiracy pending the war with Germany to publish abusive language about the form of government of the United States, laying the preparation and publishing of the first leaflet as overt acts. The second count charges a conspiracy pending the war to publish language intended to bring the form of government into contempt, laying the preparation and publishing of the two leaflets as overt acts. The third count alleges a conspiracy to encourage resistance to the United States in the same war and to attempt to effectuate the purpose by publishing the same leaflets. The fourth count lays a conspiracy to incite curtailment of production of things necessary to the prosecution of the war and to attempt to accomplish it by publishing the second leaflet to which I have referred.

The first of these leaflets says that the President's cowardly silence about the intervention in Russia reveals the hypocrisy of the plutocratic gang in Washington. It intimates that "German militarism combined with allied capitalism to crush the Russian revolution"—goes on that the tyrants of the world fight each other until they see a common enemy—working class enlightenment, when they combine to crush it; and that now militarism and capitalism combined, though not openly, to crush the Russian revolution. It says that there is only one enemy of the workers of the world and that is capitalism; that it is a crime for workers of America, &c., to fight the workers' republic of Russia, and ends "Awake! Awake, you Workers of the World! Revolutionists." A note adds "It is absurd to call us pro-German. We hate and despise German militarism more than do you hypocritical tyrants. We have more reasons for denouncing German militarism than has the coward of the White House."

The other leaflet, headed "Workers—Wake Up," with abusive language says that America together with the Allies will march for Russia to help the Czecko-Slovaks in their struggle against the Bolsheviki, and that this time the hypocrites shall not fool the Russian emigrants and friends of Russia in America. It tells the Russian emigrants that they now must spit in the face of the false military propaganda by which their sympathy and help to the prosecution of the war have been called forth and says that with the money they have lent or are going to lend "they will make bullets not only for the Germans but also for the Workers Soviets of Russia," and further, "Workers in the ammunition factories, you are producing bullets, bayonets, cannon, to murder not only the Germans, but also your dearest, best, who are in Russia and are fighting for freedom." It then appeals to the same Russian emigrants at some length not to consent to the "inquisitionary expedition to Russia," and says that the destruction of the Russian revolution is "the politics of the march to Russia." The leaflet winds up by saying "Workers, our reply to this barbaric intervention has to be a general strike!," and after a few words on the spirit of revolution, exhortations not to be afraid, and some usual tall talk ends "Woe unto those who will be in the way of progress. Let solidarity live! The Rebels." . . .

. . . It seems too plain to be denied that the suggestion to workers in the ammunition factories that they are producing bullets to murder their dearest, and the further advocacy of a general strike, both in the second leaflet, do urge curtailment of production of things necessary to the prosecution of the war within the meaning of the Act of May 16, 1918, c. 75, 40 Stat. 553, amending § 3 of the earlier Act of 1917. But to make the conduct criminal that statute requires that it should be "with intent by such curtailment to cripple or hinder the United States in the prosecution of the war." It seems to me that no such intent is proved.

I am aware of course that the word intent as vaguely used in ordinary legal discussion means no more than knowledge at the time of the act that the consequences said to be intended will ensue. Even less than that will satisfy the general principle of civil and criminal liability. A man may have to pay damages, may be sent to prison, at common law might be hanged, if at the time of his act he knew facts from which common experience showed that the consequences would follow, whether he individually could foresee them or not. But, when words are used exactly, a deed is not done with intent to produce a consequence unless that consequence is the aim of the deed. It may be obvious, and obvious to the actor, that the consequence will follow, and he may be liable for it even if he regrets it, but he does not do the act with intent to produce it unless the aim to produce it is the proximate motive of the specific act, although there may be some deeper motive behind.

It seems to me that this statute must be taken to use its words in a strict and accurate sense. They would be absurd in any other. A patriot might think that we were wasting money on aeroplanes, or making more cannon of a certain kind than we needed, and might advocate curtailment with success, yet even if it turned out that the curtailment hindered and was thought by other minds to have been obviously likely to hinder the United States in the prosecution of the war, no one would hold such conduct a crime. I admit that my illustration does not answer all that might be said but it is enough to show what I think and to let me pass to a more important aspect of the case. I refer to the First Amendment to the Constitution that Congress shall make no law abridging the freedom of speech.

I never have seen any reason to doubt that the questions of law that alone were before this Court in the cases of *Schenck, Frohwerk* and *Debs,* . . . were rightly decided. I do not doubt for a moment that by the same reasoning that would justify punishing persuasion to murder, the United States constitutionally may punish speech that produces or is intended to produce a clear and imminent danger that it will bring about forthwith certain substantive evils that the United States constitutionally may seek to prevent. The power undoubtedly is greater in time of war than in time of peace because war opens dangers that do not exist at other times.

But as against dangers peculiar to war, as against others, the principle of the right to free speech is always the same. It is only the present danger of immediate evil or an intent to bring it about that warrants Congress in setting a limit to the expression of opinion where private rights are not concerned. Congress certainly cannot forbid all effort to change the mind of the country. Now nobody can suppose that the surreptitious publishing of a silly leaflet by an unknown man, without more, would present any immediate danger that its opinions would hinder the success of the government arms or have any appreciable tendency to do so. Publishing those opinions for the very purpose of obstructing however, might indicate a greater danger and at any rate would have the quality of an attempt. So I assume that the second leaflet if published for the purposes alleged in the fourth count might be punishable. But it seems pretty clear to me that nothing less than that would bring these papers within the scope of this law. An actual intent in the sense that I have explained is necessary to constitute an attempt, where a further act of the same individual is required to complete the substantive crime, for reasons given in *Swift & Co.* v. *United States,* 196 U.S. 375, 396. It is necessary where the success of the attempt depends upon others because if that intent is not present the actor's aim may be accomplished without bringing about the evils sought to be checked. An intent to prevent interference with the revolution in Russia might have been satisfied without any hindrance to carrying on the war in which we were engaged.

I do not see how anyone can find the intent required by the statute in any of the defendants' words. The second leaflet is the only one that affords even a foundation for the charge, and there, without invoking the hatred of German militarism expressed in the former one, it is evident from the beginning to the end that the only object of the paper is to help Russia and stop American intervention there against the popular government—not to impede the United States in the war that it was carrying on. To say that two phrases taken literally might import a suggestion of conduct that would have interference with the war as an indirect and probably undesired effect seems to me by no means enough to show an attempt to produce that effect.

I return for a moment to the third count. That charges an intent to provoke resistance to the United States in its war with Germany. Taking the clause in the statute that deals with that in connection with the other elaborate provisions of the act, I think that resistance to the United States means some forcible act of opposition to some proceeding of the United States in pursuance of the war. I think the intent must be the specific intent that I have described and for the reasons that I have given I think that no such intent was proved or existed in fact. I also think that there is no hint at resistance to the United States as I construe the phrase.

In this case sentences of twenty years imprisonment have been imposed for the publishing of two leaflets that I believe the defendants had as much right to publish as the Government has to publish the Constitution of the United States now vainly invoked by them. Even if I am technically wrong and enough can be squeezed from these poor and puny anonymities to turn the color of legal litmus paper; I will add, even if what I think the necessary intent were shown; the most nominal punishment seems to me all that possibly could be inflicted, unless the defendants are to be made to suffer not for what the indictment alleges but for the creed that they avow—a creed that I believe to be the creed of ignorance and immaturity when honestly held, as I see no reason to doubt that it was held here, but which, although made the subject of examination at the trial, no one has a right even to consider in dealing with the charges before the Court.

Persecution for the expression of opinions seems to me perfectly logical. If you have no doubt of your premises or your power and want a certain result with all your heart you naturally express your wishes in law and sweep away all opposition. To allow opposition by speech seems to indicate that you think the speech impotent, as when a man says that he has squared the circle, or that you do not care whole-heartedly for the result, or that you doubt either your power or your premises. But when men have realized that time has upset many fighting faiths, they may come to believe even more than they believe the very foundations of their own conduct that the ultimate good desired is better reached by free trade in ideas—that the best test of truth is the power of the thought to get itself accepted in the competition of the market, and that truth is the only ground upon which their wishes safely can be carried out. That at any rate is the theory of our Constitution. It is an experiment, as all life is an experiment. Every year if not every day we have to wager our salvation upon some prophecy based upon imperfect knowledge. While that experiment is part of our system I think that we should be eternally vigilant against attempts to check the expression of opinions that we loathe and believe to be fraught with death, unless they so imminently threaten immediate interference with the lawful and pressing purposes of the law that an immediate check is required to save the country. I wholly disagree with the argument of the Government that the First Amendment left the common law as to seditious libel in force. History seems to me against the notion. I had conceived that the United States through many years had shown its repentance for the Sedition Act of 1798, by repaying fines that it imposed. Only the emergency that makes it immediately dangerous to leave the correction of evil counsels to time warrants making any exception to the sweeping command, "Congress shall make no law . . . abridging the freedom of speech." Of course I am speaking only of expressions of opinion and exhortations, which were all that were uttered here, but I regret that I cannot put into more impressive words my belief that in their conviction upon this indictment the defendants were deprived of their rights under the Constitution of the United States.

Mr. Justice Brandeis concurs with the foregoing opinion.

---

160   *Missouri v. Holland (1920)*

A 1916 agreement between Great Britain and the United States called for the protection of several species of migratory birds, and Congress had enacted its provisions into the Migratory Bird Act of 1918. Missouri attacked both the law and the treaty, claiming that bird hunting, essentially a local matter, lay beyond the reach of federal powers because of the Tenth Amendment. Holmes's opinion was breathtaking in scope, because he based the treaty power not on the Constitution, which had checks on government, but on the inherent powers of sovereignty, which were practically unlimited. The implications of the decision were not lost on isolationists, who saw the opinion as confirming their fears that treaty obligations could bypass constitutional limitations.

See Charles A. Lofgren, "Missouri v. Holland in Historical Perspective," 1975 *Supreme Court Review* 77 (1976); and Louis Henkin, *Foreign Affairs and the Constitution* (1972).

———

Justice Holmes delivered the opinion of the Court:
    The question raised is the general one whether the treaty and statute are void as an interference with the rights reserved to the States.

Source: 252 U.S. 416 (1920)

To answer this question it is not enough to refer to the Tenth Amendment because by Article II, § 2, the power to make treaties is delegated expressly, and by Article VI treaties made under the authority of the United States, along with the Constitution and laws of the United States made in pursuance thereof, are declared the supreme law of the land. If the treaty is valid there can be no dispute about the validity of the statute under Article I, § 8, as a necessary and proper means to execute the powers of the Government. . . .

It is said that a treaty cannot be valid if it infringes the Constitution, that there are limits, therefore, to the treaty-making power, and that one such limit is that what an act of Congress could not do unaided, in derogation of the powers reserved to the States, a treaty cannot do. . . .

Acts of Congress are the supreme law of the land only when made in pursuance of the Constitution, while treaties are declared to be so when made under the authority of the United States. It is open to question whether the authority of the United States means more than the formal acts prescribed to make the convention. We do not mean to imply that there are no qualifications to the treaty-making power; but they must be ascertained in a different way. It is obvious that there may be matters of the sharpest exigency for the national well being that an act of Congress could not deal with but that a treaty followed by such an act could, and it is not lightly to be assumed that, in matters requiring national action, "a power which must belong to and somewhere reside in every civilized government" is not to be found. We are not yet discussing the particular case before us but only are considering the validity of the test proposed. With regard to that we may add that when we are dealing with words that also are a constituent act, like the Constitution of the United States, we must realize that they have called into life a being the development of which could not have been foreseen completely by the most gifted of its begetters. It was enough for them to realize or to hope that they had created an organism; it has taken a century and has cost their successors much sweat and blood to prove that they created a nation. The case before us must be considered in the light of our whole experience and not merely in that of what was said a hundred years ago. The treaty in question does not contravene any prohibitory words to be found in the Constitution. The only question is whether it is forbidden by some invisible radiation from the general terms of the Tenth Amendment. We must consider what this country has become in deciding what that Amendment has reserved.

The State as we have intimated founds its claim of exclusive authority upon an assertion of title to migratory birds, an assertion that is embodied in statute. No doubt it is true that as between a State and its inhabitants the State may regulate the killing and sale of such birds, but it does not follow that its authority is exclusive of paramount powers. . . .

As most of the laws of the United States are carried out within the States and as many of them deal with matters which in the silence of such laws the State might regulate, such general grounds are not enough to support Missouri's claim. Valid treaties of course "are as binding within the territorial limits of the States as they are elsewhere throughout the dominion of the United States." No doubt the great body of private relations usually fall within the control of the State, but a treaty may override its power. . . .

Here a national interest of very nearly the first magnitude is involved. It can be protected only by national action in concert with that of another power. The subject matter is only transitorily within the State and has no permanent habitat therein. But for the treaty and the statute there soon might be no birds for any powers to deal with. We see nothing in the Constitution that compels the Government to sit by while a food supply is cut off and the protectors of our forests and our crops are destroyed. It is not sufficient to rely upon the States. The reliance is vain, and were it otherwise, the question is whether the United States is forbidden to act. We are of opinion that the treaty and statute must be upheld. . . .

Decree affirmed.

Mr. Justice Van Devanter and Mr. Justice Pitney dissent.

161

Federal Trade Commission v. Gratz (1920)

The Federal Trade Commission had been created in 1914 when Wilson's aides, including Louis Brandeis, had determined that it would be impossible to define specifically and by statute all the forms of unfair competition prohibited in the Clayton Antitrust Act. Instead, the FTC would interpret the law to businesses and would also have the power, through cease-and-desist orders, to force businesses to discontinue practices the agency deemed unfair. The act had been designed to allow the FTC flexibility in meeting new modes of unfair competition, and its factual findings were, like those of the Interstate Commerce Commission, supposed to be conclusive in any subsequent judicial proceedings. Justice McReynolds certainly knew the circumstances surrounding the act (he had been Wilson's first attorney general), but he picked up on the deliberate vagueness of the term "unfair competition" and maintained that courts, as a matter of law, would determine what that phrase meant. In effect, this meant that just as the Court had crippled the ICC by denying its findings of fact to be conclusive and forcing it to adjudicate each issue, it now crippled the FTC.

See Carl McFarland, *Judicial Control of the Federal Trade Commission and the Interstate Commerce Commission, 1920–1930* (1932); Robert E. Cushman, *Independent Regulatory Commissions* (1932); and G. Cullom Davis, "The Transformation of the Federal Trade Commission, 1914–1929," 49 *Mississippi Valley Historical Review* 437 (1962).

———

Justice McReynolds delivered the opinion of the Court:

It is unnecessary now to discuss conflicting views concerning validity and meaning of the act creating the commission and effect of the evidence presented. The judgment

---

Source: 253 U.S. 421 (1920)

below must be affirmed since, in our opinion, the first count of the complaint is wholly insufficient to charge respondents with practicing "unfair methods of competition in commerce" within the fair intendment of those words. We go no further and confine this opinion to the point specified.

When proceeding under § 5, it is essential, *first,* that, having reason to believe a person, partnership or corporation has used an unfair method of competition in commerce, the commission shall conclude a proceeding "in respect thereof would be to the interest of the public;" *next,* that it formulate and serve a complaint stating the charges "in that respect" and give opportunity to the accused to show why an order should not issue directing him to "cease and desist from the violation of the law so charged in said complaint." If after a hearing the commission shall deem "the method of competition in question is prohibited by this Act," it shall issue an order requiring the accused "to cease and desist from using such method of competition."

If, when liberally construed, the complaint is plainly insufficient to show unfair competition within the proper meaning of these words there is no foundation for an order to desist—the thing which may be prohibited is the method of competition specified in the complaint. Such an order should follow the complaint; otherwise it is improvident and, when challenged, will be annulled by the court.

The words "unfair method of competition" are not defined by the statute and their exact meaning is in dispute. It is for the courts, not the commission, ultimately to determine as matter of law what they include. They are clearly inapplicable to practices never heretofore regarded as opposed to good morals because characterized by deception, bad faith, fraud or oppression, or as against public policy because of their dangerous tendency unduly to hinder competition or create monopoly. The act was certainly not intended to fetter free and fair competition as commonly understood and practiced by honorable opponents in trade.

Count one alleges, in effect, that Warren, Jones & Gratz are engaged in selling, either directly to the trade or through their co-respondents, cotton ties produced by the Carnegie Steel Company and also jute bagging manufactured by the American Manufacturing Company. That P. P. Williams & Company of Vicksburg, and Charles O. Elmer of New Orleans, are the selling and distributing agents of Warren, Jones & Gratz, and as such sell and distribute their ties and bagging to jobbers and dealers who resell them to retailers, ginners and farmers. That with the purpose and effect of discouraging and stifling competition in the sale of such bagging all the respondents for more than a year have refused to sell any of such ties unless the purchaser would buy from them a corresponding amount of bagging—six yards with as many ties.

The complaint contains no intimation that Warren, Jones & Gratz did not properly obtain their ties and bagging as merchants usually do; the amount controlled by them is not stated; nor is it alleged that they held a monopoly of either ties or bagging or had ability, purpose or intent to acquire one. So far as appears, acting independently, they undertook to sell their lawfully acquired property in the ordinary course, without deception, misrepresentation, or oppression, and at fair prices, to purchasers willing to take it upon terms openly announced.

Nothing is alleged which would justify the conclusion that the public suffered injury or that competitors had reasonable ground for complaint. All question of monopoly or combination being out of the way, a private merchant, acting with entire good faith, may properly refuse to sell except in conjunction, such closely associated articles as ties and bagging. If real competition is to continue, the right of the individual to exercise reasonable discretion in respect of his own business methods must be preserved. . . .

The first count of the complaint fails to show any unfair method of competition practiced by respondents and the order based thereon was improvident.

The judgment of the court below is

Affirmed.

Mr. Justice Pitney concurs in the result.

Mr. Justice Brandeis dissenting, with whom Mr. Justice Clarke concurs.

162

Duplex Printing Press
Co. v. Deering (1921)

Following the *Danbury Hatters* case in 1908, in which the Court had applied the antitrust law to labor activity, organized labor had begun lobbying for a statutory exemption to the Sherman Act, and apparently won its battle in 1914. Section Six of the Clayton Act explicitly declared that labor did not constitute a commodity or an article of commerce and that consequently the antitrust laws should not be interpreted to forbid unions from seeking their legitimate objectives. Section Twenty prohibited courts from issuing injunctions in labor disputes "unless necessary to prevent irreparable injury to property, or to a property right." The same section also forbade injunctions against peaceful picketing or primary boycotts. The law did not come before the Court until 1921, when unions boycotted a manufacturer's products in New York to enforce a strike in Michigan. The Court handed down this decision, which turned the language of the Clayton Act upside down, almost immediately after it had struck down a state anti-injunction statute in *Truax v. Corrigan*.

See Edward Berman, *Labor and the Sherman Act* (1930); Felix Frankfurter and Nathanial V. Greene, *The Labor Injunction* (1930); and Christopher L. Tomlins, *The State and the Unions: Labor Relations, Law and the Organized Labor Movement in America, 1880–1960* (1985).

Justice Pitney delivered the opinion of the Court:

The facts . . . may be summarized as follows:

Complainant conducts its business on the "open shop" policy, without discrimination against either union or non-union men. The individual defendants and the local organizations of which they are the representatives are affiliated with the International Association of Machinists, an unincorporated association having a membership of more than 60,000, and are united in a combination, to which the International Association also is a party, having the object of compelling complainant to unionize its factory and enforce the "closed shop," the eight-hour day, and the union scale of wages, by means of interfering with and restraining its interstate trade in the products of the factory. Complainant's principal manufacture is newspaper presses of large size and complicated mechanism, varying in weight from 10,000 to 100,000 pounds, and requiring a considerable force of labor and a considerable expenditure of time—a week or more—to handle, haul, and erect them at the point of delivery. These presses are sold throughout the United States and in foreign countries; and, as they are especially designed for the production of daily papers, there is a large market for them in and about the city of New York. They are delivered there in the ordinary course of interstate commerce; the handling, hauling, and installation work at destination being done by employees of the purchaser under the supervision of a specially skilled machinist supplied by complainant. The acts complained of and sought to be restrained have nothing to do with the conduct or management of the factory in Michigan, but solely with the installation and operation of the presses by complainant's customers. None of the defendants is or ever was an employee of complainant, and complainant at no time has had relations with either of the organizations that they represent. In August, 1913 (eight months before the filing of the bill), the International Association called a strike at complainant's factory in Battle Creek, as a result of which union machinists to the number of about 11 in the factory and 3 who supervised the erection of presses in the field left complainant's employ. But the defection of so small a number did not materially interfere with the operation of the factory, and sales and shipments in interstate commerce continued.

The acts complained of made up the details of an elaborate programme adopted and carried out by defendants and their organizations in and about the city of New York as part of a country-wide programme adopted by the International Association, for the purpose of enforcing a boycott of complainant's product. . . .

All the judges of the Circuit Court of Appeals concurred in the view that defendants' conduct consisted essentially of efforts to render it impossible for complainant to carry on any commerce in printing presses between Michigan and New York and that defendants had agreed to do and were endeavoring to accomplish the very thing pronounced unlawful by this court. . . . Lawlor v. Loewe. The judges also agreed that the interference with interstate commerce was such as ought to be enjoined, unless the Clayton Act of October 15, 1914, forbade such injunction.

That act was passed after the beginning of the suit, but more than two years before it was brought to hearing. We are clear that the courts below were right in giving effect to it; the real question being whether they gave it the proper effect. In so far as the act (a) provided for relief by injunction to private suitors, (b) imposed conditions upon

Source: 254 U.S. 443 (1921)

granting such relief under particular circumstances, and (c) otherwise modified the Sherman Act, it was effective from the time of its passage, and applicable to pending suits for injunction. . . .

That complainant's business of manufacturing printing presses and disposing of them in commerce is a property right, entitled to protection against unlawful injury or interference; that unrestrained access to the channels of interstate commerce is necessary for the successful conduct of the business; that a widespread combination exists, to which defendants and the associations represented by them are parties, to hinder and obstruct complainant's interstate trade and commerce by the means that have been indicated; and that as a result of it complainant has sustained substantial damage to its interstate trade, and is threatened with further and irreparable loss and damage in the future—is proved by clear and undisputed evidence. Hence the right to an injunction is clear if the threatened loss is due to a violation of the Sherman Act as amended by the Clayton Act. . . .

Upon the question whether the provisions of the Clayton Act forbade the grant of an injunction under the circumstances of the present case, the Circuit Court of Appeals was divided; the majority holding that under section 20, "perhaps in conjunction with section 6," there could be no injunction. These sections are set forth in the margin. Defendants seek to derive from them some authority for their conduct. As to section 6, it seems to us its principal importance in this discussion is for what it does not authorize, and for the limit it sets to the immunity conferred. The section assumes the normal objects of a labor organization to be legitimate, and declares that nothing in the anti-trust laws shall be construed to forbid the existence and operation of such organizations or to forbid their members from lawfully carrying out their legitimate objects; and that such an organization shall not be held in itself—merely because of its existence and operation—to be an illegal combination or conspiracy in restraint of trade. But there is nothing in the section to exempt such an organization or its members from accountability where it or they depart from its normal and legitimate objects and engage in an actual combination or conspiracy in restraint of trade. And by no fair or permissible construction can it be taken as authorizing any activity otherwise unlawful, or enabling a normally lawful organization to become a cloak for an illegal combination or conspiracy in restraint of trade as defined by the anti-trust laws. . . .

. . . Section 20 must be given full effect according to its terms as an expression of the purpose of Congress; but it must be borne in mind that the section imposes an exceptional and extraordinary restriction upon the equity powers of the courts of the United States and upon the general operation of the anti-trust laws, a restriction in the nature of a special privilege or immunity to a particular class, with corresponding detriment to the general public; and it would violate rules of statutory construction having general application and far-reaching importance to enlarge that special privilege by resorting to a loose construction of the section, not to speak of ignoring or slighting the qualifying words that are found in it. Full and fair effect will be given to every word if the exceptional privilege be confined—as the natural meaning of the words confines it—to those who are proximately and substantially concerned as parties to an actual dispute respecting the terms or conditions of their own employment, past, present, or prospective. The extensive construction adopted by the majority of the court below virtually ignores the effect of the qualifying words. Congress had in mind particular industrial controversies, not a general class war. "Terms or conditions of employment" are the only grounds of dispute recognized as adequate to bring into play the exemptions; and it would do violence to the guarded language employed were the exemption extended beyond the parties affected in a proximate and substantial, not merely a sentimental or sympathetic, sense by the cause of dispute.

Nor can section 20 be regarded as bringing in all members of a labor organization as parties to a "dispute concerning terms or conditions of employment," which proximately affects only a few of them, with the result of conferring upon any and all members—no matter how many thousands there may be, nor how remote from the actual conflict—those exemptions which Congress in terms conferred only upon parties to the dispute. That would enlarge by construction the provisions of section 20, which contain no mention of labor organizations, so as to produce an inconsistency with section 6, which deals specifically with the subject and must be deemed to express the measure and limit of the immunity intended by Congress to be incident to mere membership in such an organization. At the same time it would virtually repeal by implication the prohibition of the Sherman Act, so far as labor organizations are concerned, notwithstanding repeals by implication are not favored, and in effect, . . . would confer upon voluntary associations of individuals formed within the states a control over commerce among the states that is denied to the governments of the states themselves. . . .

In the case of the Clayton Act, the printed committee reports are not explicit with respect to the meaning of the "ceasing to patronize" clause of what is now section 20. . . . But they contain extracts from judicial opinions and a then recent text-book sustaining the "primary boycott," and expressing an adverse view as to the secondary or coercive boycott, and, on the whole, are far from manifesting a purpose to relax the prohibition against restraints of trade in favor of the secondary boycott. . . .

. . . An ordinary controversy in a manufacturing establishment, said to concern the terms or conditions of employment there, has been held a sufficient occasion for imposing a general embargo upon the products of the establishment and a nation-wide blockade of the channels of interstate commerce against them, carried out by inciting sympathetic strikes and a secondary boycott against complainant's customers, to the great and incalculable damage of many innocent people far remote from any connection with or control over the original and actual dispute—people constituting, indeed, the general public upon whom the cost must ultimately fall, and whose vital interest in unobstructed commerce constituted the prime and paramount concern of Congress in enacting the antitrust laws, of which the section under consideration forms after all a part.

Reaching the conclusion, as we do, that complainant has a clear right to an injunction under the Sherman Act as amended by the Clayton Act, it becomes unnecessary to consider whether a like result would follow under the common law or local statutes; there being no suggestion that relief thereunder could be broader than that to which complainant is entitled under the acts of Congress. . . .

Mr. Justice Brandeis, dissenting, with whom Mr. Justice Holmes and Mr. Justice Clarke, concur.

163

Moore v. Dempsey (1923)

The criminal law provisions of the Bill of Rights, found in the Fourth through Eighth amendments, had never been applied to the states, and trial and police procedures had always been considered local matters. Some states did have guarantees in their own state constitutions, but their interpretation and enforcement had traditionally been the responsibility of state courts and officials. The racial hysteria following World War I, however, forced the Supreme Court to reexamine these premises, and in doing so it began the process that ultimately led to the application of the criminal procedure guarantees in the federal Constitution to the states as well. Another way of stating this is that the Court began to nationalize the standards of fair criminal procedure.

The first case of lynch law that had come before the Court had involved the notorious Leo Frank incident in Georgia. At that time, only Holmes and Hughes had dissented in *Frank v. Mangum* (1915) from the ruling that federal courts should examine allegations of violence surrounding the trial only in the larger context of overall fairness. In the following case, whose facts are included in the opinion, Holmes opened the door to federal courts' policing state criminal procedures to ensure fairness.

See Loren Miller, *The Petitioner* 232 (1966); and E. Overton and J. S. Waterman, "Federal Habeas Corpus Statutes and *Moore* v. *Dempsey*," 2 *Selected Essays in Constitutional Law* 1477 (1938).

———

Justice Holmes delivered the opinion of the Court:

The appellants are five negroes who were convicted of murder in the first degree and sentenced to death by the Court of the State of Arkansas. The ground of the petition for the writ [of *habeas corpus*] is that the proceedings in the State Court, although a trial in form, were only a form, and that the appellants were hurried to conviction under the pressure of a mob without any regard for their rights and without according to them due process of law.

The case stated by the petition is as follows, and it will be understood that while we put it in narrative form, we are not affirming the facts to be as stated but only what we must take them to be, as they are admitted by the demurrer: On the night of September 30, 1919, a number of colored people assembled in their church were attacked and fired upon by a body of white men, and in the disturbance that followed a white man was killed. The report of the killing caused great excitement and was followed by the hunt-

———

Source: 261 U.S. 86 (1923)

ing down and shooting of many negros and also by the killing on October 1 of one Clinton Lee, a white man, for whose murder the petitioners were indicted. They seem to have been arrested with many others on the same day. The petitioners say that Lee must have been killed by other whites, but that we leave on one side as what we have to deal with is not the petitioners' innocence or guilt but solely the question whether their constitutional rights have been preserved. They say that their meeting was to employ counsel for protection against extortions practiced upon them by the landowners and that the landowners tried to prevent their effort, but that again we pass by as not directly bearing upon the trial. . . .

A Committee of Seven was appointed by the Governor in regard to what the committee called the "insurrection" in the county. The newspapers daily published inflammatory articles. On the 7th a statement by one of the committee was made public to the effect that the present trouble was "a deliberately planned insurrection of the negroes against the whites, directed by an organization known as the 'Progressive Farmers' and Household Union of America' established for the purpose of banding negroes together for the killing of white people." According to the statement the organization was started by a swindler to get money from the blacks.

Shortly after the arrest of the petitioners a mob marched to the jail for the purpose of lynching them but were prevented by the presence of United States troops and the promise of some of the Committee of Seven and other leading officials that if the mob would refrain, as the petition puts it, they would execute those found guilty in the form of law. The Committee's own statement was that the reason that the people refrained from mob violence was "that this Committee gave our citizens their solemn promise that the law would be carried out." According to affidavits of two white men and the colored witnesses on whose testimony the petitioners were convicted, . . . the Committee made good their promise by calling colored witnesses and having them whipped and tortured until they would say what was wanted, among them being the two relied on to prove the petitioners' guilt. . . . On November 3 the petitioners were brought into Court, informed that a certain lawyer was appointed their counsel and were placed on trial before a white jury—blacks being systematically excluded from both grand and petit juries. The Court and neighborhood were thronged with an adverse crowd that threatened the most dangerous consequences to anyone interfering with the desired result. The counsel did not venture to demand delay or a change of venue, to challenge a juryman or to ask for separate trials. He had had no preliminary consultation with the accused, called no witnesses for the defence although they could have been produced, and did not put the defendants on the stand. The trial lasted about three-quarters of an hour and in less than five minutes the jury brought in a verdict of guilty of murder in the first degree. According to the allegations and affidavits there never was a chance for the petitioners to be acquitted; no juryman could have voted for an acquittal and continued to live in Phillips County and if any prisoner by any chance had been acquitted by a jury he could not have escaped the mob. . . .

In *Frank* v. *Magnum* . . . [1915] it was recognized of course that if in fact a trial is dominated by a mob so that there is an actual interference with the course of justice, there is a departure from due process of law; and that "if the State, supplying no corrective process, carries into execution a judgment of death or imprisonment based upon a verdict thus produced by mob domination, the State deprives the accused of his life or liberty without due process of law." We assume in accordance with that case that the corrective process supplied by the State may be so adequate that interference by *habeas corpus* ought not to be allowed. It certainly is true that mere mistakes of law in the course of a trial are not to be corrected in that way. But if the case is that the whole proceeding is a mask—that counsel, jury and judge were swept to the fatal end by an irresistible wave of public passion, and that the State Courts failed to correct the wrong, neither perfection in the machinery for correction nor the possibility that the trial court and counsel saw no other way of avoiding an immediate outbreak of the mob can prevent this Court from securing to the petitioners their constitutional rights.

In this case a motion for a new trial on the ground alleged in this petition was overruled and upon exceptions and appeal to the Supreme Court the judgment was affirmed. The Supreme Court said that the complaint of discrimination against petitioners by the exclusion of colored men from the jury came too late and by way of answer to the objection that no fair trial could be had in the circumstances, stated that it could not say "that this must necessarily have been the case"; that eminent counsel was appointed to defend the petitioners, that the trial was had according to law, the jury correctly charged, and the testimony legally sufficient. On June 8, 1921, two days before the date fixed for their execution, a petition for *habeas corpus* was presented to the Chancellor and he issued the writ and an injunction against the execution of the petitioners; but the Supreme Court of the State held that the Chancellor had no jurisdiction under the state law whatever might be the law of the United States. The present petition perhaps was suggested by the language of the Court: "What the result would be of an application to a Federal Court we need not inquire." It was presented to the District Court on September 21. We shall not say more concerning the corrective process afforded to the petitioners than that it does not seem to us sufficient to allow a Judge of the United States to escape the duty of examining the facts for himself when if true as alleged they make the trial absolutely void. We have confined the statement to facts admitted by the demurrer. We will not say that they cannot be met, but it appears to us unavoidable that the District Judge should find whether the facts alleged are true and whether they can be explained so far as to leave the state proceedings undisturbed.

Order reversed. The case to stand for hearing before the District Court.

[Justices McReynolds and Sutherland dissented.]

164

Adkins v. Children's Hospital (1923)

Even conservatives protested when the Court resurrected the Lochner doctrine in this case to strike down a federal statute establishing minimum wages for women in the District of Columbia. Justice Sutherland ignored two decades of court approval of protective legislation to affirm freedom of contract as "the general rule and restraint the exception . . . justified only by exceptional circumstances." Since women had been emancipated by the Nineteenth Amendment, he announced that they no longer needed special protection, and he dismissed the elaborate "Brandeis brief" prepared by Felix Frankfurter as irrelevant. Chief Justice Taft, who could hardly be labeled a liberal, found this too much, and entered one of his few dissenting opinions. Holmes entered one of his many dissents, made perhaps even more forceful by his recognition that Brandeis had recused himself because his daughter Elizabeth worked for the District Minimum Wage Board.

See Joel F. Paschal, *Mr. Justice Sutherland: A Man Against the State* (1951); Judith A. Baer, *The Chains of Protection* (1978); Robert C. Post, "Defending the Lifeworld: Substantive Due Process in the Taft Court Era," 78 *Boston University Law Review* 1489 (1998); and Thomas Reed Powell, "The Judiciality of Minimum Wage Legislation," 37 *Harvard Law Review* 545 (1924).

———

Justice Sutherland delivered the opinion of the Court:

The question presented for determination by these appeals is the constitutionality of the Act of September 19, 1918, providing for the fixing of minimum wages for women and children in the District of Columbia. . . . The purposes of the act are "to protect the women and minors of the District from conditions detrimental to their health and morals, resulting from wages which are inadequate to maintain decent standards of living; and the Act in each of its provisions and in its entirety shall be interpreted to effectuate these purposes."

The appellee in the first case is a corporation maintaining a hospital for children in the District. It employs a large number of women in various capacities, with whom it had agreed upon rates of wages and compensation satisfactory to such employees, but which in some instances were less than the minimum wage fixed by an order of the board made in pursuance of the act. The women with whom appellee had so contracted were all of full age and under no legal disability. The instant suit was brought by the appellee in the

Supreme Court of the District to restrain the board from enforcing or attempting to enforce its order on the ground that the same was in contravention of the Constitution, and particularly the due process clause of the Fifth Amendment. . . .

We come then, at once, to the substantive question involved.

The judicial duty of passing upon the constitutionality of an act of Congress is one of great gravity and delicacy. The statute here in question has successfully borne the scrutiny of the legislative branch of the government, which, by enacting it, has affirmed its validity; and that determination must be given great weight. This Court, by an unbroken line of decisions from Chief Justice Marshall to the present day, has steadily adhered to the rule that every possible presumption is in favor of the validity of an act of Congress until overcome beyond rational doubt. But if by clear and indubitable demonstration a statute be opposed to the Constitution we have no choice but to say so. The Constitution, by its own terms, is the supreme law of the land, emanating from the people, the repository of ultimate sovereignty under our form of government. A congressional statute, on the other hand, is the act of an agency of this sovereign authority and if it conflict with the Constitution must fall; for that which is not supreme must yield to that which is. To hold it invalid (if it be invalid) is a plain exercise of the judicial power—that power vested in courts to enable them to administer justice according to law. From the authority to ascertain and determine the law in a given case, there necessarily results, in case of conflict, the duty to declare and enforce the rule of the supreme law and reject that of an inferior act of legislation which, transcending the Constitution, is of no effect and binding on no one. This is not the exercise of a substantive power to review and nullify acts of Congress, for no such substantive power exists. It is simply a necessary concomitant of the power to hear and dispose of a case or controversy properly before the court, to the determination of which must be brought the test and measure of the law.

The statute now under consideration is attacked upon the ground that it authorizes an unconstitutional interference with the freedom of contract included within the guaranties of the due process clause of the Fifth Amendment. That the right to contract about one's affairs is a part of the liberty of the individual protected by this clause, is settled by the decisions of this Court and is no longer open to question. . . . Within this liberty are contracts of employment of labor. In making such contracts, generally speaking, the parties have an equal right to obtain from each other the best terms they can as the result of private bargaining. . . .

There is, of course, no such thing as absolute freedom of contract. It is subject to a great variety of restraints. But freedom of contract is, nevertheless, the general rule and restraint the exception; and the exercise of legislative authority to abridge it can be justified only by the existence of exceptional circumstances. Whether these circumstances exist in the present case constitutes the question to be answered. It will be helpful to this end to review some of the decisions where the interference has been upheld and consider the grounds upon which they rest. . . .

[Justice Sutherland reviewed those cases in which the Court upheld restrictions on freedom to contract.]

In the *Muller Case* the validity of an Oregon statute, forbidding the employment of any female in certain industries more than ten hours during any one day was upheld. The decision proceeded upon the theory that the difference between the sexes may justify a different rule respecting hours of labor in the case of women than in the case of men. It is pointed out that these consist in differences of physical structure, especially in respect of the maternal functions, and also in the fact that historically woman has always been dependent upon man, who has established his control by superior physical strength. . . . In view of the great—not to say revolutionary—changes which have taken place since that utterance, in the contractual, political and civil status of women, culminating in the Nineteenth Amendment, it is not unreasonable to say that these differences have now come almost, if not quite, to the vanishing point. In this aspect of the matter, while the physical differences must be recognized in appropriate cases, and legislation fixing hours or conditions of work may properly take them into account, we cannot accept the doctrine that women of mature age, *sui juris,* require or may be subjected to restrictions upon their liberty of contract which could not lawfully be imposed in the case of men under similar circumstances. To do so would be to ignore all the implications to be drawn from the present day trend of legislation, as well as that of common thought and usage, by which woman is accorded emancipation from the old doctrine that she must be given special protection or be subjected to special restraint in her contractual and civil relationships. In passing, it may be noted that the instant statute applies in the case of a woman employer contracting with a woman employee as it does when the former is a man. . . .

. . . This Court has been careful in every case where the question has been raised, to place its decision upon this limited authority of the legislature to regulate hours of labor and to disclaim any purpose to uphold the legislation as fixing wages, thus recognizing an essential difference between the two. It seems plain that these decisions afford no real support for any form of law establishing minimum wages.

If now, in the light furnished by the foregoing exceptions to the general rule forbidding legislative interference with freedom of contract, we examine and analyze the statute in question, we shall see that it differs from them in every material respect. It is not a law dealing with any business charged with a public interest or with public work, or to meet and tide over a temporary emergency. It has nothing to do with the character, methods or periods of wage payments. It does not prescribe hours of labor or conditions under which labor is to be done. It is not for the protection of persons under legal disability or for the prevention of fraud. It is simply and exclusively a price-fixing law, confined to adult women (for we are not now considering the provisions relating to minors), who are legally as capable of contracting for themselves as men. It forbids two parties having lawful capacity—under penalties as to the employer—to freely contract with one another in respect of the price for which one shall render service to the other in a purely private employment where both are willing, perhaps anxious, to agree, even though the consequence may be to oblige one to surrender a desirable engagement and the other to dispense with the services of a desirable employee." The price fixed by the board need have no relation to the capacity or earning power of the employee, the number of hours which may happen to constitute the day's work, the character of the place where the work is to be done, or the circumstances or surroundings of the employment; and, while it has no other basis to support its validity than the assumed necessities of the employee, it takes no account of any independent resources she may have. It is based wholly on the opinions of the members of the board and their advisers—perhaps an average of their opinions, if they do not precisely agree—as to what will be necessary to provide a living for a woman, keep her in health and preserve her morals. It applies to any and every occupation in the District, without regard to its nature or the character of the work.

The standard furnished by the statute for the guidance of the board is so vague as to be impossible of practical application with any reasonable degree of accuracy. What is sufficient to supply the necessary cost of living for a woman worker and maintain her in good health and protect her morals is obviously not a precise or unvarying sum—not even approximately so. The amount will depend upon a variety of circumstances: the individual temperament, habits of thrift, care, ability to buy necessaries intelligently, and whether the woman lives alone or with her family. To those who practice economy, a given sum will afford comfort, while to those of contrary habit the same sum will be wholly inadequate. The coöperative economies of the family group are not taken into account though they constitute an important consideration in estimating the cost of living, for it is obvious that the individual expense will be less in the case of a member of a family than in the case of one living alone. The relation between earnings and morals is not capable of standardization. It cannot be shown that well paid women safeguard their morals more carefully than those who are poorly paid. Morality rests upon other considerations than wages; and there is, certainly, no such prevalent connection between the two as to justify a broad attempt to adjust the latter with reference to the former. As a means of safeguarding morals the attempted classification, in our opinion, is without reasonable basis. . . .

The law takes account of the necessities of only one party to the contract. It ignores the necessities of the employer by compelling him to pay not less than a certain sum, not only whether the employee is capable of earning it, but irrespective of the ability of his business to sustain the burden, generously leaving him, of course, the privilege of abandoning his business as an alternative for going on at a loss. Within the limits of the minimum sum, he is precluded, under penalty of fine and imprisonment, from adjusting compensation to the differing merits of his employees. It compels him to pay at least the sum fixed in any event, because the employee needs it, but requires no service of equivalent value from the employee. . . .

The feature of this statute which, perhaps more than any other, puts upon it the stamp of invalidity is that it exacts from the employer an arbitrary payment for a purpose and upon a basis having no causal connection with his business, or the contract or the work the employee engages to do. The declared basis, as already pointed out, is not the value of the service rendered, but the extraneous circumstance that the employee needs to get a prescribed sum of money to insure her subsistence, health and morals. The ethical right of every worker, man or woman, to a living wage may be conceded. One of the declared and important purposes of trade organizations is to secure it. And with that principle and with every legitimate effort to realize it in fact, no one can quarrel; but the fallacy of the proposed method of attaining it is that it assumes that every employer is bound at all events to furnish it. The moral requirement implicit in every contract of employment, viz, that the amount to be paid and the service to be rendered shall bear to each other some relation of just equivalence, is completely ignored. The necessities of the employee are alone considered and these arise outside of the employment, are the same when there is no employment, and as great in one occupation as in another. Certainly the employer by paying a fair equivalent for the service rendered, though not sufficient to support the employee, has neither caused nor contributed to her poverty. On the contrary, to the extent of what he pays he has relieved it. In principle, there can be no difference between the case of selling labor and the case of selling goods. If one goes to the butcher, the baker or grocer to buy food, he is morally entitled to obtain the worth of his money but he is not entitled to more. If what he gets is worth what he pays he is not justified in demanding more simply because he needs more; and the shopkeeper, having dealt fairly and honestly in that transaction, is not concerned in any peculiar sense with the question of his customer's necessities. . . . A statute requiring an employer to pay in money, to pay at prescribed and regular intervals, to pay the value of the services rendered, even to pay with fair relation to the extent of the benefit obtained from the service, would be understandable. But a statute which prescribes payment without regard to any of these things and solely with relation to circumstances apart from the contract of employment, the business affected by it and the work done under it, is so clearly the product of a naked, arbitrary exercise of power that it cannot be allowed to stand under the Constitution of the United States. . . .

It has been said that legislation of the kind now under review is required in the interest of social justice, for whose ends freedom of contract may lawfully be subjected to restraint. The liberty of the individual to do as he pleases, even in innocent matters, is not absolute. It must frequently yield to the common good, and the line beyond which the power of interference may not be pressed is neither definite nor unalterable but may be made to move, within limits not well defined, with changing need and circumstance. Any attempt to fix a rigid boundary would be unwise as well as futile. But, nevertheless, there are limits to the power, and when these have been passed, it becomes the plain duty of the courts in the proper exercise of their authority to so declare. To sustain the individual freedom of action contemplated by the Constitution, is not to strike down the common good but to exalt it; for surely the good of society as a whole cannot be better served than by the preservation against arbitrary restraint of the liberties of its constituent members.

It follows from what has been said that the act in question passes the limit prescribed by the Constitution, and, accordingly, the decrees of the court below are

Affirmed.

Mr. Justice Brandeis took no part in the consideration or decision of these cases.

Chief Justice Taft, dissenting:

I regret much to differ from the Court in these cases.

The boundary of the police power beyond which its exercise becomes an invasion of the guaranty of liberty under the Fifth and Fourteenth Amendments to the Constitution is not easy to mark. Our Court has been laboriously engaged in pricking out a line in successive cases. We must be careful, it seems to me, to follow that line as well as we can and not to depart from it by suggesting a distinction that is formal rather than real.

Legislatures in limiting freedom of contract between employee and employer by a minimum wage proceed on the assumption that employees, in the class receiving least pay, are not upon a full level of equality of choice with their employer and in their necessitous circumstances are prone to accept pretty much anything that is offered. They are peculiarly subject to the overreaching of the harsh and greedy employer. The evils of the sweating system and of the long hours and low wages which are characteristic of it are well known. Now, I agree that it is a disputable question in the field of political economy how far a statutory requirement of maximum hours or minimum wages may be a useful remedy for these evils, and whether it may not make the case of the oppressed employee worse than it was before. But it is not the function of this Court to hold congressional acts invalid simply because they are passed to carry out economic views which the Court believes to be unwise or unsound.

Legislatures which adopt a requirement of maximum hours or minimum wages may be presumed to believe that when sweating employers are prevented from paying unduly low wages by positive law they will continue their business, abating that part of their profits, which were wrung from the necessities of their employees, and will concede the better terms required by the law; and that while in individual cases hardship may result, the restriction will enure to the benefit of the general class of employees in whose interest the law is passed and so to that of the community at large.

The right of the legislature under the Fifth and Fourteenth Amendments to limit the hours of employment on the score of the health of the employee, it seems to me, has been firmly established. As to that, one would think, the line had been pricked out so that it has become a well formulated rule.. . . . I have always supposed that the *Lochner Case* was thus overruled *sub silentio.* Yet the opinion of the Court herein in support of its conclusion quotes from the opinion in the *Lochner Case* as one which has been sometimes distinguished but never overruled. . . .

With deference to the very able opinion of the Court and my brethren who concur in it, it appears to me to exaggerate the importance of the wage term of the contract of employment as more inviolate than its other terms. Its conclusion seems influenced by the fear that the concession of the power to impose a minimum wage must carry with it a concession of the power to fix a maximum wage. This, I submit, is a *non sequitur.* A line of distinction like the one under discussion in this case is, as the opinion elsewhere admits, a matter of degree and practical experience and not of pure logic. Certainly the wide difference between prescribing a minimum wage and a maximum wage could as a matter of degree and experience be easily affirmed. . . .

But for my inability to agree with some general observations in the forcible opinion of Mr. Justice Holmes who follows me, I should be silent and merely record my concurrence in what he says. It is perhaps wiser for me, however, in a case of this importance, separately to give my reasons for dissenting.

I am authorized to say that Mr. Justice Sanford concurs in this opinion.

Justice Holmes, dissenting:

The question in this case is the broad one, Whether Congress can establish minimum rates of wages for women in the District of Columbia with due provision for special circumstances, or whether we must say that Congress has no power to meddle with the matter at all. To me, notwithstanding the deference due to the prevailing judgment of the Court, the power of Congress seems absolutely free from doubt. The end, to remove conditions. leading to ill health, immorality and the deterioration of the race, no one would deny to be within the scope of constitutional legislation. The means are means that have the approval of Congress, of many States, and of those governments from which we have learned our greatest lessons. When so many intelligent persons, who have studied the matter more than any of us can, have thought that the means are effective and are worth the price, it seems to me impossible to deny that the belief reasonably may be held by reasonable men. If the law encountered no other objection than that the means bore no relation to the end or that they cost too much I do not suppose that anyone would venture to say that it was bad. I agree, of course, that a law answering the foregoing requirements might be invalidated by specific provisions of the Constitution. For instance it might take private property without just compensation. But in the present instance the only objection that can be urged is found within the vague contours of the Fifth Amendment, prohibiting the depriving any person of liberty or property without due process of law. To that I turn.

The earlier decisions upon the same words in the Fourteenth Amendment began within our memory and went no farther than an unpretentious assertion of the liberty to follow the ordinary callings. Later that innocuous generality was expanded into the dogma, Liberty of Contract. Contract is not specially mentioned in the text that we have to construe. It is merely an example of doing what you want to do, embodied in the word liberty. But pretty much all law consists in forbidding men to do some things that they want to do, and contract is no more exempt from law than other acts. . . .

I confess that I do not understand the principle on which the power to fix a minimum for the wages of women can be denied by those who admit the power to fix a maximum for their hours of work. I fully assent to the proposition that here as elsewhere the distinctions of the law are distinctions of degree, but I perceive no difference in the kind or degree of interference with liberty, the only matter with which we have any concern, between the one case and the other. The bargain is equally affected whichever half you regulate. *Muller* v. *Oregon,* I take it, is as good law today as it was in 1908. It will need more than the Nineteenth Amendment to convince me that there are no differences between men and women, or that legislation cannot take those differences into account. I should not hesitate to take them into account if I thought it necessary to sustain this act. . . . But after *Bunting* v. *Oregon,* . . . I had supposed that it was not necessary, and that *Lochner* v. *New York* . . . would be allowed a deserved repose.

This statute does not compel anybody to pay anything. It simply forbids employment at rates below those fixed as the minimum requirement of health and right living. It is safe to assume that women will not be employed at even the lowest wages allowed unless they earn them, or unless the employer's business can sustain the burden. In short the law in its character and operation is like hundreds of so-called police laws that have been upheld. I see no greater objection to using a Board to apply the standard fixed by the act than there is to the other commissions with which we have become familiar, or than there is to the requirement of a license in other cases. The fact that the statute warrants classification, which like all classifications may bear hard upon some individuals, or in exceptional cases, notwithstanding the power given to the Board to issue a special license, is no greater infirmity than is incident to all law. But the ground on which the law is held to fail is fundamental and therefore it is unnecessary to consider matters of detail. . . .

I am of opinion that the statute is valid and that the decree should be reversed.

165   *Meyer v. Nebraska (1923)*

The first suggestion that the Due Process Clause of the Fourteenth Amendment might embrace the civil liberties guaranteed in the Bill of Rights as well as protection of property appeared in Brandeis's dissent in *Gilbert v. Minnesota* (1920). In early 1923, however, a majority of the Court still maintained that the Bill of Rights did not apply to the states (*Prudential Insurance Co. v. Cheek*). But the tide began to change later that year when the Court struck down a state statute that forbade the teaching of any foreign language, a World War I law that had been aimed specifically at German. To be sure, Justice McReynolds utilized the *Lochner* doctrine and found "property rights" involved, but he also noted the violation of free speech. Without using the exact words, McReynolds applied the clear and present danger test and found the statute wanting. Interestingly, the opinion came over the dissent of Justice Holmes, who found neither a threat to freedom nor any reason for the Court to question legislative policy.

Two years later, McReynolds again found property rights at stake when the Court struck down an Oregon law requiring children between eight and sixteen to attend public schools. Passed at the insistence of the Ku Klux Klan, with strong support from nativists, the law aimed to eliminate private and parochial— especially Catholic—schools in the state. For the Court, McReynolds held the statute unconstitutional, since it destroyed property rights in private schools and violated the freedom of parents to choose what sort of education their children should have (*Pierce v. Society of Sisters* [1925]).

See Orville H. Zabell, *God and Caesar in Nebraska* (1955); K. B. O'Brien, Jr., "Education, Americanization and the Supreme Court," 13 *American Quarterly* 161 (1961); and William G. Ross, *Forging New Freedoms: Nativism, Education and the Constitution, 1917–1927* (1994).

———

Mr. Justice McReynolds delivered the opinion of the Court:

Plaintiff in error was tried and convicted in the district court for Hamilton county, Nebraska, under an information which charged that on May 25, 1920, while an instructor in Zion Parochial School he unlawfully taught the subject of reading in the German language to Raymond Parpart, a child of 10 years, who had not attained and successfully passed the eighth grade. . . .

Source: 262 U.S. 390 (1923)

The problem for our determination is whether the statute as construed and applied unreasonably infringes the liberty guaranteed to the plaintiff in error by the Fourteenth Amendment:

"No state . . . shall deprive any person of life, liberty or property without due process of law."

While this court has not attempted to define with exactness the liberty thus guaranteed, the term has received much consideration and some of the included things have been definitely stated. Without doubt, it denotes not merely freedom from bodily restraint but also the right of the individual to contract, to engage in any of the common occupations of life, to acquire useful knowledge, to marry, establish a home and bring up children, to worship God according to the dictates of his own conscience, and generally to enjoy those privileges long recognized at common law as essential to the orderly pursuit of happiness by free men. . . . The established doctrine is that this liberty may not be interfered with, under the guise of protecting the public interest, by legislative action which is arbitrary or without reasonable relation to some purpose within the competency of the state to effect. Determination by the Legislature of what constitutes proper exercise of police power is not final or conclusive but is subject to supervision by the courts. . . .

The American people have always regarded education and acquisition of knowledge as matters of supreme importance which should be diligently promoted. The Ordinance of 1787 declares:

"Religion, morality and knowledge being necessary to good government and the happiness of mankind, schools and the means of education shall forever be encouraged."

Corresponding to the right of control, it is the natural duty of the parent to give his children education suitable to their station in life; and nearly all the states, including Nebraska, enforce this obligation by compulsory laws.

Practically, education of the young is only possible in schools conducted by especially qualified persons who devote themselves thereto. The calling always has been regarded as useful and honorable, essential, indeed, to the public welfare. Mere knowledge of the German language cannot reasonably be regarded as harmful. Heretofore it has been commonly looked upon as helpful and desirable. Plaintiff in error taught this language in school as part of his occupation. His right thus to teach and the right of parents to engage him so to instruct their children, we think, are within the liberty of the amendment. . . .

It is said the purpose of the legislation was to promote civic development by inhibiting training and education of the immature in foreign tongues and ideals before they could learn English and acquire American ideals, and "that the English language should be and become the mother tongue of all children reared in this state." It is also affirmed that the foreign born population is very large, that certain communities commonly use foreign words, follow foreign leaders, move in a foreign atmosphere, and that the children are thereby hindered from becoming citizens of the most useful type and the public safety is imperiled.

That the state may do much, go very far, indeed, in order to improve the quality of its citizens, physically, mentally and morally, is clear; but the individual has certain fundamental rights which must be respected. The protection of the Constitution extends to all, to those who speak other languages as well as to those born with English on the tongue. Perhaps it would be highly advantageous if all had ready understanding of our ordinary speech, but this cannot be coerced by methods which conflict with the Constitution—a desirable end cannot be promoted by prohibited means.

166   *Massachusetts v. Mellon (1923)*

Today federal grants-in-aid to states provide the bulk of the financing in many important programs. The first grant-in-aid program to states came about in 1911, when the Weeks Act sought to encourage greater state participation in forest fire prevention; in the next dozen years the idea spread to a number of programs, so that by 1925, federal grant-in-aid allocations totaled $93 million. In the reactionary mood of the 1920s, opponents of these programs claimed that the grants would destroy local self-government and extend federal power into areas reserved for the states. Massachusetts (through a suit against Secretary of the Treasury Andrew Mellon) attacked the constitutionality of the Sheppard-Towner Act, which provided grants to promote state infant and maternity care programs. The Court sustained the act indirectly by denying that the Court had jurisdiction. In his comments, however, Justice Sutherland clearly implied that there were no constitutional problems with noncoercive programs; the state had the simple option of refusing to participate and thus retaining all its prerogatives. But if it chose to take the money, then it accepted the attached conditions as well.

See Edward S. Corwin, "The Spending Power of Congress Apropos the Maternity Act," 36 *Harvard Law Review* 548 (1923).

———

Justice Sutherland delivered the opinion of the Court:
These cases . . . challenge the constitutionality of the Act of November 23, 1921, 42 Stat. 224, c. 135, commonly called the Maternity Act. Briefly, it provides for an initial appropriation and thereafter annual appropriations for a period of five years, to be apportioned among such of the several states as shall accept and comply with its provisions, for the purpose of co-operating with them to reduce maternal and infant mortality and protect the health of mothers and infants. It creates a bureau to administer the act in cooperation with state agencies, which are required to make such reports concerning their operations and expenditures as may be prescribed by the federal bureau. Whenever that

Source: 262 U.S. 447 (1923).

bureau shall determine that funds have not been properly expended in respect of any state, payments may be withheld.

It is asserted that these appropriations are for purposes not national, but local to the states, and together with numerous similar appropriations constitute an effective means of inducing the states to yield a portion of their sovereign rights. It is further alleged that the burden of the appropriations provided by this act and similar legislation falls unequally upon the several states, and rests largely upon the industrial states, such as Massachusetts; that the act is a usurpation of power not granted to Congress by the Constitution—an attempted exercise of the power of local self-government reserved to the states by the Tenth Amendment; and that the defendants are proceeding to carry the act into operation. In the Massachusetts Case it is alleged that the plaintiff's rights and powers as a sovereign state and the rights of its citizens have been invaded and usurped by these expenditures and acts, and that, although the state has not accepted the act, its constitutional rights are infringed by the passage thereof and the imposition upon the state of an illegal and unconstitutional option either to yield to the federal government a part of its reserved rights or lose the share which it would otherwise be entitled to receive of the moneys appropriated. . . .

We have reached the conclusion that the cases must be disposed of for want of jurisdiction, without considering the merits of the constitutional questions.

In the first case, the state of Massachusetts presents no justiciable controversy, either in its own behalf or as the representative of its citizens. . . .

. . . The state of Massachusetts in its own behalf, in effect, complains that the act in question invades the local concerns of the state, and is a usurpation of power, viz. the power of local self-government, reserved to the states.

Probably it would be sufficient to point out that the powers of the state are not invaded, since the statute imposes no obligation but simply extends an option which the state is free to accept or reject. But we do not rest here. Under article 3, § 2, of the Constitution, the judicial power of this court extends "to controversies . . . between a state and citizens of another state" and the court has original jurisdiction "in all cases . . . in which a state shall be a party." The effect of this is not to confer jurisdiction upon the court merely because a state is a party, but only where it is a party to a proceeding of judicial cognizance. Proceedings not of a justiciable character are outside the contemplation of the constitutional grant. . . .

What, then, is the nature of the right of the state here asserted and how is it affected by this statute? Reduced to its simplest terms, it is alleged that the statute constitutes an attempt to legislate outside the powers granted to Congress by the Constitution and within the field of local powers exclusively reserved to the states. Nothing is added to the force or effect of this assertion by the further incidental allegations that the ulterior purpose of Congress thereby was to induce the states to yield a portion of their sovereign rights; that the burden of the appropriations falls unequally upon the several states; and that there is imposed upon the states an illegal and unconstitutional option either to yield to the federal government a part of their reserved rights or lose their share of the moneys appropriated. But what burden is imposed upon the states, unequally or otherwise? Certainly there is none, unless it be the burden of taxation, and that falls upon their inhabitants, who are within the taxing power of Congress as well as that of the states where they reside. Nor does the statute require the states to do or to yield anything. If

Congress enacted it with the ulterior purpose of tempting them to yield, that purpose may be effectively frustrated by the simple expedient of not yielding.

In the last analysis, the complaint of the plaintiff state is brought to the naked contention that Congress has usurped the reserved powers of the several states by the mere enactment of the statute, though nothing has been done and nothing is to be done without their consent; and it is plain that that question, as it is thus presented, is political, and not judicial in character, and therefore is not a matter which admits of the exercise of the judicial power. . . .

It follows that, in so far as the case depends upon the assertion of a right on the part of the state to sue in its own behalf, we are without jurisdiction. In that aspect of the case we are called upon to adjudicate, not rights of person or property, not rights of dominion over physical domain, not quasi sovereign rights actually invaded or threatened, but abstract questions of political power, of sovereignty, of government. No rights of the state falling within the scope of the judicial power have been brought within the actual or threatened operation of the statute, and this court is . . . without authority to pass abstract opinions upon the constitutionality of acts of Congress. . . .

We come next to consider whether the suit may be maintained by the state as the representative of its citizens. To this the answer is not doubtful. We need not go so far as to say that a state may never intervene by suit to protect its citizens against any form of enforcement of unconstitutional acts of Congress; but we are clear that the right to do so does not arise here. Ordinarily, at least, the only way in which a state may afford protection to its citizens in such cases is through the enforcement of its own criminal statutes, where that is appropriate, or by opening its courts to the injured persons for the maintenance of civil suits or actions. But the citizens of Massachusetts are also citizens of the United States. It cannot be conceded that a state, as parens patriæ, may institute judicial proceedings to protect citizens of the United States from the operation of the statutes thereof. While the state, under some circumstances, may sue in that capacity for the protection of its citizens . . . it is no part of its duty or power to enforce their rights in respect of their relations with the federal government. In that field it is the United States, and not the state, which represents them as parens patriæ, when such representation becomes appropriate; and to the former, and not to the latter, they must look for such protective measures as flow from that status.

167

Village of Euclid v. Ambler Realty (1926)

English common law had set up elaborate provisions for the protection of one's property and even prevented one's neighbors from using their property if it interfered negatively with the use of an owner. But aside from the courts enforcing these laws, there had been little role for the state. In rural areas, the common law rules made sense, but as America became more and more urbanized, pressures on dwindling city land resources grew, with factories trying to expand into what had hitherto been primarily residential areas.

As late as 1922, in *Pennsylvania Coal Co. v. Mahon,* the Court, speaking through Justice Holmes, seemed opposed to any state interference in how private property could be used. Nonetheless, four years later, the Court upheld a modern zoning scheme and thus allowed the nation's cities and suburbs to impose rational planning standards for land use.

See Michael A. Wolf, "'Compelled by Conscientious Duty': *Village of Euclid v. Ambler Realty Co.* as Romance," 1997 *Journal of Supreme Court History* (#2) 88; Charles. M. Haar and Jerold S. Kayden, eds., *Zoning and the American Dream* (1989); and Timothy A. Fluck, "*Euclid v. Ambler:* A Retrospective," 52 *Journal of the American Planning Association* 326 (1986).

———

Mr. Justice Sutherland delivered the opinion of the Court:

The Village of Euclid is an Ohio municipal corporation. It adjoins and practically is a suburb of the City of Cleveland. Its estimated population is between 5,000 and 10,000, and its area from twelve to fourteen square miles, the greater part of which is farm lands or unimproved acreage. . . .

Appellee is the owner of a tract of land containing 68 acres, situated in the westerly end of the village, abutting on Euclid Avenue to the south and the Nickel Plate railroad to the north. Adjoining this tract, both on the east and on the west, there have been laid out restricted residential plats upon which residences have been erected.

On November 13, 1922, an ordinance was adopted by the Village Council, establishing a comprehensive zoning plan for regulating and restricting the location of trades, industries, apartment houses, two-family houses, single family houses, etc., the lot area to be built upon, the size and height of buildings, etc. . . . The enforcement of the ordinance is entrusted to the inspector of buildings, under rules and regulations of the board of zoning appeals. Meetings of the board are public, and minutes of its proceedings are kept. It is authorized to adopt rules and regulations to carry into effect provisions of the ordinance. Decisions of the inspector of buildings may be appealed to the board by any person claiming to be adversely affected by any such decision. The board is given power in specific cases of practical difficulty or unnecessary hardship to interpret the ordinance in harmony with its general purpose and intent, so that the public health, safety and general welfare may be secure and substantial justice done. Penalties are prescribed for violations, and it is provided that the various provisions are to be regarded as independent and the holding of any provision to be unconstitutional, void or ineffective shall not affect any of the others.

———

Source: 272 U.S. 365 (1926)

The ordinance is assailed on the grounds that it is in derogation of § 1 of the Fourteenth Amendment to the Federal Constitution in that it deprives appellee of liberty and property without due process of law and denies it the equal protection of the law, and that it offends against certain provisions of the Constitution of the State of Ohio. The prayer of the bill is for an injunction restraining the enforcement of the ordinance and all attempts to impose or maintain as to appellee's property any of the restrictions, limitations or conditions. The court below held the ordinance to be unconstitutional and void, and enjoined its enforcement. . . .

It is specifically averred that the ordinance attempts to restrict and control the lawful uses of appellee's land so as to confiscate and destroy a great part of its value; that it is being enforced in accordance with its terms; that prospective buyers of land for industrial, commercial and residential uses in the metropolitan district of Cleveland are deterred from buying any part of this land because of the existence of the ordinance and the necessity thereby entailed of conducting burdensome and expensive litigation in order to vindicate the right to use the land for lawful and legitimate purposes; that the ordinance constitutes a cloud upon the land, reduces and destroys its value, and has the effect of diverting the normal industrial, commercial and residential development thereof to other and less favorable locations. . . .

It is not necessary to set forth the provisions of the Ohio Constitution which are thought to be infringed. The question is the same under both Constitutions, namely, as stated by appellee: Is the ordinance invalid in that it violates the constitutional protection "to the right of property in the appellee by attempted regulations under the guise of the police power, which are unreasonable and confiscatory?"

Building zone laws are of modern origin. They began in this country about twenty-five years ago. Until recent years, urban life was comparatively simple; but with the great increase and concentration of population, problems have developed, and constantly are developing, which require, and will continue to require, additional restrictions in respect of the use and occupation of private lands in urban communities. Regulations, the wisdom, necessity and validity of which, as applied to existing conditions, are so apparent that they are now uniformly sustained, a century ago, or even half a century ago, probably would have been rejected as arbitrary and oppressive. Such regulations are sustained, under the complex conditions of our day, for reasons analogous to those which justify traffic regulations, which, before the advent of automobiles and rapid transit street railways, would have been condemned as fatally arbitrary and unreasonable. And in this there is no inconsistency, for while the meaning of constitutional guaranties never varies, the scope of their application must expand or contract to meet the new and different conditions which are constantly coming within the field of their operation. In a changing world, it is impossible that it should be otherwise. But although a degree of elasticity is thus imparted, not to the meaning, but to the application of constitutional principles, statutes and ordinances, which, after giving due weight to the new conditions, are found clearly not to conform to the Constitution, of course, must fall.

The ordinance now under review, and all similar laws and regulations, must find their justification in some aspect of the police power, asserted for the public welfare. The line which in this field separates the legitimate from the illegitimate assumption of power is not capable of precise delimitation. It varies with circumstances and conditions. A regulatory zoning ordinance, which would be clearly valid as applied to the great cities, might be clearly invalid as applied to rural communities. In solving doubts, the maxim *sic utere tuo ut alienum non laedas,* which lies at the foundation of so much of the common law of nuisances, ordinarily will furnish a fairly helpful clew. And the law of nuisances, likewise, may be consulted, not for the purpose of controlling, but for the helpful aid of its analogies in the process of ascertaining the scope of, the power. Thus the question whether the power exists to forbid the erection of a building of a particular kind or for a particular use, like the question whether a particular thing is a nuisance, is to be determined, not by an abstract consideration of the building or of the thing considered apart, but by considering it in connection with the circumstances and the locality. A nuisance may be merely a right thing in the wrong place,—like a pig in the parlor instead of the barnyard. If the validity of the legislative classification for zoning purposes be fairly debatable, the legislative judgment must be allowed to control.

There is no serious difference of opinion in respect of the validity of laws and regulations fixing the height of buildings within reasonable limits, the character of materials and methods of construction, and the adjoining area which must be left open, in order to minimize the danger of fire or collapse, the evils of over-crowding, and the like, and excluding from residential sections offensive trades, industries and structures likely to create nuisances.

Here, however, the exclusion is in general terms of all industrial establishments, and it may thereby happen that not only offensive or dangerous industries will be excluded, but those which are neither offensive nor dangerous will share the same fate. But this is no more than happens in respect of many practice-forbidding laws which this Court has upheld although drawn in general terms so as to include individual cases that may turn out to be innocuous in themselves. The inclusion of a reasonable margin to insure effective enforcement, will not put upon a law, otherwise valid, the stamp of invalidity. Such laws may also find their justification in the fact that, in some fields, the bad fades into the good by such insensible degrees that the two are not capable of being readily distinguished and separated in terms of legislation. In the light of these considerations, we are not prepared to say that the end in view was not sufficient to justify the general rule of the ordinance, although some industries of an innocent character might fall within the proscribed class. It can not be said that the ordinance in this respect "passes the bounds of reason and assumes the character of a merely arbitrary fiat." Moreover, the restrictive provisions of the ordinance in this particular may be sustained upon the principles applicable to the broader exclusion from residential districts of all business and trade structures. . . . We find no difficulty in sustaining restrictions of the kind thus far reviewed. The serious question in the case arises over the provisions of the ordinance excluding from residential districts, apartment houses, business houses, retail stores and shops, and other like establishments. This question involves the validity of what is really the crux of the more recent zoning legislation, namely, the creation and maintenance of residential districts, from which business and trade of every sort, including hotels and apartment houses, are excluded. Upon that question, this Court has not thus far spoken. The decisions of the state courts are numerous and conflicting; but those which broadly sustain the power greatly outnumber those which deny altogether or narrowly limit it; and it is very apparent that there is a constantly increasing tendency in the direction of the broader view. . . .

Under these circumstances, therefore, it is enough for us to determine, as we do, that the ordinance in its general scope and dominant features, so far as its provisions are here involved, is a valid exercise of authority, leaving other provisions to be dealt with as cases arise directly involving them. Decree reversed.

Mr. Justice Van Devanter, Mr. Justice McReynolds and Mr. Justice Butler dissent.

---

168 *Buck v. Bell (1927)*

In both America and Europe, the eugenics movement won many converts in the early decades of the twentieth century. Advocates argued that just as one bred animals to eliminate the weakest and the sickest to promote the healthiest, so weak and feeble-minded humans should not be allowed to breed and pass their deficiencies on to their offspring. Eugenicists in the United States embraced coercive sterilization with more ardor than did their European counterparts, and several states passed forced sterilization laws between 1905 and 1921. Most were struck down for procedural shortcomings, but Virginia adopted a model law that its backers believed would withstand judicial scrutiny. It then arranged a test case to carry through the courts to win judicial approval.

More than any other opinion he wrote, *Buck v. Bell* has served to undermine Holmes's reputation as a liberal. Of course, Holmes never claimed to be a liberal, and he often declared himself a Malthusian, who believed that population growth had to be curtailed. The real tragedy of this case is that there were no "three generations of imbeciles." The Buck women were illiterate, but not feeble-minded.

See Yosel Rogat, "The Judge as Spectator," 31 *University of Chicago Law Review* 213 (1964); Daniel J. Kevles, *In the Name of Eugenics: Genetics and the Uses of Human Heredity* (1985); and William E. Leuchtenburg, "Mr. Justice Holmes and Three Generations of Imbeciles," in *The Supreme Court Reborn* 3–25 (1995).

———

Mr. Justice Holmes delivered the opinion of the Court:
This is a writ of error to review a judgment of the Supreme Court of Appeals of the State of Virginia, affirming a judgment of the Circuit Court of Amherst County, by which

Source: 274 U.S. 200 (1927)

the defendant in error, the superintendent of the State Colony for Epileptics and Feeble Minded, was ordered to perform the operation of salpingectomy upon Carrie Buck, the plaintiff in error, for the purpose of making her sterile. The case comes here upon the contention that the statute authorizing the judgment is void under the Fourteenth Amendment as denying to the plaintiff in error due process of law and the equal protection of the laws.

Carrie Buck is a feeble minded white woman who was committed to the State Colony above mentioned in due form. She is the daughter of a feeble minded mother in the same institution, and the mother of an illegitimate feeble minded child. She was eighteen years old at the time of the trial of her case in the Circuit Court, in the latter part of 1924. An Act of Virginia, approved March 20, 1924, recites that the health of the patient and the welfare of society may be promoted in certain cases by the sterilization of mental defectives, under careful safeguard, &c.; that the sterilization may be effected in males by vasectomy and in females by salpingectomy, without serious pain or substantial danger to life; that the Commonwealth is supporting in various institutions many defective persons who if now discharged would become a menace but if incapable of procreating might be discharged with safety and become self-supporting with benefit to themselves and to society; and that experience has shown that heredity plays an important part in the transmission of insanity, imbecility, &c. The statute then enacts that whenever the superintendent of certain institutions including the above named State Colony shall be of opinion that it is for the best interests of the patients and of society that an inmate under his care should be sexually sterilized, he may have the operation performed upon any patient afflicted with hereditary forms of insanity, imbecility, &c., on complying with the very careful provisions by which the act protects the patients from possible abuse.

The superintendent first presents a petition to the special board of directors of his hospital or colony, stating the facts and the grounds for his opinion, verified by affidavit. Notice of the petition and of the time and place of the hearing in the institution is to be served upon the inmate, and also upon his guardian, and if there is no guardian the superintendent is to apply to the Circuit Court of the County to appoint one. If the inmate is a minor notice also is to be given to his parents if any with a copy of the petition. The board is to see to it that the inmate may attend the hearings if desired by him or his guardian. The evidence is all to be reduced to writing, and after the board has made its order for or against the operation, the superintendent, or the inmate, or his guardian, may appeal to the Circuit Court of the County. The Circuit Court may consider the record of the board and the evidence before it and such other admissible evidence as may be offered, and may affirm, revise, or reverse the order of the board and enter such order as it deems just. Finally any party may apply to the Supreme Court of Appeals, which, if it grants the appeal, is to hear the case upon the record of the trial in the Circuit Court and may enter such order as it thinks the Circuit Court should have entered. There can be no doubt that so far as procedure is concerned the rights of the patient are most carefully considered, and as every step in this case was taken in scrupulous compliance with the statute and after months of observation, there is no doubt that in that respect the plaintiff in error has had due process of law.

The attack is not upon the procedure but upon the substantive law. It seems to be contended that in no circumstances could such an order be justified. It certainly is contended that the order cannot be justified upon the existing grounds. The judgment finds the facts that have been recited and that Carrie Buck "is the probable potential parent of socially inadequate offspring, likewise afflicted, that she may be sexually sterilized without detriment to her general health and that her welfare and that of society will be promoted by her sterilization," and thereupon makes the order. In view of the general declarations of the legislature and the specific findings of the Court, obviously we cannot say as matter of law that the grounds do not exist, and if they exist they justify the result. We have seen more than once that the public welfare may call upon the best citizens for their lives. It would be strange if it could not call upon those who already sap the strength of the State for these lesser sacrifices, often not felt to be such by those concerned, in order to prevent our being swamped with incompetence. It is better for all the world, if instead of waiting to execute degenerate offspring for crime, or to let them starve for their imbecility, society can prevent those who are manifestly unfit from continuing their kind. The principle that sustains compulsory vaccination is broad enough to cover cutting the Fallopian tubes. Jacobson v. Massachusetts, 197 U.S. 11. Three generations of imbeciles are enough.

But, it is said, however it might be if this reasoning were applied generally, it fails when it is confined to the small number who are in the institutions named and is not applied to the multitudes outside. It is the usual last resort of constitutional arguments to point out shortcomings of this sort. But the answer is that the law does all that is needed when it does all that it can, indicates a policy, applies it to all within the lines, and seeks to bring within the lines all similarly situated so far and so fast as its means allow. Of course so far as the operations enable those who otherwise must be kept confined to be returned to the world, and thus open the asylum to others, the equality aimed at will be more nearly reached. Judgment affirmed.

Mr. Justice Butler dissents.

---

169   *Whitney v. California (1927)*

Anita Whitney, a member of a distinguished and affluent California family, was convicted under the state's 1919 Criminal Syndicalism Act for allegedly helping to form the Communist Labor party, a group the state charged was devoted to teaching the violent overthrow of the government. Miss Whitney claimed that it had not been her intention nor that of other organizers that the party become an instrument of violence.

Justice Sanford, speaking for the Court, upheld the conviction on three main points. First, he dismissed the due process claim that she was being convicted for joining an organization whose true purpose she could not have known at the time, saying the nature of the organization was a factual issue only, and therefore the jury decision in this matter was not open to Court review. Second, the Syndicalism Act did not fail for vagueness in defining what it made criminal. Third, the law did not unconstitutionally restrain free speech because the state has the power to punish those who abuse their right to speech "by utterances inimical to the public welfare, tending to incite crime, disturb the public peace, or endanger the foundations of organized government and threaten its overthrow."

The *Whitney* case is most noted for Justice Brandeis's concurrence (because of a technicality in the appeal, Brandeis and Holmes could not dissent from the judgment, but filed a concurrence that was in every way a dissent), which many scholars have lauded as perhaps the greatest defense of freedom of speech ever penned by a Supreme Court justice. He and Holmes concurred in the result because the federal courts could not, at that time, inquire as to whether state courts had made certain reversible errors. But there is no question that the sentiments are a distinct dissent from the views of the prevailing majority. His opinion is also a fine example of his efforts to instruct as well as to define the law. Committed as he was to judicial restraint, he here sidestepped a direct confrontation with the legislative assertion that certain types of expression are dangerous. Rather he insists on an "as applied" test, or as others have called it, a "time to answer" test; no danger flowing from speech can be considered clear and present if there is full opportunity for discussion. While upholding full and free speech, he in essence tells the legislatures that while they have the right to curb truly dangerous expressions, they must define clearly the tests for such danger. For confirmation of Brandeis's view, see Document 217.

See Eldridge F. Dowell, *History of Criminal Syndicalism Legislation in the United States* (1939); Philippa Strum, *Brandeis: Beyond Progressivism* (1993); Vincent Blasi, "The First Amendment and the Ideal of Civil Courage: The Brandeis Opinion in *Whitney v. California,*" 29 *William and Mary Law Review* 653 (1988); Pnina Lahav, "Holmes and Brandeis: Libertarian and Republican Justifications for Free Speech," 4 *Journal of Law & Politics* 451 (1987).

———

Justice Brandeis, joined by Justice Holmes, concurring:

The felony which the statute created is a crime very unlike the old felony of conspiracy or the old misdemeanor of unlawful assembly. The mere act of assisting in forming a society for teaching syndicalism, of becoming a member of it, or of assembling with others for that purpose is given the dynamic quality of crime. There is guilt although the society may not contemplate immediate promulgation of the doctrine. Thus the accused is to be punished, not for contempt, incitement or conspiracy, but for a step in preparation, which, if it threatens the public order at all, does so only remotely. The

Source: 274 U.S. 357 (1927)

novelty in the prohibition introduced is that the statute aims, not at the practice of criminal syndicalism, nor even directly at the preaching of it, but at association with those who propose to preach it.

Despite arguments to the contrary which had seemed to me persuasive, it is settled that the due process clause of the Fourteenth Amendment applies to matters of substantive law as well as to matters of procedure. Thus all fundamental rights comprised within the term liberty are protected by the Federal Constitution from invasion by the States. The right of free speech, the right to teach and the right of assembly are, of course, fundamental rights. These may not be denied or abridged. But, although the rights of free speech and assembly are fundamental, they are not in their nature absolute. Their exercise is subject to restriction, if the particular restriction proposed is required in order to protect the State from destruction or from serious injury, political, economic or moral. That the necessity which is essential to a valid restriction does not exist unless speech would produce, or is intended to produce, a clear and imminent danger of some substantive evil which the State constitutionally may seek to prevent has been settled. . . .

It is said to be the function of the legislature to determine whether at a particular time and under the particular circumstances the formation of, or assembly with, a society organized to advocate criminal syndicalism constitutes a clear and present danger of substantive evil; and that by enacting the law here in question the legislature of California determined that question in the affirmative. . . . The legislature must obviously decide, in the first instance, whether a danger exists which calls for a particular protective measure. But where a statute is valid only in case certain conditions exist, the enactment of the statute cannot alone establish the facts which are essential to its validity. Prohibitory legislation has repeatedly been held invalid because unnecessary, where the denial of liberty involved was that of engaging in a particular business. The power of the courts to strike down an offending law is no less when the interests involved are not property rights, but the fundamental personal rights of free speech and assembly.

This Court has not yet fixed the standard by which to determine when a danger shall be deemed clear; how remote the danger may be and yet be deemed present; and what degree of evil shall be deemed sufficiently substantial to justify resort to abridgment of free speech and assembly as the means of protection. To reach sound conclusions on these matters, we must bear in mind why a State is, ordinarily, denied the power to prohibit dissemination of social, economic and political doctrine which a vast majority of its citizens believes to be false and fraught with evil consequence.

Those who won our independence believed that the final end of the State was to make men free to develop their faculties; and that in its government the deliberative forces should prevail over the arbitrary. They valued liberty both as an end and as a means. They believed liberty to be the secret of happiness and courage to be the secret of liberty. They believed that freedom to think as you will and to speak as you think are means indispensable to the discovery and spread of political truth; that without free speech and assembly discussion would be futile; that with them, discussion affords ordinarily adequate protection against the dissemination of noxious doctrine; that the greatest menace to freedom is an inert people; that public discussion is a political duty; and that this should be a fundamental principle of the American government. They recognized the risks to which all human institutions are subject. But they knew that order cannot be secured merely through fear of punishment for its infraction; that it is hazardous to discourage thought, hope and imagination; that fear breeds repression; that repression breeds hate; that hate menaces stable government; that the path of safety lies in the opportunity to discuss freely supposed grievances and proposed remedies; and that the fitting remedy for evil counsels is good ones. Believing in the power of reason as applied through public discussion, they eschewed silence coerced by law—the argument of force in its worst form. Recognizing the occasional tyrannies of governing majorities, they amended the Constitution so that free speech and assembly should be guaranteed.

Fear of serious injury cannot alone justify suppression of free speech and assembly. Men feared witches and burned women. It is the function of speech to free men from the bondage of irrational fears. To justify suppression of free speech there must be reasonable ground to fear that serious evil will result if free speech is practiced. There must be reasonable ground to believe that the danger apprehended is imminent. There must be reasonable ground to believe that the evil to be prevented is a serious one. Every denunciation of existing law tends in some measure to increase the probability that there will be violation of it. Condonation of a breach enhances the probability. Expressions of approval add to the probability. Propagation of the criminal state of mind by teaching syndicalism increases it. Advocacy of lawbreaking heightens it still further. But even advocacy of violation, however reprehensible morally, is not a justification for denying free speech where the advocacy falls short of incitement and there is nothing to indicate that the advocacy would be immediately acted on. The wide difference between advocacy and incitement, between preparation and attempt, between assembling and conspiracy, must be borne in mind. In order to support a finding of clear and present danger it must be shown either that immediate serious violence was to be expected or was advocated, or that the past conduct furnished reason to believe that such advocacy was then contemplated.

Those who won our independence by revolution were not cowards. They did not fear political change. They did not exalt order at the cost of liberty. To courageous, self-reliant men, with confidence in the power of free and fearless reasoning applied through the processes of popular government, no danger flowing from speech can be deemed clear and present, unless the incidence of the evil apprehended is so imminent that it may befall before there is opportunity for full discussion. If there be time to expose through discussion the falsehood and fallacies, to avert the evil by the processes of education, the remedy to be applied is more speech, not enforced silence. Only an emergency can justify repression. Such must be the rule if authority is to be reconciled with freedom. Such, in my opinion, is the command of the Constitution. It is therefore always open to Americans to challenge a law abridging free speech and assembly by showing that there was no emergency justifying it.

Moreover, even imminent danger cannot justify resort to prohibition of these functions essential to effective democracy, unless the evil apprehended is relatively serious. Prohibition of free speech and assembly is a measure so stringent that it would be inappropriate as the means for averting a relatively trivial harm to society. A police measure may be unconstitutional merely because the remedy, although effective as a means of protection, is unduly harsh or oppressive. Thus, a State might, in the exercise of its police power, make any trespass upon the land of another a crime, regardless of the results or of the intent or purpose of the trespasser. It might, also, punish an attempt, a conspiracy, or an incitement to commit the trespass. But it is hardly conceivable that this Court would hold constitutional a statute which punished as a felony the mere voluntary assembly with a society formed to teach that pedestrians had the moral right to cross unenclosed, unposted, waste lands and to advocate their doing so, even if there was imminent danger that advocacy would lead to a trespass. The fact that speech is likely to result in some violence or in destruction of property is not enough to justify its suppression. There must be the probability of serious injury to the State. Among free men, the deterrents ordinarily to be applied to prevent crime are education and punishment for violations of the law, not abridgment of the rights of free speech and assembly.

[The California] legislative declaration satisfies the requirement of the constitution of the State concerning emergency legislation. [But] it does not preclude enquiry into the question whether, at the time and under the circumstances, the conditions existed which are essential to validity under the Federal Constitution. As a statute, even if not void on its face, may be challenged because invalid as applied, the result of such an inquiry may depend upon the specific facts of the particular case. Whenever the fundamental rights of free speech and assembly are alleged to have been invaded, it must remain open to a defendant to present the issue whether there actually did exist at the time a clear danger; whether the danger, if any, was imminent, and whether the evil apprehended was one so substantial as to justify the stringent restriction interposed by the legislature. The legislative declaration, like the fact that the statute was passed and was sustained by the highest court of the State, creates merely a rebuttable presumption that these conditions have been satisfied.

Whether in 1919, when Miss Whitney did the things complained of, there was in California such clear and present danger of serious evil, might have been made the important issue in the case. She might have required that the issue be determined either by the court or the jury. She claimed below that the statute as applied to her violated the Federal Constitution; but she did not claim that it was void because there was no clear and present danger of serious evil, nor did she request that the existence of these conditions of a valid measure thus restricting the rights of free speech and assembly be passed upon by the court or a jury. On the other hand, there was evidence on which the court or jury might have found that such danger existed. I am unable to assent to the suggestion in the opinion of the Court that assembling with a political party, formed to advocate the desirability of a proletarian revolution by mass action at some date necessarily far in the future, is not a right within the protection of the Fourteenth Amendment. In the present case, however, there was other testimony which tended to establish the existence of a conspiracy, on the part of members of the International Workers of the World, to commit present serious crimes; and likewise to show that such a conspiracy would be furthered by the activity of the society of which Miss Whitney was a member. Under these circumstances the judgment of the state court cannot be disturbed.

Our power of review in this case . . . is limited not only to the question whether a right guaranteed by the Federal Constitution was denied, but to the particular claims duly made below, and denied. We lack here the power occasionally exercised on review of judgments of lower federal courts to correct in criminal cases vital errors, although the objection was not taken in the trial court. Because we may not enquire into the errors now alleged, I concur in affirming the judgment of the state court.

170 *Olmstead v. United States (1928)*

Prohibition, by making the sale of beer, wine, and liquor illegal, spurred an enormous crime wave in the country and elicited an energetic if often futile effort by the federal and state governments to combat the bootleggers. Technology was employed by both sides, and the government used wiretaps to secure evidence against suspects without a search warrant, on the grounds that investigators had never entered the premises. By a bare five-to-four vote, the Court upheld what Holmes, in his dissent, labeled a "dirty business." Chief Justice Taft took an extremely formalist view of the Fourth Amendment, claiming it applied only to papers and other tangible items and required an actual entry into a building. The generally conservative Pierce Butler dissented and, in a careful historical study of the Fourth Amendment, repudiated Taft's view and called upon the Court to carry out the spirit of the amendment. The most impressive opinion came from Brandeis, who for many years had been interested in the issue of privacy. His dissent would be picked up and elaborated upon, by both liberals and conservatives, until the Court established a right to privacy in the 1960s (Document 212). In 1934, Congress prohibited wiretap evidence in federal courts, and in *Berger* v. *New York* (1967) the Court finally adopted the dissenters' views.

See Walter F. Murphy, *Wiretapping on Trial* (1965); and R. F. Scoular, "Wiretapping and Eavesdropping: Constitutional Development from Olmstead to Katz," 12 *St. Louis Law Journal* 513 (1968).

———

Mr. Chief Justice Taft delivered the opinion of the Court:

These cases are here by certiorari from the Circuit Court of Appeals for the Ninth Circuit. . . . They were granted with the distinct limitation that the hearing should be confined to the single question whether the use of evidence of private telephone conversations between the defendants and others, intercepted by means of wire tapping, amounted to a violation of the Fourth and Fifth Amendments.

The petitioners were convicted in the District Court for the Western District of Washington of a conspiracy to violate the National Prohibition Act by unlawfully possessing, transporting and importing intoxicating liquors and maintaining nuisances, and by selling intoxicating liquors. Seventy-two others in addition to the petitioners were indicted. Some were not apprehended, some were acquitted and others pleaded guilty. . . .

Source: 277 U.S. 438 (1928)

The information which led to the discovery of the conspiracy and its nature and extent was largely obtained by intercepting messages on the telephones of the conspirators by four federal prohibition officers. Small wires were inserted along the ordinary telephone wires from the residences of four of the petitioners and those leading from the chief office. The insertions were made without trespass upon any property of the defendants. They were made in the basement of the large office building. The taps from house lines were made in the streets near the houses. . . .

The Fourth Amendment provides—"The right of the people to be secure in their persons, houses, papers, and effects against unreasonable searches and seizures shall not be violated; and no warrants shall issue but upon probable cause; supported by oath or affirmation and particularly describing the place to be searched and the persons or things to be seized." And the Fifth: "No person . . . shall be compelled, in any criminal case, to be a witness against himself." . . .

[The Chief Justice reviewed cases previously decided by the Court explicating the Fourth Amendment.]

The Amendment itself shows that the search is to be of material things—the person, the house, his papers or his effects. The description of the warrant necessary to make the proceeding lawful, is that it must specify the place to be searched and the person or *things* to be seized. . . .

. . . The Fourth Amendment may have proper application to a sealed letter in the mail because of the constitutional provision for the Postoffice Department and the relations between the Government and those who pay to secure protection of their sealed letters. . . . It is plainly within the words of the Amendment to say that the unlawful rifling by a government agent of a sealed letter is a search and seizure of the sender's papers or effects. The letter is a paper, an effect, and in the custody of a Government that forbids carriage except under its protection.

The United States takes no such care of telegraph or telephone messages as of mailed sealed letters. The Amendment does not forbid what was done here. There was no searching. There was no seizure. The evidence was secured by the use of the sense of hearing and that only. There was no entry of the houses or offices of the defendants.

By the invention of the telephone, fifty years ago, and its application for the purpose of extending communications, one can talk with another at a far distant place. The language of the Amendment can not be extended and expanded to include telephone wires reaching to the whole world from the defendant's house or office. The intervening wires are not part of his house or office any more than are the highways along which they are stretched. . . .

Congress may of course protect the secrecy of telephone messages by making them, when intercepted, inadmissible in evidence in federal criminal trials, by direct legislation, and thus depart from the common law of evidence. But the courts may not adopt such a policy by attributing an enlarged and unusual meaning to the Fourth Amendment. The reasonable view is that one who installs in his house a telephone instrument with connecting wires intends to project his voice to those quite outside, and that the wires beyond his house and messages while passing over them are not within the protection of the Fourth Amendment. . . .

Justice Brandeis, dissenting:

When the Fourth and Fifth Amendments were adopted, "the form that evil had theretofore taken," had been necessarily simple. Force and violence were then the only means known to man by which a Government could directly effect self-incrimination. It could compel the individual to testify—a compulsion effected, if need be, by torture. It could secure possession of his papers and other articles incident to his private life—a seizure effected, if need be, by breaking and entry. Protection against such invasion of "the sanctities of a man's home and the privacies of life" was provided in the Fourth and Fifth Amendments by specific language. *Boyd* v. *United States,* 116 U. S. 616, 630. But "time works changes, brings into existence new conditions and purposes." Subtler and more far-reaching means of invading privacy have become available to the Government. Discovery and invention have made it possible for the Government, by means far more effective than stretching upon the rack, to obtain disclosure in court of what is whispered in the closet.

Moreover, "in the application of a constitution, our contemplation cannot be only of what has been but of what may be." The progress of science in furnishing the Government with means of espionage is not likely to stop with wire-tapping. Ways may some day be developed by which the Government, without removing papers from secret drawers, can reproduce them in court, and by which it will be enabled to expose to a jury the most intimate occurrences of the home. Advances in the psychic and related sciences may bring means of exploring unexpressed beliefs, thoughts and emotions. "That places the liberty of every man in the hands of every petty officer" was said by James Otis of much lesser intrusions than these. To Lord Camden, a far slighter intrusion seemed "subversive of all the comforts of society." Can it be that the Constitution affords no protection against such invasions of individual security? . . .

In *Ex parte Jackson,* [1877] . . . it was held that a sealed letter entrusted to the mail is protected by the Amendments. The mail is a public service furnished by the Government. The telephone is a public service furnished by its authority. There is, in essence, no difference between the sealed letter and the private telephone message. As Judge Rudkin said below: "True the one is visible, the other invisible; the one is tangible, the other intangible; the one is sealed and the other unsealed, but these are distinctions without a difference." The evil incident to invasion of the privacy of the telephone is far greater than that involved in tampering with the mails. Whenever a telephone line is tapped, the privacy of the persons at both ends of the line is invaded and all conversations between them upon any subject, and although proper, confidential and privileged, may be overheard. Moreover, the tapping of one man's telephone line involves the tapping of the telephone of every other person whom he may call or who may call him. As a means of espionage, writs of assistance and general warrants are but puny instruments of tyranny and oppression when compared with wire-tapping.

Time and again, this Court in giving effect to the principle underlying the Fourth Amendment, has refused to place an unduly literal construction upon it. . . .

. . . The makers of our Constitution undertook to secure conditions favorable to the pursuit of happiness. They recognized the significance of man's spiritual nature, of his feelings and of his intellect. They knew that only a part of the pain, pleasure and satisfactions of life are to be found in material things. They sought to protect Americans in their beliefs, their thoughts, their emotions and their sensations. They conferred, as against the Government, the right to be let alone—the most comprehensive of rights and the right most valued by civilized men. To protect that right, every unjustifiable intrusion by the Government upon the privacy of the individual, whatever the means employed, must be deemed a violation of the Fourth Amendment. And the use, as evidence in a criminal proceeding, of facts ascertained by such intrusion must be deemed a violation of the Fifth.

Applying to the Fourth and Fifth Amendments the established rule of construction, the defendants' objections to the evidence obtained by wiretapping must, in my opinion, be sustained. It is, of course, immaterial where the physical connection with the telephone wires leading into the defendants' premises was made. And it is also immaterial that the intrusion was in aid of law enforcement. Experience should teach us to be most on our guard to protect liberty when the Government's purposes are beneficent. Men born to freedom are naturally alert to repel invasion of their liberty by evil-minded rulers. The greatest dangers to liberty lurk in insidious encroachment by men of zeal, well-meaning but without understanding.

Independently of the constitutional question, I am of opinion that the judgment should be reversed. By the laws of Washington, wire-tapping is a crime. . . . To prove its case, the Government was obliged to lay bare the crimes committed by its officers on its behalf. A federal court should not permit such a prosecution to continue. . . .

Decency, security and liberty alike demand that government officials shall be subjected to the same rules of conduct that are commands to the citizen. In a government of laws, existence of the government will be imperilled if it fails to observe the law scrupulously. Our Government is the potent, the omnipresent teacher. For good or for ill, it teaches the whole people by its example. Crime is contagious. If the Government becomes a lawbreaker, it breeds contempt for law; it invites every man to become a law unto himself; it invites anarchy. To declare that in the administration of the criminal law the end justified the means—to declare that the Government may commit crimes in order to secure the conviction of a private criminal—would bring terrible retribution. Against that pernicious doctrine this Court should resolutely set its face.

[Justices Holmes and Butler also entered dissents.]

171   *Near v. Minnesota (1931)*

A Minnesota law authorizing suppression, as a public nuisance, of any "malicious, scandalous and defamatory newspaper, or other periodical," had been enacted specifically to silence the Saturday Press, a lurid tabloid exposing corruption in Minneapolis. The suit, by publisher Jay Near, had originally reached the Court during Chief Justice Taft's final illness, but it was not argued until Charles Evans Hughes took the center seat. Had Taft heard the case, it is likely the five-to-four decision holding prior censorship as an infringement of freedom of the press might have gone the other way. Just as Sanford had held in *Gitlow* that "it was no longer open to question" that the Fourteenth Amendment incorporated freedom of speech, so in *Near,* Chief Justice Hughes expanded the doctrine to include freedom of press as well. (For more on the idea of prior restraint, see Document 220.)

See Fred W. Friendly, *Minnesota Rag* (1981); E. Gerald, *The Press and the Constitution, 1931–1947* (1948); J. E. Hartmann, "The Minnesota Gag Law and the Fourteenth Amendment," 27 *Minnesota History* 161 (1960); and Norman Redish, "The Proper Role of the Prior Restraint Doctrine in First Amendment Theory," 70 *Virginia Law Review* 53 (1984).

Chief Justice Hughes delivered the opinion of the Court:

If we cut through mere details of procedure, the operation and effect of the statute in substance is that public authorities may bring the owner or publisher of a newspaper or periodical before a judge upon a charge of conducting a business of publishing scandalous and defamatory matter—in particular that the matter consists of charges against public officers of official dereliction—and unless the owner or publisher is able and disposed to bring competent evidence to satisfy the judge that the charges are true and are published with good motives and for justifiable ends, his newspaper or periodical is suppressed and further publication is made punishable as a contempt. This is of the essence of censorship.

The question is whether a statute authorizing such proceedings in restraint of publication is consistent with the conception of the liberty of the press as historically conceived and guaranteed. In determining the extent of the constitutional protection, it has been generally, if not universally, considered that it is the chief purpose of the guaranty to prevent previous restraints upon publication. The struggle in England, directed against the legislative power of the licenser, resulted in renunciation of the censorship of the press. The liberty deemed to be established was thus described by Blackstone: "The liberty of the press is indeed essential to the nature of a free state; but this consists in laying no *previous* restraints upon publications, and not in freedom from censure for criminal matter when published. Every freeman has an undoubted right to lay what sentiments he pleases before the public; to forbid this, is to destroy the freedom of the press; but if he publishes what is improper, mischievous or illegal, he must take the consequence of his own temerity." The criticism upon Blackstone's statement has not been because immunity from previous restraint upon publication has not been regarded as deserving of special emphasis, but chiefly because that immunity cannot be deemed to exhaust the conception of the liberty guaranteed by state and federal constitutions. . . .

Source: 283 U.S. 697 (1931)

The objection has also been made that the principle as to immunity from previous restraint is stated too broadly, if every such restraint is deemed to be prohibited. That is undoubtedly true; the protection even as to previous restraint is not absolutely unlimited. But the limitation has been recognized only in exceptional cases. No one would question but that a government might prevent actual obstruction to its recruiting service or the publication of the sailing dates of transports or the number and location of troops. On similar grounds, the primary requirements of decency may be enforced against obscene publications. The security of the community life may be protected against incitements to acts of violence and the overthrow by force of orderly government. . . . These limitations are not applicable here. . . .

The exceptional nature of its limitations places in a strong light the general conception that liberty of the press, historically considered and taken up by the Federal Constitution, has meant, principally although not exclusively, immunity from previous restraints, or censorship. . . . Public officers, whose character and conduct remain open to debate and free discussion in the press, find their remedies for false accusations in actions under libel laws providing for redress and punishment, and not in proceedings to restrain the publication of newspapers and periodicals. The fact that the liberty of the press may be abused by miscreant purveyors of scandal does not make any the less necessary the immunity of the press from previous restraint in dealing with official misconduct. Subsequent punishment for such abuses as may exist is the appropriate remedy, consistent with constitutional privilege.

The statute in question cannot be justified by reason of the fact that the publisher is permitted to show, before injunction issues, that the matter published is true and is published with good motives and for justifiable ends. If such a statute is valid, it would be equally permissible for the legislature to provide that at any time the publisher of any newspaper could be brought before a court, or even an administrative officer (as the constitutional protection may not be regarded as resting on mere procedural details), and required to produce proof of the truth of his publication, or of what he intended to publish and of his motives, or stand enjoined. If this can be done, the legislature may provide the machinery for determining in the complete exercise of its discretion what are justifiable ends and restrain publication accordingly. And it would be but a step to a complete system of censorship. We hold the statute, so far as it authorized the proceedings in this action, to be an infringement of the liberty of the press guaranteed by the Fourteenth Amendment. . . .

Judgment reversed.

172

New State Ice Co. v. Liebmann (1932)

One of the worst problems confronting small businesses during the Depression was the cutthroat competition resulting from too many firms competing in limited markets. Oklahoma tried to solve this problem in one area by declaring ice manufacture as affected with a public interest and then regulating by license the number of firms that could engage in the business. A majority of the Court rejected this view, and in addition claimed the law led to monopoly. One might have assumed that Brandeis, an inveterate foe of monopoly, would have also taken this view. But his dissent painstakingly laid out the reasons why the state had chosen this route and pragmatically accepted the fact that in certain circumstances the state might choose to foster monopoly when either the nature of the business or the public welfare demanded it. He also criticized the majority for its cramped view of business "affected with a public interest"; the state had to be free to determine to which businesses and under which circumstances that categorization should be applied. The Depression had upset many long-held views, and he eloquently called on his brethren to practice judicial restraint of legislative experimentation, a position the Court ultimately accepted as appropriate.

See Samuel J. Konefsky, *Legacy of Holmes and Brandeis* (1956); James C. Clark, "Emergencies and the Law," 39 *Political Science Review* 268 (1934); and Thomas Reed Powell, "Supreme Court and State Police Power, 1921–1930," 17 *Virginia Law Review* 529, 653, 765 (1931).

———

Justice Sutherland delivered the opinion of the Court:
The New State Ice Company, engaged in the business of manufacturing, selling and distributing ice under a license or permit duly issued by the Corporation Commission of Oklahoma, brought this suit against Liebmann in the federal district court for the western district of Oklahoma to enjoin him from manufacturing, selling and distributing ice within Oklahoma City without first having obtained a like license or permit from the commission. The license or permit is required by an act of the Oklahoma legislature, c. 147, Session Laws, 1925. That act declares that the manufacture, sale and distribution of ice is a public business; that no one shall be permitted to manufacture, sell or distribute

Source: 285 U.S. 262 (1932)

ice within the state without first having secured a license for that purpose from the commission; that whoever shall engage in such business without obtaining the license shall be guilty of a misdemeanor, punishable by fine not to exceed $25, each day's violation constituting a separate offense, and that by general order of the commission, a fine not to exceed $500 may be imposed for each violation. . . .

It must be conceded that all businesses are subject to some measure of public regulation. And that the business of manufacturing, selling or distributing ice, like that of the grocer, the dairyman, the butcher or the baker may be subjected to appropriate regulations in the interest of the public health cannot be doubted; but the question here is whether the business is so charged with a public use as to justify the particular restriction above stated. If this legislative restriction be within the constitutional power of the state legislature, it follows that the license or permit, issued to appellant, constitutes a franchise, to which a court of equity will afford protection against one who seeks to carry on the same business without obtaining from the commission a license or permit to do so. . . . In that view, engagement in the business is a privilege to be exercised only in virtue of a public grant, and not a common right to be exercised independently by any competent person conformably to reasonable regulations equally applicable to all who choose to engage therein. . . .

We have . . . with some particularity discussed the circumstances which, so far as the State of Oklahoma is concerned, afford ground for sustaining the legislative pronouncement that the business of operating cotton gins is charged with a public use, in order to put them in contrast with the completely unlike circumstances which attend the business of manufacturing, selling and distributing ice. Here we are dealing with an ordinary business, not with a paramount industry upon which the prosperity of the entire state in large measure depends. It is a business as essentially private in its nature as the business of the grocer, the dairyman, the butcher, the baker, the shoemaker, or the tailor, each of whom performs a service which, to a greater or less extent, the community is dependent upon and is interested in having maintained; but which bears no such relation to the public as to warrant its inclusion in the category of businesses charged with a public use. It may be quite true that in Oklahoma ice is not only an article of prime necessity, but indispensable; but certainly not more so than food or clothing or the shelter of a home. And this court has definitely said that the production or sale of food or clothing cannot be subjected to legislative regulation on the basis of a public use; and that the same is true in respect of the business of renting houses and apartments, except as to temporary measures to tide over grave emergencies. . . .

Stated succinctly, a private corporation here seeks to prevent a competitor from entering the business of making and selling ice. It claims to be endowed with state authority to achieve this exclusion. There is no question now before us of any regulation by the state to protect the consuming public either with respect to conditions of manufacture and distribution or to insure purity of product or to prevent extortion. The control here asserted does not protect against monopoly, but tends to foster it. The aim is not to encourage competition, but to prevent it; not to regulate the business, but to preclude persons from engaging in it. There is no difference in principle between this case and the attempt of the dairyman under state authority to prevent another from keeping cows and selling milk on the ground that there are enough dairymen in the business; or to prevent a shoemaker from making or selling shoes because shoemakers already in that occupation can make and sell all the shoes that are needed. We are not able to see anything peculiar in the business here in question which distinguishes it from ordinary manufacture and production. It is said to be recent; but it is the character of the business and not the date when it began that is determinative. It is not the case of a natural monopoly, or of an enterprise in its nature dependent upon the grant of public privileges. The particular requirement before us was evidently not imposed to prevent a practical monopoly of the business, since its tendency is quite to the contrary. Nor is it a case of the protection of natural resources. There is nothing in the product that we can perceive on which to rest a distinction, in respect of this attempted control, from other products in common use which enter into free competition, subject, of course, to reasonable regulations prescribed for the protection of the public and applied with appropriate impartiality. . . .

Justice Brandeis, dissenting:

[Justice Brandeis dissented in a lengthy (thirty-one pages) and heavily footnoted opinion showing why the Oklahoma legislature could reasonably have concluded that ice-making was affected with a public interest and should be regulated. He concluded with this often-quoted appeal for judicial restraint.]

. . . The people of the United States are now confronted with an emergency more serious than war. Misery is wide-spread, in a time, not of scarcity, but of over-abundance. The long-continued depression has brought unprecedented unemployment, a catastrophic fall in commodity prices and a volume of economic losses which threatens our financial institutions. Some people believe that the existing conditions threaten even the stability of the capitalistic system. Economists are searching for the causes of this disorder and are reëxamining the bases of our industrial structure. Business men are seeking possible remedies. Most of them realize that failure to distribute widely the profits of industry has been a prime cause of our present plight. But rightly or wrongly, many persons think that one of the major contributing causes has been unbridled competition. Increasingly, doubt is expressed whether it is economically wise, or morally right, that men should be permitted to add to the producing facilities of an industry which is already suffering from over-capacity. In justification of that doubt, men point to the excess-capacity of our productive facilities resulting from their vast expansion without corresponding increase in the consumptive capacity of the people. They assert that through improved methods of manufacture, made possible by advances in science and invention and vast accumulation of capital, our industries had become capable of producing from thirty to one hundred per cent more than was consumed even in days of vaunted prosperity; and that the present capacity will, for a long time, exceed the needs of business. All agree that irregularity in employment—the greatest of our evils—cannot be overcome unless production and consumption are more nearly balanced. Many insist there must be some form of economic control. There are plans for proration. There are many proposals for stabilization. And some thoughtful men of wide business experience insist that all projects for stabilization and proration must prove futile unless, in some way, the equivalent of the certificate of public convenience and necessity is made a prerequisite to embarking new capital in an industry in which the capacity already exceeds the production schedules.

Whether that view is sound nobody knows. The objections to the proposal are obvious and grave. The remedy might bring evils worse than the present disease. The obstacles to success seem insuperable. The economic and social sciences are largely uncharted seas. We have been none too successful in the modest essays in economic control already entered upon. The new proposal involves a vast extension of the area of control. Merely to acquire the knowledge essential as a basis for the exercise of this multitude of judgments would be a formidable task; and each of the thousands of these judgments would call for some measure of prophecy. Even more serious are the obstacles to success inherent in the demands which execution of the project would make upon human intelligence and upon the character of men. Man is weak and his judgment is at best fallible.

Yet the advances in the exact sciences and the achievements in invention remind us that the seemingly impossible sometimes happens. There are many men now living who were in the habit of using the age-old expression: "It is as impossible as flying." The discoveries in physical science, the triumphs in invention, attest the value of the process of trial and error. In large measure, these advances have been due to experimentation. In those fields experimentation has, for two centuries, been not only free but encouraged. Some people assert that our present plight is due, in part, to the limitations set by courts upon experimentation in the fields of social and economic science; and to the discouragement to which proposals for betterment there have been subjected otherwise. There must be power in the States and the Nation to remould, through experimentation, our economic practices and institutions to meet changing social and economic needs. I cannot believe that the framers of the Fourteenth Amendment, or the States which ratified it, intended to deprive us of the power to correct the evils of technological unemployment and excess productive capacity which have attended progress in the useful arts.

To stay experimentation in things social and economic is a grave responsibility. Denial of the right to experiment may be fraught with serious consequences to the Nation. It is one of the happy incidents of the federal system that a single courageous State may, if its citizens choose, serve as a laboratory; and try novel social and economic experiments without risk to the rest of the country. This Court has the power to prevent an experiment. We may strike down the statute which embodies it on the ground that, in our opinion, the measure is arbitrary, capricious or unreasonable. We have power to do this, because the due process clause has been held by the Court applicable to matters of substantive law as well as to matters of procedure. But in the exercise of this high power, we must be ever on our guard, lest we erect our prejudices into legal principles. If we would guide by the light of reason, we must let our minds be bold.

173

United States v. One Book Called "Ulysses" (1933)

Obscenity has always been considered outside the protection of the First Amendment, and a variety of state and federal laws operated to suppress the publication of allegedly obscene materials or to deny them entry into this country if published abroad. To prove that material was not obscene, one had to meet the test set forth in the English case of *Regina v. Hicklin* (1868), which judged the overall work by the effect of selected passages on particularly susceptible persons. New and sometimes shocking works, such as James Joyce's acclaimed *Ulysses,* rarely passed this test. In this important decision, District Judge John M. Woolsey not only relied on the judgment of expert witnesses, but also anticipated the later test of the Supreme Court regarding obscenity, namely, how the totality of the material affects the average person (Document 224).

See Frederick F. Schauer, *The Law of Obscenity* (1976); D. Richards, "Free Speech and Obscenity Law: Toward a Moral Theory of the First Amendment," 123 *University of Pennsylvania Law Review* 4 (1974); and Harry Kalven, Jr., "The Metaphysics of the Law of Obscenity," 1960 *Supreme Court Review* 1 (1961).

———

District Judge Woolsey:

II. I have read "Ulysses" once in its entirety and I have read those passages of which the government particularly complains several times. In fact, for many weeks, my spare time has been devoted to the consideration of the decision which my duty would require me to make in this matter.

"Ulysses"is not an easy book to read or to understand. But there has been much written about it, and in order properly to approach the consideration of it it is advisable to read a number of other books which have now become its satellites. The study of "Ulysses" is, therefore, a heavy task.

III. The reputation of "Ulysses" in the literary world, however, warranted my taking such time as was necessary to enable me to satisfy myself as to the intent with which the book was written, for, of course, in any case where a book is claimed to be obscene it must first be determined, whether the intent with which it was written was what is called, according to the usual phrase, pornographic, that is, written for the purpose of exploiting obscenity.

Source: 5 F. Supp. 182 (S.D.N.Y. 1933)

If the conclusion is that the book is pornographic, that is the end of the inquiry and forfeiture must follow.

But in "Ulysses," in spite of its unusual frankness, I do not detect anywhere the leer of the sensualist. I hold, therefore, that it is not pornographic.

IV. In writing "Ulysses," Joyce sought to make a serious experiment in a new, if not wholly novel, literary genre. He takes persons of the lower middle class living in Dublin in 1904 and seeks, not only to describe what they did on a certain day early in June of that year as they went about the city bent on their usual occupations, but also to tell what many of them thought about the while.

Joyce has attempted—it seems to me, with astonishing success—to show how the screen of consciousness with its ever-shifting kaleidoscopic impressions carries, as it were on a plastic palimpsest, not only what is in the focus of each man's observation of the actual things about him, but also in a penumbral zone residua of past impressions, some recent and some drawn up by association from the domain of the subconscious. He shows how each of these impressions affects the life and behavior of the character which he is describing.

What he seeks to get is not unlike the result of a double or, if that is possible, a multiple exposure on a cinema film, which would give a clear foreground with a background visible but somewhat blurred and out of focus in varying degrees.

To convey by words an effect which obviously lends itself more appropriately to a graphic technique, accounts, it seems to me, for much of the obscurity which meets a reader of "Ulysses." And it also explains another aspect of the book, which I have further to consider, namely, Joyce's sincerity and his honest effort to show exactly how the minds of his characters operate.

If Joyce did not attempt to be honest in developing the technique which he has adopted in "Ulysses," the result would be psychologically misleading and thus unfaithful to his chosen technique. Such an attitude would be artistically inexcusable.

It is because Joyce has been loyal to his technique and has not funked its necessary implications, but has honestly attempted to tell fully what his characters think about, that he has been the subject of so many attacks and that his purpose has been so often misunderstood and misrepresented. For his attempt sincerely and honestly to realize his objective has required him incidentally to use certain words which are generally considered dirty words and has led at times to what many think is a too poignant preoccupation with sex in the thoughts of his characters.

The words which are criticized as dirty are old Saxon words known to almost all men and, I venture, to many women, and are such words as would be naturally and habitually used, I believe, by the types of folk whose life, physical and mental, Joyce is seeking to describe. In respect of the recurrent emergence of the theme of sex in the minds of his characters, it must always be remembered that his locale was Celtic and his season spring.

Whether or not one enjoys such a technique as Joyce uses is a matter of taste on which disagreement or argument is futile, but to subject that technique to the standards of some other technique seems to me to be little short of absurd.

Accordingly, I hold that "Ulysses" is a sincere and honest book, and I think that the criticisms of it are entirely disposed of by its rationale.

V. Furthermore, "Ulysses" is an amazing tour de force when one considers the success which has been in the main achieved with such a difficult objective as Joyce set for himself. As I have stated, "Ulysses" is not an easy book to read. It is brilliant and dull, intelligible and obscure, by turns. In many places it seems to me to be disgusting, but although it contains, as I have mentioned above, many words usually considered dirty, I have not found anything that I consider to be dirt for dirt's sake. Each word of the book contributes like a bit of mosaic to the detail of the picture which Joyce is seeking to construct for his readers.

If one does not wish to associate with such folk as Joyce describes, that is one's own choice. In order to avoid indirect contact with them one may not wish to read "Ulysses"; that is quite understandable. But when such a great artist in words, as Joyce undoubtedly is, seeks to draw a true picture of the lower middle class in a European city, ought it to be impossible for the American public legally to see that picture.

To answer this question it is not sufficient merely to find, as I have found above, that Joyce did not write "Ulysses" with what is commonly called pornographic intent, I must endeavor to apply a more objective standard to his book in order to determine its effect in the result, irrespective of the intent with which it was written.

VI. The statute under which the libel is filed only denounces, in so far as we are here concerned, the importation into the United States from any foreign country of "any obscene book." Section 305 of the Tariff Act of 1930, title 19 United States Code, §1305 (19 USCA §1305). It does not marshal against books the spectrum of condemnatory adjectives found, commonly, in laws dealing with matters of this kind. I am, therefore, only required to determine whether "Ulysses" is obscene within the legal definition of that word.

The meaning of the word "obscene" as legally defined by the courts is: Tending to stir the sex impulses or to lead to sexually impure and lustful thoughts. . . .

Whether a particular book would tend to excite such impulses and thoughts must be tested by the court's opinion as to its effect on a person with average sex instincts—what the French would call *l'homme moyen sensuel*—who plays, in this branch of legal inquiry, the same role of hypothetical reagent as does the "reasonable man" in the law of torts and "the man learned in the art" on questions of invention in patent law.

The risk involved in the use of such a reagent arises from the inherent tendency of the trier of facts, however fair he may intend to be, to make his reagent too much subservient to his own idiosyncrasies. Here, I have attempted to avoid this, if possible, and to make my reagent herein more objective than he might otherwise be, by adopting the following course:

After I had made my decision in regard to the aspect of "Ulysses," now under consideration, I checked my impressions with two friends of mine who in my opinion answered to the above-stated requirement for my reagent.

These literary assessors—as I might properly describe them—were called on separately, and neither knew that I was consulting the other. They are men whose opinion on literature and on life I value most highly. They had both read "Ulysses," and, of course, were wholly unconnected with this cause.

Without letting either of my assessors know what my decision was, I gave to each of them the legal definition of obscene and asked each whether in his opinion "Ulysses" was obscene within that definition.

I was interested to find that they both agreed with my opinion: That reading "Ulysses" in its entirety, as a book must be read on such a test as this, did not tend to excite sexual impulses or lustful thoughts, but that its net effect on them was only that of a somewhat tragic and very powerful commentary on the inner lives of men and women.

It is only with the normal person that the law is concerned. Such a test as I have described, therefore, is the only proper test of obscenity in the case of a book like "Ulysses" which is a sincere and serious attempt to devise a new literary method for the observation and description of mankind.

I am quite aware that owing to some of its scenes "Ulysses" is a rather strong draught to ask some sensitive, though normal, persons to take. But my considered opinion, after long reflection, is that, whilst in many places the effect of "Ulysses" on the reader undoubtedly is somewhat emetic, nowhere does it tend to be an aphrodisiac.

"Ulysses" may, therefore, be admitted into the United States.

---

174 *Nebbia v. New York (1934)*

Conservative fears had been aroused by the Court's decision in *Home Building & Loan Association v. Blaisdell* (1934), when a five man majority approved a Minnesota statute allowing debtors greater time and flexibility in meeting their mortgage obligations. These fears seemed confirmed a few months later when, again by a bare majority, the Court upheld the New York Milk Control Act of 1933, which allowed the state to set minimum wholesale and retail milk prices in an effort to sustain the dairy industry. This time the majority opinion came not from one of the liberals, but from the moderate Owen J. Roberts, who sustained the power of the state to adopt whatever policy it deemed best to meet emergencies. The Roberts opinion seemed to carry out the proposal Brandeis made in his *New State Ice* dissent that courts defer completely to legislative judgment in economic matters. Roberts's declaration that "Neither property rights nor contract rights are absolute" horrified the conservatives, and Justice McReynolds lamented in a private letter to former Solicitor General James Beck that *Blaisdell* and *Nebbia* meant "the end of the Constitution as you and I regarded it. An Alien influence has prevailed."

Recent scholarship sees *Nebbia* as a key decision in the Court's march away from the conservative and restrictive jurisprudence of the 1920s toward a more pragmatic interpretation of the commerce power. By blurring the lines between the public and the private, Justice Roberts's opinion made it easier to rationalize and thus legitimate state interference with business.

See Barry Cushman, *Rethinking the New Deal Court: The Structure of a Constitutional Revolution* (1998); Howard Gillman, *The Constitution Besieged: The Rise and Demise of Lochner Era Police Powers Jurisprudence* (1993); and Richard Friedman, "Switching Time and Other Thought Experiments: The Hughes Court and Constitutional Transformation," 142 *University of Pennsylvania Law Review* 1891 (1994).

———

Justice Roberts delivered the opinion of the Court:

The Legislature of New York established . . . a Milk Control Board with power, among other things, to "fix minimum and maximum . . . retail prices to be charged by . . . stores to consumers for consumption off the premises where sold." The Board fixed nine cents as the price to be charged by a store for a quart of milk. Nebbia, the proprietor of a grocery store in Rochester, sold two quarts and a five cent loaf of bread for eighteen cents; and was convicted for violating the Board's order. At his trial he asserted the statute and order contravene the equal protection clause and the due process clause of the Fourteenth Amendment. . . .

Under our form of government the use of property and the making of contracts are normally matters of private and not of public concern. The general rule is that both shall be free of governmental interference. But neither property rights nor contract rights are absolute; for government cannot exist if the citizen may at will use his property to the detriment of his fellows, or exercise his freedom of contract to work them harm. Equally fundamental with the private right is that of the public to regulate it in the common interest. . . .

The milk industry in New York has been the subject of long-standing and drastic regulation in the public interest. The legislative investigation of 1932 was persuasive of the fact that for this and other reasons unrestricted competition aggravated existing evils, and the normal law of supply and demand was insufficient to correct maladjustments detrimental to the community. The inquiry disclosed destructive and demoralizing competitive conditions and unfair trade practices which resulted in retail price-cutting and reduced the income of the farmer below the cost of production. . . . [The legislature] . . . believed conditions could be improved by preventing destructive price-cutting by stores which, due to the flood of surplus milk, were able to buy at much lower prices than the larger distributors and to sell without incurring the delivery costs of the latter. In the order of which complaint is made the Milk Control Board fixed a price of ten cents per quart for sales by a distributor to a consumer, and nine cents by a store to a consumer, thus recognizing the lower costs of the store, and endeavoring to establish a differential which would be just to both. In the light of the facts the order appears not to be unreasonable or arbitrary, or without relation to the purpose to prevent ruthless competition from destroying the wholesale price structure on which the farmer depends for his livelihood, and the community for an assured supply of milk.

But we are told that because the law essays to control prices it denies due process. Notwithstanding the admitted power to correct existing economic ills by appropriate regulation of business, even though an indirect result may be a restriction of the freedom of contract or a modification of charges for services or the price of commodities, the

———

Source: 291 U.S. 502 (1934)

appellant urges that direct fixation of prices is a type of regulation absolutely forbidden. His position is that the Fourteenth Amendment requires us to hold the challenged statute void for this reason alone. The argument runs that the public control of rates or prices is *per se* unreasonable and unconstitutional, save as applied to businesses affected with a public interest; that a business so affected is one in which property is devoted to an enterprise of a sort which the public itself might appropriately undertake, or one whose owner relies on a public grant or franchise for the right to conduct the business, or in which he is bound to serve all who apply; in short, such as is commonly called a public utility; or a business in its nature a monopoly. The milk industry, it is said, possesses none of these characteristics, and, therefore, not being affected with a public interest, its charges may not be controlled by the state. Upon the soundness of this contention the appellant's case against the statute depends.

We may as well say at once that the dairy industry is not, in the accepted sense of the phrase, a public utility. We think the appellant is also right in asserting that there is in this case no suggestion of any monopoly or monopolistic practice. It goes without saying that those engaged in the business are in no way dependent upon public grants or franchises for the privilege of conducting their activities. But if, as must be conceded, the industry is subject to regulation in the public interest, what constitutional principle bars the state from correcting existing maladjustments by legislation touching prices? We think there is no such principle. The due process clause makes no mention of sales or of prices any more than it speaks of business or contracts or buildings or other incidents of property. The thought seems nevertheless to have persisted that there is something peculiarly sacrosanct about the price one may charge for what he makes or sells, and that, however able to regulate other elements of manufacture or trade, with incidental effect upon price, the state is incapable of directly controlling the price itself. This view was negatived many years ago. . . .

It is clear that there is no closed class or category of businesses affected with a public interest, and the function of courts in the application of the Fifth and Fourteenth Amendments is to determine in each case whether circumstances vindicate the challenged regulation as a reasonable exertion of governmental authority or condemn it as arbitrary or discriminatory. . . . But there can be no doubt that upon proper occasion and by appropriate measures the state may regulate a business in any of its aspects, including the prices to be charged for the products or commodities it sells.

So far as the requirement of due process is concerned, and in the absence of other constitutional restriction, a state is free to adopt whatever economic policy may reasonably be deemed to promote public welfare, and to enforce that policy by legislation adapted to its purpose. The courts are without authority either to declare such policy, or, when it is declared by the legislature, to override it. . . .

The Constitution does not secure to anyone liberty to conduct his business in such fashion as to inflict injury upon the public at large, or upon any substantial group of the people. Price control, like any other form of regulation, is unconstitutional only if arbitrary, discriminatory, or demonstrably irrelevant to the policy the legislature is free to adopt, and hence an unnecessary and unwarranted interference with individual liberty.

175 *Perry v. United States (1935)*

As part of his plan to halt the rampant deflation afflicting the country, and to forestall some of the more radical plans congressional inflationists were proposing, President Roosevelt took the country off the gold standard in April 1933. Soon afterward, Congress voided the gold repayment clauses in both private and public obligations. A series of four cases dealing with various aspects of the gold clause reached the Court in early 1935. A bare majority of the Court, fearful that an adverse decision would plunge the country into financial chaos or just be ignored by the government, sustained the administration's policy. In *Norman* v. *Baltimore & Ohio Railroad,* Chief Justice Hughes sustained the power of Congress to void private contracts in order to further public policy. But when it came to the government's own obligations, the chief justice severely rebuked the government for breaking its own word, yet because the bondholder had not suffered damage, denied him recovery. Arthur Schlesinger, Jr., later characterized the chief justice's opinion "as a masterpiece of judicial legerdemain, hardly matched in the annals of the Court since Marshall's opinion in *Marbury v. Madison.*" Justice McReynolds, speaking for the four conservatives, entered such a vitriolic dissent that the Court reporter omitted parts of it from the written record. The Constitution is gone, he lamented, "shame and humiliation are upon us."

See Henry M. Hart, Jr., "The Gold Clause in United States Bonds," 48 *Harvard Law Review* 1057 (1935); G. Nebolsine, "The Gold Clause in Private Contracts," 42 *Yale Law Journal* 1051 (1933); John P. Dawson, "The Gold Clause Decisions," 33 *Michigan Law Review* 647 (1935); and Edward S. Corwin, *Constitutional Revolution, Ltd.* (1941).

———

Chief Justice Hughes delivered the opinion of the Court:
First. The import of the obligation. The bond in suit differs from an obligation of private parties, or of States or municipalities, whose contracts are necessarily made in subjection to the dominant power of the Congress. . . . The bond now before us is an obligation of the United States. The terms of the bond are explicit. They were not only expressed in the bond itself, but they were definitely prescribed by the Congress. . . . The circular of the Treasury Department of September 28, 1918, to which the bond refers "for a statement of the further rights of the holders of bonds of said series," also provided that the principal and interest "are payable in United States gold coin of the present standard of value."

Source: 294 U.S. 330 (1935)

This obligation must be fairly construed. The *"present* standard of value" stood in contradistinction to a *lower* standard of value. The promise obviously was intended to afford protection against loss. That protection was sought to be secured by setting up a standard or measure of the Government's obligation. We think that the reasonable import of the promise is that it was intended to assure one who lent his money to the Government and took its bond that he would not suffer loss through depreciation in the medium of payment. . . .

Second. The binding quality of the obligation. The question is necessarily presented whether the Joint Resolution of June 5, 1933 (48 Stat. 113) is a valid enactment so far as it applies to the obligations of the United States. The Resolution declared that provisions requiring "payment in gold or a particular kind of coin or currency" were "against public policy," and provided that "every obligation, heretofore or hereafter incurred, whether or not any such provision is contained therein," shall be discharged "upon payment, dollar for dollar, in any coin or currency which at the time of payment is legal tender for public and private debts." This enactment was expressly extended to obligations of the United States, and provisions for payment in gold, "contained in any law authorizing obligations to be issued by or under authority of the United States," were repealed.

There is no question as to the power of the Congress to regulate the value of money, that is, to establish a monetary system and thus to determine the currency of the country. The question is whether the Congress can use that power so as to invalidate the terms of the obligations which the Government has theretofore issued in the exercise of the power to borrow money on the credit of the United States. In attempted justification of the Joint Resolution in relation to the outstanding bonds of the United States, the Government argues that "earlier Congresses could not validly restrict the 73rd Congress from exercising its constitutional powers to regulate the value of money, borrow money, or regulate foreign and interstate commerce"; and, from this premise, the Government seems to deduce the proposition that when, with adequate authority, the Government borrows money and pledges the credit of the United States, it is free to ignore that pledge and alter the terms of its obligations in case a later Congress finds their fulfillment inconvenient. The Government's contention thus raises a question of far greater importance than the particular claim of the plaintiff. On that reasoning, if the terms of the Government's bond as to the standard of payment can be repudiated, it inevitably follows that the obligation as to the amount to be paid may also be repudiated. The contention necessarily imports that the Congress can disregard the obligations of the Government at its discretion and that, when the Government borrows money, the credit of the United States is an illusory pledge.

We do not so read the Constitution. There is a clear distinction between the power of the Congress to control or interdict the contracts of private parties when they interfere with the exercise of its constitutional authority, and the power of the Congress to alter or repudiate the substance of its own engagements when it has borrowed money under the authority which the Constitution confers. In authorizing the Congress to borrow money, the Constitution empowers the Congress to fix the amount to be borrowed and the terms of payment. By virtue of the power to borrow money *"on the credit of the United States,"* the Congress is authorized to pledge that credit as an assurance of payment as stipulated,—as the highest assurance the Government can give, its plighted faith. To say that the Congress may withdraw or ignore that pledge, is to assume that the Constitution contemplates a vain promise, a pledge having no other sanction than the pleasure and convenience of the pledgor. This Court has given no sanction to such a conception of the obligations of our Government. . . .

The argument in favor of the Joint Resolution, as applied to government bonds, is in substance that the Government cannot by contract restrict the exercise of a sovereign power. But the right to make binding obligations is a competence attaching to sovereignty. In the United States, sovereignty resides in the people, who act through the organs established by the Constitution. . . . The Congress as the instrumentality of sovereignty is endowed with certain powers to be exerted on behalf of the people in the manner and with the effect the Constitution ordains. The Congress cannot invoke the sovereign power of the people to override their will as thus declared. The powers conferred upon the Congress are harmonious. The Constitution gives to the Congress the power to borrow money on the credit of the United States, an unqualified power, a power vital to the Government,—upon which in an extremity its very life may depend. The binding quality of the promise of the United States is of the essence of the credit which is so pledged. Having this power to authorize the issue of definite obligations for the payment of money borrowed, the Congress has not been vested with authority to alter or destroy those obligations. . . .

We conclude that the Joint Resolution of June 5, 1933, in so far as it attempted to override the obligation created by the bond in suit, went beyond the congressional power.

Third. The question of damages. In this view of the binding quality of the Government's obligations, we come to the question as to the plaintiff's right to recover damages. That is a distinct question. Because the Government is not at liberty to alter or repudiate its obligations, it does not follow that the claim advanced by the plaintiff should be sustained. The action is for breach of contract. As a remedy for breach, plaintiff can recover no more than the loss he has suffered and of which he may rightfully complain. He is not entitled to be enriched. Plaintiff seeks judgment for $16,931.25, in present legal tender currency, on his bond for $10,000. The question is whether he has shown damage to that extent, or any actual damage. . . .

Plaintiff computes his claim for $16,931.25 by taking the weight of the gold dollar as fixed by the President's proclamation of January 31, 1934. . . . But the change in the weight of the gold dollar did not necessarily cause loss to the plaintiff of the amount claimed. The question of actual loss cannot fairly be determined without considering the economic situation at the time the Government offered to pay him the $10,000, the face of his bond, in legal tender currency. The case is not the same as if gold coin had remained in circulation. . . . Before the change in the weight of the gold dollar in 1934, gold coin had been withdrawn from circulation. The Congress had authorized the prohibition of the exportation of gold coin and the placing of restrictions upon transactions in foreign exchange. . . .

Plaintiff demands the "equivalent" in currency of the gold coin promised. But "equivalent" cannot mean more than the amount of money which the promised gold coin would be worth to the bondholder for the purposes for which it could legally be used. That equivalence or worth could not properly be ascertained save in the light of the domestic and restricted market which the Congress had lawfully established. In the domestic transactions to which the plaintiff was limited, in the absence of special license, determination of the value of the gold coin would necessarily have regard to its use as legal tender and as a medium of exchange under a single monetary system with an established parity of all currency and coins. And in view of the control of export and foreign exchange, and the restricted domestic use, the question of value, in relation to transactions legally available to the plaintiff, would require a consideration of the purchasing power of the dollars which the plaintiff could have received. Plaintiff has not shown, or attempted to show, that in relation to buying power he has sustained any loss whatever. On the contrary, in view of the adjustment of the internal economy to the single measure of value as established by the legislation of the Congress, and the universal availability and use throughout the country of the legal tender currency in meeting all engagements, the payment to the plaintiff of the amount which he demands would appear to constitute not a recoupment of loss in any proper sense but an unjustified enrichment.

Plaintiff seeks to make his case solely upon the theory that by reason of the change in the weight of the dollar he is entitled to one dollar and sixty-nine cents in the present currency for every dollar promised by the bond, regardless of any actual loss he has suffered with respect to any transaction in which his dollars may be used. We think that position is untenable.

---

176   *Schechter Poultry Corp. v. United States (1935)*

The centerpiece of the New Deal's initial attack on the Depression was the National Industrial Recovery Act, a poorly drafted hodgepodge of proposals drawn from a variety of often opposing views. Industries were to draft code agreements to govern conduct of the marketplace, which were to include fair rules of competition, the right of labor to organize and bargain collectively, abolition of child labor, and the establishment of fair labor standards. The codes enjoyed exemption from the antitrust laws, and if businesses could not agree on a code, the president, acting through the National Recovery Administration (NRA), could draft a code and force it upon the industry. All codes, once approved by the president, had the force of law and could be enforced by federal authority. The bill had been drafted by committee in a crisis atmosphere, with the attitude of "give something to everybody," and the NRA would later sort out and resolve any conflicts or ambiguities, a course Congress had validated in its hurried approval of the measure.

The first provision to be tested in court was Section 9(c), which gave the president authority to bar shipment of so-called hot oil in interstate commerce. Several of the oil-producing states, in an effort to raise prices, had imposed production limits on wells within their borders, but they lacked any authority to stop the sale of illegal production, or hot oil, to buyers outside the state. Section 9(c) was modeled on the Webb–Kenyon Act of 1913, which utilized the federal commerce power to enforce state prohibition measures.

In *Panama Refining Co. v. Ryan* (1935), the challenge to 9(c) highlighted many of the constitutional problems facing the entire act. An astounded Court, for example, heard counsel for the oil producers tell how they could not get copies of the regulations. By an eight-to-one vote, with only Cardozo dissenting, the Court invalidated Section 9(c) on the grounds that Congress had failed to provide the president with sufficient guidelines in delegating him power over interstate commerce.

On "Black Monday," May 27, 1935, the Court struck down the Frazier–Lemke Mortgage Relief Act *(Louisville Joint Stock Land Bank v. Radford);* ruled that the president could not remove members of independent regulatory commissions *(Humphrey's Executor v. United States);* and unanimously voided the NRA. Although the Court normally limits its decisions to a single constitutional issue, Chief Justice Hughes raised three constitutional questions and answered all of them in the negative. Even the liberals on the Court considered the poorly drafted bill an abomination.

See Robert F. Himmelberg, *The Origins of the National Recovery Administration* (1976); Ellis Wayne Hawley, *The New Deal and the Problem of Monopoly* (1966); Frank Friedel, "The Sick Chicken Case," in John Garraty, ed., *Quarrels That Have Shaped the Constitution* (1975), 191; Peter H. Irons, *The New Deal Lawyers* (1982).

Chief Justice Hughes delivered the opinion of the Court:

We are told that the provision of the statute authorizing the adoption of codes must be viewed in the light of the grave national crisis with which Congress was confronted. Undoubtedly, the conditions to which power is addressed are always to be considered when the exercise of power is challenged. Extraordinary conditions may call for extraordinary remedies. But the argument necessarily stops short of an attempt to justify action which lies outside the sphere of constitutional authority. Extraordinary conditions do not create or enlarge constitutional power. The Constitution established a national government with powers deemed to be adequate, as they have proved to be both in war and peace, but these powers of the national government are limited by the constitutional grants. Those who act under these grants are not at liberty to transcend the imposed limits because they believe that more or different power is necessary. Such assertions of extra-constitutional authority were anticipated and precluded by the explicit terms of the Tenth Amendment,—"The powers not delegated to the United States by the Constitution, nor prohibited by it to the States, are reserved to the States respectively, or to the people." . . .

Source: 295 U.S. 495 (1935)

Second. *The question of the delegation of legislative power.* . . .

Accordingly we turn to the Recovery Act to ascertain what limits have been set to the exercise of the President's discretion. *First,* the President, as a condition of approval, is required to find that the trade or industrial associations or groups which propose a code, "impose no inequitable restrictions on admission to membership" and are "truly representative." That condition, however, relates only to the status of the initiators of the new laws and not to the permissible scope of such laws. *Second,* the President is required to find that the code is not "designed to promote monopolies or to eliminate or oppress small enterprises and will not operate to discriminate against them." And, to this is added a proviso that the code "shall not permit monopolies or monopolistic practices." But these restrictions leave virtually untouched the field of policy envisaged by section one, and, in that wide field of legislative possibilities, the proponents of a code, refraining from monopolistic designs, may roam at will and the President may approve or disapprove their proposals as he may see fit. . . .

Nor is the breadth of the President's discretion left to the necessary implications of this limited requirement as to his findings. As already noted, the President in approving a code may impose his own conditions, adding to or taking from what is proposed, as "in his discretion" he thinks necessary "to effectuate the policy" declared by the Act. Of course, he has no less liberty when he prescribes a code on his own motion or on complaint, and he is free to prescribe one if a code has not been approved. The Act provides for the creation by the President of administrative agencies to assist him, but the action or reports of such agencies, or of his other assistants,—their recommendations and findings in relation to the making of codes—have no sanction beyond the will of the President, who may accept, modify or reject them as he pleases. Such recommendations or findings in no way limit the authority which § 3 undertakes to vest in the President with no other conditions than those there specified. And this authority relates to a host of different trades and industries, thus extending the President's discretion to all the varieties of laws which he may deem to be beneficial in dealing with the vast array of commercial and industrial activities throughout the country.

Such a sweeping delegation of legislative power finds no support in the decisions upon which the Government especially relies. . . .

To summarize and conclude upon this point: Section 3 of the Recovery Act is without precedent. It supplies no standards for any trade, industry or activity. It does not undertake to prescribe rules of conduct to be applied to particular states of fact determined by appropriate administrative procedure. Instead of prescribing rules of conduct, it authorizes the making of codes to prescribe them. For that legislative undertaking, § 3 sets up no standards, aside from the statement of the general aims of rehabilitation, correction and expansion described in section one. In view of the scope of that broad declaration, and of the nature of the few restrictions that are imposed, the discretion of the President in approving or prescribing codes, and thus enacting laws for the government of trade and industry throughout the country, is virtually unfettered. We think that the code-making authority thus conferred is an unconstitutional delegation of legislative power.

Third. *The question of the application of the provisions of the Live Poultry Code to intrastate transactions.* . . .

The undisputed facts . . . afford no warrant for the argument that the poultry handled by defendants at their slaughterhouse markets was in a *"current"* or *"flow"* of interstate commerce and was thus subject to congressional regulation. The mere fact that there may be a constant flow of commodities into a State does not mean that the flow continues after the property has arrived and has become commingled with the mass of property within the State and is there held solely for local disposition and use. So far as the poultry here in question is concerned, the flow in interstate commerce had ceased. The poultry had come to a permanent rest within the State. It was not held, used, or sold by defendants in relation to any further transactions in interstate commerce and was not destined for transportation to other States. Hence, decisions which deal with a stream of interstate commerce—where goods come to rest within a State temporarily and are later to go forward in interstate commerce—and with the regulations of transactions involved in that practical continuity of movement, are not applicable here. . . .

Did the defendants' transactions directly *"affect"* interstate commerce so as to be subject to federal regulation? The power of Congress extends not only to the regulation of transactions which are part of interstate commerce, but to the protection of that commerce from injury. . . .

In determining how far the federal government may go in controlling intrastate transactions upon the ground that they "affect" interstate commerce, there is a necessary and well-established distinction between direct and indirect effects. The precise line can be drawn only as individual cases arise, but the distinction is clear in principle. Direct effects are illustrated by the railroad cases we have cited, as *e.g.,* the effect of failure to use prescribed safety appliances on railroads which are the highways of both interstate and intrastate commerce, injury to an employee engaged in interstate transportation by the negligence of an employee engaged in an intrastate movement, the fixing of rates for intrastate transportation which unjustly discriminate against interstate commerce. But where the effect of intrastate transactions upon interstate commerce is merely indirect, such transactions remain within the domain of state power. If the commerce clause were construed to reach all enterprises and transactions which could be said to have an indirect effect upon interstate commerce, the federal authority would embrace practically all the activities of the people and the authority of the State over its domestic concerns would exist only by sufferance of the federal government. . . .

The question of chief importance relates to the provisions of the Code as to the hours and wages of those employed in defendants' slaughterhouse markets. It is plain that these requirements are imposed in order to govern the details of defendants' management of their local business. The persons employed in slaughtering and selling in local trade are not employed in interstate commerce. Their hours and wages have no direct relation to interstate commerce. . . . If the federal government may determine the wages and hours of employees in the internal commerce of a State, because of their relation to cost and prices and their indirect effect upon interstate commerce, it would seem that a similar control might be exerted over other elements of cost, also affecting prices, such as the number of employees, rents, advertising, methods of doing business, etc. All the processes of production and distribution that enter into cost could likewise be controlled. If the cost of doing an intrastate business is in itself the permitted object of federal control, the extent of the regulation of cost would be a question of discretion and not of power. . . .

It is not the province of the Court to consider the economic advantages or disadvantages of such a centralized system. It is sufficient to say that the Federal Constitution does not provide for it. Our growth and development have called for wide use of the commerce power of the federal government in its control over the expanded activities of interstate commerce, and in protecting that commerce from burdens, interferences, and conspiracies to restrain and monopolize it. But the authority of the federal government may not be pushed to such an extreme as to destroy the distinction, which the commerce clause itself establishes, between commerce "among the several States" and the internal concerns of a State. The same answer must be made to the contention that is based upon the serious economic situation which led to the passage of the Recovery Act,—the fall in prices, the decline in wages and employment, and the curtailment of the market for commodities. Stress is laid upon the great importance of maintaining wage distributions which would provide the necessary stimulus in starting "the cumulative forces making for expanding commercial activity." Without in any way disparaging this motive, it is enough to say that the recuperative efforts of the federal government must be made in a manner consistent with the authority granted by the Constitution.

177 *United States v. Butler (1936)*

Unlike the NRA, in which the administration had relied on the commerce power, the government's agricultural program rested on the taxing power, which, according to earlier decisions (Document 145), had a far broader reach. The statute taxed processors of agricultural products and used those revenues for payments to farmers who voluntarily restricted production. Several aspects of Justice Robert's ruling were notable. First, the mechanical view of jurisprudence he set forth, the so-called T-square rule, had been rejected a decade earlier by legal scholars known as the Realists. The Realists argued that any number of nonlegal considerations, including questions of politics and economics, went into the making of a judicial decision, and judges had to be cognizant of these matters. Second, he finally resolved the century-long dispute over the nature of the general welfare clause in favor of the broader Hamiltonian view, but then denied the government the ability to use the clause. Third, of course, was the extremely narrow view of commerce, which is of a piece with the *Schechter* decision. The ruling brought forth a strong protest from Justice Stone, joined by Brandeis and Cardozo, which would be used by Roosevelt in his assault on the Court (Document 181).

See Paul L. Murphy, "The New Deal Agricultural Program and the Constitution," 29 *Agricultural History* 160 (1955); and Van L. Perkins, *Crisis in Agriculture: The A.A.A. and the New Deal* (1969).

Justice Roberts delivered the opinion of the Court:

The Government asserts that even if the respondents may question the propriety of the appropriation embodied in the statute their attack must fail because Article I, § 8 of the Constitution authorizes the contemplated expenditure of the funds raised by the tax. This contention presents the great and the controlling question in the case. . . .

There should be no misunderstanding as to the function of this court in such a case. It is sometimes said that the court assumes a power to overrule or control the action of the people's representatives. This is a misconception. The Constitution is the supreme law of the land ordained and established by the people. All legislation must conform to the principles it lays down. When an Act of Congress is appropriately challenged in the courts as not conforming to the constitutional mandate the judicial branch of the Government has only one duty,—to lay the article of the Constitution which is invoked beside the statute which is challenged and to decide whether the latter squares with the former. All the court does, or can do, is to announce its considered judgment upon the question. The only power it has, if such it may be called, is the power of judgment. This court neither approves nor condemns any legislative policy. Its delicate and difficult office is to ascertain and declare whether the legislation is in accordance with, or in contravention of, the provisions of the Constitution; and, having done that, its duty ends. . . .

The . . . [Constitution] confers upon the Congress power "to lay and collect Taxes, Duties, Imposts and Excises, to pay the Debts and provide for the common Defense and general Welfare of the United States. . . ." It is not contended that this provision grants power to regulate agricultural production upon the theory that such legislation would promote the general welfare. The Government concedes that the phrase "to provide for the general welfare" qualifies the power "to lay and collect taxes." The view that the clause grants power to provide for the general welfare, independently of the taxing power, has never been authoritatively accepted. Mr. Justice Story points out that if it were adopted "it is obvious that under color of the generality of the words, to 'provide for the common defence and general welfare,' the government of the United States is in reality, a government of general and unlimited powers, notwithstanding the subsequent enumeration of specific powers." The true construction undoubtedly is that the only thing granted is the power to tax for the purpose of providing funds for payment of the nation's debts and making provision for the general welfare.

Nevertheless, the Government asserts that warrant is found in this clause for the adoption of the Agricultural Adjustment Act. The argument is that Congress may appropriate and authorize the spending of moneys for the "general welfare"; that the phrase should be liberally construed to cover anything conducive to national welfare; that decision as to what will promote such welfare rests with Congress alone, and the courts may not review its determination; and finally that the appropriation under attack was in fact for the general welfare of the United States. . . .

Since the foundation of the Nation, sharp differences of opinion have persisted as to the true interpretation of the phrase. Madison asserted it amounted to no more than a reference to the other powers enumerated in the subsequent clauses of the same section; that, as the United States is a government of limited and enumerated powers, the grant of power to tax and spend for the general national welfare must be confined to the enu-

Source: 297 U.S. 1 (1936)

merated legislative fields committed to the Congress. In this view the phrase is mere tautology, for taxation and appropriation are or may be necessary incidents of the exercise of any of the enumerated legislative powers. Hamilton, on the other hand, maintained the clause confers a power separate and distinct from those later enumerated, is not restricted in meaning by the grant of them, and Congress consequently has a substantive power to tax and to appropriate, limited only by the requirement that it shall be exercised to provide for the general welfare of the United States. Each contention has had the support of those whose views are entitled to weight. This court has noticed the question, but has never found it necessary to decide which is the true construction. Mr. Justice Story, in his Commentaries, espouses the Hamiltonian position. We shall not review the writings of public men and commentators or discuss the legislative practice. Study of all these leads us to conclude that the reading advocated by Mr. Justice Story is the correct one. While, therefore, the power to tax is not unlimited, its confines are set in the clause which confers it, and not in those of § 8 which bestow and define the legislative powers of the Congress. It results that the power of Congress to authorize expenditure of public moneys for public purposes is not limited by the direct grants of legislative power found in the Constitution. . . .

We are not now required to ascertain the scope of the phrase "general welfare of the United States" or to determine whether an appropriation in aid of agriculture falls within it. Wholly apart from that question, another principle embedded in our Constitution prohibits the enforcement of the Agricultural Adjustment Act. The Act invades the reserved rights of the states. It is a statutory plan to regulate and control agricultural production, a matter beyond the powers delegated to the federal government. The tax, the appropriation of the funds raised, and the direction for their disbursement, are but parts of the plan. They are but means to an unconstitutional end. . . .

If the taxing power may not be used as the instrument to enforce a regulation of matters of state concern with respect to which the Congress has no authority to interfere, may it, as in the present case, be employed to raise the money necessary to purchase a compliance which the Congress is powerless to command? The Government asserts that whatever might be said against the validity of the plan if compulsory, it is constitutionally sound because the end is accomplished by voluntary co-operation. There are two sufficient answers to the contention. The regulation is not in fact voluntary. The farmer, of course, may refuse to comply, but the price of such refusal is the loss of benefits. The amount offered is intended to be sufficient to exert pressure on him to agree to the proposed regulation. The power to confer or withhold unlimited benefits is the power to coerce or destroy. If the cotton grower elects not to accept the benefits, he will receive less for his crops; those who receive payments will be able to undersell him. The result may well be financial ruin. The coercive purpose and intent of the statute is not obscured by the fact that it has not been perfectly successful. . . .

But if the plan were one for purely voluntary co-operation it would stand no better so far as federal power is concerned. At best, it is a scheme for purchasing with federal funds submission to federal regulation of a subject reserved to the states.

It is said that Congress has the undoubted right to appropriate money to executive officers for expenditure under contracts between the government and individuals. But appropriations and expenditures under contracts for proper governmental purposes cannot justify contracts which are not within federal power. And contracts for the reduction of acreage and the control of production are outside the range of that power. An appropriation to be expended by the United States under contracts calling for violation of a state law clearly would offend the Constitution. Is a statute less objectionable which authorizes expenditure of federal moneys to induce action in a field in which the United States has no power to intermeddle? The congress cannot invade state jurisdiction to compel individual action; no more can it purchase such action. . . .

Congress has no power to enforce its commands on the farmer to the ends sought by the Agricultural Adjustment Act. It must follow that it may not indirectly accomplish those ends by taxing and spending to purchase compliance. The Constitution and the entire plan of our government negative any such use of the power to tax and to spend as the act undertakes to authorize. It does not help to declare that local conditions throughout the nation have created a situation of national concern; for this is but to say that whenever there is a widespread similarity of local conditions, Congress may ignore constitutional limitations upon its own powers and usurp those reserved to the states. . . .

Justice Stone, dissenting:

The power of courts to declare a statute unconstitutional is subject to two guiding principles of decision which ought never to be absent from judicial consciousness. One is that courts are concerned only with the power to enact statutes, not with their wisdom. The other is that while unconstitutional exercise of power by the executive and legislative branches of the government is subject to judicial restraint, the only check upon our own exercise of power is our own sense of self-restraint. For the removal of unwise laws from the statute books appeal lies not to the courts but to the ballot and to the processes of democratic government. . . .

It is upon the contention that state power is infringed by purchased regulation of agricultural production that chief reliance is placed. [The] Constitution requires that public funds shall be spent for a defined purpose, the promotion of the general welfare. Their expenditure usually involves payment on terms which will insure use by the selected recipients within the limits of the constitutional purpose. Expenditures would fail of their purpose and thus lose their constitutional sanction if the terms of payment were not such that by their influence on the action of the recipients the permitted end would be attained. The power of Congress to spend is inseparable from persuasion to action over which Congress has no legislative control. Congress may not command that the science of agriculture be taught in state universities. But if it would aid the teaching of that science by grants to state institutions, it is appropriate, if not necessary, that the grant be on the condition, incorporated in the Morrill Act, that it be used for the intended purpose. Similarly it would seem to be compliance with the Constitution, not violation of it, for the government to take and the university to give a contract that the grant would be so used. It makes no difference that there is a promise to do an act which the condition is calculated to induce. Condition and promise are alike valid since both are in furtherance of the national purpose for which the money is appropriated. . . . It is a contradiction in terms to say that there is power to spend for the national welfare, while rejecting any power to impose conditions reasonably adapted to the attainment of the end which alone would justify the expenditure.

The limitation now sanctioned must lead to absurd consequences. The government may give seeds to farmers, but may not condition the gift upon their being planted in places where they are most needed or even planted at all. The government may give money to the unemployed, but may not ask that those who get it shall give labor in return, or even use it to support their families. [It] may support rural schools, [but] may not condition its grant by the requirement that certain standards be maintained. [Do] all its activities collapse because, in order to effect the permissible purpose, in myriad ways the money is paid out upon terms and conditions which influence action of the recipients within the states, which Congress cannot command? The answer would seem plain. If the expenditure is for a national public purpose, that purpose will not be thwarted because payment is on condition which will advance that purpose. The action which Congress induces by payments of money to promote the general welfare, but which it does not command or coerce, is but an incident to a specifically granted power, but a permissible means to a legitimate end. If appropriation in aid of a program of curtailment of agricultural production is constitutional, and it is not denied that it is, payment to farmers on condition that they reduce their crop acreage is constitutional. It is not any the less so because the farmer at his own option promises to fulfill the condition. . . .

A tortured construction of the Constitution is not to be justified by recourse to extreme examples of reckless congressional spending which might occur if courts could not prevent—expenditures which, even if they could be thought to effect any national purpose, would be possible only by action of a legislature lost to all sense of public responsibility. Such suppositions are addressed to the mind accustomed to believe that it is the business of courts to sit in judgment on the wisdom of legislative action. Courts are not the only agency of government that must be assumed to have capacity to govern. Congress and the courts both unhappily may falter or be mistaken in the performance of their constitutional duty. But interpretation of our great charter of government which proceeds on any assumption that the responsibility for the preservation of our institutions is the exclusive concern of any one of the three branches of government, or that it alone can save them from destruction is far more likely, in the long run, "to obliterate the constituent members" of "an indestructible union of indestructible states" than the frank recognition that language, even of a constitution, may mean what it says: that the power to tax and spend includes the power to relieve a nationwide economic maladjustment by conditional gifts of money.

Mr. Justice Brandeis and Mr. Justice Cardozo join in this opinion.

178

Ashwander v. Tennessee Valley Authority (1936)

In many ways the Tennessee Valley Authority, with which the government tried to improve a seven-state area through extensive social and economic programs, represented one of the most radical aspects of the New Deal. At the heart of the plan was a series of dams for flood control and power generation; this new source of power would benefit the residents of the largely rural area, help bring in industry, and also serve as a yardstick to measure the efficiency of private industry so that state regulatory agencies would have accurate information on which to set rates. This last aspect especially worried private power companies, which essentially challenged the right of the federal government to go into private business. The following excerpt deals with the heart of the case, and Chief Justice Hughes based his ruling on a broad reading of an extremely minor clause in the Constitution.

See C. Herman Pritchett, *The Tennessee Valley Authority* (1943); Joseph C. Swidler and R. H. Marquis, "T.V.A. in Court," 32 *Iowa Law Review* 296 (1947); G. D. Haimbaugh, Jr., "The T.V.A. Cases: A Quarter Century Later," 41 *Indiana Law Journal* 197 (1966); and Thomas K. McCraw, *TVA and the Power Fight, 1933–1939* (1971).

———

Chief Justice Hughes delivered the opinion of the Court:
Fourth. The constitutional authority to dispose of electric energy generated at the Wilson Dam. The Government acquired full title to the dam site, with all riparian rights. The power of falling water was an inevitable incident of the construction of the dam. That water power came into the exclusive control of the Federal Government. The mechanical energy was convertible into electric energy, and the water power, the right to convert it into electric energy, and the electric energy thus produced, constitute property belonging to the United States. . . .

Authority to dispose of property constitutionally acquired by the United States is expressly granted to the Congress by § 3 of Article IV of the Constitution. This section provides:

"The Congress shall have Power to dispose of and make all needful Rules and Regulations respecting the Territory or other Property belonging to the United States; and nothing in this Constitution shall be so construed as to Prejudice any Claims of the United States, or of any particular State."

Source: 297 U.S. 288 (1936)

To the extent that the power of disposition is thus expressly conferred, it is manifest that the Tenth Amendment is not applicable. And the Ninth Amendment (which petitioners also invoke) in insuring the maintenance of the rights retained by the people does not withdraw the rights which are expressly granted to the Federal Government. The question is as to the scope of the grant and whether there are inherent limitations which render invalid the disposition of property with which we are now concerned.

The occasion for the grant was the obvious necessity of making provision for the government of the vast territory acquired by the United States. The power to govern and to dispose of that territory was deemed to be indispensable to the purposes of the cessions made by the States. And yet it was a matter of grave concern because of the fear that "the sale and disposal" might become "a source of such immense revenue to the national government, as to make it independent of and formidable to the people." Story on the Constitution, §§ 1325, 1326. The grant was made in broad terms, and the power of regulation and disposition was not confined to territory, but extended to "other property belonging to the United States," so that the power may be applied, as Story says, "to the due regulation of all other personal and real property rightfully belonging to the United States." And so, he adds, "it has been constantly understood and acted upon." . . .

But when Congress thus reserved mineral lands for special disposal, can it be doubted that Congress could have provided for mining directly by its own agents, instead of giving that right to lessees on the payment of royalties? Upon what ground could it be said that the Government could not mine its own gold, silver, coal, lead, or phosphates in the public domain, and dispose of them as property belonging to the United States? That it could dispose of its land but not of what the land contained? It would seem to be clear that under the same power of disposition which enabled the Government to lease and obtain profit from sales by its lessees, it could mine and obtain profit from its own sales.

The question is whether a more limited power of disposal should be applied to the water power, convertible into electric energy, and to the electric energy thus produced at the Wilson Dam constructed by the Government in the exercise of its constitutional functions. If so, it must be by reason either of (1) the nature of the particular property, or (2) the character of the "surplus" disposed of, or (3) the manner of disposition.

(1) That the water power and the electric energy generated at the dam are susceptible of disposition as property belonging to the United States is well established. . . .

(2) The argument is stressed that, assuming that electric energy generated at the dam belongs to the United States, the Congress has authority to dispose of this energy only to the extent that it is a surplus necessarily created in the course of making munitions of war or operating the works for navigation purposes; that is, that the remainder of the available energy must be lost or go to waste. We find nothing in the Constitution which imposes such a limitation. It is not to be deduced from the mere fact that the electric energy is only potentially available until the generators are operated. The Government has no less right to the energy thus available by letting the water course over its turbines than it has to use the appropriate processes to reduce to possession other property within its control, as, for example, oil which it may recover from a pool beneath its lands, and which is reduced to possession by boring oil wells and otherwise might escape its grasp. . . . And it would hardly be contended that, when the Government reserves coal

on its lands, it can mine the coal and dispose of it only for the purpose of heating public buildings or for other governmental operations. Or, if the Government owns a silver mine, that it can obtain the silver only for the purpose of storage or coinage. Or that when the Government extracts the oil it has reserved, it has no constitutional power to sell it. Our decisions recognize no such restriction. . . . We think that the same principle is applicable to electric energy. . . .

(3) We come then to the question as to the validity of the method which has been adopted in disposing of the surplus energy generated at the Wilson Dam. The constitutional provision is silent as to the method of disposing of property belonging to the United States. That method, of course, must be an appropriate means of disposition according to the nature of the property, it must be one adopted in the public interest as distinguished from private or personal ends, and we may assume that it must be consistent with the foundation principles of our dual system of government and must not be contrived to govern the concerns reserved to the States. . . . In this instance, the method of disposal embraces the sale of surplus energy by the Tennessee Valley Authority to the Alabama Power Company, the interchange of energy between the Authority and the Power Company, and the purchase by the Authority from the Power Company of certain transmission lines.

As to the mere sale of surplus energy, nothing need be added to what we have said as to the constitutional authority to dispose. . . .

. . . We suppose that in the early days of mining in the West, if the Government had undertaken to operate a silver mine on its domain, it could have acquired the mules or horses and equipment to carry its silver to market. And the transmission lines for electric energy are but a facility for conveying to market that particular sort of property, and the acquisition of these lines raises no different constitutional question, unless in some way there is an invasion of the rights reserved to the State or to the people. We find no basis for concluding that the limited undertaking with the Alabama Power Company amounts to such an invasion. Certainly, the Alabama Power Company has no constitutional right to insist that it shall be the sole purchaser of the energy generated at the Wilson Dam; that the energy shall be sold to it or go to waste.

We limit our decision to the case before us, as we have defined it.

179

Carter v. Carter Coal Company (1936)

Congress tried to salvage part of the NRA through the Guffy–Synder Coal Conservation Act of 1935. If there was any industry that nearly everyone realized called for federal regulation, it was coal mining, which had been hard hit by the Depression and desperately needed stabilization. The act retained the NRA Bituminous Coal Code and established a commission, composed of representatives of management, labor, and the public, to control production and prices through local district boards. The act guaranteed collective bargaining and imposed union-negotiated wages and hours agreements on the entire industry; it also levied a tax on all coal produced, but remitted nine-tenths to producers abiding by the agreements. Congress tried to avoid the *Schechter* problem by declaring coal mining "affected with the public interest" and writing in a separability clause so that if one part of the act were declared invalid it would not affect the other parts. The suit challenging the law, a collusive action between company owners and shareholders, should have been dismissed, but once again the conservatives wanted to stop the New Deal in its tracks. Justice Butler's opinion not only took the narrowest view of commerce seen since *Knight* (Document 136), but even though the wages and hours provisions had not been challenged, struck down every provision of the law. Chief Justice Hughes dissented, as did Cardozo, speaking for Brandeis and Stone. The case fueled growing resentment against the Court and seemed to confirm that the conservatives were not interpreting the Constitution, but carrying out a vendetta against a program they did not like.

See Eugene V. Rostow, "Bituminous Coal and the Public Interest," 50 *Yale Law Journal* 543 (1941); T. C. Longin, "Coal, Congress and the Courts: The Bituminous Coal Industry and the New Deal," 35 *West Virginia History* 101 (1974); and James P. Johnson, *The Politics of Soft Coal* (1979).

———

Justice Sutherland delivered the opinion of the Court:

The purposes of the "Bituminous Coal Conservation Act of 1935," involved in these suits, as declared by the title, are to stabilize the bituminous coal-mining industry and promote its interstate commerce; to provide for cooperative marketing of bituminous coal; to levy a tax on such coal and provide for a drawback under certain conditions; to declare the production, distribution, and use of such coal to be affected with a national public interest; to conserve the national resources of such coal; to provide for the general welfare, and for other purposes. . . . The constitutional validity of the act is challenged in each of the suits. . . .

It is very clear that the "excise tax" is not imposed for revenue but exacted as a penalty to compel compliance with the regulatory provisions of the act. The whole purpose of the exaction is to coerce what is called an agreement—which, of course, it is not, for it lacks the essential element of consent. One who does a thing in order to avoid a monetary penalty does not agree; he yields to compulsion precisely the same as though he did so to avoid a term in jail. . . .

———

Source: 298 U.S. 238 (1936)

The ruling and firmly established principle is that the powers which the general government may exercise are only those specifically enumerated in the Constitution, and such implied powers as are necessary and proper to carry into effect the enumerated powers. Whether the end sought to be attained by an act of Congress is legitimate is wholly a matter of constitutional power and not at all of legislative discretion. Legislative congressional discretion begins with the choice of means and ends with the adoption of methods and details to carry the delegated powers into effect. The distinction between these two things—power and discretion—is not only very plain but very important. For while the powers are rigidly limited to the enumerations of the Constitution, the means which may be employed to carry the powers into effect are not restricted, save that they must be appropriate, plainly adapted to the end, and not prohibited by, but consistent with, the letter and spirit of the Constitution. . . . Thus, it may be said that to a constitutional end many ways are open; but to an end not within the terms of the Constitution, all ways are closed.

The proposition, often advanced and as often discredited, that the power of the federal government inherently extends to purposes affecting the nation as a whole with which the states severally cannot deal or cannot adequately deal, and the related notion that Congress, entirely apart from those powers delegated by the Constitution, may enact laws to promote the general welfare, have never been accepted but always definitely rejected by this court. . . .

Since the validity of the act depends upon whether it is a regulation of interstate commerce, the nature and extent of the power conferred upon Congress by the commerce clause becomes the determinative question in this branch of the case. . . .

We have seen that the word "commerce" is the equivalent of the phrase "intercourse for the purposes of trade." Plainly, the incidents leading up to and culminating in the mining of coal do not constitute such intercourse. The employment of men, the fixing of their wages, hours of labor and working conditions, the bargaining in respect of these things—whether carried on separately or collectively—each and all constitute intercourse for the purposes of production, not of trade. The latter is a thing apart from the relation of employer and employee, which in all producing occupations is purely local in character. Extraction of coal from the mine is the aim and the completed result of local activities. Commerce in the coal mined is not brought into being by force of these activities, but by negotiations, agreements, and circumstances entirely apart from production. Mining brings the subject matter of commerce into existence. Commerce disposes of it.

A consideration of the foregoing, and of many cases which might be added to those already cited, renders inescapable the conclusion that the effect of the labor provisions of the act, including those in respect of minimum wages, wage agreements, collective bargaining, and the Labor Board and its powers, primarily falls upon production and not upon commerce; and confirms the further resulting conclusion that production is a purely local activity. It follows that none of these essential antecedents of production constitutes a transaction in or forms any part of interstate commerce. . . . Everything which moves in interstate commerce has had a local origin. Without local production somewhere, interstate commerce, as now carried on, would practically disappear. Nevertheless, the local character of mining, of manufacturing and of crop growing is a fact, and remains a fact, whatever may be done with the products. . . .

... The only perceptible difference between [the *Schechter*] case and this is that in the *Schechter* case the federal power was asserted with respect to commodities which had come to rest after their interstate transportation; while here, the case deals with commodities at rest before interstate commerce has begun. That difference is without significance. The federal regulatory power ceases when interstate commercial intercourse ends; and, correlatively, the power does not attach until interstate commercial intercourse begins. There is no basis in law or reason for applying different rules to the two situations. . . . A reading of the entire opinion makes clear, what we now declare, that the want of power on the part of the federal government is the same whether the wages, hours of service, and working conditions, and the bargaining about them, are related to production before interstate commerce has begun, or to sale and distribution after it has ended. . . .

Finally, we are brought to the price-fixing provisions of the code. The necessity of considering the question of their constitutionality will depend upon whether they are separable from the labor provisions so that they can stand independently. Section 15 of the act provides:

"If any provision of this Act, or the application thereof to any person or circumstances, is held invalid, the remainder of the Act and the application of such provisions to other persons or circumstances shall not be affected thereby." . . .

The primary contemplation of the act is stabilization of the industry through the regulation of labor *and* the regulation of prices; for, since both were adopted, we must conclude that both were thought essential. The regulations of labor on the one hand and prices on the other furnish mutual aid and support; and their associated force—not one or the other but both combined—was deemed by Congress to be necessary to achieve the end sought. The statutory mandate for a code upheld by two legs at once suggests the improbability that Congress would have assented to a code supported by only one.

This seems plain enough; for Congress must have been conscious of the fact that elimination of the labor provisions from the act would seriously impair, if not destroy, the force and usefulness of the price provisions. The interdependence of wages and prices is manifest. Approximately two-thirds of the cost of producing a ton of coal is represented by wages. Fair prices necessarily depend upon the cost of production; and since wages constitute so large a proportion of the cost, prices cannot be fixed with any proper relation to cost without taking into consideration this major element. If one of them becomes uncertain, uncertainty with respect to the other necessarily ensues. . . .

The conclusion is unavoidable that the price-fixing provisions of the code are so related to and dependent upon the labor provisions as conditions, considerations or compensations, as to make it clearly probable that the latter being held bad, the former would not have been passed. The fall of the latter, therefore, carries down with it the former.

180

United States v. Curtiss-Wright Export Corporation (1936)

In 1934, Congress, by joint resolution, authorized the president to embargo arms and munitions sales to countries engaged in the armed dispute in South America's Chaco region. Soon afterward, the government indicted Curtiss-Wright for selling arms to Bolivia, one of the countries involved. The company successfully challenged the resolution in the lower courts as an unconstitutional delegation of power by Congress to the president. Although this argument had seemed to carry great weight with the Court in *Panama Refining* and *Schechter,* all the members of the Court except Justice McReynolds joined in Justice Sutherland's very expansive interpretation of the president's authority in foreign affairs. The decision would be used by Roosevelt and later chief executives to argue for an almost unlimited presidential discretion in the conduct of foreign affairs.

See Louis Henkin, ed., *Foreign Affairs and the U.S. Constitution* (1990); Robert A. Divine, "The Case of the Smuggled Bombers," in John Garraty, ed., *Quarrels That Have Shaped the Constitution* (1975), 210; and Charles A. Lofgren, *"United States v. Curtiss-Wright Export Corporation:* An Historical Assessment," 83 *Yale Law Journal* 1 (1973).

———

Justice Sutherland delivered the opinion of the Court:

Whether, if the Joint Resolution had related solely to internal affairs, it would be open to the challenge that it constituted an unlawful delegation of legislative power to the Executive, we find it unnecessary to determine. The whole aim of the resolution is to affect a situation entirely external to the United States, and falling within the category of foreign affairs. [A]ssuming (but not deciding) that the challenged delegation, if it were confined to internal affairs, would be invalid, may it nevertheless be sustained on the ground that its exclusive aim is to afford a remedy for a hurtful condition within foreign territory? . . .

[The Court examined the nature of the powers relating to internal and external affairs, and concluded that the foreign affairs powers "did not depend upon the affirmative grants of the Constitution."]

Source: 299 U.S. 304 (1936)

Not only, as we have shown, is the federal power over external affairs in origin and essential character different from that over internal affairs, but participation in the exercise of the power is significantly limited. In this vast external realm, with its important, complicated, delicate and manifold problems, the President alone has the power to speak or listen as a representative of the nation. He *makes* treaties with the advice and consent of the Senate; but he alone negotiates. Into the field of negotiation the Senate cannot intrude; and Congress itself is powerless to invade it. . . .

It is important to bear in mind that we are here dealing not alone with an authority vested in the President by an exertion of legislative power, but with such an authority plus the very delicate, plenary and exclusive power of the President as the sole organ of the federal government in the field of international relations—a power which does not require as a basis for its exercise an act of Congress, but which, of course, like every other governmental power, must be exercised in subordination to the applicable provisions of the Constitution. It is quite apparent that if, in the maintenance of our international relations, embarrassment—perhaps serious embarrassment—is to be avoided and success for our aims achieved, congressional legislation which is to be made effective through negotiation and inquiry within the international field must often accord to the President a degree of discretion and freedom from statutory restriction which would not be admissible were domestic affairs alone involved. Moreover, he, not Congress, has the better opportunity of knowing the conditions which prevail in foreign countries, and especially is this true in time of war. He has his confidential sources of information. He has his agents in the form of diplomatic, consular and other officials. Secrecy in respect of information gathered by them may be highly necessary, and the premature disclosure of it productive of harmful results. . . .

When the President is to be authorized by legislation to act in respect of a matter intended to affect a situation in foreign territory, the legislator properly bears in mind the important consideration that the form of the President's action—or, indeed, whether he shall act at all—may well depend, among other things, upon the nature of the confidential information which he has or may thereafter receive, or upon the effect which his action may have upon our foreign relations. This consideration [discloses] the unwisdom of requiring Congress in this field of governmental power to lay down narrowly definite standards by which the President is to be governed. . . .

Reversed.

181   *The Court Packing Plan (1937)*

Roosevelt's overwhelming victory in the 1936 elections convinced him that he could not allow the conservative majority of the Court to prevail over the expressed will of the people. Although he barely mentioned the Court during the campaign, soon after the election he began exploring alternatives, including a constitutional amendment, which, while the safest method (in constitutional terms) was the most dangerous in political terms. He had the example of the Child Labor Amendment, which despite great public support had been stalled for over a decade and would, in fact, never be ratified. Finally, and with great glee, he hit upon a plan originally devised by James McReynolds during his tenure as Wilson's attorney general, which allowed the appointment of additional justices to aid elderly sitting judges. Roosevelt would have been better advised to say forthrightly that he was trying to overcome the Court's political bias against the New Deal; instead, he camouflaged the issue as "court reform," which no one believed. In the end, he suffered the worst political defeat in his twelve years in office.

See William E. Leuchtenburg, *The Supreme Court Reborn: The Constitutional Revolution in the Age of Roosevelt* (1995); Barry Cushman, *Rethinking the New Deal Court: The Structure of a Constitutional Revolution* (1998); Turner Catledge, *The 168 Days* (1938); and Leonard Baker, *Back to Back: The Duel Between F.D.R. and the Supreme Court* (1967).

A. Roosevelt's Message to Congress (February 5, 1937)

At the present time the Supreme Court is laboring under a heavy burden. Its difficulties in this respect were superficially lightened some years ago by authorizing the court, in its discretion, to refuse to hear appeals in many classes of cases. This discretion was so freely exercised that in the last fiscal year, although 867 petitions for review were presented to the Supreme Court, it declined to hear 717 cases. If petitions in behalf of the Government are excluded, it appears that the court permitted private litigants to prosecute appeals in only 108 cases out of 803 applications. Many of the refusals were doubtless warranted. But can it be said that full justice is achieved when a court is forced by the sheer necessity of keeping up with its business to decline, without even an explanation, to hear 87 percent of the cases presented to it by private litigants?

It seems clear, therefore, that the necessity of relieving present congestion extends to the enlargement of the capacity of all the federal courts.

A part of the problem of obtaining a sufficient number of judges to dispose of cases is the capacity of the judges themselves. This brings forward the question of aged or infirm judges—a subject of delicacy and yet one which requires frank discussion.

In the federal courts there are in all 237 life tenure permanent judgeships. Twenty-five of them are now held by judges over seventy years of age and eligible to leave the bench on full pay. Originally no pension or retirement allowance was provided by the Congress. When after eighty years of our national history the Congress made provision

Source: 1937 *Public Papers and Addresses of Franklin D. Roosevelt* 51 (1941)

for pensions, it found a well-entrenched tradition among judges to cling to their posts, in many instances far beyond their years of physical or mental capacity. Their salaries were small. As with other men, responsibilities and obligations accumulated. No alternative had been open to them except to attempt to perform the duties of their offices to the very edge of the grave.

In exceptional cases, of course, judges, like other men, retain to an advanced age full mental and physical vigor. Those not so fortunate are often unable to perceive their own infirmities. "They seem to be tenacious of the appearance of adequacy." The voluntary retirement law of 1869 provided, therefore, only a partial solution. That law, still in force, has not proved effective in inducing aged judges to retire on a pension. . . .

. . . The modern tasks of judges call for the use of full energies.

Modern complexities call also for a constant infusion of new blood in the courts, just as it is needed in executive functions of the Government and in private business. A lowered mental or physical vigor leads men to avoid an examination of complicated and changed conditions. Little by little, new facts become blurred through old glasses fitted, as it were, for the needs of another generation; older men, assuming that the scene is the same as it was in the past, cease to explore or inquire into the present or the future. . . .

Life tenure of judges, assured by the Constitution, was designed to place the courts beyond temptations or influences which might impair their judgments; it was not intended to create a static judiciary. A constant and systematic addition of younger blood will vitalize the courts and better equip them to recognize and apply the essential concepts of justice in the light of the needs and the facts of an ever-changing world. . . .

These proposals do not raise any issue of constitutional law. They do not suggest any form of compulsory retirement for incumbent judges. Indeed, those who have reached the retirement age, but desire to continue their judicial work, would be able to do so under less physical and mental strain and would be able to play a useful part in relieving the growing congestion in the business of our courts. Among them are men of eminence and great ability whose services the Government would be loath to lose. If, on the other hand, any judge eligible for retirement should feel that his court would suffer because of an increase in its membership, he may retire or resign under already existing provisions of law if he wishes so to do. In this connection let me say that the pending proposal to extend to the Justices of the Supreme Court the same retirement privileges now available to other federal judges, has my entire approval.

One further matter requires immediate attention. We have witnessed the spectacle of conflicting decisions in both trial and appellate courts on the constitutionality of every form of important legislation. Such a welter of uncomposed differences of judicial opinion has brought the law, the courts, and, indeed, the entire administration of justice dangerously near to disrepute.

A federal statute is held legal by one judge in one district; it is simultaneously held illegal by another judge in another district. An act valid in one judicial circuit is invalid in another judicial circuit. Thus rights fully accorded to one group of citizens may be denied to others. . . .

In the uncertain state of the law, it is not difficult for the ingenious to devise novel reasons for attacking the validity of new legislation or its application. While these questions are laboriously brought to issue and debated through a series of courts, the Government must stand aside. It matters not that the Congress has enacted the law, that the Executive has signed it and that the administrative machinery is waiting to function. Government by injunction lays a heavy hand upon normal processes; and no important statute can take effect—against any individual or organization with the means to employ lawyers and engage in wide-flung litigation—until it has passed through the whole hierarchy of the courts. Thus the judiciary, by postponing the effective date of Acts of the Congress, is assuming an additional function and is coming more and more to constitute a scattered, loosely organized and slowly operating third house of the National Legislature. . . .

Now, as an immediate step, I recommend that the Congress provide that no decision, injunction, judgment or decree on any constitutional question be promulgated by any federal court without previous and ample notice to the Attorney General and an opportunity for the United States to present evidence and be heard. This is to prevent court action on the constitutionality of Acts of the Congress in suits between private individuals, where the Government is not a party to the suit, without giving opportunity to the Government of the United States to defend the law of the land.

I also earnestly recommend that in cases in which any court of first instance determines a question of constitutionality, the Congress provide that there shall be a direct and immediate appeal to the Supreme Court, and that such cases take precedence over all other matters pending in that court. Such legislation will, I am convinced, go far to alleviate the inequality, uncertainty and delay in the disposition of vital questions of constitutionality arising under our fundamental law. . . .

Draft of Proposed Bill

SEC. 1. (a) When any judge of a court of the United States, appointed to hold his office during good behavior, has heretofore or hereafter attained the age of seventy years and has held a commission or commissions as judge of any such court or courts at least ten years, continuously or otherwise, and within six months thereafter has neither resigned nor retired, the President, for each such judge who has not so resigned or retired, shall nominate, and by and with the advice and consent of the Senate, shall appoint one additional judge to the court to which the former is commissioned. Provided, That no additional judge shall be appointed hereunder if the judge who is of retirement age dies, resigns or retires prior to the nomination of such additional judge.

(b) The number of judges of any court shall be permanently increased by the number appointed thereto under the provisions of subsection (a) of this section. No more than fifty judges shall be appointed thereunder, nor shall any judge be so appointed if such appointment would result in (1) more than fifteen members of the Supreme Court of the United States, (2) more than two additional members so appointed to a circuit court of appeals, the Court of Claims, the United States Court of Customs and patent Appeals, or the Customs Court, or (3) more than twice the number of judges now authorized to be appointed for any district or, in the case of judges appointed for more than one district, for any such group of districts.

(c) That number of judges which is at least two-thirds of the number of which the Supreme Court of the United States consists, or three-fifths of the number of which the United States Court of Appeals for the District of Columbia, the Court of Claims or the United States Court of Customs and Patent Appeals consists, shall constitute a quorum of such court. . . .

SEC. 5 (a) The term "judge of retirement age" means a judge of a court of the United States, appointed to hold his office during good behavior, who has attained the age of seventy years and has held a commission or commissions as judge of any such court or courts at least ten years, continuously or otherwise, and within six months thereafter, whether or not he is eligible for retirement, has neither resigned nor retired. . . .

(d) The term "judge" includes justice.

B. Roosevelt's Fireside Chat (March 9, 1937)

Tonight, sitting at my desk in the White House, I make my first radio report to the people in my second term of office.

I am reminded of that evening in March, four years ago when I made my first radio report to you. We were then in the midst of the great banking crisis.

Soon after, with the authority of the Congress, we asked the Nation to turn over all of its privately held gold, dollar for dollar, to the Government of the United States.

Today's recovery proves how right that policy was.

But when, almost two years later, it came before the Supreme Court its constitutionality was upheld only by a five-to-four vote. The change of one vote would have thrown all the affairs of this great Nation back into hopeless chaos. In effect, four Justices ruled that the right under a private contract to exact a pound of flesh was more sacred than the main objectives of the Constitution to establish an enduring Nation. . . .

The American people have learned from the depression. For in the last three national elections an overwhelming majority of them voted a mandate that the Congress and the President begin the task of providing that protection—not after long years of debate, but now.

The Courts, however, have cast doubts on the ability of the elected Congress to protect us against catastrophe by meeting squarely our modern social and economic conditions. . . .

Last Thursday I described the American form of Government as a three horse team provided by the Constitution to the American people so that their field might be plowed. The three horses are, of course, the three branches of government—the Congress, the Executive and the Courts. Two of the horses are pulling in unison today; the third is not. Those who have intimated that the president of the United States is trying to drive that team, overlook the simple fact that the President, as Chief Executive, is himself one of the three horses.

It is the American people themselves who are in the driver's seat.

It is the American people themselves who want the furrow plowed.

It is the American people themselves who expect the third horse to pull in unison with the other two. . . .

Source: 1937 *Public Papers and Addresses of Franklin D. Roosevelt* 122 (1941)

But since the rise of the modern movement for social and economic progress through legislation, the Court has more and more often and more and more boldly asserted a power to veto laws passed by the Congress and State Legislatures in complete disregard of this original limitation.

In the last four years the sound rule of giving statutes the benefit of all reasonable doubt has been cast aside. The Court has been acting not as a judicial body, but as a policy-making body.

When the Congress has sought to stabilize national agriculture, to improve the conditions of labor, to safeguard business against unfair competition, to protect our national resources, and in many other ways, to serve our clearly national needs, the majority of the Court has been assuming the power to pass on the wisdom of these Acts of the Congress—and to approve or disapprove the public policy written into these laws.

That is not only my accusation. It is the accusation of most distinguished Justices of the present Supreme Court. I have not the time to quote to you all the language used by dissenting Justices in many of these cases. But in the case holding the Railroad Retirement Act unconstitutional, for instance, Chief Justice Hughes said in a dissenting opinion that the majority opinion was "a departure from sound principles," and placed "an unwarranted limitation upon the commerce clause." And three other Justices agreed with him. . . .

We have, therefore, reached the point as a Nation where we must take action to save the Constitution from the Court and the Court from itself. We must find a way to take an appeal from the Supreme Court to the Constitution itself. We want a Supreme Court which will do justice under the Constitution—not over it. In our Courts we want a government of laws and not of men.

I want—as all Americans want—an independent judiciary as proposed by the framers of the Constitution. That means a Supreme Court that will enforce the Constitution as written—that will refuse to amend the Constitution by the arbitrary exercise of judicial power—amendment by judicial say-so. It does not mean a judiciary so independent that it can deny the existence of facts universally recognized. . . .

What is my proposal? It is simply this: whenever a Judge or Justice of any Federal Court has reached the age of seventy and does not avail himself of the opportunity to retire on a pension, a new member shall be appointed by the President then in office, with the approval, as required by the Constitution, of the Senate of the United States.

That plan has two chief purposes. By bringing into the judicial system a steady and continuing stream of new and younger blood, I hope, first, to make the administration of all Federal justice speedier and, therefore, less costly; secondly, to bring to the decision of social and economic problems younger men who have had personal experience and contact with modern facts and circumstances under which average men have to live and work. This plan will save our national Constitution from hardening of the judicial arteries. . . .

Those opposing this plan have sought to arouse prejudice and fear by crying that I am seeking to "pack" the Supreme Court and that a baneful precedent will be established.

What do they mean by the words "packing the Court"?

Let me answer this question with a bluntness that will end all *honest* misunderstanding of my purposes.

If by that phrase "packing the Court" it is charged that I wish to place on the bench spineless puppets who would disregard the law and would decide specific cases as I wished them to be decided, I make this answer: that no President fit for his office would appoint, and no Senate of honorable men fit for their office would confirm, that kind of appointees to the Supreme Court.

But if by that phrase the charge is made that I would appoint and the senate would confirm Justices worthy to sit beside present members of the Court who understand those modern conditions, that I will appoint Justices who will not undertake to override the judgment of the Congress on legislative policy, that I will appoint Justices who will act as Justices and not as legislators—if the appointment of such Justices can be called "packing the Courts," then I say that I and with me the vast majority of the American people favor doing just that thing—now. . . .

Like all lawyers, like all Americans, I regret the necessity of this controversy. But the welfare of the United States, and indeed of the Constitution itself, is what we all must think about first. Our difficulty with the Court today rises not from the Court as an institution but from human beings within it. But we cannot yield our constitutional destiny to the personal judgment of a few men who, being fearful of the future, would deny us the necessary means of dealing with the present.

This plan of mine is no attack on the Court; it seeks to restore the Court to its rightful and historic place in our system of Constitutional Government and to have it resume its high task of building anew on the Constitution "a system of living law." The Court itself can best undo what the Court has done.

C. *Chief Justice Hughes's Letter to Senator Wheeler (March 22, 1937)*

The story of how Hughes came to write this letter is a fascinating example of how members of the Court can, when necessary, play the political game with finesse. Senator Burton K. Wheeler, an old-line Progressive who had been LaFollette's running mate in 1924, was one of the leading opponents of the Court bill. According to Alpheus T. Mason, *Brandeis: A Free Man's Life* 626 (1946):

> At the height of the battle Mrs. Brandeis, an old friend of the Wheeler family, went to call on the Senator's daughter, then living in Alexandria. In making her departure the Justice's wife commented as a sort of afterthought: "You tell your obstinate father we think he is making a courageous fight." The Senator lost no time in making an appointment with Justice Brandeis . . . [but] certain misgivings troubled him. . . . [H]e wondered whether the Justice's usual insistence on observing the proprieties of judicial office might not cause him to resent the visit. In any event, he must confine his mission solely to search for information. What he wanted to know was the actual state of the Court docket. Was it crowded? Were the Old Men worn out and behind with their work? When Brandeis suggested that the Senator's questions might more appropriately be addressed to the Chief Justice, the Senator opined: "Yes, but I don't

know the Chief Justice." "But the Chief Justice knows you, and what you're doing," commented the wily veteran of many political battles, leading Wheeler to the telephone.

For further material, see William E. Leuchtenburg, "The Nine Justices Respond to the 1937 Crisis," and Richard D. Friedman, "Chief Justice Hughes' Letter on Court-Packing," both in 1 *Journal of the Supreme Court Historical Society* at 55 and 76 (1997).

———

My Dear Senator Wheeler:

In response to your inquiries, I have the honor to present the following statement with respect to the work of the Supreme Court:

1. The Supreme Court is fully abreast of its work. When we rose on March 15 (for the present recess) we had heard argument in cases in which certiorari had been granted only four weeks before, Feb. 1.

During the current term, which began last October and which we call October Term, 1936, we have heard argument on the merits in 150 cases (180 numbers) and we have 28 cases (30 numbers) awaiting argument. We shall be able to hear all these cases, and such others as may come up for argument, before our adjournment for the term. There is no congestion of cases upon our calendar.

This gratifying condition has obtained for several years. We have been able for several terms to adjourn after disposing of all cases which are ready to be heard. . . .

3. The statute relating to our Appellate jurisdiction is the act of Feb. 13, 1925; 43 stat. 936. That act limits to certain cases the appeals which come to the Supreme Court as a matter of right. Review in other cases is made to depend upon the allowance by the Supreme Court of a writ of certiorari.

Where the appeal purports to lie as a matter of right, the rules of the Supreme Court (Rule 12) require the appellant to submit a jurisdictional statement showing that the case falls within that class of appeals and that a substantial question is involved. We examine that statement and the supporting and opposing briefs, and decide whether the court has jurisdiction. As a result, many frivolous appeals are forthright dismissed and the way is open for appeals which disclose substantial questions.

4. The act of 1925 . . . was most carefully considered by Congress. . . . That legislation was deemed to be essential to enable the Supreme Court to perform its proper function. No single court of last resort, whatever the number of judges, could dispose of all the cases which arise in this vast country and which litigants would seek to bring up if the right of appeal were unrestricted.

Hosts of litigants will take appeals so long as there is a tribunal accessible. In protracted litigation, the advantage is with those who command a long purse. Unmeritorious appeals cause intolerable delays. Such appeals clog the calendar and get in the way of those that have merit. . . .

———

Source: The New York Times, March 23, 1937

If further review [of cases] is to be had by the Supreme Court it must be because of the public interest in the questions involved. The review, for example, should be for the purpose of resolving conflicts in judicial decisions between different Circuit Courts of Appeal or between Circuit Courts of Appeal and State courts where the question is one of State law; or for the purpose of determining constitutional questions or settling the interpretation of statutes; or because of the importance of the questions of law that are involved. Review by the Supreme Court is thus in the interest of the law, not in the mere interest of the litigants.

It is obvious that if appeal as a matter of right is restricted to certain described cases, the question whether the review should be allowed in other cases must necessarily be confined to some tribunal for determination, and of course, with respect to review by the Supreme Court, that court should decide.

5. Granting certiorari is not a matter of favor but of sound judicial discretion. It is not the importance of the parties or the amount of money involved that is in any sense controlling. . . .

Furthermore, petitions for certiorari are granted if four justices think they should be. A vote by a majority is not required in such cases. Even if two or three of the justices are strongly of the opinion that certiorari should be allowed, frequently the other justices will acquiesce in their view but the petition is always granted if four so vote.

6. The work of passing upon these applications for certiorari is laborious but the court is able to perform it adequately. Observations have been made as to the vast number of pages of records and briefs that are submitted in the course of a term. The total is imposing, but the suggested conclusion is hasty and rests on an illusory basis.

Records are replete with testimony and evidence of facts. But the questions on certiorari are questions of law. So many cases turn on the facts, principles of law not being in controversy. It is only when the facts are so interwoven with the questions of law which we should review that the evidence must be examined and then only to the extent that it is necessary to decide the questions of law.

This at once disposes of a vast number of factual controversies where the parties have been fully heard in the courts below and have no right to burden the Supreme Court with the dispute which interests no one but themselves. . . .

I think it safe to say that about 60 per cent of the applications for certiorari are wholly without merit and ought never to have been made. There are probably about 20 per cent or so in addition which have a fair degree of plausibility but which fail to survive critical examination. The remainder, falling short, I believe, of 20 per cent, show substantial grounds and are granted. I think that it is the view of the members of the court that if any error is made in dealing with these applications it is on the side of liberality.

An increase in the number of justices of the Supreme Court, apart from any question of policy, which I do not discuss, would not promote the efficiency of the court. It is believed that it would impair that efficiency so long as the court acts as a unit. There would be more judges to hear, more judges to confer, more judges to discuss, more judges to be convinced and to decide.

The present number of justices is thought to be large enough so far as the prompt, adequate and efficient conduct of the work of the court is concerned. . . .

I understand that it has been suggested that with more justices the court could hear cases in divisions. It is believed that such a plan would be impracticable. A large proportion of the cases we hear are important and a decision by a part of the court would be unsatisfactory.

I may also call attention to the provision of Article III, Section 1, of the Constitution that the judicial power of the United States shall be vested "in one Supreme Court" and in such inferior courts as the Congress may from time to time ordain and establish. The Constitution does not appear to authorize two or more Supreme Courts or two or more parts of a Supreme Court functioning in effect as separate courts.

On account of the shortness of time I have not been able to consult with the members of the court generally with respect to the foregoing statement, but I am confident that it is in accord with the views of the justices. I should say, however, that I have been able to consult with Mr. Justice Van Devanter and Mr. Justice Brandeis, and I am at liberty to say that the statement is approved by them.

182   *DeJonge v. Oregon (1937)*

DeJonge was convicted under an Oregon criminal syndicalism law similar to those upheld by the Court a decade earlier. He was an admitted Communist and had been indicted for assisting in the conduct of a meeting called by the Communist party, which the state charged with "advocating criminal syndicalism." The state's highest court agreed with DeJonge that there had been no advocacy of criminal syndicalism at the meeting itself; rather he had been charged with conducting a meeting for a group advocating criminal activities; therefore proof of advocacy at the meeting was unnecessary.

The Court unanimously reversed, ruling that the First Amendment's guarantee of the right to assembly prohibited the states from outlawing meetings at which nothing illegal occurred. Chief Justice Hughes's opinion continued the incorporation of First Amendment rights to apply to the states through the Due Process Clause of the Fourteenth Amendment, and also pointed to efforts by the Court to define the core values protected by the First Amendment. This opinion would seem to follow Hand's analysis in the *Masses* case (Document 154) rather than Holmes's in *Schenck* (Document 157).

See Zechariah Chafee, Jr., *Freedom of Speech* (rev. ed., 1941); C. E. Rice, *Freedom of Association* (1962); and Eldridge F. Dowell, *History of Criminal Syndicalism Legislation in the United States* (1939).

Source: 299 U.S. 353 (1937)

Chief Justice Hughes delivered the opinion of the Court:

The broad reach of the statute as thus applied is plain. While defendant was a member of the Communist Party, that membership was not necessary to conviction on such a charge. A like fate might have attended any speaker, although not a member, who "assisted in the conduct" of the meeting. However innocuous the object of the meeting, however lawful the subjects and tenor of the addresses, however reasonable and timely the discussion, all those assisting in the conduct of the meeting would be subject to imprisonment as felons if the meeting were held by the Communist Party. This manifest result was brought out sharply at this bar by the concessions which the Attorney General made, and could not avoid, in the light of the decision of the state court. Thus if the Communist Party had called a public meeting in Portland to discuss the tariff, or the foreign policy of the Government, or taxation, or relief, or candidacies for the offices of President, members of Congress, Governor, or state legislators, every speaker who assisted in the conduct of the meeting would be equally guilty with the defendant in this case, upon the charge as here defined and sustained. The list of illustrations might be indefinitely extended to every variety of meetings under the auspices of the Communist Party although held for the discussion of political issues or to adopt protests and pass resolutions of an entirely innocent and proper character.

While the States are entitled to protect themselves from the abuse of the privileges of our institutions through an attempted substitution of force and violence in the place of peaceful political action in order to effect revolutionary changes in government, none of our decisions go to the length of sustaining such a curtailment of the right of free speech and assembly as the Oregon statute demands in its present application. . . .

Freedom of speech and of the press are fundamental rights which are safeguarded by the due process clause of the Fourteenth Amendment of the Federal Constitution. . . . The right of peaceable assembly is a right cognate to those of free speech and free press and is equally fundamental. . . . The First Amendment of the Federal Constitution expressly guarantees that right against abridgment by Congress. But explicit mention there does not argue exclusion elsewhere. For the right is one that cannot be denied without violating those fundamental principles of liberty and justice which lie at the base of all civil and political institutions,—principles which the Fourteenth Amendment embodies in the general terms of its due process clause. . . .

These rights may be abused by using speech or press or assembly in order to incite to violence and crime. The people through their legislatures may protect themselves against that abuse. But the legislative intervention can find constitutional justification only by dealing with the abuse. The rights themselves must not be curtailed. The greater the importance of safeguarding the community from incitements to the overthrow of our institutions by force and violence, the more imperative is the need to preserve inviolate the constitutional rights of free speech, free press and free assembly in order to maintain the opportunity for free political discussion, to the end that government may be responsive to the will of the people and that changes, if desired, may be obtained by peaceful means. Therein lies the security of the Republic, the very foundation of constitutional government.

It follows from these considerations that, consistently with the Federal Constitution, peaceable assembly for lawful discussion cannot be made a crime. The holding of meetings for peaceable political action cannot be proscribed. Those who assist in the conduct of such meetings cannot be branded as criminals on that score. The question, if the rights of free speech and peaceable assembly are to be preserved, is not as to the auspices under which the meeting is held but as to its purpose; not as to the relations of the speakers, but whether their utterances transcend the bounds of the freedom of speech which the Constitution protects. . . .

We are not called upon to review the findings of the state court as to the objectives of the Communist Party. Notwithstanding those objectives, the defendant still enjoyed his personal right of free speech and to take part in a peaceable assembly having a lawful purpose, although called by that Party. The defendant was none the less entitled to discuss the public issues of the day and thus in a lawful manner, without incitement to violence or crime, to seek redress of alleged grievances. That was of the essence of his guaranteed personal liberty.

We hold that the Oregon statute as applied to the particular charge as defined by the state court is repugnant to the due process clause of the Fourteenth Amendment.

183

West Coast Hotel Co. v. Parrish (1937)

The death blow to Roosevelt's Court plan came on March 29, 1937, when the Court, by a five-to-four vote, sustained a Washington State minimum wage law. Only the previous year, the Court, also by a five-to-four vote, had struck down a similar statute in *Morehead* v. *New York ex rel. Tipaldo.* Justice Roberts, who had written the opinion in *Morehead,* now joined the liberals as Chief Justice Hughes finally declared that *Adkins* (Document 164) had been wrongly decided and should be overruled.

At the time Roberts's change of vote had been described as the "switch in time that saved nine," since the Court plan had supposedly scared the brethren. In fact the plan had little to do with this particular case, which had been argued several months earlier. Roberts had been willing to overrule *Adkins* in *Morehead,* but counsel for New York had not asked the Court to reexamine that rule. When lawyers in this Washington case did challenge *Adkins,* Roberts supposedly agreed that the old rule should be abandoned. The illness of Justice Stone, however, left the Court evenly divided, and Chief Justice Hughes, rather than hand down a tie vote, held the decision until Stone could return and vote. There has been an ongoing controversy over why Roberts voted as he did, with Felix Frankfurter's article, cited below, laying the basis for the claim that Roberts did not respond to political pressure. That claim has been both challenged and defended.

See Charles A. Leonard, *A Search, for a Judicial Philosophy: Mr. Justice Roberts and the Constitutional Revolution of 1937* (1971); Felix Frankfurter, "Mr. Justice Roberts,"

104 *University of Pennsylvania Law Review* 311 (1955); John W. Chambers, "The Big Switch: Justice Roberts and the Minimum Wage Cases," 10 *Labor History* 44 (1969); Michael Ariens, "A Thrice-Told Tale, or Felix the Cat," 107 *Harvard Law Review* 620 (1994); Edward A. Purcell, Jr., "Rethinking Constitutional Change," 80 *Virginia Law Review* 279 (1994); and Barry Cushman, *Rethinking the New Deal Court* (1998).

———

Chief Justice Hughes delivered the opinion of the Court:

The violation [of due process] alleged by those attacking minimum wage regulation for women is deprivation of freedom of contract. What is this freedom? The Constitution does not speak of freedom of contract. It speaks of liberty and prohibits the deprivation of liberty without due process of law. In prohibiting that deprivation the Constitution does not recognize an absolute and uncontrollable liberty. The liberty safeguarded is liberty in a social organization which requires the protection of law against the evils which menace the health, safety, morals and welfare of the people. Liberty under the Constitution is thus necessarily subject to the restraints of due process, and regulation which is reasonable in relation to its subject and is adopted in the interests of the community is due process. This essential limitation of liberty in general governs freedom of contract in particular.

We think that [*Adkins* v. *Children's Hospital*] was a departure from the true application of the principles governing the regulation by the State of the relation of employer and employed. What can be closer to the public interest than the health of women and their protection from unscrupulous and overreaching employers? And if the protection of women is a legitimate end of the exercise of state power, how can it be said that the requirement of the payment of a minimum wage fairly fixed in order to meet the very necessities of existence is not an admissible means to that end? The legislature of the State was clearly entitled to consider that women are in the class receiving the least pay, that their bargaining power is relatively weak, and that they are the ready victims of those who would take advantage of their necessitous circumstances. The legislature was entitled to adopt measures to reduce the evils of the "sweating system," the exploiting of workers at wages so low as to be insufficient to meet the bare cost of living, thus making their very helplessness the occasion of a most injurious competition. The legislature had the right to consider that its minimum wage requirements would be an important aid in carrying out its policy of protection. The adoption of similar requirements by many States evidences a deep-seated conviction both as to the presence of the evil and as to the means adapted to check it. Legislative response to that conviction cannot be regarded as arbitrary or capricious, and that is all we have to decide. . . .

There is an additional and compelling consideration which recent economic experience has brought into a strong light. The exploitation of a class of workers who are in an unequal position with respect to bargaining power and are thus relatively defenceless against the denial of a living wage is not only detrimental to their health and well being

Source: 300 U.S. 379 (1937)

but casts a direct burden for their support upon the community. What these workers lose in wages the taxpayers are called upon to pay. The bare cost of living must be met. We may take judicial notice of the unparalleled demands for relief which arose during the recent period of depression. The community is not bound to provide what is in effect a subsidy for unconscionable employers. The community may direct its law-making power to correct the abuse which springs from their selfish disregard of the public interest. [*Adkins* is] overruled.

Affirmed.

184

National Labor Relations Board v. Jones & Laughlin Steel Corporation (1937)

Two weeks after *West Coast Hotel,* the Court, again by five-to-four vote, decided several cases that sustained the National Labor Relations Act. In that law, Congress had explicitly extended protection over labor's right to organize and bargain collectively, and it had set up an administrative agency to ensure that right as well as to police labor practices. In the past, the Court had denied the federal government power over labor relations, insisting it did not constitute part of interstate commerce. Chief Justice Hughes revived the stream of commerce theory, and in doing so wrote a broad mandate for the federal government's exercise of the Commerce Clause. The ruling opened the way for the New Deal to extend its labor program and to provide statutory support for workers' efforts to organize into unions and to bargain collectively.

See Richard C. Cortner, *The Wagner Act Cases* (1964) and *The Jones & Laughlin Case* (1970); Paul R. Benson, Jr., *The Supreme Court and the Commerce Clause, 1937–1970* (1970); and James A. Gross, *The Making of the National Labor Relations Board,* 2 vols. (1974–1981).

———

Chief Justice Hughes delivered the opinion of the Court:
    The corporation is engaged in the business of manufacturing iron and steel in plants situated in Pittsburgh and nearby Aliquippa, Pennsylvania. It manufactures and distrib-

Source: 301 U.S. 1 (1937)

utes a widely diversified line of steel and pig iron, being the fourth largest producer of steel in the United States. With its subsidiaries—nineteen in number—it is a completely integrated enterprise, owning and operating ore, coal and limestone properties, lake and river transportation facilities and terminal railroads located at its manufacturing plants. It owns or controls mines in Michigan and Minnesota. It operates four ore steamships on the Great Lakes, used in the transportation of ore to its factories. It owns coal mines in Pennsylvania. It operates towboats and steam barges used in carrying coal to its factories. It owns limestone properties in various places in Pennsylvania and West Virginia. . . . Much of its product is shipped to its warehouses in Chicago, Detroit, Cincinnati and Memphis,—to the last two places by means of its own barges and transportation equipment. In Long Island City, New York, and in New Orleans it operates structural steel fabricating shops in connection with the warehousing of semi-finished materials sent from its works. Through one of its wholly-owned subsidiaries it owns, leases and operates stores, warehouses and yards for the distribution of equipment and supplies for drilling and operating oil and gas wells and for pipe lines, refineries and pumping stations. It has sales offices in twenty cities in the United States and a wholly-owned subsidiary which is devoted exclusively to distributing its product in Canada. Approximately 75 per cent of its product is shipped out of Pennsylvania.

Summarizing these operations, the Labor Board concluded that the works in Pittsburgh and Aliquippa "might be likened to the heart of a self-contained, highly integrated body. They draw in the raw materials from Michigan, Minnesota, West Virginia, Pennsylvania in part through arteries and by means controlled by the respondent; they transform the materials and then pump them out to all parts of the nation through the vast mechanism which the respondent has elaborated."

To carry on the activities of the entire steel industry, 33,000 men mine ore, 44,000 men mine coal, 4,000 men quarry limestone, 16,000 men manufacture coke, 343,000 men manufacture steel, and 83,000 men transport its product. Respondent has about 10,000 employees in its Aliquippa plant, which is located in a community of about 30,000 persons. . . .

First. The scope of the Act.—The Act is challenged in its entirety as an attempt to regulate all industry, thus invading the reserved powers of the States over their local concerns. It is asserted that the Act is not a true regulation of commerce or of matters which directly affect it but on the contrary has the fundamental object of placing under the compulsory supervision of the federal government all industrial labor relations within the nation. . . .

We think it clear that the National Labor Relations Act may be construed so as to operate within the sphere of constitutional authority. The jurisdiction conferred upon the Board, and invoked in this instance, is found in §10(a), which provides: "Sec. 10(a). The Board is empowered, as hereinafter provided, to prevent any person from engaging in any unfair labor practice (listed in section 8) affecting commerce."

The critical words of this provision, prescribing the limits of the Board's authority in dealing with the labor practices, are "affecting commerce." The Act specifically defines the "commerce" to which it refers (§ 2(6)): "The term 'commerce' means trade, traffic, commerce, transportation, or communication among the several States. . . ."

There can be no question that the commerce thus contemplated by the Act is interstate and foreign commerce in the constitutional sense. The Act also defines the term "affecting commerce" (§ 2(7)): "The term 'affecting commerce' means in commerce, or burdening or obstructing commerce or the free flow of commerce, or having led or tending to lead to a labor dispute burdening or obstructing commerce or the free flow of commerce." . . .

Third. The application of the Act to employees engaged in production.—The principle involved.—Respondent says that whatever may be said of employees engaged in interstate commerce, the industrial relations and activities in the manufacturing department of respondent's enterprise are not subject to federal regulation. The argument rests upon the proposition that manufacturing in itself is not commerce. . . .

. . . The congressional authority to protect interstate commerce from burdens and obstructions is not limited to transactions which can be deemed to be an essential part of a "flow" of interstate or foreign commerce. Burdens and obstructions may be due to injurious action springing from other sources. The fundamental principle is that the power to regulate commerce is the power to enact "all appropriate legislation" for "its protection and advancement"; to adopt measures "to promote its growth and insure its safety"; "to foster, protect, control and restrain." That power is plenary and may be exerted to protect interstate commerce "no matter what the source of the dangers which threaten it." Although activities may be intrastate in character when separately considered, if they have such a close and substantial relation to interstate commerce that their control is essential or appropriate to protect that commerce from burdens and obstructions, Congress cannot be denied the power to exercise that control. . . . Undoubtedly the scope of this power must be considered in the light of our dual system of government and may not be extended so as to embrace effects upon interstate commerce so indirect and remote that to embrace them, in view of our complex society, would effectually obliterate the distinction between what is national and what is local and create a completely centralized government. The question is necessarily one of degree. That intrastate activities, by reason of close and intimate relation to interstate commerce, may fall within federal control is demonstrated in the case of carries who are engaged in both interstate and intrastate transportation. . . .

The close and intimate effect which brings the subject within the reach of federal power may be due to activities in relation to productive industry although the industry when separately viewed is local. The fact that the employees here concerned were engaged in production is not determinative. The question remains as to the effect upon interstate commerce of the labor practice involved. In the Schechter case, we found that the effect there was so remote as to be beyond the federal power. . . .

Fourth. Effects of the unfair labor practice in respondent's enterprise.—Giving full weight to respondent's contention with respect to a break in the complete continuity of the "stream of commerce" by reason of respondent's manufacturing operations, the fact remains that the stoppage of those operations by industrial strife would have a most serious effect upon interstate commerce. In view of respondent's far-flung activities, it is idle to say that the effect would be indirect or remote. It is obvious that it would be immediate and might be catastrophic. We are asked to shut our eyes to the plainest facts of our national life and to deal with the question of direct and indirect effects in an intellectual vacuum. Because there may be but indirect and remote effects upon interstate commerce in connection with a host of local enterprises throughout the country, it does not follow that other industrial activities do not have such a close and intimate relation to interstate commerce as to make the presence of industrial strife a matter of the most urgent national concern. When industries organize themselves on a national scale, making their relation to interstate commerce the dominant factor in their activities, how can it be maintained that their industrial labor relations constitute a forbidden field into which Congress may not enter when it is necessary to protect interstate commerce from the paralyzing consequences of industrial war? We have often said that interstate commerce itself is a practical conception. It is equally true that interferences with that commerce must be appraised by a judgment that does not ignore actual experience.

Experience has abundantly demonstrated that the recognition of the right of employees to self-organization and to have representatives of their own choosing for the purpose of collective bargaining is often an essential condition of industrial peace. Refusal to confer and negotiate has been one of the most prolific causes of strife. This is such an outstanding fact in the history of labor disturbances that it is a proper subject of judicial notice and requires no citation of instances. . . .

Our conclusion is that the order of the Board was within its competency and that the Act is valid as here applied. . . .

Reversed.

---

185   *Stewart Machine Company v. Davis (1937)*

Before the 1930s, the Court had taken a relatively liberal view of the federal government's taxing power, as well as the concomitant power to spend (see, for examples, Documents 145 and 166). In cases like the second child labor case, *Bailey* v. *Drexel Furniture Co.* (1922), and especially *Butler* (Document 177), however, the Court had apparently allowed its distaste for particular programs to outweigh its normal deference to legislative choices regarding the use of an admittedly broad power.

In this case, a five-man majority upheld major provisions of the Social Security Act, especially the unique arrangement for unemployment compensation. Because some states had already initiated such programs, Congress chose to set national standards and then leave administration to local authorities. To encourage the states, Congress allowed tax credits for employers already enrolled in state plans, a provision that opponents claimed violated states' rights by coercing the states to join.

Justice Cardozo, in a section of his opinion not reproduced below, went to great lengths in taking judicial notice of the critical conditions accompanying the Depression that had led to this law, conditions that the four-member conservative bloc had consistently denied had anything to do with the Court's review of legislation.

See William Anderson, *The Nation and the States: Rivals or Partners* (1974); Joseph E. Kallenbach, *Federal Cooperation with the States under the Commerce Clause* (1942); and T. R. McCoy and B. Friedman, "Conditional Spending: Federalism's Trojan Horse," 1988 *Supreme Court Review* 85.

Justice Cardozo delivered the opinion of the Court:

The assault on the statute proceeds on an extended front. Its assailants take the ground that the tax is not an excise; that it is not uniform throughout the United States as excises are required to be; that its exceptions are so many and arbitrary as to violate the Fifth Amendment; that its purpose was not revenue, but an unlawful invasion of the reserved powers of the states; and that the states in submitting to it have yielded to coercion and have abandoned governmental functions which they are not permitted to surrender.

The objections will be considered seriatim with such further explanation as may be necessary to make their meaning clear.

First. The tax, which is described in the statute as an excise, is laid with uniformity throughout the United States as a duty, an impost or an excise upon the relation of employment.

1. We are told that the relation of employment is one so essential to the pursuit of happiness that it may not be burdened with a tax. Appeal is made to history. From the precedents of colonial days we are supplied with illustrations of excises common in the colonies. They are said to have been bound up with the enjoyment of particular commodities. Appeal is also made to principle or the analysis of concepts. An excise, we are told, imports a tax upon a privilege; employment, it is said, is a right, not a privilege, from which it follows that employment is not subject to an excise. Neither the one appeal nor the other leads to the desired goal.

As to the argument from history: Doubtless there were many excises in colonial days and later that were associated, more or less intimately, with the enjoyment or the use of property. This would not prove, even if no others were then known, that the forms then accepted were not subject to enlargement. . . .

The historical prop failing, the prop or fancied prop of principle remains. We learn that employment for lawful gain is a "natural" or "inherent" or "inalienable" right, and not a "privilege" at all. But natural rights, so called, are as much subject to taxation as rights of less importance. An excise is not limited to vocations or activities that may be prohibited altogether. It is not limited to those that are the outcome of a franchise. It extends to vocations or activities pursued as of common right. What the individual does

Source: 301 U.S. 548 (1937)

in the operation of a business is amenable to taxation just as much as what he owns, at all events if the classification is not tyrannical or arbitrary. . . .

The statute books of the states are strewn with illustrations of taxes laid on occupations pursued of common right. We find no basis for a holding that the power in that regard which belongs by accepted practice to the legislatures of the states, has been denied by the Constitution to the Congress of the nation.

2. The tax being an excise, its imposition must conform to the canon of uniformity. There has been no departure from this requirement. According to the settled doctrine the uniformity exacted is geographical, not intrinsic. . . .

Second. The excise is not invalid under the provisions of the Fifth Amendment by force of its exemptions.

The statute does not apply, as we have seen, to employers of less than eight. It does not apply to agricultural labor, or domestic service in a private home or to some other classes of less importance. Petitioner contends that the effect of these restrictions is an arbitrary discrimination vitiating the tax. . . .

. . . The states, though subject to [the equal protection] clause, are not confined to a formula of rigid uniformity in framing measures of taxation. . . . They may tax some kinds of property at one rate, and others at another, and exempt others altogether. . . . If this latitude of judgment is lawful for the states, it is lawful, *a fortiori,* in legislation by the Congress, which is subject to restraints less narrow and confining. . . .

The classifications and exemptions directed by the statute now in controversy have support in considerations of policy and practical convenience that cannot be condemned as arbitrary. The classifications and exemptions would therefore be upheld if they had been adopted by a state and the provisions of the Fourteenth Amendment were invoked to annul them. . . . The act of Congress is therefore valid, so far at least as its system of exemptions is concerned. . . .

Third. The excise is not void as involving the coercion of the States in contravention of the Tenth Amendment or of restrictions implicit in our federal form of government. . . .

. . . The case for the petitioner is built on the contention that here an ulterior aim is wrought into the very structure of the act, and what is even more important that the aim is not only ulterior, but essentially unlawful. In particular, the 90 per cent credit is relied upon as supporting that conclusion. But before the statute succumbs to an assault upon these lines, two propositions must be made out by the assailant. . . . There must be a showing in the first place that separated from the credit the revenue provisions are incapable of standing by themselves. There must be a showing in the second place that the tax and the credit in combination are weapons of coercion, destroying or impairing the autonomy of the states. The truth of each proposition being essential to the success of the assault, we pass for convenience to a consideration of the second, without pausing to inquire whether there has been a demonstration of the first. . . .

The Social Security Act is an attempt to find a method by which all these public agencies may work together to a common end. Every dollar of the new taxes will continue in all likelihood to be used and needed by the nation as long as states are unwilling, whether through timidity or for other motives, to do what can be done at home. At least the inference is permissible that Congress so believed, though retaining undiminished freedom to spend the money as it pleased. On the other hand fulfilment of the home duty will be lightened and encouraged by crediting the taxpayer upon his account with the Treasury of the nation to the extent that his contributions under the laws of the locality have simplified or diminished the problem of relief and the probable demand upon the resources of the fisc. Duplicated taxes, or burdens that approach them, are recognized hardships that government, state or national, may properly avoid. . . .

Who then is coerced through the operation of this statute? Not the taxpayer. He pays in fulfillment of the mandate of the local legislature. Not the state. Even now she does not offer a suggestion that in passing the unemployment law she was affected by duress. . . . For all that appears she is satisfied with her choice, and would be sorely disappointed if it were now to be annulled. The difficulty with the petitioner's contention is that it confuses motive with coercion. "Every tax is in some measure regulatory. To some extent it interposes an economic impediment to the activity taxed as compared with others not taxed." . . . In like manner every rebate from a tax when conditioned upon conduct is in some measure a temptation. But to hold that motive or temptation is equivalent to coercion is to plunge the law in endless difficulties. The outcome of such a doctrine is the acceptance of a philosophical determinism by which choice becomes impossible. Till now the law has been guided by a robust common sense which assumes the freedom of the will as a working hypothesis in the solution of its problems. The wisdom of the hypothesis has illustration in this case. Nothing in the case suggests the exertion of a power akin to undue influence, if we assume that such a concept can ever be applied with fitness to the relations between state and nation. Even on that assumption the location of the point at which pressure turns into compulsion, and ceases to be inducement, would be a question of degree,—at times, perhaps, of fact. The point had not been reached when Alabama made her choice. We cannot say that she was acting, not of her unfettered will, but under the strain of a persuasion equivalent to undue influence, when she chose to have relief administered under laws of her own making, by agents of her own selection, instead of under federal laws, administered by federal officers, with all the ensuing evils, at least to many minds, of federal patronage and power. There would be a strange irony, indeed, if her choice were now to be annulled on the basis of an assumed duress in the enactment of a statute which her courts have accepted as a true expression of her will. . . . We think the choice must stand.

186   *Palko v. Connecticut (1937)*

In this case, Justice Cardozo put forward his famous explanation of "selective incorporation," which greatly affected the Court's nationalization of the First Amendment as well as the Fourth through Seventh amendments. Connecticut allowed the prosecution to take appeals in criminal cases. After a jury had convicted Palko of second-degree murder, the state appealed, and the state supreme court ordered a retrial, in which Palko was found guilty of first-degree murder. He correctly claimed that such a procedure would be barred in federal courts under the Fifth Amendment's ban against double jeopardy. He further argued that all of the guarantees of the Bill of Rights now extended to the states through the Fourteenth Amendment.

Justice Cardozo rejected this claim and denied that the Fourteenth Amendment automatically carried all of the Bill of Rights into effect against the state. Rather, it applied only to those that are "of the very essence of a scheme of ordered liberty," and it would be the courts that determined which rights met this criterion.

Although "selective incorporation" had been the dominant theme in the Court's expansion of protected rights, it would be challenged a decade later by Justice Black, who called for "total incorporation" in the *Adamson case* (Document 192). The Court nonetheless has incorporated nearly all of the Bill of Rights, while adhering to the Cardozo rationale.

See Charles Fairman, "Does the Fourteenth Amendment Incorporate the Bill of Rights? The Original Understanding," 2 *Stanford Law Review* 5 (1949); Louis Henkin, "'Selective Incorporation' in the 14th Amendment," 73 *Yale Law Journal* 74 (1963); and Richard Cortner, *The Supreme Court and the Second Bill of Rights* (1981).

———

Justice Cardozo delivered the opinion of the Court:

1. The execution of the sentence will not deprive appellant of his life without the process of law assured to him by the Fourteenth Amendment of the Federal Constitution.

The argument for appellant is that whatever is forbidden by the Fifth Amendment is forbidden by the Fourteenth also. . . . His thesis is even broader. Whatever would be a violation of the original bill of rights (Amendments I to VIII) if done by the federal government is now equally unlawful by force of the Fourteenth Amendment if done by a state. There is no such general rule.

The Fifth Amendment provides, among other things, that no person shall be held to answer for a capital or otherwise infamous crime unless on presentment or indictment of a grand jury. This court has held that, in prosecutions by a state, presentment or indictment by a grand jury may give way to informations at the instance of a public officer. . . . The Fifth Amendment provides also that no person shall be compelled in any criminal case to be a witness against himself. This court has said that, in prosecutions by a state, the exemption will fail if the state elects to end it. . . . The Sixth Amendment calls for a jury trial in criminal cases and the Seventh for a jury trial in civil cases at common law where the value in controversy shall exceed twenty dollars. This court has ruled that consistently with those amendments trial by jury may be modified by a state or abolished altogether. . . .

Source: 302 U.S. 419 (1937)

On the other hand, the due process clause of the Fourteenth Amendment may make it unlawful for a state to abridge by its statutes the freedom of speech which the First Amendment safeguards against encroachment by the Congress . . . or the like freedom of the press . . . or the free exercise of religion . . . or the right of peaceable assembly, without which speech would be unduly trammeled . . . or the right of one accused of crime to the benefit of counsel. . . . In these and other situations immunities that are valid as against the federal government by force of the specific pledges of particular amendments have been found to be implicit in the concept of ordered liberty, and thus, through the Fourteenth Amendment, become valid as against the states.

The line of division may seem to be wavering and broken if there is a hasty catalogue of the cases on the one side and the other. Reflection and analysis will induce a different view. There emerges the perception of a rationalizing principle which gives to discrete instances a proper order and coherence. The right to trial by jury and the immunity from prosecution except as the result of an indictment may have value and importance. Even so, they are not of the very essence of a scheme of ordered liberty. . . . Few would be so narrow or provincial as to maintain that a fair and enlightened system of justice would be impossible without them. What is true of jury trials and indictments is true also, as the cases show, of the immunity from compulsory self-incrimination. . . . This too might be lost, and justice still be done. . . .

We reach a different plane of social and moral values when we pass to the privileges and immunities that have been taken over from the earlier articles of the federal bill of rights and brought within the Fourteenth Amendment by a process of absorption. These in their origin were effective against the federal government alone. If the Fourteenth Amendment has absorbed them, the process of absorption has had its source in the belief that neither liberty nor justice would exist if they were sacrificed. . . . This is true, for illustration, of freedom of thought, and speech. Of that freedom one may say that it is the matrix, the indispensable condition, of nearly every other form of freedom. With rare aberrations a pervasive recognition of that truth can be traced in our history, political and legal. . . . Fundamental too in the concept of due process, and so in that of liberty, is the thought that condemnation shall be rendered only after trial. . . . The hearing, moreover, must be a real one, not a sham or a pretense. . . . For that reason, ignorant defendants in a capital case were held to have been condemned unlawfully when in truth, though not in form, they were refused the aid of counsel. . . . The decision did not turn upon the fact that the benefit of counsel would have been guaranteed to the defendants by the provisions of the Sixth Amendment if they had been prosecuted in a federal court. The decision turned upon the fact that in the particular situation laid before us in the evidence the benefit of counsel was essential to the substance of a hearing.

Our survey of the cases serves, we think, to justify the statement that the dividing line between them, if not unfaltering throughout its course, has been true for the most part to a unifying principle. On which side of the line the case made out by the appellant has appropriate location must be the next inquiry and the final one. Is that kind of double jeopardy to which the statute has subjected him a hardship so acute and shocking that our polity will not endure it? Does it violate those "fundamental principles of liberty and justice which lie at the base of all our civil and political institutions"? . . . The answer surely must be "no." What the answer would have to be if the state were permitted after a trial free from error to try the accused over again or to bring another case against him, we have no occasion to consider. We deal with the statute before us and no other. The state is not attempting to wear the accused out by a multitude of cases with accumulated trials. It asks no more than this, that the case against him shall go on until there shall be a trial free from the corrosion of substantial legal error. . . . This is not cruelty at all, nor even vexation in any immoderate degree. If the trial had been infected with error adverse to the accused, there might have been review at his instance, and as often as necessary to purge the vicious taint. A reciprocal privilege, subject at all times to the discretion of the presiding judge . . . has now been granted to the state. There is here no seismic innovation. The edifice of justice stands, its symmetry, to many, greater than before.

---

187   *United States v. Carolene Products Co. (1938)*

In both *Nebbia* (Document 174) and *West Coast Hotel* (Document 183), the Court indicated that while it would defer to legislative judgment, it would still exercise review of economic legislation. Following the Court packing battle (Document 181) and the appointment of new judges, the Court began to abandon review of economic legislation, a process completed in *Williamson v. Lee Optical Co.* (1955). By then it had adopted the so-called rational basis test for economic legislation: if the legislature had the power, then all it needed was a rational basis for choosing to exercise it in any given manner, and courts would not interfere, even if they disagreed with the wisdom of the policy.

In the *Carolene Products* case, the Court rejected a due process challenge to a federal prohibition against the interstate shipment of so-called filled milk, which was skimmed milk mixed with nonmilk fats. In his opinion for the Court, Justice Stone essentially adopted the rational-basis test, indicating that if in its judgment Congress deemed filled milk unhealthy, then that provided the necessary rationale for it to exercise its commerce powers.

Immediately following this statement, Justice Stone inserted his famous Footnote 4, which asserted that in noneconomic regulation cases, the Court might adopt a higher level of scrutiny. That footnote has been the basis for judicial activism in matters that restrict the free play of the political process or involve so-called suspect classifications, such as race, creed, alienage, and gender.

The footnote can be seen as a demarcation point in the previously mentioned shift of the Court's attention from matters dealing with property rights to those affecting civil liberties and civil rights. It provided the rationale for a double standard of judicial review, with a low-level review of economic matters and a high-level review for statutes affecting individual liberties and rights.

See Alpheus T. Mason, *Harlan Fiske Stone: Pillar of the Law* (1956); Lewis F. Powell, Jr., "Carolene Products Revisited," 82 *Columbia Law Review* 1087 (1982); and Michael Perry, "Mr. Justice Stone and Footnote 4," 6 *George Mason University Civil Rights Law Journal* 35 (1996).

———

Footnote 4

There may be narrower scope for operation of the presumption of constitutionality when legislation appears on its face to be within a specific prohibition of the Constitution, such as those of the first ten Amendments, which are deemed equally specific when held to be embraced within the 14th. See *Stromberg* v. *California* [1931], *Lovell* v. *Griffin* [1938].

It is unnecessary to consider now whether legislation which restricts those political processes which can ordinarily be expected to bring about repeal of undesirable legislation, is to be subjected to more exacting judicial scrutiny under the general prohibitions of the 14th Amendment than are most other types of legislation. On restrictions upon the right to vote, see *Nixon* v. *Herndon* [1927]; *Nixon* v. *Condon* [1932]; on restraints upon the dissemination of information, *see Near* v. *Minnesota* [1932]; *Grosjean* v. *American Press Co.* [1936]; *Lovell* v. *Griffin;* on interference with political organizations, see *Stromberg* v. *California,;* *Fiske* v. *Kansas* [1972]; *Whitney* v. *California* [1927]; *Herndon* v. *Lowry* [1937]; and see Holmes, J., *in Gitlow* v. *New York* [1925]; as to prohibition of peaceable assembly, see *De Jonge* v. *Oregon* [1937].

Nor need we enquire whether similar considerations enter into the review of statutes directed at particular religious, *Pierce* v. *Society of Sisters* [1925], or national, *Meyer* v. *Nebraska* [1923]; *Bartels* v. *Iowa; Farrington* v. *Tokushige;* or racial minorities, *Nixon* v. *Herndon; Nixon* v. *Condon;* whether prejudice against discrete and insular minorities may be a special condition, which tends seriously to curtail the operation of those political processes ordinarily to be relied upon to protect minorities, and which may call for a correspondingly more searching judicial inquiry. Compare *McCulloch* v. *Maryland* [1819]; *South Carolina* v. *Barnwell Bros.,* and cases cited.

———

Source: 304 U.S. 144 (1938)

188   *United States v. Darby (1941)*

In 1938, Congress passed the last major piece of New Deal legislation, the Fair Labor Standards Act. It prohibited the shipment of goods in interstate commerce that had been produced in plants violating maximum hours, minimum wage, and child labor standards. Darby, a Georgia lumber manufacturer, successfully challenged the law in the lower courts, claiming that it intruded into local manufacturing, and therefore exceeded congressional power to regulate interstate commerce, the rule that had prevailed since *Hammer v. Dagenhart* (Document 155).

    Darby, along with *Wickard v. Filburn* (next document), extended the reach of the Commerce Clause to the point where practically any commercial activity would be considered within governmental reach. *Wickard* confirmed direct powers of regulation; *Darby* confirmed the so-called commerce excluding power, the ability to keep certain items out of commerce because they are either noxious or produced in violation of certain principles of public policy.

See Charles Fahy, "Notes on Developments in Constitutional Law, 1936–1949," 38 *Georgetown Law Journal* 1 (1949); and Edward S. Corwin, "The Passing of Dual Federalism," 36 *Virginia Law Review* 1 (1950).

———

Justice Stone delivered the opinion of the Court:

    The two principal questions in this case are, *first,* whether Congress has constitutional power to prohibit the shipment in interstate commerce of lumber manufactured by employees whose wages are less than a prescribed minimum or whose weekly hours of labor at that wage are greater than a prescribed maximum, and, *second,* whether it has power to prohibit the employment of workmen in the production of goods "for interstate commerce" at other than prescribed wages and hours. . . .

    The prohibition of shipment of the proscribed goods in interstate commerce. §15(a)(1) prohibits, and the indictment charges, the shipment in interstate commerce, of goods produced for interstate commerce by employees whose wages and hours of employment do not conform to the requirements of the Act. The only question arising under the commerce clause with respect to such shipments is whether Congress has the constitutional power to prohibit them.

    While manufacture is not of itself interstate commerce the shipment of manufactured goods interstate is such commerce and the prohibition of such shipment by Congress is indubitably a regulation of the commerce. The power to regulate commerce is

Source: 312 U.S. 100 (1941)

the power "to prescribe the rule by which commerce is governed." . . . It extends not only to those regulations which aid, foster and protect the commerce, but embraces those which prohibit it. It is conceded that the power of Congress to prohibit transportation in interstate commerce includes noxious articles, stolen articles, kidnapped persons, and articles such as intoxicating liquor or convict made goods, traffic in which is forbidden or restricted by the laws of the state of destination. . . .

But it is said that the present prohibition falls within the scope of none of these categories; that while the prohibition is nominally a regulation of the commerce its motive or purpose is regulation of wages and hours of persons engaged in manufacture, the control of which has been reserved to the states and upon which Georgia and some of the states of destination have placed no restriction; that the effect of the present statute is not to exclude the prescribed articles from interstate commerce in aid of state regulation . . . but instead, under the guise of a regulation of interstate commerce, it undertakes to regulate wages and hours within the state contrary to the policy of the state which has elected to leave them unregulated.

The power of Congress over interstate commerce can neither be enlarged nor diminished by the exercise or non-exercise of state power. Congress, following its own conception of public policy concerning the restrictions which may appropriately be imposed on interstate commerce, is free to exclude from the commerce articles whose use in the states for which they are destined it may conceive to be injurious to the public health, morals or welfare, even though the state has not sought to regulate their use. Such regulation is not a forbidden invasion of state power merely because either its motive or its consequence is to restrict the use of articles of commerce within the states of destination. It is no objection to the assertion of the power to regulate interstate commerce that its exercise is attended by the same incidents which attend the exercise of the police power of the states. . . .

The motive and purpose of the present regulation is plainly to make effective the Congressional conception of public policy that interstate commerce should not be made the instrument of competition in the distribution of goods produced under substandard labor conditions, which competition is injurious to the commerce and to the states from and to which the commerce flows. The motive and purpose of a regulation of interstate commerce are matters for the legislative judgment upon the exercise of which the Constitution places no restriction and over which the courts are given no control. . . . Whatever their motive and purpose, regulations of commerce which do not infringe some constitutional prohibition are within the plenary power conferred on Congress by the Commerce Clause. Subject only to that limitation, presently to be considered, we conclude that the prohibition of the shipment interstate of goods produced under the forbidden substandard labor conditions is within the constitutional authority of Congress.

These principles of constitutional interpretation have been so long and repeatedly recognized by this Court as applicable to the Commerce Clause, that there would be little occasion for repeating them now were it not for the decision of this Court twenty-two years ago in Hammer v. Dagenhart. In that case it was held by a bare majority of the Court over the powerful and now classic dissent of Mr. Justice Holmes setting forth the fundamental issues involved, that Congress was without power to exclude the products of child labor from interstate commerce. The reasoning and conclusion of the Court's opinion there cannot be reconciled with the conclusion which we have reached, that the power of Congress under the Commerce Clause is plenary to exclude any article from interstate commerce subject only to the specific prohibitions of the Constitution.

Hammer v. Dagenhart has not been followed. The distinction on which the decision was rested that Congressional power to prohibit interstate commerce is limited to articles which in themselves have some harmful or deleterious property—a distinction which was novel when made and unsupported by any provision of the Constitution—has long since been abandoned. The thesis of the opinion that the motive of the prohibition or its effect to control in some measure the use or production within the states of the article thus excluded from the commerce can operate to deprive the regulation of its constitutional authority has long since ceased to have force. The conclusion is inescapable that Hammer v. Dagenhart was a departure from the principles which have prevailed in the interpretation of the Commerce Clause both before and since the decision and that such vitality, as a precedent, as it then had has long since been exhausted. It should be and now is overruled.

Validity of the wage and hour requirements. Section 15(a)(2) and §§ 6 and 7 require employers to conform to the wage and hour provisions with respect to all employees engaged in the production of goods for interstate commerce. As appellees' employees are not alleged to be "engaged in interstate commerce" the validity of the prohibition turns on the question whether the employment, under other than the prescribed labor standards, of employees engaged in the production of goods for interstate commerce is so related to the commerce and so affects it as to be within the reach of the power of Congress to regulate it. . . .

Congress, having by the present Act adopted the policy of excluding from interstate commerce all goods produced for the commerce which do not conform to the specified labor standards, it may choose the means reasonably adapted to the attainment of the permitted end, even though they involve control of intrastate activities. Such legislation has often been sustained with respect to powers, other than the commerce power granted to the national government, when the means chosen, although not themselves within the granted power, were nevertheless deemed appropriate aids to the accomplishment of some purpose within an admitted power of the national government. A familiar like exercise of power is the regulation of intrastate transactions which are so commingled with or related to interstate commerce that all must be regulated if the interstate commerce is to be effectively controlled. . . .

. . . The evils aimed at by the Act are the spread of substandard labor conditions through the use of the facilities of interstate commerce for competition by the goods so produced with those produced under the prescribed or better labor conditions; and the consequent dislocation of the commerce itself caused by the impairment or destruction of local businesses by competition made effective through interstate commerce. The Act is thus directed at the suppression of a method or kind of competition in interstate commerce which it has in effect condemned as "unfair," as the Clayton Act has condemned other "unfair methods of competition" made effective through interstate commerce. . . .

The means adopted by § 15(a)(2) for the protection of interstate commerce by the suppression of the production of the condemned goods for interstate commerce is so related to the commerce and so affects it as to be within the reach of the commerce power. Congress, to attain its objective in the suppression of nationwide competition in interstate commerce by goods produced under substandard labor conditions, has made no distinction as to the volume or amount of shipments in the commerce or of production for commerce by any particular shipper or producer. It recognized that in present day industry, competition by a small part may affect the whole and that the total effect of the competition of many small producers may be great. . . .

Our conclusion is unaffected by the Tenth Amendment which provides: "The powers not delegated to the United States by the Constitution, nor prohibited by it to the States, are reserved to the States respectively, or to the people." The amendment states but a truism that all is retained which has not been surrendered. There is nothing in the history of its adoption to suggest that it was more than declaratory of the relationship between the national and state governments as it had been established by the Constitution before the amendment or that its purpose was other than to allay fears that the new national government might seek to exercise powers not granted, and that the states might not be able to exercise fully their reserved powers. . . .

Reversed.

189   *Wickard v. Filburn (1942)*

The Agricultural Adjustment Act of 1938 gave the secretary of agriculture power to set grain quotas for each year. After the secretary set the national figures, they would then be apportioned to states and then counties, and eventually to individual farms. Farmers who exceeded their assignments, even if the food had been grown for use on their own farms, were penalized. Filburn, an Ohio farmer, sued Secretary of Agriculture Wickard to enjoin enforcement of the penalties, claiming that control of agriculture, a local undertaking, exceeded the commerce power, the same argument that had prevailed in *United States v. Butler* (Document 177).

Justice Jackson's strong opinion essentially obliterated any distinction between production (allegedly local in nature) and commerce, as well as that between direct and indirect effects of regulation. For all practical purposes, the federal government could now regulate just about any type of commercial activity in the nation. This decision, coming after the United States entered the war, indicated that the federal government would not have to rely on emergency war powers as a justification for those war programs regulating industry.

See Paul R. Benson, Jr., *The Supreme Court and the Commerce Clause, 1937–1970* (1970); J. E. Baskette, Jr., "Agricultural Marketing Agreement and Order Programs, 1933–1943," 33 *Georgetown Law Journal* 123 (1945); and Barry Cushman, *Rethinking the New Deal Court* (1998).

Justice Jackson delivered the opinion of the Court:

The general scheme of the [Act] as related to wheat is to control the volume moving in interstate and foreign commerce in order to avoid surpluses and shortages and the consequent abnormally low or high wheat prices and obstructions to commerce. The Secretary of Agriculture is directed to ascertain and proclaim each year a national acreage allotment for the next crop of wheat, which is then apportioned to the states and their counties, and is eventually broken up into allotments for individual farms. . . .

It is urged that under the Commerce Clause, Congress does not possess the power it has in this instance sought to exercise. The question would merit little consideration . . . except for the fact that this Act extends federal regulation to production not intended in any part for commerce but wholly for consumption on the farm. . . . Marketing quotas not only embrace all that may be sold without penalty but also what may be consumed on the premises. The sum of this is that the Federal Government fixes a quota including all that the farmer may harvest for sale or for his own farm needs, and declares that wheat produced on excess acreage may neither be disposed of nor used except upon payment of the penalty, or except it is stored as required by the Act or delivered to the Secretary of Agriculture.

Appellee says that this is a regulation of production and consumption of wheat. Such activities are, he urges, beyond the reach of Congressional power under the Commerce Clause, since they are local in character, and their effects upon interstate commerce are at most "indirect." In answer the Government argues that the statute regulates neither production nor consumption, but only marketing; and, in the alternative, that if the Act does go beyond the regulation of marketing it is sustainable as a "necessary and proper" implementation of the power of Congress over interstate commerce.

The Government's concern lest the Act be held to be a regulation of production or consumption, rather than of marketing, is attributable to a few dicta and decisions of this Court which might be understood to lay it down that activities such as "production," "manufacturing," and "mining" are strictly "local" and, except in special circumstances which are not present here, cannot be regulated under the commerce power because their effects upon interstate commerce are, as matter of law, only "indirect." Even today, when this power has been held to have great latitude, there is no decision of this Court that such activities may be regulated where no part of the product is intended for interstate commerce or intermingled with the subjects thereof. We believe that a review of the course of decision under the Commerce Clause will make plain, however, that questions of the power of Congress are not to be decided by reference to any formula which would give controlling force to nomenclature such as "production" and "indirect" and foreclose consideration of the actual effects of the activity in question upon interstate commerce. . . .

The Court's recognition of the relevance of the economic effects in the application of the Commerce Clause . . . has made the mechanical application of legal formulas no longer feasible. Once an economic measure of the reach of the power granted to Congress in the Commerce Clause is accepted, questions of federal power cannot be decided simply by finding the activity in questions to be "production" not can consideration of its economic effects be foreclosed by calling them "indirect." Whether the subject of the

Source: 317 U.S. 111 (1942).

regulation in question was "production," "consumption," or "marketing" is, therefore, not material for purposes of deciding the question of federal power before us. That an activity is of local character may help in a doubtful case to determine whether Congress intended to reach it. But even if appellee's activity be local and though it may not be regarded as commerce, it may still, whatever its nature, be reached by Congress if it exerts a substantial economic effect on interstate commerce, and this irrespective of whether such effect is what might at some earlier time have been defined as "direct" or "indirect." . . .

The wheat industry has been a problem industry for some years. Largely as a result of increased foreign production and import restrictions, annual exports of wheat and flour from the United States during the ten-year period ending in 1940 averaged less than 10 per cent of total production, while during the 1920's they averaged more than 25 per cent. The decline in the export trade has left a large surplus in production which, in connection with an abnormally large supply of wheat and other grains in recent years, caused congestion in a number of markets; tied up railroad cars; and caused elevators in some instances to turn away grains, and railroads to institute embargoes to prevent further congestion. . . .

In the absence of regulation the price of wheat in the United States would be much affected by world conditions. During 1941, producers who cooperated with the Agricultural Adjustment program received an average price on the farm of about $1.16 a bushel, as compared with the world market price of 40 cents a bushel. . . .

The effect of consumption of homegrown wheat on interstate commerce is due to the fact that it constitutes the most variable factor in the disappearance of the wheat crop. Consumption on the farm where grown appears to vary in an amount greater than 20 per cent of average production. The total amount of wheat consumed as food varies but relatively little, and use as seed is relatively constant.

The maintenance by government regulation of a price for wheat undoubtedly can be accomplished as effectively by sustaining or increasing the demand as by limiting the supply. The effect of the statute before us is to restrict the amount which may be produced for market and the extent as well to which one may forestall resort to the market by producing to meet his own needs. That appellee's own contribution to the demand for wheat may be trivial by itself is not enough to remove him from the scope of federal regulation where, as here, his contribution, taken together with that of many others similarly situated, is far from trivial. . . .

It is well established by decisions of this Court that the power to regulate commerce includes the power to regulate the prices at which commodities in that commerce are dealt in and practices affecting such prices. One of the primary purposes of the Act in question was to increase the market price of wheat, and to that end to limit the volume thereof that could affect the market. It can hardly be denied that a factor of such volume and variability as home-consumed wheat would have a substantial influence on price and market conditions. This may arise because being in marketable condition such [homegrown] wheat overhangs the market and, if induced by rising prices, tends to flow into the market and check price increases. But if we assume that it is never marketed, it supplies a need of the man who grew it which would otherwise be reflected by purchases in the open market. Home grown wheat in this sense competes with wheat in commerce. The stimulation of commerce is a use of the regulatory function quite as definitely as prohibitions or restrictions thereon. This record leaves us in no doubt that Congress may properly have considered that wheat consumed on the farm where grown, if wholly outside the scheme of regulation, would have a substantial effect in defeating and obstructing its purpose to stimulate trade therein at increased prices. . . .

Reversed.

190

West Virginia Board of Education v. Barnette (1943)

Just as there had been no First Amendment case law on speech prior to *Schenck* (Document 157), so there was little case law on the First Amendment's religion clauses before World War II. The first concerted exploration of what the religion clauses meant came with a series of challenges against state and local restrictions litigated by the Jehovah's Witnesses.

The Witnesses made household solicitations, sold their publications, and held parades, among other things, to proselytize their beliefs. None of these activities was in itself noxious, but all were regulated in one way or another by local ordinances or required permits. The Witnesses could easily have secured the necessary permits, but refused to apply for them, denying that the secular authorities had any power in this area. The Witnesses won their first battle solely on the basis of the Free Exercise Clause in *Cantwell v. Connecticut* (1940), when a unanimous Court struck down as arbitrary a state law prohibiting solicitation without official approval.

The Witnesses also refused to salute the American flag, claiming that such a salute violated the biblical injunction against worshiping graven images. In *Minersville School District v. Gobitis* (1940), Justice Frankfurter upheld the local requirement. With Europe already at war and America rearming, patriotism had to be encouraged, and in balancing community interests against individual rights, Frankfurter found in favor of the community. Only Justice Stone dissented, charging the required salute violated freedom of speech and of religion.

The Witnesses refused to compromise, and in spite of enormous public hostility clung to their outspoken religious beliefs. Over the next few years, they lost a series of court cases. In *Cox v. New Hampshire* (1940), a unanimous bench upheld a state regulation requiring parade permits, and in *Chaplinsky v. New Hampshire* (1942), the Court sustained the conviction of a Witness who had gotten into a fight after calling a city marshal "a damned fascist." In another Witness case that year, *Jones v. Opelika*, the Court upheld municipal license fees for transient merchants or book peddlers, but three of the *Gobitis* majority—Black, Douglas, and Murphy—now joined with Stone in dissent. Moreover, many Americans had begun to rethink the meaning of a mandatory flag salute in light of revelations about indoctrination methods in Nazi Germany. The climax came in the second flag salute case when Justice Jackson, who rarely supported minority rights, joined the dissenters and wrote one of the most eloquent opinions of his career. Frankfurter entered an anguished dissent, objecting especially to Jackson's use of the Holmes clear-and-present-danger test, and called for increased judicial restraint.

See Leo Pfeffer, *Church, State and Freedom* (rev. ed., 1967); David Manwaring, *Render unto Caesar: The Flag Salute Cases* (1962); Irving Dillard, "The Flag Salute Cases," in John Garraty, ed., *Quarrels That Have Shaped the Constitution* (1975), 222; and Shawn Francis Peters, *Judging Jehovah's Witnesses* (2000).

————

Justice Jackson delivered the opinion of the Court:

Appellees, citizens of the United States and of West Virginia, brought suit in the United States District Court for themselves and others similarly situated asking its injunction to restrain enforcement of these [flag salute] laws and regulations against Jehovah's Witnesses. The Witnesses are an unincorporated body teaching that the obligation imposed by law of God is superior to that of laws enacted by temporal government. Their religious beliefs include a literal version of Exodus, Chapter 20, verses 4 and 5, which says: "Thou shalt not make unto thee any graven image, or any likeness of anything that is in heaven above, or that is in the earth beneath, or that is in the water under the earth; thou shalt not bow down thyself to them nor serve them." They consider that the flag is an "image" within this command. For this reason they refuse to salute it.

Children of this faith have been expelled from school and are threatened with exclusion for no other cause. Officials threaten to send them to reformatories maintained for criminally inclined juveniles. Parents of such children have been prosecuted and are threatened with prosecutions for causing delinquency. . . .

There is no doubt that, in connection with the pledges, the flag salute is a form of utterance. Symbolism is a primitive but effective way of communicating ideas. The use of an emblem or flag to symbolize some system, idea, institution, or personality, is a short cut from mind to mind. Causes and nations, political parties, lodges and ecclesiastical groups seek to knit the loyalty of their followings to a flag or banner, a color or design. The State announces rank, function, and authority through crowns and maces, uniforms and black robes; the church speaks through the Cross, the Crucifix, the altar and shrine, and clerical raiment. Symbols of State often convey political ideas just as religious symbols come to convey theological ones. Associated with many of these sym-

Source: 319 U.S. 624 (1943)

bols are appropriate gestures of acceptance or respect: a salute, a bowed or bared head, a bended knee. A person gets from a symbol the meaning he puts into it, and what is one man's comfort and inspiration is another's jest and scorn. . . .

It is also to be noted that the compulsory flag salute and pledge requires affirmation of a belief and an attitude of mind. It is not clear whether the regulation contemplates that pupils forego any contrary convictions of their own and become unwilling converts to the prescribed ceremony or whether it will be acceptable if they simulate assent by words without belief and by a gesture barren of meaning. It is now a commonplace that censorship or suppression of expression of opinion is tolerated by our Constitution only when the expression presents a clear and present danger of action of a kind the State is empowered to prevent and punish. It would seem that involuntary affirmation could be commanded only on even more immediate and urgent grounds than silence. But here the power of compulsion is invoked without any allegation that remaining passive during a flag salute ritual creates a clear and present danger that would justify an effort even to muffle expression. To sustain the compulsory flag salute we are required to say that a Bill of Rights which guards the individual's right to speak his own mind, left it open to public authorities to compel him to utter what is not in his mind.

Whether the First Amendment to the Constitution will permit officials to order observance of ritual of this nature does not depend upon whether as a voluntary exercise we would think it to be good, bad or merely innocuous. Any credo of nationalism is likely to include what some disapprove or to omit what others think essential, and to give off different overtones as it takes on different accents or interpretations. If official power exists to coerce acceptance of any patriotic creed, what it shall contain cannot be decided by courts, but must be largely discretionary with the ordaining authority, whose power to prescribe would no doubt include power to amend. Hence validity of the asserted power to force an American citizen publicly to profess any statement of belief or to engage in any ceremony of assent to one, presents questions of power that must be considered independently of any idea we may have as to the utility of the ceremony in question. . . .

Government of limited power need not be anemic government. Assurance that rights are secure tends to diminish fear and jealousy of strong government, and by making us feel safe to live under it makes for its better support. Without promise of a limiting Bill of Rights it is doubtful if our Constitution could have mustered enough strength to enable its ratification. To enforce those rights today is not to choose weak government over strong government. It is only to adhere as a means of strength to individual freedom of mind in preference to officially disciplined uniformity for which history indicates a disappointing and disastrous end.

The subject now before us exemplifies this principle. Free public education, if faithful to the ideal of secular instruction and political neutrality, will not be partisan or enemy of any class, creed, party, or faction. If it is to impose any ideological discipline, however, each party or denomination must seek to control, or failing that, to weaken the influence of the educational system. Observance of the limitations of the Constitution will not weaken government in the field appropriate for its exercise. . . .

The *Gobitis* opinion reasoned that this is a field "where courts possess no marked and certainly no controlling competence," that it is committed to the legislatures as well as the courts to guard cherished liberties and that it is constitutionally appropriate to "fight out the wise use of legislative authority in the forum of public opinion and before legislative assemblies rather than to transfer such a contest to the judicial arena," since all the "effective means of inducing political changes are left free." . . .

The very purpose of a Bill of Rights was to withdraw certain subjects from the vicissitudes of political controversy, to place them beyond the reach of majorities and officials and to establish them as legal principles to be applied by the courts. One's right to life, liberty, and property, to free speech, a free press, freedom of worship and assembly, and other fundamental rights may not be submitted to vote; they depend on the outcome of no elections.

In weighing arguments of the parties it is important to distinguish between the due process clause of the Fourteenth Amendment as an instrument for transmitting the principles of the First Amendment and those cases in which it is applied for its own sake. The test of legislation which collides with the Fourteenth Amendment, because it also collides with the principles of the First, is much more definite than the test when only the Fourteenth is involved. Much of the vagueness of the due process clause disappears when the specific prohibitions of the First become its standard. The right of a State to regulate, for example, a public utility may well include, so far as the due process test is concerned, power to impose all of the restrictions which a legislature may have a "rational basis" for adopting. But freedoms of speech and of press, of assembly, and of worship may not be infringed on such slender grounds. They are susceptible of restriction only to prevent grave and immediate danger to interests which the State may lawfully protect. It is important to note that while it is the Fourteenth Amendment which bears directly upon the State it is the more specific limiting principles of the First Amendment that finally govern this case.

Nor does our duty to apply the Bill of Rights to assertions of official authority depend upon our possession of marked competence in the field where the invasion of rights occurs. True, the task of translating the majestic generalities of the Bill of Rights, conceived as part of the pattern of liberal government in the eighteenth century, into concrete restrains on officials dealing with the problems of the twentieth century, is one to disturb self-confidence. These principles grew in soil which also produced a philosophy that the individual was the center of society, that his liberty was attainable through mere absence of governmental restraints, and that government should be entrusted with few controls and only the mildest supervision over men's affairs. We must transplant these rights to a soil in which the *laissez-faire* concept or principle of non-interference has withered at least as to economic affairs, and social advancements are increasingly sought through closer integration of society and through expanded and strengthened governmental controls. These changed conditions often deprive precedents of reliability and cast us more than we would choose upon our own judgment. But we act in these matters not by authority of our competence but by force of our commissions. We cannot, because of modest estimates of our competence in such specialties as public education, withhold the judgment that history authenticates as the function of this Court when liberty is infringed. . . .

Lastly, and this is the very heart of the *Gobitis* opinion, it reasons that "National unity is the basis of national security," that the authorities have "the right to select appropriate means for its attainment," and hence reaches the conclusion that such compulsory measures toward "national unity" are constitutional. . . . Upon the verity of this assumption depends our answer in this case.

National unity as an end which officials may foster by persuasion and example is not in question. The problem is whether under our Constitution compulsion as here employed is a permissible means for its achievement.

Struggles to coerce uniformity of sentiment in support of some end thought essential to their time and country have been waged by many good as well as by evil men. Nationalism is a relatively recent phenomenon but at other times and places the ends have been racial or territorial security, support of a dynasty or regime, and particular plans for saving souls. As first and moderate methods to attain unity have failed, those bent on its accomplishment must resort to an ever-increasing severity. As governmental pressure toward unity becomes greater, so strife becomes more bitter as to whose unity it shall be. Probably no deeper division of our people could proceed from any provocation than from finding it necessary to choose what doctrine and whose program public educational officials shall compel youth to unite in embracing. Ultimate futility of such attempts to compel coherence is the lesson of every such effort from the Roman drive to stamp out Christianity as a disturber of its pagan unity, the Inquisition, as a means to religious and dynastic unity, the Siberian exiles as a means to Russian unity, down to the fast failing efforts of our present totalitarian enemies. Those who begin coercive elimination of dissent soon find themselves exterminating dissenters. Compulsory unification of opinion achieves only the unanimity of the graveyard.

It seems trite but necessary to say that the First Amendment to our Constitution was designed to avoid these ends by avoiding these beginnings. There is no mysticism in the American concept of the State or of the nature or origin of its authority. We set up government by consent of the governed, and the Bill of Rights denies those in power any legal opportunity to coerce that consent. Authority here is to be controlled by public opinion, not public opinion by authority.

The case is made difficult not because the principles of its decision are obscure but because the flag involved is our own. Nevertheless, we apply the limitations of the Constitution with no fear that freedom to be intellectually and spiritually diverse or even contrary will disintegrate the social organization. To believe that patriotism will not flourish if patriotic ceremonies are voluntary and spontaneous instead of a compulsory routine is to make an unflattering estimate of the appeal of our institutions to free minds. We can have intellectual individualism and the rich cultural diversities that we owe to exceptional minds only at the price of occasional eccentricity and abnormal attitudes. When they are so harmless to others or to the State as those we deal with here, the price is not too great. But freedom to differ is not limited to things that do not matter much. That would be a mere shadow of freedom. The test of its substance is the right to differ as to things that touch the heart of the existing order.

If there is any fixed star in our constitutional constellation, it is that no official, high or petty, can prescribe what shall be orthodox in politics, nationalism, religion, or other matters of opinion or force citizens to confess by word or act their faith therein. If there are any circumstances which permit an exception, they do not now occur to us.

We think the action of the local authorities in compelling the flag salute and pledge transcends constitutional limitations on their power and invades the sphere of intellect and spirit which it is the purpose of the First Amendment to our Constitution to reserve from all official control.

The decision of this Court in *Minersville School District* v. *Gobitis* and the holdings of those few *per curiam* decisions which preceded and foreshadowed it are overruled, and the judgment enjoining enforcement of the West Virginia Regulation is Affirmed.

Justice Frankfurter, dissenting:

One who belongs to the most vilified and persecuted minority in history is not likely to be insensible to the freedoms guaranteed by our Constitution. Were my purely personal attitude relevant I should wholeheartedly associate myself with the general libertarian views in the Court's opinion, representing as they do the thought and action of a lifetime. But as judges we are neither Jew nor Gentile, neither Catholic nor agnostic. We owe equal attachment to the Constitution and are equally bound by our judicial obligations whether we derive our citizenship from the earliest or the latest immigrants to these shores. As a member of this Court I am not justified in writing my private notions of policy into the Constitution, no matter how deeply I may cherish them or how mischievous I may deem their disregard. The duty of a judge who must decide which of two claims before the Court shall prevail, that of a State to enact and enforce laws within its general competence or that of an individual to refuse obedience because of the demands of his conscience, is not that of the ordinary person. It can never be emphasized too much that one's own opinion about the wisdom or evil of a law should be excluded altogether when one is doing one's duty on the bench. The only opinion of our own even looking in that direction that is material is our opinion whether legislators could in reason have enacted such a law. In the light of all the circumstances, including the history of this question in this Court, it would require more daring than I possess to deny that reasonable legislators could have taken the action which is before us for review. Most unwillingly, therefore, I must differ from my brethren with regard to legislation like this. I cannot bring my mind to believe that the "liberty" secured by the Due Process Clause gives this Court authority to deny to the State of West Virginia the attainment of that which we all recognize as a legitimate legislative end, namely, the promotion of good citizenship, by employment of the means here chosen. . . .

. . . Practically we are passing upon the political power of each of the forty-eight states. Moreover, since the First Amendment has been read into the Fourteenth, our problem is precisely the same as it would be if we had before us an Act of Congress for the District of Columbia. To suggest that we are here concerned with the heedless action of some village tyrants is to distort the augustness of the constitutional issue and the reach of the consequences of our decision.

Under our constitutional system the legislature is charged solely with civil concerns of society. If the avowed or intrinsic legislative purpose is either to promote or to discourage some religious community or creed, it is clearly within the constitutional restrictions imposed on legislatures and cannot stand. But it by no means follows that legislative power is wanting whenever a general non-discriminatory civil regulation in fact touches conscientious scruples or religious beliefs of an individual or a group. Regard for such scruples or beliefs undoubtedly presents one of the most reasonable claims for the exertion of legislative accommodation. It is, of course, beyond our power to rewrite the State's requirement, by providing exemptions for those who do not wish to participate in the flag salute or by making some other accommodations to meet their scruples. That wisdom might suggest the making of such accommodations and that school administration would not find it too difficult to make them and yet maintain the ceremony for those not refusing to conform, is outside our province to suggest. Tact, respect, and generosity toward variant views will always commend themselves to those charged with the duties of legislation so as to achieve a maximum of good will and to require a minimum of unwilling submission to a general law. But the real question is, who is to make such accommodations, the courts or the legislature?

191 *Korematsu v. United States (1944)*

Shortly after Pearl Harbor, military officials and West Coast residents began demanding that Japanese and Japanese-Americans be removed from the area, on grounds that fifth-columnists and spies could easily hide within that population. Giving in to these demands, President Roosevelt signed Executive Order 9066 on February 19, 1942, authorizing the secretary of war and certain military officers to designate parts of the country as "military areas," from which any and all persons could be excluded. All told, some 110,000 persons of Japanese origin, nearly all of them loyal to the United States and most U.S. citizens, were relocated into camps in the interior of the country.

In the three cases challenging the relocation program, the Court carefully skirted both the racial aspects that had inspired the removal and the constitutional basis for the program. Had they confronted the racial nature of the program, they justices might have been forced to apply a strict scrutiny test, the highest level of constitutional evaluation, and it is doubtful if the government could have met that standard. In the following case, the majority came as close as it ever would to these issues; the dissent by Justice Murphy is notable for its sensitivity to the underlying problems.

Even before the war ended, the relocation program came under attack from civil libertarians and constitutional scholars, and the verdict of history is that it was wrong and unnecessary. Various efforts are still underway to have the program retroactively declared unconstitutional.

See Eugene V. Rostow, "The Japanese-American Cases—A Disaster," 54 *Yale Law Journal* 489 (1945); Peter Irons, *Justice at War* (1983); Commission on Wartime Relocation, *Personal Justice Denied* (1983); and Page Smith, *Democracy on Trial: The*

Japanese American Evacuation and Relocation in World War II (1995). The critical documents are in Peter Irons, *Justice Delayed* (1989).

———

Justice Black delivered the opinion of the Court:

It should be noted, to begin with, that all legal restrictions which curtail the civil rights of a single racial group are immediately suspect. That is not to say that all such restrictions are unconstitutional. It is to say that courts must subject them to the most rigid scrutiny. Pressing public necessity may sometimes justify the existence of such restrictions; racial antagonism never can. . . .

Exclusion of those of Japanese origin was deemed necessary because of the presence of an unascertained number of disloyal members of the group, most of whom we have no doubt were loyal to this country. It was because we could not reject the finding of the military authorities that it was impossible to bring about an immediate segregation of the disloyal from the loyal that we sustained the validity of the curfew order as applying to the whole group. In the instant case, temporary exclusion of the entire group was rested by the military on the same ground. The judgment that exclusion of the whole group was for the same reason a military imperative answers the contention that the exclusion was in the nature of group punishment based on antagonism to those of Japanese origin. That there were members of the group who retained loyalties in Japan has been confirmed by investigations made subsequent to the exclusion. Approximately five thousand American citizens of Japanese ancestry refused to swear unqualified allegiance to the United States and to renounce allegiance to the Japanese Emperor, and several thousand evacuees requested repatriation to Japan.

We uphold the exclusion order as of the time it was made and when the petitioner violated it. . . . In doing so, we are not unmindful of the hardships imposed by it upon a large group of American citizens. . . . But hardships are part of war, and war is an aggregation of hardships. All citizens alike, both in and out of uniform, feel the impact of war in greater or lesser measure. Citizenship has its responsibilities as well as its privileges, and in time of war the burden is always heavier. Compulsory exclusion of large groups of citizens from their homes, except under circumstances of direct emergency and peril, is inconsistent with our basic governmental institutions. But when under conditions of modern warfare our shores are threatened by hostile forces, the power to protect must be commensurate with the threatened danger. . . .

It is said that we are dealing here with the case of imprisonment of a citizen in a concentration camp solely because of his ancestry, without evidence or inquiry concerning his loyalty and good disposition towards the United States. Our task would be simple, our duty clear, were this a case involving the imprisonment of a loyal citizen in a concentration camp because of racial prejudice. Regardless of the true nature of the assembly and relocation centers—and we deem it unjustifiable to call them concentration camps with all the ugly connotations that term implies—we are dealing specifically with nothing but an exclusion order. To cast this case into outlines of racial prejudice, with-

Source: 323 U.S. 214 (1944)

out reference to the real military dangers which were presented, merely confuses the issue. Korematsu was not excluded from the Military Area because of hostility to him or his race. He *was* excluded because we are at war with the Japanese Empire, because the properly constituted military authorities feared an invasion of our West Coast and felt constrained to take proper security measures, because they decided that the military urgency of the situation demanded that all citizens of Japanese ancestry be segregated from the West Coast temporarily, and finally, because Congress, reposing its confidence in this time of war in our military leaders—as inevitably it must—determined that they should have the power to do just this. There was evidence of disloyalty on the part of some, the military authorities considered that the need for action was great, and time was short. We cannot—by availing ourselves of the calm perspective of hindsight—now say that at that time these actions were unjustified.

Justice Murphy, dissenting:

This exclusion of "all persons of Japanese ancestry, both alien and nonalien," from the Pacific Coast area on a plea of military necessity in the absence of martial law ought not to be approved. Such exclusion goes over "the very brink of constitutional power" and falls into the ugly abyss of racism.

In dealing with matters relating to the prosecution and progress of a war, we must accord great respect and consideration to the judgments of the military authorities who are on the scene and who have full knowledge of the military facts. The scope of their discretion must, as a matter of necessity and common sense, be wide. And their judgments ought not to be overruled lightly by those whose training and duties ill-equip them to deal intelligently with matters so vital to the physical security of the nation.

At the same time, however, it is essential that there be definite limits to military discretion, especially where martial law has not been declared. Individuals must not be left impoverished of their constitutional rights on a plea of military necessity that has neither substance nor support. . . .

That this forced exclusion was the result in good measure of this erroneous assumption of racial guilt rather than bona fide military necessity is evidenced by the Commanding General's Final Report on the evacuation from the Pacific Coast area. In it he refers to all individuals of Japanese descent as "subversive," as belonging to "an enemy race" whose "racial strains are undiluted," and as constituting "over 112,000 potential enemies . . . at large today" along the Pacific Coast. In support of this blanket condemnation of all persons of Japanese descent, however, no reliable evidence is cited to show that such individuals were generally disloyal, or had generally so conducted themselves in this area as to constitute a special menace to defense installations or war industries, or had otherwise by their behavior furnished reasonable ground for their exclusion as a group.

Justification for the exclusion is sought, instead, mainly upon questionable racial and sociological grounds not ordinarily within the realm of expert military judgment, supplemented by certain semi-military conclusions drawn from an unwarranted use of circumstantial evidence. . . .

No one denies, of course, that there were some disloyal persons of Japanese descent on the Pacific Coast who did all in their power to aid their ancestral land. Similar disloyal activities have been engaged in by many persons of German, Italian and even more pioneer stock in our country. But to infer that examples of individual disloyalty prove group disloyalty and justify discriminatory action against the entire group is to deny that under our system of law individual guilt is the sole basis for deprivation of rights. . . . To give constitutional sanction to that inference in this case, however well-intentioned may have been the military command on the Pacific Coast, is to adopt one of the cruelest of the rationales used by our enemies to destroy the dignity of the individual and to encourage and open the door to discriminatory actions against other minority groups in the passions of tomorrow. . . .

I dissent, therefore, from this legalization of racism. Racial discrimination in any form and in any degree has no justifiable part whatever in our democratic way of life. It is unattractive in any setting but it is utterly revolting among a free people who have embraced the principles set forth in the Constitution of the United States. All residents of this nation are kin in some way by blood or culture to a foreign land. Yet they are primarily and necessarily a part of the new and distinct civilization of the United States. They must accordingly be treated at all times as the heirs of the American experiment and as entitled to all the rights and freedoms guaranteed by the Constitution.

---

192 *Adamson v. California (1947)*

Adamson claimed that his conviction for murder violated the Fourteenth Amendment because, under state law, the prosecution had been allowed to comment on his failure to take the stand at his trial. The majority, speaking through Justice Reed, agreed that in federal proceedings, the prosecution's comments would have violated the Fifth Amendment's privilege against self-incrimination. Moreover, the Fourteenth Amendment's Due Process Clause did include the right to a fair trial. But following Cardozo's reasoning in *Palko* (Document 186), Reed found no grounds to apply that provision of the Fifth Amendment to the states.

Justice Black's dissent in this case, in which he was joined by Justice Douglas, contains the fullest exposition of his belief that the Fourteenth Amendment "totally" incorporates the guarantees of the entire Bill of Rights. To buttress his opinion, Black appended a lengthy history of the Fourteenth Amendment, which became the focus of a lively—and continuing—academic debate. Justice Frankfurter, who had become alarmed at what he perceived as growing judicial activism by the Court's liberal wing, entered a concurrence with the majority strongly endorsing Cardozo's view of selective incorporation.

See Richard C. Cortner, *The Supreme Court and the Second Bill of Rights* (1981); Felix Frankfurter, "Memorandum on 'Incorporation'" 78 *Harvard Law Review* 746 (1965);

Jeffrey D. Hockett, *New Deal Justice: The Constitutional Jurisprudence of Hugo L. Black, Felix Frankfurter, and Robert H. Jackson* (1996).

Justice Black, dissenting:

This decision reasserts a constitutional theory spelled out in *Twining* v. *New Jersey* . . . that this Court is endowed by the Constitution with boundless power under "natural law" periodically to expand and contract constitutional standards to conform to the Court's conception of what at a particular time constitutes "civilized decency" and "fundamental liberty and justice." Invoking this *Twining* rule, the Court concludes that although comment upon testimony in a federal court would violate the Fifth Amendment, identical comment in a state court does not violate today's fashion in civilized decency and fundamentals and is therefore not prohibited by the Federal Constitution as amended.

The *Twining* case was the first, as it is the only, decision of this Court which has squarely held that states were free, notwithstanding the Fifth and Fourteenth Amendments, to extort evidence from one accused of crime. I agree that if *Twining* be reaffirmed, the result reached might appropriately follow. But I would not reaffirm the *Twining* decision. I think that decision and the "natural law" theory of the Constitution upon which it relies degrade the constitutional safeguards of the Bill of Rights and simultaneously appropriate for this Court a broad power which we are not authorized by the Constitution to exercise. . . .

The first ten amendments were proposed and adopted largely because of fear that Government might unduly interfere with prized individual liberties. The people wanted and demanded a Bill of Rights written into their Constitution. The amendments embodying the Bill of Rights were intended to curb all branches of the Federal Government in the fields touched by the amendments—Legislative, Executive, and Judicial. The Fifth, Sixth, and Eighth Amendments were pointedly aimed at confining exercise of power by courts and judges within precise boundaries, particularly in the procedure used for the trial of criminal cases. Past history provided strong reasons for the apprehensions which brought these procedural amendments into being and attest the wisdom of their adoption. For the fears of arbitrary court action sprang largely from the past use of courts in the imposition of criminal punishments to suppress speech, press, and religion. Hence the constitutional limitations of courts' powers were, in the view of the Founders, essential supplements to the First Amendment, which was itself designed to protect the widest scope for all people to believe and to express the most divergent political, religious, and other views. . . .

My study of the historical events that culminated in the Fourteenth Amendment, and the expressions of those who sponsored and favored, as well as those who opposed its submission and passage, persuades me that one of the chief objects that the provisions of the Amendment's first section, separately, and as a whole, were intended to accomplish was to make the Bill of Rights, applicable to the states. With full knowledge of the

---

Source: 332 U.S. 46 (1947)

import of the *Barron* decision, the framers and backers of the Fourteenth Amendment proclaimed its purpose to be to overturn the constitutional rule that case had announced. This historical purpose has never received full consideration or exposition in any opinion of this Court interpreting the Amendment. . . .

For this reason, I am attaching to this dissent an appendix which contains a résumé, by no means complete, of the Amendment's history. In my judgment that history conclusively demonstrates that the language of the first section of the Fourteenth Amendment, taken as a whole, was thought by those responsible for its submission to the people, and by those who opposed its submission, sufficiently explicit to guarantee that thereafter no state could deprive its citizens of the privileges and protections of the Bill of Rights. Whether this Court ever will, or whether it now should, in the light of past decisions, give full effect to what the Amendment was intended to accomplish is not necessarily essential to a decision here. However that may be, our prior decisions, including *Twining,* do not prevent our carrying out that purpose, at least to the extent of making applicable to the states, not a mere part, as the Court has, but the full protection of the Fifth Amendment's provision against compelling evidence from an accused to convict him of crime. And I further contend that the "natural law" formula which the Court uses to reach its conclusion in this case should be abandoned as an incongruous excrescence on our Constitution. I believe that formula to be itself a violation of our Constitution, in that it subtly conveys to courts, at the expense of legislatures, ultimate power over public policies in fields where no specific provision of the Constitution limits legislative power. And my belief seems to be in accord with the views expressed by this Court, at least for the first two decades after the Fourteenth Amendment was adopted. . . .

[Justice Black summarized the history of the Fourteenth Amendment from the *Slaughterhouse* cases to *Lochner* v. *New York.*]

The foregoing constitutional doctrine, judicially created and adopted by expanding the previously accepted meaning of "due process," marked a complete departure from the *Slaughter-House* philosophy of judicial tolerance of state regulation of business activities. Conversely, the new formula contracted the effectiveness of the Fourteenth Amendment as a protection from state infringement of individual liberties enumerated in the Bill of Rights. Thus the Court's second-thought interpretation of the Amendment was an about-face from the *Slaughter-House* interpretation and represented a failure to carry out the avowed purpose of the Amendment's sponsors. This reversal is dramatized by the fact that the *Hurtado* case, which had rejected the due process clause as an instrument for preserving Bill of Rights liberties and privileges, was cited as authority for expanding the scope of that clause so as to permit this Court to invalidate all state regulatory legislation it believed to be contrary to "fundamental" principles.

The *Twining* decision, rejecting the compelled testimony clause of the Fifth Amendment, and indeed rejecting all the Bill of Rights, is the end product of one phase of this philosophy. At the same time, that decision consolidated the power of the Court assumed in past cases by laying broader foundations for the Court to invalidate state and even federal regulatory legislation. For the *Twining* decision, giving separate consideration to "due process" and "privileges or immunities," went all the way to say that the "privileges or immunities" clause of the Fourteenth Amendment "did not forbid the States to abridge the personal rights enumerated in the first eight Amendments. . . ." And in order to be certain, so far as possible, to leave this Court wholly free to reject all the Bill of Rights as specific restraints upon state action, the decision declared that even if this Court should decide that the due process clause forbids the states to infringe personal liberties guaranteed by the Bill of Rights, it would do so, not "because those rights are enumerated in the first eight Amendments, but because they are of such a nature that they are included in the conception of due process of law." . . .

I cannot consider the Bill of Rights to be an outworn 18th Century "strait jacket" as the *Twining* opinion did. Its provisions may be thought outdated abstractions by some. And it is true that they were designed to meet ancient evils. But they are the same kind of human evils that have emerged from century to century wherever excessive power is sought by the few at the expense of the many. In my judgment the people of no nation can lose their liberty so long as a Bill of Rights like ours survives and its basic purposes are conscientiously interpreted, enforced and respected so as to afford continuous protection against old, as well as new, devices and practices which might thwart those purposes. I fear to see the consequences of the Court's practice of substituting its own concepts of decency and fundamental justice for the language of the Bill of Rights as its point of departure in interpreting and enforcing that Bill of Rights. If the choice must be between the selective process of the *Palko* decision applying some of the Bill of Rights to the States, or the *Twining* rule applying none of them, I would choose the *Palko* selective process. But rather than accept either of these choices, I would follow what I believe was the original purpose of the Fourteenth Amendment—to extend to all the people of the nation the complete protection of the Bill of Rights. To hold that this Court can determine what, if any, provisions of the Bill of Rights will be enforced, and if so to what degree, is to frustrate the great design of a written Constitution.

193

Everson v. Board of Education (1947)

A New Jersey law authorized local school districts to arrange for transportation of pupils to and from schools, including the transportation of children attending private and parochial schools. In one district, the board voted to reimburse the parents of parochial school students for the expenses of transporting them to school. A local taxpayer challenged the payments as a violation of the First Amendment's ban on an establishment of religion.

Justice Black's opinion for the narrow five-man majority is noteworthy because, even though he lauded the Jeffersonian notion of a "wall of separation" and seemed to indicate compelling reasons against any form of aid to parochial schools, he nonetheless upheld the statute. Although Catholic groups applauded the decision, Protestants and civil libertarians condemned it. The conclusion itself, in this first instance of the Court's dealing with the Establishment Clause, has not withstood the test of time, but the arguments Black marshaled in support of a wall of separation have often been quoted by subsequent courts.

See Richard E. Morgan, *The Supreme Court and Religion* (1972); Frank J. Sorauf, *The Wall of Separation* (1976); Jesse Choper, "The Establishment Clause and Aid to Parochial Schools," 56 *California Law Review* 260 (1968); and John T. Noonan, Jr., *The Lustre of Our Country* (1998).

———

Justice Black delivered the opinion of the Court:

The only contention here is that the state statute and the resolution, insofar as they authorized reimbursement to parents of children attending parochial schools, violate the Federal Constitution in two respects, which to some extent overlap. *First.* They authorize the State to take by taxation the private property of some and bestow it upon others, to be used for their own private purposes, [in violation of the due process clause]. *Second.* The statute and the resolution forced inhabitants to pay taxes to help support and maintain schools which are dedicated to, and which regularly teach, the Catholic Faith. This is alleged to be a use of state power to support church schools contrary to the prohibition of the First Amendment which the Fourteenth Amendment made applicable to the states.

First. It is much too late to argue that legislation intended to facilitate the opportunity of children to get a secular education serves no public purpose. . . . [The] same thing is no less true of legislation to reimburse needy parents, or all parents, for payment of the fares of their children so that they can ride in public busses to and from schools rather than run the risk of traffic and other hazards incident to walking or "hitchhiking." . . .

Second. The New Jersey statute is challenged as a "law respecting an establishment of religion." [Whether this law] is one respecting an "establishment of religion" requires an understanding of the meaning of that language, particularly with respect to the imposition of taxes. . . .

[Justice Black then examined at length the historical antecedents of the Establishment Clause.]

The "establishment of religion" clause of the First Amendment means at least this: Neither a state nor the Federal Government can set up a church. Neither can pass laws which aid one religion, aid all religions, or prefer one religion over another. Neither can force nor influence a person to go to or to remain away from church against his will or force him to profess a belief or disbelief in any religion. No person can be punished for entertaining or professing religious beliefs or disbeliefs, for church attendance or nonattendance. No tax in any amount, large or small, can be levied to support any religious

Source: 330 U.S. 1 (1947)

activities or institutions, whatever they may be called, or whatever form they may adopt to teach or practice religion. Neither a state nor the Federal Government can, openly or secretly, participate in the affairs of any religious organizations or groups and vice versa. In the words of Jefferson, the clause against establishment of religion by law was intended to erect "a wall of separation between church and State."

We must [sustain the New Jersey law] if it is within the State's constitutional power even though it approaches the verge of the power. New Jersey cannot consistently with the "establishment of religion" clause of the First Amendment contribute tax-raised funds to the support of an institution which teaches the tenets and faith of any church. On the other hand, other language of the amendment commands that New Jersey cannot hamper its citizens in the free exercise of their own religion. Consequently, it cannot exclude individual Catholics, Lutherans, Mohammedans, Baptists, Jews, Methodists, Non-believers, Presbyterians, or the members of any other faith, *because of their faith, or lack of it,* from receiving the benefits of public welfare legislation. While we do not mean to intimate that a state could not provide transportation only to children attending public schools, we must be careful, in protecting the citizens of New Jersey against state-established churches, to be sure that we do not inadvertently prohibit New Jersey from extending its general state law benefits to all its citizens without regard to their religious belief.

Measured by these standards, we cannot say that the First Amendment prohibits New Jersey from spending tax-raised funds to pay the bus fares of parochial school pupils as a part of a general program under which it pays the fares of pupils attending public and other schools. It is undoubtedly true that children are helped to get to church schools. There is even a possibility that some of the children might not be sent to the church schools if the parents were compelled to pay their children's bus fares out of their own pockets when transportation to a public school would have been paid for by the State. . . . The [First] Amendment requires the state to be a neutral in its relations with groups of religious believers and non-believers; it does not require the state to be their adversary. State power is no more to be used so as to handicap religions than it is to favor them.

This Court has said that parents may, in the discharge of their duty under state compulsory education laws, send their children to a religious rather than a public school if the school meets the secular educational requirements which the state has power to impose. See Pierce v. Society of Sisters. . . . It appears that these parochial schools meet New Jersey's requirements. The State contributes no money to the schools. It does not support them. Its legislation, as applied, does no more than provide a general program to help parents get their children, regardless of their religion, safely and expeditiously to and from accredited schools.

The First Amendment has erected a wall between church and state. That wall must be kept high and impregnable. We could not approve the slightest breach. New Jersey has not breached it here.

Affirmed.

Justice Jackson, joined by Justice Frankfurter, dissenting:

The Court's opinion marshals every argument in favor of state aid and puts the case in its most favorable light, but much of its reasoning confirms my conclusions that there are no good grounds upon which to support the present legislation. In fact, the undertones of the opinion, advocating complete and uncompromising separation of Church from State, seem utterly discordant with its conclusion yielding support to their commingling in educational matters. The case which irresistibly comes to mind as the most fitting precedent is that of Julia who, according to Byron's reports, "whispering 'I will ne'er consent,'—consented."

Mr. Justice Rutledge, with whom Mr. Justice Frankfurter, Mr. Justice Jackson and Mr. Justice Burton agree, dissenting.

194   *Executive Order 9981 (1948)*

HARRY S. TRUMAN

During World War II, blacks complained that discrimination at home could not be squared with the fight against intolerance overseas. President Roosevelt issued an executive order in June 1941, directing that blacks be accepted into job-training programs in defense plants, forbade discrimination by defense contractors, and established a Fair Employment Practices Commission. Civil rights, however, remained a low priority during the war.

Congress killed the wartime agency after the end of hostilities and refused President Truman's request to create a permanent FEPC. Truman nonetheless established a Presidential Commission on Civil Rights to explore the problem, and its report, "To Secure These Rights," issued in October 1947, defined the nation's civil rights agenda for the next generation. Truman, in a courageous act, asked Congress in early 1948 to implement the commission's recommendations. When the Southern delegations threatened to block any civil rights bills by filibustering, Truman used his executive authority to bolster the Civil Rights section of the Justice Department, named blacks to high-ranking positions, and by executive order abolished segregation in the armed forces and directed military leaders to integrate the branches.

See Richard Dalfiume, *Desegregation in the U.S. Armed Forces* (1953); Donald R. McCoy and Richard T. Ruetten, *Quest and Response: Minority Rights in the Truman Administration* (1973); and William C. Berman, *Politics of Civil Rights in the Truman Administration* (1970).

Establishing the President's Committee on Equality of Treatment and Opportunity in the Armed Services

Whereas it is essential that there be maintained in the armed services of the United States the highest standards of democracy, with equality of treatment and opportunity for all those who serve in our country's defense:

Now therefore, by virtue of the authority vested in me as President of the United States, by the Constitution and the statutes of the United States, and as Commander in Chief of the armed services, it is hereby ordered as follows:

1. It is hereby declared to be the policy of the President that there shall be equality of treatment and opportunity for all persons in the armed services without regard to race, color, religion or national origin. This policy shall be put into effect as rapidly as possible, having due regard to the time required to effectuate any necessary changes without impairing efficiency or morale.

2. There shall be created in the National Military Establishment an advisory committee to be known as the President's Committee on Equality of Treatment and Opportunity in the Armed Services, which shall be composed of seven members to be designated by the President.

3. The Committee is authorized on behalf of the President to examine into the rules, procedures and practices of the armed services in order to determine in what respect such rules, procedures and practices may be altered or improved with a view to carrying out the policy of this order. The Committee shall confer and advise with the Secretary of Defense, the Secretary of the Army, the Secretary of the Navy, and the Secretary of the Air Force, and shall make such recommendations to the President and to said Secretaries as in the judgment of the Committee will effectuate the policy hereof.

4. All executive departments and agencies of the Federal Government are authorized and directed to cooperate with the Committee in its work, and to furnish the Committee such information or the services of such persons as the Committee may require in the performance of its duties.

5. When requested by the Committee to do so, persons in the armed services or in any of the executive departments and agencies of the Federal Government shall testify before the Committee and shall make available for the use of the Committee such documents and other information as the Committee may require.

6. The Committee shall continue to exist until such time as the President shall terminate its existence by Executive order.

Harry S. Truman
The White House,
July 26, 1948.

Source: 13 *Fed. Register* 4313 (1948)

195 *Shelley v. Kraemer (1948)*

Following the invalidation of racially discriminatory zoning ordinances in *Buchanan v. Warley* (1917), residential segregation depended upon restrictive covenants, in which buyers agreed, as a condition of purchase written into the deed, not to sell their houses to blacks. (Some restrictive covenants also applied to Jews, Catholics, Indians, Asians, and Hispanics.) Although these covenants could be enforced in court, most people considered them private agreements, and the Supreme Court had on several occasions ruled private discrimination beyond the reach of the Fourteenth Amendment.

In this case, the Court did not abandon the view that private discrimination remained beyond constitutional reach; the covenants themselves, as private agreements, were not illegal. But the covenants could only be enforced in state courts, and that invoked the state action doctrine. So long as the state sanctioned and enforced the agreements, it violated the Fourteenth Amendment. Following this case, segregation in residential neighborhoods relied on custom and informal agreements—certainly powerful by themselves—but those who chose to ignore the covenants could not be legally forced to observe them.

In a companion case, *Hurd v. Hodge,* Vinson applied the ruling to the District of Columbia, although the Fourteenth Amendment did not apply to the national government. The chief justice found that enforcement of the covenants violated the 1866 Civil Rights Act and that it went against public policy to allow a federal court to enforce a discriminatory agreement that was unenforceable in state courts.

See Louis Henkin, *"Shelley v. Kraemer:* Notes for a Revised Opinion," 110 *University of Pennsylvania Law Review* 473 (1962); Mark V. Tushnet, *"Shelley v. Kraemer* and Theories of Equality," 33 *New York Law School Review* 383 (1988); and Clement E. Vose, *Caucasians Only: The Supreme Court, the N.A.A.C.P. and the Restrictive Covenant Cases* (1959).

———

Chief Justice Vinson delivered the opinion of the Court:

It cannot be doubted that among the civil rights intended to be protected from discriminatory state action by the 14th Amendment are the rights to acquire, enjoy, own and dispose of property. Equality in the enjoyment of property rights was regarded by the framers of that Amendment as an essential precondition to the realization of other basic civil rights and liberties which the Amendment was intended to guarantee. Thus, § 1978

Source: 334 U.S. 1 (1948)

of the Revised Statutes . . . derived from § 1 of the Civil Rights Act of 1866 which was enacted by Congress while the Fourteenth Amendment was also under consideration, provides: "All citizens of the United States shall have the same right, in every State and Territory, as is enjoyed by white citizens thereof to inherit, purchase, lease, sell, hold, and convey real and personal property." This Court has given specific recognition to the same principle. Buchanan v. Warley . . . (1917). It is likewise clear that restrictions on the right of occupancy of the sort sought to be created by the private agreements in these cases could not be squared with the requirements of the 14th Amendment if imposed by state statute or local ordinance. . . .

But the present cases do not involve action by state legislatures or city councils. Here the particular patterns of discrimination and the areas in which the restrictions are to operate, are determined, in the first instance, by the terms of agreements among private individuals. Participation of the State consists in the enforcement of the restrictions so defined. The crucial issue is whether this distinction removes these cases from [the reach of the Fourteenth Amendment].

Since the Civil Rights Cases, the principle has become firmly embedded in our constitutional law that the action inhibited by the first section of the 14th Amendment is only such action as may fairly be said to be that of the States. That Amendment erects no shield against merely private conduct, however discriminatory or wrongful. We conclude, therefore, that the restrictive agreements standing alone cannot be regarded as violative of any rights guaranteed to petitioners by the 14th Amendment. So long as the purposes of those agreements are effectuated by voluntary adherence to their terms, it would appear clear that there has been no action by the State and the provisions of the Amendment have not been violated.

But here there was more. These are cases in which the purposes of the agreements were secured only by judicial enforcement by state courts of the restrictive terms of the agreements. The respondents urge that judicial enforcement of private agreements does not amount to state action; or, in any event, the participation of the State is so attenuated in character as not to amount to state action within the meaning of the 14th Amendment. Finally, it is suggested, even if the States in these cases may be deemed to have acted in the constitutional sense, their action did not deprive petitioners of rights guaranteed by the 14th Amendment. . . .

That the action of state courts and judicial officers in their official capacities is to be regarded as action of the State within the meaning of the 14th Amendment, is a proposition which has long been established by decisions of this Court. . . .

We have no doubt that there has been state action in these cases in the full and complete sense of the phrase. The undisputed facts disclose that petitioners were willing purchasers of properties upon which they desired to establish homes. The owners of the properties were willing sellers; and contracts of sale were accordingly consummated. It is clear that but for the active intervention of the state courts, supported by the full panoply of state power, petitioners would have been free to occupy the properties in question without restraint. These are not cases, as has been suggested, in which the States have merely abstained from action, leaving private individuals free to impose such discriminations as they see fit. Rather, these are cases in which the States have made available to such individuals the full coercive power of government to deny to petitioners, on the grounds of race or color, the enjoyment of property rights in premises which petitioners are willing and financially able to acquire and which the grantors are willing to sell. The difference between judicial enforcement and non-enforcement of the restrictive covenants is the difference to petitioners between being denied rights of property available to other members of the community and being accorded full enjoyment of those rights on an equal footing.

The enforcement of the restrictive agreements by the state courts in these cases was directed pursuant to the common-law policy of the States as formulated by those courts in earlier decisions. The judicial action in each case bears the clear and unmistakable imprimatur of the State. We have noted that previous decisions of this Court have established the proposition that judicial action is not immunized from the operation of the 14th Amendment simply because it is taken pursuant to the state's common-law policy. Nor is the Amendment ineffective simply because the particular pattern of discrimination, which the State has enforced, was defined initially by the terms of a private agreement. State action, as that phrase is understood for the purposes of the 14th Amendment, refers to exertions of state power in all forms. And when the effect of that action is to deny rights subject to the protection of the 14th Amendment, it is the obligation of this Court to enforce the constitutional commands. We hold that in granting judicial enforcement of the restrictive agreements in these cases, the States have denied petitioners the equal protection of the laws and that, therefore, the action of the state courts cannot stand. We have noted that freedom from discrimination by the States in the enjoyment of property rights was among the basic objectives sought to be effectuated by the framers of the 14th Amendment. That such discrimination has occurred in these cases is clear.

---

196   *Dennis v. United States (1951)*

Anticommunist fears following World War II, whipped up by right-wing demagogues such as Wisconsin Senator Joseph L. McCarthy, led to a number of prosecutions based on the Smith Act (1940), which made it a crime to teach or advocate the overthrow of the government by force or to belong to any group advocating such a course. In 1948, the government indicted twelve leaders of the Communist party, and the following year, in an explosive trial before Judge Harold Medina, all twelve were found guilty.

Their first appeal had gone to Chief Judge Learned Hand of the Second Circuit, who had wrestled with the problem of free speech since the World War I *Masses* case (Document 154). He distinguished this case from earlier cases in which the defendants had been prosecuted for verbal protests alone. "It is quite another matter to say that an organized effort to inculcate the duty of revolution may not be suppressed."

A majority of the Court agreed, but Chief Justice Vinson's opinion reflected anticommunist sentiment as much as legal reasoning. Justice Black's dissent relied on his belief in the preferred position of First Amendment rights, and recalled Brandeis's warnings about limiting speech when emotions run high. The dissent by Justice Douglas carried on the civil liberties tradition of Holmes and Brandeis, and he castigated the majority for making the test rely on the intent of the speaker, thus punishing not the speech but the thought.

Scholarly and civil libertarian criticism of the case, the waning of the McCarthy Red Scare, and the death of Chief Justice Vinson led the Court to abandon *Dennis* without ever specifically overruling it (see Document 198).

See Stanley I. Kutler, *The American Inquisition* (1982); Michal R. Belknap, *Cold War Political Justice* (1977); Wallace Mendelson, "Clear and Present Danger—From *Schenck* to *Dennis,*" 52 *Columbia Law Review* 313 (1952); C. J. Antieu, *"Dennis v. United States:* Precedent, Principle, or Perversion?" 5 *Vanderbilt Law Review* 141 (1952); and R. Mollen, "Smith Act Prosecutions," 26 *University of Pittsburgh Law Review* 705 (1965).

———

Chief Justice Vinson announced the judgment of the Court and an opinion in which Justice Reed, Justice Burton and Justice Minton joined:

The indictment charged the petitioners with wilfully and knowingly conspiring (1) to organize as the Communist Party of the United States of America a society, group and assembly of persons who teach and advocate the overthrow and destruction of the Government of the United States by force and violence, and (2) knowingly and wilfully to advocate and teach the duty and necessity of overthrowing and destroying the Government of the United States by force and violence. . . .

The trial of the case extended over nine months, six of which were devoted to the taking of evidence, resulting in a record of 16,000 pages. Our limited grant of the writ of certiorari has removed from our consideration any question as to the sufficiency of the evidence to support the jury's determination that petitioners are guilty of the offense charged. The Court of Appeals held that the record supports the following broad conclusions: [that] the Communist Party is a highly disciplined organization, adept at infiltration into strategic positions, use of aliases, and double-meaning language; that the Party is rigidly controlled; that Communists, unlike other political parties, tolerate no dissension from the policy laid down by the guiding forces; that the literature of the Party and the statements and activities of its leaders, petitioners here, advocate, and the general goal of the Party was, during the period in question, to achieve a successful overthrow of the existing order by force and violence. . . .

Whatever theoretical merit there may be to the argument that there is a "right" to rebellion against dictatorial governments is without force where the existing structure of the government provides for peaceful and orderly change. We reject any principle of governmental helplessness in the face of preparation for revolution. No one could con-

Source: 341 U.S. 494 (1951)

ceive that it is not within the power of Congress to prohibit acts intended to overthrow the Government by force and violence. The question with which we are concerned here is not whether Congress has such *power,* but whether the *means* which it has employed conflict with the First and Fifth Amendments to the Constitution.

One of the bases for the contention that the means which Congress has employed are invalid takes the form of an attack on the face of the statute on the grounds that by its terms it prohibits academic discussion of the merits of Marxism-Leninism, that it stifles ideas and is contrary to all concepts of a free speech and a free press. The very language of the Smith Act negates the interpretation which petitioners would have us impose on that Act. It is directed at advocacy, not discussion. . . . This case has resulted in convictions for the teaching and advocacy of the overthrow of the Government by force and violence, which, even though coupled with the intent to accomplish that overthrow, contains an element of speech. For this reason, we must pay special heed to the demands of the First Amendment marking out the boundaries of speech.

The basis of the First Amendment is the hypothesis that speech can rebut speech, propaganda will answer propaganda, free debate of ideas will result in the wisest governmental policies. An analysis of the leading cases in this Court which have involved direct limitations on speech, however, will demonstrate that both the majority of the Court and the dissenters in particular cases have recognized that this is not an unlimited, unqualified right, but that the societal value of speech must, on occasion, be subordinated to other values and considerations. Although no case subsequent to Whitney and Gitlow has expressly overruled the majority opinions in those cases, there is little doubt that subsequent opinions have inclined toward the Holmes-Brandeis rationale. But neither Justice Holmes nor Justice Brandeis ever envisioned that a shorthand phrase should be crystallized into a rigid rule to be applied inflexibly without regard to the circumstances of each case. Speech is not an absolute, above and beyond control by the legislature when its judgment, subject to review here, is that certain kinds of speech are so undesirable as to warrant criminal sanction. . . .

In this case we are squarely presented with the application of the "clear and present danger" test, and must decide what that phrase imports. We first note that many of the cases in which this Court has reversed convictions by use of this or similar tests have been based on the fact that the interest which the State was attempting to protect was itself too insubstantial to warrant restriction of speech. Overthrow of the Government by force and violence is certainly a substantial enough interest for the Government to limit speech. [If], then, this interest may be protected, the literal problem which is presented is what has been meant by the use of the phrase "clear and present danger" of the utterances bringing about the evil within the power of Congress to punish.

Obviously, the words cannot mean that before the Government may act, it must wait until the putsch is about to be executed, the plans have been laid and the signal is awaited. If Government is aware that a group aiming at its overthrow is attempting to indoctrinate its members and to commit them to a course whereby they will strike when the leaders feel the circumstances permit, action by the Government is required. The argument that there is no need for Government to concern itself, for Government is strong, it possesses ample powers to put down a rebellion, it may defeat the revolution with ease needs no answer. For that is not the question. Certainly an attempt to overthrow the Government by force, even though doomed from the outset because of inadequate numbers or power of the revolutionists, is a sufficient evil for Congress to prevent. The damage which such attempts create both physically and politically to a nation makes it impossible to measure the validity in terms of the probability of success, or the immediacy of a successful attempt. In the instant case the trial judge charged the jury that they could not convict unless they found that petitioners intended to overthrow the Government "as speedily as circumstances would permit." This does not mean, and could not properly mean, that they would not strike until there was certainty of success. What was meant was that the revolutionists would strike when they thought the time was ripe. We must therefore reject the contention that success or probability of success is the criterion.

The situation with which Justices Holmes and Brandeis were concerned in Gitlow was a comparatively isolated event, bearing little relation in their minds to any substantial threat to the safety of the community. They were not confronted with any situation comparable to the instant one—the development of an apparatus designed and dedicated to the overthrow of the Government, in the context of world crisis after crisis.

Chief Judge Learned Hand, writing for the majority below, interpreted the phrase as follows: "In each case [courts] must ask whether the gravity of the 'evil,' discounted by its improbability, justifies such invasion of free speech as is necessary to avoid the danger." We adopt this statement of the rule. As articulated by Chief Judge Hand, it is as succinct and inclusive as any other we might devise at this time. . . .

[Petitioners] intended to overthrow the Government of the United States as speedily as the circumstances would permit. Their conspiracy to organize the Communist Party and to teach and advocate the overthrow of the Government of the United States by force and violence created a "clear and present danger" of an attempt to overthrow the Government by force and violence. . . .

Affirmed.

Justice Douglas, dissenting:

If this were a case where those who claimed protection under the First Amendment were teaching the techniques of sabotage, the assassination of the President, the filching of documents from public files, the planting of bombs, the art of street warfare, and the like, I would have no doubts. The freedom to speak is not absolute; the teaching of methods of terror and other seditious conduct should be beyond the pale along with obscenity and immorality. This case was argued as if those were the facts. The argument imported much seditious conduct into the record. That is easy and it has popular appeal, for the activities of Communists in plotting and scheming against the free world are common knowledge. But the fact is that no such evidence was introduced at the trial. There is a statute which makes a seditious conspiracy unlawful. Petitioners, however, were not charged with a "conspiracy to overthrow" the Government. They were charged with a conspiracy to form a party and groups and assemblies of people who teach and advocate the overthrow of our Government by force or violence and with a conspiracy to advocate and teach its overthrow by force and violence. It may well be that indoctrination in the techniques of terror to destroy the Government would be indictable under either statute. But the teaching which is condemned here is of a different character.

So far as the present record is concerned, what petitioners did was to organize people to teach and themselves teach the Marxist-Leninist doctrine contained chiefly in four books: Foundations of Leninism by Stalin (1924), The Communist Manifesto by Marx and Engels (1848), State and Revolution by Lenin (1917), History of the Communist Party of the Soviet Union (B) (1939). Those books are to Soviet Communism what Mein Kampf was to Nazism. If they are understood, the ugliness of Communism is revealed, its deceit and cunning are exposed, the nature of its activities becomes apparent, and the chances of its success less likely. That is not, of course, the reason why petitioners chose these books for their classrooms. They are fervent Communists to whom these volumes are gospel. They preached the creed with the hope that some day it would be acted upon.

The opinion of the Court does not outlaw these texts nor condemn them to the fire, as the Communists do literature offensive to their creed. But if the books themselves are not outlawed, if they can lawfully remain on library shelves, by what reasoning does their use in a classroom become a crime? [The] Act, as construed, requires the element of intent—that those who teach the creed believe in it. The crime then depends not on what is taught but on who the teacher is. That is to make freedom of speech turn not on *what is said,* but on the *intent* with which it is said. Once we start down that road we enter territory dangerous to the liberties of every citizen. . . .

There comes a time when even speech loses its constitutional immunity. Speech innocuous one year may at another time fan such destructive flames that it must be halted in the interests of the safety of the Republic. That is the meaning of the clear and present danger test. When conditions are so critical that there will be no time to avoid the evil that the speech threatens, it is time to call a halt. Otherwise, free speech which is the strength of the Nation will be the cause of its destruction. Yet free speech is the rule, not the exception. The restraint to be constitutional must be based on more than fear, on more than passionate opposition against the speech, on more than a revolted dislike for its contents. There must be some immediate injury to society that is likely if speech is allowed. . . .

The nature of Communism as a force on the world scene would, of course, be relevant to the issue of clear and present danger of petitioners' advocacy within the United States. But the primary consideration is the strength and tactical position of petitioners and their converts in this country. On that there is no evidence in the record. If we are to take judicial notice of the threat of Communists within the nation, it should not be difficult to conclude that *as a political party* they are of little consequence. Communism in the world scene is no bogeyman; but Communism as a political faction or party in this country plainly is. Communism has been so thoroughly exposed in this country that it has been crippled as a political force. Free speech has destroyed it as an effective political party. How it can be said that there is a clear and present danger that this advocacy will succeed is, therefore, a mystery. In America [Communists] are miserable merchants of unwanted ideas; their wares remain unsold. If we are to proceed on the basis of judicial notice, it is impossible for me to say that the Communists in this country are so potent or so strategically deployed that they must be suppressed for their speech. This is my view if we are to act on the basis of judicial notice. But the mere statement of the opposing views indicates how important it is that we know the facts before we act. Neither prejudice nor hate nor senseless fear should be the basis of this solemn act. Free speech should not be sacrificed on anything less than plain and objective proof of danger that the evil advocated is imminent.

197

Youngstown Sheet & Tube Co. v. Sawyer (1952)

In April 1952, President Truman ordered seizure of the nation's steel mills in order to forestall a strike, which, he claimed, would have seriously harmed the nation during the Korean conflict. He chose not to use the Taft-Hartley Act provision for an eighty-day "cooling-off period," nor to ask Congress for special legislation.

The steel companies did not deny that the government could take over their property in emergencies. Rather, they claimed that the wrong branch of the government had proceeded against them; in essence, they sued the president on behalf of Congress in the name of separation of powers. Six members of the Court agreed, and Justice Black's opinion flatly denied that the president had any authority.

In a concurring opinion, Justice Frankfurter suggested that a president could act in the absence of statutory permission if there was a historical record that the legislature had acquiesced in similar previous actions or had left the executive discretionary power. But he found neither condition present in this case. Chief Justice Vinson (who had privately assured Truman of the legitimacy of the seizure), joined by Reed and Minton, dissented and argued for a strong executive discretion, limited only by specific congressional restraints. Where Black said the president could act only with congressional approval, they argued he could act except when Congress specifically disapproved.

See Edward S. Corwin, "The Steel Seizure Case—A Judicial Brick Without Straw," 53 *Columbia Law Review* 53 (1953); and Maeva Marcus, *Truman and the Steel Seizure Case: The Limits of Presidential Power* (1977).

———

Justice Black delivered the opinion of the Court:

We are asked to decide whether the President . . . was acting within his constitutional power when he issued an order directing the Secretary of Commerce to take possession of and operate most of the Nation's steel mills. The mill owners argue that the President's order amounts to lawmaking, a legislative function which the Constitution has expressly confided to the Congress and not to the President. The Government's position is that the order was made on findings of the President that his action was necessary

———
Source: 343 U.S. 579 (1952).

to avert a national catastrophe which would inevitably result from a stoppage of steel production, and that in meeting this grave emergency the President was acting within the aggregate of his constitutional powers as the Nation's Chief Executive and the Commander in Chief of the Armed Forces of the United States. . . .

The President's power, if any, to issue the order must stem either from an act of Congress or from the Constitution itself. There is no statute that expressly authorizes the President to take possession of property as he did here. Nor is there any act of Congress to which our attention has been directed from which such a power can fairly be implied. There are two statutes which do authorize the President to take both personal and real property under certain conditions. . . . However, the Government admits that these conditions were not met and that the President's order was not rooted in either of the statutes. . . .

Moreover, the use of the seizure technique to solve labor disputes in order to prevent work stoppages was not only unauthorized by any congressional enactment; prior to this controversy, Congress had refused to adopt that method of settling labor disputes. When the Taft-Hartley Act was under consideration in 1947, Congress rejected an amendment which would have authorized such governmental seizures in cases of emergency. Instead, the plan sought to bring about settlements by use of the customary devices of mediation, conciliation, investigations by boards of inquiry, and public reports. In some instances temporary injunctions were authorized to provide cooling-off periods. All this failing, unions were left free to strike. . . .

It is clear that if the President had authority to issue the order he did, it must be found in some provision of the Constitution. And it is not claimed that express constitutional language grants this power to the President. The contention is that presidential power should be implied from the aggregate of his powers under the Constitution. Particular reliance is placed on provisions in Article II which say that "The executive Power shall be vested in a President"; that "he shall take Care that the Laws be faithfully executed"; and that he "shall be Commander in Chief of the Army and Navy of the United States."

The order cannot properly be sustained as an exercise of the President's military power as Commander in Chief of the Armed Forces. The Government attempts to do so by citing a number of cases upholding broad powers in military commanders engaged in day-to-day fighting in a theater of war. Such cases need not concern us here. Even though "theater of war" be an expanding concept, we cannot with faithfulness to our constitutional system hold that the Commander in Chief of the Armed Forces has the ultimate power as such to take possession of private property in order to keep labor disputes from stopping production. This is a job for the Nation's lawmakers, not for its military authorities.

Nor can the seizure order be sustained because of the several constitutional provisions that grant executive power to the President. In the framework of our Constitution, the President's power to see that the laws are faithfully executed refutes the idea that he is to be a lawmaker. The Constitution limits his functions in the law-making process to the recommending of laws he thinks wise and the vetoing of laws he thinks bad. And the Constitution is neither silent nor equivocal about who shall make laws which the President is to execute. . . .

The President's order does not direct that a congressional policy be executed in a manner prescribed by Congress—it directs that a presidential policy be executed in a manner prescribed by the President. The preamble of the order itself, like that of many statutes, sets out reasons why the President believes certain policies should be adopted, proclaims these policies as rules of conduct to be followed, and again, like a statute, authorizes a government official to promulgate additional rules and regulations consistent with the policy proclaimed and needed to carry that policy into execution. The power of Congress to adopt such public policies as those proclaimed by the order is beyond question. It can authorize the taking of private property for public use. It can make laws regulating the relationships between employers and employees, prescribing rules designed to settle labor disputes, and fixing wages and working conditions in certain fields of our economy. The Constitution does not subject this lawmaking power of Congress to presidential or military supervision or control.

It is said that other Presidents without congressional authority have taken possession of private business enterprises in order to settle labor disputes. But even if this be true, Congress has not thereby lost its exclusive constitutional authority to make laws necessary and proper to carry out the powers vested by the Constitution "in the Government of the United States, or any Department or Officer thereof."

The Founders of this Nation entrusted the lawmaking power to the Congress alone in both good and bad times. It would do no good to recall the historical events, the fears of power and the hopes for freedom that lay behind their choice. Such a review would but confirm our holding that this seizure order cannot stand.

Affirmed.

---

198   *Yates v. United States (1957)*

After *Dennis* (Document 196), the government brought a number of prosecutions against lower-level leaders of the Communist party. The Court, however, showed itself to be quite sensitive to the criticism that had greeted *Dennis* among civil libertarians and in the scholarly community, where there was widespread agreement that the Court had seriously distorted the clear-and-present-danger test. It would have been politically disadvantageous for the Court to have reversed *Dennis,* so Justice Harlan came up with a useful solution that in effect nullified the earlier case. In *Yates,* he concluded that the lower courts had given too broad a meaning to the term "organize" in the Smith Act, and that a high level of evidence would be required to support a conviction under the Smith Act criteria. In *Noto v. United States* (1961), the Court found that the evidentiary level had been met, but voided the conviction because proof of illegal advocacy was insufficient. Between the two decisions, it became almost impossible to prosecute under the Smith Act for speech alone. Some commentators

726 DOCUMENTS OF AMERICAN CONSTITUTIONAL AND LEGAL HISTORY

have suggested that the decision in *Yates* was a belated confirmation of Learned Hand's opinion in *Masses* (Document 154).

See R. Mollen, "Smith Act Prosecutions," 26 *University of Pittsburgh Law Review* 705 (1965); and Harry Kalven, Jr., *A Worthy Tradition: Freedom of Speech in America* (1988).

———

Justice Harlan delivered the opinion of the Court:

We brought these cases here to consider certain questions arising under the Smith Act which have not heretofore been passed upon by this Court, and otherwise to review the convictions of these petitioners for conspiracy to violate that Act. Among other things, the convictions are claimed to rest upon an application of the Smith Act which is hostile to the principles upon which its constitutionality was upheld in *Dennis v. United States.* . . .

These 14 petitioners stand convicted, after a jury trial in the United States District Court for the Southern District of California, upon a single count indictment charging them with conspiring (1) to advocate and teach the duty and necessity of overthrowing the Government of the United States by force and violence, and (2) to organize, as the Communist Party of the United States, a society of persons who so advocate and teach, all with the intent of causing the overthrow of the Government by force and violence as speedily as circumstances would permit. . . .

Upon conviction each of the petitioners was sentenced to five years' imprisonment and a fine of $10,000. . . .

In the view we take of this case, it is necessary for us to consider only the following of petitioners' contentions: (1) that the term "organize" as used in the Smith Act was erroneously construed by the two lower courts; (2) that the trial court's instructions to the jury erroneously excluded from the case the issue of "incitement to action"; (3) that the evidence was so insufficient as to require this Court to direct the acquittal of these petitioners. . . . For reasons given hereafter, we conclude that these convictions must be reversed and the case remanded to the District Court with instructions to enter judgments of acquittal as to certain of the petitioners, and to grant a new trial as to the rest.

I. The Term "Organize"

One object of the conspiracy charged was to violate the third paragraph of 18 U.S.C. § 2385, which provides:

Whoever organizes or helps or attempts to organize any society, group, or assembly of persons who teach, advocate, or encourage the overthrow or destruction of any [government in the United States] by force or violence . . . [s]hall be fined not more than $10,000 or imprisoned not more than ten years, or both. . . .

———

Source: 354 U.S. 298 (1957)

Petitioners claim that "organize" means to "establish," "found," or "bring into existence," and that in this sense the Communist Party was organized by 1945 at the latest. On this basis petitioners contend that this part of the indictment, returned in 1951, was barred by the three-year statute of limitations. The Government, on the other hand, says that "organize" connotes a continuing process which goes on throughout the life of an organization, and that, in the words of the trial court's instructions to the jury, the term includes such things as "the recruiting of new members and the forming of new units, and the regrouping or expansion of existing clubs, classes and other units of any society, party, group or other organization." The two courts below accepted the Government's position. We think, however, that petitioners' position must prevail. . . .

We conclude, therefore, that since the Communist Party came into being in 1945, and the indictment was not returned until 1951, the three-year statute of limitations had run on the "organizing" charge, and required the withdrawal of that part of the indictment from the jury's consideration. . . .

II. Instructions to the Jury

Petitioners contend that the instructions to the jury were fatally defective in that the trial court refused to charge that, in order to convict, the jury must find that the advocacy which the defendants conspired to promote was of a kind calculated to "incite" persons to action for the forcible overthrow of the Government. It is argued that advocacy of forcible overthrow as mere *abstract doctrine* is within the free speech protection of the First Amendment; that the Smith Act, consistently with that constitutional provision, must be taken as proscribing only the sort of advocacy which incites to illegal *action;* and that the trial court's charge, by permitting conviction for mere advocacy, unrelated to its tendency to produce forcible action, resulted in an unconstitutional application of the Smith Act. The Government, which at the trial also requested the court to charge in terms of "incitement," now takes the position, however, that the true constitutional dividing line is not between inciting and abstract advocacy of forcible overthrow, but rather between advocacy as such, irrespective of its inciting qualities, and the mere discussion or exposition of violent overthrow as an abstract theory. . . .

There can be no doubt from the record that in so instructing the jury the court regarded as immaterial, and intended to withdraw from the jury's consideration, any issue as to the character of the advocacy in terms of its capacity to stir listeners to forcible action. Both the petitioners and the Government submitted proposed instructions which would have required the jury to find that the proscribed advocacy was not of a mere abstract doctrine of forcible overthrow, but of action to that end, by the use of language reasonably and ordinarily calculated to incite persons to such action. The trial court rejected these proposed instructions on the ground that any necessity for giving them which may have existed at the time the *Dennis* case was tried was removed by this Court's subsequent decision in that case. The court made it clear in colloquy with counsel that in its view the illegal advocacy was made out simply by showing that what was said dealt with forcible overthrow and that it was uttered with a specific intent to accomplish that purpose, insisting that all such advocacy was punishable "whether it is language of incitement or not." . . .

We are thus faced with the question whether the Smith Act prohibits advocacy and teaching of forcible overthrow as an abstract principle, divorced from any effort to instigate action to that end, so long as such advocacy or teaching is engaged in with evil intent. We hold that it does not.

The distinction between advocacy of abstract doctrine and advocacy directed at promoting unlawful action is one that has been consistently recognized in the opinions of this Court. . . .

We need not, however, decide the issue before us in terms of constitutional compulsion, for our first duty is to construe this statute. In doing so we should not assume that Congress chose to disregard a constitutional danger zone so clearly marked, or that it used the words "advocate" and "teach" in their ordinary dictionary meanings when they had already been construed as terms of art carrying a special and limited connotation. . . . The legislative history of the Smith Act and related bills shows beyond all question that Congress was aware of the distinction between the advocacy or teaching of abstract doctrine and the advocacy or teaching of action, and that it did not intend to disregard it. The statute was aimed at the advocacy and teaching of concrete action for the forcible overthrow of the Government, and not of principles divorced from action.

The Government's reliance on this Court's decision in *Dennis* is misplaced. . . .

In failing to distinguish between advocacy of forcible overthrow as an abstract doctrine and advocacy of action to that end, the District Court appears to have been led astray by the holding in *Dennis* that advocacy of violent action to be taken at some future time was enough. It seems to have considered that, since "inciting" speech is usually thought of as something calculated to induce immediate action, and since *Dennis* held advocacy of action for future overthrow sufficient, this meant that advocacy, irrespective of its tendency to generate action, is punishable, provided only that it is uttered with a specific intent to accomplish overthrow. In other words, the District Court apparently thought that *Dennis* obliterated the traditional dividing line between advocacy of abstract doctrine and advocacy of action.

This misconceives the situation confronting the Court in *Dennis* and what was held there. Although the jury's verdict, interpreted in light of the trial court's instructions, did not justify the conclusion that the defendants' advocacy was directed at, or created any danger of, immediate overthrow, it did establish that the advocacy was aimed at building up a seditious group and maintaining it in readiness for action at a propitious time. . . . That sort of advocacy, even though uttered with the hope that it may ultimately lead to violent revolution, is too remote from concrete action to be regarded as the kind of indoctrination preparatory to action which was condemned in *Dennis*. As one of the concurring opinions in *Dennis* put it:

> "Throughout our decisions there has recurred a distinction between the statement of an idea which may prompt its hearers to take unlawful action, and advocacy that such action be taken." . . .

There is nothing in *Dennis* which makes that historic distinction obsolete. . . .

In light of the foregoing we are unable to regard the District Court's charge upon this aspect of the case as adequate. The jury was never told that the Smith Act does not denounce advocacy in the sense of preaching abstractly the forcible overthrow of the Government. We think that the trial court's statement that the proscribed advocacy must include the "urging," "necessity," and "duty" of forcible overthrow, and not merely its "desirability" and "propriety," may not be regarded as a sufficient substitute for charging that the Smith Act reaches only advocacy of action for the overthrow of government by force and violence. The essential distinction is that those to whom the advocacy is addressed must be urged to *do* something, now or in the future, rather than merely to *believe* in something. . . .

We recognize that distinctions between advocacy or teaching of abstract doctrines, with evil intent, and that which is directed to stirring people to action, are often subtle and difficult to grasp, for in a broad sense, as Mr. Justice Holmes said in his dissenting opinion in *Gitlow*, . . . "Every idea is an incitement." But the very subtlety of these distinctions required the most clear and explicit instructions with reference to them, for they concerned an issue which went to the very heart of the charges against these petitioners. The need for precise and understandable instructions on this issue is further emphasized by the equivocal character of the evidence in this record, with which we deal in Part III of this opinion. Instances of speech that could be considered to amount to "advocacy of action" are so few and far between as to be almost completely overshadowed by the hundreds of instances in the record in which overthrow, if mentioned at all, occurs in the course of doctrinal disputation so remote from action as to be almost wholly lacking in probative value. Vague references to "revolutionary" or "militant" action of an unspecified character, which are found in the evidence, might in addition be given too great weight by the jury in the absence of more precise instructions. Particularly in light of this record, we must regard the trial court's charge in this respect as furnishing wholly inadequate guidance to the jury on this central point in the case. We cannot allow a conviction to stand on such "an equivocal direction to the jury on a basic issue."

199

Brown v. Board of Education (1954)

The NAACP had never accepted the legitimacy of the "separate-but-equal" rule, and in the 1940s and 1950s, it had brought a series of cases designed to show that separate facilities did not meet the equality criterion. In *McLaurin v. Oklahoma State Regents* (1950), a unanimous Court had struck down University of Oklahoma rules that had permitted McLaurin to attend classes but fenced him off from other students. The same day, the Court ruled in *Sweatt* v. *Painter* that a makeshift law school the state of Texas had created did not come near providing a facility equal to the top-of-the-line school at the University of Texas in Austin. Whatever else the justices knew about segregated facilities, they did know what made a good law school; for the first time, the Court ordered a black student admitted into a previously all-white school, even though the state had an all-black school the student could attend. The opinion gave the NAACP hope that the justices were finally ready to tackle the basic question of whether segregated facilities could in fact be equal.

In 1952, the NAACP brought five cases before the Court specifically challenging the *Plessy* doctrine. Unable to reach agreement, the Court asked the parties to reargue the cases in the October 1953 term. The justices particularly wanted both sides to discuss whether Congress in proposing the Fourteenth Amendment, and the states in ratifying it, had intended to ban racial segregation in schools.

From all reports, the Court was then divided over whether it could or should overrule *Plessy,* with Chief Justice Vinson allegedly opposed to such a radical move. But he died unexpectedly a few weeks before the reargument, and the new chief justice, Earl Warren, skillfully steered the Court to the historic and unanimous ruling that came down on May 17, 1954.

A politically astute man, Warren kept the opinion short, focused only on the plight of young black schoolchildren, and delayed implementation orders until a rehearing the following term (see the next document).

See Mark V. Tushnet, *The NAACP's Strategy Against Segregated Education, 1925–1950* (1987); Jack Greenburg, *Crusaders in the Courts* (1994); Juan Williams, *Thurgood Marshall: American Revolutionary* (1998); and especially Richard Kluger, *Simple Justice: The History of Brown v. Board of Education and Black America's Struggle for Equality* (1976).

———

Chief Justice Warren delivered the opinion of the Court:

These cases come to us from the States of Kansas, South Carolina, Virginia, and Delaware. In each of the cases, minors of the Negro race seek the aid of the courts in obtaining admission to the public schools of their community on a nonsegregated basis. In each instance, they had been denied admission to schools attended by white children under laws requiring or permitting segregation according to race. This segregation was alleged to deprive the plaintiffs of the equal protection of the laws under the 14th Amendment. . . . The plaintiffs contend that segregated public schools are not "equal" and cannot be made "equal," and that hence they are deprived of the equal protection of the laws. Argument was heard in the 1952 Term, and reargument was heard this Term on certain questions propounded by the Court.

Reargument was largely devoted to the circumstances surrounding the adoption of the 14th Amendment in 1868. It covered exhaustively consideration of the Amendment in Congress, ratification by the states, then existing practices in racial segregation, and the views of proponents and opponents of the Amendment. This discussion and our own

———

Source: 347 U.S. 483 (1954)

investigation convince us that, although these sources cast some light, it is not enough to resolve the problem with which we are faced. At best, they are inconclusive. The most avid proponents of the post-War Amendments undoubtedly intended them to remove all legal distinctions among "all persons born or naturalized in the United States." Their opponents, just as certainly, were antagonistic to both the letter and the spirit of the Amendments and wished them to have the most limited effect. What others in Congress and the state legislatures had in mind cannot be determined with any degree of certainty.

An additional reason for the inconclusive nature of the Amendment's history, with respect to segregated schools, is the status of public education at that time. In the South, the movement toward free common schools, supported by general taxation, had not yet taken hold. Education of white children was largely in the hands of private groups. Education of Negroes was almost nonexistent, and practically all of the race were illiterate. In fact, any education of Negroes was forbidden by law in some states. Today, in contrast, many Negros have achieved outstanding success in the arts and sciences as well as in the business and professional world. It is true that public school education had advanced further in the North, but the effect of the Amendment on Northern States was generally ignored in the congressional debates. Even in the North, the conditions of public education did not approximate those existing today. The curriculum was usually rudimentary; ungraded schools were common in rural areas; the school term was but three months a year in many states; and compulsory school attendance was virtually unknown. As a consequence, it is not surprising that there should be so little in the history of the 14th Amendment relating to its intended effect on public education.

In the first cases in this Court construing the 14th Amendment, decided shortly after its adoption, the Court interpreted it as proscribing all state-imposed discriminations against the Negro race. The doctrine of "separate but equal" did not make its appearance in this Court until 1896, . . . involving not education but transportation. In this Court, there have been six cases involving the "separate but equal" doctrine in the field of public education. In Cumming v. County Board of Education . . . and Gong Lum v. Rice, . . . the validity of the doctrine itself was not challenged. In more recent cases, all on the graduate school level, inequality was found in that specific benefits enjoyed by white students were denied to Negro students of the same educational qualifications. . . . In none of these cases was it necessary to reexamine the doctrine to grant relief to the Negro plaintiff. And in Sweatt v. Painter, the Court expressly reserved decision on the question whether Plessy v. Ferguson should be held inapplicable to public education. In the instant cases, that question is directly presented. Here, unlike Sweatt v. Painter, there are findings below that the Negro and white schools involved have been equalized or are being equalized, with respect to buildings, curricula, qualifications and salaries of teachers, and other "tangible" factors. Our decision, therefore, cannot turn on merely a comparison of these tangible factors in the Negro and white schools involved in each of the cases. We must look instead to the effect of segregation itself on public education.

In approaching this problem, we cannot turn the clock back to 1868 when the Amendment was adopted, or even to 1896 when Plessy was written. We must consider public education in the light of its full development and its present place in American life throughout the Nation. Only in this way can it be determined if segregation in public schools deprives these plaintiffs of the equal protection of the laws. Today, education is perhaps the most important function of state and local governments. Compulsory school attendance laws and the great expenditures for education both demonstrate our recognition of the importance of education to our democratic society. It is required in the performance of our most basic public responsibilities, even service in the armed forces. It is the very foundation of good citizenship. Today it is a principal instrument in awakening the child to cultural values, in preparing him for later professional training, and in helping him to adjust normally to his environment. In these days, it is doubtful that any child may reasonably be expected to succeed in life if he is denied the opportunity of an education. Such an opportunity, where the state has undertaken to provide it, is a right which must be made available to all on equal terms.

We come then to the question presented: Does segregation of children in public schools solely on the basis of race, even though the physical facilities and other "tangible" factors may be equal, deprive the children of the minority group of equal educational opportunities? We believe that it does. In Sweatt in finding that a segregated law school for Negroes could not provide them equal educational opportunities, this Court relied in large part on "those qualities which are incapable of objective measurement but which make for greatness in a law school." In McLaurin, the Court, in requiring that a Negro admitted to a white graduate school be treated like all other students, again resorted to intangible considerations: "[his] ability to study, to engage in discussions and exchange views with other students, and, in general, to learn his profession." Such considerations apply with added force to children in grade and high schools. To separate them from others of similar age and qualifications solely because of their race generates a feeling of inferiority as to their status in the community that may affect their hearts and minds in a way unlikely ever to be undone. The effect of this separation on their educational opportunities was well stated by a finding in the Kansas case by a court which nevertheless felt compelled to rule against the Negro plaintiffs: "Segregation of white and colored children in public schools has a detrimental effect upon the colored children. The impact is greater when it has the sanction of the law; for the policy of separating the races is usually interpreted as denoting the inferiority of the negro group. A sense of inferiority affects the motivation of a child to learn. Segregation with the sanction of law, therefore, has a tendency to retard the educational and mental development of negro children and to deprive them of some of the benefits they would receive in a [racially] integrated school system." Whatever may have been the extent of psychological knowledge at the time of Plessy v. Ferguson, this finding is amply supported by modern authority. Any language in Plessy v. Ferguson contrary to this finding is rejected.

We conclude that in the field of public education the doctrine of "separate but equal" has no place. Separate educational facilities are inherently unequal. Therefore, we hold that the plaintiffs and others similarly situated for whom the actions have been brought are, by reason of the segregation complained of, deprived of the equal protection of the laws guaranteed by the 14th Amendment. This disposition makes unnecessary any discussion whether such segregation also violates the Due Process Clause of the 14th Amendment. Because these are class actions, because of the wide applicability of this decision, and because of the great variety of local conditions, the formulation of decrees in these cases presents problems of considerable complexity. On reargument, the consideration of appropriate relief was necessarily subordinated to the primary question—the constitutionality of segregation in public education. We have now announced that such segregation is a denial of the equal protection of the laws. In order that we may have the full assistance of the parties in formulating decrees, the cases will be restored to the docket, and the parties are requested to present further argument. . . .

It is so ordered.

200

Brown v. Board of Education II (1955)

Following *Brown I,* the Court asked the parties to the original suits to reargue what methods the Court should use to implement the decision. It also invited amicus briefs from the federal government and from all states that had segregated schools. The NAACP pushed for full integration in the shortest possible time; Southern states, on the other hand, urged the Court to face "reality" and to go slowly—very slowly. The federal government urged a middle position between "integration now" and "segregation forever."

The Court pretty much followed the federal government's proposal that integration had to begin with states submitting timetables, but it left oversight to federal district courts, which, exercising their traditional powers of equity, could make adjustments, when necessary. Desegregation, however, had to begin and proceed "with all deliberate speed."

See sources listed for previous document, as well as Daniel M. Berman, *It Is So Ordered* (1966); and Numan V. Bartley, *The Rise of Massive Resistance* (1969).

Chief Justice Warren delivered the opinion of the Court:

These cases were decided on May 17, 1954. The opinions of that date, declaring the fundamental principle that racial discrimination in public education is unconstitutional, are incorporated herein by reference. All provisions of federal, state, or local law requiring or permitting such discrimination must yield to this principle. There remains for consideration the manner in which relief is to be accorded. Because these cases arose under different local conditions and their disposition will involve a variety of local problems, we requested further argument on the question of relief. In view of the nationwide importance of the decision, we invited the Attorney General of the United States and the Attorneys General of all states requiring or permitting racial discrimination in public

---

Source: 349 U.S. 294 (1955)

education to present their views on that question. The parties, the United States, and the States of Florida, North Carolina, Arkansas, Oklahoma, Maryland, and Texas filed briefs and participated in the oral argument. . . .

Full implementation of these constitutional principles may require solution of varied local school problems. School authorities have the primary responsibility for elucidating, assessing, and solving these problems; courts will have to consider whether the action of school authorities constitutes good faith implementation of the governing constitutional principles. Because of their proximity to local conditions and the possible need for further hearings, the courts which originally heard these cases can best perform this judicial appraisal. Accordingly, we believe it appropriate to remand the cases to those courts.

In fashioning and effectuating the decrees, the courts will be guided by equitable principles. Traditionally, equity has been characterized by a practical flexibility in shaping its remedies and by a facility for adjusting and reconciling public and private needs. These cases call for the exercise of these traditional attributes of equity power. At stake is the personal interest of the plaintiffs in admission to public schools as soon as practicable on a nondiscriminatory basis. To effectuate this interest may call for elimination of a variety of obstacles in making the transition to school systems operated in accordance with the constitutional principles set forth in our May 17, 1954, decision. Courts of equity may properly take into account the public interest in the elimination of such obstacles in a systematic and effective manner. But it should go without saying that the vitality of these constitutional principles cannot be allowed to yield simply because of disagreement with them.

While giving weight to these public and private considerations, the courts will require that the defendants make a prompt and reasonable start toward full compliance with our May 17, 1954, ruling. Once such a start has been made, the courts may find that additional time is necessary to carry out the ruling in an effective manner. The burden rests upon the defendants to establish that such time is necessary in the public interest and is consistent with good faith compliance at the earliest practicable date. To that end, the courts may consider problems related to administration, arising from the physical condition of the school plant, the school transportation system, personnel, revision of school districts and attendance areas into compact units to achieve a system of determining admission to the public schools on a nonracial basis, and revision of local laws and regulations which may be necessary in solving the foregoing problems. They will also consider the adequacy of any plans the defendants may propose to meet these problems and to effectuate a transition to a racially nondiscriminatory school system. During this period of transition, the courts will retain jurisdiction of these cases. The . . . lower courts are to take such proceedings and enter such orders and decrees consistent with this opinion as are necessary and proper to admit to public schools on a racially nondiscriminatory basis with all deliberate speed the parties to these cases.

201

Southern Manifesto on Integration (1956)

Initial Southern reaction to *Brown* was moderate, but within a short time critics mounted a full-scale assault against the decision. Legal scholars attacked the reasoning, claiming the Fourteenth Amendment had never intended blacks to be equal to whites; sociologists denounced the studies the Court had utilized to justify its assertion that segregation harmed black children. White Citizens Councils spread across the South, claiming 500,000 members in eleven states, and Southern political leaders began to resurrect theories of states' rights. Harry Byrd of Virginia called for "massive resistance," the Alabama legislature declared it had the power of "interposition" to protect its citizens from unlawful federal activity, and although South Carolina avoided using the word "nullification," it too passed a resolution that in effect tried to nullify *Brown.*

One of the most powerful protests against the desegregation decisions came when 101 members of Congress, including all but three of the senators from the former Confederate states, signed the belligerent Southern Manifesto. In it they set out the main constitutional objections to *Brown,* including matters of original intent, historic tradition, states' rights, and the limited nature of the federal government, especially the judiciary.

See Neil R. McMillen, *The Citizens Council* (1971); James F. Byrnes, "The Supreme Court Must Be Curbed," *U.S. News* (May 18, 1956); Numan V. Bartley, *The Rise of Massive Resistance* (1969); and Benjamin Muse, *Ten Years of Prelude* (1964).

———

We regard the decision of the Supreme Court in the school cases as clear abuse of judicial power. It climaxes a trend in the Federal judiciary undertaking to legislate, in derogation of the authority of Congress, and to encroach upon the reserved rights of the states and the people.

The original Constitution does not mention education. Neither does the Fourteenth Amendment nor any other amendment. The debates preceding the submission of the Fourteenth Amendment clearly show that there was no intent that it should affect the systems of education maintained by the states.

The very Congress which proposed the amendment subsequently provided for segregated schools in the District of Columbia.

Source: New York Times, March 12, 1956

When the amendment was adopted in 1868, there were thirty-seven states of the Union. Every one of the twenty-six states that had any substantial racial differences among its people either approved the operation of segregated schools already in existence or subsequently established such schools by action of the same law-making body which considered the Fourteenth Amendment.

As admitted by the Supreme Court in the public school case (Brown v. Board of Education), the doctrine of separate but equal schools "apparently originated in Roberts v. City of Boston (1849), upholding school segregation against attack as being violative of a state constitutional guarantee of equality." This constitutional doctrine began in the North—not in the South—and it was followed not only in Massachusetts but in Connecticut, New York, Illinois, Indiana, Michigan, Minnesota, New Jersey, Ohio, Pennsylvania and other northern states until they, exercising their rights as states through the constitutional processes of local self-government, changed their school systems.

In the case of Plessy v. Ferguson in 1896 the Supreme Court expressly declared that under the Fourteenth Amendment no person was denied any of his rights if the states provided separate but equal public facilities. This decision has been followed in many other cases. It is notable that the Supreme Court, speaking through Chief Justice Taft, a former President of the United States, unanimously declared in 1927 in Lum v. Rice that the "separate but equal" principle is " . . . within the discretion of the state in regulating its public schools and does not conflict with the Fourteenth Amendment."

This interpretation, restated time and again, became a part of the life of the people of many of the states and confirmed their habits, customs, traditions and way of life. It is founded on elemental humanity and common sense, for parents should not be deprived by Government of the right to direct the lives and education of their own children.

Though there has been no constitutional amendment or act of Congress changing this established legal principle almost a century old, the Supreme Court of the United States, with no legal basis for such action, undertook to exercise their naked judicial power and substituted their personal political and social ideas for the established law of the land.

This unwarranted exercise of power by the court, contrary to the Constitution, is creating chaos and confusion in the states principally affected. It is destroying the amicable relations between the white and Negro races that have been created through ninety years of patient effort by the good people of both races. It has planted hatred and suspicion where there has been heretofore friendship and understanding.

Without regard to the consent of the governed, outside agitators are threatening immediate and revolutionary changes in our public school systems. If done, this is certain to destroy the system of public education in some of the states.

With the gravest concern for the explosive and dangerous condition created by this decision and inflamed by outside meddlers:

We reaffirm our reliance on the Constitution as the fundamental law of the land.

We decry the Supreme Court's encroachments on rights reserved to the states and to the people, contrary to established law and to the Constitution.

We commend the motives of those states which have declared the intention to resist forced integration by any lawful means.

We appeal to the states and people who are not directly affected by these decisions to consider the constitutional principles involved against the time when they too, on issues vital to them, may be the victims of judicial encroachment.

Even though we constitute a minority in the present Congress, we have full faith that a majority of the American people believe in the dual system of government which has enabled us to achieve our greatness and will in time demand that the reserved rights of the states and of the people be made secure against judicial usurpation.

We pledge ourselves to use all lawful means to bring about a reversal of this decision which is contrary to the Constitution and to prevent the use of force in its implementation.

In this trying period, as we all seek to right this wrong, we appeal to our people not to be provoked by the agitators and troublemakers invading our states and to scrupulously refrain from disorder and lawless acts.

---

202 *Cooper v. Aaron (1958)*

In the fall of 1957, the Little Rock, Arkansas, school board agreed to abide by a court order to admit nine black students to Central High School. Governor Orville Faubus, who had previously acted moderately in regard to desegregation, decided to cast his lot with the hard-line opposition and called out the National Guard to prevent integration. Faubus withdrew the troops following another court order, but when black students attempted to enroll in Central High, a mob attacked the school and drove them off. President Dwight Eisenhower, who had tried to keep his administration out of the desegregation controversy, was forced to act in the light of open defiance of a federal court order. He federalized the Arkansas National Guard and ordered in a thousand paratroopers to Little Rock to maintain order.

The Supreme Court had been silent since *Brown II,* preferring to let the Southern states attempt to work out peaceful desegregation under the oversight of the lower federal courts. It now decided that it should once again reassert the unconstitutionality of segregation, and as it did throughout the Warren years, it spoke in one voice. In an opinion signed by all nine justices, the Court not only reaffirmed the *Brown* ruling, but reasserted its own role as ultimate arbiter of the Constitution.

See Tony Freyer, *The Little Rock Crisis: A Constitutional Interpretation* (1984); and Benjamin Muse, *Ten Years of Prelude* (1964).

Opinion of the Court by the Chief Justice and Justices Black, Frankfurter, Douglas, Burton, Clark, Harlan, Brennan, and Whittaker.

As this case reaches us it raises questions of the highest importance to the maintenance of our federal system of government. It necessarily involves a claim by the Governor and Legislature of a State that there is no duty on state officials to obey federal court orders resting on this Court's considered interpretation of the United States Constitution. Specifically it involves actions by the Governor and Legislature of Arkansas upon the premise that they are not bound by our holding in *Brown v. Board of Education*. . . . That holding was that the Fourteenth Amendment forbids States to use their governmental powers to bar children on racial grounds from attending schools where there is state participation through any arrangement, management, funds or property. We are urged to uphold a suspension of the Little Rock School Board's plan to do away with segregated public schools in Little Rock until state laws and efforts to upset and nullify our holding in *Brown v. Board of Education* have been further challenged and tested in the courts. We reject these contentions.

The case was argued before us on September 11, 1958. On the following day we unanimously affirmed the judgment of the Court of Appeals for the Eighth Circuit, . . . which had reversed a judgment of the District Court for the Eastern District of Arkansas. . . . The District Court had granted the application of the petitioners, the Little Rock School Board and School Superintendent, to suspend for two and one-half years the operation of the School Board's court-approved desegregation program. In order that the School Board might know, without doubt, its duty in this regard before the opening of school, which had been set for the following Monday, September 15, 1958, we immediately issued the judgment, reserving the expression of our supporting views to a later date. This opinion of all of the members of the Court embodies those views. . . .

In affirming the judgment of the Court of Appeals which reversed the District Court we have accepted without reservation the position of the School Board, the Superintendent of Schools, and their counsel that they displayed entire good faith in the conduct of these proceedings and in dealing with the unfortunate and distressing sequence of events which has been outlined. We likewise have accepted the findings of the District Court as to the conditions at Central High School during the 1957–1958 school year, and also the findings that the educational progress of all the students, white and colored, of that school has suffered and will continue to suffer if the conditions which prevailed last year are permitted to continue.

The significance of these findings, however, is to be considered in light of the fact, indisputably revealed by the record before us, that the conditions they depict are directly traceable to the actions of legislators and executive officials of the State of Arkansas, taken in their official capacities, which reflect their own determination to resist this Court's decision in the *Brown* case and which have brought about violent resistance to that decision in Arkansas. In its petition for certiorari filed in this Court, the School Board itself describes the situation in this language: "The legislative, executive, and judicial departments of the state government opposed the desegregation of Little Rock schools by enacting laws, calling out troops, making statements villifying federal law

Source: 358 U.S. 1 (1958)

and federal courts, and failing to utilize state law enforcement agencies and judicial processes to maintain public peace."

One may well sympathize with the position of the Board in the face of the frustrating conditions which have confronted it, but, regardless of the Board's good faith, the actions of the other state agencies responsible for those conditions compel us to reject the Board's legal position. Had Central High School been under the direct management of the State itself, it could hardly be suggested that those immediately in charge of the school should be heard to assert their own good faith as a legal excuse for delay in implementing the constitutional rights of these respondents, when vindication of those rights was rendered difficult or impossible by the actions of other state officials. The situation here is in no different posture because the members of the School Board and the Superintendent of Schools are local officials; from the point of view of the Fourteenth Amendment, they stand in this litigation as the agents of the State.

The constitutional rights of respondents are not to be sacrificed or yielded to the violence and disorder which have followed upon the actions of the Governor and Legislature. As this Court said some 41 years ago in a unanimous opinion in a case involving another aspect of racial segregation: "It is urged that this proposed segregation will promote the public peace by preventing race conflicts. Desirable as this is, and important as is the preservation of the public peace, this aim cannot be accomplished by laws or ordinances which deny rights created or protected by the Federal Constitution." *Buchanan v. Warley* . . . Thus law and order are not here to be preserved by depriving the Negro children of their constitutional rights. The record before us clearly establishes that the growth of the Board's difficulties to a magnitude beyond its unaided power to control is the product of state action. Those difficulties, as counsel for the Board forthrightly conceded on the oral argument in this Court, can also be brought under control by state action.

The controlling legal principles are plain. The command of the Fourteenth Amendment is that no "State" shall deny to any person within its jurisdiction the equal protection of the laws. . . .

What has been said, in the light of the facts developed, is enough to dispose of the case. However, we should answer the premise of the actions of the Governor and Legislature that they are not bound by our holding in the *Brown* case. It is necessary only to recall some basic constitutional propositions which are settled doctrine.

Article VI of the Constitution makes the Constitution the "supreme Law of the Land." In 1803, Chief Justice Marshall, speaking for a unanimous Court, referring to the Constitution as "the fundamental and paramount law of the nation," declared in the notable case of *Marbury v. Madison,* 1 Cranch 137, 177, that "It is emphatically the province and duty of the judicial department to say what the law is." This decision declared the basic principle that the federal judiciary is supreme in the exposition of the law of the Constitution, and that principle has ever since been respected by this Court and the Country as a permanent and indispensable feature of our constitutional system. It follows that the interpretation of the Fourteenth Amendment enunciated by this Court in the *Brown* case is the supreme law of the land, and Art. VI of the Constitution makes it of binding effect on the States "any Thing in the Constitution or Laws of any State to the Contrary notwithstanding." Every state legislator and executive and judicial officer is solemnly committed by oath taken pursuant to Art. VI, cl. 3, "to support this Constitution." . . .

No state legislator or executive or judicial officer can war against the Constitution without violating his undertaking to support it. Chief Justice Marshall spoke for a unanimous Court in saying that: "If the legislatures of the several states may, at will, annul the judgments of the courts of the United States, and destroy the rights acquired under those judgments, the constitution itself becomes a solemn mockery . . ." *United States v. Peters.* . . . A Governor who asserts a power to nullify a federal court order is similarly restrained. If he had such power, said Chief Justice Hughes, in 1932, also for a unanimous Court, "it is manifest that the fiat of a state Governor, and not the Constitution of the United States, would be the supreme law of the land; that the restrictions of the Federal Constitution upon the exercise of state power would be but impotent phrases . . ." *Sterling v. Constantin.* . . .

It is, of course, quite true that the responsibility for public education is primarily the concern of the States, but it is equally true that such responsibilities, like all other state activity, must be exercised consistently with federal constitutional requirements as they apply to state action. The Constitution created a government dedicated to equal justice under law. The Fourteenth Amendment embodied and emphasized that ideal. State support of segregated schools through any arrangement, management, funds, or property cannot be squared with the amendment's command that no State shall deny to any person within its jurisdiction the equal protection of the laws. The right of a student not to be segregated on racial grounds in schools so maintained is indeed so fundamental and pervasive that it is embraced in the concept of due process of law. . . . The basic decision in *Brown* was unanimously reached by this Court only after the case had been briefed and twice argued and the issues had been given the most serious consideration. Since the first *Brown* opinion three new Justices have come to the Court. They are at one with the Justices still on the Court who participated in that basic decision as to its correctness, and that decision is now unanimously reaffirmed. The principles announced in that decision and the obedience of the States to them, according to the command of the Constitution, are indispensable for the protection of the freedom guaranteed by our fundamental charter for all of us. Our constitutional ideal of equal justice under law is thus made a living truth.

203   *Mapp v. Ohio (1961)*

Following the introduction of the exclusionary rule in *Weeks* (Document 150), the Supreme Court had applied the rule only to exclude illegally seized evidence from use in federal trials. The issue of its use in state trials arose in *Wolf v. Colorado* (1949), but Justice Frankfurter there expounded a doctrine of selective incorporation, and the Court refused to apply the rule to the states.

This was the state of the law when Ohio police raided Dolltree Mapp's apartment without a warrant and during the search accidentally discovered pornographic materials, for possession of which she was later indicted and convicted. When the case came up to the Supreme Court, both sides of the litigation saw it as a First Amendment case, and neither side briefed nor argued the exclusionary rule. But between *Wolf* and *Mapp*, six new members had come onto the bench, and several of them joined with the *Wolf* minority to apply the exclusionary rule, for the first time, to the states.

See Roger Traynor, "*Mapp v. Ohio* at Large in the 50 States," 1962 *Duke Law Journal* 319 (1962); Fred Graham, *The Due Process Revolution: The Warren Court's Impact on Criminal Law* (1970); R. E. Burns, "*Mapp v. Ohio:* An All-American Mistake," 19 *DePaul Law Review* 80 (1969); and P. E. Wilson, "Perspective on *Mapp v. Ohio*," 11 *University of Kansas Law Review* 423 (1963).

———

Justice Clark delivered the opinion of the Court:

[I]n the year 1914, in the *Weeks* case, this Court "for the first time" held that "in a federal prosecution the Fourth Amendment barred the use of evidence secured through an illegal search and seizure." This Court has ever since required of federal law officers a strict adherence to that command which this Court has held to be a clear, specific, and constitutionally required—even if judicially implied—deterrent safeguard without insistence upon which the Fourth Amendment would have been reduced to "a form of words." It meant, quite simply, that "conviction by means of unlawful seizures and enforced confessions . . . should find no sanction in the judgments of the courts," . . . Weeks v. United States . . . and that such evidence "shall not be used at all." Silverthorne Lumber Co. v. United States. . . .

. . . In Byars v. United States . . . (1927), a unanimous Court declared that "the doctrine [cannot] . . . be tolerated *under our constitutional system,* that evidences of crime discovered by a federal officer in making a search without lawful warrant may be used against the victim of the unlawful search where a timely challenge has been interposed." . . .

. . . Only last Term, after again carefully re-examining the *Wolf* doctrine in Elkins v. United States, the Court pointed out that "the controlling principles" as to search and seizure and the problem of admissibility "seemed clear" until the announcement in *Wolf* "that the Due Process Clause of the Fourteenth Amendment does not itself require state courts to adopt the exclusionary rule" of the *Weeks* case. At the same time, the Court pointed out, "the underlying constitutional doctrine which *Wolf* established . . . that the Federal Constitution . . . prohibits unreasonable searches and seizures by state officers" had undermined the "foundation upon which the admissibility of state seized evidence in a federal trial originally rested. . . ." The Court concluded that it was therefore obliged to hold, although it chose the narrower ground on which to do so, that all evidence obtained by an unconstitutional search and seizure was inadmissible in a federal court

Source: 367 U.S. 643 (1961)

regardless of its source. Today we once again examine *Wolf's* constitutional documentation of the right to privacy free from unreasonable state intrusion, and, after its dozen years on our books, are led by it to close the only courtroom door remaining open to evidence secured by official lawlessness in flagrant abuse of that basic right, reserved to all persons as a specific guarantee against that very same unlawful conduct. We hold that all evidence obtained by searches and seizures in violation of the Constitution is, by that same authority, inadmissible in a state court.

Since the Fourth Amendment's right of privacy has been declared enforceable against the States through the Due Process Clause of the Fourteenth, it is enforceable against them by the same sanction of exclusion as is used against the Federal Government. Were it otherwise, then just as without the *Weeks* rule the assurance against unreasonable federal searches and seizures would be "a form of words," valueless and undeserving of mention in a perpetual charter of inestimable human liberties, so too, without that rule the freedom from state invasions of privacy would be so ephemeral and so neatly severed from its conceptual nexus with the freedom from all brutish means of coercing evidence as not to merit this Court's high regard as a freedom "implicit in the concept of ordered liberty." . . .

. . . This Court has not hesitated to enforce as strictly against the States as it does against the Federal Government the rights of free speech and of a free press, the rights to notice and to a fair, public trial, including, as it does, the right not to be convicted by use of a coerced confession, however logically relevant it be, and without regard to its reliability. And nothing could be more certain than that when a coerced confession is involved, "the relevant rules of evidence" are overridden without regard to "the incidence of such conduct by the police," slight or frequent. Why should not the same rule apply to what is tantamount to coerced testimony by way of unconstitutional seizure of goods, papers, effects, documents, etc.? . . .

Moreover, our holding that the exclusionary rule is an essential part of both the Fourth and Fourteenth Amendments is not only the logical dictate of prior cases, but it also makes very good sense. There is no war between the Constitution and common sense. Presently, a federal prosecutor may make no use of evidence illegally seized, but a State's attorney across the street may, although he supposedly is operating under the enforceable prohibitions of the same Amendment. Thus the State, by admitting evidence unlawfully seized, serves to encourage disobedience to the Federal Constitution which it is bound to uphold. Moreover, as was said in *Elkins,* "[t]he very essence of a healthy federalism depends upon the avoidance of needless conflict between state and federal courts." . . .

There are those who say, as did Justice (then Judge) Cardozo, that under our constitutional exclusionary doctrine "[t]he criminal is to go free because the constable has blundered." . . . In some cases this will undoubtedly be the result. But, as was said in *Elkins,* "there is another consideration—the imperative of judicial integrity." . . . The criminal goes free, if he must, but it is the law that sets him free. Nothing can destroy a government more quickly than its failure to observe its own laws, or worse, its disregard of the charter of its own existence. As Mr. Justice Brandeis, dissenting, said in Olmstead v. United States, 277 U.S. 438, 485 (1928): "Our Government is the potent, the omnipresent teacher. For good or for ill, it teaches the whole people by its example. . . . If the Government becomes a lawbreaker, it breeds contempt for law; it invites every man to become a law unto himself; it invites anarchy."

---

204 *Baker v. Carr (1962)*

The Constitution assigns two senators to each state, and a number of representatives according to the state's share of the total population determined in the decennial census, but it is silent as to how these representatives are to be assigned within each state. James Madison had implied that the arrangements should be equitable, and many states did in fact periodically redraw their congressional as well as state assembly district lines to ensure rough equity among the voters.

But twelve states had not redrawn their lines for more than three decades; Alabama had not reapportioned its legislature since 1901, and Delaware since 1897. A minority of the voters could thus block majority will and could not even be forced to redistrict. In *Colgrove v. Green* (1946) the Court rejected an appeal from Illinois voters to mandate reapportionment under the Guaranty Clause of the Constitution (Article IV, Section 4). Justice Frankfurter labeled the matter a "political question" and declared the requested relief beyond the Court's "competence to grant."

The first hint of change came in *Gomillion v. Lightfoot* (1960), when Justice Frankfurter, relying solely on the Fifteenth Amendment, struck down a blatant gerrymander scheme in Alabama designed to disenfranchise black voters. Frankfurter, however, carefully avoided implying that the case had any relation to issues of reapportionment. Nonetheless two years later, the Court accepted jurisdiction in this case, brought by urban voters in Tennessee, where there had been no redistricting since 1901, despite a provision in the state constitution requiring reapportionment every ten years.

In his decision for a six-to-two majority, Justice Brennan ruled only that questions of reapportionment were in fact justiciable and therefore could be entertained by the courts, thus overruling *Colgrove*. But he then referred the issue to the district court for adjudication and remedy, in much the same fashion as the high court had delegated responsibility for implementing *Brown* to the lower courts. It would be only a matter of time, however, before the Court would be asked to review the lower courts' orders (see Document 207).

See Richard C. Cortner, *The Apportionment Cases* (1970); Robert G. Dixon, Jr., *Democratic Representation: Representative Reapportionment in Law and Politics* (1968); and

Robert McKay, "Reapportionment: Success Story of the Warren Court," 67 *Michigan Law Review* 223 (1968).

———

Justice Brennan delivered the opinion of the Court:

This civil action was brought under 42 U. S. C. §§ 1983 and 1988 to redress the alleged deprivation of federal constitutional rights. The complaint, alleging that by means of a 1901 statute of Tennessee apportioning the members of the General Assembly among the State's 95 counties, "these plaintiffs and others similarly situated, are denied the equal protection of the laws accorded them by the Fourteenth Amendment to the Constitution of the United States by virtue of the debasement of their votes," was dismissed by a three-judge court convened under 28 U. S. C. § 2281 in the Middle District of Tennessee. The court held that it lacked jurisdiction of the subject matter and also that no claim was stated upon which relief could be granted. . . . We noted probable jurisdiction of the appeal. . . . We hold that the dismissal was error, and remand the cause to the District Court for trial and further proceedings consistent with this opinion. . . .

Tennessee's standard for allocating legislative representation among her counties is the total number of qualified voters resident in the respective counties, subject only to minor qualifications. Decennial reapportionment in compliance with the constitutional scheme was effected by the General Assembly each decade from 1871 to 1901. The 1871 apportionment was preceded by an 1870 statute requiring an enumeration. The 1881 apportionment involved three statutes, the first authorizing an enumeration, the second enlarging the Senate from 25 to 33 members and the House from 75 to 99 members, and the third apportioning the membership of both Houses. In 1891 there were both an enumeration and an apportionment. In 1901 the General Assembly abandoned separate enumeration in favor of reliance upon the Federal Census and passed the Apportionment Act here in controversy. In the more than 60 years since that action, all proposals in both Houses of the General Assembly for reapportionment have failed to pass. . . .

Jurisdiction of the Subject Matter

The District Court was uncertain whether our cases withholding federal judicial relief rested upon a lack of federal jurisdiction or upon the inappropriateness of the subject matter for judicial consideration—what we have designated "nonjusticiability." The distinction between the two grounds is significant. In the instance of nonjusticiability, consideration of the cause is not wholly and immediately foreclosed; rather, the Court's inquiry necessarily proceeds to the point of deciding whether the duty asserted can be judicially identified and its breach judicially determined, and whether protection for the right asserted can be judicially molded. In the instance of lack of jurisdiction the cause either does not "arise under" the Federal Constitution, laws or treaties (or fall within one

Source: 369 U.S. 186 (1962)

of the other enumerated categories of Art. III, § 2), or is not a "case or controversy" within the meaning of that section; or the cause is not one described by any jurisdictional statute. Our conclusion . . . that this cause presents no nonjusticiable "political question" settles the only possible doubt that it is a case or controversy. Under the present heading of "Jurisdiction of the Subject Matter" we hold only that the matter set forth in the complaint does arise under the Constitution and is within 28 U. S. C. § 1343.

Article III, § 2, of the Federal Constitution provides that "The judicial Power shall extend to all Cases, in Law and Equity, arising under this Constitution, the Laws of the United States, and Treaties made, or which shall be made, under their Authority. . . ." It is clear that the cause of action is one which "arises under" the Federal Constitution. The complaint alleges that the 1901 statute effects an apportionment that deprives the appellants of the equal protection of the laws in violation of the Fourteenth Amendment. . . .

The appellees refer to *Colegrove v. Green,* 328 U.S. 549, as authority that the District Court lacked jurisdiction of the subject matter. Appellees misconceive the holding of that case. The holding was precisely contrary to their reading of it. Seven members of the Court participated in the decision. Unlike many other cases in this field which have assumed without discussion that there was jurisdiction, all three opinions filed in *Colegrove* discussed the question. Two of the opinions expressing the views of four of the Justices, a majority, flatly held that there was jurisdiction of the subject matter. Mr. Justice Black joined by Mr. Justice Douglas and Mr. Justice Murphy stated: "It is my judgment that the District Court had jurisdiction. . . ." Mr. Justice Rutledge, writing separately, expressed agreement with this conclusion. . . .

We hold that the District Court has jurisdiction of the subject matter of the federal constitutional claim asserted in the complaint.

Justiciability

The mere fact that the suit seeks protection of a political right does not mean it presents a political question. Such an objection "is little more than a play upon words." . . .

Our discussion, even at the price of extending this opinion, requires review of a number of political question cases, in order to expose the attributes of the doctrine — attributes which, in various settings, diverge, combine, appear, and disappear in seeming disorderliness. . . . That review reveals that in the Guaranty Clause cases and in the other "political question" cases, it is the relationship between the judiciary and the coordinate branches of the Federal Government, and not the federal judiciary's relationship to the States, which gives rise to the "political question."

We have said that "In determining whether a question falls within [the political question] category, the appropriateness under our system of government of attributing finality to the action of the political departments and also the lack of satisfactory criteria for a judicial determination are dominant considerations." *Coleman v. Miller,* 307 U.S. 433, 454–455. The nonjusticiability of a political question is primarily a function of the separation of powers. Much confusion results from the capacity of the "political question" label to obscure the need for case-by-case inquiry. Deciding whether a matter has in any measure been committed by the Constitution to another branch of government, or whether the action of that branch exceeds whatever authority has been committed, is itself a delicate exercise in constitutional interpretation, and is a responsibility of this Court as ultimate interpreter of the Constitution. To demonstrate this requires no less than to analyze representative cases and to infer from them the analytical threads that make up the political question doctrine. . . .

We come, finally, to the ultimate inquiry whether our precedents as to what constitutes a nonjusticiable "political question" bring the case before us under the umbrella of that doctrine. A natural beginning is to note whether any of the common characteristics which we have been able to identify and label descriptively are present. We find none: The question here is the consistency of state action with the Federal Constitution. We have no question decided, or to be decided, by a political branch of government coequal with this Court. Nor do we risk embarrassment of our government abroad, or grave disturbance at home if we take issue with Tennessee as to the constitutionality of her action here challenged. Nor need the appellants, in order to succeed in this action, ask the Court to enter upon policy determinations for which judicially manageable standards are lacking. Judicial standards under the Equal Protection Clause are well developed and familiar, and it has been open to courts since the enactment of the Fourteenth Amendment to determine, if on the particular facts they must, that a discrimination reflects *no* policy, but simply arbitrary and capricious action. . . .

We conclude that the complaint's allegations of a denial of equal protection present a justiciable constitutional cause of action upon which appellants are entitled to a trial and a decision. The right asserted is within the reach of judicial protection under the Fourteenth Amendment.

The judgment of the District Court is reversed and the cause is remanded for further proceedings consistent with this opinion.

Justice Frankfurter, whom Justice Harlan joined, dissenting:

The Court today reverses a uniform course of decision established by a dozen cases, including one by which the very claim now sustained was unanimously rejected only five years ago. The impressive body of rulings thus cast aside reflected the equally uniform course of our political history regarding the relationship between population and legislative representation—a wholly different matter from denial of the franchise to individuals because of race, color, religion or sex. Such a massive repudiation of the experience of our whole past in asserting destructively novel judicial power demands a detailed analysis of the role of this Court in our constitutional scheme. Disregard of inherent limits in the effective exercise of the Court's "judicial Power" not only presages the futility of judicial intervention in the essentially political conflict of forces by which the relation between population and representation has time out of mind been and now is determined. It may well impair the Court's position as the ultimate organ of "the supreme Law of the Land" in that vast range of legal problems, often strongly entangled in popular feeling, on which this Court must pronounce. The Court's authority—possessed neither of the purse nor the sword—ultimately rests on sustained public confidence in its moral sanction. Such feeling must be nourished by the Court's complete detachment, in fact and in appearance, from political entanglements and by abstention from injecting itself into the clash of political forces in political settlements.

A hypothetical claim resting on abstract assumptions is now for the first time made the basis for affording illusory relief for a particular evil even though it foreshadows deeper and more pervasive difficulties in consequence. The claim is hypothetical and the assumptions are abstract because the Court does not vouchsafe the lower courts—state and federal—guidelines for formulating specific, definite, wholly unprecedented remedies for the inevitable litigations that today's umbrageous disposition is bound to stimulate in connection with politically motivated reapportionments in so many States. In such a setting, to promulgate jurisdiction in the abstract is meaningless. It is devoid of reality as "a brooding omnipresence in the sky" for it conveys no intimation what relief, if any, a District Court is capable of affording that would not invite legislatures to play ducks and drakes with the judiciary. For this Court to direct the District Court to enforce a claim to which the Court has over the years consistently found itself required to deny legal enforcement and at the same time to find it necessary to withhold any guidance to the lower court how to enforce this turnabout, new legal claim, manifests an odd— indeed an esoteric—conception of judicial propriety. One of the Court's supporting opinions, as elucidated by commentary, unwittingly affords a disheartening preview of the mathematical quagmire (apart from diverse judicially inappropriate and elusive determinants), into which this Court today catapults the lower courts of the country without so much as adumbrating the basis for a legal calculus as a means of extrication. Even assuming the indispensable intellectual disinterestedness on the part of judges in such matters, they do not have accepted legal standards or criteria or even reliable analogies to draw upon for making judicial judgments. To charge courts with the task of accommodating the incommensurable factors of policy that underlie these mathematical puzzles is to attribute, however flatteringly, omnicompetence to judges. The Framers of the Constitution persistently rejected a proposal that embodied this assumption.

---

205   *Engel v. Vitale (1962)*

New York public schools opened each school day with a prayer, a "nonsectarian" prayer composed by the Board of Regents. Other states and localities used other invocations, such as the Lord's Prayer, or in some cases borrowed from sectarian services. In *Engel,* the Court ruled that any mandatory prayer violated the First Amendment's ban on an establishment of religion.

The decision created a huge uproar, because many Americans had become used to beginning school days and public functions with a prayer. Many people, and nearly all the mainstream religious groups, accepted Justice Black's argument that a prescribed prayer violated the Establishment Clause, but many fundamentalist sects did not. They claimed that there had always been a national commitment to prayer. Now the Court had banned God from the schools, and they intended to use all possible means to get around the ruling.

See Frank J. Sorauf, *The Wall of Separation* (1976); John H. Laubach, *School Prayers: Congress, the Court, and the Public* (1969); and Kenneth M. Dolbeare and Phillip E. Hammond, *The School Prayer Decision: From Court Policy to Local Practice* (1970).

———

Justice Black delivered the opinion of the Court:

The respondent Board of Education of Union Free School District No. 9, New Hyde Park, New York, acting in its official capacity under state law, directed the School District's principal to cause the following prayer to be said aloud by each class in the presence of a teacher at the beginning of each school day:

"Almighty God, we acknowledge our dependence upon Thee, and we beg Thy blessings upon us, our parents, our teachers and our Country."

This daily procedure was adopted on the recommendation of the State Board of Regents, a governmental agency created by the State Constitution to which the New York Legislature has granted broad supervisory, executive, and legislative powers over the State's public school system. These state officials composed the prayer which they recommended and published as a part of their "Statement on Moral and Spiritual Training in the Schools," saying: "We believe that this Statement will be subscribed to by all men and women of good will, and we call upon all of them to aid in giving life to our program." . . .

We think that by using its public school system to encourage recitation of the Regents' prayer, the State of New York has adopted a practice wholly inconsistent with the Establishment Clause. There can, of course, be no doubt that New York's program of daily classroom invocation of God's blessings as prescribed in the Regents' prayer is a religious activity. It is a solemn avowal of divine faith and supplication for the blessings of the Almighty. The nature of such a prayer has always been religious, none of the respondents has denied this and the trial court expressly so found. . . .

The petitioners contend among other things that the state laws requiring or permitting use of the Regents' prayer must be struck down as a violation of the Establishment Clause because that prayer was composed by governmental officials as a part of a governmental program to further religious beliefs. For this reason, petitioners argue, the State's use of the Regents' prayer in its public school system breaches the constitutional wall of separation between Church and State. We agree with that contention since we think that the constitutional prohibition against laws respecting an establishment of religion must at least mean that in this country it is no part of the business of government to compose official prayers for any group of the American people to recite as a part of a religious program carried on by government.

It is a matter of history that this very practice of establishing governmentally composed prayers for religious services was one of the reasons which caused many of our

———

early colonists to leave England and seek religious freedom in America. The Book of Common Prayer, which was created under governmental direction and which was approved by Acts of Parliament in 1548 and 1549, set out in minute detail the accepted form and content of prayer and other religious ceremonies to be used in the established, tax-supported Church of England. . . .

It is an unfortunate fact of history that when some of the very groups which had most strenuously opposed the established Church of England found themselves sufficiently in control of colonial governments in this country to write their own prayers into law, they passed laws making their own religion the official religion of their respective colonies. Indeed, as late as the time of the Revolutionary War, there were established churches in at least eight of the thirteen former colonies and established religions in at least four of the other five. But the successful Revolution against English political domination was shortly followed by intense opposition to the practice of establishing religion by law. This opposition crystallized rapidly into an effective political force in Virginia where the minority religious groups such as Presbyterians, Lutherans, Quakers and Baptists had gained such strength that the adherents to the established Episcopal Church were actually a minority themselves. In 1785–1786, those opposed to the established Church, led by James Madison and Thomas Jefferson, who, though themselves not members of any of these dissenting religious groups, opposed all religious establishments by law on grounds of principle, obtained the enactment of the famous "Virginia Bill for Religious Liberty" by which all religious groups were placed on an equal footing so far as the State was concerned. Similar though less far-reaching legislation was being considered and passed in other States. . . .

The First Amendment was added to the Constitution to stand as a guarantee that neither the power nor the prestige of the Federal Government would be used to control, support or influence the kinds of prayer the American people can say—that the people's religions must not be subjected to the pressures of government for change each time a new political administration is elected to office. Under that Amendment's prohibition against governmental establishment of religion, as reinforced by the provisions of the Fourteenth Amendment, government in this country, be it state or federal, is without power to prescribe by law any particular form of prayer which is to be used as an official prayer in carrying on any program of governmentally sponsored religious activity.

There can be no doubt that New York's state prayer program officially establishes the religious beliefs embodied in the Regents' prayer. The respondents' argument to the contrary, which is largely based upon the contention that the Regents' prayer is "nondenominational" and the fact that the program, as modified and approved by state courts, does not require all pupils to recite the prayer but permits those who wish to do so to remain silent or be excused from the room, ignores the essential nature of the program's constitutional defects. Neither the fact that the prayer may be denominationally neutral nor the fact that its observance on the part of the students is voluntary can serve to free it from the limitations of Establishment Clause, as it might from the Free Exercise Clause, of the First Amendment, both of which are operative against the States by virtue of the Fourteenth Amendment. Although these two clauses may in certain instances overlap, they forbid two quite different kinds of governmental encroachment upon religious freedom. The Establishment Clause, unlike the Free Exercise Clause, does not depend upon any showing of direct governmental compulsion and is violated by the enactment of laws which establish an official religion whether those laws operate directly to coerce nonobserving individuals or not. This is not to say, of course, that laws officially prescribing a particular form of religious worship do not involve coercion of such individuals. When the power, prestige and financial support of government is placed behind a particular religious belief, the indirect coercive pressure upon religious minorities to conform to the prevailing officially approved religion is plain. But the purposes underlying the Establishment Clause go much further than that. Its first and most immediate purpose rested on the belief that a union of government and religion tends to destroy government and to degrade religion. The history of governmentally established religion, both in England and in this country, showed that whenever government had allied itself with one particular form of religion, the inevitable result had been that it had incurred the hatred, disrespect and even contempt of those who held contrary beliefs. That same history showed that many people had lost their respect for any religion that had relied upon the support of government to spread its faith. The Establishment Clause thus stands as an expression of principle on the part of the Founders of our Constitution that religion is too personal, too sacred, too holy, to permit its "unhallowed perversion" by a civil magistrate. Another purpose of the Establishment Clause rested upon an awareness of the historical fact that governmentally established religions and religious persecutions go hand in hand. The Founders knew that only a few years after the Book of Common Prayer became the only accepted form of religious services in the established Church of England, an Act of Uniformity was passed to compel all Englishmen to attend those services and to make it a criminal offense to conduct or attend religious gatherings of any other kind—a law which was consistently flouted by dissenting religious groups in England and which contributed to widespread persecutions of people like John Bunyan who persisted in holding "unlawful [religious] meetings . . . to the great disturbance and distraction of the good subjects of this kingdom. . . ." And they knew that similar persecutions had received the sanction of law in several of the colonies in this country soon after the establishment of official religions in those colonies. It was in large part to get completely away from this sort of systematic religious persecution that the Founders brought into being our Nation, our Constitution, and our Bill of Rights with its prohibition against any governmental establishment of religion. The New York laws officially prescribing the Regents' prayer are inconsistent both with the purposes of the Establishment Clause and with the Establishment Clause itself.

It has been argued that to apply the Constitution in such a way as to prohibit state laws respecting an establishment of religious services in public schools is to indicate a hostility toward religion or toward prayer. Nothing, of course, could be more wrong. The history of man is inseparable from the history of religion. And perhaps it is not too much to say that since the beginning of that history many people have devoutly believed that "More things are wrought by prayer than this world dreams of." It was doubtless largely due to men who believed this that there grew up a sentiment that caused men to leave the crosscurrents of officially established state religions and religious persecution in Europe and come to this country filled with the hope that they could find a place in which they could pray when they pleased to the God of their faith in the language they chose. And there were men of this same faith in the power of prayer who led the fight for adoption of our Constitution and also for our Bill of Rights with the very guarantees of religious freedom that forbid the sort of governmental activity which New York has attempted here. These men knew that the First Amendment, which tried to put an end to governmental control of religion and of prayer, was not written to destroy either. They knew rather that it was written to quiet well-justified fears which nearly all of them felt arising out of an awareness that governments of the past had shackled men's tongues to make them speak only the religious thoughts that government wanted them to speak and to pray only to the God that government wanted them to pray to. It is neither sacrilegious nor antireligious to say that each separate government in this country should stay out of the business of writing or sanctioning official prayers and leave that purely religious function to the people themselves and to those the people choose to look to for religious guidance. . . .

The judgment of the Court of Appeals of New York is reversed and the cause remanded for further proceedings not inconsistent with this opinion.

Reversed and remanded.

---

206   *Gideon v. Wainwright (1963)*

In *Betts v. Brady* (1942), the Court had ruled that the Fourteenth Amendment did not apply the Sixth Amendment's right to counsel to the states. The due process criterion, however, might require an attorney in certain circumstances; for example, in highly technical cases or when the defendant was illiterate. The next twenty years saw both state and federal courts deluged with appeals by persons claiming special circumstances. In the cases reaching the Supreme Court the justices, without overruling *Betts,* usually managed to reverse convictions by finding the existence of special circumstances. Many of the states in the meantime adopted the simpler expedient of providing counsel to poor defendants in all felony cases.

Clarence Earl Gideon did not claim special circumstances. He was not illiterate or mentally retarded or the victim of racial prejudice, and the question of law was not complicated. He had been accused and convicted of breaking and entering a poolroom to commit petit larceny. He wanted a lawyer, and since he had no money, he wanted the state of Florida to provide one for him, but Florida still operated under the *Betts* rule.

His appeal came at an opportune moment, when the brethren believed *Betts* should be overturned. Justice Black, who dissented in the *Betts* case, saw that dissent vindicated when he delivered the Court's opinion in *Gideon.* Moreover, in an unusual ruling, the Court made the decision retroactive, so that thousands of prisoners in Florida and elsewhere who had been tried without an attorney had to be either retried or released. In Gideon's case, a retrial with an attorney led to his acquittal.

See the classic case study by Anthony Lewis, *Gideon's Trumpet* (1964); J. F. Decker and T. J. Lorigan, "Right to Counsel: The Impact of *Gideon v. Wainwright* in the Fifty States," 3 *Creighton Law Review* 103 (1969); and the works cited for Document 214.

———

Justice Black delivered the opinion of the Court:

Petitioner was charged in a Florida state court with having broken and entered a poolroom with intent to commit a misdemeanor. This offense is a felony under Florida law. Appearing in court without funds and without a lawyer, petitioner asked the court to appoint counsel for him, whereupon the following colloquy took place:

> "The Court: Mr. Gideon, I am sorry, but I cannot appoint Counsel to represent you in this case. Under the laws of the State of Florida, the only time the Court can appoint Counsel to represent a Defendant is when that person is charged with a capital offense. I am sorry, but I will have to deny your request to appoint Counsel to defend you in this case.
>
> The Defendant: The United States Supreme Court says I am entitled to be represented by Counsel."

Put to trial before a jury, Gideon conducted his defense about as well as could be expected from a layman. He made an opening statement to the jury, cross-examined the State's witnesses, presented witnesses in his own defense, declined to testify himself, and made a short argument "emphasizing his innocence to the charge contained in the information field in this case." The jury returned a verdict of guilty, and petitioner was sentenced to serve five years in the state prison. Later, petitioner filed in the Florida Supreme Court this habeas corpus petition attacking his conviction and sentence on the ground that the trial court's refusal to appoint counsel for him denied him rights "guaranteed by the Constitution and the Bill of Rights by the United States Government." Treating the petition for habeas corpus as properly before it, the State Supreme Court, "upon consideration thereof" but without an opinion, denied all relief. Since 1942, when *Betts v. Brady* was decided by a divided Court, the problem of a defendant's federal constitutional right to counsel in a state court has been a continuing source of controversy and litigation in both state and federal courts. To give this problem another review here, we granted certiorari. . . .

The Sixth Amendment provides, "In all criminal prosecutions, the accused shall enjoy the right . . . to have the Assistance of Counsel for his defense." We have construed this to mean that in federal courts counsel must be provided for defendants unable to employ counsel unless the right is competently and intelligently waived. *Betts* argued that this right is extended to indigent defendants in state courts by the Fourteenth Amendment. In response the Court stated that, while the Sixth Amendment laid down "no rule for the conduct of the States, the question recurs whether the constraint laid by the Amendment upon the national courts expresses a rule so fundamental and essential to a fair trial, and so, to due process of law, that it is made obligatory upon the States by the Fourteenth Amendment." In order to decide whether the Sixth Amendment's guar-

Source: 372 U.S. 335 (1963)

antee of counsel is of this fundamental nature, the Court in *Betts* set out and considered "relevant data on the subject . . . afforded by constitutional and statutory provisions subsisting in the colonies and the States prior to the inclusion of the Bill of Rights in the national Constitution, and in the constitutional, legislative, and judicial history of the States to the present date." On the basis of this historical data the Court concluded that "appointment of counsel is not a fundamental right, essential to a fair trial." It was for this reason the *Betts* Court refused to accept the contention that the Sixth Amendment's guarantee of counsel for indigent federal defendants was extended to or, in the words of that Court, "made obligatory upon the States by the Fourteenth Amendment." Plainly, had the Court concluded that appointment of counsel for an indigent criminal defendant was "a fundamental right, essential to a fair trial," it would have held that the Fourteenth Amendment requires appointment of counsel in a state court, just as the Sixth Amendment requires in a federal court. . . .

We accept *Betts v. Brady's* assumption, based as it was on our prior cases, that a provision of the Bill of Rights which is "fundamental and essential to a fair trial" is made obligatory upon the States by the Fourteenth Amendment. We think the Court in *Betts* was wrong, however, in concluding that the Sixth Amendment's guarantee of counsel is not one of these fundamental rights. Ten years before *Betts v. Brady,* this Court, after full consideration of all the historical data examined in *Betts,* had unequivocally declared that "the right to the aid of counsel is of this fundamental character." *Powell v. Alabama* (1932). While the Court at the close of its *Powell* opinion did by its language, as this Court frequently does, limit its holding to the particular facts and circumstances of that case, its conclusions about the fundamental nature of the right to counsel are unmistakable. . . .

. . . The fact is that in deciding as it did—that "appointment of counsel is not a fundamental right, essential to a fair trial"—the Court in *Betts v. Brady* made an abrupt break with its own well-constituted precedents. In returning to these old precedents, sounder we believe than the new, we but restore constitutional principles established to achieve a fair system of justice. Not only these precedents but also reason and reflection require us to recognize that in our adversary system of criminal justice, any person haled into court, who is too poor to hire a lawyer, cannot be assured a fair trial unless counsel is provided for him. This seems to us to be an obvious truth. Governments, both state and federal, quite properly spend vast sums of money to establish machinery to try defendants accused of crime. Lawyers to prosecute are everywhere deemed essential to protect the public's interest in an orderly society. Similarly, there are few defendants charged with crime, few indeed, who fail to hire the best lawyers they can get to prepare and present their defenses. That government hires lawyers to prosecute and defendants who have the money hire lawyers to defend are the strongest indications of the widespread belief that lawyers in criminal courts are necessities, not luxuries. The right of one charged with crime to counsel may not be deemed fundamental and essential to fair trials in some countries, but it is in ours. From the very beginning, our state and national constitutions and laws have laid great emphasis on procedural and substantive safeguards designed to assure fair trials before impartial tribunals in which every defendant stands equal before the law. This noble ideal cannot be realized if the poor man charged with crime has to face his accusers without a lawyer to assist him. . . .

The Court in *Betts v. Brady* departed from the sound wisdom upon which the Court's holding in *Powell v. Alabama* rested. Florida, supported by two other States, has asked that *Betts v. Brady* be left intact. Twenty-two States, as friends of the Court, argue that *Betts* was "an anachronism when handed down" and that it should now be overruled. We agree.

The judgment is reversed and the case is remanded to the Supreme Court of Florida for further action not inconsistent with this opinion.

207

Reynolds v. Sims (1964)

In *Baker* (Document 204), the Court had ruled only that apportionment questions were justiciable; in *Reynolds,* the Court dealt directly with the problem, and its decision completely altered the face of state government. There were six companion cases, representing different apportionment schemes, including one in which voters had approved a system of disproportional representation. In his strenuous dissent in *Baker,* Frankfurter had warned the Court of the dangers of getting involved in the political thicket, especially if it could not, as he feared, fashion "judicially manageable standards" to govern resolution of the issue. But Justice Douglas, in a challenge to the Georgia county unit system, had come up with a simple standard of "one man, one vote," which immediately impressed the nation as eminently fair, and which the Court adopted here.. Following the case, there was a brief and spasmodic attempt to overturn the decision by constitutional amendment, but that failed as soon as new state governments, elected under the decision, came into power.

See items cited in Document 204.

———

Chief Justice Warren delivered the opinion of the Court:
Wesberry clearly established that the fundamental principle of representative government in this country is one of equal representation for equal numbers of people, without regard to race, sex, economic status, or place of residence within a State. Our problem, then, is to ascertain, in the instant cases, whether there are any constitutionally cognizable principles which would justify departures from the basic standard of equality among voters in the apportionment of seats in state legislatures. A predominant consideration in determining whether a State's legislative apportionment scheme constitutes an invidious discrimination violative of rights asserted under the Equal Protection

Source: 377 U.S. 533 (1964)

Clause is that the rights allegedly impaired are individual and personal in nature. Undoubtedly, the right of suffrage is a fundamental matter in a free and democratic society. Especially since the right to exercise the franchise in a free and unimpaired manner is preservative of other basic civil and political rights, any alleged infringement of the right of citizens to vote must be carefully and meticulously scrutinized. . . .

Legislators represent people, not trees or acres. Legislators are elected by voters, not farms or cities or economic interests. As long as ours is a representative form of government, the right to elect legislators in a free and unimpaired fashion is a bedrock of our political system. It could hardly be gainsaid that a constitutional claim had been asserted by an allegation that certain otherwise qualified voters had been entirely prohibited from voting for members of their state legislature. And, if a State should provide that the votes of citizens in one part of the State should be given two times, or five times, or ten times the weight of votes of citizens in another part of the State, it could hardly be contended that the right to vote of those residing in the disfavored areas had not been effectively diluted. Of course, the effect of state legislative distracting schemes which give the same number of representatives to unequal numbers of constituents is identical. Weighting the votes of citizens differently, by any method or means, merely because of where they happen to reside, hardly seems justifiable. . . .

Logically, in a society ostensibly grounded on representative government, it would seem reasonable that a majority of the people of a State could elect a majority of that State's legislators. To sanction minority control of state legislative bodies would appear to deny majority rights in a way that far surpasses any possible denial of minority rights that might otherwise be thought to result. And the concept of equal protection has been traditionally viewed as requiring the uniform treatment of persons standing in the same relation to the governmental action questioned or challenged. With respect to the allocation of legislative representation, all voters, as citizens of a State, stand in the same relation regardless of where they live. Any suggested criteria for the differentiation of citizens are insufficient to justify any discrimination, as to the weight of their votes, unless relevant to the permissible purposes of legislative apportionment. Since the achieving of fair and effective representation for all citizens is concededly the basic aim of legislative apportionment, we conclude that the Equal Protection Clause guarantees the opportunity for equal participation by all voters in the election of state legislators. Diluting the weight of votes because of place of residence impairs basic constitutional rights under the Fourteenth Amendment just as much as invidious discriminations based upon factors such as race or economic status. . . . Our constitutional system amply provides for the protection of minorities by means other than giving them majority control of state legislatures.

We are told that the matter of apportioning representation in a state legislature is a complex and many-faceted one. We are advised that States can rationally consider factors other than population. We are admonished not to restrict the power of the States to impose differing views as to political philosophy on their citizens. We are cautioned about the dangers of entering into political thickets and mathematical quagmires. Our answer is this: a denial of constitutionally protected rights demands judicial protection; our oath and our office require no less of us. To the extent that a citizen's right to vote is debased, he is that much less a citizen. The weight of a citizen's vote cannot be made to depend on where he lives. Population is, of necessity, the starting point for consideration and the controlling criterion for judgment in legislative apportionment controversies. A citizen, a qualified voter, is no more nor no less so because he lives in the city or on the farm. This is the clear and strong command of our Constitution's Equal Protection Clause. This is an essential part of the concept of a government of laws and not men. This is at the heart of Lincoln's vision of "government of the people, by the people, . . . for the people." We hold that, as a basic constitutional standard, the Equal Protection Clause requires that the seats in both houses of a bicameral state legislature must be apportioned on a population basis. Simply stated, an individual's right to vote for state legislators is unconstitutionally impaired when its weight is in a substantial fashion diluted when compared with votes of citizens living in other parts of the state.

208   *Gulf of Tonkin Resolution (1964)*

Following the French withdrawal from Vietnam, the United States had taken an increasingly active role in trying to prevent a Communist takeover of Southeast Asia. By the fall of 1963, there were about 16,500 American "advisors" in South Vietnam, and since they often went into battle with ARVN troops, there had been casualties. Following his unexpected accession to the presidency, an unprepared Lyndon Johnson had to make a fateful decision regarding further American involvement. Mindful of the criticism heaped upon Roosevelt and Truman for "losing" China, Johnson determined to step up the American involvement. He did all this without any formal declaration of war, but following an alleged attack by North Vietnamese gunboats on American destroyers in the Gulf of Tonkin, Congress passed the following resolution.

Despite claims by antiwar protesters that the war was illegal because Congress had never authorized it, most constitutional scholars believe that the Tonkin Gulf Resolution was a de facto declaration of war, especially when taken in conjunction with continuing authorizations of money by Congress to support the military venture. This view was certainly held by Johnson, who had been responsible for drafting the resolution.

See Francis D. Wormuth, *The Vietnam, War: The President vs. the Constitution* (1974); W. Taylor Reveley, *War Powers of the President and Congress* (1981); Note, "Congress, the President, and the Power to Commit Forces to Combat," 81 *Harvard Law Review* 1771 (1968); and Louis Fisher, *Presidential War Power* (1995).

Source: H. J. Res. 1145, 73 *Statutes at Large* 384 (1964)

Joint Resolution to Promote the Maintenance of International Peace and Security in Southeast Asia

Whereas naval units of the Communist regime in Vietnam, in violation of the principles of the Charter of the United Nations and of international law, have deliberately and repeatedly attacked United States naval vessels lawfully present in international waters, and have thereby created a serious threat to international peace; and

Whereas these attacks are part of a deliberate and systematic campaign of aggression that the Communist regime in North Vietnam has been waging against its neighbors and the nations joined with them in the collective defense of their freedom; and

Whereas the United States is assisting the peoples of southeast Asia to protect their freedom and has no territorial, military or political ambitions in that area, but desires only that these peoples should be left in peace to work out their own destinies in their own way: Now, therefore, be it

Resolved by the Senate and House of Representatives of the United States of America in Congress assembled, That the Congress approves and supports the determination of the President, as Commander in Chief, to take all necessary measures to repel any armed attack against the forces of the United States and to prevent further aggression.

SEC. 2. The United States regards as vital to its national interest and to world peace the maintenance of international peace and security in southeast Asia. Consonant with the Constitution of the United States and the Charter of the United Nations and in accordance with its obligations under the Southeast Asia Collective Defense Treaty, the United States is, therefore, prepared, as the President determines, to take all necessary steps, including the use of armed force, to assist any member or protocol state of the Southeast Asia Collective Defense Treaty requesting assistance in defense of its freedom.

SEC. 3. This resolution shall expire when the President shall determine that the peace and security of the area is reasonably assured by international conditions created by action of the United Nations or otherwise, except that it may be terminated earlier by concurrent resolution of the Congress.

Approved August 10, 1964.

209

New York Times v. Sullivan (1964)

Among areas traditionally considered outside First Amendment protection, libel had always been viewed as an abuse of speech or press, and the common law had punished libelers severely. This particular libel action grew out of an advertisement placed in the *Times* in December 1960 by a group protesting an alleged "unprecedented wave of terror" against blacks engaged in nonviolent demonstrations in the South. Sullivan, the elected police and fire commissioner of Montgomery, Alabama, sued the *Times* and several of the ad's sponsors, claiming that his reputation had been injured and that the ad contained a number of factual errors. The ad, for example, claimed that Martin Luther King, Jr., had been arrested seven times; he had been arrested four times. A local jury awarded Sullivan $500,000, and the paper appealed. There were ten other similar judgments pending against the *Times,* and it was clear that these suits intended to put the newspaper out of business. In this landmark opinion, the Court extended freedom of speech and press to invalidate much of the traditional law of libel, and except in very limited circumstances, made criticism of public figures immune from legal retaliation.

See Harry Kalven, *"The New York Times* Case: A Note on 'The Central Meaning' of the First Amendment," 1964 *Supreme Court Review*191 (1965); Alexander Meikeljohn, "Public Speech in the Supreme Court Since *New York Times v. Sullivan,"* 26 *Syracuse Law Review* 819 (1975); and Anthony Lewis, *Make No Law: The Sullivan Case and the First Amendment* (1991).

―――――

Justice Brennan delivered the opinion of the Court:

We are required in this case to determine for the first time the extent to which the constitutional protections for speech and press limit a State's power to award damages in a libel action brought by a public official against critics of his official conduct. . . .

Under Alabama law, a publication is "libelous per se" if the words "tend to injure a person in his reputation" or to "bring him into public contempt"; the trial court stated that the standard was met if the words are such as to "injure him in his public office, or impute misconduct to him in his office, or want of official integrity, or want of fidelity to a public trust." The jury must find that the words were published "of and concerning" the plaintiff, but where the plaintiff is a public official his place in the governmental hierarchy is sufficient evidence to support a finding that his reputation has been affected by statements that reflect upon the agency of which he is in charge. Once "libel per se" has been established, the defendant has no defense as to stated facts unless he can persuade the jury that they were true in all their particulars. Unless he can discharge the burden of proving truth, general damages are presumed, and may be awarded without proof of pecuniary injury. The question before us is whether this rule of liability, as applied to an action brought by a public official against critics of his official conduct, abridges the freedom of speech and of the press. . . .

. . . Alabama courts [rely] on statements of this Court to the effect that the Constitution does not protect libelous publications. Those statements do not foreclose our

Source: 376 U.S. 254 (1964)

inquiry here. None of the cases sustained the use of libel laws to impose sanctions upon expression critical of the official conduct of public officials. Like insurrection, contempt, advocacy of unlawful acts, breach of the peace, obscenity, solicitation of legal business, and the various other formulae for the repression of expression that have been challenged in this Court, libel can claim no talismanic immunity from constitutional limitations. It must be measured by standards that satisfy the First Amendment. . . .

We consider this case against the background of a profound national commitment to the principle that debate on public issues should be uninhibited, robust, and wide-open, and that it may well include vehement, caustic, and sometimes unpleasantly sharp attacks on government and public officials. The present advertisement, as an expression of grievance and protest on one of the major public issues of our time, would seem clearly to qualify for the constitutional protection. The question is whether it forfeits that protection by the falsity of some of its factual statements and by its alleged defamation of respondent. Authoritative interpretations of the First Amendment guarantees have consistently refused to recognize an exception for any test of truth—whether administered by judges, juries, or administrative officials—and especially not one that puts the burden of proving truth on the speaker. "The constitutional protection does not turn upon the truth, popularity, or social utility of the ideas and beliefs which are offered." . . . Injury to official reputation affords no more warrant for repressing speech that would otherwise be free than does factual error. . . . Criticism of their official conduct does not lose its constitutional protection merely because it is effective criticism and hence diminishes their official reputations.

If neither factual error nor defamatory content suffices to remove the constitutional shield from criticism of official conduct, the combination of the two elements is no less inadequate. This is the lesson to be drawn from the great controversy over the Sedition Act of 1798, 1 Stat. 596, which first crystallized a national awareness of the central meaning of the First Amendment. . . . The Sedition Act was never tested in this Court, [but] the attack upon its validity has carried the day in the court of history. Fines levied in its prosecution were repaid by Act of Congress . . . Jefferson, as President, pardoned those who had been convicted and sentenced under the Act and remitted their fines. These views reflect a broad consensus that the Act, because of the restraint it imposed upon criticism of government and public officials, was inconsistent with the First Amendment. . . .

The state rule of law is not saved by its allowance of the defense of truth. A defense for erroneous statements honestly made is no less essential here than was the requirement of proof of guilty knowledge which . . . we held indispensable to a valid conviction of a bookseller for possessing obscene writings for sale. A rule compelling the critic of official conduct to guarantee the truth of all his factual assertions—and to do so on pain of libel judgments virtually unlimited in amount—leads to a comparable "self-censorship." Allowance of the defense of truth, with the burden of proving it on the defendant, does not mean that only false speech will be deterred. Under such a rule, would-be critics of official conduct may be deterred from voicing their criticism, even though it is believed to be true and even though it is in fact true, because of doubt whether it can be proved in court or fear of the expense of having to do so. The rule thus dampens the vigor and limits the variety of public debate. It is inconsistent with the First Amendment. The constitutional guarantees require, we think, a federal rule that prohibits a public official from recovering damages for a defamatory falsehood relating to his official conduct unless he proves that the statement was made with "actual malice"—that is, with knowledge that it was false or with reckless disregard of whether it was false or not. . . .

Reversed and remanded.

210 — *Title II, Civil Rights Act (1964)*

Several months before his death, President John F. Kennedy came to the conclusion that in order to combat racial discrimination, the federal government needed greater statutory authority, and on June 11, 1963, he asked Congress for legislation to provide "the kind of equality of treatment which we would want ourselves." The bill he proposed would ban discrimination in public accommodations, on the grounds that such businesses were affected with a public interest. He also sought power for the Justice Department to initiate suits when it had reason to believe that private parties were unable or afraid to sue on their own.

Southerners blocked the bill for the rest of the year, but following Kennedy's assassination in late November 1963, the new president, Lyndon Baines Johnson, called upon Congress to enact the bill as a memorial to Kennedy. Brilliantly using his extensive legislative skills, Johnson guided the bill through both houses of Congress and signed it into law on July 2, 1964.

Title II, parts of which are reprinted here, is the public accommodations section. For court challenges, see next document.

See Carl M. Brauer, *John F. Kennedy and the Second Reconstruction* (1977); Charles W. Quick, "Public Accommodations: A Justification of Title II," 16 *Western Reserve Law Review* 660 (1965); and Clifford M. Lytle, "History of the Civil Rights Bill of 1964," 51 *Journal of Negro History* 275 (1966).

———

SEC. 201. (a) All persons shall be entitled to the full and equal enjoyment of the goods, services, facilities, privileges, advantages, and accommodations of any place of public accommodation, as defined in this section, without discrimination or segregation on the ground of race, color, religion, or national origin.

Source: 78 Statutes at Large 241

(b) Each of the following establishments which serves the public is a place of public accommodation within the meaning of this title if its operations affect commerce, or if discrimination or segregation by it is supported by State action:

(1) any inn, hotel, motel, or other establishment which provides lodging to transient guests, other than an establishment located within a building which contains not more than five rooms for rent or hire and which is actually occupied by the proprietor of such establishment as his residence;

(2) any restaurant, cafeteria, lunchroom, lunch counter, soda fountain, or other facility principally engaged in selling food for consumption on the premises, including, but not limited to, any such facility located on the premises of any retail establishment; or any gasoline station;

(3) any motion picture house, theater, concert hall, sports arena, stadium or other place of exhibition or entertainment; and

(4) any establishment (A)(i) which is physically located within the premises of any establishment otherwise covered by this subsection, or (ii) within the premises of which is physically located any such covered establishment, and (B) which holds itself out as serving patrons of such covered establishment.

(c) The operations of an establishment affect commerce within the meaning of this title if (1) it is one of the establishments described in paragraph (1) of subsection (b); (2) in the case of an establishment described in paragraph (2) of subsection (b), it serves or offers to serve interstate travelers or a substantial portion of the food which it serves, or gasoline or other products which it sells, has moved in commerce; (3) in the case of an establishment described in paragraph (3) of subsection (b), it customarily presents films, performances, athletic teams, exhibitions, or other sources of entertainment which move in commerce; and (4) in the case of an establishment described in paragraph (4) of subsection (b), it is physically located within the premises of, or there is physically located within its premises, an establishment the operations of which affect commerce within the meaning of this subsection. For purposes of this section, "commerce" means travel, trade, traffic, commerce, transportation, or communication among the several States, or between the District of Columbia and any State, or between any foreign country or any territory or possession and any State or the District of Columbia, or between points in the same State but through any other State or the District of Columbia or a foreign country.

(d) Discrimination or segregation by an establishment is supported by State action within the meaning of this title if such discrimination or segregation (1) is carried on under color of any law, statute, ordinance, or regulation; or (2) is carried on under color of any custom or usage required or enforced by officials of the State or political subdivision thereof; or (3) is required by action of the State or political subdivision thereof. . . .

(e) The provisions of this title shall not apply to a private club or other establishment not in fact open to the public, except to the extent that the facilities of such establishment are made available to the customers or patrons of an establishment within the scope of subsection (b).

SEC. 202. All persons shall be entitled to be free, at any establishment or place, from discrimination or segregation of any kind on the ground of race, color, religion, or national origin, if such discrimination or segregation is or purports to be required by any law, statute, ordinance, regulation, rule, or order of a State or any agency or political sub-division thereof.

Sec. 203.   No person shall (a) withhold, deny, or attempt to withhold or deny, or deprive or attempt to deprive, any person of any right or privilege secured by section 201 or 202, or (b) intimidate, threaten, or coerce, or attempt to intimidate, threaten, or coerce any person with the purpose of interfering with any right or privilege secured by section 201 or 202, or (c) punish or attempt to punish any person for exercising or attempting to exercise any right or privilege secured by section 201 or 202.

211

Heart of Atlanta Motel v. United States (1964)

The justices had closely followed the 1964 Civil Rights Act, aware that its passage would align all three branches of the government in advocating equal rights for all Americans. Within six months after Lyndon Johnson had signed the bill into law, the Court heard two expedited test cases that questioned the validity of the public accommodations sections. In the following case, a unanimous Court upheld congressional power to legislate in this area under the Commerce Clause. In a companion case, *Katzenbach v. McClung,* the Court sustained the law's application to restaurants that had a primarily local trade, because a significant portion of the food supplies bought by Ollie's Barbecue in Birmingham, Alabama, came from outside the state. The decisions are important not only for the impact they had on the civil rights movement, but also for the Court's broad view of congressional power under the Commerce Clause.

See sources listed in previous document, and also Donald B. King and Charles W. Quick, eds., *Legal Aspects of the Civil Rights Movement* (1965).

———

Justice Clark delivered the opinion of the Court:
Appellant owns and operates the Heart of Atlanta Motel which has 216 rooms available to transient guests. The motel is located on Courtland Street, two blocks from downtown Peachtree Street. It is readily accessible to interstate highways 75 and 85 and state highways 23 and 41. Appellant solicits patronage from outside the State of Georgia

Source: 379 U.S. 241 (1964)

through various national advertising media, including magazines of national circulation; it maintains over 50 billboards and highway signs within the State, soliciting patronage for the motel; it accepts convention trade from outside Georgia and approximately 75% of its registered guests are from out of State. Prior to passage of the Act the motel had followed a practice of refusing to rent rooms to Negroes, and it alleged that it intended to continue to do so. In an effort to perpetuate that policy this suit was filed. . . .

. . . The sole question posed is the constitutionality of [the 1964 Civil Rights Act] as applied to these facts. The legislative history of the Act indicates that Congress based the Act on § 5 and the Equal Protection Clause of the Fourteenth Amendment as well as its power to regulate interstate commerce. . . .

The Senate Commerce Committee made it quite clear that the fundamental object of Title II was to vindicate "the deprivation of personal dignity that surely accompanies denials of equal access to public establishments." At the same time, however, it noted that such an objective has been and could be readily achieved "by congressional action based on the commerce power of the Constitution." Our study of the legislative record, made in the light of prior cases, has brought us to the conclusion that Congress possessed ample power in this regard, and we have therefore not considered the other grounds relied upon. This is not to say that the remaining authority upon which it acted was not adequate, a question upon which we do not pass, but merely that since the commerce power is sufficient for our decision here we have considered it alone. . . .

While the Act as adopted carried no congressional findings the record of its passage through each house is replete with evidence of the burdens that discrimination by race or color places upon interstate commerce. This testimony included the fact that our people have become increasingly mobile with millions of all races traveling from State to State; that Negroes in particular have been the subject of discrimination in transient accommodations, having to travel great distances to secure the same; that often they have been unable to obtain accommodations and have had to call upon friends to put them up overnight; [and] that these conditions had become so acute as to require the listing of available lodging for Negroes in a special guidebook which was itself "dramatic testimony of the difficulties" Negroes encounter in travel. . . .

The power of Congress to deal with these obstructions depends on the meaning of the Commerce Clause. The determinative test of the exercise of power by the Congress under the Commerce Clause is simply whether the activity sought to be regulated is "commerce which concerns more States than one" and has a real and substantial relation to the national interest. . . .

The same interest in protecting interstate commerce which led Congress to deal with segregation in interstate carriers and the white slave traffic has prompted it to extend the exercise of its power to gambling; to criminal enterprises; to deceptive practices in the sale of products; to fraudulent security transactions; to misbranding of drugs; to wages and hours; to members of labor unions; to crop control; to discrimination against shippers; to the protection of small business from injurious price cutting; to resale price maintenance; to professional football; and to racial discrimination by owners and managers of terminal restaurants. That Congress was legislating against moral wrongs in many of these areas rendered its enactments no less valid. In framing Title II of this Act Congress was also dealing with what it considered a moral problem. But that fact does not detract from the overwhelming evidence of the disruptive effect that racial discrimination has had on commercial intercourse. It was this burden which empowered Congress to enact appropriate legislation, and given this basis for the exercise of its power, Congress was not restricted by the fact that the particular obstruction to interstate commerce with which it was dealing was also deemed a moral and social wrong.

It is said that the operation of the motel here is of a purely local character. But, assuming this to be true, "if it is interstate commerce that feels the pinch, it does not matter how local the operation that applies the squeeze." . . . Thus the power of Congress to promote interstate commerce also includes the power to regulate the local incidents thereof, including local activities in both the States of origin and destination, which might have a substantial and harmful effect upon that commerce. One need only examine the evidence which we have discussed above to see that Congress may—as it has— prohibit racial discrimination by motels serving travelers, however "local" their operations may appear. . . .

We, therefore, conclude that the action of the Congress in the adoption of the Act as applied here to a motel which concededly serves interstate travelers is within the power granted it by the Commerce Clause of the Constitution, as interpreted by this Court for 140 years. . . .

Affirmed.

212   *Griswold v. Connecticut (1965)*

The Warren Court's expansion of the enumerated liberties in the Bill of Rights led litigants to seek still further expansion of the so-called nonenumerated rights. Some of these rights had been recognized within the common law, but in a form often attached to property. The right to privacy, for example, could best be tied to the old adage, "a man's home is his castle." In the United States, the law of privacy remained poorly defined; Justice Brandeis had referred to privacy in several of his opinions in the 1920s and 1930s, but there was no constitutionally recognized right to privacy until 1965. *Griswold* is truly a landmark case, in which the Court resurrected substantive due process not to protect property, but to safeguard privacy and other individual "liberty interests."

Connecticut had an 1879 statute prohibiting the use of any drug or device to prevent contraception and penalizing any person who advised or provided contraceptive materials. Civil libertarians had previously brought the law to the high court, but in *Poe v. Ullman* (1961), Justice Frankfurter for a plurality had denied justiciability, primarily because the law had never been enforced. Soon afterward, the state prosecuted officials of the Planned Parenthood League, and the Court accepted jurisdiction. *Griswold* has been praised on one hand for its creative jurisprudence and damned on the other for its judicial activism.

See Allan F. Westin, *Privacy and Freedom* (1967); R. H. Clark, "Constitutional Sources of the Penumbral Right to Privacy," 19 *Villanova Law Review* 833 (1974); Adam C. Breckenridge, *The Right to Privacy* (1970); and David J. Garrow, *Liberty and Sexuality* (1994).

———

Justice Douglas delivered the opinion of the Court:

We are met with a wide range of questions that implicate the Due Process Clause of the 14th Amendment. Overtones of some arguments suggest that *Lochner* should be our guide. But we decline that invitation. . . . We do not sit as a super-legislature to determine the wisdom, need, and propriety of laws that touch economic problems, business affairs, or social conditions. This law, however, operates directly on an intimate relation of husband and wife and their physician's role in one aspect of that relation.

The association of people is not mentioned in the Constitution nor in the Bill of Rights. The right to educate a child in a school of the parents' choice—whether public or private or parochial—is also not mentioned. Nor is the right to study any particular subject or any foreign language. Yet the First Amendment has been construed to include certain of those rights. . . . The right to educate one's children as one chooses is made applicable to the States. . . . The same dignity is given the right to study the German language in a private school. In other words, the State may not, consistently with the spirit of the First Amendment, contract the spectrum of available knowledge. The right of freedom of speech and press includes not only the right to utter or to print, but the right to distribute, the right to receive, the right to read and freedom of inquiry, freedom of thought, and freedom to teach—indeed the freedom of the entire university community. Without those peripheral rights the specific rights would be less secure. . . .

The foregoing cases suggest that specific guarantees in the Bill of Rights have penumbras, formed by emanations from those guarantees that help give them life and substance. . . . Various guarantees create zones of privacy. The right of association contained in the penumbra of the First Amendment is one, as we have seen. The Third Amendment in its prohibition against the quartering of soldiers "in any house" in time of peace without the consent of the owner is another facet of that privacy. The Fourth Amendment explicitly affirms the "right of the people to be secure in their persons, houses, papers, and effects against unreasonable searches and seizures." The Fifth Amendment in its Self-Incrimination Clause enables the citizen to create a zone of privacy which government may not force him to surrender to his detriment. The Ninth Amendment provides: "The enumeration in the Constitution, of certain rights, shall not be construed to deny or disparage others retained by the people." The Fourth and Fifth Amendments were described in Boyd v. United States . . . [1886], as protection against all governmental invasions "of the sanctity of a man's home and the privacies of life." We recently referred in [Mapp v. Ohio . . . (1961)] to the Fourth Amendment as creating a "right to privacy, no less important than any other right carefully and particularly reserved to the people." We have had many controversies over these penumbral rights of

Source: 381 U.S. 419 (1965)

"privacy and repose." . . . These cases bear witness that the right of privacy which presses for recognition here is a legitimate one.

The present case, then, concerns a relationship lying within the zone of privacy created by several fundamental constitutional guarantees. And it concerns a law which, in forbidding the *use* of contraceptives rather than regulating their manufacture or sale, seeks to achieve its goals by means having a maximum destructive impact upon that relationship. Such a law cannot stand in light of the familiar principle, so often applied by this Court, that a "governmental purpose to control or prevent activities constitutionally subject to state regulation may not be achieved by means which sweep unnecessarily broadly and thereby invade the area of protected freedoms." . . . Would we allow the police to search the sacred precincts of marital bedrooms for telltale signs of the use of contraceptives? The very idea is repulsive to the notions of privacy surrounding the marriage relationship.

We deal with a right of privacy older than the Bill of Rights—older than our political parties, older than our school system. Marriage is a coming together for better or for worse, hopefully enduring, and intimate to the degree of being sacred. The association promotes a way of life, not causes; a harmony in living, not political faiths; a bilateral loyalty, not commercial or social projects. Yet it is an association for as noble a purpose as any involved in our prior decisions.

Reversed.

213

South Carolina v. Katzenbach (1966)

Following the passage of the 1964 Civil Rights Act (Document 210), leaders of the black community urged Congress to pass a measure protecting the right to vote. In Alabama, for example, although blacks made up about half of the state's population, they accounted for only 1 percent of the registered voters. In 1965, Congress responded with the Voting Rights Act, which authorized the attorney general to send federal registrars into any county where discrimination was suspected suspended the use of literacy tests; and allowed the attorney general, in essence, to supervise voting registration. The act worked; two months after federal registrars arrived in Selma, Alabama, the percentage of voting-age blacks on the rolls rose from 10 to 60. Eventually, these figures translated into elected black legislators, sheriffs, and mayors.

The law had been passed under authority of Section 2 of the Fifteenth Amendment, which gave Congress power to enforce Section 1, which prohibited the denial to any person of the right to vote on the basis of race. Southern states quickly challenged the law, claiming that Section 2 gave Congress only

the general power to forbid violations of voting rights, not the authority to fashion specific remedies. The Supreme Court took this case on original jurisdiction, and it unanimously upheld all the provisions of the law; Justice Black dissented on one minor point. A few weeks later, in *Katzenbach v. Morgan,* the
Court upheld Section 4(e), which provided that anyone who had completed
sixth grade in a Spanish-speaking Puerto Rican school could not be denied the
right to vote because of inability to read or write English.

See Donald S. Strong, *Negroes, Ballots, and Judges* (1968); Ward E. Y. Elliot, *The Rise
of Guardian Democracy* (1974); Alexander M. Bickel, "The Voting Rights Cases," 1966
Supreme Court Review 79 (1967); and Stephen F. Lawson, *In Pursuit of Power: Southern Blacks and Electoral Politics, 1965–1982* (1985).

Chief Justice Warren delivered the opinion of the Court:

The Voting Rights Act [of 1965] was designed by Congress to banish the blight of
racial discrimination in voting, which has infected the electoral process in parts of our
country for nearly a century. The Act creates stringent new remedies for voting discrimination where it persists on a pervasive scale, and in addition the statute strengthens
existing remedies for pockets of voting discrimination elsewhere in the country. Congress assumed the power to prescribe these remedies from Sec. 2 of the Fifteenth
Amendment, which authorizes the National Legislature to effectuate by "appropriate"
measures the constitutional prohibition against racial discrimination in voting. We hold
that the sections of the Act which are properly before us are an appropriate means for
carrying out Congress' constitutional responsibilities and are consonant with all other
provisions of the Constitution. We therefore deny South Carolina's request that enforcement of these sections of the Act be enjoined.

I

The constitutional propriety of the Voting Rights Act of 1965 must be judged with reference to the historical experience which it reflects. Before enacting the measure, Congress explored with great care the problem of racial discrimination in voting. . . .

Two points emerge vividly from the voluminous legislative history of the Act contained in the committee hearings and floor debates. First: Congress felt itself confronted
by an insidious and pervasive evil which had been perpetuated in certain parts of our
country through unremitting and ingenious defiance of the Constitution. Second: Congress concluded that the unsuccessful remedies which it had prescribed in the past would
have to be replaced by sterner and more elaborate measures in order to satisfy the clear
commands of the Fifteenth Amendment. . . .

Source: 383 U.S. 307 (1966)

According to the evidence in recent Justice Department voting suits, [discriminatory application of voting tests] is now the principal method used to bar Negroes from the polls. Discriminatory administration of voting qualifications has been found in all eight Alabama cases, in all nine Louisiana cases, and in all nine Mississippi cases which have gone to final judgment. Moreover, in almost all of these cases, the courts have held that the discrimination was pursuant to a widespread "pattern or practice." White applicants for registration have often been excused altogether from the literacy and understanding tests or have been given easy versions, have received extensive help from voting officials, and have been registered despite serious errors in their answers. Negroes, on the other hand, have typically been required to pass difficult versions of all the tests, without any outside assistance and without the slightest error. The good-morals requirement is so vague and subjective that it has constituted an open invitation to abuse at the hands of voting officials. Negroes obliged to obtain vouchers from registered voters have found it virtually impossible to comply in areas where almost no Negroes are on the rolls.

In recent years, Congress has repeatedly tried to cope with the problem by facilitating case-by-case litigation against voting discrimination. . . .

Despite the earnest efforts of the Justice Department and of many federal judges, these new laws have done little to cure the problem of voting discrimination. . . . Voting suits are unusually onerous to prepare, sometimes requiring as many as 6,000 man-hours spent combing through registration records in preparation for trial. Litigation has been exceedingly slow, in part because of the ample opportunities for delay afforded voting officials and others involved in the proceedings. Even when favorable decisions have finally been obtained, some of the States affected have merely switched to discriminatory devices not covered by the federal decrees or have enacted difficult new tests designed to prolong the existing disparity between white and Negro registration. Alternatively, certain local officials have defied and evaded court orders or have simply closed their registration offices to freeze the voting rolls. The provision of the 1960 law authorizing registration by federal officers has had little impact on local maladministration because of its procedural complexities. . . .

II

The Voting Rights Act of 1965 reflects Congress' firm intention to rid the country of racial discrimination in voting. The heart of the Act is a complex scheme of stringent remedies aimed at areas where voting discrimination has been most flagrant. The first of the remedies, contained in Sec. 4(a), is the suspension of literacy tests and similar voting qualifications for a period of five years from the last occurrence of substantial voting discrimination. Section 5 prescribes a second remedy, the suspension of all new voting regulations pending review by federal authorities to determine whether their use would perpetuate voting discrimination. The third remedy, covered in Secs. 6(b), 7, 9, and 13(a), is the assignment of federal examiners on certification by the Attorney General to list qualified applicants who are thereafter entitled to vote in all elections. . . .

III

These provisions of the Voting Rights Act of 1965 are challenged on the fundamental ground that they exceed the powers of Congress and encroach on an area reserved to the States by the Constitution. South Carolina and certain of the *amici curiae* also attack specific sections of the Act for more particular reasons. They argue that the coverage formula prescribed in Sec. 4(a)–(d) violates the principle of the equality of States, denies due process by employing an invalid presumption and by barring judicial review of administrative findings, constitutes a forbidden bill of attainder, and impairs the separation of powers by adjudicating guilt through legislation. They claim that the review of new voting rules required in Sec. 5 infringes Article III by directing the District Court to issue advisory opinions. They contend that the assignment of federal examiners authorized in Sec. 6(b) abridges due process by precluding judicial review of administrative findings and impairs the separation of powers by giving the Attorney General judicial functions; also that the challenge procedure prescribed in Sec. 9 denies due process on account of its speed. Finally, South Carolina and certain of the *amici curiae* maintain that Secs. 4(a) and 5, buttressed by Sec. 14(b) of the Act, abridge due process by limiting litigation to a distant forum.

Some of these contentions may be dismissed at the outset. The word "person" in the context of the Due Process Clause of the Fifth Amendment cannot, by any reasonable mode of interpretation, be expanded to encompass the States of the Union, and to our knowledge this has never been done by any court. Likewise, courts have consistently regarded the Bill of Attainder Clause of Article I and the principle of the separation of powers only as protections for individual persons and private groups, those who are peculiarly vulnerable to non-judicial determinations of guilt. Nor does a State have standing as the parent of its citizens to invoke these constitutional provisions against the Federal Government, the ultimate (*patriae*) of every American citizen. The objections to the Act which are raised under these provisions may therefore be considered only as additional aspects of the basic question presented by the case: Has Congress exercised its powers under the Fifteenth Amendment in an appropriate manner with relation to the States?

The ground rules for resolving this question are clear. The language and purpose of the Fifteenth Amendment, the prior decisions construing its several provisions, and the general doctrines of constitutional interpretation, all point to one fundamental principle. As against the reserved powers of the States, Congress may use any rational means to effectuate the constitutional prohibition of racial discrimination in voting.

Section 1 of the Fifteenth Amendment declares that "the right of citizens of the United States to vote shall not be denied or abridged by the United States or by any State on account of race, color, or previous condition of servitude." This declaration has always been treated as self-executing and has repeatedly been construed, without further legislative specification, to invalidate state voting qualifications or procedures which are discriminatory on their face or in practice. These decisions have been rendered with full respect for the general rule that States "have broad powers to determine the conditions under which the right of suffrage may be exercised." The gist of the matter is that the

Fifteenth Amendment supersedes contrary exertions of state power. "When a State exercises power wholly within the domain of state interest, it is insulated from federal judicial review. But such insulation is not carried over when state power is used as an instrument for circumventing a federally protected right."

South Carolina contends that the cases cited above are precedents only for the authority of the judiciary to strike down state statutes and procedures—that to allow an exercise of this authority by Congress would be to rob the courts of their rightful constitutional role. On the contrary, Sec. 2 of the Fifteenth Amendment expressly declares that "Congress shall have power to enforce this article by appropriate legislation." By adding this authorization, the Framers indicated that Congress was to be chiefly responsible for implementing the rights created in Sec. 1. "It is the power of Congress which has been enlarged. Congress is authorized to *enforce* the prohibitions by appropriate legislation. Some legislation is contemplated to make the amendments fully effective." Accordingly, in addition to the courts, Congress has full remedial powers to effectuate the constitutional prohibition against racial discrimination in voting. . . .

The basic test to be applied in a case involving Sec. 2 of the Fifteenth Amendment is the same as in all cases concerning the express powers of Congress with relation to the reserved powers of the States. Chief Justice Marshall laid down the classic formulation, 50 years before the Fifteenth Amendment was ratified:

> "Let the end be legitimate, let it be within the scope of the constitution, and all means which are appropriate, which are plainly adapted to that end, which are not prohibited, but consist with the letter and spirit of the constitution, are constitutional."

The Court has subsequently echoed his language in describing each of the Civil War Amendments. . . .

We therefore reject South Carolina's argument that Congress may appropriately do no more than to forbid violations of the Fifteenth Amendment in general terms—that the task of fashioning specific remedies or of applying them to particular localities must necessarily be left entirely to the courts. Congress is not circumscribed by any such artificial rules under Sec. 2 of the Fifteenth Amendment. In the oft-repeated words of Chief Justice Marshall, referring to another specific legislative authorization in the Constitution, "This power, like all others vested in Congress, is complete in itself, may be exercised to its utmost extent, and acknowledges no limitations, other than are prescribed in the constitution."

IV

Congress exercised its authority under the Fifteenth Amendment in an inventive manner when it enacted the Voting Rights Act of 1965. First: The measure prescribes remedies for voting discrimination which go into effect without any need for prior adjudication. This was clearly a legitimate response to the problem, for which there is ample precedent under other constitutional provisions. Congress had found that case-by-case litigation was inadequate to combat widespread and persistent discrimination in voting, because of the inordinate amount of time and energy required to overcome the obstructionist tactics invariably encountered in these lawsuits. After enduring nearly a century of systematic resistance to the Fifteenth Amendment, Congress might well decide to shift the advantage of time and inertia from the perpetrators of the evil to its victims. The question remains, of course, whether the specific remedies prescribed in the Act were an appropriate means of combatting the evil, and to this question we shall presently address ourselves.

Second: The Act intentionally confines these remedies to a small number of States and political subdivisions which in most instances were familiar to Congress by name. This, too, was a permissible method of dealing with the problem. Congress had learned that substantial voting discrimination presently occurs in certain sections of the country, and it knew no way of accurately forecasting whether the evil might spread elsewhere in the future. In acceptable legislative fashion, Congress chose to limit its attention to the geographic areas where immediate action seemed necessary. The doctrine of the equality of States, invoked by South Carolina, does not bar this approach, for that doctrine applies only to the terms upon which States are admitted to the Union, and not to the remedies for local evils which have subsequently appeared. . . . [The Court then examined, and upheld, the particular sections of the Act.]

214 *Miranda v. Arizona (1966)*

The Fifth Amendment's right against self-incrimination means more than the right not to testify against oneself at trial, but just what the right does mean has been the subject of several court cases over the years. In *Malloy v. Hogan* (1964), the Court applied the privilege to the states, and later that year it tied the Fifth Amendment protection against self-incrimination to the Sixth Amendment's right to counsel in *Escobedo v. Illinois.*

In this case, two years later, a seriously divided Court attempted to give police and the legal profession clear guidance on what due process required. A suspect had to be informed in clear and unequivocal language that he or she had the right to remain silent, that anything said might be used in a court proceeding, and that a lawyer, if requested, would be provided. If the police interrogated a person without these warnings, any resulting confession would be invalid. The *Miranda* decision triggered a firestorm of criticism against the Court for "coddling" criminals and "handcuffing" the police. Yet as most responsible police officers noted at that time, although they were unheard in the noise, good police departments had already adopted similar rules, and they had not proven a deterrent; if anything, they fostered better police work.

Despite much initial criticism, the decision has gained widespread acceptance, and in 2000, the Court reaffirmed the *Miranda* rule in *Dickerson v. United States,* with Chief Justice William Rehnquist, once a critic, delivering the 7–2 opinion.

See Fred Graham, *The Due Process Revolution* (1970); Yale Kamisar, *Police Interrogation and* Confessions (1980); Richard A. Seeburger and R. Stanton Wettick, Jr., "Miranda in Pittsburgh—A Statistical Study," 29 *University of Pittsburgh Law Review* 1 (1967); and Leonard Baker, *Miranda, Crime, Law and Order* (1983).

———

Chief Justice Warren delivered the opinion of the Court:

The cases before us raise questions which go to the roots of our concepts of American criminal jurisprudence: the restraints society must observe consistent with the Federal Constitution in prosecuting individuals for crime. More specifically, we deal with the admissibility of statements obtained from an individual who is subjected to custodial police interrogation and the necessity for procedures which assure that the individual is accorded his privilege under the Fifth Amendment to the Constitution not to be compelled to incriminate himself.

We start here, as we did in *Escobedo,* with the premise that our holding is not an innovation in our jurisprudence, but is an application of principles long recognized and applied in other settings. We have undertaken a thorough re-examination of the *Escobedo* decision and the principles it announced, and we reaffirm it. That case was but an explication of basic rights that are enshrined in our Constitution—that "No person . . . shall be compelled in any criminal case to be a witness against himself," and that "the accused shall . . . have the Assistance of Counsel"—rights which were put in jeopardy in that case through official overbearing. These precious rights were fixed in our Constitution only after centuries of persecution and struggle. And in the words of Chief Justice Marshall, they were secured "for ages to come, and . . . designed to approach immortality as nearly as human institutions can approach it."

Our holding will be spelled out with some specificity in the pages which follow but briefly stated it is this: the prosecution may not use statements, whether exculpatory or inculpatory, stemming from custodial interrogation of the defendant unless it demonstrates the use of procedural safeguards effective to secure the privilege against self-incrimination. By custodial interrogation, we mean questioning initiated by law enforcement officers after a person has been taken into custody or otherwise deprived of his freedom of action in any significant way. As for the procedural safeguards to be employed, unless other fully effective means are devised to inform accused persons of their right of silence and to assure a continuous opportunity to exercise it, the following measures are required. Prior to any questioning, the person must be warned that he has a right to remain silent, that any statement he does make may be used as evidence against him, and that he has a right to the presence of an attorney, either retained or appointed. The defendant may waive effectuation of these rights, provided the waiver is made voluntarily, knowingly and intelligently. If, however, he indicates in any manner and at any stage of the process that he wishes to consult with an attorney before speaking there can be no questioning. Likewise, if the individual is alone and indicates in any manner that he does not wish to be interrogated, the police may not question him. The mere fact that

Source: 384 U.S. 436 (1966)

he may have answered some questions or volunteered some statements on his own does not deprive him of the right to refrain from answering any further inquiries until he has consulted with an attorney and thereafter consents to be questioned.

The constitutional issue we decide in each of these cases is the admissibility of statements obtained from a defendant questioned while in custody or otherwise deprived of his freedom of action in any significant way. In each, the defendant was questioned by police officers, detectives, or a prosecuting attorney in a room in which he was cut off from the outside world. In none of these cases was the defendant given a full and effective warning of his rights at the outset of the interrogation process. In all the cases, the questioning elicited oral admissions, and in three of them, signed statements as well which were admitted at their trials. They all thus share salient features—incommunicado interrogation of individuals in a police-dominated atmosphere, resulting in self-incriminating statements without full warning of constitutional rights. . . .

It is obvious that such an interrogation environment is created for no purpose other than to subjugate the individual to the will of his examiner. This atmosphere carries its own badge of intimidation. To be sure, this is not physical intimidation, but it is equally destructive of human dignity. The current practice of incommunicado interrogation is at odds with one of our Nation's most cherished principles—that the individual may not be compelled to incriminate himself. Unless adequate protective devices are employed to dispel the compulsion inherent in custodial surroundings, no statement obtained from the defendant can truly be the product of his free choice.

From the foregoing, we can readily perceive an intimate connection between the privilege against self-incrimination and police custodial questioning. . . . An individual swept from familiar surrounding into police custody, surrounded by antagonistic forces, and subjected to the techniques of persuasion described above cannot be otherwise than under compulsion to speak. As a practical matter, the compulsion to speak in the isolated setting of the police station may well be greater than in courts or other official investigations, where there are often impartial observers to guard against intimidation or trickery. . . .

Today, then, there can be no doubt that the Fifth Amendment privilege is available outside of criminal court proceedings and serves to protect persons in all settings in which their freedom of action is curtailed in any significant way from being compelled to incriminate themselves. We have concluded that without proper safeguards the process of in-custody interrogation of persons suspected or accused of crime contains inherently compelling pressures which work to undermine the individual's will to resist and to compel him to speak where he would not otherwise do so freely. In order to combat these pressures and to permit a full opportunity to exercise the privilege against self-incrimination, the accused must be adequately and effectively apprised of his rights and the exercise of those rights must be fully honored.

It is impossible for us to foresee the potential alternatives for protecting the privilege which might be devised by Congress or the States in the exercise of their creative rule-making capacities. Therefore we cannot say that the Constitution necessarily requires adherence to any particular solution for the inherent compulsions of the interrogation process as it is presently conducted. Our decision in no way creates a constitutional straitjacket which will handicap sound efforts at reform, nor is it intended to have this effect. We encourage Congress and the States to continue their laudable search for increasingly effective ways of protecting the rights of the individual while promoting efficient enforcement of our criminal laws. However, unless we are shown other procedures which are at least as effective in apprising accused persons of their right of silence and in assuring a continuous opportunity to exercise it, the following safeguards must be observed.

At the outset, if a person in custody is to be subjected to interrogation, he must first be informed in clear and unequivocal terms that he has the right to remain silent. For those unaware of the privilege, the warning is needed simply to make them aware of it—the threshold requirement for an intelligent decision as to its exercise. More important, such a warning is an absolute prerequisite in overcoming the inherent pressures of the interrogation atmosphere. It is not just the subnormal or woefully ignorant who succumb to an interrogator's imprecations, whether implied or expressly stated, that the interrogation will continue until a confession is obtained or that silence in the face of accusation is itself damning and will bode ill when presented to a jury. Further, the warning will show the individual that his interrogators are prepared to recognize his privilege should he choose to exercise it.

The Fifth Amendment privilege is so fundamental to our system of constitutional rule and the expedient of giving an adequate warning as to the availability of the privilege so simple, we will not pause to inquire in individual cases whether the defendant was aware of his rights without a warning being given. Assessments of the knowledge the defendant possessed, based on information as to his age, education, intelligence, or prior contact with authorities, can never be more than speculation; a warning is a clearcut fact. More important, whatever the background of the person interrogated, a warning at the time of the interrogation is indispensable to overcome its pressures and to insure that the individual knows he is free to exercise the privilege at that point in time.

The warning of the right to remain silent must be accompanied by the explanation that anything said can and will be used against the individual in court. This warning is needed in order to make him aware not only of the privilege, but also of the consequences of foregoing it. It is only through an awareness of these consequences that there can be any assurance of real understanding and intelligent exercise of the privilege. Moreover, this warning may serve to make the individual more acutely aware that he is faced with a phase of the adversary system—that he is not in the presence of persons acting solely in his interest.

The circumstances surrounding in-custody interrogation can operate very quickly to overbear the will of one merely made aware of this privilege by his interrogators. Therefore, the right to have counsel present at the interrogation is indispensable to the protection of the Fifth Amendment privilege under the system we delineate today. Our aim is to assure that the individual's right to choose between silence and speech remains unfettered throughout the interrogation process. A once-stated warning, delivered by those who will conduct the interrogation, cannot itself suffice to that end among those who most require knowledge of their rights. A mere warning given by the interrogators is not alone sufficient to accomplish that end. Prosecutors themselves claim that the admonishment of the right to remain silent without more "will benefit only the recidivist and the professional." Even preliminary advice given to the accused by his own attorney can be swiftly overcome by the secret interrogation process. Thus, the need for counsel to protect the Fifth Amendment privilege comprehends not merely a right to consult with counsel prior to questioning, but also to have counsel present during any questioning if the defendant so desires. . . .

An individual need not make a pre-interrogation request for a lawyer. While such request affirmatively secures his right to have one, his failure to ask for a lawyer does not constitute a waiver. No effective waiver of the right to counsel during interrogation can be recognized unless specifically made after the warnings we here delineate have been given. The accused who does not know his rights and therefore does not make a request may be the person who most needs counsel. . . .

Accordingly we hold that an individual held for interrogation must be clearly informed that he has the right to consult with a lawyer and to have the lawyer with him during interrogation under the system for protecting the privilege we delineate today. As with the warnings of the right to remain silent and that anything stated can be used in evidence against him, this warning is an absolute prerequisite to interrogation. No amount of circumstantial evidence that the person may have been aware of this right will suffice to stand in its stead. Only through such a warning is there ascertainable assurance that the accused was aware of this right.

If an individual indicates that he wishes the assistance of counsel before any inter-rogation occurs, the authorities cannot rationally ignore or deny his request on the basis that the individual does not have or cannot afford a retained attorney. The financial abil-ity of the individual has no relationship to the scope of the rights involved here. The priv-ilege against self-incrimination secured by the Constitution applies to all individuals. The need for counsel in order to protect the privilege exists for the indigent as well as the affluent. In fact, were we to limit these constitutional rights to those who can retain an attorney, our decisions today would be of little significance. The cases before us as well as the vast majority of confession cases with which we have dealt in the past involve those unable to retain counsel. While authorities are not required to relieve the accused of his poverty, they have the obligation not to take advantage of indigence in the admin-istration of justice. Denial of counsel to the indigent at the time of interrogation while allowing an attorney to those who can afford one would be no more supportable by rea-son or logic than the similar situation at trial and on appeal. . . .

In order fully to apprise a person interrogated of the extent of his rights under this system then, it is necessary to warn him not only that he has the right to consult with an attorney, but also that if he is indigent a lawyer will be appointed to represent him. With-out this additional warning, the admonition of the right to consult with counsel would often be understood as meaning only that he can consult with a lawyer if he has one or has the funds to obtain one. The warning of a right to counsel would be hollow if not couched in terms that would convey to the indigent—the person most often subjected to interrogation—the knowledge that he too has a right to have counsel present. As with the warnings of the right to remain silent and of the general right to counsel, only by effec-tive and express explanation to the indigent of this right can there be assurance that he was truly in a position to exercise it.

Once warnings have been given, the subsequent procedure is clear. If the individual indicates in any manner, at any time prior to or during questioning, that he wishes to remain silent, the interrogation must cease. At this point he has shown that he intends to exercise his Fifth Amendment privilege; any statements taken after the person invokes his privilege cannot be other than the product of compulsion, subtle or otherwise. Without the right to cut off questioning, the setting of in-custody interrogation operates on the individual to overcome free choice in producing a statement after the privilege has been once invoked. If the individual states that he wants an attorney, the interrogation must cease until an attorney is present. At that time, the individual must have an opportunity to confer with the attorney and to have him present during any subsequent questioning. If the individual cannot obtain an attorney and he indicates that he wants one before speaking to police, they must respect his decision to remain silent.

This does not mean, as some have suggested, that each police station must have a "station house lawyer" present at all times to advise prisoners. It does mean, however, that if police propose to interrogate a person they must make known to him that he is entitled to a lawyer and that if he cannot afford one, a lawyer will be provided for him prior to any interrogation. If authorities conclude that they will not provide counsel during a reasonable period of time in which investigation in the field is carried out, they may refrain from doing so without violating the person's Fifth Amendment privilege so long as they do not question him during that time.

If the interrogation continues without the presence of an attorney and a statement is taken, a heavy burden rests on the government to demonstrate that the defendant knowingly and intelligently waived his privilege against self-incrimination and his right to retained or appointed counsel. This Court has always set high standards of proof for the waiver of constitutional rights, and we reassert these standards as applied to in-custody interrogation. Since the State is responsible for establishing the isolated circumstances under which the interrogation takes place and has the only means of making available corroborated evidence of warning given during incommunicado interrogation, the burden is rightly on its shoulders. . . .

In announcing these principles, we are not unmindful of the burdens which law enforcement officials must bear, often under trying circumstances. We also fully recognize the obligation of all citizens to aid in enforcing the criminal laws. This Court, while protecting individual rights, has always given ample latitude to law enforcement agencies in the legitimate exercise of their duties. The limits we have placed on the interrogation process should not constitute an undue interference with a proper system of law enforcement. As we have noted, our decision does not in any way preclude police from carrying out their traditional investigatory functions. Although confessions may play an important role in some convictions, the cases before us present graphic examples of the overstatement of the "need" for confessions. In each case authorities conducted interrogations ranging up to five days in duration despite the presence, through standard investigating practices, of considerable evidence against each defendant. . . .

Justice Harlan, with whom Justices Stewart and White join, dissenting:

I believe the decision for the Court represents poor constitutional law and entails harmful consequences for the country at large. How serious these consequences may prove to be only time can tell. But the basic flaws in the Court's justification seem to me readily apparent now once all sides of the problem are considered. . . .

The thrust of the new rules is to negate all pressures, to reinforce the nervous or ignorant suspect, and ultimately to discourage any confession at all. The aim in short is toward "voluntariness" in a utopian sense, or to view it from a different angle, voluntariness with a vengeance.

To incorporate this notion into the Constitution requires a strained reading of history and precedent and a disregard of the very pragmatic concerns that alone may on occasion justify such strains. I believe that reasoned examination will show that the Due Process Clauses provide an adequate tool for coping with confessions and that, even if the Fifth Amendment privilege against self-incrimination be invoked, its precedents taken as a whole do not sustain the present rules. Viewed as a choice based on pure policy, these new rules prove to be a highly debatable, if not one-sided, appraisal of the competing interests, imposed over widespread objection, at the very time when judicial restraint is most called for by the circumstances. . . .

I turn now to the Court's asserted reliance on the Fifth Amendment, an approach which I frankly regard as a *trompe l'oeil.* The Court's opinion in my view reveals no adequate basis for extending the Fifth Amendment's privilege against self-incrimination to the police station. Far more important, it fails to show that the Court's new rules are well supported, let alone compelled, by Fifth Amendment precedents. Instead, the new rules actually derive from quotation and analogy drawn from precedents under the Sixth Amendment, which should properly have no bearing on police interrogation. . . .

Having decided that the Fifth Amendment privilege does apply in the police station, the Court reveals that the privilege imposes more exacting restrictions than does the Fourteenth Amendment's voluntariness test. It then emerges from a discussion of *Escobedo* that the Fifth Amendment requires for an admissible confession that it be given by one distinctly aware of his right not to speak and shielded from "the compelling atmosphere" of interrogation. From these key premises, the Court finally develops the safeguards of warning, counsel, and so forth. I do not believe these premises are sustained by precedents under the Fifth Amendment.

The more important premise is that pressure on the suspect must be eliminated though it be only the subtle influence of the atmosphere and surroundings. The Fifth Amendment, however, has never been thought to forbid *all* pressure to incriminate one's self in the situations covered by it. . . . This is not to say that short of jail or torture any sanction is permissible in any case; policy and history alike may impose sharp limits. However, the Court's unspoken assumption that *any* pressure violates the privilege is not supported by the precedents and it has failed to show why the Fifth Amendment prohibits that relatively mild pressure the Due Process Clause permits.

The Court appears similarly wrong in thinking that precise knowledge of one's rights is a settled prerequisite under the Fifth Amendment to the loss of its protections. . . . No Fifth Amendment precedent is cited for the Court's contrary view. There might of course be reasons apart from Fifth Amendment precedent for requiring warning or any other safeguard on questioning but that is a different matter entirely. . . .

Examined as an expression of public policy, the Court's new regime proves so dubious that there can be no due compensation for its weakness in constitutional law. . . . Precedent reveals that the Fourteenth Amendment in practice has been construed to strike a different balance, that the Fifth Amendment gives the Court little solid support in this context, and that the Sixth Amendment should have no bearing at all. Legal history has been stretched before to satisfy deep needs of society. In this instance, however, the Court has not and cannot make the powerful showing that its new rules are plainly desirable in the context of our society, something which is surely demanded before those rules are engrafted onto the Constitution and imposed on every State and country in the land.

Without at all subscribing to the generally black picture of police conduct painted by the Court, I think it must be frankly recognized at the outset that police questioning allowable under due process precedents may inherently entail some pressure on the suspect and may seek advantage in his ignorance or weaknesses. . . . Until today, the role of the Constitution has been only to sift out *undue* pressure, not to assure spontaneous confessions.

The Court's new rules aim to offset these minor pressures and disadvantages intrinsic to any kind of police interrogation. The rules do not serve due process interests in preventing blatant coercion since, as I noted earlier, they do nothing to contain the policeman who is prepared to lie from the start. The rules work for reliability in confessions almost only in the Pickwickian sense that they can prevent some from being given at all.

---

215   *Loving v. Virginia (1967)*

Virginia, like many Southern states, had antimiscegenation laws dating back to slave times. In the post–Civil War era, the states expanded their earlier laws barring interracial sexual relations to prohibit racial intermarriage as well. A black woman and a white man, both residents of Virginia, had been married in the District of Columbia; after returning to Virginia, they were arrested, convicted of violating the state's ban on interracial marriage, and had their one-year jail sentence suspended for twenty-five years on condition that they leave the state and not return to Virginia for twenty-five years.

The state claimed that there was no racial discrimination here, since the statue applied evenhandedly to both whites and blacks. That had been the rationale in the *Naim* case mentioned in the decision, and the Supreme Court had been criticized because it had refused to review the *Naim* decision. In 1955, however, the Court wanted to focus its attention on the issue of school desegregation, and only later did it begin to spread the equal protection doctrine to cover other areas of racial discrimination.

See Harvey M. Applebaum, "Miscegenation Statutes: A Constitutional and Social Problem," 53 *Georgetown Law Review* 49 (1964); Walter Wadlington, "The *Loving* Case: Virginia's Antimiscegenation Statute in Historical Perspective," 52 *Virginia Law Review* 1189 (1966); and Peter Wallenstein, "Race, Marriage, and the Supreme Court: From

Pace v. Alabama (1883) to *Loving v. Virginia* (1967)," *Journal of Supreme Court History* 65 (1998).

———

Chief Justice Warren delivered the opinion of the Court:

Virginia is now one of 16 States which prohibit and punish marriages on the basis of racial classifications. Penalties for miscegenation arose as an incident to slavery and have been common in Virginia since the colonial period. In upholding the constitutionality of these provisions, [the Virginia Supreme Court] referred to its 1955 decision in Naim v. Naim as stating the reasons supporting the validity of these laws. In Naim, the state court concluded that the State's legitimate purposes were "to preserve the racial integrity of its citizens," and to prevent "the corruption of blood," "a mongrel breed of citizens," and "the obliteration of racial pride," obviously an endorsement of the doctrine of White Supremacy. The State does not contend that its powers to regulate marriage are unlimited notwithstanding the commands of the 14th Amendment but argues that the meaning of the Equal Protection Clause, as illuminated by the statements of the Framers, is only that state penal laws containing an interracial element as part of the definition of the offense must apply equally to whites and Negroes in the sense that members of each race are punished to the same degree. Thus, the State contends that, because its miscegenation statutes punish equally both the white and the Negro participants in an interracial marriage, these statutes, despite their reliance on racial classifications, do not constitute an invidious discrimination based upon race. . . .

Because we reject the notion that the mere "equal application" of a statute containing racial classifications is enough to remove the classifications from the 14th Amendment's proscription of all invidious racial discriminations, we do not accept the State's contention that these statutes should be upheld if there is any possible basis for concluding that they serve a rational purpose. We deal with statutes containing racial classifications, and the fact of equal application does not immunize the statute from the very heavy burden of justification which the 14th Amendment has traditionally required of state statutes drawn according to race.

The State argues that statements in the Thirty-ninth Congress about the time of the passage of the 14th Amendment indicate that the Framers did not intend the Amendment to make unconstitutional state miscegenation laws. We have said in connection with a related problem that although these historical sources "cast some light" they are not sufficient to resolve the problem; "at best, they are inconclusive." . . . We have rejected the proposition that the debates in the Thirty-ninth Congress or in the State legislatures which ratified the 14th Amendment supported the theory that the requirement of equal protection of the laws is satisfied by penal laws defining offenses based on racial classifications so long as white and Negro participants in the offense were similarly published. . . .

The State finds support for its "equal application" theory in the decision of the Court in Pace v. Alabama, . . . (1883). In that case, the Court upheld a conviction under an

Source: 388 U.S. 1 (1967)

Alabama statute forbidding adultery or fornication between a white person and a Negro which imposed a greater penalty than that of a statute proscribing similar conduct by members of the same race. The Court reasoned that the statute could not be said to discriminate against Negroes because the punishment for each participant in the offense was the same. However, as recently as the 1964 Term, in rejecting the reasoning of that case, we stated: "Pace represents a limited view of the Equal Protection Clause which has not withstood analysis in the subsequent decisions of this Court." . . . The clear and central purpose of the 14th Amendment was to eliminate all official state sources of invidious racial discrimination in the States. There can be no question but that Virginia's miscegenation statutes rest solely upon distinctions drawn according to race. The statutes proscribe generally accepted conduct if engaged in by members of different races. At the very least, the Equal Protection Clause demands that racial classifications, especially suspect in criminal statutes, be subjected to the "most rigid scrutiny" . . . and, if they are ever to be upheld, they must be shown to be necessary to the accomplishment of some permissible state objective, independent of the racial discrimination which it was the object of the 14th Amendment to eliminate. There is patently no legitimate overriding purpose independent of invidious racial discrimination which justifies this classification. The fact that Virginia prohibits only interracial marriages involving white persons demonstrates that the racial classifications must stand on their own justification, as measures designed to maintain White Supremacy. We have consistently denied the constitutionality of measures which restrict the rights of citizens on account of race. There can be no doubt that restricting the freedom to marry solely because of racial classifications violates the central meaning of the Equal Protection Clause.

Reversed.

---

216   *Epperson v. Arkansas (1968)*

In the famous "Monkey Trial" of 1927, John Scopes had been convicted in Dayton, Tennessee, for violating the state's ban on teaching evolution in his biology class. Scopes's conviction had been thrown out in the Tennessee Supreme Court on a technicality, thus preventing a challenge to the antievolution law from going on to the United States Supreme Court. As a result, the constitutionality of antievolution statutes in Tennessee and other states had never been tested. Forty years after the Scopes trial, a schoolteacher in Arkansas sought a declaratory judgment on the constitutionality of that state's law, which prohibited the teaching in state-supported schools of "the theory or doctrine that mankind is ascended or descended from a lower order of animals." She claimed she could not teach her biology course from the assigned syllabus without running afoul of the law. The state's high court evaded the issue, but a unanimous Supreme

Court, speaking through Justice Fortas, faced the establishment issue squarely. The decision, however, did not end efforts to ban evolution from the schools.

See Richard E. Morgan, *The Supreme Court and Religion* (1972); Frank J. Sorauf, *The Wall of Separation: The Constitutional Politics of Church and State* (1976); and C. R. Ledbetter, Jr., "The Antievolution Law: Church and State in Arkansas," 38 *Arkansas Historical Quarterly* 299 (1979).

———

Justice Fortas delivered the opinion of the Court:

The Arkansas law makes it unlawful for a teacher in any state-supported school or university "to teach the theory or doctrine that mankind ascended or descended from a lower order of animals," or "to adopt or use in any such institution a textbook that teaches" this theory. Violation is a misdemeanor and subjects the violator to dismissal from his position. . . .

Only Arkansas and Mississippi have such "antievolution" or "monkey" laws on their books. There is no record of any prosecutions in Arkansas under its statute. It is possible that the statute is presently more of a curiosity than a vital fact of life in these States. Nevertheless, the present case was brought, the appeal as of right is properly here, and it is our duty to decide the issues presented.

At the outset, it is urged upon us that the challenged statute is vague and uncertain and therefore within the condemnation of the Due Process Clause of the Fourteenth Amendment. The contention that the Act is vague and uncertain is supported by language in the brief opinion of Arkansas' Supreme Court. That court, perhaps reflecting the discomfort which the statute's quixotic prohibition necessarily engenders in the modern mind, stated that it "expresses no opinion" as to whether the Act prohibits "explanation" of the theory of evolution or merely forbids "teaching that the theory is true." Regardless of this uncertainty, the court held that the statute is constitutional.

On the other hand, counsel for the State, in oral argument in this Court, candidly stated that, despite the State Supreme Court's equivocation, Arkansas would interpret the statute "to mean that to make a student aware of the theory . . . just to teach that there was such a theory" would be grounds for dismissal and for prosecution under the statute; and he said "that the Supreme Court of Arkansas' opinion should be interpreted in that manner." He said: "If Mrs. Epperson would tell her students that 'Here is Darwin's theory, that man ascended or descended from a lower form of being,' then I think she would be under this statute liable for prosecution."

In any event, we do not rest our decision upon the asserted vagueness of the statute. On either interpretation of its language, Arkansas' statute cannot stand. It is of no moment whether the law is deemed to prohibit mention of Darwin's theory, or to forbid any or all of the infinite varieties of communication embraced within the term "teaching." Under either interpretation, the law must be stricken because of its conflict with the

Source: 393 U.S. 97 (1968)

constitutional prohibition of state laws respecting an establishment of religion or prohibiting the free exercise thereof. The overriding fact is that Arkansas' law selects from the body of knowledge a particular segment which it proscribes for the sole reason that it is deemed to conflict with a particular religious doctrine; that is, with a particular interpretation of the Book of Genesis by a particular religious group.

The antecedents of today's decision are many and unmistakable. They are rooted in the foundation soil of our Nation. They are fundamental to freedom.

Government in our democracy, state and national, must be neutral in matters of religious theory, doctrine, and practice. It may not be hostile to any religion or to the advocacy of no-religion; and it may not aid, foster, or promote one religion or religious theory against another or even against the militant opposite. The First Amendment mandates governmental neutrality between religion and religion, and between religion and nonreligion. . . .

The earliest cases in this Court on the subject of the impact of constitutional guarantees upon the classroom were decided before the Court expressly applied the specific prohibitions of the First Amendment to the States. But as early as 1923, the Court did not hesitate to condemn under the Due Process Clause "arbitrary" restrictions upon the freedom of teachers to teach and of students to learn. In that year, the Court, in an opinion by Justice McReynolds, held unconstitutional an Act of the State of Nebraska making it a crime to teach any subject in any language other than English to pupils who had not passed the eighth grade. The state's purpose in enacting the law was to promote civic cohesiveness by encouraging the learning of English and to combat the "baneful effect" of permitting foreigners to rear and educate their children in the language of the parents' native land. The Court recognized these purposes, and it acknowledged the State's power to prescribe the school curriculum, but it held that these were not adequate to support the restriction upon the liberty of teacher and pupil. The challenged statute it held, unconstitutionally interfered with the right of the individual, guaranteed by the Due Process Clause, to engage in any of the common occupations of life and to acquire useful knowledge.

For purposes of the present case, we need not reenter the difficult terrain which the Court, in 1923, traversed without apparent misgivings. We need not take advantage of the broad premise which the Court's decision in *Meyer* furnishes, nor need we explore the implications of that decision in terms of the justiciability of the multitude of controversies that beset our campuses today. Today's problem is capable of resolution in the narrower terms of the First Amendment's prohibition of laws respecting an establishment of religion or prohibiting the free exercise thereof.

There is and can be no doubt that the First Amendment does not permit the State to require that teaching and learning must be tailored to the principles or prohibitions of any religious sect of dogma. . . .

In the present case, there can be no doubt that Arkansas has sought to prevent its teachers from discussion of the theory of evolution because it is contrary to the belief of some that the Book of Genesis must be the exclusive source of doctrine as to the origin of man. No suggestion has been made that Arkansas' law may be justified by considerations of state policy other than the religious views of some of its citizens. It is clear that fundamentalist sectarian conviction was and is the law's reason for existence. . . .

Arkansas' law cannot be defended as an act of religious neutrality. Arkansas did not seek to excise from the curricula of its schools and universities all discussion of the origin of man. The law's effort was confined to an attempt to blot out a particular theory because of its supposed conflict with the Biblical account, literally read. Plainly, the law is contrary to the mandate of the First, and in violation of the Fourteenth, Amendments to the Constitution.

The judgment of the Supreme Court of Arkansas is reversed.

217   *Brandenburg v.*
                                                    Ohio (1969)

In the 1960s, a number of states still had criminal syndicalism laws on their books, some of them dating back to the Red Scare following World War I. The Ohio statute outlawed "advocating the duty, necessity, or propriety of crime, sabotage, violence, or unlawful methods of terrorism as a means of accomplishing industrial or political reform," as well as "voluntarily assembling with any society, group, or assemblage of persons formed to teach or advocate the doctrines of criminal syndicalism."

Brandenburg, the leader of a Ku Klux Klan group, had been convicted under this statute for advocating terrorism as a means of political reform. Most of the prosecution's case rested on videotapes showing Brandenburg addressing two small groups (one of six persons, the other of twelve), mumbling obscenities against Jews and blacks, and urging Caucasians to fight for their rights.

The Court voided the statute (and all similar state statutes) because of the overly vague definition of criminal activities, which restricted the rights of assembly and advocacy. It was applauded as combining the best of Holmes, Brandeis, and Hand, in that in areas of speech it made freedom the rule and restriction the restraint, permitted restriction only when a clear connection could be shown between speech and an illegal activity, and required the state to spell out its rules clearly.

See Frank R. Strong, "Fifty Years of 'Clear and Present Danger': From *Schenck* to *Brandenburg*—and Beyond," 1969 *Supreme Court Review* 41 (1970); and Harry Kalven, *A Worthy Tradition* (1988).

Per Curiam

The record shows that a man, identified at trial as the appellant, telephoned an announcer-reporter on the staff of a Cincinnati television station and invited him to come to a Ku Klux Klan "rally" to be held at a farm in Hamilton County. With the cooperation of the organizers, the reporter and a cameraman attended the meeting and filmed the events. Portions of the films were later broadcast on the local station and on a national network. The prosecution's case rested on the films and on testimony identifying the appellant as the person who communicated with the reporter and who spoke at the rally. . . .

One film showed 12 hooded figures, some of whom carried firearms. They were gathered around a large wooden cross, which they burned. No one was present other than the participants and the newsmen who made the film. Most of the words uttered during the scene were incomprehensible when the film was projected, but scattered phrases could be understood that were derogatory of Negroes and, in one instance, of Jews. Another scene on the same film showed the appellant, in Klan regalia, making a speech. The speech, in full, was as follows: "This is an organizers' meeting. We have had quite a few members here today which are—we have hundreds, hundreds of members throughout the State of Ohio. I can quote from a newspaper clipping from the Columbus, Ohio Dispatch, five weeks ago Sunday morning. The Klan has more members in the State of Ohio than does any other organization. We're not a revengent organization, but if our President, our Congress, our Supreme Court, continues to suppress the white, Caucasian race, it's possible that there might have to be some revengeance taken. We are marching on Congress July the Fourth, four hundred thousand strong. From there we are dividing into two groups, one group to march on St. Augustine, Florida, the other group to march into Mississippi. Thank you."

The second film showed six hooded figures one of whom, later identified as the appellant, repeated a speech very similar to that recorded on the first film. The reference to the possibility of "revengeance" was omitted, and one sentence was added: "Personally, I believe the nigger should be returned to Africa, the Jew returned to Israel." Though some of the figures in the films carried weapons, the speaker did not.

The Ohio Criminal Syndicalism Statute was enacted in 1919. From 1917 to 1920, identical or quite similar laws were adopted by 20 States and two territories. [In 1927], this Court sustained the constitutionality of California's Criminal Syndicalism Act, the text of which is quite similar to that of the laws of Ohio [in *Whitney* v. *California*]. The Court upheld the statute on the ground that, without more, "advocating" violent means to effect political and economic change involves such danger to the security of the State that the State may outlaw it. . . . But Whitney has been thoroughly discredited by later decisions. . . . These later decisions have fashioned the principle that the constitutional guarantees of free speech and free press do not permit a State to forbid or proscribe advocacy of the use of force or of law violation except where such advocacy is directed to inciting or producing imminent lawless action and is likely to incite or produce such action. As we said, . . . "the mere abstract teaching of the moral propriety or even moral necessity for a resort to force and violence, is not the same as preparing a group for vio-

---

Source: 395 U.S. 444 (1969)

lent action and steeling it to such action." . . . A statute which fails to draw this distinction impermissibly intrudes upon the freedoms guaranteed by the First and Fourteenth Amendments. It sweeps within its condemnation speech which our Constitution has immunized from governmental control. . . .

Measured by this test, Ohio's Criminal Syndicalism Act cannot be sustained. The Act punishes persons who "advocate or teach the duty, necessity, or propriety" of violence "as a means of accomplishing industrial or political reform"; or who publish or circulate or display any book or paper containing such advocacy; or who "justify" the commission of violent acts "with intent to exemplify, spread or advocate the propriety of the doctrines of criminal syndicalism"; or who "voluntarily assemble" with a group formed "to teach or advocate the doctrines of criminal syndicalism." Neither the indictment nor the trial judge's instructions to the jury in any way refined the statute's bald definition of the crime in terms of mere advocacy not distinguished from incitement to imminent lawless action.

Accordingly, we are here confronted with a statute which, by its own words and as applied, purports to punish mere advocacy and to forbid, on pain of criminal punishment, assembly with others merely to advocate the described type of action. Such a statute falls within the condemnation of the First and Fourteenth Amendments. The contrary teaching of [*Whitney*] cannot be supported, and that decision is therefore overruled.

Reversed.

---

218   *Swann v. Charlotte-Mecklenburg Board of Education (1971)*

The Warren Court's activism left a number of unresolved issues for its successor, especially in the area of school desegregation. In one of the last decisions of the Warren Court, *United States v. Montgomery County Board of Education* (1969), Justice Black set down guidelines to achieve racial mixes of faculty at individual schools that would reflect a ratio of white to black teachers in an entire system—the first time the Court had endorsed numerical goals as a remedy. But the decision was vague regarding specifics and apparently left the lower courts a great deal of leeway in framing equitable remedies.

In a case arising in North Carolina, the federal district court prescribed a specific mix of white (71 percent) to black students (29 percent) and ordered extensive busing to achieve that goal. Previous cases had dealt primarily with rural districts and small towns where blacks and whites lived in relatively close proximity. In the cities, school officials claimed, racial segregation resulted from longstanding residential patterns and not from legal prescription. The Court, in its last unanimous school desegregation decision, rejected that reasoning. Chief Justice Burger declared that the current segregation pattern resulted from previous discrimination and was therefore subject to correction. Moreover, he reaffirmed the great flexibility that the district courts had in fashioning appropriate remedies to achieve integration, including busing.

See J. Harvey Wilkinson, III, *From Brown to Bakke* (1979); Raymond Wolters, *The Burden of Brown: Thirty Years of School Desegregation* (1984); George R. Metcalf, *From Little Rock to Boston: The History of School Desegregation* (1983); Bernard Schwartz, *Swann's Way* (1986); and Gary Orfield, *Must We Bus? Segregated Schools and National Policy* (1978).

———

Chief Justice Burger delivered the opinion of the Court:

The problems encountered by the [lower courts] make plain that we should now try to amplify guidelines, however incomplete and imperfect, for the assistance of school authorities and courts. [Desegregation] has been rendered more difficult by changes since 1954 in the structure and patterns of communities, the growth of student population, movement of families, and other changes, some of which had marked impact on school planning, sometimes neutralizing or negating remedial action before it was fully implemented. Rural areas accustomed for half a century to the consolidated school systems implemented by bus transportation could make adjustments more readily than metropolitan areas. The objective today remains to eliminate from the public schools all vestiges of state-imposed segregation. If school authorities fail in their affirmative obligations . . . judicial authority may be invoked. Once a right and a violation have been shown, the scope of a district court's equitable powers to remedy past wrongs is broad. The task is to correct, by a balancing of the individual and collective interests, the condition that offends the Constitution. But it is important to remember that judicial powers may be exercised only on the basis of a constitutional violation.

[Local school boards] are traditionally charged with broad power to formulate and implement educational policy and might well conclude, for example, that in order to prepare students to live in a pluralistic society each school should have a prescribed ratio of Negro to white students reflecting the proportion for the district as a whole. To do this as an educational policy is within the broad discretionary powers of school authorities; absent a finding of a constitutional violation, however, that would not be within the authority of a federal court. . . .

(1) *Racial Balances or Racial Quotas.* . . . If we were to read the holding of the District Court to require, as a matter of substantive constitutional right, any particular degree of racial balance or mixing, that approach would be disapproved and we would be obliged to reverse. The constitutional command to desegregate schools does not mean that every school in every community must always reflect the racial composition of the school system as a whole. But the use made of mathematical ratios was no more than a starting point in the process of shaping a remedy, rather than an inflexible requirement.

———

Source: 402 U.S. 1 (1971)

[As] we said in Green, a school authority's remedial plan or a district court's remedial decree is to be judged by its effectiveness. Awareness of the racial composition of the whole school system is likely to be a useful starting point in shaping a remedy to correct past constitutional violations. In sum, the very limited use made of mathematical ratios was within the equitable remedial discretion of the District Court.

(2) *One-Race Schools.* The record in this case reveals the familiar phenomenon that in metropolitan areas minority groups are often found concentrated in one part of the city. In some circumstances certain schools may remain all or largely of one race until new schools can be provided or neighborhood patterns change. Schools all or predominantly of one race in a district of mixed population will require close scrutiny to determine that school assignments are not part of state-enforced segregation. In light of the above, it should be clear that the existence of some small number of one-race, or virtually one-race, schools within a district is not in and of itself the mark of a system which still practices segregation by law. [Courts] should scrutinize such schools, and the burden upon the school authorities will be to satisfy the court that their racial composition is not the result of present or past discriminatory action on their part. . . .

(3) *Remedial Altering of Attendance Zones.* The maps submitted in these cases graphically demonstrate that one of the principal tools employed by school planners and by courts to break up the dual school system has been a frank—and sometimes drastic—gerrymandering of school districts and attendance zones. An additional step was pairing, "clustering," or "grouping" of schools with attendance assignments made deliberately to accomplish the transfer of Negro students out of formerly segregated Negro schools and transfer of white students to formerly all-Negro schools. More often than not, these zones are neither compact nor contiguous; indeed they may be on opposite ends of the city. As an interim corrective measure, this cannot be said to be beyond the broad remedial powers of a court.

Absent a constitutional violation there would be no basis for judicially ordering assignment of students on a racial basis. All things being equal, with no history of discrimination, it might well be desirable to assign pupils to schools nearest their homes. But all things are not equal in a system that has been deliberately constructed and maintained to enforce racial segregation. The remedy for such segregation may be administratively awkward, inconvenient, and even bizarre in some situations and may impose burdens on some; but all awkwardness and inconvenience cannot be avoided in the interim period when remedial adjustments are being made to eliminate the dual school systems. No fixed or even substantially fixed guidelines can be established as to how far a court can go, but it must be recognized that there are limits. The objective is to dismantle the dual school system. . . . When school authorities present a district court with a "loaded game board," affirmative action in the form of remedial altering of attendance zones is proper to achieve truly nondiscriminatory assignments. [We] hold that the pairing and grouping of non-contiguous school zones is a permissible tool and such action is to be considered in light of the objectives sought. . . .

(4) *Transportation of Students.* . . . Eighteen million of the Nation's public school children, approximately 39%, were transported to their schools by bus in 1969–1970 in all parts of the country. The importance of bus transportation as a normal and accepted tool of educational policy is readily discernible in this and the companion case. The decree provided that . . . trips for elementary school pupils average about seven miles

and the District Court found that they would take "not over 35 minutes at the most." This system compares favorably with the transportation plan previously operated in Charlotte under which each day 23,600 students on all grade levels were transported an average of 15 miles one way for an average trip requiring over an hour. In these circumstances, we find no basis for holding that the local school authorities may not be required to employ bus transportation as one tool of school desegregation. Desegregation plans cannot be limited to the walk-in school. An objection to transportation of students may have validity when the time or distance of travel is so great as to risk either the health of the children or significantly impinge on the educational process. District courts must weigh the soundness of any transportation plan in light of what is said in subdivisions (1), (2), and (3) above. The reconciliation of competing values in a desegregation case is, of course, a difficult task with many sensitive facets but fundamentally no more so than remedial measures courts of equity have traditionally employed. . . .

At some point, these school authorities and others like them should have achieved full compliance with this Court's decision in Brown I. The systems will then be "unitary" in the sense required by our decisions in Green and Alexander. It does not follow that the communities served by such systems will remain demographically stable, for in a growing, mobile society, few will do so. Neither school authorities nor district courts are constitutionally required to make year-by-year adjustments of the racial composition of student bodies once the affirmative duty to desegregate has been accomplished and racial discrimination through official action is eliminated from the system. This does not mean that federal courts are without power to deal with future problems; but in the absence of a showing that either the school authorities or some other agency of the State has deliberately attempted to fix or alter demographic patterns to affect the racial composition of the schools, further intervention by a district court should not be necessary.

---

219   *Lemon v. Kurtzman (1971)*

The enormous educational aid programs initiated by the Johnson administration led to corresponding increases in funding by the states, as well as to a demand by parochial schools that they be allowed to share in the aid programs, since they carried the burden of educating a large number of children. The Court had been dealing with the problem of aid to parochial schools since 1947 (Document 193), and during the Warren years had developed a two-pronged test of whether legislative aid violated the Establishment Clause: The activity must have a secular legislative purpose and must neither advance nor hinder religion. In this case, the Burger Court added a third prong: The aid must avoid excessive governmental entanglement with religion. The *Lemon* test has been the standard criterion by which state aid programs have been judged ever since, but in recent years, the exact meaning of the test has become somewhat clouded. In a number of cases, both the majority and the minority have invoked *Lemon* to justify their support for or opposition to specific aid programs.

See Leonard W. Levy, *The Establishment Clause: Religion and the First Amendment* (2nd ed., 1994); Leo Pfeffer, "Freedom and/or Separation," 64 *Minnesota Law Review* 561 (1980); Jesse Choper, "The Religion Clauses of the First Amendment," 41 *University of Pittsburgh Law Review* 673 (1980); Kenneth F. Ripple, "The Entanglement Test of the Religion Clauses—A Ten Year Assessment," 27 *UCLA Law Review* 1195 (1980).

———

Chief Justice Burger delivered the opinion of the Court:

These two appeals raise questions as to Pennsylvania and Rhode Island statutes providing state aid to church-related elementary and secondary schools. Both statutes are challenged as violative of the Establishment and Free Exercise Clauses of the First Amendment and the Due Process Clause of the Fourteenth Amendment.

Pennsylvania has adopted a statutory program that provides financial support to nonpublic elementary and secondary schools by way of reimbursement for the cost of teachers' salaries, 0textbooks, and instructional materials in specified secular subjects. Rhode Island has adopted a statute under which the State pays directly to teachers in nonpublic elementary schools a supplement of 15% of their annual salary. Under each statute state aid has been given to church-related educational institutions. We hold that both statutes are unconstitutional. . . .

In Everson v. Board of Education . . . (1947), this Court upheld a state statute that reimbursed the parents of parochial school children for bus transportation expenses. There Mr. Justice Black, writing for the majority, suggested that the decision carried to "the verge" of forbidden territory under the Religion Clauses. . . . Candor compels acknowledgment, moreover, that we can only dimly perceive the lines of demarcation in this extraordinarily sensitive area of constitutional law.

The language of the Religion Clauses of the First Amendment is at best opaque, particularly when compared with other portions of the Amendment. Its authors did not simply prohibit the establishment of a state church or a state religion, an area history shows they regarded as very important and fraught with great dangers. Instead they commanded that there should be "no law *respecting* an establishment of religion." A law may be one "respecting" the forbidden objective while falling short of its total realization. A law "respecting" the proscribed result, that is, the establishment of religion, is not always easily identifiable as one violative of the Clause. A given law might not *establish* a state religion but nevertheless be one "respecting" that end in the sense of being a step that could lead to such establishment and hence offend the First Amendment.

In the absence of precisely stated constitutional prohibitions, we must draw lines with reference to the three main evils against which the Establishment Clause was intended to afford protection: "sponsorship, financial support, and active involvement of the sovereign in religious activity." . . .

———

Source: 403 U.S. 602 (1971)

Every analysis in this area must begin with consideration of the cumulative criteria developed by the Court over many years. Three such tests may be gleaned from our cases. First, the statute must have a secular legislative purpose; second, its principal or primary effect must be one that neither advances nor inhibits religion; . . . finally, the statute must not foster "an excessive government entanglement with religion." . . .

Inquiry into the legislative purposes of the Pennsylvania and Rhode Island statutes affords no basis for a conclusion that the legislative intent was to advance religion. On the contrary, the statutes themselves clearly state that they are intended to enhance the quality of the secular education in all schools covered by the compulsory attendance laws. There is no reason to believe the legislatures meant anything else. . . .

The two legislatures, however, have also recognized that church-related elementary and secondary schools have a significant religious mission and that a substantial portion of their activities is religiously oriented. They have therefore sought to create statutory restrictions designed to guarantee the separation between secular and religious educational functions and to ensure that State financial aid supports only the former. All these provisions are precautions taken in candid recognition that these programs approached, even if they did not intrude upon, the forbidden areas under the Religion Clauses. We need not decide whether these legislative precautions restrict the principal or primary effect of the programs to the point where they do not offend the Religion Clauses, for we conclude that the cumulative impact of the entire relationship arising under the statutes in each State involves excessive entanglement between government and religion.

In Waltz v. Tax Commission [1970], the Court upheld state tax exemptions for real property owned by religious organizations and used for religious worship. That holding, however, tended to confine rather than enlarge the area of permissible state involvement with religious institutions by calling for close scrutiny of the degree of entanglement involved in the relationship. The objective is to prevent, as far as possible, the intrusion of either into the precincts of the other.

Our prior holdings do not call for total separation between church and state; total separation is not possible in an absolute sense. Some relationship between government and religious organizations is inevitable. . . . Judicial caveats against entanglement must recognize that the line of separation, far from being a "wall," is a blurred, indistinct, and variable barrier depending on all the circumstances of a particular relationship.

This is not to suggest, however, that we are to engage in a legalistic minuet in which precise rules and forms must govern. A true minuet is a matter of pure form and style, the observance of which is itself the substantive end. Here we examine the form of the relationship for the light that it casts on the substance.

In order to determine whether the government entanglement with religion is excessive, we must examine the character and purposes of the institutions that are benefited, the nature of the aid that the State provides, and the resulting relationship between the government and the religious authority. Mr. Justice Harlan, in a separate opinion in *Walz*, . . . echoed the classic warning as to "programs, whose very nature is apt to entangle the state in details of administration." . . . Here we find that both statutes foster an impermissible degree of entanglement. . . .

We need not and do not assume that teachers in parochial schools will be guilty of bad faith or any conscious design to evade the limitations imposed by the statute and the First Amendment. We simply recognize that a dedicated religious person, teaching in a school affiliated with his or her faith and operated to inculcate its tenets, will inevitably experience great difficulty in remaining religiously neutral. Doctrines and faith are not inculcated or advanced by neutrals. With the best of intentions such a teacher would find it hard to make a total separation between secular teaching and religious doctrine. What would appear to some to be essential to good citizenship might well for others border on or constitute instruction in religion. Further difficulties are inherent in the combination of religious discipline and the possibility of disagreement between teacher and religious authorities over the meaning of the statutory restrictions.

We do not assume, however, that parochial school teachers will be unsuccessful in their attempts to segregate their religious beliefs from their secular educational responsibilities. But the potential for impermissible fostering of religion is present. . . .

A comprehensive, discriminating, and continuing state surveillance will inevitably be required to ensure that these restrictions are obeyed and the First Amendment otherwise respected. Unlike a book, a teacher cannot be inspected once so as to determine the extent and intent of his or her personal beliefs and subjective acceptance of the limitations imposed by the First Amendment. These prophylactic contacts will involve excessive and enduring entanglement between state and church. . . .

. . . The very restrictions and surveillance necessary to ensure that teachers play a strictly nonideological role give rise to entanglements between church and state. The Pennsylvania statute, like that of Rhode Island, fosters this kind of relationship. Reimbursement is not only limited to courses offered in the public schools and materials approved by state officials, but the statute excludes "any subject matter expressing religious teaching, or the morals or forms of worship of any sect." In addition, schools seeking reimbursement must maintain accounting procedures that require the State to establish the cost of the secular as distinguished from the religious instruction.

The Pennsylvania statute, moreover, has the further defect of providing state financial aid directly to the church-related schools. . . . The history of government grants of a continuing cash subsidy indicates that such programs have almost always been accompanied by varying measures of control and surveillance. The government cash grants before us now provide no basis for predicting that comprehensive measures of surveillance and controls will not follow. In particular the government's post-audit power to inspect and evaluate a church-related school's financial records and to determine which expenditures are religious and which are secular creates an intimate and continuing relationship between church and state.

A broader base of entanglement of yet a different character is presented by the divisive political potential of these state programs. In a community where such a large number of pupils are served by church-related schools, it can be assumed that state assistance will entail considerable political activity. Partisans of parochial schools, understandably concerned with rising costs and sincerely dedicated to both the religious and secular educational missions of their schools, will inevitably champion this cause and promote political action to achieve their goals. Those who oppose state aid, whether for constitutional, religious, or fiscal reasons, will inevitably respond and employ all of the usual political campaign techniques to prevail. Candidates will be forced to declare and voters to choose. It would be unrealistic to ignore the fact that many people confronted with issues of this kind will find their votes aligned with their faith. . . .

Finally, nothing we have said can be construed to disparage the role of church-related elementary and secondary schools in our national life. Their contribution has been and is enormous. Nor do we ignore their economic plight in a period of rising costs

and expanding need. Taxpayers generally have been spared vast sums by the maintenance of these educational institutions by religious organizations, largely by the gifts of
faithful adherents.

The merit and benefits of these schools, however are not the issue before us in these
cases. The sole question is whether state aid to these schools can be squared with the dictates of the Religion Clauses. Under our system the choice has been made that government is to be entirely excluded from the area of religious instruction and churches
excluded from the affairs of government. The Constitution decrees that religion must be
a private matter for the individual, the family, and the institutions of private choice, and
that while some involvement and entanglement are inevitable, lines must be drawn.

220

New York Times Co. v. United States (1971)

Portions of secret Defense Department studies and reports regarding the Vietnam War had been illegally copied and made available to the press. *The New
York Times* began publication of the so-called Pentagon Papers on June 13,
1971; the *Washington Post* followed on the eighteenth. The Nixon administration immediately sought to restrain publication, and between June 15 and 23,
the case went through two district and two circuit courts, one district court
issued an injunction, while the other did not. The Supreme Court granted certiorari on an expedited basis on June 25, heard arguments the next day, and
issued its opinion on June 30. By a six-to-three vote, the justices struck down
the injunctions, but could not agree on the reasoning. So the Court issued a very
brief *per curiam* decision, holding the injunctions invalid as prior restraints,
and the justices each wrote out his own reasons for the opinion. Although
hailed by the press as a resounding victory for the First Amendment, the decision broke no new ground, but reaffirmed the landmark ruling in *Near v. Minnesota* (Document 171).

See Louis Henkin, "The Right to Know and the Duty to Withhold: The Case of the Pentagon Papers," 120 *University of Pennsylvania Law Review* 271 (1971); Sanford J.
Ungar, *The Papers and the Paper* (1972); and Anthony Lewis, "A Public Right to Know
about Public Institutions: The First Amendment as a Sword," 1980 *Supreme Court
Review* 1 (1981).

Source: 403 U.S. 713 (1971)

Per Curiam

We granted certiorari in these cases in which the United States seeks to enjoin the New York Times and the Washington Post from publishing the contents of a classified study entitled "History of U.S. Decision-Making Process on Viet Nam Policy."

"Any system of prior restraints of expression comes to this Court bearing a heavy presumption against its constitutional validity." . . . The Government "thus carries a heavy burden of showing justification for the enforcement of such a restraint." . . . The District Court in the New York Times case and the District Court and the Court of Appeals in the Washington Post case held that the Government had not met that burden. We agree.

The judgment of the Court of Appeals for the District of Columbia Circuit is therefore affirmed. The order of the Court of Appeals for the Second Circuit is reversed and the case is remanded with directions to enter a judgment affirming the judgment of the District Court. The stays entered June 25, 1971, by the Court are vacated. The mandates shall issue forthwith.

So ordered.

Justice Black, with whom Justice Douglas joins, concurring:

I adhere to the view that the Government's case against the Washington Post should have been dismissed and that the injunction against the New York Times should have been vacated without oral argument when the cases were first presented to this Court. I believe that every moment's continuance of the injunctions against these newspapers amounts to a flagrant, indefensible, and continuing violation of the First Amendment. . . . In my view it is unfortunate that some of my Brethren are apparently willing to hold that the publication of news may sometimes be enjoined. Such a holding would make a shambles of the First Amendment. . . . Only a free and unrestrained press can effectively expose deception in government. To find that the President has "inherent power" to halt the publication of news by resort to the courts would wipe out the First Amendment. The word "security" is a broad, vague generality whose contours should not be invoked to abrogate the fundamental law embodied in the First Amendment. . . .

Justice Douglas, with whom Justice Black joins, concurring:

[The First Amendment] leaves, in my view, no room for governmental restraint on the press. There is, moreover, no statute barring the publication by the press of the material which the Times and Post seek to use. . . . [I]t is apparent that Congress was capable of and did distinguish between publishing and communication in the various sections of the Espionage Act.

So any power that the Government possesses must come from its "inherent power." The power to wage war is "the power to wage war successfully." But the war power stems from a declaration of war. The Constitution by Article I, § 8, gives Congress, not the President, power "to declare War." Nowhere are presidential wars authorized. We need not decide therefore what leveling effect the war power of Congress might have.

These disclosures may have a serious impact. But that is no basis for sanctioning a previous restraint on the press. . . . The dominant purpose of the First Amendment was

to prohibit the widespread practice of governmental suppression of embarrassing information. A debate of large proportions goes on in the Nation over our posture in Vietnam.
Open debate and discussion of public issues are vital to our national health. The stays in
these cases that have been in effect for more than a week constitute a flouting of the principles of the First Amendment as interpreted in [*Near* v. *Minnesota*].

Justice Brennan, concurring:
    The error that has pervaded these cases from the outset was the granting of any
injunctive relief whatsoever, interim or otherwise. The entire thrust of the Government's
claim throughout these cases has been that publication of the material sought to be
enjoined "could," or "might," or "may" prejudice the national interest in various ways.
But the First Amendment tolerates absolutely no prior judicial restraints of the press
predicated upon surmise or conjecture that untoward consequences may result. Our
cases, it is true, have indicated that there is a single, extremely narrow class of cases in
which the First Amendment's ban on prior judicial restraint may be overridden. Our
cases have thus far indicated that such cases may arise only when the Nation "is at
war" . . . during which times "no one would question but that a government might prevent actual obstruction to its recruiting service or the publication of the sailing dates of
transports or the number and location of troops." . . . Even if the present world situation
were assumed to be tantamount to a time of war, or if the power of presently available
armaments would justify even in peacetime the suppression of information that would
set in motion a nuclear holocaust, in neither of these actions has the Government presented or even alleged that publication of items from or based upon the material at issue
would cause the happening of an event of that nature. . . . Until the Government has
clearly made out its case, the First Amendment commands that no injunction may issue.

Justice Stewart, with whom Justice White joins, concurring:
    The only effective restraint upon executive policy and power in the areas of national
defense and international affairs may lie in an enlightened citizenry. For this reason, it is
perhaps here that a press that is alert, aware, and free most vitally serves the basic purpose of the First Amendment. Yet it is elementary that the successful conduct of international diplomacy and the maintenance of an effective national defense require both
confidentiality and secrecy. I think there can be but one answer to this dilemma, if
dilemma it be. The responsibility must be where the power is. The Executive must have
the largely unshared duty to determine and preserve the degree of internal security necessary to exercise . . . power successfully. It is the constitutional duty of the Executive—
as a matter of sovereign prerogative and not as a matter of law as the courts know law—
through the promulgation and enforcement of executive regulations to protect the
confidentiality necessary to carry out its responsibilities in the fields of international
relations and national defense. This is not to say that Congress and the courts have no
role to play. Undoubtedly Congress has the power to enact specific and appropriate criminal laws to protect government property and preserve government secrets. . . .
    But in the cases before us we are asked neither to construe specific regulations nor
to apply specific laws. We are asked, instead, to perform a function that the Constitution

gave to the Executive, not the Judiciary. We are asked, quite simply, to prevent the publication by two newspapers of material that the Executive Branch insists should not, in the national interest, be published. I am convinced that the Executive is correct with respect to some of the documents involved. But I cannot say that disclosure of any of them will surely result in direct, immediate, and irreparable damage to our Nation or its people. That being so, there can under the First Amendment be but one judicial resolution of the issues before us. I join the judgments of the Court.

Justice White, with whom Justice Stewart joins, concurring:
I concur in today's judgments, but only because of the concededly extraordinary protection against prior restraints enjoyed by the press under our constitutional system. I do not say that in no circumstances would the First Amendment permit an injunction against publishing information about government plans or operations. Nor, after examining the materials the Government characterizes as the most sensitive and destructive, can I deny that revelation of these documents will do substantial damage to public interests. Indeed, I am confident that their disclosure will have that result. But I nevertheless agree that the United States has not satisfied the very heavy burden which it must meet to warrant an injunction against publication in these cases, at least in the absence of express and appropriately limited congressional authorization for prior restraints in circumstances such as these. . . .

Justice Marshall, concurring:
The ultimate issue in this case is whether this Court or the Congress has the power to make law. [I]n some situations it may be that . . . there is a basis for the invocation of the equity jurisdiction of this Court as an aid to prevent the publication of material damaging to "national security," however that term may be defined. It would, however, be utterly inconsistent with the concept of separation of powers for this Court to use its power of contempt to prevent behavior that Congress has specifically declined to prohibit. There would be a similar damage to the basic concept of these co-equal branches of Government if when the [executive] had adequate authority granted by Congress to protect "national security" it can choose instead to invoke the contempt power of a court to enjoin the threatened conduct. . . . It is plain that Congress has specifically refused to grant the authority the Government seeks from this Court. It is not for this Court to fling itself into every breach perceived by some Government official. . . .

Justice Harlan, with whom the Chief Justice and Justice Blackmun join, dissenting:
[I] consider that the Court has been almost irresponsibly feverish in dealing with these cases.
Both the Court of Appeals for the Second Circuit and the Court of Appeals for the District of Columbia Circuit rendered judgment on June 23. The New York Times' petition for certiorari, its motion for accelerated consideration thereof, and its application for interim relief were filed in this Court on June 24, at about 11 A.M. The application of the United States for interim relief in the Post case was also filed here on June 24, at about

7:15 P.M. This Court's order setting a hearing before us on June 26 at 11 A.M., a course which I joined only to avoid the possibility of even more peremptory action by the Court, was issued less than 24 hours before. The record in the Post case was filed with the Clerk shortly before 1 P.M. on June 25; the record in the Times case did not arrive until 7 or 8 o'clock that same night. The briefs of the parties were received less than two hours before argument on June 26.

[The] frenzied train of events . . . took place in the name of the presumption against prior restraints created by the First Amendment. Due regard for the extraordinarily important and difficult questions involved in these litigations should have led the Court to shun its precipitate timetable. . . .

These are difficult questions of fact, of law, and of judgment; the potential consequences of erroneous decision are enormous. The time which has been available to us, to the lower courts, and to the parties has been wholly inadequate for giving these cases the kind of consideration they deserve. It is a reflection on the stability of the judicial process that these great issues—as important as any that have arisen during my time on the Court—should have been decided under the pressures engendered by the torrent of publicity that has attended these litigations from their inception.

Forced as I am to reach the merits of these cases, I dissent from the opinion and judgments of the Court. Within the severe limitations imposed by the time constraints under which I have been required to operate, I can only state my reasons in telescoped form. It is plain to me that the scope of the judicial function in passing upon the activities of the Executive Branch of the Government in the field of foreign affairs is very narrowly restricted. This view is, I think, dictated by the concept of separation of powers upon which our constitutional system rests. I agree that, in performance of its duty to protect the values of the First Amendment against political pressures, the judiciary must review the initial Executive determination to the point of satisfying itself that the subject matter of the dispute does lie within the proper compass of the President's foreign relations power. Constitutional considerations forbid "a complete abandonment of judicial control." Moreover, the judiciary may properly insist that the determination that disclosure of the subject matter would irreparably impair the national security be made by the head of the Executive Department concerned—here the Secretary of State or the Secretary of Defense—after actual personal consideration by that officer. But in my judgment the judiciary may not properly go beyond these two inquiries and redetermine for itself the probable impact of disclosure on the national security. . . .

Even if there is some room for the judiciary to override the executive determination, it is plain that the scope of review must be exceedingly narrow. . . . [Pending] further hearings in each case conducted under the appropriate ground rules, I would continue the restraints on publication. I cannot believe that the doctrine prohibiting prior restraints reaches to the point of preventing courts from maintaining the status quo long enough to act responsibly in matters of such national importance as those involved here.

221 *Branzburg v. Hayes (1972)*

Journalists had long claimed that in order to secure news effectively, they had to be protected against legal orders to divulge confidential sources, and they sought a "reporter's privilege" akin to the old common law protection afforded priest and penitent, doctor and patient, or lawyer and client. Some states had enacted such a privilege, but the press sought grounding for it in the First Amendment. In this case, three separate instances of reporters being penalized for refusing to divulge confidential sources to a grand jury led to the only Supreme Court examination of the issue. The six-man majority held that the Press Clause did not provide such protection. Potter Stewart, joined by Justices Marshall and Brennan, dissented; he had on other occasions referred to the "institutional" role of a free press in democratic societies and was willing to extend constitutional protections in order to facilitate the work of the press.

See Potter Stewart, "Or of the Press," 26 *Hastings Law Journal* 631 (1975); Benno C. Schmidt, Jr., "Journalists' Privilege: One Year After *Branzburg*," in Warren Symposium, *The First Amendment and the News Media* (1973); Harold Nelson., "The Newsman's Privilege," 24 *Vanderbilt Law Review* 667 (1971); and Vincent Blasi, *Press Subpoenas: An Empirical and Legal Analysis* (1971).

———

Justice White delivered the Opinion of the Court:

The issue in these cases is whether requiring newsmen to appear and testify before state or federal grand juries abridges the freedom of speech and press guaranteed by the First Amendment. We hold that it does not.

[The three journalists] press First Amendment claims that may be simply put; that to gather news it is often necessary to agree either not to identify the source of information published or to publish only part of the facts revealed, or both; that if the reporter is nevertheless forced to reveal these confidences to a grand jury, the source so identified and other confidential sources of other reporters will be measurably deterred from furnishing publishable information, all to the detriment of the free flow of information protected by the First Amendment. Although [they] do not claim an absolute privilege against official interrogation in all circumstances, they assert that the reporter should not be forced either to appear or to testify before a grand jury or at trial until and unless sufficient grounds are shown for believing that the reporter possesses information relevant to a crime the grand jury is investigating, that the information the reporter has is unavailable from other sources, and that the need for the information is sufficiently compelling to override the claimed invasion of First Amendment interests occasioned by the disclosure. Principally relied upon are [cases] requiring that official action with adverse impact on First Amendment rights be justified by a public interest that is "compelling" or "paramount," and those precedents establishing the principle that justifiable governmental goals may not be achieved by unduly broad means having an unnecessary impact on protected rights of speech, press, or association. The heart of the claim is that the burden on news gathering from compelling reporters to disclose confidential information outweighs any public interest in obtaining the information.

News gathering qualifies for First Amendment protection; without some protection for seeking out the news, freedom of the press could be eviscerated. But this case involves no intrusions upon speech or assembly; no penalty, civil or criminal, related to the content of published material, is at issue here. The use of confidential sources by the press is not forbidden or restricted. No attempt is made to require the press to publish its sources of information or indiscriminately to disclose them on request. The sole issue is the obligation of reporters to respond to grand jury subpoenas as other citizens do and to answer questions relevant to an investigation into the commission of crime. . . .

The First Amendment does not invalidate every incidental burdening of the press that may result from the enforcement of civil or criminal statutes of general applicability. It has generally been held that the First Amendment does not guarantee the press a constitutional right of special access to information not available to the public generally. Despite the fact that news gathering may be hampered, the press is regularly excluded from grand jury proceedings, our own conferences, the meetings of other official bodies gathered in executive session, and the meetings of private organizations. Newsmen have no constitutional right of access to the scenes of crime or disaster when the general public is excluded, and they may be prohibited from attending or publishing information about trials if such restrictions are necessary to assure a defendant a fair trial before an impartial tribunal. It is thus not surprising that the great weight of authority is that newsmen are not exempt from the normal duty of appearing before a grand jury and answering questions relevant to a criminal investigation. . . .

This conclusion [does not] threaten the vast bulk of confidential relationships between reporters and their sources. Only where news sources themselves are implicated in crime or possess information relevant to the grand jury's task need they or the reporter be concerned about grand jury subpoenas. Nothing before us indicates that a large number or percentage of *all* confidential news sources fall into either category and would in any way be deterred by our holding. . . .

We are admonished that refusal to provide a First Amendment reporter's privilege will undermine the freedom of the press to collect and disseminate news. But this is not the lesson history teaches us. From the beginning of our country the press has operated without constitutional protection for press informants, and the press has flourished. It is said that currently press subpoenas have multiplied, that mutual distrust and tension between press and officialdom have increased, that reporting styles have changed, and that there is now more need for confidential sources, particularly where the press seeks news about minority cultural and political groups or dissident organizations suspicious of the law and public officials. These developments, even if true, are treacherous grounds for a far-reaching interpretation of the First Amendment. . . .

The argument for such a constitutional privilege rests heavily on those cases holding that the infringement of protected First Amendment rights must be no broader than necessary to achieve a permissible governmental purpose. We do not deal, however, with a governmental institution that has abused its proper function, as a legislative committee does when it "expose[s] for the sake of exposure." . . . Nothing in the record indicates that these grand juries were "prob[ing] at will and without relation to existing need." . . . Nor did the grand juries attempt to invade protected First Amendment rights by forcing wholesale disclosure of names and organizational affiliations for a purpose which was not germane to the determination of whether crime has been committed . . . and the characteristic secrecy of grand jury proceedings is a further protection against the undue invasion of such rights. . . . As we have indicated, the investigation of crime by the grand jury implements a fundamental governmental role of securing the safety of the person and property of the citizen, and it appears to us that calling reporters to give testimony in the manner and for the reasons that other citizens are called "bears a reasonable relationship to the achievement of the governmental purpose asserted as its justification." . . .

We are unwilling to embark the judiciary on a long and difficult journey to such an uncertain destination. The administration of a constitutional newsman's privilege would present practical and conceptual difficulties of a high order. Sooner or later, it would be necessary to define those categories of newsmen who qualified for the privilege, a questionable procedure in light of the traditional doctrine that liberty of the press is the right of the lonely pamphleteer who uses carbon paper or a mimeograph just as much as of the large metropolitan publisher who utilizes the latest photocomposition methods. The informative function asserted by representatives of the organized press in the present cases is also performed by lecturers, political pollsters, novelists, academic researchers, and dramatists. Almost any author may quite accurately assert that he is contributing to the flow of information to the public, that he relies on confidential sources of information, and that these sources will be silenced if he is forced to make disclosures before a grand jury. In each instance where a reporter is subpoenaed to testify, the courts would also be embroiled in preliminary factual and legal determinations with respect to whether the proper predicate had been laid for the reporter's appearance. In the end, by considering whether enforcement of a particular law served a "compelling" governmental interest, the courts would be inextricably involved in distinguishing between the value of enforcing different criminal laws. By requiring testimony from a reporter in investigations involving some crimes but not in others, they would be making a value judgment which a legislature had declined to make. At the federal level, Congress has freedom to determine whether a statutory newsman's privilege is necessary and desirable and to fashion standards and rules as narrow or broad as deemed necessary and, equally important, to re-fashion those rules as experience from time to time may dictate. There is also merit in leaving state legislatures free, within First Amendment limits, to fashion their own standards. . . . There is much force in the pragmatic view that the press has at its disposal powerful mechanisms of communication and is far from helpless to protect itself from harassment or substantial harm. . . .

. . . Grand jury investigations if instituted or conducted other than in good faith, would pose wholly different issues for resolution under the First Amendment. Official harassment of the press undertaken not for purposes of law enforcement but to disrupt a reporter's relationship with his news sources would have no justification. Grand juries are subject to judicial control and subpoenas to motions to quash. We do not expect courts will forget that grand juries must operate within the limits of the First Amendment as well as the Fifth.

So ordered.

---

222   *Furman v. Georgia (1972)*

The question of whether capital punishment violated the Eighth Amendment ban on cruel and unusual punishment had been pushed upon the Court for nearly a decade before the justices agreed to tackle the issue in late 1971. At the time, a subcommittee of the Court sifted through literally dozens of petitions for review in capital punishment cases to pick out a handful that could serve as useful test cases. In June 1972, by a vote of five to four, the Court vacated approximately 600 death sentences on the grounds that capital punishment schemes, as then structured, violated the Eighth and Fourteenth amendments. The majority, however, could agree only on a one-paragraph *per curiam* opinion; each of the justices then explained his vote. Although the Eighth Amendment is frequently referred to, the analysis used is really the Cardozo reasoning in *Palko* (Document 186), seeking to determine the contours of due process within an ordered scheme of liberty. The decision did not declare the death sentence *per se* unconstitutional, although two justices, Marshall and Brennan, continued to voice that view in other capital punishment cases. When states revised their sentencing guidelines, the Court held capital punishment, with appropriate procedural safeguards, constitutional (Document 232).

See Hugo Bedau, *The Courts, the Constitution, and Capital Punishment* (1977); Walter Burns, *For Capital Punishment* (1979); Jack Greenburg, "Capital Punishment as a System," 91 *Yale Law Journal* 908 (1982); William Schabas, *The Abolition of the Death Penalty in International Law* (1993); and Louis P. Pojman, *The Death Penalty—For and Against* (1998).

Source: 408 U.S. 238 (1972)

Per Curiam

The Court holds that the imposition and carrying out of the death penalty in these cases constitutes cruel and unusual punishment in violation of the Eighth and Fourteenth Amendments. The judgment in each case is therefore reversed insofar as it leaves undisturbed the death sentence imposed, and the cases are remanded for further proceedings. So ordered.

Judgment in each case reversed in part and cases remanded. . . .

Justice Douglas, concurring:

In these three cases the death penalty was imposed, one of them for murder, and two for rape. In each the determination of whether the penalty should be death or a lighter punishment was left by the State to the discretion of the judge or of the jury. In each of the three cases the trial was to a jury. . . .

In this country there was almost from the beginning a "rebellion against the common-law rule imposing a mandatory death sentence on all convicted murderers." The first attempted remedy was to restrict the death penalty to defined offenses such as "premeditated" murder. But juries took "the law into their own hands" and refused to convict on the capital offense.

> "In order to meet the problem of jury nullification, legislatures did not try, as before, to refine further the definition of capital homicides. Instead they adopted the method of forthrightly granting juries the discretion which they had been exercising in fact."

The Court [in *McGautha v. California* (1971)] concluded "In light of history, experience, and the present limitations of human knowledge, we find it quite impossible to say that committing to the untrammeled discretion of the jury the power to pronounce life or death in capital cases is offensive to anything in the Constitution."

The Court refused to find constitutional dimensions in the argument that those who exercise their discretion to send a person to death should be given standards by which that discretion should be exercised. . . . We are now imprisoned in the *McGautha* holding. Indeed the seeds of the present cases are in *McGautha*. Juries (or judges, as the case may be) have practically untrammeled discretion to let an accused live or insist that he die. . . .

A law that stated that anyone making more than $50,000 would be exempt from the death penalty would plainly fail, as would a law that in terms said that Blacks, those who never went beyond the fifth grade in school, or those who made less than $3,000 a year, or those who were unpopular or unstable should be the only people executed. A law which in the overall view reaches that result in practice has no more sanctity than a law which in terms provides the same.

Thus, these discretionary statutes are unconstitutional in their operation. They are pregnant with discrimination and discrimination is an ingredient not compatible with the idea of equal protection of the laws that is implicit in the ban on "cruel and unusual" punishments.

Any law which is nondiscriminatory on its face may be applied in such a way as to violate the Equal Protection Clause of the Fourteenth Amendment. Such conceivably might be the fate of a mandatory death penalty, where equal or lesser sentences were imposed on the elite, a harsher one on the minorities or members of the lower castes. Whether a mandatory death penalty would otherwise be constitutional is a question I do not reach.

I concur in the judgments of the Court.

Justice Brennan, concurring:

At bottom, then, the Cruel and Unusual Punishments Clause prohibits the infliction of uncivilized and inhuman punishments. The State, even as it punishes, must treat its members with respect for their intrinsic worth as human beings. A punishment is "cruel and unusual," therefore, if it does not comport with human dignity.

This formulation, of course, does not of itself yield principles for assessing the constitutional validity of particular punishments. Nevertheless, even though "this Court has had little occasion to give precise content to the [Clause]," there are principles recognized in our cases and inherent in the clause sufficient to permit a judicial determination whether a challenged punishment comports with human dignity.

The primary principle is that a punishment must not be so severe as to be degrading to the dignity of human beings. . . .

In determining whether a punishment comports with human dignity, we are aided also by a second principle inherent in the Clause—that the State must not arbitrarily inflict a severe punishment. This principle derives from the notion that the State does not respect human dignity when, without reason, it inflicts upon some people a severe punishment that it does not inflict upon others. . . .

A third principle inherent in the Clause is that a severe punishment must not be unacceptable to contemporary society. . . .

The final principle inherent in the Clause is that a severe punishment must not be excessive. A punishment is excessive under this principle if it is unnecessary: the infliction of a severe punishment by the State cannot comport with human dignity when it is nothing more than the pointless infliction of suffering. If there is a significantly less severe punishment adequate to achieve the purposes for which the punishment is inflicted, the punishment inflicted is unnecessary and therefore excessive. . . .

When the punishment of death is inflicted in a trivial number of the cases in which it is legally available, the conclusion is virtually inescapable that it is being inflicted arbitrarily. Indeed, it smacks of little more than a lottery system. The States claim, however, that this rarity is evidence not of arbitrariness, but of informed selectivity: Death is inflicted, they say, only in "extreme" cases.

Informed selectivity, of course, is a value not to be denigrated. Yet presumably the State could make precisely the same claim if there were 10 executions per year, or five, or even if there were but one. That there may be as many as 50 per year does not strengthen the claim. When the rate of infliction is at this low level, it is highly implausible that only the worst criminals or the criminals who commit the worst crimes are selected for this punishment. No one has yet suggested a rational basis that could differentiate in those terms the few who die from the many who go to prison. Crimes and criminals simply do not admit of a distinction that can be drawn so finely as to explain, on that ground, the execution of such a tiny sample of those eligible. Certainly the laws that provide for this punishment do not attempt to draw that distinction; all cases to which the laws apply are necessarily "extreme." Nor is the distinction credible in fact. If, for example, petitioner Furman or his crime illustrate the "extreme," then nearly all murderers and their murders are also "extreme." Furthermore, our procedures in death cases, rather than resulting in the selection of "extreme" cases for this punishment, actually sanction an arbitrary selection. For this Court has held that juries may, as they do, make the decision whether to impose a death sentence wholly unguided by standards governing that decision. In other words, our procedures are not constructed to guard against the totally capricious selection of criminals for the punishment of death.

Although it is difficult to imagine what further facts would be necessary in order to prove that death is, as my Brother STEWART puts it, "wantonly and freakishly" inflicted, I need not conclude that arbitrary infliction is patently obvious. I am not considering this punishment by the isolated light of one principle. The probability or arbitrariness is sufficiently substantial that it can be relied upon, in combination with the other principles, in reaching a judgment on the constitutionality of this punishment. . . .

Justice Stewart, concurring:

Legislatures—state and federal—have sometimes specified that the penalty of death shall be the mandatory punishment for every person convicted of engaging in certain designated criminal conduct. Congress, for example, has provided that anyone convicted of acting as a spy for the enemy in time of war shall be put to death. The Rhode Island Legislature has ordained the death penalty for a life term prisoner who commits murder. Massachusetts has passed a law imposing the death penalty upon anyone convicted of murder in the commission of a forcible rape. An Ohio law imposes the mandatory penalty of death upon the assassin of the President of the United States or the Governor of the State.

If we were reviewing death sentences imposed under these or similar laws, we would be faced with the need to decide whether capital punishment is unconstitutional for all crimes and under all circumstances. We would need to decide whether a legislature—state or federal—could constitutionally determine that certain criminal conduct is so atrocious that society's interest in deterrence and retribution wholly outweighs any considerations of reform or rehabilitation of the perpetrator, and that, despite the inconclusive empirical evidence, only the automatic penalty of death will provide maximum deterrence.

On that score I would say only that I cannot agree that retribution is a constitutionally impermissible ingredient in the imposition of punishment. The instinct for retribution is part of the nature of man, and channeling that instinct in the administration of criminal justice serves an important purpose in promoting the stability of a society governed by law. When people begin to believe the organized society is unwilling or unable to impose upon criminal offenders the punishment they "deserve," then there are sown the seeds of anarchy—of self-help, vigilante justice, and lynch law.

The constitutionality of capital punishment in the abstract is not, however, before us in these cases. For the Georgia and Texas legislatures have not provided that the death penalty shall be imposed upon all those who are found guilty of forcible rape. And the Georgia Legislature has not ordained that death shall be the automatic punishment for murder. In a word, neither State has made a legislative determination that forcible rape and murder can be deterred only by imposing the penalty of death upon all who perpetrate those offenses. As Mr. Justice White so tellingly puts it, "legislative will is not frustrated if the penalty is never imposed."

Instead, the death sentences now before us are the product of a legal system that brings them, I believe, within the very core of the Eighth Amendment's guarantee against cruel and unusual punishments, a guarantee applicable against the States through the Fourteenth Amendment. In the first place, it is clear that these sentences are "cruel" in the sense that they excessively go beyond, not in degree but in kind, the punishments that the state legislatures have determined to be necessary. In the second place, it is equally clear that these sentences are "unusual" in the sense that the penalty of death is infrequently imposed for murder, and that its imposition for rape is extraordinarily rare. But I do not rest by conclusion upon these two propositions alone.

These death sentences are cruel and unusual in the same way that being struck by lightening is cruel and unusual. For, of all the people convicted of rapes and murders in 1967 and 1968, many just as reprehensible as these, the petitioners are among a capriciously selected random handful upon whom the sentence of death has in fact been imposed. My concurring Brothers have demonstrated that, if any basis can be discerned for the selection of these few to be sentenced to die, it is the constitutionally impermissible basis of race. But racial discrimination has not been proved, and I put it to one side. I simply conclude that the Eighth and Fourteenth Amendments cannot tolerate the infliction of a sentence of death under legal systems that permit this unique penalty to be so wantonly and so freakishly imposed.

For these reasons I concur in the judgments of the Court.

Justice White, concurring:

The facial constitutionality of statutes requiring the imposition of the death penalty for first degree murder, for more narrowly defined categories of murder or for rape would present quite different issues under the Eighth Amendment than are posed by the cases before us. In joining the Court's judgment, therefore, I do not at all intimate that the death penalty is unconstitutional *per se* or that there is no system of capital punishment that would comport with the Eighth Amendment. That question, ably argued by several of my Brethren, is not presented by these cases and need not be decided.

The narrower question to which I address myself concerns the constitutionality of capital punishment statutes under which (1) the legislature authorizes the imposition of the death penalty for murder or rape; (2) the legislature does not itself mandate the penalty in any particular class or kind of case (that is, legislative will is not frustrated if the penalty is never imposed) but delegates to judges or juries the decisions as to those cases, if any, in which the penalty will be utilized; and (3) judges and juries have ordered the death penalty with such infrequency that the odds are now very much against imposition and execution of the penalty with respect to any convicted murderer or rapist. It is in this context that we must consider whether the execution of these petitioners violates the Eighth Amendment.

I begin with what I consider a near truism: that the death penalty could so seldom be imposed that it would cease to be a credible deterrent or measurably to contribute to any other end of punishment in the criminal justice system. It is perhaps true that no matter how infrequently those convicted of rape or murder are executed, the penalty so imposed is not disproportionate to the crime and those executed may deserve exactly what they received. It would also be clear that executed defendants are finally and completely incapacitated from again committing rape or murder or any other crime. But when imposition of the penalty reaches a certain degree of infrequency, it would be very doubtful that any existing general need for retribution would be measurably satisfied. Nor could it be said with confidence that society's need for specific deterrence justifies death for so few when for so many in like circumstances life imprisonment or shorter prison terms are judged sufficient, or that community values are measurably reenforced by authorizing a penalty so rarely invoked.

Most important, a major goal of the criminal law—to deter others by punishing the convicted criminal—would not be substantially served where the penalty is so seldom invoked that it ceases to be the credible threat essential to influence the conduct of others. For present purposes I accept the morality and utility of punishing one person to influence another. I accept also the effectiveness of punishment generally and need not reject the death penalty as a more effective deterrent than a lesser punishment. But common sense and experience tell us that seldom-enforced laws become ineffective measures for controlling human conduct and that the death penalty, unless imposed with sufficient frequency, will make little contribution to deterring those crimes for which it may be exacted. . . .

It is also my judgment that this point has been reached with respect to capital punishment as it is presently administered under the statutes involved in these cases. Concededly, it is difficult to prove as a general proposition that capital punishment, however administered, more effectively serves the ends of the criminal law than does imprisonment. But however that may be, I cannot avoid the conclusion that as the statutes before us are now administered, the penalty is so infrequently imposed that the threat of execution is too attenuated to be of substantial service to criminal justice.

I need not restate the facts and figures that appear in the opinion of my Brethren. Nor can I "prove" my conclusion from these data. But like my Brethren, I must arrive at judgment; and I can do no more than state a conclusion based on 10 years of almost daily exposure to the facts and circumstances of hundreds and hundreds of federal and state criminal cases involving crimes for which death is the authorized penalty. That conclusion, as I have said, is that the death penalty is exacted with great infrequency even for the most atrocious crimes and that there is no meaningful basis for distinguishing the few cases in which it is imposed from the many cases in which it is not. The short of it is that the policy of vesting sentencing authority primarily in juries—a decision largely motivated by the desire to mitigate the harshness of the law and to bring community judgment to bear on the sentence as well as guilt or innocence—has so effectively achieved its aims that capital punishment within the confines of the statutes now before us has for all practical purposes run its course. . . .

I concur in the judgments of the Court.

Justice Marshall, concurring:

A punishment may be deemed cruel and unusual for any one of four distinct reasons.

First, there are certain punishments which inherently involve so much physical pain and suffering that civilized people cannot tolerate them—e.g., use of the rack, the thumbscrew, or other modes of torture. Regardless of public sentiment with respect to imposition of one of these punishments in a particular case or at any one moment in history, the Constitution prohibits it. These are punishments that have been barred since the adoption of the Bill of Rights.

Second, there are punishments which are unusual, signifying that they were previously unknown as penalties for a given offense. . . .

Third, a penalty may be cruel and unusual because it is excessive and serves no valid legislative purpose. The decisions previously discussed are replete with assertions that one of the primary functions of the cruel and unusual punishments clause is to prevent excessive or unnecessary penalties. . . .

Fourth, where a punishment is not excessive and serves a valid legislative purpose, it still may be invalid if popular sentiment abhors it. . . .

There is but one conclusion that can be drawn from all of this—i.e., the death penalty is an excessive and unnecessary punishment which violates the Eighth Amendment. The statistical evidence is not convincing beyond all doubt, but, it is persuasive. It is not improper at this point to take judicial notice of the fact that for more than 200 years men have labored to demonstrate that capital punishment serves no purpose that life imprisonment could not serve equally as well. And they have done so with great success. Little if any evidence has been adduced to prove the contrary. The point has now been reached at which deference to the legislatures is tantamount to abdication of our judicial roles as factfinders, judges, and ultimate arbiters of the Constitution. We know that at some point the presumption of constitutionality accorded legislative acts gives way to a realistic assessment of those acts. This point comes when there is sufficient evidence available so that judges can determine not whether the legislature acted wisely, but whether it had any rational basis whatsoever for acting. We have this evidence before us now. There is no rational basis for concluding that capital punishment is not excessive. It therefore violates the Eighth Amendment.

In addition, even if capital punishment is not excessive, it nonetheless violates the Eighth Amendment because it is morally unacceptable to the people of the United States at this time in their history. . . .

Chief Justice Burger, with whom Justices Blackmun, Powell, and Rehnquist join, dissenting:

While I cannot endorse the process of decisionmaking that has yielded today's result and the restraints which that result imposes on legislative action, I am not altogether displeased that legislative bodies have been given the opportunity, and indeed unavoidable responsibility, to make a thorough re-evaluation of the entire subject of capital punishment. If today's opinions demonstrate nothing else, they starkly show that this is an area where legislatures can act far more effectively than courts.

The legislatures are free to eliminate capital punishment for specific crimes or to carve out limited exceptions to a general abolition of the penalty, without adherence to the conceptual strictures of the Eighth Amendment. The legislatures can and should make an assessment of the deterrent influence of capital punishment, both generally and as affecting the commission of specific types of crimes. If legislatures come to doubt the effi-cacy of capital punishment, they can abolish it, either completely or on a selective basis. If new evidence persuades them that they have acted unwisely, they can reverse their field and reinstate the penalty to the extent it is thought warranted. An Eighth Amendment rul-ing by judges cannot be made with such flexibility or discriminating precision. . . .

The five opinions in support of the judgment differ in many respects, but they share a willingness to make sweeping factual assertions, unsupported by empirical data, con-cerning the manner of imposition and effectiveness of capital punishment in this coun-try. Legislatures will have the opportunity to make a more penetrating study of these claims with the familiar and effective tools available to them as they are not to us.

---

233 *Equal Rights Amendment (1972–1973)*

The women's movement realized that to secure permanent and protected equal-ity, it needed more than congressional statutes (which could be rescinded), state equal rights amendments (which had limited applicability), or even Court inter-pretations of the Equal Protection Clause (which could vary as personnel on the bench changed). There had been demands for an equal rights for women amendment since the 1920s, but Congress did not respond to the demand of women's groups for fifty years, until it approved a constitutional amendment and sent it to the states for ratification on March 22, 1972.

About half the necessary number of states ratified within three months after submission, but then opposition to the ERA coalesced and managed to stall the process. In October 1978, Congress extended the period for ratification (originally seven years) until June 30, 1982. In July 1980, the ERA needed only three more states to ratify it, but it still lacked those three states when the extended deadline ran out.

During the 1970s and early 1980s, exchanges between supporters and opponents of the ERA could be found in newspapers, magazines, and scholarly journals, as well as on radio and television. The following exchange between Phyllis Schlafly, one of the national leaders in the anti-ERA drive, and Senator Marlow Cook of Kentucky, is typical.

See Janet K. Boles, *The Politics of the Equal Rights Amendment* (1979); Donald G. Mathews and Jane S. DeHart, *Sex, Gender, and the Politics of the ERA* (1990); and Mary Frances Berry, *Why ERA Failed* (1986).

A. *Proposed Equal Rights Amendment (1972)*

SECTION 1. Equality of rights under law shall not be denied or abridged by the United States or by any State on account of sex.

SECTION 2. The Congress shall have the power to enforce, by appropriate legislation, the provisions of this article.

SECTION 3. This amendment shall take effect two years after the date of ratification.

B. *Against the ERA (1973)*

PHYLLIS SCHLAFLY

The Equal Rights Amendment will not give women anything which they do not already have, or have a way of getting, but it will take away from women some of their most important legal rights, benefits and exemptions. It is like trying to kill a fly with a sledge-hammer; you probably won't kill the fly, but you surely will break up some of the furniture.

Most people who supported ERA as it sailed through Congress by big margins did so because they believed it would give women "equal pay for equal work." The fact is, however, that ERA will not do anything whatsoever for women in the field of employment. In not a single one of the 15 state legislative hearings where I have testified have the pro-ERA lawyers claimed that ERA will help women in this vital area. When I stated that ERA will do nothing for women in the field of employment, in a live debate with the leading Congressional proponent of ERA, Congresswoman Martha Griffiths, on the Lou Gordon television show in Detroit, she replied, "I never claimed it would."

One of the reasons why this is so is the existence of the Equal Employment Opportunity Act of 1972, a law which is very specific in requiring equality for women in hiring, pay and promotions. There is nothing more, constitutionally or legislatively, that women could reasonably want. The only thing remaining is implementation, and this is proceeding rapidly. For example, the $38 million settlement which the Equal Employment Opportunity Act forced on American Telephone and Telegraph required back payments not only to women who hadn't been paid as much as they should have been, but also to women who hadn't been promoted as they thought they should have been, and even to women who never applied for jobs because they didn't think they would get them!

In the various state legislative hearings, the pro-ERA lawyers have not cited any state laws which adversely discriminate against women which ERA will remedy. In state after state, the proponents say: There is nothing wrong with the laws in *this* state, but we want to help those poor discriminated against women in other states. Those "other" states have never been identified.

Sources: A. 2 *Enc. of Am. Const.* 647 (1986). B. Adapted with permission from *Trial* 18 (Nov/Dec 1973). Copyright 1973 by the Association of Trial Lawyers of America.

Congresswoman Leonor Sullivan, distinguished member of Congress for some 20 years, who voted against ERA in Congress, answered this point very well. She said: "What is the matter with women in any state who permit a state law to remain on the books which is clearly discriminatory? Missouri has no such laws. Our women were instrumental in eliminating them. I suggest the women in other states do likewise."

The women in Illinois have just done exactly this. On September 13, 1973, the Governor signed ten bills which eliminate every vestige of discrimination against women in Illinois, including such areas as credit cards, home loans, housing and bigamy. These bills went through the General Assembly quickly and without controversy, and they take effect immediately, without the two-year waiting period ERA would require. These new laws prove that specific legislation to meet particular problems is the practical, proper, and prompt procedure—rather than the blunderbuss language of the Federal Equal Rights Amendment which would, at the same time, deprive women of the legal rights, benefits, and exemptions they now possess.

ERA will not even do anything for women in the field of education. Women are already fully guaranteed equality in educational opportunities, admissions, and employment through Title VII of the Civil Rights Act of 1964, the Equal Pay Act of 1963, the Education Amendments of June 1972, and Executive Order 11246 which authorizes broad administrative power to enforce corrective goals, timetables and affirmative action plans.

The major effort of ERA in the field of family relations is that it will invalidate the state laws which impose the obligation on the husband to support his wife. These laws are fundamental to the institution of the family and an essential part of the marriage contract. They give the wife her legal right to be a full-time wife and mother, in her own home, taking care of her own babies. . . .

Typical of the state laws guaranteeing the wife her legal right to be supported is the Ohio statute: "The husband must support himself, his wife, and his minor children out of his property or by his labor. If he is unable to do so, the wife must assist him so far as she is able. If he neglects to support his wife, any other person, in good faith, may supply her with necessities for her support, and recover the reasonable value thereof from the husband unless she abandons him without cause." . . .

These are the present rights which wives will lose if ERA is ratified because ERA will mandate a doctrinaire legal equality between the sexes, and will make unconstitutional any law which imposes an obligation on one sex that it does not impose on the other. Under ERA, all laws which say the *husband* must support his *wife* will immediately become unconstitutional. Either the state legislatures will be forced to rewrite the state laws on marital support and make them "sex-neutral," (that is, replace "husband" and "wife" with the word "spouse"), or, if the legislatures fail to act, the courts will nullify the present wording. Pro-ERA lawyers have not denied this in testimony at the state legislative hearings around the country.

Pro-ERA lawyers have attempted to answer this point by claiming that "sex-neutral" language could still impose an obligation on the "wage-earning spouse" to support the spouse who remains at home. However, this would reduce the wife's legal rights even further. This would mean that, if the husband is lazy and wants to watch television all day, and the wife conscientiously takes a job to feed her hungry children, then she, as the "principal wage-earning spouse," would acquire the obligation to support her lazy husband, subject to criminal penalties if she failed to support him and pay all his debts!

ERA proponents usually try to divert the argument from the rights of the wife to the plight of the divorced woman, which is a different matter altogether. A divorced woman does not have the rights of a wife, but only the rights given in the divorce decree. There is, however, one dramatic way that ERA will reduce the rights of a divorced woman: She will lose her present presumption of custody of the children. Pro-ERA lawyers admit that the divorce court will be required to award custody of the children on the new constitutional principle of equality between the sexes—instead of on the present presumption (in the absence of evidence of bad character) that the mother should keep her children, which is enshrined in custom.

ERA proponents claim that the courts will not interfere in an on-going marriage to guarantee a wife's right to support. In most cases, a wife does not need to go to court to get support from her husband. The husband knows that he is responsible to pay for his wife's necessaries according to their standard of living, and that, to fulfill this obligation, his wages may be garnisheed, his bank account attached, he may have to post a bond, or ultimately go to jail. Case law proves that the courts will require a husband in an on-going marriage to pay his wife's bills even though he tries to get out of it by saying that the credit is extended without his knowledge or consent, and even though the wife has separate funds of her own and can afford to pay the bill. . . .

The second large area of legal rights enjoyed by women which ERA would take away pertains to the draft and military service. The majority US House Judiciary Committee *Report on the Equal Rights Amendment* states: "Not only would women, including mothers, be subject to the draft, but the military would be compelled to place them in combat units alongside the men."

The ERA proponents say that they want women to serve in the military on an absolutely equal basis with men. . . .

At the state legislative hearings around the country, ERA proponents have confirmed this and stated that this is what they want. For example, at the Virginia General Assembly's Task Force Hearings on September 18, 1973, an ERA proponent claimed that it would be unfair discrimination if women were kept out of combat or off warships because this might prevent them from winning Congressional Medals of Honor!

The present exemption for women does prevent them from having to fight a jungle war in Vietnam, or from being POWs or MIAs. There are a few radicals who think this is "discrimination," but not many.

One of the favorite dodges of the ERA proponents is to say that Congress *now* has the power to draft women. This is true—but Congress has used its power to exempt women, and that is the way the overwhelming majority of American men and women want it. If ERA is ratified, Congress will no longer have this option. If we have a national emergency and ERA is in effect, Congress will be constitutionally compelled to draft women on the same basis as men. If the emergency requires the drafting of fathers, as it did during World War II, then Congress would be compelled to draft mothers. There can, of course, be exemptions on the basis of age, physical disability, etc., but not on the basis of sex.

The third group of rights and benefits which ERA will take away from women concerns protective labor legislation, that is, the various state laws designed to give women employees particular benefits and protections not granted to men. These laws include such provisions as protecting women from being compelled to work too many hours a day or week or at night, the weight-lifting restrictions, provisions which mandate rest areas, rest periods, protective equipment, or a chair for a woman who stands on her feet all day, laws which protect women from being forced to work in dangerous jobs such as mining, and the laws which grant more generous workmen's compensation for injuries to a woman than to a man.

Women have worked hard over many generations to achieve such legislation to protect and benefit women whom economic necessity requires to work in a paying job. If ERA is ratified, all these laws will be wiped out with one stroke of the pen. ERA proponents cannot, and do not, dispute this fundamental fact.

Some ERA proponents argue that protective labor legislation is already outlawed by Title VII of the Civil Rights Act of 1964. It is true that *some* labor legislation in *some* states has been invalidated by the courts, but this is no reason to use the sledgehammer approach and knock it all out. To any extent that labor legislation has been knocked out by the Civil Rights Act, it can be restored by another amendment to the Civil Rights Act. But if it is knocked out by the Constitution, it cannot be restored except by the long and laborious process of repealing a constitutional amendment.

The business and professional women who have appeared as witnesses for ERA before state legislatures usually argue that protective labor legislation doesn't "protect" but instead discriminates adversely, and that protective legislation is obsolete and unnecessary in this modern technological age. This is the attitude of a business or professional woman who sits at a comfortable desk in a clean office and finds intellectual fulfillment in her job.

Only if ERA is permanently rejected will women be protected in their right to have overtime on a voluntary basis and their right to reject heavy and dangerous work without penalty.

One part of the Equal Rights Amendment which the proponents seldom, if ever, mention is Section 2, which states, "The Congress shall have the power to enforce, by appropriate legislation, the provisions of this article." Section 2 will transfer jurisdiction over women's rights, domestic relations, and criminal law and property law pertaining to women, out of the hands of the state legislatures and into the hands of the federal government: the Congress, the Executive branch, and the federal courts.

This grab of power by the federal government would involve matters that heretofore have been generally acknowledged to be the primary and, in some cases, the exclusive legislative responsibility of the states. These would include family law, divorce, child custody, alimony, minimum marriageable age limits, dower rights, inheritance, survivor's benefits, insurance rates, welfare, prison regulations, and protective labor legislation. All state and local laws, policies and regulations involving any difference of treatment between the sexes will be over-ridden by federal legislation, which means, ultimately, administrative regulations.

During most of the time that the Equal Rights Amendment was being considered by the US Congress, it had attached to it the Hayden Modification which stated: "The provisions of this article shall not be construed to impair any rights, benefits or exemptions conferred by law upon persons of the female sex." The Hayden Modification was deleted under pressure from the women's liberationists who lobbied for ERA.

Professor Paul A. Freund of the Harvard Law School, whose study of the Equal Rights Amendment covers 25 years, wrote in the March 1971 issue of the *Harvard Civil*

Rights-Civil Liberties Law Review: "The real issue is not the legal status of women. The issue is the integrity and responsibility of the law-making process itself." Professor Philip B. Kurland of the University of Chicago Law School told the Illinois General Assembly on June 5, 1972: "I think that it is largely misrepresented as a women's rights amendment when in fact the primary beneficiary will be men."

Thus it is clear, that ERA will do absolutely nothing for women in the field of employment, but will take away from women their present superior rights, benefits, and exemptions. The devastating effects of ERA on women's rights were forecast on September 19, 1973, when the Pennsylvania Superior Court held that Pennsylvania's new state equal rights amendment invalidates Pennsylvania laws giving special marital rights and remedies to women only. The court specifically rejected the argument that ERA was meant to apply only to jobs, wages, and education, and stated that the "plain meaning" of ERA does not permit any exemptions.

The tally on the Equal Rights Amendment is impressive. Thirty states ratified, most of those very quickly, without the debate and study which a constitutional amendment deserves. Twenty states have refused to ratify. Of the 30 states which ratified, the Nebraska Legislature has already rescinded its previous ratification, and resolutions to rescind have been introduced in 12 other states. Wisconsin, which passed ERA early and without much debate, subsequently resoundingly defeated an ERA amendment to the state constitution in a statewide referendum. Since it takes 38 states to put a new amendment in the Constitution, ERA can be considered a terminal case.

C. For the ERA (1973)

MARLOW W. COOK

In a 1776 letter to her husband, Abigail Adams requested that US laws be formulated to no longer treat women as "vassals." She wrote:

" . . . and by the way in the new Code of Laws which I suppose it will be necessary for you to make I desire you would Remember the Ladies, and be more generous and favourable to them than your ancestors. Do not put such unlimited power into the hands of the Husbands. Remember all Men would by tyrants if they could. If particular care and attention is not paid to the Ladies we are determined to foment a Rebellion, and will not hold ourselves bound by any Laws in which we have no voice, or Representation."

Two hundred years later, America has finally begun to take Mrs. Adams' request seriously. Congress has proposed, and 30 states have ratified the Equal Rights Amendment, which simply states:

"Equality of rights under the law shall not be denied or abridged by the United States or by any State on account of sex."

To become law, the Amendment must be ratified by 38 states.

Source: Adapted with permission from *Trial* 19 (Nov/Dec 1973). Copyright 1973 by the Association of Trial Lawyers of America.

A number of state legislatures will decide, when they reconvene in January, whether to ratify the Equal Rights Amendment. In so deciding, two basic questions must be faced once the effects of the Amendment are understood.

First is the threshold question of whether we want to eliminate sex discrimination in federal, state and local law and governmental actions. The second is whether we want a constitutional amendment to accomplish this equalization. The two are interrelated, in view of recent Supreme Court decisions and the trend toward equality in America. But let us try to explore them separately.

I believe there is practical unanimity among Americans that women should be extended equality of status, rights and opportunities in our laws. What controversy there is concerns extending equal responsibilities to women. As a matter of simple justice and common sense, equal rights and *responsibilities* must be extended to all citizens without discrimination.

I say this for a number of reasons, the primary being that one is not possible without the other. Any exceptions used to escape the responsibilities of citizenship can be just as easily used to deny equality of rights of citizenship.

Another reason that equal rights and responsibilities should be extended to women is the psychology of inferiority that results when classes of persons otherwise equally capable are not treated equally. The Supreme Court recognized this psychological effect in *Brown v. Board of Education* with regard to race. Others have explored the phenomenon with regard to sex.

But the equalization that is so necessary is the coming trend in this country in any event. America has already recognized that its women citizens have not been receiving equality of treatment under the law. The Supreme Court in its most recent statement on this issue, has stated:

"There can be no doubt that our Nation has had a long and unfortunate history of sex discrimination. Traditionally, such discrimination was rationalized by an attitude of "romantic paternalism" which, in practical effect, put women not on a pedestal, but in a cage." . . .

Thus, I think it safe to say that sex is no longer considered a rational classification, reasonably related to any legitimate state interest. Four members of the Court in *Frontiero* went further to find that sex, like race, alienage and national origin, is a "suspect classification," requiring close judicial scrutiny and a compelling state interest to uphold. This is the test that I believe should be used under the 14th Amendment for classifications based on sex. But this test has not yet been accepted by a majority of the Court in regard to sex classifications in our laws.

The important point is that the current trend in formulating and interpreting our laws is that the sex characteristic bears no relation to ability to perform or contribute to society. This means that nearly every argument opposing the Equal Rights Amendment overlooks the present trend toward equality which could accomplish much of what the ERA will. Those who would opt for "protecting" women have already lost the war.

Although current developments in the law are very favorable toward women gaining equality of rights, I must stress how far those developments are from the ideal of total equality for women.

The majority of the Supreme Court may have found that sex is an "invidious" classification, but *not* that sex is a "suspect" classification. Thus, the constitutional test to be used in judging future cases is in doubt. No one knows how important a governmental interest is needed to uphold a statute or governmental practice that discriminates on the basis of sex.

We need a more definite standard by which judges, legislatures and public officials can act. We need a standard which cannot be abrogated by future courts or public officials. We need a constitutional amendment, particularly in view of the legislative history of the Equal Rights Amendment, which elucidates with specificity how its requirements can be met.

The ERA would become effective two years after the date of ratification. During those two years, the federal and state legislatures would have a tremendous incentive to re-examine their laws in light of the new and definite standard of equality for women and men. Judges would have to take judicial notice of the new standard rather than follow the concededly bad history of discriminatory precedents adhered to in the past. . . .

There is confusion on the part of some, as to how the declaration of equality, ordered by the ERA, will be translated into statutes, court decisions and governmental actions.

The purpose of the amendment is simply to end the unequal treatment under the law to which women have been subjected since the Constitution was first adopted. It is important to note that the only kind of sex discrimination which this would forbid is that which exists in law. Interpersonal relationships and customs of chivalry will, of course, remain as they always have been, a matter of individual choice. The adoption of this amendment will neither make a man a gentleman nor will it require him to stop being one.

It has been stated by some, that the ERA would deny women the "automatic" right to support, custody and alimony in the area of domestic relations law. These rights under present law are often illusory if they are granted at all. The Senate Judiciary Committee *Report on the Equal Rights Amendment* in explaining the effect of the ERA in family law, quoted the report of the Association of the Bar of the City of New York:

"The Amendment would bar a state from imposing a greater liability on one spouse than on the other merely because of sex. It is clear that the Amendment would not require both a husband and wife to contribute identical amounts of money to a marriage. The support obligation of each spouse would be defined in functional terms based, for example, on each spouse's earning power, current resources and nonmonetary contributions to the family welfare."

"Thus, if spouses have equal resources and earning capacities, each would be equally liable for the support of the other—or in practical effect, neither would be required to support the other. On the other hand, where one spouse is the primary wage earner and the other runs the home, the wage earner would have a duty to support the spouse who stays at home in compensation for the performance of her or his duties." . . .

The Equal Rights Amendment will require laws that discriminate on the basis of sex to be rewritten, but not drastically changed. Rather, the rights of spouses and parents will simply be viewed more equitably under the ERA than under present laws.

In other areas of domestic relations law, women stand to gain a great deal: the right of a separate domicile, the right to contract when married, the right to consortium, the right to one's own name, and the right to marry or divorce on an equal basis with men.

In community property states the power of management and control over the community property could not remain with the husband alone, as is the present case in all community property states except Texas. In the forty-two common law property states, a greater deference would be given the contribution to common property by a spouse who works in the home.

Thus, it can be seen that no great change in the American social structure would follow from adoption of the Equal Rights Amendment. No women who wish to remain in the home would be driven out, and the legal obligations persons assume upon marriage would remain. The only change would be a more equitable treatment for persons under the law.

A second area of supposed "protections" that women would lose under the Equal Rights Amendment concerns the draft-exempt status that women have held up to this time. This is indeed a policy question, just as drafting of men is. The Senate Report and Senate floor debate in defeating riders to the Equal Rights Amendment make clear that any draft law under the ERA could not discriminate on the basis of sex.

As in the past, only those qualified would be drafted, and exemptions for parents could be implemented. Service to one's country in the armed services is an obligation of citizenship. In return, many benefits of service are extended to veterans and servicemen and women: training, education, medical care, G.I. benefits, upward mobility for the poor, and preference in hiring.

Much of the wind has been sucked from the sails of the opponents of the ERA by the outstanding performance of our military women in combat areas of Southeast Asia. The *Frontiero* decision and the new assignment policies of the services point in the direction toward increased equality for women in the military.

Without a draft, women would have to be allowed to volunteer for service on an equal basis with men. Assignments of personnel would remain as they always have been, on the basis of individual capability and the needs of the service.

One recurring "red herring" opponents have argued is in the area of the right to privacy. As the Senate Report states and floor debate further attests to, the legislative intent of the ERA is that the right to privacy in private bodily functions such as sleeping, disrobing, and bathing will remain, even if this means separation of the sexes in state dormitories, prisons, military barracks or ships.

This is a narrow exception to the rule of equality laid down by the Equal Rights Amendment.

It has been said that women will forfeit "protective" labor legislation under the Equal Rights Amendment, such as hours, weight-lifting and mandatory rest period laws. Just as the Supreme Court has already recognized, some such protective laws do not protect, but in reality, restrain working women from progressing in their employment. Progress is already being made in this area under federal legislation, state law and court decisions.

Under the ERA, any state would be free to enact legislation that truly protects persons from dangerous working conditions and courts could extend benefits to discriminated classes of workers, rather than denying benefits (if they are truly beneficial) to men.

In the area of criminal law, it has been said that women will lose the protection of rape laws under the ERA. The legislative history of the Amendment is clearly contrary to that opinion.

The Senate Committee *Report* states, "But the Amendment will not invalidate laws which punish rape, for such laws are designed to protect women in a way that they are uniformly distinct from men." Senate floor debate also made this point clear. The Senate was satisfied as to the effect of the Equal Rights Amendment, and voted down a change to the Amendment's wording, with regard to sexual offenses.

Women stand to gain a great deal in the criminal law area under the ERA, and such discriminatory treatment as outlined in the Senate Committee Report below, could no longer be perpetrated:

"There is also invidious discrimination against women in the criminal laws of some states. One state has a statute allowing women to be jailed for three years for habitual drunkenness, while a man can receive only 30 days for the same offense. In two states, the defense of "passion killing" is allowed to the wronged husband, but not to the deceived wife. And in another state, female juvenile offenders can be declared "persons in need of supervision" for non-criminal acts until they are 18, while males are covered by the statute only until age 16."

Women have faced widespread discrimination in the area of education and stand to lose no "protections" here. Discrimination in admission to college, graduate and professional schools is widespread, as is discrimination against women in every level of the teaching profession.

The Senate Committee *Report* explained the effect of the ERA in this area as follows:

"With respect to education, the Equal Rights Amendment will require that state supported schools at all levels eliminate laws of regulations or official practices which exclude women or limit their numbers. The Amendment would not require quotas for men and women, nor would it require that schools accurately reflect the sex distribution of the population; rather admission would turn on the basis of ability or other relevant characteristics, and not on the basis of sex."

The Report also stated that scholarship funds would have to be distributed on a nondiscriminatory basis; state schools limited to one sex would have to allow both sexes to attend; and employment and promotion in public schools would, as in other cases of governmental action, have to be free from sex discrimination.

Congress, through legislation, has already taken steps to assure equality in schools receiving federal funds, with limited exceptions. But it is time to assure, through a constitutional amendment, that no one will be denied equal educational opportunity by the state.

The policy question of eliminating sex discrimination from federal and state law and governmental acts is being answered affirmatively with greater certainty with each passing day. Women are anxious to share in the fullness of citizenship, and have been since our country was founded. As a matter of simple justice and common sense, equality of rights and responsibilities must be shared by all.

Once the effects of the ERA are understood, it can be readily seen that no real "protections" will be lost by women, but many rights and opportunities will be gained.

As our country prepares to celebrate our second century of existence, I think it most fitting to rededicate ourselves to the principle of equality of all citizens. It is unfortunate that equal rights for men and women is a cause whose time has come. For, as Abigail Adams pointed out, this is a cause that should have always been.

224 *Miller v. California (1973)*

The modern Supreme Court had begun dealing with the problem of obscenity in two 1957 cases, *Roth v. United* States and *Alberts v. California.* Justice Brennan had reaffirmed the traditional rule that obscene materials did not enjoy constitutional protection, but any idea having the "slightest redeeming social importance" could claim First Amendment protection. He also rejected the old test for obscenity, an 1868 English standard that judged material by the effect of selected passages on particularly susceptible persons, and replaced it with the contemporary standard of whether, "to the average person, applying contemporary community standards, the dominant theme of the material taken as a whole appeals to prurient interests." (Compare this to the test used in the *Ulysses* case, Document 173.)

Over the next dozen years, the courts were flooded with obscenity cases as the society underwent the so-called sexual revolution. Publishers proved extremely innovative in demonstrating "redeeming social importance," and both judges and legislators found it increasingly difficult to define obscene materials with any precision. There is more than a touch of frustration in Justice Stewart's comment regarding pornography, "I know it when I see it, and this is not it!"

The Warren Court's allegedly lax attitude toward pornography became an issue in the 1968 presidential campaign, and Richard Nixon promised that if elected he would appoint tough-minded men to the bench. With four Nixon appointees on the Court in 1973, the justices tried again to find a precise definition, and Chief Justice Burger attempted to give lower courts and state legislatures judicially manageable standards for control of pornographic materials. In lieu of the *Roth* test, he suggested that obscene material be defined as material "lacking serious literary, artistic, political or scientific value," and the trier of fact, in evaluating the material, would apply "contemporary community standards." It appeared that Burger was willing for different standards to apply in different parts of the country and in different types of communities.

Justice Brennan entered a lengthy dissent covering *Miller* and a companion case, *Paris Adult Theatre I v. Slaton,* in which he reviewed the Court's attempts to draw a clear line between free expression and order. He reluctantly concluded that the effort could never succeed, and he suggested that the Court adopt the recommendations of the recent report by the United States Commission on Obscenity and Pornography. With the exception of obstrusive advertising and distribution to minors, the First Amendment would prevent governmental suppression of allegedly obscene materials; the states, however, would retain power over modes of distribution. Otherwise, he warned, the courts would be bogged down in endless cases of definition. Brennan's prediction proved accurate, and eventually the Burger Court washed its hands, so to speak, and refused to take any more obscenity cases.

See Andrea Dworkin, *Pornography: Men Possessing Women* (1981); Richard F. Hixson, *Pornography and the Justices: The Supreme Court and the Intractable Obscenity Problem* (1996); Rochelle Gurstein, *The Repeal of Reticence* (1996); and Susan M. Easton, *The Problem of Pornography* (1994).

———

Chief Justice Burger delivered the opinion of the Court:

This is one of a group of "obscenity-pornography" cases being reviewed by the Court in a re-examination of standards enunciated in earlier cases involving what Mr. Justice Harlan called "the intractable obscenity problem." This case involves the application of a State's criminal obscenity statute to a situation in which sexually explicit materials have been thrust by aggressive sales action upon unwilling recipients who had in no way indicated any desire to receive such materials. This Court has recognized that the States have a legitimate interest in prohibiting dissemination or exhibition of obscene material when the mode of dissemination carries with it a significant danger of offending the sensibilities of unwilling recipients or of exposure to juveniles. It is in this context that we are called on to define the standards which must be used to identify obscene material that a State may regulate.

Since the Court now undertakes to formulate standards more concrete than those in the past, it is useful for us to focus on two of the landmark cases in the somewhat tortured history of the Court's obscenity decisions. While *Roth* presumed "obscenity" to be "utterly without redeeming social value," *Memoirs v. Massachusetts* [1966] required that to prove obscenity it must be affirmatively established that the material is "*utterly* without redeeming social value." Thus, even as they repeated the words of *Roth,* the *Memoirs* plurality produced a drastically altered test that called on the prosecution to prove a negative, i.e., that the material was "*utterly* without redeeming social value"—a burden virtually impossible to discharge. Apart from the initial formulation in the *Roth* case, no majority of the Court has at any given time been able to agree on a standard to determine what constitutes obscene, pornographic material subject to regulation under the States' police power. The variety of views is not remarkable, for in the area of freedom of speech and press the courts must always remain sensitive to any infringement on genuinely serious literary, artistic, political, or scientific expression. This is an area in which there are few eternal verities. . . .

This much has been categorically settled by the Court, that obscene material is unprotected by the First Amendment. We acknowledge, however, the inherent dangers of undertaking to regulate any form of expression. State statutes designed to regulate obscene materials must be carefully limited. As a result, we now confine the permissible scope of such regulation to works which depict or describe sexual conduct. That conduct must be specifically defined by the applicable state law, as written or authoritatively construed. A state offense must also be limited to works which, taken as a whole, appeal to the prurient interest in sex, which portray sexual conduct in a patently offensive way, and which, taken as a whole, do not have serious literary, artistic, political, or scientific value.

The basic guidelines for the trier of fact must be: (a) whether "the average person, applying contemporary community standards" would find that the work, taken as a whole, appeals to the prurient interest, (b) whether the work depicts or describes, in a patently offensive way, sexual conduct specifically defined by the applicable state law, and (c) whether the work, taken as a whole, lacks serious literary, artistic, political, or scientific value. We do not adopt as a constitutional standard the "*utterly* without redeeming social value" test; that concept has never commanded the adherence of more than three Justices at one time. If a state law that regulates obscene material is thus limited, as written or construed, First Amendment values are adequately protected by the ultimate power of appellate courts to conduct an independent review of constitutional claims when necessary.

We emphasize that it is not our function to propose regulatory schemes for the States. It is possible, however, to give a few plain examples of what a state statute could define for regulation under the second part (b) of the standard announced in this opinion: (a) patently offensive representations or descriptions of ultimate sexual acts, normal or perverted, actual or simulated (b) patently offensive representations or descriptions of masturbation, excretory functions, and lewd exhibition of the genitals.

Sex and nudity may not be exploited without limit by films or pictures exhibited or sold in places of public accommodation any more than live sex and nudity can be exhibited or sold without limit in such public places. At a minimum, prurient, patently offensive depiction or description of sexual conduct must have serious literary, artistic, political, or scientific value to merit First Amendment protection. For example, medical books for the education of physicians and related personnel necessarily use graphic illustrations and descriptions of human anatomy. In resolving the inevitably sensitive questions of fact and law, we must continue to rely on the jury system, accompanied by the safeguards that judges, rules of evidence, presumption of innocence and other protective features provide, as we do with rape, murder and a host of other offenses against society and its individual members.

Mr. Justice Brennan, author of the opinions of the Court, or the plurality opinions, in [several cases] has abandoned his former position and now maintains that no formulation of this Court, the Congress, or the States can adequately distinguish obscene material unprotected by the First Amendment from protected expression. Paradoxically, he indicates that suppression of unprotected obscene material is permissible to avoid exposure to unconsenting adults, as in this case, and to juveniles, although he gives no indication of how the division between protected and nonprotected materials may be drawn with greater precision for these purposes than for regulation of commercial exposure to consenting adults only. Nor does he indicate where in the Constitution he finds the authority to distinguish between a willing "adult" one month past the state law age of majority and a willing "juvenile" one month younger.

Under the holdings announced today, no one will be subject to prosecution for the sale or exposure of obscene materials unless these materials depict or describe patently offensive "hard core" sexual conduct specifically defined by the regulating state law, as written or construed. We are satisfied that these specific prerequisites will provide fair notice to a dealer in such materials that his public and commercial activities may bring prosecution. If the inability to define regulated materials with ultimate, god-like precision altogether removes the power of the States or the Congress to regulate, then "hard core" pornography may be exposed without limit to the juvenile, the passerby, and the consenting adult alike, as, indeed, Mr. Justice Douglas contends. In this belief, however, he now stands alone. Today, for the first time since *Roth,* a majority of this Court has agreed on concrete guidelines to isolate "hard core" pornography from expression protected by the First Amendment. . . .

Under a national Constitution, fundamental First Amendment limitations on the powers of the States do not vary from community to community, but this does not mean that there are, or should or can be, fixed, uniform national standards of precisely what appeals to the "prurient interest" or is "patently offensive." These are essentially questions of fact, and our nation is simply too big and too diverse for this Court to reasonably expect that such standards could be articulated for all 50 States in a single formulation, even assuming the prerequisite consensus exists. To require a State to structure obscenity proceedings around evidence of a *national* "community standard" would be an exercise in futility. Neither the State's alleged failure to offer evidence of "national standards," nor the trial court's charge that the jury consider state community standards, were constitutional errors in this case. It is neither realistic nor constitutionally sound to read the First Amendment as requiring that the people of Maine or Mississippi accept public depiction of conduct found tolerable in Las Vegas, or New York City. People in different States vary in their tastes and attitudes, and this diversity is not to be strangled by the absolutism of imposed uniformity. . . .

In sum we (a) reaffirm the *Roth* holding that obscene material is not protected by the First Amendment; (b) hold that such material can be regulated by the States, subject to the specific safeguards enunciated above, without a showing that the material is "*utterly* without redeeming social value"; and (c) hold that obscenity is to be determined by applying "contemporary community standards," not "national standards." . . .

Vacated and remanded.

Justice Douglas, dissenting:

To send men to jail for violating standards they cannot understand, construe, and apply is a monstrous thing to do in a Nation dedicated to fair trials and due process. We deal with highly emotional, not rational, questions. To many the Song of Solomon is obscene. I do not think we, the judges, were ever given the constitutional power to make definitions of obscenity. If it is to be defined, let the people debate and decide by a constitutional amendment what they want to ban as obscene and what standards they want the legislatures and the courts to apply. Whatever the choice, the courts will have some guidelines. Now we have none except our own predilections.

Justice Brennan, with whom Justice Stewart and Justice Marshall join, dissenting:

In my dissent [in *Paris Adult Theatre I v. Slaton*] I noted that I had no occasion to consider the extent of state power to regulate the distribution of sexually oriented material to juveniles or the offensive exposure of such material to unconsenting adults. I need not now decide whether a statute might be drawn to impose, within the requirements of the First Amendment, criminal penalties for the precise conduct at issue here. For it is clear that under my dissent in *Paris,* the statute here is unconstitutionally overbroad, and therefore invalid on its face.

---

225   *Roe v. Wade (1973)*

With the exception of the *Brown* decision (Document 199), no Court decision of the past half-century has been as controversial as that which interpreted a woman's right to privacy to include the right to have an abortion. The original ruling in *Griswold* had found a majority of the justices affirming a right to privacy but disagreeing on its source and reach. The abortion cases presented these issues squarely.

At that time, most states, like Texas had a law making it a crime to "procure an abortion" except by "medical advice for the purpose of saving the life of the mother." The Texas suit involved challenges from a pregnant single woman (Jane Roe) and from a licensed physician, Dr. Hallford. A number of states were then in the process of revising their abortion statutes, and in a companion case, *Doe v. Bolton,* the Court also struck down Georgia's "modern" statute.

Justice Blackmun's majority opinion not only declared that privacy included autonomy over one's body, but also did what Justice Douglas had avoided doing in *Griswold,* namely, identified a new substantive due process as the basis for noneconomic individual rights.

The decision touched off a public debate that has not subsided. Even some people who favored abortion criticized the Court for its judicial activism and for having involved itself before the political processes at the state level had had sufficient time to work out the problem. Where *Brown* had a series of precedents leading away from *Plessy,* aside from *Griswold* (Document 212), there was no precedential history for the Court to rely on in *Roe.* Defenders of the decision, on the other hand, have praised the Court, claiming it is necessary constantly to revise and update our understanding of individual liberties.

See John H. Ely, "The Wages of Crying Wolf: A Commentary on *Roe v. Wade,*" 82 *Yale Law Journal* 920 (1973); Marian Faux, *Roe v. Wade* (1988); Lawrence H. Tribe, *Abortion: The Clash of Absolutes* (1990); David J. Garrow, *Liberty and Sexuality: The Right to Privacy and the Making of Roe v. Wade* (1994); and Sarah Weddington, *A Question of Choice* (1992)

Justice Blackmun delivered the opinion of the Court:

We forthwith acknowledge our awareness of the sensitive and emotional nature of the abortion controversy, of the vigorous opposing views, even among physicians, and of the deep and seemingly absolute convictions that the subject inspires. One's philosophy, one's experience, one's exposure to the raw edges of human existence, one's religious training, one's attitudes toward life and family and their values, and the moral standards one establishes and seeks to observe, are all likely to influence and to color one's thinking and conclusions about abortion. In addition, population growth, pollution, poverty, and racial overtones tend to complicate and not to simplify the problem. Our task, of course, is to resolve the issue by constitutional measurement, free of emotion and of predilection. We seek earnestly to do this, and, because we do, we have inquired into, and in this opinion place some emphasis upon, medical and medical-legal history and what that history reveals about man's attitudes toward the abortion procedure over the centuries. . . .

The principal thrust of appellant's attack on the Texas statutes is that they improperly invade a right, said to be possessed by the pregnant woman, to choose to terminate her pregnancy. . . .

The Constitution does not explicitly mention any right of privacy. However, the Court has recognized that a right of personal privacy, or a guarantee of certain areas or zones of privacy, does exist under the Constitution. In varying contexts, the Court or individual Justices have, indeed, found at least the roots of that right in the First Amendment, in the Fourth and Fifth Amendments; in the penumbras of the Bill of Rights; in the Ninth Amendment; or in the concept of liberty guaranteed by the first section of the 14th Amendment. These decisions make it clear that only personal rights that can be deemed "fundamental" or "implicit in the concept of ordered liberty" are included in this guarantee of personal privacy. They also make it clear that the right has some extension to activities relating to marriage, procreation, contraception, family relationships, and child rearing and education.

This right of privacy, whether it be founded in the 14th Amendment's concept of personal liberty and restrictions upon state action, as we feel it is, or, as the District Court determined, in the Ninth Amendment's reservation of rights to the people, is broad enough to encompass a woman's decision whether or not to terminate her pregnancy. The detriment that the State would impose upon the pregnant woman by denying this choice altogether is apparent. Specific and direct harm medically diagnosable even in early pregnancy may be involved. Maternity, or additional offspring, may force upon the woman a distressful life and future. Psychological harm may be imminent. Mental and physical health may be taxed by child care. There is also the distress, for all concerned, associated with the unwanted child, and there is a problem of bringing a child into a family already unable, psychologically and otherwise, to care for it. In other cases, as in this one, the additional difficulties and continuing stigma of unwed motherhood may be involved. All these are factors the woman and her responsible physician necessarily will consider in consultation.

On the basis of elements such as these, appellants and some *amici* argue that the woman's right is absolute and that she is entitled to terminate her pregnancy at whatever

Source: 410 U.S. 113 (1973)

time, in whatever way, and for whatever reason she alone chooses. With this we do not agree. The Court's decision recognizing a right of privacy also acknowledge that some state regulation in areas protected by that right is appropriate. A state may properly assert important interests in safeguarding health, in maintaining medical standards, and in protecting potential life. At some point in pregnancy, these respective interests become sufficiently compelling to sustain regulation of the factors that govern the abortion decision. The privacy right involved, therefore, cannot be said to be absolute. In fact, it is not clear to us that the claim asserted by some *amici* that one has an unlimited right to do with one's body as one pleases bears a close relationship to the right of privacy previously articulated in the Court's decisions. The Court has refused to recognize an unlimited right of this kind in the past. We, therefore, conclude that the right of personal privacy includes the abortion decision, but that this right is not unqualified and must be considered against important state interests in regulation.

A. The appellee and certain *amici* argue that the fetus is a "person" within the language and meaning of the 14th Amendment. In support of this, they outline at length and in detail the well-known facts of fetal development. If this suggestion of personhood is established, the appellant's case, of course, collapses, for the fetus' right to life is then guaranteed specifically by the Amendment. On the other hand, the appellee conceded that no case could be cited that holds that a fetus is a person within the meaning of the 14th Amendment. . . .

B. The pregnant woman cannot be isolated in her privacy. She carries an embryo and, later, a fetus, if one accepts the medical definitions of the developing young in the human uterus. The situation therefore is inherently different from marital intimacy, or bedroom possession of obscene material, or marriage, or procreation, or education, with which these other cases were concerned. It is reasonable and appropriate for a State to decide that at some point in time another interest, that of health of the mother or that of potential human life, becomes significantly involved. The woman's privacy is no longer sole and any right of privacy she possesses must be measured accordingly.

Texas argues that, apart from the 14th Amendment, life begins at conception and is present throughout pregnancy, and that, therefore, the State has a compelling interest in protecting that life from and after conception. We need not resolve the difficult question of when life begins. When those trained in the respective disciplines of medicine, philosophy, and theology are unable to arrive at any consensus, the judiciary, at this point in the development of man's knowledge, is not in a position to speculate as to the answer. It should be sufficient to note briefly the wide divergence of thinking on this most sensitive and difficult question. There has always been strong support for the view that life does not begin until live birth. This was the belief of the Stoics. It appears to be the predominant, though not the unanimous, attitude of the Jewish faith. It may be taken to represent also the position of a large segment of the Protestant community. The common law found greater significance in quickening. Physicians and their scientific colleagues have regarded that event with less interest and have tended to focus either upon conception, upon live birth, or upon the interim point at which the fetus becomes "viable," that is, potentially able to live outside the mother's womb, albeit with artificial aid. Viability is usually placed at about seven months (28 weeks) but may occur earlier, even at 24 weeks. The Aristotelian theory of "mediate animation," that held sway throughout the

Middle Ages and the Renaissance in Europe, continued to be official Roman Catholic dogma until the 19th century, despite opposition to this "ensoulment" theory from those in the church who would recognize the existence of life from the moment of conception. The latter is now, of course, the official belief of the Catholic Church. This is a view strongly held by many non-Catholics as well, and by many physicians. Substantial problems for precise definition of this view are posed, however, by new embryological data that purport to indicate that conception is a "process" over time, rather than an event, and by new medical techniques such as menstrual extraction, the "morning-after" pill, implantation of embryos, artificial insemination, and even artificial wombs. In areas other than criminal abortion, the law has been reluctant to endorse any theory that life, as we recognize it, begins before live birth or to accord legal rights to the unborn except in narrowly defined situations and except when the rights are contingent upon live birth. . . . In short, the unborn have never been recognized in the law as persons in the whole sense.

In view of all this, we do not agree that, by adopting one theory of life, Texas may override the rights of the pregnant woman that are at stake. We repeat, however, that the State does have an important and legitimate interest in preserving and protecting the health of the pregnant woman, whether she be a resident of the State or a nonresident who seeks medical consultation and treatment there, and that it has still *another* important and legitimate interest in protecting the potentiality of human life. These interests are separate and distinct. Each grows in substantiality as the woman approaches term and, at a point during pregnancy, each becomes "compelling."

With respect to the State's important and legitimate interest in the health of the mother, the "compelling" point, in the light of present medical knowledge, is at approximately the end of the first trimester. This is so because of the now established medical fact that until the end of the first trimester mortality in abortion is less than mortality in normal childbirth. It follows that, from and after this point, a State may regulate the abortion procedure to the extent that the regulation reasonably relates to the preservation and protection of maternal health. Examples of permissible state regulation in this area are requirements as to the qualifications of the person who is to perform the abortion; as to the licensure of that person; as to the facility in which the procedure is to be performed, that is, whether it must be a hospital or may be a clinic or some other place of less-than-hospital status; as to the licensing of the facility; and the like. This means, on the other hand, that for the period of pregnancy prior to this "compelling" point, the attending physician, in consultation with his patient, is free to determine, without regulation by the State, that, in his medical judgment, the patient's pregnancy should be terminated. If that decision is reached, the judgment may be effectuated by an abortion free of interference by the State.

With respect to the State's important and legitimate interest in potential life, the "compelling" point is at viability. This is so because the fetus then presumably has the capability of meaningful life outside the mother's womb. State regulation protective of fetal life after viability thus has both logical and biological justifications. If the State is interested in protecting fetal life after viability, it may go so far as to proscribe abortion during that period, except when it is necessary to preserve the life or health of the mother.

Measured against these standards, the Texas law sweeps too broadly. The statute makes no distinction between abortions performed early in pregnancy and those per-

formed later, and it limits to a single reason, "saving" the mother's life, the legal justification for the procedure. The statute, therefore, cannot survive the constitutional attack
made upon it here. . . .

This holding, we feel, is consistent with the relative weights of the respective interests involved, with the lessons and examples of medical and legal history, with the lenity
of the common law, and with the demands of the profound problems of the present day.
The decision leaves the State free to place increasing restrictions on abortion as the
period of pregnancy lengthens, so long as those restrictions are tailored to the recognized
state interests. The decision vindicates the right of the physician to administer medical
treatment according to his professional judgment up to the points where important state
interests provide compelling justifications for intervention. Up to those points, the abortion decision in all its aspects is inherently, and primarily, a medical decision, and basic
responsibility for it must rest with the physician. If an individual practitioner abuses the
privilege of exercising proper medical judgment, the usual remedies, judicial and
intraprofessional, are available. . . .

It is so ordered.

Justice Stewart, concurring:

In 1963, this Court purported to sound the death knell for the doctrine of substantive
due process. Barely two years later, [in *Griswold*], the Court held a Connecticut birth control law unconstitutional. In view of what had been so recently said in *Skrupa*, the Court's
opinion in *Griswold* understandably did its best to avoid reliance on the Due Process
Clause. Yet, the Connecticut law did not violate any specific provision of the Constitution. So it was clear to me then, and it is equally clear to me now, that the *Griswold* decision can be rationally understood only as a holding that the Connecticut statute substan-
tively invaded the "liberty" that is protected by the Due Process Clause of the 14th
Amendment. As so understood *Griswold* stands as one in a long line of pre-*Skrupa* cases
decided under the doctrine of substantive due process, and I now accept it as such. The
"liberty" protected by the Due Process Clause of the 14th Amendment covers more than
those freedoms explicitly named in the Bill of Rights. Several decisions of this Court
make clear that freedom of personal choice in matters of marriage and family life is one
of the liberties protected by the Due Process Clause of the 14th Amendment. . . . As
recently as last Term, in *Eisenstadt v. Baird,* we recognized "the right of the *individual,*
married or single, to be free from unwarranted governmental intrusion into matters so
fundamentally affecting a person as the decision whether to bear or beget a child." That
right necessarily includes the right of a woman to decide whether or not to terminate her
pregnancy. . . .

Justice Douglas, concurring:

The Ninth Amendment obviously does not create federally enforceable rights. It
merely says, "The enumeration in the Constitution, of certain rights, shall not be construed to deny or disparage others retained by the people." But a catalogue of these rights
includes customary, traditional, and time-honored rights, amenities, privileges, and
immunities that come within the sweep of "the Blessings of Liberty" mentioned in the

preamble to the Constitution. Many of them in my view come within the meaning of the term "liberty" as used in the 14th Amendment.

First is the autonomous control over the development and expression of one's intellect, interests, tastes, and personality. These are rights protected by the First Amendment and in my view they are absolute, permitting of no exception. . . .

Second is freedom of choice in the basic decisions of one's life respecting marriage, divorce, procreation, contraception, and the education and upbringing of children. These "fundamental" rights, unlike those protected by the First Amendment, are subject to some control by the police power. . . .

Third is the freedom to care for one's health and person, freedom from bodily restraint or compulsion, freedom to walk, stroll, or loaf. These rights, though fundamental, are likewise subject to regulation on a showing of "compelling state interest." . . .

A woman is free to make the basic decision whether to bear an unwanted child. Childbirth may deprive a woman of her preferred life style and force upon her a radically different and undesired future. Such reasoning is, however, only the beginning of the problem. The State has interests to protect. While childbirth endangers the lives of some women, voluntary abortion at any time and place regardless of medical standards would impinge on a rightful concern of society. The women's health is part of that concern; as is the life of the fetus after quickening. These concerns justify the State in treating the procedure as a medical one. . . .

Justice White, with whom Justice Rehnquist joins, dissenting:

At the heart of the controversy in these cases are those recurring pregnancies that pose no danger whatsoever to the life or health of the mother but are nevertheless unwanted for any one or more of a variety of reasons—convenience, family planning, economics, dislike of children, the embarrassment of illegitimacy, etc. The common claim before us is that for any one of such reasons, or for no reason at all, and without asserting or claiming any threat to life or health, any woman is entitled to an abortion at her request if she is able to find a medical advisor willing to undertake the procedure. The Court for the most part sustains this position: During the period prior to the time the fetus becomes viable, the Constitution of the United States values the convenience, whim or caprice of the putative mother more than the life or potential life of the fetus; the Constitution, therefore, guarantees the right to an abortion as against any state law or policy seeking to protect the fetus from an abortion not prompted by more compelling reasons of the mother.

With all due respect, I dissent. I find nothing in the language or history of the Constitution to support the Court's judgment. The Court simply fashions and announces a new constitutional right for pregnant mothers and, with scarcely any reason or authority for its action, invests that right with sufficient substance to override most existing state abortion statutes. The upshot is that the people and the legislatures of the 50 States are constitutionally disentitled to weigh the relative importance of the continued existence and development of the fetus on the one hand against a spectrum of possible impacts on the mother on the other hand. As an exercise of raw judicial power, the court perhaps has authority to do what it does today; but in my view its judgment is an improvident and extravagant exercise of the power of judicial review that the Constitution extends to this Court. . . .

Justice Rehnquist, dissenting:

I have difficulty in concluding that the right of "privacy" is involved in this case. Texas bars the performance of a medical abortion by a licensed physician on a plaintiff such as Roe. A transaction resulting in an operation such as this is not "private" in the ordinary usage of that word. . . . If the Court means by the term "privacy" no more than that the claim of a person to be free from unwanted state regulation of consensual transactions may be a form of "liberty" protected by the 14th Amendment, there is no doubt that similar claims have been upheld in our earlier decisions on the basis of that liberty. I agree that "liberty" embraces more than the rights found in the Bill of Rights. But that liberty is not guaranteed absolutely against deprivation, but only against deprivation without due process of law. The test traditionally applied in the area of social and economic legislation is whether or not a law such as that challenged has a rational relation to a valid state objective. The Due Process Clause of the 14th Amendment undoubtedly does place a limit, albeit a broad one, on legislative power to enact laws such as this. If the Texas statute were to prohibit an abortion even where the mother's life is in jeopardy, I have little doubt that such a statute would lack a rational relation to a valid state objective under the test stated. But the Court's sweeping invalidation of any restrictions on abortion during the first trimester is impossible to justify under that standard, and the conscious weighing of competing factors which the Court's opinion apparently substitutes for the established test is far more appropriate to a legislative judgment than to a judicial one.

---

226   *War Powers Act (1973)*

Revelations about the unilateral exercise of presidential power in both the Johnson and Nixon administrations led Congress to reassert its claim to have a constitutional role in making foreign policy. In 1967, the Senate had passed the "National Commitments" resolution, reaffirming the importance of the congressional war power. In 1969, a Senate Foreign Relations subcommittee began investigating the extent of secret commitments made by the executive without informing or seeking the advice of Congress. The announcement of the Christmas bombing of North Vietnam finally pushed Congress to act, and the War Powers Resolution, passed over Richard Nixon's veto, set up procedures to require the president to consult Congress before committing troops overseas. In the fifteen years following the passage of the resolution, it proved neither as crippling of the executive as its critics had warned nor as effective in involving Congress as its proponents had promised.

See Jacob Javits, *Who Makes War?* (1973); Thomas Eagleton, *War and Presidential Power* (1974); Walter Van Alstyne, "Congress, the President, and the Power to Declare War," 121 *University of Pennsylvania Law Review* 1 (1972); Alexander Bickel, "Congress, the President, and the Power to Wage War," 48 *Chicago-Kent Law Review* 131 (1971); Louis Fisher, *Presidential War Power* (1995); and David G. Adler and Larry N. George, Eds., *The Constitution and the Conduct of American Foreign Policy* (1996).

———

Short Title

Section 1. This joint resolution may be cited as the "War Powers Resolution."

Purpose and Policy

Sec. 2. (a) It is the purpose of this joint resolution to fulfill the intent of the framers of the Constitution of the United States and insure that the collective judgment of both the Congress and the President will apply to the introduction of United States Armed Forces into hostilities, or into situations where imminent involvement in hostilities is clearly indicated by the circumstances, and to the continued use of such forces in hostilities or in such situations.

(b) Under article I, section 8, of the Constitution, it is specifically provided that the Congress shall have the power to make all laws necessary and proper for carrying into execution, not only its own powers but also all other powers vested by the Constitution in the Government of the United States, or in any department or officer thereof.

(c) The constitutional powers of the President as Commander-in-Chief to introduce United States Armed Forces into hostilities, or into situations where imminent involvement in hostilities is clearly indicated by the circumstances, are exercised only pursuant to (1) a declaration of war, (2) specific statutory authorization, or (3) a national emergency created by attack upon the United States, its territories or possessions, or its armed forces.

Consultation

Sec. 3. The President in every possible instance shall consult with Congress before introducing United States Armed Forces into hostilities or into situations where imminent involvement in hostilities is clearly indicated by the circumstances, and after every such introduction shall consult regularly with the Congress until United States Armed Forces are no longer engaged in hostilities or have been removed from such situations.

Source: 87 *Statutes at Large* 55 (1973)

Reporting

Sec 4. (a) In the absence of a declaration of war, in any case in which United States Armed Forces are introduced—

(1) into hostilities or into situations where imminent involvement in hostilities is clearly indicated by the circumstances;

(2) into the territory, airspace or waters of a foreign nation, while equipped for combat, except for deployments which relate solely to supply, replacement, repair, or training of such forces; or

(3) in numbers which substantially enlarge United States Armed Forces equipped for combat already located in a foreign nation;

the President shall submit within 48 hours to the Speaker of the House of Representatives and to the President pro tempore of the Senate a report, in writing, setting forth—

(A) the circumstances necessitating the introduction of United States Armed Forces;

(B) the constitutional and legislative authority under which such introduction took place; and

(C) the estimated scope and duration of the hostilities or [involvement].

Congressional Action

Sec. 5 . . . (b) Within sixty calendar days after a report is submitted or is required to be submitted pursuant to section 4(a)(1), whichever is earlier, the President shall terminate any use of United States Armed Forces with respect to which such report was submitted (or required to be submitted), unless the Congress (1) has declared war or has enacted a specific authorization for such use of United States Armed Forces, (2) has extended by law such sixty-day period, or (3) is physically unable to meet as a result of an armed attack upon the United States. Such sixty-day period shall be extended for not more than an additional thirty days if the President determines and certifies to the Congress in writing that unavoidable military necessity respecting the safety of United States Armed Forces requires the continued use of such armed forces in the course of bringing about a prompt removal of such forces.

(c) Notwithstanding subsection (b), at any time that United States Armed Forces are engaged in hostilities outside the territory of the United States, its possessions and territories without a declaration of war or specific statutory authorization, such forces shall be removed by the President if the Congress so directs by concurrent resolution. . . .

Interpretation of Joint Resolution

Sec. 8. (a) Authority to introduce United States Armed Forces into hostilities or into situations wherein involvement in hostilities is clearly indicated by the circumstances shall not be inferred—

(1) from any provision of law (whether or not in effect before the date of the enactment of this joint resolution), including any provision contained in any appropriation Act, unless such provision specifically authorizes the introduction of United States Armed Forces into hostilities or into such situations and states that it is intended to constitute specific statutory authorization within the meaning of this joint resolution; or

(2) from any treaty heretofore or hereafter ratified unless such treaty is implemented by legislation specifically authorizing the introduction of United States Armed Forces into hostilities or into such situations and stating that it is intended to constitute specific statutory authorization within the meaning of this joint resolution. . . .

(d) Nothing in this joint resolution—

(1) is intended to alter the constitutional authority of the Congress or of the President, or the provisions of existing treaties; or

(2) shall be construed as granting any authority to the President with respect to the introduction of United States Armed Forces into hostilities or into situations wherein involvement in hostilities is clearly indicated by the circumstances which authority he would not have had in the absence of this joint resolution.

227   *Frontiero v. Richardson (1973)*

The success of blacks in invoking the Equal Protection Clause to invalidate racial discrimination led other groups to seek similar results. Women attacked long standing patterns of classification that imposed an inferior status upon them and secured major legislative achievements in Title VII of the 1964 Civil Rights Act and the Equal Pay Act of 1973.

In the Supreme Court, the justices struck down a number of gender-based distinctions, but as in this case, shied away from declaring sex a constitutionally suspect classification akin to race. The case involved an attack on a longstanding army regulation that denied married servicewomen the same fringe benefits paid to their male counterparts. Justice Brennan, along with Justices Douglas, White, and Marshall, indicated his willingness to bring gender discrimination within the Equal Protection Clause, but he lacked one vote. Nonetheless, although the Court has not utilized the strict scrutiny in gender cases that it employs for racial classification, there is no doubt that it applies a higher standard than mere rational basis and also that it does not automatically defer to legislative judgment on these matters.

See Ruth Bader Ginsburg, "Gender and the Constitution," 44 *University of Cincinnati Law Review* 1 (1975); A. E. Freedman, "Sex Equality, Sex Differences, and the Supreme

Court, 92 *Yale Law Journal* 913 (1983); and Gerald Gunther, "In Search of Evolving Doctrine," 86 *Harvard Law Review* 1 (1972).

Justice Brennan announced the judgment of the Court in an opinion in which Justices Douglas, White, and Marshall joined:

The question before us concerns the right of a female member of the uniformed service to claim her spouse as a "dependent" for the purposes of obtaining increased quarters allowances and medical and dental benefits on an equal footing with male members. Under the statutes, a serviceman may claim his wife as a "dependent" without regard to whether she is in fact dependent upon him for any part of her support but a servicewoman may not claim her husband as a "dependent" unless he is in fact dependent upon her for over one-half of his support. . . .

At the outset, appellants contend that classifications based upon sex, like classifications based upon race, alienage, and national origin, are inherently suspect and must therefore be subjected to close judicial scrutiny. We agree. . . .

There can be no doubt that our Nation has had a long and unfortunate history of sex discrimination. Traditionally, such discrimination was rationalized by an attitude of "romantic paternalism" which, in practical effect put women, not on a pedestal, but in a cage. As a result of notions such as these, our statute books gradually became laden with gross, stereotyped distinctions between the sexes and, indeed, throughout much of the 19th century the position of women in our society was, in many respects, comparable to that of blacks under the pre-Civil War slave codes. Neither slaves nor women could hold office, serve on juries, or bring suit in their own names, and married women traditionally were denied the legal capacity to hold or convey property or to serve as legal guardians of their own children. And although blacks were guaranteed the right to vote in 1870, women were denied even that right until adoption of the 19th Amendment half a century later.

It is true, of course, that the position of women in America has improved markedly in recent decades. Nevertheless, it can hardly be doubted that, in part because of the high visibility of the sex characteristic, women still face pervasive, although at times more subtle, discrimination in our educational institutions, in the job market and, perhaps most conspicuously, in the political arena. Moreover, since sex, like race and national origin, is an immutable characteristic determined solely by the accident of birth, the imposition of special disabilities upon the members of a particular sex because of their sex would seem to violate "the basic concept of our system that legal burdens should bear some relationship to individual responsibility." And what differentiates sex from such nonsuspect statuses as intelligence or physical disability, and aligns it with the recognized suspect criteria, is that the sex characteristic frequently bears no relation to ability to perform or contribute to society. As a result, statutory distinctions between the sexes often have the effect of invidiously relegating the entire class of females to inferior legal status without

Source: 411 U.S. 677 (1973)

regard to the actual capabilities of its individual members. . . . We can only conclude that classifications based upon sex, like classifications based upon race, alienage, or national origin, are inherently suspect, and must therefore be subjected to strict judicial scrutiny. Applying the analysis mandated by that stricter standard of review, it is clear that the statutory scheme now before us is constitutionally invalid.

The Government concedes that the differential treatment accorded men and women under these statutes serves no purpose other than mere "administrative convenience." It maintains that, as an empirical matter, wives in our society frequently are dependent upon their husbands, while husbands rarely are dependent upon their wives. Thus, the Government argues that Congress might reasonably have concluded that it would be both cheaper and easier simply conclusively to presume that wives of male members are financially dependent upon their husbands, while burdening female members with the task of establishing dependency in fact. The Government offers no concrete evidence, however, tending to support its view that such differential treatment in fact saves the Government any money. In order to satisfy the demands of strict judicial scrutiny, the Government must demonstrate, for example, that it is actually cheaper to grant increased benefits with respect to *all* male members, than it is to determine which male members are in fact entitled to such benefits and to grant increased benefits only to those members whose wives actually meet the dependency requirement. In any case, our prior decisions make clear that, although efficacious administration of governmental programs is not without some importance, "the Constitution recognizes higher values than speed and efficiency." When we enter the realm of "strict judicial scrutiny," there can be no doubt that "administrative convenience" is not a shibboleth. On the contrary, any statutory scheme which draws a sharp line between the sexes, *solely* for the purpose of achieving administrative convenience, necessarily commands "dissimilar treatment for men and women who are similarly situated," and therefore involves the "very kind of arbitrary legislative choice" forbidden by the Constitution.

Reversed.

Mr. Justice Stewart concurs in the judgment, agreeing that the statutes before us work an invidious discrimination in violation of the Constitution.

Justice Powell, with whom Chief Justice Burger and Justice Blackmun joined, concurred in the judgment:

It is unnecessary for the Court in this case to characterize sex as a suspect classification, with all of the far-reaching implications of such a holding. *Reed,* which abundantly supports our decision today, did not add sex to the narrowly limited group of classifications which are inherently suspect. In my view, we can and should decide this case on the authority of *Reed* and reserve for the future any expansion of its rationale.

There is another, and I find compelling, reason for deferring a general categorizing of sex classifications as invoking the strictest test of judicial scrutiny. The Equal Rights Amendment, which if adopted will resolve the substance of this precise question, has been approved by the Congress. By acting prematurely and unnecessarily, as I view it, the Court has assumed a decisional responsibility at the very time when state legislatures, functioning within the traditional democratic process, are debating the proposed

Amendment. It seems to me that this reaching out to preempt by judicial action a major political decision which is currently in process of resolution does not reflect appropriate respect for duly prescribed legislative process. . . .

[Justice REHNQUIST dissented, citing the opinion of District Court Judge Rives, who doubted that the statute had a sex classification, and even if it did, it made no difference, since gender did not constitute a "suspect" classification.]

228

San Antonio Independent School District v. Rodriguez (1973)

By the time of his assassination, Martin Luther King had begun to draw the nation's attention to the relationship between civil rights and poverty, arguing that poor people could never enjoy full status as citizens. The Court had in the past ruled that basic rights could not be denied because of lack of money; this had been the main argument in striking down the poll tax in *Harper v. Virginia Board of Elections* (1966).

In this case, the petitioners attacked the Texas system of financing public schools, which relied primarily on local property taxes. As a result, rich residential districts as well as districts with large amounts of valuable industrial real estate spent considerably more than poorer areas on schools. Parents of Mexican-American children initiated the suit on behalf of all children residing in districts with a low property tax base, claiming violation of equal protection. The District Court accepted the argument and, exercising strict scrutiny, ruled poverty a suspect classification and education a fundamental right.

Although the Court declined, by a narrow majority, to accept this reasoning and to constitutionalize a right to equal education, a number of state constitutions did include education as a listed basic right. In those states, similar lawsuits proved successful in state courts, forcing New Jersey and other states to completely overhaul their systems of financing public education to equalize spending among districts.

See Barbara Brudno, *Poverty, Inequality and the Law* (1976); Harold Silver, *An Educational War on Poverty* (1991); and Arnold Lewis, *Power, Poverty and Education* (1979).

Mr. Justice POWELL delivered the opinion of the [Court]:

I. [We] must decide, first whether the Texas system of financing public education operates to the disadvantage of some suspect class or impinges upon a fundamental right explicitly or implicitly protected by the Constitution, thereby requiring strict judicial scrutiny. If so, the judgment of the District Court should be affirmed. If not, the Texas scheme must still be examined to determine whether it rationally furthers some legitimate, articulated state purpose and therefore does not constitute an invidious discrimination in violation of [equal protection].

II. We find neither the suspect-classification nor the fundamental-interest analysis persuasive.

A. The wealth discrimination discovered by the District Court, [and] by several other courts that have recently struck down school financing laws in other States is quite unlike any of the forms of wealth discrimination heretofore reviewed by this Court. [The] individuals or groups of individuals who constituted the class discriminated against in our prior cases shared two distinguishing characteristics: because of their impecunity they were completely unable to pay for some desired benefit, and as a consequence, they sustained an absolute deprivation of a meaningful opportunity to enjoy that benefit. Even a cursory examination, however, demonstrates that neither of the two distinguishing characteristics of wealth classifications can be found here. First, there is reason to believe that the poorest families are not necessarily clustered in the poorest property districts. A recent Connecticut study found, not surprisingly, that the poor were clustered around commercial and industrial areas—those same areas that provide the most attractive sources of property tax income for school districts. There is no basis on the record for assuming that the poorest people are concentrated in the poorest districts in Texas. Second, lack of personal resources has not occasioned an absolute deprivation of the desired benefit. The argument here is not that the children are receiving no public education; rather, it is that they are receiving a poorer quality education than children in districts having more assessible wealth. Apart from the unsettled and disputed question whether the quality of education may be determined by the amount of money expended for it, a sufficient answer to appellees' argument is that, at least where wealth is involved, equal protection does not require absolute equality or precisely equal advantages. Nor, indeed, in view of the infinite variables affecting the educational process, can any system assure equal quality of education except in the most relative sense. For these two reasons, the disadvantaged class is not susceptible of identification in traditional terms.

This brings us to the third way in which the classification scheme might be defined—*district* wealth discrimination. Since the only correlation indicated by the evidence is between district property wealth and expenditures, it may be argued that discrimination might be found without regard to the individual income characteristics of district residents. However described, it is clear that appellees' suit asks this Court to extend its most exacting scrutiny to review a system that allegedly discriminates against a large, diverse, and amorphous class, unified only by the common factor of residence in districts that happen to have less taxable wealth than other districts. The system of alleged discrimination and the class it defines have none of the traditional indicia of sus-

Source: 411 U.S. 1 (1973)

pectness: the class is not saddled with such disabilities, or subjected to such a history of purposeful unequal treatment, or relegated to such a position of political powerlessness as to command extraordinary protection from the majoritarian political process. We thus conclude that the Texas system does not operate to the peculiar disadvantage of any suspect class. Recognizing that this Court has never heretofore held that wealth discrimination alone provides an adequate basis for invoking strict scrutiny, appellees also assert that the State's system impermissibly interferes with the exercise of a "fundamental" right requiring the strict standard of judicial review.

B. In *Brown v. Board of Education,* a unanimous Court recognized that "education is perhaps the most important function of state and local governments." Nothing this Court holds today in any way detracts from our historic dedication to public education. But the importance of a service performed by the State does not determine whether it must be regarded as fundamental for purposes of examination under equal protection. . . . It is not the province of this Court to create substantive constitutional rights in the name of guaranteeing equal protection. Thus the key to discovering whether education is "fundamental" is not to be found in comparisons of the relative societal significance of education as opposed to subsistence or housing. Nor is it to be found by weighing whether education is as important as the right to travel. Rather, the answer lies in assessing whether there is a right to education explicitly or implicitly guaranteed by the Constitution.

Education, of course, is not among the rights afforded explicit protection under our Federal Constitution. Nor do we find any basis for saying it is implicitly so protected. As we have said, the undisputed importance of education will not alone cause this Court to depart from the usual standard for reviewing a State's social and economic legislation. It is appellees' contention, however, that education is distinguishable from other services and benefits provided by the State because it bears a peculiarly close relationship to other rights and liberties accorded protection under the Constitution. Specifically, they insist that education is itself a fundamental personal right because it is essential to the effective exercise of First Amendment freedoms and to intelligent utilization of the right to vote. In asserting a nexus between speech and education, appellees urge that the right to speak is meaningless unless the speaker is capable of articulating his thoughts intelligently and persuasively. The "marketplace of ideas" is an empty forum for those lacking basic communicative tools. A similar line of reasoning is pursued with respect to the right to vote. Exercise of the franchise, it is contended, cannot be divorced from the educational foundation of the voter. We need not dispute any of these propositions. Yet we have never presumed to possess either the ability or the authority to guarantee to the citizenry the most *effective* speech or the most *informed* electoral choice. That these may be desirable goals [is] not to be doubted. [But] they are not values to be implemented by judicial intrusion into otherwise legitimate state activities.

C. We need not rest our decision, however, solely on the inappropriateness of the strict scrutiny test. A century of adjudication under equal protection affirmatively supports the application of the traditional standard of review, which requires only that the State's system be shown to bear some rational relationship to legitimate state purposes. We have here nothing less than a direct attack on the way in which Texas has chosen to raise and disburse state and local tax revenues. Appellees would have the Court intrude in an area in which it has traditionally deferred to state legislatures. This Court has often admonished against such interferences with the State's fiscal policies under equal protection. Thus we stand on familiar ground when we continue to acknowledge that the Justices of this Court lack both the expertise and the familiarity with local problems so necessary to the making of wise decisions with respect to the raising and disposition of public revenues. No scheme of taxation has yet been devised which is free of all discriminatory impact. In such a complex arena in which no perfect alternatives exist, the Court does well not to impose too rigorous a standard of scrutiny lest all local fiscal schemes become subjects of criticism under equal protection. And this case also involves the most persistent and difficult questions of educational policy, another area in which this Court's lack of specialized knowledge and experience counsels against premature interference with the informed judgments made at the state and local levels. Education, perhaps even more than welfare assistance, presents a myriad of "intractable economic, social, and even philosophical problems." In such circumstances, the judiciary is well advised to refrain from imposing on the States inflexible constitutional restraints that could circumscribe continued research and experimentation. . . .

IV. A cautionary postscript seems appropriate. Affirmance here would occasion in Texas and elsewhere an unprecedented upheaval in public education. The complexity of the problems is demonstrated by the lack of consensus with respect to whether it may be said with any assurance that the poor, the racial minorities, or the children in overburdened core-city school districts would be benefitted by abrogation of traditional modes of financing education. We hardly need add that this Court's action today is not to be viewed as placing its judicial imprimatur on the status quo. The need is apparent for reform in tax systems which may well have relied too long and too heavily on the local property tax. But the ultimate solutions must come from the lawmakers and from the democratic pressures of those who elect them.

Reversed.

Mr. Justice WHITE, with whom Mr. Justice DOUGLAS and Mr. Justice BRENNAN join, dissenting:

This case would be quite different if it were true that the Texas system, while insuring minimum educational expenditures in every district through state funding, extended a meaningful option to all local districts to increase their per-pupil expenditures. But for districts with a low per-pupil real estate tax base, the Texas system utterly fails to extend a realistic choice to parents because the property tax, which is the only revenue-raising mechanism extended to school districts, is practically and legally unavailable. Requiring the State to establish only that unequal treatment is in furtherance of a permissible goal, without also requiring the State to show that the means chosen to effectuate that goal are rationally related to its achievement, makes equal protection analysis no more than an empty gesture.

Mr. Justice MARSHALL, with whom Mr. Justice DOUGLAS concurs, dissenting:

I must once more voice my disagreement with the Court's rigidified approach to equal protection analysis. The Court apparently seeks to establish today that equal protection cases fall into one of two neat categories which dictate the appropriate standard of review—strict scrutiny or mere rationality. But this Court's decisions defy such easy categorization. A principled reading of what this Court has done reveals that it has applied a spectrum of standards in reviewing discrimination allegedly violative of equal protection. This spectrum clearly comprehends variations in the degree of care with which the Court will scrutinize particular classifications, depending, I believe, on the constitutional and societal importance of the interest adversely affected and the recognized invidiousness of the basis upon which the particular classification is drawn. In fact, many of the Court's recent decisions embody the very sort of reasoned approach to equal protection for which I previously argued. I therefore cannot accept the majority's labored efforts to demonstrate that fundamental interests, which call for strict scrutiny, encompass only established rights which we are somehow bound to recognize from the text of the Constitution itself. To be sure, some interests which the Court has deemed to be fundamental for purposes of equal protection are themselves constitutionally protected rights. But it will not do to suggest that the "answer" to whether an interest is fundamental for purposes of equal protection analysis is always determined by whether that interest "is a right explicitly or implicitly guaranteed by the Constitution." I would like to know where the Constitution guarantees the right to procreate, or the right to vote in state elections or the right to an appeal from a criminal conviction. These are instances in which, due to the importance of the interests at stake, the Court has displayed a strong concern with the existence of discriminatory state treatment. But the Court has never said or indicated that these are interests which independently enjoy full-blown constitutional protection. . . .

It seems to me inescapably clear that this Court has consistently adjusted the care with which it will review state discrimination in light of the constitutional significance of the interests affected and the invidiousness of the particular classification. The majority suggests, however, that a variable standard of review would give this Court the appearance of a "super-legislature." I cannot agree. Such an approach seems to me a part of the guarantees of our Constitution and of the historic experiences with oppression of and discrimination against discrete, powerless minorities which underlie that document. In truth, the Court itself will be open to the criticism raised by the majority so long as it continues on its present course of effectively selecting in private which cases will be afforded special consideration without acknowledging the true basis of its action. It is true that this Court has never deemed the provision of free public education to be required by the Constitution. Nevertheless, the fundamental importance of education is amply indicated by the prior decisions of this Court, by the unique status accorded public education by our society, and by the close relationship between education and some of our most basic constitutional values. Education directly affects the ability of a child to exercise his First Amendment interests. Of particular importance is the relationship between education and the political process and the demonstrated effect of education on the exercise of the franchise by the electorate. It is this very sort of intimate relationship between a particular personal interest and specific constitutional guarantees that has heretofore caused the Court to attach special significance, for purposes of equal protection analysis, to individual interests such as procreation and the exercise of the state franchise. These factors compel us to recognize the fundamentality of education and to scrutinize with appropriate care the bases for state discrimination affecting equality of educational opportunity in Texas school districts—a conclusion which is only strengthened when we consider the character of the classification in this case.

When evaluated with these considerations in mind, it seems to me that discrimination on the basis of group wealth in this case likewise calls for careful judicial scrutiny. First, local district wealth bears no relationship whatsoever to the interest of Texas school children in the educational opportunity afforded them by Texas. Given the importance of that interest, we must be particularly sensitive to the invidious characteristics of any form of discrimination that is not clearly intended to serve it, as opposed to some other distinct state interest. Discrimination on the basis of group wealth may not, to be sure, reflect the social stigma frequently attached to personal poverty. Nevertheless, insofar as group wealth discrimination involves wealth over which the disadvantaged individual has no significant control, it represents in fact a more serious basis of discrimination than does personal wealth. For such discrimination is no reflection of the individual's characteristics or his abilities. We have previously treated discrimination on a basis which the individual cannot control as constitutionally disfavored. Moreover, prior cases have dealt with discrimination on the basis of indigency which was attributable to the operation of the private sector. But we have no such simple de facto wealth discrimination here. The means for financing public education in Texas are specified by the State. At the same time, governmentally imposed land use controls have undoubtedly encouraged and rigidified natural trends in the allocation of particular areas for residential or commercial use, and thus determined each district's amount of taxable property wealth. In short, this case, in contrast to the Court's previous wealth discrimination decisions, can only be seen as "unusual in the extent to which governmental action is the cause of the wealth classifications."

Here, both the nature of the interest and the classification dictate close judicial scrutiny of the purposes which Texas seeks to serve with its present educational financing scheme and of the means it has selected to serve that purpose. I need not now decide how I might ultimately strike the balance were we confronted with a situation where the State's sincere concern for local control inevitably produced educational inequality. For on this record, it is apparent that the State's purported concern with local control is offered primarily as an excuse rather than as a justification for interdistrict inequality. School districts cannot choose to have the best education in the State by imposing the highest tax rate. Instead, the quality of the educational opportunity offered by any particular district is largely determined by the amount of taxable property located in the district—a factor over which local voters can exercise no control. In my judgment, any substantial degree of scrutiny reveals that the State has selected means wholly inappropriate to secure its purported interest in assuring its school districts local fiscal control. At the same time, appellees have pointed out a variety of alternative financing schemes which may serve the State's purported interest in local control as well as, if not better than, the present scheme without the current impairment of the educational opportunity of vast numbers of Texas school children. . . .

229

Articles of Impeachment Against Richard M. Nixon (1974)

Following his overwhelming reelection as president in 1972, the administration of Richard M. Nixon began deteriorating. News of his secret bombing of Cambodia and efforts to nullify congressional spending authorizations led to increasingly bitter confrontations with Congress. Then the Watergate scandal, which had been simmering ever since the arrest of burglars at the Democratic National Committee offices in Washington before the election, exploded and not only involved Nixon in the coverup of the break-in, but also raised allegations that he had misused presidential authority over the Internal Revenue Service and other government agencies in vendettas against those he considered his "enemies," including prominent journalists and politicians.

On March 1, 1974, a federal grand jury indicted seven of Nixon's aides for conspiracy to obstruct justice in relation to the Watergate investigations and named the president as an unindicted coconspirator. In the meantime, the special prosecutor sought tapes and documents concerning meetings at the White House, which Nixon refused to release. The prosecutor went into federal court, asking for a *subpoena duces tecum* to force the president to hand over the materials; Nixon countered with a claim of executive privilege. On appeal to the Supreme Court, the justices (with Rehnquist not participating) denied the claim of executive authority against the need for effective law enforcement. (In *United States v. Nixon,* the Court admitted that executive privilege existed, but held that the judiciary would decide when it could be appropriately invoked.)

Once the tapes were made available, they indicated that Nixon had indeed known about the break-in and had participated in the cover-up. Until this point, his defenders had declared that the president could not be found guilty by circumstance; there had to be a "smoking gun." With these tapes, a consensus rapidly developed in Congress that Nixon would have to be removed from office. A special House committee drew up and adopted three articles of impeachment at the end of July 1974; the first dealt with Watergate, the second dealt with misuse of his powers, and the third accused him of not cooperating with Congress. While it is unlikely that he could have been convicted on the third count, either of the first two commanded enough votes in the Senate. Rather than be impeached and convicted, Nixon resigned as president on August 8, 1974, to be succeeded by Gerald Ford.

The impeachment proceedings raised again the controversy that had swirled around Andrew Johnson a century earlier (Document 122 in Volume I): Was impeachment designed only for criminal acts or was it also designed for political malfeasance? What did "high crimes and misdemeanors" mean? Where did the limits of congressional and executive authority collide?

See Gerald Gunther, "Judicial Hegemony and Legislative Autonomy: The Nixon Case and the Impeachment Process," 23 *UCLA Law Review* 30 (1974); Michael J. Gerhardt, *The Federal Impeachment Process: A Constitutional and Historical Analysis* (1996); and Symposium, "*United States v. Nixon:* Presidential Power and Executive Privilege Twenty-Five Years Later," 83 *Minnesota Law Review* 1061 (May 1999).

———

Impeaching Richard M. Nixon, President of the United States, of high crimes and misdemeanors.

Resolved, That Richard M. Nixon, President of the United States, is impeached for high crimes and misdemeanors, and that the following articles of impeachment be exhibited to the Senate:

Articles of impeachment exhibited by the House of Representatives of the United States of America in the name of itself and of all of the people of the United States of America, against Richard M. Nixon, President of the United States of America, in maintenance and support of its impeachment against him for high crimes and misdemeanors.

Article I

In his conduct of the office of President of the United States, Richard M. Nixon, in violation of his constitutional oath faithfully to execute the office of President of the United States and, to the best of his ability, preserve, protect, and defend the Constitution of the United States, and in violation of his constitutional duty to take care that the laws be faithfully executed, has prevented, obstructed, and impeded the administration of justice, in that:

On June 17, 1972, and prior thereto, agents of the Committee for the Re-election of the President committed unlawful entry of the headquarters of the Democratic National Committee in Washington, District of Columbia, for the purpose of securing political intelligence. Subsequent thereto, Richard M. Nixon, using the powers of his high office, engaged personally and through his subordinates and agents, in a course of conduct or plan designed to delay, impede, and obstruct the investigation of such unlawful entry; to cover up, conceal, and protect those responsible; and to conceal the existence and scope of other unlawful covert activities.

The means used to implement this course of conduct or plan included one or more of the following:

(1) making or causing to be made false or misleading statements to lawfully authorized investigative officers and employees of the United States;

(2) withholding relevant and material evidence or information from lawfully authorized investigative officers and employees of the United States;

Source: House Judiciary Committee, *Report on the Impeachment of Richard M. Nixon, President of the United States,* House Report No. 1035, 93rd Cong., 2d Sess. (1974)

(3) approving, condoning, acquiescing in, and counseling witnesses with respect to the giving of false or misleading statements . . . ;

(4) interfering or endeavoring to interfere with the conduct of investigations by the Department of Justice of the United States, the Federal Bureau of Investigation, the Office of Watergate Special Prosecution Force, and Congressional Committees;

(5) approving, condoning, and acquiescing in, the surreptitious payment of substantial sums of money for the purpose of obtaining the silence or influencing the testimony of witnesses, potential witnesses or individuals who participated in such unlawful entry and other illegal activities;

(6) endeavoring to misuse the Central Intelligence Agency, an agency of the United States;

(7) disseminating information received from officers [of] the Department of Justice of the United States to subjects of investigations [for] the purpose of aiding and assisting such subjects in their attempts to avoid criminal liability;

(8) making false or misleading public statements for the purpose of deceiving the people of the United States into believing that a thorough and complete investigation had been conducted with respect to allegations of misconduct on the part of personnel of the executive branch of the United States and personnel of the Committee for the Re-election of the President, and that there was no involvement of such personnel in such misconduct; or

(9) endeavoring to cause prospective defendants, and individuals duly tried and convicted, to expect favored treatment and consideration in return for their silence or false testimony, or rewarding individuals for their silence or false testimony.

In all of this, Richard M. Nixon has acted in a manner contrary to his trust as President and subversive of constitutional government, to the great prejudice of the cause of law and justice and to the manifest injury of the people of the United States.

Wherefore Richard M. Nixon, by such conduct, warrants impeachment and trial, and removal from office.

Article II

Using the powers of the office of President of the United States, Richard M. Nixon, in violation of his constitutional oath faithfully to execute the office of President of the United States and, to the best of his ability, preserve, protect, and defend the Constitution of the United States, and in disregard of his constitutional duty to take care that the laws be faithfully executed, has repeatedly engaged in conduct violating the constitutional rights of citizens, impairing the due and proper administration of justice and the conduct of lawful inquiries, or contravening the laws governing agencies of the executive branch and the purposes of these agencies.

This conduct has included one or more of the following:

(1) He has, acting personally and through his subordinates and agents, endeavored to obtain from the Internal Revenue Service, in violation of the constitutional rights of citizens, confidential information contained in income tax returns for purposes not authorized by law, and to cause, in violation of the constitutional rights of citizens, income tax

audits or other income tax investigations to be initiated or conducted in a discriminatory manner.

(2) He misused the Federal Bureau of Investigation, the Secret Service, and other executive personnel, in violation or disregard of the constitutional rights of citizens, by directing or authorizing such agencies or personnel to conduct or continue electronic surveillance or other investigations for purposes unrelated to national security, the enforcement of laws, or any other lawful function of his office; he did direct, authorize, or permit the use of information obtained thereby for purposes unrelated to national security, the enforcement of laws, or any other lawful function of his office; and he did direct the concealment of certain records made by the Federal Bureau of Investigation of electronic surveillance.

(3) He has, acting personally and through his subordinates and agents, in violation or disregard of the constitutional rights of citizens, authorized and permitted to be maintained a secret investigative unit within the office of the President, financed in part with money derived from campaign contributions, which unlawfully utilized the resources of the Central Intelligence Agency, engaged in covert and unlawful activities, and attempted to prejudice the constitutional right of an accused to a fair trial.

(4) He has failed to take care that the laws were faithfully executed by failing to act when he knew or had reason to know that his close subordinates endeavored to impede and frustrate lawful inquiries by duly constituted executive, judicial, and legislative entities concerning the unlawful entry into the headquarters of the Democratic National Committee, and the cover-up thereof, and concerning other unlawful activities, including those relating to the confirmation of Richard Kleindienst as Attorney General of the United States, the electronic surveillance of private citizens, the break-in into the offices of Dr. Lewis Fielding, and the campaign financing practices of the Committee to Re-elect the President.

(5) In disregard of the rule of law, he knowingly misused the executive power by interfering with agencies of the executive branch, including the Federal Bureau of Investigation, the Criminal Division, and the Office of Watergate Special Prosecution Force, of the Department of Justice, and the Central Intelligence Agency, in violation of his duty to take care that the laws be faithfully executed.

In all of this, Richard M. Nixon has acted in a manner contrary to his trust as President and subversive of constitutional government, to the great prejudice of the cause of law and justice and to the manifest injury of the people of the United States.

Wherefore Richard M. Nixon, by such conduct, warrants impeachment and trial, and removal from office.

Article III

In his conduct of the office of President of the United States, Richard M. Nixon, contrary to his oath faithfully to execute the office of President of the United States and, to the best of his ability, preserve, protect, and defend the Constitution of the United States, and in violation of his constitutional duty to take care that the laws be faithfully executed, has failed without lawful cause or excuse to produce papers and things as directed by duly authorized subpoenas issued by the Committee on the Judiciary of the House of

Representatives on April 11, 1974, May 15, 1974, May 30, 1974, and June 24, 1974, and willfully disobeyed such subpoenas. The subpoenaed papers and things were deemed necessary by the Committee in order to resolve by direct evidence fundamental, factual questions relating to Presidential direction, knowledge, or approval of actions demonstrated by other evidence to be substantial grounds for impeachment of the President. In refusing to produce these papers and things, Richard M. Nixon, substituting his judgment as to what materials were necessary for the inquiry, interposed the powers of the Presidency against the lawful subpoenas of the House of Representatives, thereby assuming to himself functions and judgments necessary to the exercise of the sole power of impeachment vested by the Constitution in the House of Representatives.

In all of this, Richard M. Nixon has acted in a manner contrary to his trust as President and subversive of constitutional government, to the great prejudice of the cause of law and justice, and to the manifest injury of the people of the United States.

Wherefore Richard M. Nixon, by such conduct, warrants impeachment and trial, and removal from office.

---

230   *People v. Brisendine (1975)*

Four men had been arrested for illegally camping and having an open fire. When the four were arrested, the police, without a warrant, searched their backpacks for weapons, a legitimate procedure since it was a search incident to an arrest. They did not find weapons, but did find drugs, and the four men were later convicted on drug charges as well. On appeal, they claimed that the California constitution protected them against such a warrantless search and established a higher level of protection than did federal standards enunciated by the Supreme Court. In its decision, the California court agreed, and enunciated its rationale for following state rather than federal standards.

See Richard Falk, "The State Constitution: A More than 'Adequate' Nonfederal Ground," 61 *California Law Review* 273 (1973); Note, "Rediscovering the California Declaration of Rights," 26 *Hastings Law Journal* 481 (1974); and Note, "The New Federalism: Toward a Principled Interpretation of the State Constitution," 29 *Stanford Law Review* 297 (1977).

———

Judge Mosk:

We conclude there was substantial evidence to support the trial court's finding that the search was legitimately concerned with weapons and not contraband. Similarly,

Source: 13 Cal. 3d 528 (1975)

since it was necessary for the officers to be in close proximity with defendant and his companions for a prolonged period of time, we are of the view that the circumstances reasonably warranted such a weapons search; that being the case, the officers were justified in investigating further when a pat-down of defendant's knapsack proved inadequate to disclose if it contained weapons. However, we hold that the officers' subsequent intrusion into the opaque bottle and envelopes inside the knapsack cannot be justified by the limited purpose which validated the search in its inception. Accordingly, we hold these items were obtained by means of an unreasonable search and seizure in violation of article I, section 13, of the California Constitution. . . .

. . . It is well settled that "a search which is reasonable at its inception may violate the Fourth Amendment by virtue of its intolerable intensity and scope." . . . The issue is thus dual: "whether the officer's action was justified at its inception, and whether it was reasonably related in scope to the circumstances which justified the interference in the first place." . . .

Defendant contends that the search of his knapsack exceeded the legitimate purpose for which a search was authorized. Yet rather than presenting a single "scope" issue the search of the pack poses three such problems, a fact only cursorily alluded to by either party. The first is the question of the validity of any search of defendant's effects, including the pack: second, the search of the interior of the pack; and third, the search of the bottle and envelopes containing the contraband. As each involves different considerations we will discuss them seriatim.

The People cite Chimel v. California (1969) . . . for the proposition that "it is reasonable for the arresting officer to search the person arrested or an area within which he might reach for weapons in order to remove any weapons the latter might seek to use in order to resist arrest or effect escape." . . .

Defendant contends that *Chimel* is inapposite, and that even assuming the right to search his person for weapons, the patdown of the pack was not authorized because (1) there was no evidence the pack contained weapons and (2) if the officers feared the possibility that a weapon was contained therein they should have simply removed the pack from his area of control.

Preliminarily, it should be noted that the traditional rationale of warrantless searches incident to arrests is the two-fold need to uncover evidence of the crime and weapons which might be used [to] injure the arresting officer or effect an escape.

When Officer Denney opened the side pocket of the knapsack he found a frosted, opaque plastic bottle and a pair of envelopes. Because of the translucent but no transparent nature of the bottle, the People could not rely on the exception to the warrant requirement for objects or contraband found in plain view. . . .

Nor can the People's burden be discharged by the assertion that the bottle and envelopes might possibly contain unusual or atypical weapons. In People v. Collins (1970) . . . we rejected that contention as applied to a "little lump" felt during the course of a pat-down. We there expressly disapproved of the approach taken in People v. Armenta (1968) . . . in which it was fancifully theorized that such a soft object might have been a "rubber water pistol loaded with carbolic acid." *Collins* made explicit the rule that "an officer who exceeds a pat-down without first discovering an object which feels reasonably like a knife, gun, or club must be able to point to specific and articulable facts which reasonably support a suspicion that the particular suspect is armed with an atypical weapon which would feel like the object felt during the patdown." . . .

Conversely, of course, if the pat-down discloses an object which reasonably feels like a weapon, further intrusion may be necessary and permissible. . . .

To briefly summarize our holding: Typically in cases of warrantless weapons searches the police must be able to point to specific and articulable facts which reasonably justify a belief that the suspect is armed. In the ordinary citation situation the fact of the arrest alone will not supply this justification and additional facts must be shown. In the case of transportation in the police vehicle, however, or in the analogous circumstance here, the necessity of close proximity will itself provide the needed basis for a protective pat-down of the person. To intrude further than a pat-down, the officer must provide additional specific and articulable facts necessitating the additional intrusion.

Here these additional facts were present by reason of necessity that the campers' effects accompany the officers and the impossibility of securing them in a place where access was precluded. Thus the officers could go beyond a pat-down of the outer clothing and conduct a similarly limited search of the relevant items. Indeed, even an inquiry into the interior of the pack was permissible when the pat-down of the exterior proved impractical. But once confronted with a purely innocent interior it was again incumbent upon the officers to explain why still further intrusion was required. As to such explanation, the record is silent.

Accordingly, since the contraband was illegally seized in violation of article I, section 13, of the California Constitution, we hold that it was erroneously received in evidence. . . .

Inasmuch as it constituted the sole evidence against defendant, its admission was prejudicial error and the judgment (order granting probation) must be reversed. . . .

There remains for consideration whether we should adhere to our precedential decisions on this point even though they impose a higher standard than is now required by [the United States Supreme Court]. Our right to do so cannot be seriously questioned. In Cooper v. California (1967) . . . the Supreme Court recognized this well-known principle: "Our holding, of course, does not affect the State's power to impose higher standards on searches and seizures than required by the Federal Constitution if it chooses to do so." . . .

This court has always assumed the independent vitality of our state Constitution. In the search and seizure area our decisions have often comported with federal law, yet there has never been any question that this similarity was a matter of choice and not compulsion. As Chief Justice Wright stated in People v. Triggs (1973) . . . : "At least since the advent of Wolf v. Colorado (1949) . . . we have treated the law under article I, section 19 [now §13], of our state Constitution as 'substantially equivalent' to the Supreme Court's construction of the Fourth Amendment." . . .

The foregoing cases illustrate the incontrovertible conclusion that the California Constitution is, and always has been, a document of independent force. Any other result would contradict not only the most fundamental principles of federalism but also the historic bases of state charters. It is a fiction too long accepted that provisions in state constitutions textually identical to the Bill of Rights were intended to mirror their federal counterpart. The lesson of history is otherwise: the Bill of Rights was based upon the corresponding provisions of the first state constitutions, rather than the reverse. "By the end of the Revolutionary period, the concept of a Bill of Rights had been fully developed in the American system. Eleven of the 13 states (and Vermont as well) had enacted Constitutions to fill in the political gap caused by the overthrow of British authority. . . . Eight of the Revolutionary Constitutions were prefaced by Bills of Rights, while four contained guarantees of many of the most important individual rights in the body of their texts. Included in these Revolutionary constitutional provisions were *all of the rights that were to be protected in the federal Bill of Rights.* By the time of the Treaty of Paris (1783) then, the American inventory of individual rights had been virtually completed and included in the different state Constitutions whether in separate Bills of Rights or the organic texts themselves." . . . In particular, the Rights of the Colonists (Boston, 1772) declared for the first time "the right against unreasonable searches and seizures that was to ripen into the Fourth Amendment" . . . and that protection was embodied in every one of the eight state constitutions adopted prior to 1789 which contained a separate bill of rights. . . .

We need not further extend this opinion to trace to their remote origins the historical roots of state constitutional provisions. Yet we have no doubt that such inquiry would confirm our view of the matter. The federal Constitution was designed to guard the states as sovereignties against potential abuses of centralized government; state charters, however, were conceived as the first and at one time the only line of protection of the individual against the excesses of local officials. Thus in determining that California citizens are entitled to greater protection under the California Constitution against unreasonable searches and seizures than that required by the United States Constitution, we are embarking on no revolutionary course. Rather we are simply reaffirming a basic principle of federalism—that the nation as a whole is composed of distinct geographical and political entities bound together by a fundamental federal law but nonetheless independently responsible for safeguarding the rights of their citizens.

---

231   *Darrin v. Gould (1975)*

Although the federal Equal Rights Amendment went down to defeat, over a third of the states adopted state ERAs, thus allowing state courts to set a higher standard against which to measure gender discrimination than that available under the Fourteenth Amendment. In this case, the Washington state court struck down rules prohibiting qualified girls from participating in interscholastic sports. It was just this type of decision that opponents of the ERA used to alarm people, claiming that if adopted, the ERA would do away with all sensible distinctions between males and females. To proponents of the ERA, the results of this decision were to be applauded, as they wiped away still another artificial barrier between the sexes.

See Note, "Sex Discrimination in Interscholastic High School Athletics," 25 *Syracuse Law Review* 535 (1974); and Peter J. Galie, "The Other Supreme Courts: Judicial Activism among State Supreme Courts," 33 *Syracuse Law Review* 731 (1982).

———

Washington has used the rational relationship test in invalidating statutory classifications . . . in construing Const. art. 1, § 12, in light of the Fourteenth Amendment and the Due Process Clause of the Fifth Amendment, held sex to be a suspect classification requiring a showing of a compelling state interest to uphold it. . . .

The Supreme Court of Washington has not yet expressly held that education free of discrimination based upon sex is a fundamental right within the meaning of Const. art. 1, § 12 so as to call for strict scrutiny of a classification claimed to infringe upon that right. That in Washington, education (physical and cultural), free from discrimination based on sex, is a fundamental constitutional right, is a conclusion properly drawn from Const. art. 9, § 1 adopted in 1889. That article provides:

It is the paramount duty of the state to make ample provision for the education of all children residing within its borders, without distinction or preference on account of race, color, caste, or sex.

When the Darrin girls were denied permission to play in the fall of 1973, Const. art. 31, § 1, Washington's Equal Rights Amendment provided:

Equality of rights and responsibility under the law *shall not* be denied or abridged on account of sex.

(Italics ours.)

Const. art. 31, provided the latest expression of the constitutional law of the state, dealing with sex discrimination, as adopted by the people themselves. Presumably the people in adopting Const. art. 31 intended to do more than repeat what was already contained in the otherwise governing constitutional provisions, federal and state, by which discrimination based on sex was permissible under the rational relationship and strict scrutiny tests. Any other view would mean the people intended to accomplish no change in the existing constitutional law governing sex discrimination, except possibly to make the validity of a classification based on sex come within the suspect class under Const. art. 1, § 12. Had such a limited purpose been intended, there would have been no necessity to resort to the broad, sweeping, mandatory language of the Equal Rights Amendment. . . .

Source: 85 Wash. 2d 859 (1975)

In sum, the WIAA rule discriminating against girls on account of their sex violates Const. art. 31, if not the Equal Protection Clause of the Fourteenth Amendment, Const. art. 1, § 12 and Const. art. 9, § 1. No compelling state interest requires a holding to the contrary. The overriding compelling state interest as adopted by the people of this state in 1972 is that: "Equality of rights and responsibility under the law shall not be denied or abridged on account of sex." We agree with the rationale of *Commonwealth v. Pennsylvania Interscholastic Athletic Ass'n,* that under our ERA discrimination on account of sex is forbidden. The WIAA rule forbidding qualified girls from playing on the high school football team in interscholastic competition cannot be used to deny the Darrin girls, and girls like them, the right to participate as members of that team. This is all the more so when the school provides no corresponding girls' football team on which girls may participate as players.

Reversed.

Judge Horowitz:

This case involves a claim of illegal discrimination against girls in the field of high school interscholastic football competition. The trial court denied relief against the discrimination claimed and this appeal followed.

The question is whether a school district operating a high school in this state may constitutionally deny two of its fully qualified high school students permission to play on the high school football team in interscholastic competition solely on the ground the students are girls. We hold the denial a prohibited discrimination based on sex and reverse.

Carol and Delores Darrin were students at the Wishkah Valley High School in Grays Harbor County, Washington, during the fall of 1973. Carol was then a junior, 16 years of age, 5 feet 6 inches tall, weighing about 170 pounds. Delores was then a freshman, 14 years of age, 5 feet 9 inches tall, weighing about 212 pounds. The girls wished to play contact football. The high school had no girls' contact football team. The school did, however, have a high school football team eligible for interstate competition, all members of the team being boys. The high school football coach found both girls complied with all eligibility requirements and permitted them to play on the team in practice sessions. The girls passed the required physical examinations, met the medical insurance requirements and played the necessary number of practice sessions required by the rules of the Washington Interscholastic Activities Association (WIAA) for football players. . . .

Just prior to the start of the football season, WIAA informed the football coach that WIAA regulations prohibited girls from participating in interscholastic contact football on boys' teams. For that reason only, the school board of the Wishkah Valley School District prohibited the Darrin girls from playing on the high school team. . . .

Two basic questions arise:

(1) Does the denial of permission to the Darrin girls to play on the boys' high school football team in interscholastic competition constitute a discrimination by state action based on sex per se or is the denial based on inability to play?

(2) If the denial is a discrimination based on sex per se is it prohibited by law, constitutional, statutory, or both? . . .

We must consider first to what extent sex discrimination was forbidden by the Equal Protection Clauses of the Fourteenth Amendment and corresponding art. 1, § 12 of the State Constitution. The Equal Protection Clause of the Fourteenth Amendment as construed by the Supreme Court of the United States has been increasingly and somewhat more aggressively used to invalidate classifications based on sex in determining whether there exists a rational relationship between the classification and the lawfully permissible object of the statute. . . .

Const. art. 1, § 12, the state's version of the Equal Protection Clause, has been construed in a manner similar to that of the Equal Protection Clause of the Fourteenth Amendment. . . . Such construction, however, is not automatically compelled. Const. art. 1, § 12 may be construed to provide greater protection to individual rights than that provided by the Equal Protection Clause.

---

232   *Gregg v. Georgia (1976)*

Following *Furman* (Document 222), much to the chagrin of opponents of capital punishment, all thirty-seven states that had previously imposed the death penalty rewrote their statutes to meet the imprecise constitutional standards implied in that case. With this case, the Court began to sort through those statutes and reaffirmed the constitutionality of the death sentence when accompanied by appropriate procedural safeguards.

The new Georgia statute provided that in a jury trial, the jury would first determine guilt or innocence; if it found the defendant guilty, it would then vote separately on punishment. The prosecution could then introduce aggravating circumstances and the defense mitigating factors. The state supreme court would automatically review all death sentences to protect against excessive or disproportionate punishment.

The division of the Court would be repeated in nearly all of the capital punishment cases heard in the next few years. Brennan and Marshall opposed the death penalty as cruel and unusual punishment *per se;* White, Rehnquist, Blackmun, and Burger were most willing to allow the legislature discretion in determining the criteria and procedures; in the middle Stewart, Powell, and Stevens sought to ensure sufficient procedural safeguards in imposing a sentence that all members of the Court recognized as significantly different from all other forms of punishment. Blackmun, it should be noted, later changed his views, and in his latter years on the Court, drew closer to the Brennan/Marshall position.

See materials noted for Document 222; and Jane C. England, "Capital Punishment in the Light of Constitutional Evolution: An Analysis of Distinctions between *Furman* and *Gregg*," 52 *Notre Dame Lawyer* 596 (1977).

———————

Judgment of the Court, and opinion of Justices Stewart, Powell, and Stevens, announced by Justice Stewart:

The issue in this case is whether the imposition of the sentence of death for the crime of murder under the law of Georgia violates the Eighth and Fourteenth Amendments. . . .

Before considering the issues presented it is necessary to understand the Georgia statutory scheme for the imposition of the death penalty. The Georgia statute, as amended after our decision in *Furman v. Georgia* . . . (1972), retains the death penalty for six categories of crime: murder, kidnapping for ransom or where the victim is harmed, armed robbery, rape, treason, and aircraft hijacking. . . . The capital defendant's guilt or innocence is determined in the traditional manner, either by a trial judge or a jury, in the first stage of a bifurcated trial.

If trial is by jury, the trial judge is required to charge lesser included offenses when they are supported by any view of the evidence. . . . After a verdict, finding, or plea of guilty to a capital crime, a presentence hearing is conducted before whoever made the determination of guilt. The sentencing procedures are essentially the same in both bench and jury trials. . . .

In the assessment of the appropriate sentence to be imposed the judge is also required to consider or to include in his instructions to the jury "any mitigating circumstances or aggravating circumstances otherwise authorized by law and any of [10] statutory aggravating circumstances which may be supported by the evidence. . . ." The scope of the non-statutory aggravating or mitigating circumstances is not delineated in the statute. Before a convicted defendant may be sentenced to death, however, except in cases of treason or aircraft hijacking, the jury, or the trial judge in cases tried without a jury, must find beyond a reasonable doubt one of the 10 aggravating circumstances specified in the statute. The sentence of death may be imposed only if the jury (or judge) finds one of the statutory aggravating circumstances and then elects to impose that sentence. . . . If the verdict is death, the jury or judge must specify the aggravating circumstance(s) found. . . . In jury cases, the trial judge is bound by the jury's recommended sentence. . . .

In addition to the conventional appellate process available in all criminal cases, provision is made for special expedited direct review by the Supreme Court of Georgia of the appropriateness of imposing the sentence of death in the particular case. The court is directed to consider "the punishment as well as any errors enumerated by way of appeal." . . . If the court affirms a death sentence, it is required to include in its decision reference to similar cases that it has taken into consideration. . . . Under its special review authority, the court may either affirm the death sentence or remand the case for resentencing. In cases in which the death sentence is affirmed there remains the possibility of executive clemency.

———————

Source: 428 U.S. 153 (1976)

We address initially the basic contention that the punishment of death for the crime of murder is, under all circumstances, "cruel and unusual" in violation of the Eighth and Fourteenth Amendments of the Constitution. . . .

The Court on a number of occasions has both assumed and asserted the constitutionality of capital punishment. In several cases that assumption provided a necessary foundation for the decision, as the Court was asked to decide whether a particular method of carrying out a capital sentence would be allowed to stand under the Eighth Amendment. But until *Furman v. Georgia* . . . the Court never confronted squarely the fundamental claim that the punishment of death always, regardless of the enormity of the offense or the procedure followed in imposing the sentence, is cruel and unusual punishment in violation of the Constitution. Although this issue was presented and addressed in *Furman,* it was not resolved by the Court. Four Justices would have held that capital punishment is not unconstitutional *per se;* two Justices would have reached the opposite conclusion; and three Justices, while agreeing that the statutes then before the Court were invalid as applied, left open the question whether such punishment may ever be imposed. We now hold that the punishment of death does not invariably violate the Constitution.

The history of the prohibition of "cruel and unusual" punishment already has been reviewed at length. . . . The American draftsmen, who adopted the English phrasing in drafting the Eighth Amendment, were primarily concerned, however, with proscribing "tortures" and other "barbarous" methods of punishment." . . .

In the earliest cases raising Eighth Amendment claims, the Court focused on particular methods of execution to determine whether they were too cruel to pass constitutional muster. The constitutionality of the sentence of death itself was not at issue, and the criterion used to evaluate the mode of execution was its similarity to "torture" and other "barbarous" methods. . . .

But the Court has not confined the prohibition embodied in the Eighth Amendment to "barbarous" methods that were generally outlawed in the 18th century. Instead, the Amendment has been interpreted in a flexible and dynamic manner. The Court early recognized that "a principle to be vital, must be capable of wider application than the mischief which gave it birth." . . . Thus the Clause forbidding "cruel and unusual" punishments "is not fastened to the obsolete but may acquire meaning as public opinion becomes enlightened by a humane justice." . . .

. . . Our cases also make clear that public perceptions of standards of decency with respect to criminal sanctions are not conclusive. A penalty also must accord with "the dignity of man," which is the "basic concept underlying the Eighth Amendment." . . . This means, at least, that the punishment not be "excessive." When a form of punishment in the abstract (in this case, whether capital punishment may ever be imposed as a sanction for murder) rather than in the particular (the propriety of death as a penalty to be applied to a specific defendant for a specific crime) is under consideration, the inquiry into "excessiveness" has two aspects. First, the punishment must not involve the unnecessary and wanton infliction of pain. . . . Second, the punishment must not be grossly out of proportion to the severity of the crime. . . .

Of course, the requirements of the Eighth Amendment must be applied with an awareness of the limited role to be played by the courts. This does not mean that judges have no role to play, for the Eighth Amendment is a restraint upon the exercise of legislative power. . . .

Therefore, in assessing a punishment selected by a democratically elected legislature against the constitutional measure, we presume its validity. We may not require the legislature to select the least severe penalty possible so long as the penalty selected is not cruelly inhumane or disproportionate to the crime involved. And a heavy burden rests on those who would attack the judgment of the representatives of the people.

This is true in part because the constitutional test is intertwined with an assessment of contemporary standards and the legislative judgment weighs heavily in ascertaining such standards. "[I]n a democratic society legislatures, not courts, are constituted to respond to the will and consequently the moral values of the people." . . .

A decision that a given punishment is impermissible under the Eighth Amendment cannot be reversed short of a constitutional amendment. The ability of the people to express their preference through the normal democratic processes, as well as through ballot referenda, is shut off. Revisions cannot be made in the light of further experience. . . .

In the discussion to this point we have sought to identify the principles and considerations that guide a court in addressing an Eighth Amendment claim. We now consider specifically whether the sentence of death for the crime of murder is a *per se* violation of the Eighth and Fourteenth Amendments to the Constitution. We note first that history and precedent strongly support a negative answer to this question. . . .

Four years ago, the petitioners in *Furman* and its companion cases predicated their argument primarily upon the asserted proposition that standards of decency had evolved to the point where capital punishment no longer could be tolerated. The petitioners in those cases said, in effect, that the evolutionary process had come to an end, and that standards of decency required that the Eighth Amendment be construed finally as prohibiting capital punishment for any crime regardless of its depravity and impact on society. This view was accepted by two Justices. Three other Justices were unwilling to go so far; focusing on the procedures by which convicted defendants were selected for the death penalty rather than on the actual punishment inflicted, they joined in the conclusion that the statutes before the Court were constitutionally invalid.

The petitioners in the capital cases before the Court today renew the "standards of decency" argument, but developments during the four years since *Furman* have undercut substantially the assumptions upon which their argument rested. Despite the continuing debate, dating back to the 19th century, over the morality and utility of capital punishment, it is now evident that a large proportion of American society continues to regard it as an appropriate and necessary criminal sanction.

The most marked indication of society's endorsement of the death penalty for murder is the legislative response to *Furman*. The legislatures of at least 35 States have enacted new statutes that provide for the death penalty for at least some crimes that result in the death of another person. And the Congress of the United States, in 1974, enacted a statute providing the death penalty for aircraft piracy that results in death. These recently adopted statutes have attempted to address the concerns expressed by the Court in *Furman* primarily (i) by specifying the factors to be weighed and the procedures to be followed in deciding when to impose a capital sentence, or (ii) by making the death penalty mandatory for specified crimes. But all of the post-*Furman* statutes make clear that capital punishment itself has not been rejected by the elected representatives of the people.

In the only statewide referendum occurring since *Furman* and brought to our attention, the people of California adopted a constitutional amendment that authorized capital punishment, in effect negating a prior ruling by the Supreme Court of California in *People v. Anderson* . . . (1972), that the death penalty violated the California Constitution. . . .

In sum, we cannot say that the judgment of the Georgia Legislature that capital punishment may be necessary in some cases is clearly wrong. Considerations of federalism, as well as respect for the ability of a legislature to evaluate, in terms of its particular State, the moral consensus concerning the death penalty and its social utility as a sanction, require us to conclude, in the absence of more convincing evidence, that the infliction of death as a punishment for murder is not without justification and thus is not unconstitutionally severe.

Finally, we must consider whether the punishment of death is disproportionate in relation to the crime for which it is imposed. There is no question that death as a punishment is unique in its severity and irrevocability. . . . When a defendant's life is at stake, the Court has been particularly sensitive to insure that every safeguard is observed. . . . But we are concerned here only with the imposition of capital punishment for the crime of murder, and when a life has been taken deliberately by the offender, we cannot say that the punishment is invariably disproportionate to the crime. It is an extreme sanction, suitable to the most extreme of crimes.

We hold that the death penalty is not a form of punishment that may never be imposed, regardless of the circumstances of the offense, regardless of the character of the offender, and regardless of the procedure followed in reaching the decision to impose it.

We now consider whether Georgia may impose the death penalty on the petitioner in this case.

[The Court found that the Georgia procedure in general, and its application in this case, met constitutional requirements.]

---

233   *Regents of the University of California v. Bakke (1978)*

This case arose from a preferential admissions program at the University of California Davis Medical School, which annually reserved 16 spaces out of 100 for minority candidates. In effect, Davis ran two admissions programs, one to choose 84 "regular" candidates out of an applicant pool of nearly 3,000 persons, and another to choose 16 out of a smaller pool with lower criteria. Allan Bakke, a white male, failed to win admission in 1973 and again in 1974, even though his grades and MCAT scores were higher than many of the students accepted under the minority program. After a third rejection, he successfully sued in state court, claiming he had been denied his rights, and that the Davis program violated both the Equal Protection Clause and Title VI of the 1964 Civil Rights Act. On appeal, four members of the high court believed that race could be a factor in admissions decisions in order to correct previous injustices; four others believed that any racial considerations violated Title VI. Justice Powell then crafted a classic transitional decision, holding that race could be a factor, but only one of many, used to seek a balanced class; race, however, had been used improperly here, so Bakke should be granted admission. The case did not answer the larger questions, but paved the way for Court approval of other affirmative action programs.

See symposium on this case, 67 *California Law Review* 1 (1979); Allan P. Sindler, *Bakke, DeFunis and Minority Admissions: The Quest for Equal Opportunity* (1978); Bernard Schwartz, *Behind Bakke: Affirmative Action and the Supreme Court* (1988); Herman Belz, *Equality Transformed: A Quarter-Century of Affirmative Action* (1991); and Ronald J. Fiscus, *The Constitutional Logic of Affirmative Action* (1992).

———

Justice Powell announced the judgment of the Court:

This case presents a challenge to the special admissions program of the petitioner, the Medical School of the University of California at Davis, which is designed to assure the admission of a specified number of students from certain minority groups. The Supreme Court of California held the special admissions program unlawful, enjoined petitioner from considering the race of any applicant, and ordered Bakke's admission. For the reasons stated in the following opinion, I believe that so much of the judgment of the California court as holds petitioner's special admissions program unlawful and directs that respondent be admitted to the Medical School must be affirmed. For the reasons expressed in a separate opinion, my Brother The Chief Justice, Mr. Justice Stewart, Mr. Justice Rehnquist, and Mr. Justice Stevens concur in this judgment. I also conclude for the reasons stated in the following opinion that the portion of the court's judgment enjoining petitioner from according any consideration to race in its admissions process must be reversed. For reasons expressed in separate opinions, my Brothers Mr. Justice Brennan, Mr. Justice White, Mr. Justice Marshall, and Mr. Justice Blackmun concur in this judgment.

Affirmed in part and reversed in part. . . .

Because the special admissions program involved a racial classification, the supreme court [of California] held itself bound to apply strict scrutiny. It then turned to the goals the University presented as justifying the special program. Although the court

Source: 438 U.S. 265 (1978)

agreed that the goals of integrating the medical profession and increasing the number of physicians willing to serve members of minority groups were compelling state interests, it concluded that the special admissions program was not the least intrusive means of achieving those goals. Without passing on the state constitutional or the federal statutory grounds cited in the trial court's judgment, the California court held that the Equal Protection Clause required that "no applicant may be rejected because of his race, in favor of another who is less qualified, as measured by standards applied without regard to race." . . .

III. A. The parties disagree as to the level of judicial scrutiny to be applied to the special admissions program. En route to this crucial battle over the scope of judicial review, the parties fight a sharp preliminary action over the proper characterization of the special admissions program. Petitioner prefers to view it as establishing a "goal" of minority representation in the medical school. Respondent, echoing the courts below, labels it a racial quota. This semantic distinction is beside the point: the special admissions program is undeniably a classification based on race and ethnic background. To the extent that there existed a pool of at least minimally qualified minority applicants to fill the 16 special admissions seats, white applicants could compete only for 84 seats in the entering class, rather than the 100 open to minority applicants. Whether this limitation is described as a quota or a goal, it is a line drawn on the basis of race and ethnic status.

The guarantees of the 14th Amendment extend to persons. Its language is explicit. The guarantee of equal protection cannot mean one thing when applied to one individual and something else when applied to a person of another color. If both are not accorded the same protection, then it is not equal. Nevertheless, petitioner argues that the court below erred in applying strict scrutiny because white males are not a "discrete and insular minority" requiring extraordinary protection from the majoritarian political process. This rationale, however, has never been invoked in our decisions as a prerequisite to subjecting racial or ethnic distinctions to strict scrutiny. Nor has this Court held that discreteness and insularity constitute necessary pre-conditions to holding that a particular classification is invidious. . . . Racial and ethnic classifications, however, are subject to stringent examination without regard to these additional characteristics. We declared as much in the first cases explicitly to recognize racial distinctions as suspect. Racial and ethnic distinctions of any sort are inherently suspect and thus call for the most exacting judicial examination.

B. . . . Over the past 30 years, this Court has embarked upon the crucial mission of interpreting the Equal Protection Clause with the view of assuring to all persons "the protection of equal laws," in a Nation confronting a legacy of slavery and racial discrimination. Because the landmark decisions in this area arose in response to the continued exclusion of Negroes from the mainstream of American society, they could be characterized as involving discrimination by the "majority" white race against the Negro minority. But they need not be read as depending upon that characterization for their results. It suffices to say that "over the years, this Court consistently repudiated 'distinctions between citizens solely because of their ancestry' as being 'odious to a free people whose institutions are founded upon the doctrine of equality.'" Petitioner urges us to adopt for the first time a more restrictive view of the Equal Protection Clause and hold that discrimination against members of the white "majority" cannot be suspect if its purpose can be characterized as "benign." The clock of our liberties, however, cannot be turned back to 1868. It is far too late to argue that the guarantee of equal protection to *all* persons permits the recognition of special wards entitled to a degree of protection greater than that accorded others. "The 14th Amendment is not directed solely against discrimination due to a 'two-class theory'—that is, based upon differences between 'white' and Negro."

Once the artificial line of a "two-class theory" of the 14th Amendment is put aside, the difficulties entailed in varying the level of judicial review according to a perceived "preferred" status of a particular racial or ethnic minority are intractable. The concepts of "majority" and "minority" necessarily reflect temporary arrangements and political judgments. As observed above, the white "majority" itself is composed of various minority groups, most of which can lay claim to a history of prior discrimination at the hands of the state and private individuals. Not all of these groups can receive preferential treatment and corresponding judicial tolerance of distinctions drawn in terms of race and nationality, for then the only "majority" left would be a new minority of White Anglo-Saxon Protestants. There is no principled basis for deciding which groups would merit "heightened judicial solicitude" and which would not. Courts would be asked to evaluate the extent of the prejudice and consequent harm suffered by various minority groups. Those whose societal injury is thought to exceed some arbitrary level of tolerability then would be entitled to preferential classifications at the expense of individuals belonging to other groups. Those classifications would be free from exacting judicial scrutiny. As these preferences began to have their desired effect, and the consequences of past discrimination were undone, new judicial rankings would be necessary. The kind of variable sociological and political analysis necessary to produce such rankings simply does not lie within the judicial competence—even if they otherwise were politically feasible and socially desirable.

Moreover, there are serious problems of justice connected with the idea of preference itself. First, it may not always be clear that a so-called preference is in fact benign. Courts may be asked to validate burdens imposed upon individual members of particular groups in order to advance the group's general interest. Nothing in the Constitution supports the notion that individuals may be asked to suffer otherwise impermissible burdens in order to enhance the societal standing of their ethnic groups. Second, preferential programs may only reinforce common stereotypes holding that certain groups are unable to achieve success without special protection based on a factor having no relationship to individual worth. Third, there is a measure of inequity in forcing innocent persons in respondent's position to bear the burdens of redressing grievances not of their making. By hitching the meaning of the Equal Protection Clause to these transitory considerations, we would be holding, as a constitutional principle, that judicial scrutiny of classifications touching on racial and ethnic background may vary with the ebb and flow of political forces. Disparate constitutional tolerance of such classifications well may serve to exacerbate racial and ethnic antagonisms rather than alleviate them. Also, the mutability of a constitutional principle, based upon shifting political and social judgments, undermines the chances for consistent application of the Constitution from one generation to the next, a critical feature of its coherent interpretation. . . .

If it is the individual who is entitled to judicial protection against classifications based upon his racial or ethnic background because such distinctions impinge upon personal rights, rather than the individual only because of his membership in a particular group, then constitutional standards may be applied consistently. Political judgments regarding the necessity for the particular classification may be weighed in the constitutional balance but the standard of justification will remain constant. This is as it should be, since those political judgments are the product of rough compromise struck by contending groups within the democratic process. When they touch upon an individual's race or ethnic background, he is entitled to a judicial determination that the burden he is asked to bear on that basis is precisely tailored to serve a compelling governmental interest. . . .

IV. We have held that in "order to justify the use of a suspect classification, a State must show that its purpose or interest is both constitutionally permissible and substantial, and that its use of the classification is 'necessary to the accomplishment' of its purpose or the safeguarding of its interest." The special admissions program purports to serve the purposes of: (i) "reducing the historic deficit of traditionally disfavored minorities in medical schools and the medical profession;" (ii) countering the effects of societal discrimination; (iii) increasing the number of physicians who will practice in communities currently underserved; and (iv) obtaining the educational benefits that flow from an ethnically diverse student body. It is necessary to decide which, if any, of these purposes is substantial enough to support the use of a suspect classification.

A. If petitioner's purpose is to assure within its student body some specified percentage of a particular group merely because of its race or ethnic origin, such a preferential purpose must be rejected not as insubstantial but as facially invalid. Preferring members of any one group for no reason other than race or ethnic origin is discrimination for its own sake. This the Constitution forbids.

B. The State certainly has a legitimate and substantial interest in ameliorating, or eliminating where feasible, the disabling effects of identified discrimination. The school desegregation cases attest to the importance of this state goal, which is far more focused than the remedying of the effects of "societal discrimination," an amorphous concept of injury that may be ageless in its reach into the past. We have never approved a classification that aids persons perceived as members of relatively victimized groups at the expense of other innocent individuals in the absence of judicial, legislative, or administrative findings of constitutional or statutory violations. . . . Without such findings of constitutional or statutory violations, it cannot be said that the government has any greater interest in helping one individual than in refraining from harming another. Thus, the government has no compelling justification for inflicting such harm.

Petitioner does not purport to have made, and is in no position to make, such findings. Its broad mission is education, not the formulation of any legislative policy or the adjudication of particular claims of illegality. . . .

C. Petitioner identifies, as another purpose of its program, improving the delivery of health care services to communities currently underserved. It may be assumed that in some situations a State's interest in facilitating the health care of its citizens is sufficiently compelling to support the use of suspect classification. But there is virtually no evidence in the record indicating that petitioner's special admissions program is either needed or geared to promote that goal. Petitioner simply has not carried its burden of demonstrating that it must prefer members of particular ethnic groups over all other individuals in order to promote better health care delivery to deprived citizens. Indeed, petitioner has not shown that its preferential classification is likely to have any significant effect on the problem.

D. The fourth goal asserted by petitioner is the attainment of a diverse student body. This clearly is a constitutionally permissible goal for an institution of higher education. Academic freedom, though not a specifically enumerated constitutional right, long has been viewed as a special concern of the First Amendment. The freedom of a university to make its own judgments as to education includes the selection of its student body. Thus, in arguing that its universities must be accorded the right to select those students who will contribute the most to the "robust exchange of ideas," petitioner invokes a countervailing constitutional interest, that of the First Amendment. In this light, petitioner must be viewed as seeking to achieve a goal that is of paramount importance in the fulfillment of its mission. It may be argued that there is greater force to these views at the undergraduate level than in a medical school where the training is centered primarily on professional competency. But even at the graduate level, our tradition and experience lend support to the view that the contribution of diversity is substantial. Physicians serve a heterogeneous population. An otherwise qualified medical student with a particular background—whether it be ethnic, geographic, culturally advantaged or disadvantaged—may bring to a professional school of medicine experiences, outlooks and ideas that enrich the training of its student body and better equip its graduates to render with understanding their vital service to humanity.

Ethnic diversity, however, is only one element in a range of factors a university properly may consider in attaining the goal of a heterogeneous student body. Although a university must have wide discretion in making the sensitive judgments as to who should be admitted, constitutional limitations protecting individual rights may not be disregarded. Respondent urges—and the courts below have held—that petitioner's dual admissions program is a racial classification that impermissibly infringes his rights under the 14th Amendment. As the interest of diversity is compelling in the context of a university's admissions program, the question remains whether the program's racial classification is necessary to promote this interest.

V. A. It may be assumed that the reservation of a specified number of seats in each class for individuals from the preferred ethnic groups would contribute to the attainment of considerable ethnic diversity in the student body. But petitioner's argument that this is the only effective means of serving the interest of diversity is seriously flawed. . . .

The experience of other university admissions programs, which take race into account in achieving the educational diversity valued by the First Amendment, demonstrates that the assignment of a fixed number of places to a minority group is not a necessary means toward that end. . . . In such an admissions program, race or ethnic background may be deemed a "plus" in a particular applicant's file, yet it does not insulate the individual from comparison with all other candidates for the available seats. The file of a particular black applicant may be examined for his potential contribution to diversity without the factor of race being decisive when compared, for example, with that of an applicant identified as an Italian-American if the latter is thought to exhibit qualities more likely to promote beneficial educational pluralism. Such qualities could include exceptional personal talents, unique work or service experience, leadership potential, maturity, demonstrated compassion, a history of overcoming disadvantage, ability to communicate with the poor, or other qualifications deemed important. In short, an admissions program operated in this way is flexible enough to consider all pertinent elements of diversity in light of the particular qualifications of each applicant, and to place them on the same footing for consideration, although not necessarily according them the same weight. Indeed, the weight attributed to a particular quality may vary from year to year depending upon the "mix" both of the student body and the applicants for the incoming class.

B. In summary, it is evident that the Davis special admissions program involves the use of an explicit racial classification never before countenanced by this Court. It tells applicants who are not Negro, Asian, or "Chicano" that they are totally excluded from a specific percentage of the seats in an entering class. No matter how strong their qualifications, quantitative and extracurricular, including their own potential for contribution to educational diversity, they are never afforded the chance to compete with applicants from the preferred groups for the special admission seats. At the same time, the preferred applicants have the opportunity to compete for every seat in the class. The fatal flaw in petitioner's program is its disregard of individual rights as guaranteed by the 14th Amendment. Such rights are not absolute. But when a State's distribution of benefits or imposition of burdens hinges on the color of a person's skin or ancestry, that individual is entitled to a demonstration that the challenged classification is necessary to promote a substantial state interest. Petitioner has failed to carry this burden. For this reason, that portion of the California court's judgment holding petitioner's special admissions programs invalid under the 14th Amendment must be affirmed.

C. In enjoining petitioner from ever considering the race of any applicant, however, the courts below failed to recognize that the State has a substantial interest that legitimately may be served by a properly devised admissions program involving the competitive consideration of race and ethnic origin. For this reason, so much of the California court's judgment as enjoins petitioner from any consideration of the race of any applicant must be reversed.

VI. With respect to respondent's entitlement to an injunction directing his admission to the Medical School, petitioner has conceded that it could not carry its burden of proving that, but for the existence of its unlawful special admissions program, respondent still would not have been admitted. Hence, respondent is entitled to the injunction, and that portion of the judgment must be affirmed.

---

234 *State v. Schmid (1980)*

When questions involving issues such as free speech are raised in state courts, the judges can approach the matter either from a federal or a state viewpoint. They may follow the First Amendment precedents of the U.S. Supreme Court, or if the state has a comparable Bill of Rights, they may look to state precedents. States must, under the federal system, provide at least the protection mandated by the First Amendment; but they may also provide a higher level. In this case, and in Documents 230 and 231, we can see that state courts have been at least as protective as federal courts, if not more so, of constitutional rights.

In this case a nonstudent was convicted of trespassing after he had sold and distributed political materials on the campus of Princeton University, a private school. In his appeal, he invoked not only the First Amendment, but also the rights of free speech and assembly in the New Jersey constitution. The state court agreed that the New Jersey constitution provided more comprehensive rights than did the First Amendment.

See Note, "Private Abridgement of Speech and the State Constitutions," 90 *Yale Law Journal* 165 (1980); and Peter J. Galie, "The Other Supreme Courts: Judicial Activism among State Supreme Courts," 33 *Syracuse Law Review* 731 (1982).

Judge Handler:

While distributing political literature on the campus of Princeton University, defendant Chris Schmid, a member of the United States Labor Party, was arrested and charged by the University with trespass upon private property. He was subsequently convicted under the State's penal trespass statute. On this appeal he challenges the conviction on the grounds that it stems from a violation of his federal and state constitutional rights to freedom of speech and assembly.

It is clear that public colleges and universities, as instrumentalities of state government, are not beyond the reach of the First Amendment. . . . A public college or university, created or controlled by the state itself, is an arm of state government and, thus, by definition, implicates state action. . . .

A private college or university, however, stands upon a different footing in relationship to the state. Such an institution is not the creature or instrument of state government. Even though such an institution may conduct itself identically to its state-operated counterparts and, in terms of educational purposes and activities, may be virtually indistinguishable from a public institution, . . . a private college or university does not thereby either operate under or exercise the authority of state government. Hence, the state nexus requirement that triggers the application of the First Amendment is not readily met in the case of a private educational institution. . . .

Notwithstanding the primary thrust of the First Amendment against state governmental interference with expressional freedoms, the guarantees of this Amendment may under appropriate conditions be invoked against nongovernmental bodies. In particular settings, private entities, including educational institutions, may so impact upon the public or share enough of the essential features of governmental bodies as to be engaged functionally in "state action" for First Amendment purposes. The more focused inquiry therefore must be turned to those circumstances that can subject an entity of essentially

Source: 84 N.J. 535 (1980)

nongovernmental or private character to the requirements imposed by the First Amendment. . . .

[Judge Handler reviewed ties between the State and Princeton University.]

Nonetheless, this congeries of facts does not equate with state action on the part of Princeton University. . . . Princeton University is, indisputably, predominantly private, unregulated and autonomous in its character and functioning as an institution of higher education. The interface between the University and the State is not so extensive as to demonstrate a joint and mutual participation in higher education or to establish an inter-dependent or symbiotic relationship between the two in the field of education. . . .

Defendant asserts that under the State Constitution he is afforded protection of his expressional rights even if it is not clear that the First Amendment would serve to grant that protection. The United States Supreme Court has recently acknowledged in the most clear and unmistakable terms that a state's organic and general law can independently furnish a basis for protecting individual rights of speech and assembly. . . . The view that state constitutions exist as a cognate source of individual freedoms and that state con-stitutional guarantees of these rights may indeed surpass the guarantees of the federal Constitution has received frequent judicial expression. . . .

On numerous occasions our own courts have recognized the New Jersey Constitu-tion to be an alternative and independent source of individual rights. . . . Justice Sullivan had observed that although the New Jersey constitutional provision relating to searches and seizures was identical to the federal Fourth Amendment provisions, "'we have the right to construe our State constitutional provision in accordance with what we conceive to be its plain meaning.'"

The guarantees of our State Constitution have been found to extend to a panoply of rights deemed to be most essential to both the quality of individual life and the preser-vation of personal liberty. . . .

A basis for finding exceptional vitality in the New Jersey Constitution with respect to individual rights of speech and assembly is found in part in the language employed. Our Constitution affirmatively recognizes these freedoms, *viz.:*

> Every person may freely speak, write and publish his sentiments on all subjects, being responsible for the abuse of that right. No law shall be passed to restrain or abridge the liberty of speech or of the press. . . .
>
> The people have the right freely to assemble together, to consult for the common good, to make known their opinions to their representatives, and to petition for redress of grievances. . . .

Although our own courts have seldom been invited or required to view the New Jer-sey Constitution as a separate basis for delineating the scope of individual speech and assembly freedoms, the philosophy recognizing the importance of such rights has been frequently voiced. In a case decided last term dealing with such expressional rights in the context of municipal zoning restrictions, Justice Clifford observed as follows:

> [P]olitical speech . . . occupies a preferred position in our system of constitutionally-protected interests. [*State* v. *Miller* . . . (1980).]
>
> Where political speech is involved, our tradition insists that government "allow the widest room for discussion, the narrowest range for its restriction." [*Id.*] . . .

. . . The rights of speech and assembly guaranteed by the State Constitution are protectable not only against governmental or public bodies, but under some circumstances against private persons as well. It has been noted that in our interpretation of fundamental State constitutional rights, there are no constraints arising out of principles of federalism.

. . . Hence, federal requirements concerning "state action," founded primarily in the language of the Fourteenth Amendment and in principles of federal-state relations, do not have the same force when applied to state-based constitutional rights.

It is also clear that while state constitutions may be distinct repositories of fundamental rights independent of the federal Constitution, there nonetheless exist meaningful parallels between the federal Constitution and state constitutions, especially in the areas where constitutional values are shared, such as speech and assembly. Indicative of such mutuality, our State Constitution not only affirmatively guarantees to individuals the rights of speech and assembly, but also expressly prohibits government itself, in a manner analogous to the federal First and Fourteenth Amendments, from unlawfully restraining or abridging "the liberty of speech." . . .

We conclude, therefore, that the State Constitution furnishes to individuals the complementary freedoms of speech and assembly and protects the reasonable exercise of those rights. These guarantees extend directly to governmental entities as well as to persons exercising governmental powers. They are also available against unreasonably restrictive or oppressive conduct on the part of private entities that have otherwise assumed a constitutional obligation not to abridge the individual exercise of such freedoms because of the public use of their property. The State Constitution in this fashion serves to thwart inhibitory actions which unreasonably frustrate, infringe, or obstruct the expressional and associational rights of individuals exercised under Article I, paragraphs 6 and 18 thereof.

Against this constitutional backdrop must be addressed the question of whether the State Constitution's guarantees of speech and assembly under Article I, paragraphs 6 and 18 apply to the distribution of political materials by defendant Schmid upon the Princeton University campus on April 5, 1978. This question brings us to the heart of the problem—the need to balance within a constitutional framework legitimate interests in private property with individual freedoms of speech and assembly. . . .

The application of the appropriate standard in this case must commence with an examination of the primary use of the private property, namely, the campus and facilities of Princeton University. Princeton University itself has furnished the answer to this inquiry in expansively expressing its overriding educational goals, *viz:*

> The central purposes of a University are the pursuit of truth, the discovery of new knowledge through scholarship and research, the teaching and general development of students, and the transmission of knowledge and learning to society at large. Free inquiry and free expression within the academic community are indispensable to the achievement of these goals. The freedom to teach and to learn depends upon the creation of appropriate conditions and opportunities on the campus as a whole as well as in classrooms and lecture halls. All members of the academic community share the responsibility for securing and sustaining the general conditions conducive to this freedom. . . .
>
> Free Speech and peaceable assembly are basic requirements of the University as a center for free inquiry and the search for knowledge and insight. . . .

No one questions that Princeton University has honored this grand ideal and has in fact dedicated its facilities and property to achieve the educational goals expounded in this compelling statement.

In examining next the extent and nature of a public invitation to use its property, we note that a public presence within Princeton University is entirely consonant with the University's expressed educational mission. Princeton University, as a private institution of higher education, clearly seeks to encourage both a wide and continuous exchange of opinions and ideas and to foster a policy of openness and freedom with respect to the use of its facilities. The commitment of its property, facilities, and resources to educational purposes contemplates substantial public involvement and participation in the academic life of the University. The University itself has endorsed the educational value of an open campus and the full exposure of the college community to the "outside world," *i.e.,* the public at large. Princeton University has indeed invited such public uses of its resources in fulfillment of its broader educational ideals and objectives.

The further question is whether the expressional activities undertaken by the defendant in this case are discordant in any sense with both the private and public uses of the campus and facilities of the University. There is nothing in the record to suggest that Schmid was evicted because the purpose of his activities, distributing political literature, offended the University's educational policies. The reasonable and normal inference thus to be extracted from the record in the instant case is that defendant's attempt to disseminate political material was not incompatible with either Princeton University's professed educational goals or the University's overall use of its property for educational purposes. Further, there is no indication that even under the terms of the University's own regulations, Schmid's activities in any way, directly or demonstrably "disrupt[ed] the regular and essential operations of the University" or that in either the time, the place, or the manner of Schmid's distribution of the political materials, he "significantly infringed on the rights of others" or caused any interference or inconvenience with respect to the normal use of University property and the normal routine and activities of the college community. . . .

In this case, however, the University regulations that were applied to Schmid (in contrast to those subsequently adopted) contained no standards, aside from the requirement for invitation and permission, for governing the actual exercise of expressional freedom. Indeed, there were no standards extant regulating the granting or withholding of such authorization, nor did the regulations deal adequately with the time, place, or manner for individuals to exercise their rights of speech and assembly. Regulations thus devoid of reasonable standards designed to protect both the legitimate interests of the University as an institution of higher education and the individual exercise of expressional freedom cannot constitutionally be invoked to prohibit the otherwise noninjurious and reasonable exercise of such freedoms. . . . In these circumstances, given the absence of adequate reasonable regulations, the required accommodation of Schmid's expressional and associational rights, otherwise reasonably exercised, would not constitute an unconstitutional abridgment of Princeton University's property rights . . . (absent any regulations governing expressional activity, such activity reasonably exercised on private property devoted to public use is protectable under state constitution and does not constitute impermissible infringement upon private property rights). It follows that in the absence of a reasonable regulatory scheme, Princeton University did in fact violate defendant's State constitutional rights of expression in evicting him and securing his arrest for distributing political literature upon its campus.

We are mindful that Princeton University's regulatory policies governing the time, place, and manner for the exercise of constitutionally-protected speech and associational rights have been modified substantially since the events surrounding Schmid's arrest and now more fully and adequately define the nature of these restrictions. As we have indicated, the content of such regulations, recognizing and controlling the right to engage in expressional activities, may be molded by the availability of alternative means of communication. . . . These current amended regulations exemplify the approaches open to private educational entities seeking to protect their institutional integrity while at the same time recognizing individual rights of speech and assembly and accommodating the public whose presence nurtures academic inquiry and growth. As noted, however, these regulations were not in place when the University interfered with Schmid's reasonable efforts to communicate his political views to those present on its campus in April 1978. Hence, Schmid suffered a constitutional impairment of his State constitutional rights of speech and assembly and his conviction for trespass must therefore be undone.

Accordingly, for the reasons set forth, the judgment below is reversed.

235   *Richmond Newspapers, Inc. v. Virginia (1980)*

In the 1970s, courts reluctantly opened their doors to the media, fearing that flash bulbs and cameras would disrupt the pursuit of justice. The prospect of graphic press accounts also disturbed jurists who believed that impartial justice demanded an isolated courtroom. These concerns came to the fore in a Richmond, Virginia, courtroom where, for a variety of reasons, the trial of a person on a single charge of murder had ended in mistrial or had otherwise been aborted three times. Both defense and prosecution agreed to the trial judge's suggestion that the courtroom be closed to everyone to ensure that the fourth trial went to completion. The judge had that power under state law, but he never held hearings to determine if it was necessary, or if there might be a better way to proceed. Local newspapers, barred from the trial, brought suit.

The case raised an issue the Court had previously skirted, the relationship between the First Amendment's Press Clause and the Sixth Amendment right to a public trial. In this case, the Court found the two complementary, since the press by its reporting of criminal trials informed the public, who could not attend, how well the criminal justice system was working. The decision did not mean that all cases had to be open to full press coverage. The Court specifically pointed out that judges always retained power to ensure fair trials and had a variety of measures they could apply to that end. But henceforth the presumption would be in favor of the press having access to the trial.

Although only Justices White and Stevens joined Chief Justice Burger's opinion, Justices Brennan, Marshall, Stewart, and Blackmun concurred in the result; only Justice Rehnquist dissented.

See Anthony Lewis, "A Public Right to Know About Public Institutions: The First Amendment as a Sword," 1980 *Supreme Court Review* 1 (1981); William J. Brennan, "Address," 32 *Rutgers Law Review* 173 (1979); and Note, "*Richmond Newspapers, Inc. v. Virginia* and the Emerging Right of Access," 61 *Journalism Quarterly* 615 (1984).

———

Chief Justice Burger announced the judgment of the Court and delivered an opinion, in which Justices White and Stevens joined:

The narrow question presented in this case is whether the right of the public and press to attend criminal trials is guaranteed under the United States Constitution. . . .

[The Chief justice traced the evolution and justification of open criminal trials from the Norman Conquest to the present era.]

The origins of the proceeding which has become the modern criminal trial in Anglo-American justice can be traced back beyond reliable historical records. We need not here review all details of its development, but a summary of that history is instructive. What is significant for present purposes is that throughout its evolution, the trial has been open to all who care to observe.

In the days before the Norman Conquest, cases in England were generally brought before moots, such as the local court of the hundred or the county court, which were attended by the freemen of the community. Somewhat like modern jury duty, attendance at these early meetings was compulsory on the part of the freemen, who were called upon to render judgment.

With the gradual evolution of the jury system in the years after the Norman Conquest, the duty of all freemen to attend trials to render judgment was relaxed, but there is no indication that criminal trials did not remain public. When certain groups were excused from compelled attendance, the statutory exemption did not prevent them from attending; Lord Coke observed that those excused "are not compellable to come, but left to their own liberty."

From this unbroken, uncontradicted history, supported by reasons as valid today as in centuries past, we are bound to conclude that a presumption of openness inheres in the very nature of a criminal trial under our system of justice. This conclusion is hardly novel; without a direct holding on the issue, the Court has voiced its recognition of it in a variety of contexts over the years. . . .

Source: 448 U.S. 555 (1980)

Despite the history of criminal trials being presumptively open since long before the Constitution, the State presses its contention that neither the Constitution nor the Bill of Rights contains any provision which by its terms guarantees to the public the right to attend criminal trials. Standing alone, this is correct, but there remains the question whether, absent an explicit provision, the Constitution affords protection against exclusion of the public from criminal trials.

The First Amendment, in conjunction with the Fourteenth, prohibits governments from "abridging the freedom of speech, or of the press; or the right of the people peaceably to assemble, and to petition the Government for a redress of grievances." These expressly guaranteed freedoms share a common core purpose of assuring freedom of communication on matters relating to the functioning of government. Plainly it would be difficult to single out any aspect of government of higher concern and importance to the people than the manner in which criminal trials are conducted; as we have shown, recognition of this pervades the centuries-old history of open trials and the opinions of this Court.

The Bill of Rights was enacted against the backdrop of the long history of trials being presumptively open. Public access to trials was then regarded as an important aspect of the process itself; the conduct of trials "before as many of the people as chose to attend" was regarded as one of "the inestimable advantages of a free English constitution of government." In guaranteeing freedoms such as those of speech and press, the First Amendment can be read as protecting the right of everyone to attend trials so as to give meaning to those explicit guarantees. "The First Amendment goes beyond protection of the press and the self-expression of individuals to prohibit government from limiting the stock of information from which members of the public may draw." Free speech carries with it some freedom to listen. "In a variety of contexts this Court has referred to a First Amendment right to receive information and ideas." What this means in the context of trials is that the First Amendment guarantees of speech and press, standing alone, prohibit government from summarily closing courtroom doors which had long been open to the public at the time that Amendment was adopted. "For the First Amendment does not speak equivocally. . . . It must be taken as a command of the broadest scope that explicit language, read in the context of a liberty-loving society, will allow."

It is not crucial whether we describe this right to attend criminal trials to hear, see and communicate observations concerning them as a "right of access," or a "right to gather information," for we have recognized that "without some protection for seeking out the news, freedom of the press could be eviscerated." The explicit, guaranteed rights to speak and to publish concerning what takes place at a trial would lose much meaning if access to observe the trial could, as it was here, be foreclosed arbitrarily.

The right of access to places traditionally open to the public, as criminal trials have long been, may be seen as assured by the amalgam of the First Amendment guarantees of speech and press; and their affinity to the right of assembly is not without relevance. From the outset, the right of assembly was regarded not only as an independent right but also as a catalyst to augment the free exercise of the other First Amendment rights with which it was deliberately linked by the draftsmen. . . .

The State argues that the Constitution nowhere spells out a guarantee for the right of the public to attend trials, and that accordingly no such right is protected. The possibility that such a contention could be made did not escape the notice of the Constitution's draftsmen; they were concerned that some important rights might be thought disparaged because not specifically guaranteed. It was even argued that because of this danger no Bill of Rights should be adopted. In a letter to Thomas Jefferson in October 1788, James Madison explained why he, although "in favor of a bill of rights," had "not viewed it in an important light" up to that time: "I conceive that in a certain degree . . . the rights in question are reserved by the manner in which the federal powers are granted." He went on to state that "there is great reason to fear that a positive declaration of some of the most essential rights could not be obtained in the requisite latitude."

But arguments such as the State makes have not precluded recognition of important rights not enumerated. Notwithstanding the appropriate caution against reading into the Constitution rights not explicitly defined, the Court has acknowledged that certain unarticulated rights are implicit in enumerated guarantees. For example, the rights of association and of privacy, the right to be presumed innocent, and the right to be judged by a standard of proof beyond a reasonable doubt in a criminal trial, as well as the right to travel, appear nowhere in the Constitution or Bill of Rights. Yet these important but unarticulated rights have nonetheless been found to share constitutional protection in common with explicit guarantees. The concerns expressed by Madison and others have thus been resolved; fundamental rights, even though not expressly guaranteed, have been recognized by the Court as indispensable to the enjoyment of rights explicitly defined.

We hold that the right to attend criminal trials is implicit in the guarantees of the First Amendment; without the freedom to attend such trials, which people have exercised for centuries, important aspects of freedom of speech and "of the press could be eviscerated."

Having concluded there was a guaranteed right of the public under the First and Fourteenth Amendments to attend the trial of Stevenson's case, we return to the closure order challenged by appellants. The Court in *Gannett* made clear that although the Sixth Amendment guarantees the accused a right to a public trial, it does not give a right to a private trial. Despite the fact that this was the fourth trial of the accused, the trial judge made no findings to support closure; no inquiry was made as to whether alternative solutions would have met the need to ensure fairness; there was no recognition of any right under the Constitution for the public or press to attend the trial. In contrast to the pretrial proceeding dealt with in *Gannett,* there exist in the context of the trial itself various tested alternatives to satisfy the constitutional demands of fairness. There was no suggestion that any problems with witnesses could not have been dealt with by their exclusion from the courtroom or their sequestration during the trial. Nor is there anything to indicate that sequestration of the jurors would not have guarded against their being subjected to any improper information. All of the alternatives admittedly present difficulties for trial courts, but none of the factors relied on here was beyond the realm of the manageable. Absent an overriding interest articulated in findings, the trial of a criminal case must be open to the public. Accordingly, the judgment under review is

Reversed.

236
Mississippi University for Women v. Hogan (1982)

In their attack on gender discrimination, women have often protested programs that traditionally excluded them, such as military academies and intercollegiate sports. Their argument paralleled that of the civil rights movement, namely, that segregation on the basis of gender could never be anything but unequal. But there have always been single-sex schools in the United States that educated women students, and these included some of the finest colleges, such as the "Seven Sisters"—the sister schools to the Ivy League, such as Radcliffe and Barnard. Feminist activists often struck conflicting notes about these schools. On the one hand, they objected to segregation based on gender; on the other, they recognized the value of all-women schools, as well as the fact that in no instance did the state force women to attend them.

To some people, the following case should never have been brought, because the Civil Rights Act had specifically excluded traditional single-sex schools from its coverage. In addition, there seemed little principle involved; Joe Hogan had not been denied an education, but merely wanted one more convenient to where he lived. Justice O'Connor's decision also went well beyond the facts of the case, and seemed to require a strict scrutiny examination in gender discrimination cases, something the Court had never before done. Compare this opinion to that of Justice Ginsburg in the VMI decision (Document 259).

See Kenneth L. Karst, "Women's Constitution," 1984 *Duke Law Journal* 477 (1984); Ruth Bader Ginsburg, "Gender and the Constitution," 44 *University of Cincinnati Law Review* 1 (1975); and A. E. Freedman, "Sex Equality, Sex Differences and the Supreme Court," 92 *Yale Law Journal* 913 (1983).

———

Justice O'CONNOR delivered the opinion of the Court:

This case presents the narrow issue of whether a state statute that excludes males from enrolling in a state-supported professional nursing school violates the Equal Protection Clause of the Fourteenth Amendment.

The facts are not in dispute. In 1884, the Mississippi Legislature created the Mississippi Industrial Institute and College for the Education of White Girls of the State of Mississippi, now the oldest state-supported all-female college in the United States. The

Source: 458 U.S. 718 (1982)

school, known today as Mississippi University for Women (MUW), has from its inception limited its enrollment to women.

In 1971, MUW established a School of Nursing, initially offering a 2-year associate degree. Three years later, the school instituted a 4-year baccalaureate program in nursing and today also offers a graduate program. The School of Nursing has its own faculty and administrative officers and establishes its own criteria for admission.

Respondent, Joe Hogan, is a registered nurse but does not hold a baccalaureate degree in nursing. Since 1974, he has worked as a nursing supervisor in a medical center in Columbus, the city in which MUW is located. In 1979, Hogan applied for admission to the MUW School of Nursing's baccalaureate program. Although he was otherwise qualified, he was denied admission to the School of Nursing solely because of his sex. School officials informed him that he could audit the courses in which he was interested, but could not enroll for credit.

Hogan filed an action in the United States District Court for the Northern District of Mississippi, claiming the single-sex admissions policy of MUW's School of Nursing violated the Equal Protection Clause of the Fourteenth Amendment. . . .

We begin our analysis aided by several firmly established principles. Because the challenged policy expressly discriminates among applicants on the basis of gender, it is subject to scrutiny under the Equal Protection Clause of the Fourteenth Amendment. That this statutory policy discriminates against males rather than against females does not exempt it from scrutiny or reduce the standard of review. Our decisions also establish that the party seeking to uphold a statute that classifies individuals on the basis of their gender must carry the burden of showing an "exceedingly persuasive justification" for the classification. The burden is met only by showing at least that the classification serves "important governmental objectives and that the discriminatory means employed" are "substantially related to the achievement of those objectives."

Although the test for determining the validity of a gender-based classification is straightforward, it must be applied free of fixed notions concerning the roles and abilities of males and females. Care must be taken in ascertaining whether the statutory objective itself reflects archaic and stereotypic notions. Thus, if the statutory objective is to exclude or "protect" members of one gender because they are presumed to suffer from an inherent handicap or to be innately inferior, the objective itself is illegitimate.

If the State's objective is legitimate and important, we next determine whether the requisite direct, substantial relationship between objective and means is present. The purpose of requiring that close relationship is to assure that the validity of a classification is determined through reasoned analysis rather than through the mechanical application of traditional, often inaccurate, assumptions about the proper roles of men and women. The need for the requirement is amply revealed by reference to the broad range of statutes already invalidated by this Court, statutes that relied upon the simplistic, outdated assumption that gender could be used as a "proxy for other, more germane basis of classification," to establish a link between objective and classification.

Applying this framework, we now analyze the arguments advanced by the State to justify its refusal to allow males to enroll for credit in MUW's School of Nursing.

The State's primary justification for maintaining the single-sex admissions policy of MUW's School of Nursing is that it compensates for discrimination against women and, therefore, constitutes educational affirmative action. As applied to the School of Nursing, we find the State's argument unpersuasive.

In limited circumstances, a gender-based classification favoring one sex can be justified if it intentionally and directly assists members of the sex that is disproportionately burdened. However, we consistently have emphasized that "the mere recitation of a benign, compensatory purpose is not an automatic shield which protects against any inquiry into the actual purposes underlying a statutory scheme. . . ."

Mississippi has made no showing that women lacked opportunities to obtain training in the field of nursing or to attain positions of leadership in that field when the MUW School of Nursing opened its door or that women currently are deprived of such opportunities. In fact, in 1970, the year before the School of Nursing's first class enrolled, women earned 94 percent of the nursing baccalaureate degrees conferred in Mississippi and 98.6 percent of the degrees earned nation-wide. As one would expect, the labor force reflects the same predominance of women in nursing. When MUW's School of Nursing began operation, nearly 98 percent of all employed registered nurses were female.

Rather than compensate for discriminatory barriers faced by women, MUW's policy of excluding males from admission to the School of Nursing tends to perpetuate the stereotyped view of nursing as an exclusively woman's job. By assuring that Mississippi allots more openings in its state-supported nursing schools to women than it does to men, MUW's admissions policy lends credibility to the old view that women, not men, should become nurses, and makes the assumption that nursing is a field for women a self-fulfilling prophecy. Thus, we conclude that, although the State recited a "benign, compensatory purpose," it failed to establish that the alleged objective is the actual purpose underlying the discriminatory classification.

The policy is invalid also because it fails the second part of the equal protection test, for the State has made no showing that the gender-based classification is substantially and directly related to its proposed compensatory objective. To the contrary, MUW's policy of permitting men to attend classes as auditors fatally undermines its claim that women, at least those in the School of Nursing, are adversely affected by the presence of men.

MUW permits men who audit to participate fully in classes. Additionally, both men and women take part in continuing education courses offered by the School of Nursing, in which regular nursing students also can enroll. The uncontroverted record reveals that admitting men to nursing classes does not affect teaching style, that the presence of men in the classroom would not affect the performance of the female nursing students, and that men in coeducational nursing schools do not dominate the classroom. In sum the record in this case is flatly inconsistent with the claim that excluding men from the School of Nursing is necessary to reach any of MUW's educational goals.

Thus, considering both the asserted interest and the relationship between the interest and the methods used by the State, we conclude that the State has fallen far short of establishing the "exceedingly persuasive justification" needed to sustain the gender-based classification. Accordingly, we hold that MUW's policy of denying males the right to enroll for credit in its School of Nursing violates the Equal Protection Clause of the Fourteenth Amendment. . . .

Because we concluded that the State's policy of excluding males from MUW's School of Nursing violates the Equal Protection Clause of the Fourteenth Amendment, we affirm the judgment of the Court of Appeals.

It is so ordered.

Justice POWELL, with whom Justice REHNQUIST joins, dissenting:

The Court's opinion bows deeply to conformity. Left without honor—indeed, held unconstitutional—is an element of diversity that has characterized much of American education and enriched much of American life. The Court in effect holds today that no State now may provide even a single institution of higher learning open only to women students. It gives no heed to the efforts of the State of Mississippi to provide abundant opportunities for young men and young women to attend coeducational institutions, and none to the preferences of the more than 40,000 young women who over the years have evidenced their approval of an all-women's college by choosing Mississippi University for Women (MUW) over seven coeducational universities within the State. The Court decides today that the Equal Protection Clause makes it unlawful for the State to provide women with a traditionally popular and respected choice of educational environment. It does so in a case instituted by one man, who represents no class, and whose primary concern is personal convenience.

It is undisputed that women enjoy complete equality of opportunity in Mississippi's public system of higher education. Of the State's 8 universities and 16 junior colleges, all except MUW are coeducational. At least two other Mississippi universities would have provided respondent with the nursing curriculum that he wishes to pursue. No other male has joined in his complaint. The only groups with any personal acquaintance with MUW to file *amicus* briefs are female students and alumnae of MUW. And they have emphatically rejected respondent's arguments, urging that the State of Mississippi be allowed to continue offering the choice from which they have benefitted.

Nor is respondent significantly disadvantaged by MUW's all-female tradition. His constitutional complaint is based upon a single asserted harm: that he must *travel* to attend the state-supported nursing schools that concededly are available to him. The Court characterizes this injury as one of "inconvenience." This description is fair and accurate, though somewhat embarrassed by the fact that there is, of course, no constitutional right to attend a state-supported university in one's home town. Thus the Court, to redress respondent's injury of inconvenience, must rest its invalidation of MUW's single-sex program on a mode of "sexual stereotype" reasoning that has no application whatever to the respondent or the "wrong" of which he complains. At best this is anomalous. And ultimately the anomaly reveals legal error—that of applying a heightened equal protection standard, developed in cases of genuine sexual stereotyping, to a narrowly utilized state classification that provides an *additional* choice for women. Moreover, I believe that Mississippi's educational system should be upheld in the case even if this inappropriate method of analysis is applied.

Coeducation, historically, is a novel educational theory. From grade school through high school, college, and graduate and professional training, much of the Nation's population during much of our history has been educated in sexually segregated classrooms.

At the college level, for instance, until recently some of the most prestigious colleges and universities—including most of the Ivy League—had long histories of single-sex education. As Harvard, Yale, and Princeton remained all-male colleges well into the second half of this century, the "Seven Sister" institutions established a parallel standard of excellence for women's colleges. Mount Holyoke, Smith, and Wellesley recently have made considered decisions to remain essentially single-sex institutions. Barnard retains its independence from Columbia, its traditional coordinate institution. Harvard and Radcliffe maintained separate admissions policies as recently as 1975.

The sexual segregation of students has been a reflection of, rather than an imposition upon, the preference of those subject to the policy. It cannot be disputed, for example, that the highly qualified women attending the leading women's colleges could have earned admission to virtually any college of their choice. Women attending such colleges have chosen to be there, usually expressing a preference for the special benefits of single-sex institutions. Similar decisions were made by the colleges that elected to remain open to women only.

The arguable benefits of single-sex colleges also continue to be recognized by students of higher education. The Carnegie Commission on Higher Education has reported that it "favor[s] the continuation of colleges for women. They provide an element of diversity . . . and [an environment in which women] generally . . . speak up more in their classes, . . . hold more positions of leadership on campus, . . . and . . . have more role models and mentors among women teachers and administrators." A 10-year empirical study by the Cooperative Institutional Research Program of the American Council of Education and the University of California, Los Angeles, also has affirmed the distinctive benefits of single-sex colleges and universities. . . .

Despite the continuing expressions that single-sex institutions may offer singular advantages to their students, there is no doubt that coeducational institutions are far more numerous. But their numerical predominance does not establish—in any sense properly cognizable by a court—that individual preferences for single-sex education are misguided or illegitimate, or that a State may not provide its citizens with a choice.

The issue in this case is whether a State transgresses the Constitution when—within the context of a public system that offers a diverse range of campuses, curricula, and educational alternatives—it seeks to accommodate the legitimate personal preferences of those desiring the advantages of an all-women's college. In my view, the Court errs seriously by assuming—without argument or discussion—that the equal protection standard generally applicable to sex discrimination is appropriate here. That standard was designed to free women from "archaic and overbroad generalizations. . . ." In no previous case have we applied it to invalidate state efforts to *expand* women's choices. Nor are there prior sex discrimination decisions by this Court in which a male plaintiff, as in this case, had the choice of an equal benefit. . . .

By applying heightened equal protection analysis to this case, the Court frustrates the liberating spirit of the Equal Protection Clause. It prohibits the States from providing women with an opportunity to choose the type of university they prefer. And yet it is these women whom the Court regards as the *victims* of an illegal, stereotyped perception of the role of women in our society. The Court reasons this way in a case in which no woman has complained, and the only complainant is a man who advances no claims on behalf of anyone else. His claim, it should be recalled, is not that he is being denied a substantive educational opportunity, or even the right to attend an all-male or a coeducational college. It is *only* that the colleges open to him are located at inconvenient distances.

The Court views this case as presenting a serious equal protection claim of sex discrimination. I do not, and I would sustain Mississippi's right to continue MUW on a rational-basis analysis. But I need not apply this "lowest tier" of scrutiny. I can accept for present purposes the standard applied by the Court: that there is a gender-based distinction that must serve an important governmental objective by means that are substantially related to its achievement. The record in this case reflects that MUW has a historic position in the State's educational system dating back to 1884. More than 2,000 women presently evidence their preference to MUW by having enrolled there. The choice is one that discriminated invidiously against no one. And the State's purpose in preserving that choice is legitimate and substantial. Generations of our finest minds, both among educators and students, have believed that single-sex, college-level institutions afford distinctive benefits. There are many persons, of course, who have different views. But simply because there are these differences is no reason—certainly none of constitutional dimension—to conclude that no substantial state interest is served when such a choice is made available. . . .

A distinctive feature of America's tradition has been respect for diversity. This has been characteristic of the peoples from numerous lands who have built our country. It is the essence of our democratic system. At stake in this case as I see it is the preservation of a small aspect of this diversity. But that aspect is by no means insignificant, given our heritage of available choice between single-sex and coeducational institutions of higher learning. The Court answers that there is discrimination—not just that which may be tolerable, as for example between those candidates for admission able to contribute most to an educational institution and those able to contribute less—but discrimination of constitutional dimension. But, having found "discrimination," the Court finds it difficult to identify the victims. It hardly can claim that women are discriminated against. A constitutional case is held to exist solely because one man found it inconvenient to travel to any of the other institutions made available to him by the State of Mississippi. In essence he insists that he has a right to attend a college in his home community. This simply is not a sex discrimination case. The Equal Protection Clause was never intended to be applied to this kind of case.

[Chief Justice BURGER and Justice BLACKMUN dissented separately.]

237

Immigration and Naturalization Service v. Chadha (1983)

Congress has long delegated a variety of powers to the executive, but one device it used to retain control was the so-called legislative veto. Through this device, one or both houses could either approve or disapprove of certain executive or administrative decisions. Although not mentioned in the Constitution, the legislative veto had been used since 1932, and served the useful purpose of allowing Congress to respond to changing circumstances and make adjustments in continuing programs without having to pass new legislation or trying to anticipate all future contingencies. But presidents normally opposed the device, and Jimmy Carter wanted a test case to determine the constitutionality of the legislative veto. The test came when the INS ruled that Jagdish Rai Chadha could stay in the United States, but had that ruling canceled when one member of the House, without explaining his reasons, secured a resolution barring residency to Chadha and several others. Chadha sued, and the case went all the way to the Supreme Court. The chief justice's opinion is noteworthy not only for striking down the legislative veto, but also for its implication that there is no longer any such thing as a "political question" that can avoid court scrutiny.

In the opinion, Chief Justice Burger spoke for a 7–2 Court, with Justices White and Rehnquist dissenting.

See Barbara H. Craig, *Chadha: The Story of an Epic Constitutional Struggle* (1988); Robert G. Dixon, Jr., "The Congressional Veto," 56 *North Carolina Law Review* 423 (1978); Jacob Javits and Gary Klein, "Congressional Oversight and the Legislative Veto: A Constitutional Analysis," 52 *N.Y.U. Law Review* 455 (1977); and Peter L. Straus, "Was There a Baby in the Bathwater?" 1983 *Duke Law Journal* 79 (1983).

———

Chief Justice Burger delivered the opinion of the Court:

It is also argued that these cases present a nonjusticiable political question because Chadha is merely challenging Congress' authority under the Naturalization Clause, U.S. Const., Art. I, § 8, cl. 4, and the Necessary and Proper Clause, U.S. Const., Art. I, § 8, cl. 18. It is argued that Congress' Art. I power "To establish an uniform Rule of Naturalization," combined with the Necessary and Proper Clause, grants it unreviewable authority over the regulation of aliens. The plenary authority of Congress over aliens under Art. I,

§ 8, cl. 4, is not open to question, but what is challenged here is whether Congress has chosen a constitutionally permissible means of implementing that power. As we made clear in *Buckley v. Valeo* . . . (1976): "Congress has plenary authority in all cases in which it has substantive legislative jurisdiction . . . so long as the exercise of that authority does not offend some other constitutional restriction." . . .

A brief review of those factors which may indicate the presence of a nonjusticiable political question satisfies us that our assertion of jurisdiction over these cases does no violence to the political question doctrine. . . .

It is correct that this controversy may, in a sense, be termed "political." But the presence of constitutional issues with significant political overtones does not automatically invoke the political question doctrine. Resolution of litigation challenging the constitutional authority of one of the three branches cannot be evaded by courts because the issues have political implications in the sense urged by Congress. *Marbury v. Madison* . . . (1803), was also a "political" case, involving as it did claims under a judicial commission alleged to have been duly signed by the President but not delivered. But "courts cannot reject as 'no law suit' a bona fide controversy as to whether some action denominated 'political' exceeds constitutional authority." . . .

The contentions on standing and justiciability have been fully examined, and we are satisfied the parties are properly before us. The important issues have been fully briefed and twice argued. . . . The Court's duty in these cases, as Chief Justice Marshall declared in *Cobens v. Virginia* . . . (1821), is clear:

> "Questions may occur which we would gladly avoid; but we cannot avoid them. All we can do is, to exercise our best judgment, and conscientiously to perform our duty."

III

A

We turn now to the question whether action of one House of Congress under § 244(c) (2) violates strictures of the Constitution. We begin, of course, with the presumption that the challenged statute is valid. Its wisdom is not the concern of the courts; if a challenged action does not violate the Constitution, it must be sustained. . . .

By the same token, the fact that a given law or procedure is efficient, convenient, and useful in facilitating functions of government, standing alone, will not save it if it is contrary to the Constitution. Convenience and efficiency are not the primary objectives—or the hallmarks—of democratic government and our inquiry is sharpened rather than blunted by the fact that congressional veto provisions are appearing with increasing frequency in statutes which delegate authority to executive and independent agencies. . . .

Justice WHITE undertakes to make a case for the proposition that the one-House veto is a useful "political invention," . . . and we need not challenge that assertion. We can even concede this utilitarian argument although the long-range political wisdom of this "invention" is arguable. It has been vigorously debated, and it is instructive to compare the views of the protagonists. . . . But policy arguments supporting even useful "political inventions" are subject to the demands of the Constitution which defines powers and, with respect to this subject, sets out just how those powers are to be exercised.

Explicit and unambiguous provisions of the Constitution prescribe and define the respective functions of the Congress and of the Executive in the legislative process. Since the precise terms of those familiar provisions are critical to the resolution of these cases, we set them out verbatim. Article I provides:

> "All legislative Powers herein granted shall be vested in a Congress of the United States, which shall consist of a Senate *and* House of Representatives." Art. I, § 1. (Emphasis added.)
>
> "Every Bill which shall have passed the House of Representatives *and* the Senate, *shall,* before it becomes a law, be presented to the President of the United States. . . ." Art. I, § 7, cl. 2. (Emphasis added.)
>
> "*Every* Order, Resolution, or Vote to which the Concurrence of the Senate and House of Representatives may be necessary (except on a question of Adjournment) *shall* be presented to the President of the United States; and before the Same shall take Effect, *shall be* approved by him, or being disapproved by him, *shall be* repassed by two thirds of the Senate and House of Representatives, according to the Rules and Limitations prescribed in the Case of a Bill." Art. I, § 7, cl. 3. (Emphasis added.)

These provisions of Art. I are integral parts of the constitutional design for the separation of powers. We have recently noted that "[t]he principle of separation of powers was not simply an abstract generalization in the minds of the Framers: it was woven into the document that they drafted in Philadelphia in the summer of 1787." *Buckley v. Valeo.* . . . Just as we relied on the textual provision of Art. II, § 2, cl. 2, to vindicate the principle of separation of powers in *Buckley,* we see that the purposes underlying the Presentment Clauses, Art. I, § 7, cls. 2, 3, and the bicameral requirement of Art. I, §1, and § 7, cl. 2, guide our resolution of the important question presented in these cases. The very structure of the Articles delegating and separating powers under Arts. I, II, and III exemplifies the concept of separation of powers, and we now turn to Art. I.

B

THE PRESENTMENT CLAUSES

The records of the Constitutional Convention reveal that the requirement that all legislation be presented to the President before becoming law was uniformly accepted by the Framers. Presentment to the President and the Presidential veto were considered so imperative that the draftsmen took special pains to assure that these requirements could not be circumvented. . . .

The decision to provide the President with a limited and qualified power to nullify proposed legislation by veto was based on the profound conviction of the Framers that the powers conferred on Congress were the powers to be most carefully circumscribed. It is beyond doubt that lawmaking was a power to be shared by both Houses and the President. . . .

We see therefore that the Framers were acutely conscious that the bicameral requirement and the Presentment Clauses would serve essential constitutional functions. The President's participation in the legislative process was to protect the Executive

Branch from Congress and to protect the whole people from improvident laws. The division of the Congress into two distinctive bodies assures that the legislative power would be exercised only after opportunity for full study and debate in separate settings. The President's unilateral veto power, in turn, was limited by the power of two-thirds of both Houses of Congress to overrule a veto thereby precluding final arbitrary action of one person. See *id.,* at 99–104. It emerges clearly that the prescription for legislative action in Art. I, §§ 1, 7, represents the Framers' decision that the legislative power of the Federal Government be exercised in accord with a single, finely wrought and exhaustively considered, procedure.

IV

The Constitution sought to divide the delegated powers of the new Federal Government into three defined categories, Legislative, Executive, and Judicial, to assure, as nearly as possible, that each Branch of government would confine itself to its assigned responsibility. The hydraulic pressure inherent within each of the separate Branches to exceed the outer limits of its power, even to accomplish desirable objectives, must be resisted.

Although not "hermetically" sealed from one another, . . . the powers delegated to the three Branches are functionally identifiable. When any Branch acts, it is presumptively exercising the power the Constitution has delegated to it. . . . When the Executive acts, he presumptively acts in an executive or administrative capacity as defined in Art. II. And when, as here, one House of Congress purports to act, it is presumptively acting within its assigned sphere.

Beginning with this presumption, we must nevertheless establish that the challenged action under § 244(c)(2) is of the kind to which the procedural requirements of Art. I, § 7, apply. Not every action taken by either House is subject to the bicameralism and presentment requirements of Art. I. . . . Whether actions taken by either House are, in law and fact, an exercise of legislative power depends not on their form but upon "whether they contain matter which is properly to be regarded as legislative in its character and effect." . . .

Examination of the action taken here by one House pursuant to § 244(c)(2) reveals that it was essentially legislative in purpose and effect. In purporting to exercise power defined in Art. I, § 8, cl. 4, to "establish an uniform Rule of Naturalization," the House took action that had the purpose and effect of altering the legal rights, duties, and relations of persons, including the Attorney General, Executive Branch officials and Chadha, all outside the Legislative Branch. Section 244(c)(2) purports to authorize one House of Congress to require the Attorney General to deport an individual alien whose deportation otherwise would be canceled under § 244. The one-House veto operated in these cases to overrule the Attorney General and mandate Chadha's deportation; absent the House action, Chadha would remain in the United States. Congress has *acted* and its action has altered Chadha's status. . . .

The nature of the decision implemented by the one-House veto in these cases further manifests its legislative character. After long experience with the clumsy, time-consuming private bill procedure, Congress made a deliberate choice to delegate to the Executive Branch, and specifically to the Attorney General, the authority to allow deportable aliens to remain in this country in certain specified circumstances. It is not disputed that this choice to delegate authority is precisely the kind of decision that can be implemented only in accordance with the procedures set out in Art. I. Disagreement with the Attorney General's decision on Chadha's deportation—that is, Congress' decision to deport Chadha—no less than Congress' original choice to delegate to the Attorney General the authority to make that decision, involves determinations of policy that Congress can implement in only one way; bicameral passage followed by presentment to the President. Congress must abide by its delegation of authority until that delegation is legislatively altered or revoked.

Since it is clear that the action by the House under § 244(c)(2) was not within any of the express constitutional exceptions authorizing one House to act alone, and equally clear that it was an exercise of legislative power, that action was subject to the standards prescribed in Art. I. The bicameral requirement, the Presentment Clauses, the President's veto, and Congress' power to override a veto were intended to erect enduring checks on each Branch and to protect the people from the improvident exercise of power by mandating certain prescribed steps. To preserve those checks, and maintain the separation of powers, the carefully defined limits on the power of each Branch must not be eroded. To accomplish what has been attempted by one House of Congress in this case requires action in conformity with the express procedures of the Constitution's prescription for legislative action: passage by a majority of both Houses and presentment to the President.

The veto authorized by § 244(c)(2) doubtless has been in many respects a convenient shortcut; the "sharing" with the Executive by Congress of its authority over aliens in this manner is, on its face, an appealing compromise. In purely practical terms, it is obviously easier for action to be taken by one House without submission to the President; but it is crystal clear from the records of the Convention, contemporaneous writings and debates, that the Framers ranked other values higher than efficiency. The records of the Convention and debates in the states preceding ratification underscore the common desire to define and limit the exercise of the newly created federal powers affecting the states and the people. There is unmistakable expression of a determination that legislation by the national Congress be a step-by-step, deliberate and deliberative process.

The choices we discern as having been made in the Constitutional Convention impose burdens on governmental processes that often seem clumsy, inefficient, even unworkable, but those hard choices were consciously made by men who had lived under a form of government that permitted arbitrary governmental acts to go unchecked. There is no support in the Constitution or decisions of this Court for the proposition that the cumbersomeness and delays often encountered in complying with explicit constitutional standards may be avoided, either by the Congress or by the President. . . . With all the obvious flaws of delay, untidiness, and potential for abuse, we have not yet found a better way to preserve freedom than by making the exercise of power subject to the carefully crafted restraints spelled out in the Constitution.

V

We hold that the congressional veto provision in § 244(c)(2) is severable from the Act and that it is unconstitutional. Accordingly, the judgment of the Court of Appeals is

Affirmed.

---

238   *Wallace v. Jaffree (1985)*

Following *Engel v. Vitale* (Document 205), and the Bible-reading decision in *Abington School District v. Schempp* (1963), people and groups who wanted prayer and Bible-reading in schools mounted a number of campaigns to over-turn the Court's rulings. Senator Robert C. Byrd of West Virginia summed up the feelings of many when he complained that "some one is tampering with America's soul." Beginning in 1963, proposed constitutional amendments have been introduced into each session of Congress to permit Bible-reading or prayers in public schools, and a prayer amendment came within nine votes of Senate passage in 1966.

The revival of a strong fundamentalist Christian movement in the 1980s led to repeated efforts to introduce a variety of religious activities into the public school system. In 1980, the Court struck down a Kentucky statute requiring the posting of the Ten Commandments in all public school classrooms. The *per curiam* opinion in *Stone v. Graham* characterized the law as plainly religious. The decision led President Reagan and others to call once again for an amendment to permit prayer in school.

In Alabama, the legislature tried to get around the *Engel* rule with a series of laws. The first, in 1978, simply provided for a one-minute period of silent meditation; a 1981 amendment authorized "meditation or voluntary prayer." In 1982, however, the legislature directed teachers to lead "willing students" in a prescribed prayer. The decision dealt primarily with the 1981 law, which was obviously religious in intent, and left to a future decision the question of whether silence that could be devoted to prayer was constitutional.

See Norman Redlich, "Separation of Church and State: The Burger Court's Tortuous Journey," 60 *Notre Dame Law Review* 1094 (1985); Leonard W. Levy, *The Establishment Clause: Religion and the First Amendment* (1986); and Michael W. McConnell, "Accommodation of Religion," 1985 *Supreme Court Review* 1 (1986).

Justice Stevens delivered the opinion of the Court:

The narrow question for decision is whether § 16-1-20.1, which authorizes a period of silence for "meditation or voluntary prayer," is a law respecting the establishment of religion within the meaning of the First Amendment.

I. Appellee Ishmael Jaffree is a resident of Mobile County, Alabama. On May 28, 1982, he filed a complaint on behalf of three of his minor children; two of them were second-grade students and the third was then in kindergarten. [The complaint alleged] that two of the children had been subjected to various acts of religious indoctrination "from the beginning of the school year in September, 1981"; that the defendant teachers had "on a daily basis" led their classes in saying certain prayers in unison; that the minor children were exposed to ostracism from their peer group class members if they did not participate; and that Ishmael Jaffree had repeatedly but unsuccessfully requested that the devotional services be stopped. . . .

On August 2, 1982, the District Court held an evidentiary hearing on appellees' motion for a preliminary injunction. At that hearing, State Senator Donald G. Holmes testified that he was the "prime sponsor" of the bill that was enacted in 1981 as § 16-1-20.1. He explained that the bill was an "effort to return voluntary prayer to our public schools . . . it is a beginning and a step in the right direction." Apart from the purpose to return voluntary prayer to public school, Senator Holmes unequivocally testified that he had "no other purpose in mind." . . .

II. Our unanimous affirmance of the Court of Appeals' judgment . . . makes it unnecessary to comment at length on the District Court's remarkable conclusion that the Federal Constitution imposes no obstacle to Alabama's establishment of a state religion. Before analyzing the precise issue that is presented to us, it is nevertheless appropriate to recall how firmly embedded in our constitutional jurisprudence is the proposition that the several States have no greater power to restrain the individual freedoms protected by the First Amendment than does the Congress of the United States.

As is plain from its text, the First Amendment was adopted to curtail the power of Congress to interfere with the individual's freedom to believe, to worship, and to express himself in accordance with the dictates of his own conscience. Until the Fourteenth Amendment was added to the Constitution, the First Amendment's restraints on the exercise of federal power simply did not apply to the States. But when the Constitution was amended to prohibit any State from depriving any person of liberty without due process of law, that Amendment imposed the same substantive limitations on the States' power to legislate that the First Amendment had always imposed on the Congress' power. This Court has confirmed and endorsed this elementary proposition of law time and time again.

Just as the right to speak and the right to refrain from speaking are complimentary components of a broader concept of individual freedom of mind, so also the individual's freedom to choose his own creed is the counterpart of his right to refrain from accepting the creed established by the majority. At one time it was thought that this right merely proscribed the preference of one Christian sect over another, but would not require equal respect for the conscience of the infidel, the atheist, or the adherent of a non-Christian faith such as Mohammedism or Judaism. But when the underlying principle has been

Source: 472 U.S. 38 (1985)

examined in the crucible of litigation, the Court has unambiguously concluded that the individual freedom of conscience protected by the First Amendment embraces the right to select any religious faith or none at all. This conclusion derives support not only from the interest in respecting the individual's freedom of conscience, but also from the conviction that religious beliefs worthy of respect are the product of free and voluntary choice by the faithful, and from recognition of the fact that the political interest in forestalling intolerance extends beyond intolerance among Christian sects—or even intolerance among "religions"—to encompass intolerance of the disbeliever and the uncertain. The State of Alabama, no less than the Congress of the United States, must respect that basic truth.

III. It is the first of [the *Lemon*] criteria that is most plainly implicated by this case. As the District Court correctly recognized, no consideration of the second or third criteria is necessary if a statute does not have a clearly secular purpose. . . . The First Amendment requires that a statute must be invalidated if it is entirely motivated by a purpose to advance religion.

In applying the purpose test, it is appropriate to ask "whether government's actual purpose is to endorse or disapprove of religion." . . . In this case, the answer to that question is dispositive. For the record not only provides us with an unambiguous affirmative answer, but it also reveals that the enactment of § 16-1-20.1 was not motivated by any clearly secular purpose—indeed, the statute had *no* secular purpose.

IV. The sponsor of the bill that became § 16-1-20.1, Senator Donald Holmes, inserted into the legislative record—apparently without dissent—a statement indicating that the legislation was an "effort to return voluntary prayer" to the public schools. Later Senator Holmes confirmed this purpose before the District Court. In response to the question whether he had any purpose for the legislation other than returning voluntary prayer to public schools, he stated, "No, I did not have no other purpose in mind." The State did not present evidence of *any* secular purpose. . . .

. . . The Legislature enacted § 16-1-20.1 . . . for the sole purpose of expressing the State's endorsement of prayer activities for one minute at the beginning of each school day. The addition of "or voluntary prayer" indicates that the State intended to characterize prayer as a favored practice. Such an endorsement is not consistent with the established principle that the Government must pursue a course of complete neutrality toward religion.

The importance of that principle does not permit us to treat this as an inconsequential case involving nothing more than a few words of symbolic speech on behalf of the political majority. For whenever the State itself speaks on a religious subject, one of the questions that we must ask is "whether the Government intends to convey a message of endorsement or disapproval of religion." The well-supported concurrent findings of the District Court and the Court of Appeals—that § 16-1-20.1 was intended to convey a message of State-approval of prayer activities in the public schools—make it unnecessary, and indeed inappropriate, to evaluate the practical significance of the addition of the words "or voluntary prayer" to the statute. Keeping in mind, as we must, "both the fundamental place held by the Establishment Clause in our constitutional scheme and the myriad, subtle ways in which Establishment Clause values can be eroded," . . . we conclude that § 16-1-20.1 violates the First Amendment.

The judgment of the Court of Appeals is affirmed.

239   Construing the
                                          Constitution (1985)

Years ago, John Marshall declared that the Constitution is a law and therefore subject to judicial interpretation; but, as he also noted, it is more than just a law, it is an organic outline of government. In recent years, there has been considerable debate in political arenas as well as in the academic world over how judges should interpret the Constitution. One group believes in a strict adherence to the intent of the Framers and claims that there is sufficient contemporary evidence to tell judges just what the Founding Fathers meant in particular clauses of the Constitution. Another group believes that times have changed so dramatically since the Philadelphia Convention of 1787 that the documents of that time are at best only a starting point in constitutional construction. This latter group, often termed judicial activists, also believes that it is the Court's responsibility to make sure that the Constitution remains relevant to contemporary social needs. Associate Justice William J. Brennan, Jr., who served on the Court from 1956 to 1990, was considered by many as the leading exponent of judicial activism. Edwin Meese III, attorney general in the Reagan administration, has also been outspoken in his belief that judges had gone too far in imposing their views rather than accepting the clear intent of the Framers. The following colloquy sets out the main tenets of both schools of jurisprudence.

See Raoul Berger, *Government by Judiciary* (1977); Michael Perry, *The Constitution, The Courts, and Human* Rights (1982); William H. Rehnquist, "The Notion of a Living Constitution," 54 *Texas Law Review* 693 (1976); John Hart Ely, *A Theory of Judicial Review* (1980); Jesse Choper, *The Supreme Court and the Political Branches* (1980); and Sanford Levinson, *Constitutional Faith* (1988).

———

A. WILLIAM J. BRENNAN, JR.

My encounters with the constitutional text are not purely or even primarily introspective; the Constitution cannot be for me simply a contemplative haven for private moral reflection. My relation to this great text is inescapably public. That is not to say that my

Source: 19 *University of California Davis Law Review* 2 (1985)

reading of the text is not a personal reading, only that the personal reading perforce occurs in a public context, and is open to critical scrutiny from all quarters.

The Constitution is fundamentally a public text—the monumental charter of a government and a people—and a Justice of the Supreme Court must apply it to resolve public controversies. For, from our beginnings, a most important consequence of the constitutionally created separation of powers has been the American habit, extraordinary to other democracies, of casting social, economic, philosophical and political questions in the form of lawsuits, in an attempt to secure ultimate resolution by the Supreme Court. In this way, important aspects of the most fundamental issues confronting our democracy may finally arrive in the Supreme Court for judicial determination. Not infrequently, these are the issues upon which contemporary society is most deeply divided. They arouse our deepest emotions. The main burden of my twenty-nine Terms on the Supreme Court has thus been to wrestle with the Constitution in this heightened public context, to draw meaning from the text in order to resolve public controversies.

Two other aspects of my relation to this text warrant mention. First, constitutional interpretation for a federal judge is, for the most part, obligatory. When litigants approach the bar of court to adjudicate a constitutional dispute, they may justifiably demand an answer. Judges cannot avoid a definitive interpretation because they feel unable to, or would prefer not to, penetrate to the full meaning of the Constitution's provisions. Unlike literary critics, judges cannot merely savor the tensions or revel in the ambiguities inhering in the text—judges must resolve them.

Second, consequences flow from a Justice's interpretation in a direct and immediate way. A judicial decision respecting the incompatibility of Jim Crow with a constitutional guarantee of equality is not simply a contemplative exercise in defining the shape of a just society. It is an order—supported by the full coercive power of the State—that the present society change in a fundamental aspect. Under such circumstances the process of deciding can be a lonely, troubling experience for fallible human beings conscious that their best may not be adequate to the challenge. We Justices are certainly aware that we are not final because we are infallible; we know that we are infallible only because we are final. One does not forget how much may depend on the decision. More than the litigants may be affected. The course of vital social, economic and political currents may be directed.

These three defining characteristics of my relation to the constitutional text—its public nature, obligatory character, and consequentialist aspect—cannot help but influence the way I read that text. When Justices interpret the Constitution they speak for their community, not for themselves alone. The act of interpretation must be undertaken with full consciousness that it is, in a very real sense, the community's interpretation that is sought. Justices are not platonic guardians appointed to wield authority according to their personal moral predilections. Precisely because coercive force must attend any judicial decision to countermand the will of a contemporary majority, the Justices must render constitutional interpretations that are received as legitimate. The source of legitimacy is, of course, a wellspring of controversy in legal and political circles. At the core of the debate is what the late Yale Law School professor Alexander Bickel labeled "the counter-majoritarian difficulty." Our commitment to self-governance in a representative democracy must be reconciled with vesting in electorally unaccountable Justices the power to invalidate the expressed desires of representative bodies on the ground of inconsistency with higher law. Because judicial power resides in the authority to give meaning to the Constitution, the debate is really a debate about how to read the text, about constraints on what is legitimate interpretation.

There are those who find legitimacy in fidelity to what they call "the intentions of the Framers." In its most doctrinaire incarnation, this view demands that Justices discern exactly what the Framers thought about the question under consideration and simply follow that intention in resolving the case before them. It is a view that feigns self-effacing deference to the specific judgments of those who forged our original social compact. But in truth it is little more than arrogance cloaked as humility. It is arrogant to pretend that from our vantage we can gauge accurately the intent of the Framers on application of principle to specific, contemporary questions. All too often, sources of potential enlightenment such as records of the ratification debates provide sparse or ambiguous evidence of the original intention. Typically, all that can be gleaned is that the Framers themselves did not agree about the application or meaning of particular constitutional provisions, and hid their differences in cloaks of generality. Indeed, it is far from clear whose intention is relevant—that of the drafters, the congressional disputants, or the ratifiers in the states?—or even whether the idea of an original intention is a coherent way of thinking about a jointly drafted document drawing its authority from a general assent of the states. And apart from the problematic nature of the sources, our distance of two centuries cannot but work as a prism refracting all we perceive. One cannot help but speculate that the chorus of lamentations calling for interpretation faithful to "original intention"—and proposing nullification of interpretations that fail this quick litmus test—must inevitably come from persons who have no familiarity with the historical record.

Perhaps most importantly, while proponents of this facile historicism justify it as a depoliticization of the judiciary, the political underpinnings of such a choice should not escape notice. A position that upholds constitutional claims only if they were within the specific contemplation of the Framers in effect establishes a presumption of resolving textual ambiguities against the claim of constitutional right. It is far from clear what justifies such a presumption against claims of right. Nothing intrinsic in the nature of interpretation—if there is such a thing as the "nature" of interpretation—commands such a passive approach to ambiguity. This is a choice no less political than any other; it expresses antipathy to claims of the minority to rights against the majority. Those who would restrict claims of right to the values of 1789 specifically articulated in the Constitution turn a blind eye to social progress and eschew adaptation of overarching principles to changes of social circumstances.

Another, perhaps more sophisticated, response to the potential power of judicial interpretation stresses democratic theory: because ours is a government of the people's elected representatives, substantive value choices should by and large be left to them. This view emphasizes not the transcendent historical authority of the framers but the predominant contemporary authority of the elected branches of government. Yet it has similar consequences for the nature of proper judicial interpretation. Faith in the majoritarian process counsels restraint. Even under more expansive formulations of this approach, judicial review is appropriate only to the extent of ensuring that our democratic process functions smoothly. Thus, for example, we would protect freedom of speech merely to ensure that the people are heard by their representatives, rather than as a separate, substantive value. When, by contrast, society tosses up to the Supreme Court a dispute that would require invalidation of a legislature's substantive policy choice, the Court generally would stay its hand because the Constitution was meant as a plan of government and not as an embodiment of fundamental substantive values. . . .

. . . Faith in democracy is one thing, blind faith quite another. Those who drafted our Constitution understood the difference. One cannot read the text without admitting that it embodies substantive value choices; it places certain values beyond the power of any legislature. Obvious are the separation of powers; the privilege of the Writ of Habeas Corpus; prohibition of Bills of Attainder and ex post facto laws; prohibition of cruel and unusual punishments; the requirement of just compensation for official taking of property; the prohibition of laws tending to establish religion or enjoining the free exercise of religion; and, since the Civil War, the banishment of slavery and official race discrimination. With respect to at least such principles, we simply have not constituted ourselves as strict utilitarians. While the Constitution may be amended, such amendments require an immense effort by the People as a whole.

To remain faithful to the content of the Constitution, therefore, an approach to interpreting the text must account for the existence of these substantive value choices, and must accept the ambiguity inherent in the effort to apply them to modern circumstances. The Framers discerned fundamental principles through struggles against particular malefactions of the Crown; the struggle shapes the particular contours of the articulated principles. But our acceptance of the fundamental principles has not and should not bind us to those precise, at times anachronistic contours. Successive generations of Americans have continued to respect these fundamental choices and adopt them as their own guide to evaluating quite different historical practices. Each generation has the choice to overrule or add to the fundamental principles enunciated by the Framers; the Constitution can be amended or it can be ignored. Yet with respect to its fundamental principles, the text has suffered neither fate. Thus, if I may borrow the words of an esteemed predecessor, Justice Robert Jackson, the burden of judicial interpretation is to translate "the majestic generalities of the Bill of Rights, conceived as part of the pattern of liberal government in the eighteenth century, into concrete restraints on officials dealing with the problems of the twentieth century."

We current Justices read the Constitution in the only way that we can: as Twentieth Century Americans. We look to the history of the time of framing and to the intervening history of interpretation. But the ultimate question must be, what do the words of the text mean in our time? For the genius of the Constitution rests not in any static meaning it might have had in a world that is dead and gone, but in the adaptability of its great principles to cope with current problems and current needs. What the constitutional fundamentals meant to the wisdom of other times cannot be their measure to the vision of our time. Similarly, what those fundamentals mean for us, our descendants will learn, cannot be their measure to the vision of their time. . . .

If we are to be as a shining city upon a hill, it will be because of our ceaseless pursuit of the constitutional ideal of human dignity. For the political and legal ideals that form the foundation of much that is best in American institutions—ideals jealously preserved and guarded throughout our history—still form the vital force in creative political thought and activity within the nation today. As we adapt our institutions to the ever-changing conditions of national and international life, those ideals of human dignity—liberty and justice for all individuals—will continue to inspire and guide us because they are entrenched in our Constitution. The Constitution with its Bill of Rights thus has a bright future, as well as a glorious past, for its spirit is inherent in the aspirations of our people.

B. EDWIN MEESE III

A large part of American history has been the history of constitutional debate. From the Federalists and the Anti-Federalists, to Webster and Calhoun, to Lincoln and Douglas, we find many examples. Now, as we approach the Bicentennial of the framing of the Constitution, we are witnessing another debate concerning our fundamental law. It is not simply a ceremonial debate, but one that promises to have a profound effect on the future of our Republic.

The current debate is a sign of a healthy nation. Unlike people of many other countries, we are free both to discover the defects of our laws and our government through open discussion and to correct them through our political system.

This debate on the Constitution involves great and fundamental issues. It invites the participation of the best minds the bar, the academy, and the bench have to offer. In recent weeks there have been important new contributions to this debate from some of the most distinguished scholars and jurists in the land. Representatives of the three branches of the federal government have entered the debate, journalistic commentators too. . . .

It is easy to forget what a young country America really is. The bicentennial of our independence was just a few years ago, that of the Constitution still two years off.

The period surrounding the creation of the Constitution is not a dark and mythical realm. The young America of the 1780's and 90's was a vibrant place, alive with pamphlets, newspapers, and books chronicling and commenting upon the great issues of the day. We know how the Founding Fathers lived, and much of what they read, thought, and believed. The disputes and compromises of the Constitutional Convention were carefully recorded. The minutes of the Convention are a matter of public record. Several of the most important participants—including James Madison, the "father" of the Constitution—wrote comprehensive accounts of the Convention. Others, Federalists and Anti-Federalists alike, committed their arguments for and against ratification, as well as their understandings of the Constitution, to paper, so that their ideas and conclusions could be widely circulated, read, and understood.

In short, the Constitution is not buried in the mists of time. We know a tremendous amount of the history of its genesis. The Bicentennial is encouraging even more scholarship about its origins. We know who did what, when, and many times why. One can talk intelligently about a "founding generation."

With these thoughts in mind, I would like to discuss the administration's approach to constitutional interpretation which has been led by President Reagan and which we at the Department of Justice and my colleagues in other agencies have advanced. But to begin, it may be useful to say what it is not.

Our approach does not view the Constitution as some kind of super municipal code, designed to address merely the problems of a particular era—whether those of 1787, 1789, or 1868. There is no question that the Constitutional Convention grew out of widespread dissatisfaction with the Articles of Confederation. But the delegates at Philadelphia moved beyond the job of patching that document to write a *Constitution*. Their intention was to write a document not just for their times but for posterity.

The language they employed clearly reflects this. For example, they addressed *commerce,* not simply shipping or barter. Later the Bill of Rights spoke, through the fourth amendment, to "unreasonable searches and seizures," not merely the regulation of specific law enforcement practices of 1789. Still later, the Framers of the fourteenth amendment were concerned not simply about the rights of black citizens to personal security, but also about the equal protection of the law for all persons within the states.

The Constitution is not a legislative code bound to the time in which it was written. Neither, however, is it a mirror that simply reflects the thoughts and ideas of those who stand before it.

Our approach to constitutional interpretation begins with the document itself. The plain fact is, it exists. It is something that has been written down. Walter Berns of the American Enterprise Institute has noted that the central object of American constitutionalism was "the effort" of the Founders "to express fundamental governmental arrangements in a legal document—to 'get it in writing.'"

Indeed, judicial review has been grounded in the fact that the Constitution is a written, as opposed to an unwritten, document. In *Marbury v. Madison* John Marshall rested his rationale for judicial review on the fact that we have a written constitution with meaning that is binding upon judges. "[I]t is apparent," he wrote, "that the framers of the constitution contemplated that instrument as a rule for the government of *courts,* as well as of the legislature. Why otherwise does it direct the judges to take an oath to support it?" . . .

We know that those who framed the Constitution chose their words carefully. They debated at great length the most minute points. The language they chose meant something. They proposed, they substituted, they edited, and they carefully revised. Their words were studied with equal care by state ratifying conventions.

This is not to suggest that there was unanimity among the Framers and ratifiers on all points. The Constitution and the Bill of Rights, and some of the subsequent amendments, emerged after protracted debate. Nobody got everything they wanted. What's more, the Framers were not clairvoyants—they could not foresee every issue that would be submitted for judicial review. Nor could they predict how all foreseeable disputes would be resolved under the Constitution. But the point is, the meaning of the Constitution can be known.

What does this written Constitution mean? In places it is exactingly specific. Where it says that Presidents of the United States must be at least thirty-five years of age it means exactly that. (I have not heard of any claim that thirty-five means thirty or twenty-five or twenty). Where it specifies how the House and Senate are to be organized, it means what it says.

The Constitution, including its twenty-six amendments, also expresses particular principles. One is the right to be free of an unreasonable search or seizure. Another concerns religious liberty. Another is the right to equal protection of the laws.

Those who framed these principles meant something by them. And the meanings can be found, understood, and applied.

The Constitution itself is also an expression of certain general principles. These principles reflect the deepest purpose of the Constitution—that of establishing a political system through which Americans can best govern themselves consistent with the goal of securing liberty.

The text and structure of the Constitution are instructive. It contains very little in the way of specific political solutions. It speaks volumes on how problems should be approached, and by *whom.* For example, the first three articles set out clearly the scope and limits of three distinct branches of national government, the powers of each being carefully and specifically enumerated. In this scheme it is no accident to find the legislative branch described first, as the Framers had fought and sacrificed to secure the right of democratic self-governance. Naturally, this faith in republicanism was not unbounded, as the next two articles make clear.

Yet the Constitution remains a document of powers and principles. And its undergirding premise remains that democratic self-government is subject only to the limits of certain constitutional principles. This respect for the political process was made explicit early on. When John Marshall upheld the act of Congress chartering a national bank in *McCulloch v. Maryland* he wrote: "The Constitution [was] intended to endure for ages to come, and, consequently, to be adapted to the various crises of human affairs." But to use *McCulloch,* as some have tried, as support for the idea that the Constitution is a protean, changeable thing is to stand history on its head. Marshall was keeping faith with the original intention that Congress be free to elaborate and apply constitutional powers and principles. He was not saying the the Court must invent some new constitutional value in order to keep pace with the times. In Walter Berns' words: "Marshall's meaning is not that the Constitution may be adapted to the 'various crises of human affairs,' but that the legislative powers granted by the Constitution are adaptable to meet these crises."

The approach this administration advocates is rooted in the text of the Constitution as illuminated by those who drafted, proposed, and ratified it. In his famous "Commentary on the Constitution of the United States" Justice Joseph Story explained that "[t]he first and fundamental rule in the interpretation of all instruments is, to construe them according to the sense of the terms, and the intention of the parties."

Our approach understands the significance of a written document and seeks to discern the particular and general principles it expresses. It recognizes that there may be debate at times over the application of these principles. But it does not mean these principles cannot be identified.

Constitutional adjudication is obviously not a mechanical process. It requires an appeal to reason and discretion. The text and intention of the Constitution must be understood to constitute the banks within which constitutional interpretation must flow. As James Madison said, if "the sense in which the Constitution was accepted and ratified by the nation . . . be not the guide in expounding it, there can be no security for a consistent and stable, more than for a faithful exercise of its powers."

Thomas Jefferson, so often cited incorrectly as a framer of the Constitution, in fact shared Madison's view: "Our peculiar security is in the possession of a written Constitution. Let us not make it a blank paper by construction." . . .

In the main a jurisprudence that seeks to be faithful to our Constitution—a jurisprudence of original intention, as I have called it—is not difficult to describe. Where the language of the Constitution is specific, it must be obeyed. Where there is a demonstrable consensus among the Framers and ratifiers as to a principle stated or implied by the Constitution, it should be followed. Where there is ambiguity as to the precise meaning or reach of a constitutional provision, it should be interpreted and applied in a manner so as to at least not contradict the text of the Constitution itself.

Sadly, while almost everyone participating in the current constitutional debate would give assent to these propositions, the techniques and conclusions of some of the debaters do violence to them. What is the source of this violence? In large part I believe that it is the misuse of history stemming from the neglect of the idea of a written constitution.

There is a frank proclamation by some judges and commentators that what matters most about the Constitution is not its words but its so-called "spirit." These individuals focus less on the language of specific provisions than on what they describe as the "vision" or "concepts of human dignity" they find embodied in the Constitution. . . .

. . . In recent decades many have come to view the Constitution—more accurately, part of the Constitution, provisions of the Bill of Rights and the fourteenth amendment—as a charter for judicial activism on behalf of various constituencies. Those who hold this view often have lacked demonstrable textual or historical support for their conclusions. Instead they have grounded their rulings in appeals to social theories, to moral philosophies or personal notions of human dignity, or to "penumbras," somehow emanating ghostlike from various provisions—identified and not identified—in the Bill of Rights. The problem with this approach, as John Hart Ely, Dean of Stanford Law School, has observed with respect to one such decision, is not that it is bad constitutional law, but that it is not constitutional law in any meaningful sense at all.

Despite this fact, the perceived popularity of some results in particular cases has encouraged some observers to believe that any critique of the methodology of those decisions is an attack on the results. This perception is sufficiently widespread that it deserves an answer. My answer is to look at history.

When the Supreme Court, in *Brown v. Board of Education*, sounded the death knell for official segregation in the country, it earned all the plaudits it received. But the Supreme Court in that case was not giving new life to old words, or adapting a "living," "flexible" Constitution to new reality. It was restoring the original principle of the Constitution to constitutional law. The *Brown* Court was correcting the damage done fifty years earlier, when in *Plessy v. Ferguson* an earlier Supreme Court had disregarded the clear intent of the Framers of the civil war amendments to eliminate the legal degradation of blacks, and had contrived a theory of the Constitution to support the charade of "separate but equal" discrimination.

It is amazing how so much of what passes for social and political progress is really the undoing of old judicial mistakes. . . .

A jurisprudence that seeks fidelity to the Constitution—a jurisprudence of original intention—is not a jurisprudence of political results. It is very much concerned with process, and it is a jurisprudence that in our day seeks to depoliticize the law. The great genius of the constitutional blueprint is found in its creation and respect for spheres of authority and the limits it places on governmental power. In this scheme the Framers did not see the courts as the exclusive custodians of the Constitution. Indeed, because the document posits so few conclusions it leaves to the more political branches the matter of adapting and vivifying its principles in each generation. It also leaves to the people of the states, in the tenth amendment, those responsibilities and rights not committed to federal care. The power to declare acts of Congress and laws of the states null and void is truly awesome. This power must be used when the Constitution clearly speaks. It should not be used when the Constitution does not. . . .

In summary, I would emphasize that what is at issue here is not an agenda of issues or a menu of results. At issue is a way of government. A jurisprudence based on first principles is neither conservative nor liberal, neither right nor left. It is a jurisprudence that cares about committing and limiting to each organ of government the proper ambit of its responsibilities. It is a jurisprudence faithful to our Constitution.

By the same token, an activist jurisprudence, one which anchors the Constitution only in the consciences of jurists, is a chameleon jurisprudence, changing color and form in each era. The same activism hailed today may threaten the capacity for decision through democratic consensus tomorrow, as it has in many yesterdays. Ultimately, as the early democrats wrote into the Massachusetts state constitution, the best defense of our liberties is a government of laws and not men.

---

240   *Bowsher v. Synar (1986)*

In an effort to gain control of a runaway federal budget, Congress in 1985 adopted the Gramm-Rudman Resolution, which called for scheduled step reductions in the annual deficit until a balanced budget had been achieved. If Congress failed to take the necessary steps, either by cutting expenditures or by raising revenues, the comptroller general could impose across-the-board cuts on all programs.

The Court struck down Gramm-Rudman by a seven-to-two vote, but the decision seemed aimed more at where the power to cut had been lodged than at the logic of the bill. In what is clearly a separation of powers decision, the Court left unclear whether a similar measure that assigned these functions completely to an executive officer would pass constitutional muster.

See "Symposium," 72 *Cornell Law Review* 421 (1987); exchange between Paul W. Kahn, 13 *Hastings Constitutional Law Quarterly* 185 (1986), and William D. Popkin, 14 *Hastings Constitutional Law Quarterly* 205 (1987); and Paul R. Verkuil, "Status of Independent Agencies After *Bowsher,*" 1986 *Duke Law Journal* 779 (1986).

———

Source: 478 U.S. 714 (1986)

Chief Justice Burger delivered the opinion of the Court:

The question presented by these appeals is whether the assignment by Congress to the Comptroller General of the United States of certain functions under the Balanced Budget and Emergency Deficit Control Act of 1985 violates the doctrine of separation of powers. . . .

III. The declared purpose of separating and dividing the powers of government [was] to "diffus[e] power the better to secure liberty." . . . Justice Jackson's words echo the famous warning of Montesquieu, quoted by James Madison in The Federalist No. 47, that "there can be no liberty where the legislative and executive powers are united in the same person, or body of magistrates.' . . ."

Even a cursory examination of the Constitution reveals the influence of Montesquieu's thesis that checks and balances were the foundation of a structure of government that would protect liberty. The Framers provided a vigorous legislative branch and a separate and wholly independent executive branch, with each branch responsible ultimately to the people. The Framers also provided for a judicial branch equally independent. . . .

That this system of division and separation of powers produces conflicts, confusion, and discordance at times is inherent, but it was deliberately so structured to assure full, vigorous and open debate on the great issues affecting the people and to provide avenues for the operation of checks on the exercise of governmental power.

The Constitution does not contemplate an active role for Congress in the supervision of officers charged with the execution of the laws it enacts. The President appoints "Officers of the United States" with the "Advice and Consent of the Senate. . . ." Article II, § 2. Once the appointment has been made and confirmed, however, the Constitution explicitly provides for removal of Officers of the United States by Congress only upon impeachment by the House of Representatives and conviction by the Senate. An impeachment by the House and trial by the Senate can rest only on "Treason, Bribery or other high Crimes and Misdemeanors." Article II, § 4. A direct congressional role on the removal of officers charged with the execution of the laws beyond this limited one is inconsistent with separation of powers. . . .

In light of [our] precedents, we conclude that Congress cannot reserve for itself the power of removal of an officer charged with the execution of the laws except by impeachment. To permit the execution of the laws to be vested in an officer answerable only to Congress would, in practical terms, reserve in Congress control over the execution of the laws. As the District Court observed, "Once an officer is appointed, it is only the authority that can remove him, and not the authority that appointed him, that he must fear and, in the performance of his functions, obey." The structure of the Constitution does not permit Congress to execute the laws; it follows that Congress cannot grant to an officer under its control what it does not possess.

Our decision in [Chadha] supports this conclusion. [To] permit an officer controlled by Congress to execute the laws would be, in essence, to permit a congressional veto. Congress could simply remove, or threaten to remove, an officer for executing the laws in any fashion found to be unsatisfactory to Congress. This kind of congressional control over the execution of the laws, Chadha makes clear, is constitutionally impermissible. With these principles in mind, we turn to consideration of whether the Comptroller General is controlled by Congress.

IV. Appellants urge that the Comptroller General performs his duties independently and is not subservient to Congress. We agree with the District Court that this contention does not bear close scrutiny.

The critical factor lies in the provisions of the statute defining the Comptroller General's office relating to removability. Although the Comptroller General is nominated by the President from a list of three individuals recommended by the Speaker of the House of Representatives and the President pro tempore of the Senate, see 31 U.S.C. § 703(a)(2), and confirmed by the Senate, he is removable only at the initiative of Congress. He may be removed not only by impeachment but also by Joint Resolution of Congress "at any time" resting on any one of [several] bases. . . .

It is clear that Congress has consistently viewed the Comptroller General as an officer of the Legislative Branch. The Reorganization Acts of 1945 and 1949, for example, both stated that the Comptroller General and the GAO are "a part of the legislative branch of the Government." Similarly, in the Accounting and Auditing Act of 1950, Congress required the Comptroller General to conduct audits "as an agent of the Congress." Over the years, the Comptrollers General have also viewed themselves as part of the Legislative Branch. In one of the early Annual Reports of Comptroller General, the official seal of his office was described as reflecting: "the independence of judgment to be exercised by the General Accounting Office, subject to the control of the legislative branch. . . . The combination represents an agency of the Congress independent of other authority auditing and checking the expenditures of the Government as required by law and subjecting any questions arising in that connection to quasi-judicial determination." Later, Comptroller General Warren, who had been a member of Congress for 15 years before being appointed Comptroller General, testified that: "During most of my public life, . . . I have been a member of the legislative branch. Even now, although heading a great agency, it is an agency of the Congress, and I am an agent of the Congress."

[Against] this background, we see no escape from the conclusion that, because Congress had retained removal authority over the Comptroller General, he may not be entrusted with executive powers. The remaining question is whether the Comptroller General has been assigned such powers in the Balanced Budget and Emergency Deficit Control Act of 1985.

V. The primary responsibility of the Comptroller General under the instant Act is the preparation of a "report." This report must contain detailed estimates of projected federal revenues and expenditures. The report must also specify the reductions, if any, necessary to reduce the deficit to the target for the appropriate fiscal year. The reductions must be set forth on a program by-program basis.

In preparing the report, the Comptroller General is to have "due regard" for the estimates and reductions set forth in a joint report submitted to him by the Director of CBO and the Director of OMB, the President's fiscal and budgetary advisor. However, the Act plainly contemplates that the Comptroller General will exercise his independent judgment and evaluation with respect to those estimates. The Act also provides that the Comptroller General's report "shall explain fully any differences between the contents of such report and the report of the Directors."

Appellants suggest that the duties assigned to the Comptroller General in the Act are essentially ministerial and mechanical so that their performance does not constitute "execution of the law" in a meaningful sense. On the contrary, we view these functions as plainly entailing execution of the law in constitutional terms. Interpreting a law enacted by Congress to implement the legislative mandate is the very essence of "execution" of the law. Under §251, the Comptroller General must exercise judgment concerning facts that affect the application of the Act. He must also interpret the provisions of the Act to determine precisely what budgetary calculations are required. Decisions of that kind are typically made by officers charged with executing a statute. . . .

. . . By placing the responsibility for execution of the [Act] in the hands of an officer who is subject to removal only by itself, Congress in effect has retained control over the execution of the Act and has intruded into the executive function. The Constitution does not permit such intrusion.

241   *Bowers v. Hardwick (1986)*

The announcement of a constitutionally protected right to privacy (Documents 212 and 225) left many unanswered questions about how far this right extended, and whether it was near absolute or subject to certain state restrictions. In *Stanley v. Georgia* (1969), the Court reversed a conviction for "possession of obscene matter," holding that the First and Fourteenth amendments "prohibit making the private possession of obscene material a crime." This decision was interpreted by some groups to mean that within one's home, almost any activity engaged in by consenting adults would be protected from state interference.

Most states, however, have laws regulating sexual conduct, some of which date back to colonial times. For the most part, when the activity is confined to consenting adults, the state avoids involvement, and the laws are rarely enforced. There are some who claim that the only reason many of these laws are still on the statute books is that legislators are afraid to sponsor repealing proposals lest they be labeled advocates of or participants in the conduct in question.

Even in this case, where the police inadvertently entered a bedroom and caught the defendant engaged in sodomy, the state did not prosecute. In effect the respondent sought a declaratory judgment that laws regulating private consensual sexual conduct were unconstitutional invasions of his privacy and that of other practicing homosexuals.

Given that such laws are rarely enforced, the Court could have dismissed the suit since it did not constitute a valid "case or controversy" as required by Article III. But a bare majority of the Court wanted to send a message, both to the public and to the lower courts, namely, that the right to privacy first adumbrated in *Griswold* is not absolute. The justices also recognized that homosexual sodomy, unlike marital privacy, had little public support, and by taking this stand they could rebut some of the charges that they had gone too far in allow-ing so-called permissive behavior. What the rather harsh majority opinion by Justice White does not take into account, however, is the issue raised by Justice Blackmun in his dissent—namely, that the Georgia law criminalized types of behavior engaged in not only by homosexuals, but to a far larger extent by het-erosexual couples as well.

As was usual in the mid-eighties, the fifth man comprising the majority was Lewis F. Powell, who apparently had a difficult time making up his mind on this case. After his retirement, he told a reporter that he had probably made a mistake, and should have voted to strike down the Georgia law. (See a some-what different approach to gay rights in Document 258).

See comments in D. A. J. Richards, "History, Homosexuals and Homophobia," 19 *Connecticut Law Review* 129 (1986); Charles Fried, *Order and Law* (1991); Richard Pos-ner, *Sex and Reason* (1992); and Cass Sunstein, "Sexual Orientation and the Constitu-tion," 55 *University of Chicago Law Review* 1161 (1988).

―――――

Justice White delivered the opinion of the Court:

In August 1982, respondent was charged with violating the Georgia statute crimi-nalizing sodomy by committing that act with another adult male in the bedroom of respondent's home. After a preliminary hearing, the District Attorney decided not to present the matter to the grand jury unless further evidence developed.

Respondent then brought suit in the Federal District Court, challenging the consti-tutionality of the statute insofar as it criminalized consensual sodomy. He asserted that he was a practicing homosexual, that the Georgia sodomy statute, as administered by the defendants, placed him in imminent danger of arrest, and that the statute for several rea-sons violates the Federal Constitution.

A divided panel of the Court of Appeals for the Eleventh Circuit went on to hold that the Georgia statute violated respondent's fundamental rights because his homosex-ual activity is a private and intimate association that is beyond the reach of state regula-tion by reason of the Ninth Amendment and the Due Process Clause of the Fourteenth Amendment. The case was remanded for trial, at which, to prevail, the State would have to prove that the statute is supported by a compelling interest and is the most narrowly drawn means of achieving that end.

Because other Courts of Appeals have arrived at judgments contrary to that of the Eleventh Circuit in this case, we granted the State's petition for certiorari questioning the holding that its sodomy statute violates the fundamental rights of homosexuals. We agree with the state that the Court of Appeals erred, and hence reverse its judgment.

This case does not require a judgment on whether laws against sodomy between consenting adults in general, or between homosexuals in particular, are wise or desirable. It raises no question about the right or propriety of state legislative decisions to repeal their laws that criminalize homosexual sodomy, or of state court decisions invalidating those laws on state constitutional grounds. The issue presented is whether the Federal Constitution confers a fundamental right upon homosexuals to engage in sodomy and hence invalidates the laws of the many States that still make such conduct illegal and have done so for a very long time. The case also calls for some judgment about the limits of the Court's role in carrying out its constitutional mandate. . . .

We think it evident that none of the rights announced in [our earlier cases dealing with privacy] bears any resemblance to the claimed constitutional right of homosexuals to engage in acts of sodomy that is asserted in this case. No connection between family, marriage, or procreation on the one hand and homosexual activity on the other has been demonstrated, either by the Court of Appeals or by respondent. Moreover, any claim that these cases nevertheless stand for the proposition that any kind of private sexual conduct between consenting adults is constitutionally insulated from state proscription is unsupportable. Indeed, the Court's opinion in *Carey* twice asserted that the privacy right, which the *Griswold* line of cases found to be one of the protections provided by the Due Process Clause, did not reach so far.

Precedent aside, however, respondent would have us announce, as the Court of Appeals did, a fundamental right to engage in homosexual sodomy. This we are quite unwilling to do. It is true that despite the language of the Due Process Clauses of the Fifth and Fourteenth Amendments, which appears to focus only on the processes by which life, liberty, or property is taken, the cases are legion in which those Clauses have been interpreted to have substantive content, subsuming rights that to a great extent are immune from federal or state regulation or proscription. Among such cases are those recognizing rights that have little or no textual support in the constitutional language.

Striving to assure itself and the public that announcing rights not readily identifiable in the Constitution's text involves much more than the imposition of the Justices' own choice of values on the States and the Federal Government, the Court has sought to identify the nature of the rights qualifying for heightened judicial protection. In *Palko v. Connecticut* (1937), it was said that this category includes those fundamental liberties that are "implicit in the concept of ordered liberty," such that "neither liberty nor justice would exist if [they] were sacrificed." A different description of fundamental liberties appeared in *Moore v. East Cleveland* (1977), where they are characterized as those liberties that are "deeply rooted in this Nation's history and tradition."

It is obvious to us that neither of these formulations would extend a fundamental right to homosexuals to engage in acts of consensual sodomy. Proscriptions against that conduct have ancient roots. Sodomy was a criminal offense at common law and was forbidden by the laws of the original thirteen States when they ratified the Bill of Rights. In 1868, when the Fourteenth Amendment was ratified, all but 5 of the 37 States in the Union had criminal sodomy laws. In fact, until 1961, all 50 States outlawed sodomy, and today, 24 States and the District of Columbia continue to provide criminal penalties for sodomy performed in private and between consenting adults. Against this background, to claim that a right to engage in such conduct is "deeply rooted in this Nation's history and tradition" or "implicit in the concept of ordered liberty" is, at best, facetious.

Nor are we inclined to take a more expansive view of our authority to discover new fundamental rights embedded in the Due Process Clause. The Court is most vulnerable and comes nearest to illegitimacy when it deals with judge-made constitutional law having little or no cognizable roots in the language or design of the Constitution. That this is so was painfully demonstrated by the face-off between the Executive and the Court in the 1930's, which resulted in the repudiation of much of the substantive gloss that the Court had placed on the Due Process Clause of the Fifth and Fourteenth Amendments. There should be, therefore, great resistance to expand the substantive reach of those Clauses, particularly if it requires redefining the category of rights deemed to be fundamental. Otherwise, the Judiciary necessarily takes to itself further authority to govern the country without express constitutional authority. The claimed right pressed on us today falls far short of overcoming this resistance. . . .

Even if the conduct at issue here is not a fundamental right, respondent asserts that there must be a rational basis for the law and that there is none in this case other than the presumed belief of a majority of the electorate in Georgia that homosexual sodomy is immoral and unacceptable. This is said to be an inadequate rationale to support the law. The law, however, is constantly based on notions of morality, and if all laws representing essentially moral choices are to be invalidated under the Due Process Clause, the courts will be very busy indeed. Even respondent makes no such claim, but insists that majority sentiments about the morality of homosexuality should be declared inadequate. We do not agree, and are unpersuaded that the sodomy laws of some 25 States should be invalidated on this basis.

Chief Justice Burger, concurring:

I join the Court's opinion, but I write separately to underscore my view that in constitutional terms there is no such thing as a fundamental right to commit homosexual sodomy.

As the Court notes, the proscriptions against sodomy have very "ancient roots." Decisions of individuals relating to homosexual conduct have been subject to state intervention throughout the history of Western Civilization. Condemnation of those practices is firmly rooted in Judeao-Christian moral and ethical standards. . . . To hold that the act of homosexual sodomy is somehow protected as a fundamental right would be to cast aside millennia of moral teaching.

This is essentially not a question of personal "preferences" but rather that of the legislative authority of the State. I find nothing in the Constitution depriving a State of the power to enact the statute challenged here.

Justice Blackmun, with whom Justices Brennan, Marshall, and Stevens join, dissenting:

This case is no more about "a fundamental right to engage in homosexual sodomy," as the Court purports to declare, than *Stanley v. Georgia* (1969), was about a fundamental right to watch obscene movies, or *Katz v. United States* (1967), was about a fundamental right to place interstate bets from a telephone booth. Rather, this case is about "the most comprehensive of rights and the right most valued by civilized men," namely "the right to be let alone." . . .

In its haste to reverse the Court of Appeals and hold that the Constitution does not "confer a fundamental right upon homosexuals to engage in sodomy," the Court relegates the actual statute being challenged to a footnote and ignores the procedural posture of the case before it. A fair reading of the statute and of the complaint clearly reveals that the majority has distorted the question this case presents.

First, the Court's almost obsessive focus on homosexual activity is particularly hard to justify in light of the broad language Georgia has used. Unlike the Court, the Georgia Legislature has not proceeded on the assumption that homosexuals are so different from other citizens that their lives may be controlled in a way that would not be tolerated if it limited the choices of those other citizens. Rather, Georgia has provided that "[a] person commits the offense of sodomy when he performs or submits to any sexual act involving the sex organs of one person and the mouth or anus of another." The sex or status of the persons who engage in the act is irrelevant as a matter of state law. In fact, to the extent I can discern a legislative purpose for Georgia's 1968 enactment, that purpose seems to have been to broaden the coverage of the law to reach heterosexual as well as homosexual activity. Michael Hardwick's standing may rest in significant part on Georgia's apparent willingness to enforce against homosexuals a law it seems not to have any desire to enforce against heterosexuals. But his claim that [the Georgia law] involves an unconstitutional intrusion into his privacy and his right of intimate association does not depend in any way on his sexual orientation. . . .

In construing the right to privacy, the Court has proceeded along two somewhat distinct, albeit complementary, lines. First, it has recognized a privacy interest with reference to certain *decisions* that are properly for the individual to make. Second, it has recognized a privacy interest with reference to certain *places* without regard for the particular activities in which the individuals who occupy them are engaged. The case before us implicates both the decisional and the spatial aspects of the right to privacy.

The Court concludes today that none of our prior cases dealing with various decisions that individuals are entitled to make free of governmental interference "bears any resemblance to the claimed constitutional right of homosexuals to engage in acts of sodomy that is asserted in this case." While it is true that these cases may be characterized by their connection to protection of the family, the Court's conclusion that they extend no further than this boundary ignores the warning against "closing our eyes to the basic reasons why certain rights associated with the family have been accorded shelter under the Fourteenth Amendment's Due Process Clause." We protect those rights not because they contribute, in some direct and material way, to the general public welfare, but because they form so central a part of an individual's life. "The concept of privacy embodies the 'moral fact that a person belongs to himself and not others nor to society as a whole.'" And so we protect the decision whether to marry precisely because marriage "is an association that promotes a way of life, not causes; a harmony in living, not political faiths; a bilateral loyalty, not commercial or social projects." We protect the decision whether to have a child because parenthood alters so dramatically an individual's self-definition, not because of demographic considerations or the Bible's command to be fruitful and multiply. And we protect the family because it contributes so powerfully to the happiness of individuals, not because of a preference for stereotypical households. . . .

Only the most willful blindness could obscure the fact that sexual intimacy is "a sensitive, key relationship of human existence, central to family life, community welfare, and the development of human personality." The fact that individuals define themselves in a significant way through their intimate sexual relationships with others suggests, in a Nation as diverse as ours, that there may be many "right" ways of conducting those relationships, and that much of the richness of a relationship will come from the freedom an individual has to *choose* the form and nature of these intensely personal bonds.

In a variety of circumstances we have recognized that a necessary corollary of giving individuals freedom to choose how to conduct their lives is acceptance of the fact that different individuals will make different choices. For example, in holding that the clearly important state interest in public education should give way to a competing claim by the Amish to the effect that extended formal schooling threatened their way of life, the Court declared: "There can be no assumption that today's majority is 'right' and the Amish and others like them are 'wrong.' A way of life that is odd or even erratic but interferes with no rights or interests of others is not to be condemned because it is different." The Court claims that its decision today merely refuses to recognize a fundamental right to engage in homosexual sodomy; what the Court really has refused to recognize is the fundamental interest all individuals have in controlling the nature of their intimate associations with others.

The behavior for which Hardwick faces prosecution occurred in his own home, a place to which the Fourth Amendment attaches special significance. The Court's treatment of this aspect of the case is symptomatic of its overall refusal to consider the broad principles that have informed our treatment of privacy in specific cases. Just as the right to privacy is more than the mere aggregation of a number of entitlements to engage in specific behavior, so too, protecting the physical integrity of the home is more than merely a means of protecting specific activities that often take place there. . . .

It took but three years for the Court to see the error in its analysis in *Minersville School District v. Gobitis* (1940), and to recognize that the threat to national cohesion posed by a refusal to salute the flag was vastly outweighed by the threat to those same values posed by compelling such a salute. See *West Virginia Board of Education v. Barnette* (1943). I can only hope that here, too, the Court soon will reconsider its analysis and conclude that depriving individuals of the right to choose for themselves how to conduct their intimate relationships poses a far greater threat to the values most deeply rooted in our Nation's history than tolerance of nonconformity could ever do. Because I think the Court today betrays those values, I dissent.

242   *Edwards v. Aguillard (1987)*

The growth of a powerful conservative religious and social movement in the 1980s led to a number of legislative attempts to undo what militant religious leaders viewed as the dreadful mistakes of the Court. As seen in Document 238, the Alabama legislature tried to overturn the ban on state-sponsored school prayer. In this instance, Louisiana resumed the fundamentalist fight against evolution, by mandating that if a school taught "evolution science" it had to give equal time to so-called creation science. Most reputable scientists dismissed creation science as a blind for teaching the creation as told in Genesis; science, they maintained, is a system built on doubt and questioning, not on blind faith.

The majority dismissed the law as a ploy, although newly named Chief Justice William Rehnquist, joined by Justice Scalia, continued his pattern of deferring to the legislative will and calling for a greater accommodation of religion with the state.

See Michael McConnell, "The Origins and Historical Understanding of Free Exercise of Religion," 103 *Harvard Law Review* 1409 (1990); Derek Davis, *Original Intent: Chief Justice Rehnquist and the Course of Church/State Relations* (1991); Gregg Ivers, *Lowering the Wall: Religion and the Supreme Court in the 1980s* (1991); and Edward J. Larson, *Summer for the Gods* (1997).

———

Justice BRENNAN delivered the opinion of the Court:

The Creationism Act forbids the teaching of the theory of evolution in public schools unless accompanied by instruction in "creation science." No school is required to teach evolution or creation science. If either is taught, however, the other must also be taught. The theories of evolution and creation science are statutorily defined as "the scientific evidences for [creation or evolution] and inferences from those scientific evidences."

Appellees, who include parents of children attending Louisiana public schools, Louisiana teachers, and religious leaders, challenged the constitutionality of the Act in District court, seeking an injunction and declaratory relief. Appellants, Louisiana officials charged with implementing the Act, defended on the ground that the purpose of the Act is to protect a legitimate secular interest, namely, academic freedom. . . .

The Establishment Clause forbids the enactment of any law "respecting an establishment of religion." The Court has applied a three-pronged test to determine whether legislation comports with the Establishment Clause. First, the legislature must have adopted the law with a secular purpose. Second, the statute's principle of primary effect

Source: 482 U.S. 578 (1987)

must be one that neither advances nor prohibits religion. Third, the statute must not result in an excessive entanglement of government with religion. State action violates the Establishment Clause if it fails to satisfy any of these prongs. . . .

The Court has been particularly vigilant in monitoring compliance with the Establishment Clause in elementary and secondary schools. . . . Students in such institutions are impressionable and their attendance is involuntary. . . . Furthermore, "the public school is at once the symbol of our democracy and the most pervasive means for promoting our common destiny. In no activity of the State is it more vital to keep out divisive forces than in its schools. . . ."

Consequently, the Court has been required often to invalidate statutes which advance religion in public elementary and secondary schools. . . .

Therefore, in employing the three-pronged *Lemon* test, we must do so mindful of the particular concerns that arise in the context of public elementary and secondary schools. We now turn to the evolution of the Act under the *Lemon* test. . . .

"The purpose prong of the *Lemon* test asks whether government's actual purpose is to endorse or disapprove of religion." A governmental intention to promote religion is clear when the State enacts a law to serve a religious purpose. . . . If the law was enacted for the purpose of endorsing religion, "no consideration of the second or third criteria is necessary." In this case, the petitioners have identified no clear secular purpose for the Louisiana Act.

True, the Act's stated purpose is to protect academic freedom. . . . However, even if "academic freedom" is read to mean "teaching all of the evidence" with respect to the origin of human beings, the Act does not further this purpose. The goal of providing a more comprehensive science curriculum is not furthered either by outlawing the teaching of evolution or by requiring the teaching of creation science.

While the Court is normally deferential to a State's articulation of a secular purpose, it is required that the statement of such purpose be sincere and not a sham. . . .

It is clear from the legislative history that the purpose of the legislative sponsor, Senator Bill Keith, was to narrow the science curriculum. During the legislative hearings, Senator Keith stated: "My preference would be that neither [creationism nor evolution] be taught." . . . It is clear that requiring schools to teach creation science with evolution does not advance academic freedom. . . . As the president of the Louisianan Science Teachers Association testified, "any scientific concept that's based on established fact can be included in our curriculum already, and no legislation allowing this is necessary." The Act provides Louisiana schoolteachers with no new authority. Thus the stated purpose is not furthered by it.

If the Louisiana legislature's purpose was solely to maximize the comprehensiveness and effectiveness of science instruction, it would have encouraged the teaching of all scientific theories about the origins of humankind. But under the Act's requirements, teachers who were once free to teach any and all facets of this subject are now unable to do so. Moreover, the Act fails even to ensure that creation science will be taught, but instead requires the teaching of this theory only when the theory of evolution is taught. . . . Thus the Act does not serve to protect academic freedom, but has the distinctly different purpose of discrediting "evolution by counterbalancing its teaching at every turn with teaching of creation science. . . ."

The preeminent purpose of the Louisiana legislature was clearly to advance the religious viewpoint that a supernatural being created humankind. . . . Furthermore, it is not happenstance that the legislature required the teaching of a theory that coincided with this religious view. The legislative history documents that the Act's primary purpose was to change the science curriculum of public schools in order to provide persuasive advantage to a particular religious doctrine that rejects the factual basis of evolution in its entirety. . . .

The Creationism Act is designed *either* to promote the theory of creation science which embodies a particular religious tenet by requiring that creation science be taught whenever evolution is taught or to prohibit the teaching of a scientific theory disfavored by certain religious sects by forbidding the teaching of evolution when creation science is not also taught. The Establishment Clause, however, forbids *alike* the preference of a religious doctrine or the prohibition of theory which is deemed antagonistic to a particular dogma. Because the primary purpose of the Creationism Act is to advance a particular religious belief, the Act endorses religion in violation of the First Amendment.

We do not imply that a legislature could never require that scientific critiques of prevailing scientific theories be taught. . . . Teaching a variety of scientific theories about the origins of humankind to schoolchildren might be validly done with the clear secular intent of enhancing the effectiveness of science instruction. But because the primary purpose of the Creationism Act is to endorse a particular religious doctrine, the Act furthers religion in violation of the Establishment Clause.

The judgment of the Court of Appeals therefore is Affirmed.

Justice POWELL, with whom Justice O'CONNOR joins, concurring:

I write separately to note certain aspects of the legislative history, and to emphasize that nothing in the Court's opinion diminishes the traditionally broad discretion accorded state and local school officials in the selection of the public school curriculum. . . .

When, as here, "both courts below are unable to discern an arguably valid secular purpose, the Court normally should hesitate to find one." My examination of the language and the legislative history of the Balanced Treatment Act confirms that the intent of the Louisiana legislature was to promote a particular religious belief. . . .

Here, it is clear that religious belief is the Balanced Treatment Act's "reason for existence." The tenets of creation-science parallel the Genesis story of creation, and this is a religious belief. "No legislative recitation of a supposed secular purpose can blind us to that fact. . . ."

The legislature acted with the unconstitutional purpose of structuring the public school curriculum to make it compatible with a particular religious belief: the "divine creation of man." . . .

Whatever the academic merit of particular subjects or theories, the Establishment Clause limits the discretion of state officials to pick and choose among them for the purpose of promoting a particular religious belief. The language of the statute and its legislative history convince me that the Louisiana legislature exercised its discretion for this purpose in the case.

A decision respecting the subject matter to be taught in public schools does not violate the Establishment Clause simply because the material to be taught " 'happens to consider or harmonize with the tenets of some or all religions.' "

As matter of history, school children can and should properly be informed of all aspects of this Nation's religious heritage. I would see no constitutional problem if school children were taught the nature of the Founding Fathers' religious beliefs and how these beliefs affected the attitudes of the times and the structure of our government. Courses in comparative religion of course are customary and constitutionally appropriate. In fact, since religion permeates our history, a familiarity with the nature of religious beliefs is necessary to understand many historical as well as contemporary events. In addition, it is worth noting that the Establishment Clause does not prohibit *per se* the educational use of religious documents in public school education. . . . The Establishment Clause is properly understood to prohibit the use of the Bible and other religious documents in public school education only when the purpose of the use is to advance a particular religious belief.

Justice SCALIA, with whom The Chief Justice joins, dissenting:
Even if I agreed with the questionable premise that legislation can be invalidated under the Establishment Clause on the basis of its motivation alone, without regard to its effects, I would still find no justification for today's decision. The Louisiana legislators who passed the "Balanced Treatment for Creation-Science and Evolution-Science Act," each of whom had sworn to support the Constitution, were well aware of the potential Establishment Clause problems and considered that aspect of the legislation with great care. After seven hearings and several months of study, resulting in substantial revision of the original proposal, they approved the Act overwhelmingly and specifically articulated the secular purpose they meant it to serve. Although the record contains abundant evidence of the sincerity of that purpose (the only issue pertinent to this case), the Court today holds, essentially on the basis of "its visceral knowledge regarding what *must* have motivated the legislators," that the members of the Louisiana Legislature knowingly violated their oaths and then lied about it. I dissent. . . .

We have relatively little information upon which to judge the motives of those who supported the Act. About the only direct evidence is the statute itself and transcripts of the seven committee hearings at which it was considered. Unfortunately, several of those hearings were sparsely attended, and the legislators who were present revealed little about their motives. We have no committee reports, no floor debates, no remarks inserted into the legislative history, no statement from the Governor, and no post-enactment statements or testimony from the bill's sponsor of any other legislators. Nevertheless, there is ample evidence that the majority is wrong in holding that the Balanced Treatment Act is without secular purpose. . . .

Our task is not to judge the debate about teaching the origins of life, but to ascertain what the members of the Louisiana Legislature believed. The vast majority of them voted to approve a bill which explicitly stated a secular purpose; what is crucial is not their wisdom in believing that purpose would be achieved by the bill, but their *sincerity* in believing it would be. . . .

Striking down a law approved by the democratically elected representatives of the people is no minor matter. "The cardinal principle of statutory construction is to save and not to destroy. We have repeatedly held that as between two possible interpretations of a statute, by one of which it would be unconstitutional and by the other valid, our plain duty is to adopt that which will save the act." So, too, it seems to me, with discerning statutory purpose. Even if the legislative history were silent or ambiguous about the existence of a secular purpose—and here it is not—the statute should survive *Lemon's* purpose test. But even more validation than mere legislative history is present here. The Louisiana Legislature explicitly set forth its secular purpose ("protecting academic freedom") in the very text of the Act.

The legislative history gives ample evidence of the sincerity of the Balanced Treatment Act's articulated purpose. Witness after witness urged the legislators to support the Act so that students would not be "indoctrinated" but would instead be free to decide for themselves, based upon a fair presentation of the scientific evidence, about the origin of life. . . .

It is undoubtedly true that what prompted the Legislature to direct its attention to the misrepresentation of evolution in the schools (rather than the inaccurate presentation of other topics) was its awareness of the tension between evolution and the religious beliefs of many children. But even appellees concede that a valid secular purpose is not rendered impermissible simply because its pursuit is promoted by concern for religious sensitivities. . . .

In sum, even if one concedes, for the sake of argument, that a majority of the Louisiana Legislature voted for the Balanced Treatment Act partly in order to foster (rather than merely eliminate discrimination against) Christian fundamentalist beliefs, our cases establish that that alone would not suffice to invalidate the Act, so long as there was a genuine secular purpose as well. We have, moreover, no adequate basis for disbelieving the secular purpose set forth in the Act itself, or for concluding that it is a sham enacted to conceal the legislators' violation of their oaths of office. . . .

I have to this point assumed the validity of the *Lemon* "purpose" test. . . . In the past we have attempted to justify our embarrassing Establishment Clause jurisprudence on the ground that it "sacrifices clarity and predictability for flexibility." . . . I think it is time that we sacrifice some "flexibility" for "clarity and predictability." Abandoning *Lemon's* purpose test—a test which exacerbates the tension between the Free Exercise and Establishment Clauses, has no basis in the language or history of the amendment, and, as today's decision shows, has wonderfully flexible consequences—would be a good place to start.

243

Nollan v. California Coastal Commission (1987)

The constitutional controversy of the 1930s (see Documents 178–181 and 183) and the emergence of a rights-based agenda had led the Court to ignore what had once been its primary concern—property rights. But the nation's shift to the right in the 1980s saw the appointment of more conservative justices to both state and federal benches, and litigants claiming that their property rights had been violated began to appear in the courtroom.

Although the Court had approved the power of the state to issue zoning requirements, there had been very few challenges to that power that would have explicated its amplitude as well as its limits. In this instance, the California commission had required public access to private beachfront property as a condition for issuing a building permit. In the decision, the Court emphasized the government's permanent occupation of private property as well as the absence of any direct connection between the permit condition and the public interest. The permanent physical occupation by the state of private property is, in general, a taking.

The condition imposed in *Nollan* is called an "exaction," and is quite common in a number of circumstances. Developers and landowners are often required to meet certain conditions, such as improvements of roadways or drainage systems, in order to get building permits. Challenges to exactions had usually been fought out in state courts, since the exactions were imposed under either state law or local laws deriving their authority from the state. Most state courts required some sort of nexus between the exaction and the conditions to be created by development. The Nollans, aware that state courts tended to interpret state claims liberally, decided to challenge the exaction in federal court. Although the fact of property rights resurfacing in the high court after five decades made some headlines, in essence the important holding is that the high court constitutionalized the state court requirement of a nexus between exactions and the public interest in order to justify the conditions imposed.

See Matthew S. Watson, "The Scope of the Supreme Court's Heightened Scrutiny Takings Doctrine and Its Impact on Development Exactions," 20 *Whittier Law Review* 181 (1998); Noreen Murphy, "The Viability of Impact Fees After Nollan," 31 *New England Law Review* 203 (1996); and Richard Epstein, "The Harms and Benefits of Nollan," 15 *Northern Illinois University Law Review* 479 (1995).

———

Justice SCALIA delivered the opinion of the Court:

James and Marilyn Nollan appeal from a decision of the California Court of Appeals ruling that the California Coastal Commission could condition its grant of permission to rebuild their house on their transfer to the public of an easement across their beachfront property. The California court rejected their claim that imposition of that condition violates the Takings Clause of the Fifth Amendment, as incorporated against the States by the Fourteenth Amendment. . . .

The Nollans own a beachfront lot in Ventura County, California. A quarter-mile north of their property is Faria County Park, an oceanside public park with a public

Source: 483 U.S. 825 (1987)

beach and recreation area. Another public beach area, known locally as "the Cove," lies 1,800 feet south of their lot. A concrete seawall approximately eight feet high separates the beach portion of the Nollans' property from the rest of the lot. The historic mean high tide line determines the lot's oceanside boundary.

The Nollans originally leased their property with an option to buy. The building on the lot was a small bungalow, totaling 504 square feet, which for a time they rented to summer vacationers. After years of rental use, however, the building had fallen into disrepair, and could no longer be rented out.

The Nollans' option to purchase was conditioned on their promise to demolish the bungalow and replace it. In order to do so, . . . they were required to obtain a coastal development permit from the California Coastal Commission. On February 25, 1982, they submitted a permit application to the Commission in which they proposed to demolish the existing structure and replace it with a three-bedroom house in keeping with the rest of the neighborhood.

The Nollans were informed that their application had been placed on the administrative calendar, and that the Commission staff had recommended that the permit be granted subject to the condition that they allow the public an easement to pass across a portion of their property bounded by the mean high tide line on one side, and their seawall on the other side. This would make it easier for the public to get to Faria County Park and the Cove. The Nollans protested imposition of the condition, but the Commission overruled their objections and granted the permit subject to their recordation of a deed restriction granting the easement. . . .

Had California simply required the Nollans to make an easement across their beachfront available to the public on a permanent basis in order to increase public access to the beach, rather than conditioning their permit to rebuild their house on their agreeing to do so, we have no doubt there would have been a taking. To say that the appropriation of a public easement across a landowner's premises does not constitute the taking of a property interest but rather (as Justice BRENNAN contends) "a mere restriction on its use" . . . is to use words in a manner that deprives them of all their ordinary meaning. Indeed, one of the principal uses of the eminent domain power is to assure that the government be able to require conveyance of just such interests, so long as it pays for them. . . . We have repeatedly held that, as to property reserved by its owner for private use, "the right to exclude [others is] 'one of the most essential sticks in the bundle of rights that are commonly characterized as property'". . . . Where governmental action results in "a permanent physical occupation" of the property, by the government itself or by others . . . "our cases uniformly have found a taking to the extent of the occupation, without regard to whether the action achieves an important public benefit or has only minimal economic impact on the owner." We think a "permanent physical occupation" has occurred, for purposes of that rule, where individuals are given a permanent and continuous right to pass to and fro, so that the real property may continuously be traversed, even though no particular individual is permitted to station himself permanently upon the premises.

Justice BRENNAN argues that while this might ordinarily be the case, the California Constitution's prohibition on any individual's "exclu[ding] the right of way to [any navigable] water whenever it is required for any public purpose," Art. X, Section 4, produces a different result here. . . . There are a number of difficulties with that argument.

Most obviously, the right of way sought here is not naturally described as one to navigable water (from the street to the sea) but along it; it is at least highly questionable whether the text of the California Constitution has any prima facie application to the situation before us. . . .

Given, then, that requiring uncompensated conveyance of the easement outright would violate the Fourteenth Amendment, the question becomes whether requiring it to be conveyed as a condition for issuing a land-use permit alters the outcome. We have long recognized that land-use regulation does not effect a taking if it "substantially advances legitimate state interests" and does not "deny an owner economically viable use of his land," *Agins v. Tiburon.* . . . Our cases have not elaborated on the standards for determining what constitutes a "legitimate state interest" or what type of connection between the regulation and the state interest satisfies the requirement that the former "substantially advance" the latter. They have made clear, however, that a broad range of governmental purposes and regulations satisfies these requirements. . . . The Commission argues that among these permissible purposes are protecting the public's ability to see the beach, assisting the public in overcoming the "psychological barrier" to using the beach created by a developed shorefront, and preventing congestion on the public beaches. We assume, without deciding, that this is so—in which case the Commission unquestionably would be able to deny the Nollans their permit outright if their new house (alone, or by reason of the cumulative impact produced in conjunction with other construction) would substantially impede these purposes, unless the denial would interfere so drastically with the Nollans' use of their property as to constitute a taking. . . .

The Commission argues that a permit condition that serves the same legitimate police-power purpose as a refusal to issue the permit should not be found to be a taking if the refusal to issue the permit would not constitute a taking. We agree. Thus, if the Commission attached to the permit some condition that would have protected the public's ability to see the beach notwithstanding construction of the new house—for example, a height limitation, a width restriction, or a ban on fences—so long as the Commission could have exercised its police power (as we have assumed it could) to forbid construction of the house altogether, imposition of the condition would also be constitutional. Moreover (and here we come closer to the facts of the present case), the condition would be constitutional even if it consisted of the requirement that the Nollans provide a viewing spot on their property for passersby with whose sighting of the ocean their new house would interfere. Although such a requirement, constituting a permanent grant of continuous access to the property, would have to be considered a taking if it were not attached to a development permit, the Commission's assumed power to forbid construction of the house in order to protect the public's view of the beach must surely include the power to condition construction upon some concession by the owner, even a concession of property rights, that serves the same end. If a prohibition designed to accomplish that purpose would be a legitimate exercise of the police power rather than a taking, it would be strange to conclude that providing the owner an alternative to that prohibition which accomplishes the same purpose is not.

The evident constitutional propriety disappears, however, if the condition substituted for the prohibition utterly fails to further the end advanced as the justification for the prohibition. When that essential nexus is eliminated, the situation becomes the same as if California law forbade shouting fire in a crowded theater, but granted dispensations to those willing to contribute $100 to the state treasury. While a ban on shouting fire can be a core exercise of the State's police power to protect the public safety, and can thus meet even our stringent standards for regulation of speech, adding the unrelated condition alters the purpose to one which, while it may be legitimate, is inadequate to sustain the ban. Therefore, even though, in a sense, requiring a $100 tax contribution in order to shout fire is a lesser restriction on speech than an outright ban, it would not pass constitutional muster. Similarly here, the lack of nexus between the condition and the original purpose of the building restriction converts that purpose to something other than what it was. The purpose then becomes, quite simply, the obtaining of an easement to serve some valid governmental purpose, but without payment of compensation. Whatever may be the outer limits of "legitimate state interests" in the takings and land-use context, this is not one of them. In short, unless the permit condition serves the same governmental purpose as development ban, the building restriction is not a valid regulation of land use but "an out-and-out plan of extortion." *J.E.D. Associates, Inc. v. Atkinson.* . . .

The Commission claims that it concedes as much, and that we may sustain the condition at issue here by finding that it is reasonably related to the public need or burden that the Nollans' new house creates or to which it contributes. We can accept, for purposes of discussion, the Commission's proposed test as to how close a "fit" between the condition and the burden is required, because we find that this case does not meet even the most untailored standards. . . .

It is quite impossible to understand how a requirement that people already on the public beaches be able to walk across the Nollans' property reduces any obstacles to viewing the beach created by the new house. It is also impossible to understand how it lowers any "psychological barrier" to using the public beaches, or how it helps to remedy any additional congestion on them caused by construction of the Nollans' new house. We therefore find that the Commission's imposition of the permit condition cannot be treated as an exercise of its land-use power for any of these purposes. Our conclusion on this point is consistent with the approach taken by every other court that has considered the question, with the exception of the California state courts. . . .

As indicated earlier, our cases describe the condition for abridgement of property rights through the police power as a "substantial advancing" of a legitimate state interest. We are inclined to be particularly careful about the adjective where the actual conveyance of property is made a condition to the lifting of a land-use restriction, since in that context there is heightened risk that the purpose is avoidance of the compensation requirement, rather than the stated police-power objective. . . .

Reversed.

Justice BRENNAN, with whom Justice MARSHALL joins, dissenting:

. . . The Court's conclusion that the permit condition imposed on appellants is unreasonable cannot withstand analysis. First, the Court demands a degree of exactitude that is inconsistent with our standard for reviewing the rationality of a State's exercise of its police power for the welfare of its citizens. Second, even if the nature of the public-access condition imposed must be identical to the precise burden on access created by appellants, this requirement is plainly satisfied.

There can be no dispute that the police power of the States encompasses the authority to impose conditions on private development. . . . The Coastal Commission, if it had so chosen, could have denied the Nollans' request for a development permit, since the property would have remained economically viable without the requested new development. Instead, the State sought to accommodate the Nollans' desire for new development, on the condition that the development not diminish the overall amount of public access to the coastline. . . .

The Court finds fault with this measure because it regards the condition as insufficiently tailored to address the precise type of reduction in access produced by the new development. . . . Such a narrow conception of rationality, however, has long since been discredited as a judicial arrogation of legislative authority. "To make scientific precision a criterion of constitutional power would be to subject the State to an intolerable supervision hostile to the basic principles of our Government." *Sproles v. Binford* (1932). . . .

Even if we accept the Court's unusual demand for a precise match between the condition imposed and the specific type of burden on access created by the appellants, the State's action easily satisfies this requirement. First, the lateral access condition serves to dissipate the impression that the beach that lies behind the wall of homes along the shore is for private use only. It requires no exceptional imaginative powers to find plausible the Commission's point that the average person passing along the road in front of a phalanx of imposing permanent residences, including the appellants' new home, is likely to conclude that this particular portion of the shore is not open to the public. . . . The burden produced by the diminution in visual access—the impression that the beach is not open to the public—is thus directly alleviated by the provision for public access over the dry sand. The Court therefore has an unrealistically limited conception of what measures could reasonably be chosen to mitigate the burden produced by a diminution of visual access.

The second flaw in the Court's analysis of the fit between burden and exaction is more fundamental. The Court assumes that the only burden with which the Coastal Commission was concerned was blockage of visual access to the beach. This is incorrect. The Commission specifically stated in its report in support of the permit condition that "[t]he Commission finds that the applicants' proposed development would present an increase in view blockage, *an increase in private use of the shorefront,* and that this impact would burden the public's ability to traverse to and along the shorefront." (emphasis added). It declared that the possibility that "the public may get the impression that the beachfront is no longer available for public use" would be "due to *the encroaching nature of private use immediately adjacent to the public use, as well as* the visual 'block' of increased residential build-out impacting the visual quality of the beachfront." (emphasis added). . . .

Finally, the character of the regulation in this case is not unilateral government action, but a condition on approval of a development request submitted by appellants. The State has not sought to interfere with any pre-existing property interest, but has responded to appellants' proposal to intensify development on the coast. . . .

Examination of the economic impact of the Commission's action reinforces the conclusion that no taking has occurred. . . . Appellants have been allowed to replace a one-story, 521-square-foot beach home with a two-story, 1,674-square-foot residence and an attached two-car garage, resulting in development covering 2,464 square feet of the lot. Such development obviously significantly increases the value of appellants' property; appellants make no contention that this increase is offset by any diminution in value resulting from the deed restriction, much less that the restriction made the property less valuable than it would have been without the new construction. Furthermore, appellants gain an additional benefit from the Commission's permit condition program. They are able to walk along the beach beyond the confines of their own property only because the Commission has required deed restrictions as a condition of approving other new beach developments. Thus, appellants benefit both as private landowners and as members of the public from the fact that new development permit requests are conditioned on preservation of public access. . . .

---

244 *Texas v. Johnson (1989)*

The American flag, like the emblems of all countries, carries profound emotional significance; it is the banner under which Americans have fought and died to preserve freedom. We salute it and pledge allegiance to it, and there is an extensive protocol for its handling, display, and disposal. It is not surprising, therefore, that many states had laws on the books prohibiting the desecration of the flag, either through defacing, burning, damaging, or generally treating the flag with disrespect. During the Vietnam War, a number of protesters were arrested under these statutes, but no case on this issue ever reached the high court for full argument; like the civil rights sit-in cases, the justices dismissed the convictions on technicalities without ever reaching the merits.

Gregory Lee Johnson had been arrested after burning an American flag at the Republican National Convention in Dallas in 1984. He claimed, and Texas state courts agreed, that his act had been one of political protest, and that the First Amendment protected symbolic as well as articulated speech. A bare majority of the justices agreed that the state could not make peaceful protest a crime, even where the focus of the protest was the flag.

The decision triggered an enormous public outcry, and Congress initially tried to fashion a constitutional amendment to overturn the Court's decision. Instead, it eventually passed a much narrower statute, which was in turn declared unconstitutional almost as soon as President Bush had signed the law (see Document 246).

See Frank I. Michelson, "Saving Old Glory: On Constitutional Iconography," 42 *Stanford Law Review* 1337 (1990); Kent Greenawalt, "O'er the Land of the Free: Flag Burning as Speech," 37 *UCLA Law Review* 925 (1990); Murray Dry, "Flag Burning and the Constitution," 1990 *Supreme Court Review* 69; and Michael Kent Curtis, *The Constitution and the Flag,* 2 vols. (1993)

Justice BRENNAN delivered the opinion of the Court:

After publicly burning an American flag as a means of political protest, Gregory Lee Johnson was convicted of desecrating a flag in violation of Texas law. This case presents the question whether his conviction is consistent with the First Amendment. We hold that it is not.

Johnson was convicted of flag desecration for burning the flag rather than for uttering insulting words. This fact somewhat complicates our consideration of his conviction under the First Amendment. We must first determine whether Johnson's burning of the flag constituted expressive conduct, permitting him to invoke the First Amendment in challenging his conviction. If his conduct was expressive, we next decide whether the State's regulation is related to the suppression of free expression. If the State's regulation is not related to expression, then the less stringent standard we announced in *United States v. O'Brien* for regulations of noncommunicative conduct controls. If it is, then we are outside of *O'Brien*'s test, and we must ask whether this interest justifies Johnson's conviction under a more demanding standard. A third possibility is that the State's asserted interest is simply not implicated on these facts, and in that event the interest drops out of the picture.

The First Amendment literally forbids the abridgement only of "speech," but we have long recognized that its protection does not end at the spoken or written word. While we have rejected "the view that an apparently limitless variety of conduct can be labeled 'speech' whenever the person engaging in the conduct intends thereby to express an idea," we have acknowledged that conduct may be "sufficiently imbued with elements of communication to fall within the scope of the First and Fourteenth Amendments."

In deciding whether particular conduct possesses sufficient communicative elements to bring the First Amendment into play, we have asked whether "an intent to convey a particularized message was present, and [whether] the likelihood was great that the message would be understood by those who viewed it." Hence, we have recognized the expressive nature of students' wearing of black armbands to protest American military involvement in Vietnam, *Tinker v. Des Moines Independent Community School Dist.*; of a sit-in by blacks in a "whites only" area to protest segregation, *Brown v. Louisiana;* of the wearing of American military uniforms in a dramatic presentation criticizing American involvement in Vietnam, *Schacht v. United States;* and of picketing about a wide variety of causes, see, e.g., *Food Employees v. Logan Valley Plaza, Inc.; United States v. Grace.*

Especially pertinent to this case are our decisions recognizing the communicative nature of conduct relating to flags. Attaching a peace sign to the flag, saluting the flag, and displaying a red flag, we have held, all may find shelter under the First Amendment. That we have had little difficulty identifying an expressive element in conduct relating to flags should not be surprising. The very purpose of a national flag is to serve as a symbol of our country; it is, one might say, "the one visible manifestation of two hundred years of nationhood." Thus, we have observed:

> The flag salute is a form of utterance. Symbolism is a primitive but effective way of communicating ideas. The use of an emblem or flag to symbolize some system, idea,

Source: 491 U.S. 397 (1989)

institution, or personality, is a short cut from mind to mind. Causes and nations, political parties, lodges and ecclesiastical groups seek to knit the loyalty of their followings to a flag or banner, a color or design.

Pregnant with expressive content, the flag as readily signifies this Nation as does the combination of letters found in "America."

We have not automatically concluded, however, that any action taken with respect to the flag is expressive. Instead, in characterizing such action for First Amendment purposes, we have considered the context in which it occurred. In [*Spence v. Washington*], for example, we emphasized that Spence's taping of a peace sign to his flag was "roughly simultaneous with and concededly triggered by the Cambodian incursion and the Kent State tragedy." The State of Washington had conceded, in fact, that Spence's conduct was a form of communication, and we stated that "the State's concession is inevitable on this record."

The State of Texas conceded for purposes of its oral argument in this case that Johnson's conduct was expressive conduct, and this concession seems to us as prudent as was Washington's in *Spence*. Johnson burned an American flag as part—indeed, as the culmination—of a political demonstration that coincided with the convening of the Republican Party and its renomination of Ronald Reagan for President. The expressive, overtly political nature of this conduct was both intentional and overwhelmingly apparent. At his trial, Johnson explained his reasons for burning the flag as follows: "The American Flag was burned as Ronald Reagan was being renominated as President. And a more powerful statement of symbolic speech, whether you agree with it or not, couldn't have been made at that time. It's quite a just position [juxtaposition]. We had new patriotism and no patriotism." In these circumstances, Johnson's burning of the flag was conduct "sufficiently imbued with elements of communication," to implicate the First Amendment.

The Government generally has a freer hand in restricting expressive conduct than it has in restricting the written or spoken word. It may not, however, proscribe particular conduct *because* it has expressive elements. "What might be termed the more generalized guarantee of freedom of expression makes the communicative nature of conduct an inadequate *basis* for singling out that conduct for proscription. A law *directed at* the communicative nature of conduct must, like a law directed at speech itself, be justified by the substantial showing of need that the First Amendment requires." It is, in short, not simply the verbal or nonverbal nature of the expression, but the governmental interest at stake, that helps to determine whether a restriction on that expression is valid.

Thus, although we have recognized that where " 'speech' and 'nonspeech' elements are combined in the same course of conduct, a sufficiently important governmental interest in regulating the nonspeech element can justify incidental limitations on First Amendment freedoms," we have limited the applicability of *O'Brien's* relatively lenient standard to those cases in which "the governmental interest is unrelated to the suppression of free expression." In stating, moreover, that *O'Brien's* test "in the last analysis is little, if any, different from the standard applied to time, place, or manner restrictions," we have highlighted the requirement that the governmental interest in question be unconnected to expression in order to come under *O'Brien's* less demanding rule.

In order to decide whether *O'Brien's* test applies here, therefore, we must decide whether Texas has asserted an interest in support of Johnson's conviction that is unrelated to the suppression of expression. If we find that an interest asserted by the State is simply not implicated on the facts before us, we need not ask whether *O'Brien's* test applies. The State offers two separate interests to justify this conviction: preventing breaches of the peace, and preserving the flag as a symbol of nationhood and national unity. We hold that the first interest is not implicated on this record and that the second is related to the suppression of expression.

Texas claims that its interest in preventing the breaches of the peace justifies Johnson's conviction for flag desecration. However, no disturbance of the peace actually occurred or threatened to occur because of Johnson's burning of the flag. Although the State stresses the disruptive behavior of the protestors during their march toward City Hall, it admits that "no actual breach of the peace occurred at the time of the flagburning or in response to the flagburning." The State's emphasis on the protestors' disorderly actions prior to arriving at City Hall is not only somewhat surprising given that no charges were brought on the basis of this conduct, but it also fails to show that a disturbance of the peace was a likely reaction to *Johnson's* conduct. The only evidence offered by the State at trial to show the reaction to Johnson's actions was the testimony of several persons who had been seriously offended by the flag-burning.

The State's position, therefore, amounts to a claim that an audience that takes serious offense at particular expression is necessarily likely to disturb the peace and that the expression may be prohibited on this basis. Our precedents do not countenance such a presumption. On the contrary, they recognize that a principal "function of free speech under our system of government is to invite dispute. It may indeed best serve its high purpose when it induces a condition of unrest, creates dissatisfaction with conditions as they are, or even stirs people to anger." It would be odd indeed to conclude *both* that "if it is the speaker's opinion that gives offense, that consequence is a reason for according it constitutional protection," *and* that the Government may ban the expression of certain disagreeable ideas on the unsupported presumption that their very disagreeableness will provoke violence.

Thus, we have not permitted the Government to assume that every expression of a provocative idea will incite a riot, but have instead required careful consideration of the actual circumstances surrounding such expression, asking whether the expression "is directed to inciting or producing imminent lawless action and is likely to incite or produce such action." To accept Texas' arguments that it need only demonstrate "the potential for the breach of the peace," and that every flag-burning necessarily possesses that potential, would be to eviscerate our holding in *Brandenburg [v. Ohio]*. This we decline to do.

Nor does Johnson's expressive conduct fall within that small class of "fighting words" that are "likely to provoke the average person to retaliation, and thereby cause a breach of the peace." No reasonable onlooker would have regarded Johnson's generalized expression of dissatisfaction with the policies of the Federal Government as a direct personal insult or an invitation to exchange fisticuffs.

We thus conclude that the State's interest in maintaining order is not implicated on these facts. The State need not worry that our holding will disable it from preserving the peace. We do not suggest that the First Amendment forbids a State to prevent "imminent lawless action." And, in fact, Texas already has a statute specifically prohibiting breaches of the peace, which tends to confirm that Texas need not punish this flag desecration in order to keep the peace.

The State also asserts an interest in preserving the flag as a symbol of nationhood and national unity. In *Spence,* we acknowledged that the Government's interest in preserving the flag's special symbolic value "is directly related to expression in the context of activity" such as affixing a peace symbol to a flag. We are equally persuaded that this interest is related to expression in the case of Johnson's burning of the flag. The State, apparently, is concerned that such conduct will lead people to believe either that the flag does not stand for nationhood and national unity, but instead reflects other, less positive concepts, or that the concepts reflected in the flag do not in fact exist, that is, we do not enjoy unity as a Nation. These concerns blossom only when a person's treatment of the flag communicates some message, and thus are related "to the suppression of free expression" within the meaning of *O'Brien.* We are thus outside of *O'Brien*'s test altogether.

It remains to consider whether the State's interest in preserving the flag as a symbol of nationhood and national unity justifies Johnson's conviction.

As in *Spence,* "we are confronted with a case of prosecution for the expression of an idea through activity," and "accordingly, we must examine with particular care the interests advanced by [petitioner] to support its prosecution." Johnson was not, we add, prosecuted for the expression of just any idea; he was prosecuted for his expression of dissatisfaction with the policies of this country, expression situated at the core of our First Amendment values.

Moreover, Johnson was prosecuted because he knew that his politically charged expression would cause "serious offense." If he had burned the flag as a means of disposing of it because it was dirty or torn, he would not have been convicted of flag desecration under this Texas law: federal law designates burning as the preferred means of disposing of a flag "when it is in such condition that it is no longer a fitting emblem for display," and Texas has no quarrel with this means of disposal. The Texas law is thus not aimed at protecting the physical integrity of the flag in all circumstances, but is designed instead to protect it only against impairments that would cause serious offense to others. Texas concedes as much: "Section 42.09(b) reaches only those severe acts of physical abuse of the flag carried out in way likely to be offensive. The statute mandates intentional or knowing abuse, that is, the kind of mistreatment that is not innocent, but rather is intentionally designed to seriously offend other individuals."

If there is a bedrock principle underlying the First Amendment, it is that the Government may not prohibit the expression of an idea simply because society finds the idea itself offensive or disagreeable.

We have not recognized an exception to this principle even where our flag has been involved. In *Street v. New York* (1969), we held that a State may not criminally punish a person for uttering words critical of the flag. Rejecting the argument that the conviction could be sustained on the ground that Street had "failed to show the respect for our national symbol which may properly be demanded of every citizen," we concluded that "the constitutionally guaranteed 'freedom to be intellectually . . . diverse or even contrary,' and the 'right to differ as to things that touch the heart of the existing order,' encompass the freedom to express publicly one's opinion about our flag, including those opinions which are defiant or contemptuous." Nor may the Government, we have held, compel conduct that would evince respect for the flag. "To sustain the compulsory flag salute we are required to say that a Bill of Rights which guards the individual's right to speak his own mind, left it open to public authorities to compel him to utter what is not in his mind."

It is not the State's ends, but its means, to which we object. It cannot be gainsaid that there is a special place reserved for the flag in this Nation, and thus we do not doubt that the Government has a legitimate interest in making efforts to "preserve the national flag as an unalloyed symbol for our country." We reject the suggestion, urged at oral argument by counsel for Johnson, that the Government lacks "any state interest whatsoever" in regulating the manner in which the flag may be displayed. Congress has, for example, enacted precatory regulations describing the proper treatment of the flag, and we cast no doubt on the legitimacy of its interest in making such recommendations. To say that the Government has an interest in encouraging proper treatment for the flag, however, is not to say that it may criminally punish a person for burning a flag as a means of political protest. "National unity as an end which officials may foster by persuasion and example is not in question. The problem is whether under our Constitution compulsion as here employed is a permissible means for its achievement."

We are fortified in today's conclusion by our conviction that forbidding criminal punishment for conduct such as Johnson's will not endanger the special role played by our flag or the feelings it inspires. To paraphrase Justice Holmes, we submit that nobody can suppose that this one gesture of an unknown man will change our Nation's attitude towards its flag. Indeed, Texas' argument that the burning of an American flag "is an act having a high likelihood to cause a breach of the peace," and its statute's implicit assumption that physical mistreatment of the flag will lead to "serious offense," tend to confirm that the flag's special role is not in danger; if it were, no one would riot or take offense because a flag had been burned.

We are tempted to say, in fact, that the flag's deservedly cherished place in our community will be strengthened, not weakened, by our holding today. Our decision is a reaffirmation of the principles of freedom and inclusiveness that the flag best reflects, and of the conviction that our toleration of criticism such as Johnson's is a sign and source of our strength. Indeed, one of the proudest images of our flag, the one immortalized in our own national anthem, is of the bombardment it survived at Fort McHenry. It is the Nation's resilience, not its rigidity, that Texas sees reflected in the flag—and it is that resilience that we reassert today.

The way to preserve the flag's special role is not to punish those who feel differently about these matters. It is to persuade them that they are wrong. "To courageous, self-reliant men, with confidence in the power of free and fearless reasoning applied through the processes or popular government, no danger flowing from speech can be deemed clear and present, unless the incidence of the evil apprehended is so imminent that it may befall before there is opportunity for full discussion. If there be time to expose through discussion the falsehood and fallacies, to avert the evil by the processes of education, the remedy to be applied is more speech, not enforced silence." And, precisely because it is our flag that is involved, one's response to the flag-burner may exploit the uniquely persuasive power of the flag itself. We can imagine no more appropriate response to burning a flag than waving one's own, no better way to counter a flag-burner's message than by saluting the flag that burns, no surer means of preserving the dignity even of the flag that burned than by—as one witness here did—according its remains a respectful burial. We do not consecrate the flag by punishing its desecration, for in doing so we dilute the freedom that this cherished emblem represents.

Johnson was convicted for engaging in expressive conduct. The State's interest in preventing breaches of the peace does not support his conviction because Johnson's con-

duct did not threaten to disturb the peace. Nor does the State's interest in preserving the flag as a symbol of nationhood and national unity justify his criminal conviction for engaging in political expression. The judgment of the Texas Court of Criminal Appeals is therefore
Affirmed.

Justice KENNEDY, concurring:

I write not to qualify the words Justice Brennan chooses so well, for he says with power all that is necessary to explain our ruling. I join his opinion without reservation, but with a keen sense that this case, like others before us from time to time, exacts its personal toll. This prompts me to add to our pages these few remarks.

The case before us illustrates better than most that the judicial power is often difficult in its exercise. We cannot here ask another branch to share responsibility, as when the argument is made that a statute is flawed or incomplete. For we are presented with a clear and simple statute to be judged against a pure command of the Constitution. The outcome can be laid at no door but ours.

The hard fact is that sometimes we must make decisions we do not like. We make them because they are right, right in the sense that the law and the Constitution, as we see them, compel the result. And so great is our commitment to the process that, except in the rare case, we do not pause to express distaste for the result, perhaps for fear of undermining a valued principle that dictates the decision. This is one of those rare cases.

Our colleagues in dissent advance powerful arguments why respondent may be convicted for his expression, reminding us that among those who will be dismayed by our holding will be some who have had the singular honor of carrying the flag in battle. And I agree that the flag holds a lonely place of honor in an age when absolutes are distrusted and simple truths are burdened by unneeded apologetics.

With all respect to those views, I do not believe the Constitution gives us the right to rule as the dissenting members of the Court urge, however painful this judgment is to announce. Though symbols often are what we ourselves make of them, the flag is constant in expressing beliefs Americans share, beliefs in law and peace and that freedom which sustains the human spirit. The case here today forces recognition of the costs to which those beliefs commit us. It is poignant but fundamental that the flag protects those who hold it in contempt.

For all the record shows, this respondent was not a philosopher and perhaps did not even possess the ability to comprehend how repellent his statements must be to the Republic itself. But whether or not he could appreciate the enormity of the offense he gave, the fact remains that his acts were speech, in both the technical and the fundamental meaning of the Constitution. So I agree with the Court that he must go free.

Chief Justice REHNQUIST, with whom Justice WHITE and Justice O'CONNOR join, dissenting:

In holding this Texas statute unconstitutional, the Court ignores Justice Holmes' familiar aphorism that "a page of history is worth a volume of logic." *New York Trust Co. v. Eisner,* (1921). For more than 200 years, the American flag has occupied a unique position as the symbol of our Nation, a uniqueness that justifies a governmental prohibition against flag burning in the way respondent Johnson did here.

The American flag, then, throughout more than 200 years of our history, has come to be the visible symbol embodying our Nation. It does not represent the views of any particular political party, and it does not represent any particular political philosophy. The flag is not simply another "idea" or "point of view" competing for recognition in the marketplace of ideas. Millions and millions of Americans regard it with an almost mystical reverence regardless of what sort of social, political, or philosophical beliefs they may have. I cannot agree that the First Amendment invalidates the Act of Congress, and the laws of 48 of the 50 States, which make criminal the public burning of the flag.

Here it may equally well be said that the public burning of the American flag by Johnson was no essential part of any exposition of ideas, and at the same time it had a tendency to incite a breach of the peace. Johnson was free to make any verbal denunciation of the flag that he wished; indeed, he was free to burn the flag in private. He could publicly burn other symbols of the Government or effigies of political leaders. He did lead a march through the streets of Dallas, and conducted a rally in front of the Dallas City Hall. He engaged in a "die-in" to protest nuclear weapons. He shouted out various slogans during the march including: "Reagan, Mondale, which will it be? Either one means World War III"; "Ronald Reagan, killer of the hour, Perfect example of U.S. power"; and "red, white and blue, we spit on you, you stand for plunder, you will go under." For none of these acts was he arrested or prosecuted; it was only when he proceeded to burn publicly an American flag stolen from its rightful owner that he violated the Texas statute.

The Court concludes its opinion with a regrettably patronizing civics lecture, presumably addressed to the Members of both Houses of Congress, the members of the 48 state legislatures that enacted prohibitions against flag burning, and the troops fighting under the flag in Vietnam who objected to its being burned: "The way to preserve the flag's special role is not to punish those who feel differently about these matters. It is to persuade them that they are wrong." The Court's role as the final expositor of the Constitution is well established, but its role as a platonic guardian admonishing those responsible to public opinion as if they were truant school children has no similar place in our system of government. The cry of "no taxation without representation" animated those who revolted against the English Crown to found our Nation—the idea that those who submitted to government should have some say as to what kind of laws would be passed. Surely one of the high purposes of a democratic society is to legislate against conduct that is regarded as evil and profoundly offensive to the majority of the people—whether it be murder, embezzlement, pollution, or flag burning.

Our Constitution wisely places limits on the powers of legislative majorities to act, but the declaration of such limits by this Court, "is, at all times, a question of much delicacy, which ought seldom, if ever, to be decided in the affirmative, in a doubtful case." *Fletcher v. Peck* (1810) (Marshall, C.J.) Uncritical extension of constitutional protection to the burning of the flag risks the frustration of the very purpose for which organized governments are instituted. The Court decides that the American flag is just another symbol, about which not only must opinions pro and con be tolerated, but for which the most minimal public respect may not be enjoined. The government may conscript men into the Armed Forces where they must fight and perhaps die for the flag, but the government may not prohibit the public burning of the banner under which they fight. I would uphold the Texas statute as applied in this case.

245

City of Richmond v. J.A. Croson Company (1989)

Affirmative action has been a major flashpoint in the civil rights debate. How much preference, if any, should society provide groups that historically have been the victims of discrimination in order to help them compete in the future on an equal basis. Both Congress and the executive branch have adopted various programs incorporating preferences for minorities, and in many instances these became the models for state and local affirmative action programs.

Beginning with *Bakke* (Document 233), the Court upheld the idea of affirmative action, although it ruled some programs impermissible under the Equal Protection Clause. But in a major 1981 decision, *Fullilove v. Klutznik,* the justices had approved a congressionally mandated set-aside program, in which a certain percentage of contracts in federally financed programs had to be reserved for minority contractors, which Congress defined with some specificity.

The black majority city council in Richmond, Virginia (a predominantly black city), established a set-aside program and adopted the same definitions of minorities as had Congress. The Croson Company tried diligently to find a minority contractor to work with, but none could meet the city's bonding requirements. When Croson informed the city of this, the council decided to rebid a contract initially awarded to Croson, and the company went into federal court.

The decision in the case has often been misinterpreted. The Court did not find all affirmative action programs unconstitutional, but rather declared that there had to be sufficient evidence of past discrimination in order to justify set-asides. The city council had in fact drawn a sloppy proposal, and could not document the discrimination. The Court also drew a sharp distinction between Congress, which had enforcement powers under the Fourteenth Amendment, and state and local governments which did not.

See Paul Brest et al., "Constitutional Scholars' Statement on Affirmative Action After *Croson,*" 98 *Yale Law Journal* 1711 (1989); Ronald J. Fiscus, *The Constitutional Logic of Affirmative Action* (1992); and Melvin I. Urofsky, "Richmond v. J.A. Croson Company," in A. E. Dick Howard and Melvin I. Urofsky, eds., *Virginia and the Constitution* (1992), 192–207.

———

Justice O'CONNOR announced the judgment of the Court:

In this case, we confront once again the tension between the Fourteenth Amend-

Source: 488 U.S. 469 (1989)

ment's guarantee of equal treatment to all citizens, and the use of race-based measures to ameliorate the effects of past discrimination on the opportunities enjoyed by members of minority groups in our society. In *Fullilove v. Klutznick* (1980), we held that a congressional program requiring that 10% of certain federal construction grants be awarded to minority contractors did not violate the equal protection principles embodied in the Due Process Clause of the Fifth Amendment. Relying largely on our decision in *Fullilove,* some lower federal courts have applied a similar standard of review in assessing the constitutionality of state and local minority set-aside provisions under the Equal Protection Clause of the Fourteenth Amendment. Since our decision two Terms ago in *Wygant v. Jackson Board of Education* (1986), the lower federal courts have attempted to apply its standards in evaluating the constitutionality of state and local programs which allocate a portion of public contracting opportunities exclusively to minority-owned businesses. We noted probable jurisdiction in this case to consider the applicability of our decision in *Wygant* to a minority set-aside program adopted by the city of Richmond, Virginia.

On April 11, 1983, the Richmond City Council adopted the Minority Business Utilization Plan (the Plan). The Plan required prime contractors to whom the city awarded construction contracts to subcontract at least 30% of the dollar amount of the contract to one or more Minority Business Enterprises (MBEs). The 30% set-aside did not apply to city contracts awarded to minority-owned prime contractors.

The Plan defined an MBE as "a business at least fifty-one (51) percent of which is owned and controlled . . . by minority group members." "Minority group members" were defined as "citizens of the United States who are Blacks, Spanish-speaking, Orientals, Indians, Eskimos, or Aleuts." There was no geographic limit to the Plan; an otherwise qualified MBE from anywhere in the United States could avail itself of the 30% set-aside. The Plan declared that it was "remedial" in nature, and enacted "for the purpose of promoting wider participation by minority business enterprises in the construction of public projects." The Plan expired on June 30, 1988, and was in effect for approximately five years.

The Plan authorized the Director of the Department of General Services to promulgate rules which "shall allow waivers in those individual situations where a contractor can prove to the satisfaction of the director that the requirements herein cannot be achieved." To this end, the Director promulgated Contract Clauses, Minority Business Utilization Plan. . . .

Opponents of the ordinance questioned both its wisdom and its legality. They argued that a disparity between minorities in the population of Richmond and the number of prime contracts awarded to MBEs had little probative value in establishing discrimination in the construction industry. Representatives of various contractors' associations questioned whether there were enough MBEs in the Richmond area to satisfy the 30% set-aside requirement. Mr. Murphy noted that only 4.7% of all construction firms in the United States were minority owned and that 41% of these were located in California, New York, Illinois, Florida, and Hawaii. He predicted that the ordinance would thus lead to a windfall for the few minority firms in Richmond.

The parties and their supporting *amici* fight an initial battle over the scope of the city's power to adopt legislation designed to address the effects of past discrimination. Relying on our decision in *Wygant,* appellee argues that the city must limit any race-based remedial efforts to eradicating the effects of its own prior discrimination. This is essentially the position taken by the Court of Appeals below. Appellant argues that our decision in *Fullilove* is controlling, and that as a result the city of Richmond enjoys sweeping legislative power to define and attack the effects of prior discrimination in its local construction industry. We find that neither of these two rather stark alternatives can withstand analysis.

In *Fullilove,* we upheld the minority set-aside contained in the Public Works Employment Act of 1977 against a challenge based on the equal protection component of the Due Process Clause. The Act authorized a four billion dollar appropriation for federal grants to state and local governments for use in public works projects. The primary purpose of the Act was to give the national economy a quick boost in a recessionary period; funds had to be committed to state or local grantees by September 30, 1977. The Act also contained the following requirement: "Except to the extent the Secretary determines otherwise, no grant shall be made under this Act . . . unless the applicant gives satisfactory assurance to the Secretary that at least 10 per centum of the amount of each grant shall be expended for minority business enterprises." MBEs were defined as businesses effectively controlled by "citizens of the United States who are Negroes, Spanish-speaking, Orientals, Indians, Eskimos, and Aleuts."

The principal opinion in *Fullilove,* written by Chief Justice Burger, did not employ "strict scrutiny" or any other traditional standard of equal protection review. The Chief Justice noted at the outset that although racial classifications call for close examination, the Court was at the same time, "bound to approach [its] task with appropriate deference to the Congress, a co-equal branch charged by the Constitution with the power to 'provide for the . . . general Welfare of the United States' and 'to enforce by appropriate legislation,' the equal protection guarantees of the Fourteenth Amendment."

Appellant and its supporting *amici* rely heavily on *Fullilove* for the proposition that a city council, like Congress, need not make specific findings of discrimination to engage in race-conscious relief. Thus, appellant argues "it would be a perversion of federalism to hold that the federal government has a compelling interest in remedying the effects of racial discrimination in its own public works program, but a city government does not."

What appellant ignores is that Congress, unlike any State or political subdivision, has a specific constitutional mandate to enforce the dictates of the Fourteenth Amendment. The power to "enforce" may at times also include the power to define situations which *Congress* determines threatened principles of equality and to adopt prophylactic rules to deal with those situations. The Civil War Amendments themselves worked a dramatic change in the balance between congressional and state power over matters of race. Speaking of the Thirteenth and Fourteenth Amendments in *Ex Parte Virginia* (1880), the Court stated: "They were intended to be, what they really are, limitations of the powers of the States and enlargements of the power of Congress."

That Congress may identify and redress the effects of society-wide discrimination does not mean that, *a fortiori,* the States and their political subdivisions are free to decide that such remedies are appropriate. Section 1, of the Fourteenth Amendment is an explicit *constraint* on state power, and the States must undertake any remedial efforts in accordance with that provision. To hold otherwise would be to cede control over the content of the Equal Protection Clause to the 50 state legislatures and their myriad political subdivisions. The mere recitation of a benign or compensatory purpose for the use of a racial classification would essentially entitle the States to exercise the full power of Congress under § 5 of the Fourteenth Amendment and insulate any racial classification from judicial scrutiny under § 1. We believe that such a result would be contrary to the intentions of the Framers of the Fourteenth Amendment, who desired to place clear limits on the States' use of race as a criterion for legislative action, and to have the federal courts enforce those limitations.

The Equal Protection Clause of the Fourteenth Amendment provides that "No state shall . . . deny to *any person* within its jurisdiction the equal protection of laws" (emphasis added). As this Court has noted in the past, the "rights created by the first section of the Fourteenth Amendment are, by its terms, guaranteed to the individual. The rights established are personal rights." The Richmond Plan denies certain citizens the opportunity to compete for a fixed percentage of public contracts bases solely upon their race. To whatever racial group these citizens belong, their "personal rights" to be treated with equal dignity and respect are implicated by a rigid rule erecting race as the sole criterion in an aspect of public decisionmaking.

Appellant argues that it is attempting to remedy various forms of past discrimination that are alleged to be responsible for the small number of minority businesses in the local contracting industry. Among these the city cites the exclusion of blacks from skilled construction trade unions and training programs. This past discrimination has prevented them "from following the traditional path from laborer to entrepreneur." The city also lists a host of nonracial factors which would seem to face a member of any racial group attempting to establish a new business enterprise, such as deficiencies in working capital, inability to meet bonding requirements, unfamiliarity with bidding procedures, and disability caused by an inadequate track record.

While there is no doubt that the sorry history of both private and public discrimination in this country has contributed to a lack of opportunities for black entrepreneurs, this observation, standing alone, cannot justify a rigid racial quota in the awarding of public contracts in Richmond, Virginia. Like the claim that discrimination in primary and secondary schooling justifies a rigid racial preference in medical school admissions, an amorphous claim that there has been past discrimination in a particular industry cannot justify the use of an unyielding racial quota.

It is sheer speculation how many minority firms there would be in Richmond absent past societal discrimination, just as it was sheer speculation how many minority medical students would have been admitted to the medical school at Davis absent past discrimination in educational opportunities. Defining these sorts of injuries as "identified discrimination" would give local governments license to create a patchwork of racial preferences based on statistical generalizations about any particular field of endeavor.

Reliance on the disparity between the number of prime contracts awarded to minority firms and the minority population of the city of Richmond is similarly misplaced. There is no doubt that "where gross statistical disparities can be shown, they alone in a proper case may constitute prima facie proof of a pattern or practice of discrimination" under Title VII. But it is equally clear that "when special qualifications are required to fill particular jobs, comparisons to the general population (rather than to the smaller group of individuals who possess the necessary qualifications) may have little probative value."

In the employment context, we have recognized that for certain entry level positions requiring minimal training, statistical comparisons of the racial composition of an employer's workforce to the racial composition of the relevant population may be probative of a pattern of discrimination. But where special qualifications are necessary, the relevant statistical pool for purposes of demonstrating discriminatory exclusion must be the number of minorities qualified to undertake the particular task.

In this case, the city does not even know how many MBEs in the relevant market are qualified to undertake prime or subcontracting work in public construction projects. Nor does the city know what percentage of total city construction dollars minority firms now receive as subcontractors on prime contracts let by the city.

To a large extent, the set-aside of subcontracting dollars seems to rest on the unsupported assumption that white prime contractors simply will not hire minority firms. Indeed, there is evidence in this record that overall minority participation in city contracts in Richmond is seven to eight percent, and that minority contractor participation in Community Block Development Grant *construction* projects is 17% to 22%. Without any information on minority participation in subcontracting, it is quite simply impossible to evaluate overall minority representation in the city's construction expenditures. . . .

In sum, none of the evidence presented by the city points to any identified discrimination in the Richmond construction industry. We, therefore, hold that the city has failed to demonstrate a compelling interest in apportioning public contracting opportunities on the basis of race. To accept Richmond's claim that past societal discrimination alone can serve as the basis for rigid racial preferences would be to open the door to competing claims for "remedial relief" for every disadvantaged group. The dream of a Nation of equal citizens in a society where race is irrelevant to personal opportunity and achievement would be lost in a mosaic of shifting preferences based on inherently unmeasurable claims of past wrongs. "Courts would be asked to evaluate the extent of the prejudice and consequent harm suffered by various minority groups. Those whose societal injury is thought to exceed some arbitrary level of tolerablity then would be entitled to preferential classifications. . . ." We think such a result would be contrary to both the letter and spirit of a constitutional provision whose central command is equality.

The foregoing analysis applies only to the inclusion of blacks within the Richmond set-aside program. There is *absolutely no evidence* of past discrimination against Spanish-speaking, Oriental, Indian, Eskimo, or Aleut persons in any aspect of the Richmond construction industry. The District Court took judicial notice of the fact that the vast majority of "minority" persons in Richmond were black. It may well be that Richmond has never had an Aleut or Eskimo citizen. The random inclusion of racial groups that, as a practical matter, may never have suffered from discrimination in the construction industry in Richmond, suggests that perhaps the city's purpose was not in fact to remedy past discrimination.

Because the city of Richmond has failed to identify the need for remedial action in the awarding of its public construction contracts, its treatment of its citizens on a racial basis violates the dictates of the Equal Protection Clause. Accordingly, the judgment of the Court of Appeals for the Fourth Circuit is

AFFIRMED.

Justices BRENNAN, MARSHALL and BLACKMUN dissented.

---

246   *United States v. Eichman (1990)*

Following the decision in *Texas v. Johnson* (Document 244), Congress passed a law that it hoped would prove constitutional on the grounds that the federal government had national powers more suited to the protection of the flag. The Court found the same First Amendment objections.

See readings at Document 244, and Douglas W. Kmiec, "In the Aftermath of Johnson and Eichman," 90 *Brigham Young University Law Review* 577 (1990).

———

Justice BRENNAN delivered the opinion of the Court:

After our decision in *Johnson,* Congress passed the Flag Protection Act of 1989. The Act provides in relevant part:

(a)(1) Whoever knowingly mutilates, defaces, physically defiles, burns, maintains on the floor or ground, or tramples upon any flag of the United States shall be fined under this title or imprisoned for not more than one year, or both.

(2) This subsection does not prohibit any conduct consisting of the disposal of a flag when it has become worn or soiled.

(b) As used in this section, the term 'flag of the United States' means any flag of the United States, or any part thereof, made of any substance, of any size, in a form that is commonly displayed.

The Government concedes in this case, as it must, that appellees' flag-burning constituted expressive conduct; but invites us to reconsider our rejection in *Johnson* of the claim that flag-burning as a mode of expression, like obscenity or "fighting words," does not enjoy the full protection of the First Amendment. This we decline to do. The only remaining question is whether the Flag Protection Act is sufficiently distinct from the

Source: 496 U.S. 310 (1990)

Texas statute that it may constitutionally be applied to proscribe appellees' expressive conduct.

The Government contends that the Flag Protection Act is constitutional because, unlike the statute addressed in *Johnson,* the Act does not target expressive conduct on the basis of the content of its message. The Government asserts an interest in "protecting the physical integrity of the flag under all circumstances" in order to safeguard the flag's identity "'as the unique and unalloyed symbol of the Nation.'" The Act proscribes conduct (other than disposal) that damages or mistreats the flag, without regard to the actor's motive, his intended message, or the likely effects of his conduct on onlookers. By contrast, the Texas statute expressly prohibited only those acts of physical flag desecration "that the actor knows will seriously offend" onlookers, and the former federal statute prohibited only those acts of desecration that "cast contempt upon" the flag.

Although the Flag Protection Act contains no explicit content-based limitation on the scope of prohibited conduct, it is nevertheless clear that the Government's asserted *interest* is "related 'to the suppression of free expression,'" and concerned with the content of such expression. The Government's interest in protecting the "physical integrity" of a privately owned flag rests upon the perceived need to preserve the flag's status as a symbol of our Nation and certain national ideals. But the mere destruction or disfigurement of a particular physical manifestation of the symbol, without more, does not diminish or otherwise affect the symbol itself in any way. For example, the secret destruction of a flag in one's basement would not threaten the flag's recognized meaning. Rather, the Government's desire to preserve the flag as a symbol for certain national ideals is implicated "only when a person's treatment of the flag communicates [a] message" to others that is inconsistent with those ideals.

Moreover, the precise language of the Act's prohibitions confirms Congress' interest in the communicative impact of flag destruction. The Act criminalizes the conduct of anyone who "knowingly mutilates, defaces, physically defiles, burns, maintains on the floor or ground, or tramples upon any flag." Each of the specified terms—with the possible exception of "burns"—unmistakably connotes disrespectful treatment of the flag and suggests a focus on those acts likely to damage the flag's symbolic value. And the explicit exemption for disposal of "worn or soiled" flags protects certain acts traditionally associated with patriotic respect for the flag.

As we explained in *Johnson:* "If we were to hold that a State may forbid flag-burning wherever it is likely to endanger the flag's symbolic role—as where, for example, a person ceremoniously burns a dirty flag—we would be . . . permitting a State to 'prescribe what shall be orthodox' by saying that one may burn the flag to convey one's attitude toward it and its referents only if one does not endanger the flag's representation of nationhood and national unity." Although Congress cast the Flag Protection Act in somewhat broader terms than the Texas statute at issue in *Johnson,* the Act still suffers from the same fundamental flaw: it suppresses expression out of concern for its likely communicative impact. Despite the Act's wider scope, its restriction on expression cannot be "'justified without reference to the content of the regulated speech.'" (State's interest in protecting flag's symbolic value is directly related to suppression of expression and thus *O'Brien* test is inapplicable even where statute declared "simply . . . that *nothing* may be affixed or superimposed on a United States flag"). The Act therefore must be subjected to "the most exacting scrutiny," and for the reasons stated in *Johnson,* the Government's interest cannot justify its infringement on First Amendment rights. We decline the Government's invitation to reassess this conclusion in light of Congress' recent recognition of a purported "national consensus" favoring a prohibition on flag-burning. Even assuming such a consensus exists, any suggestion that the Government's interest in suppressing speech becomes more weighty as popular opposition to that speech grows is foreign to the First Amendment.

247

Cruzan v. Director, Missouri Department of Health (1990)

The development of a constitutionally recognized right to privacy, and the limits—if any—upon it, constitute one of the major jurisprudential issues of our time. Beginning with cases such as *Griswold* (Document 212) and *Roe* (Document 225), the Court has struggled to define exactly what privacy in a rights context means. Conservatives oppose the notion, but even they have recognized that some matters are so important that some constitutional protection is necessary.

The "right to die" issue burst upon the scene in 1976 in the case of Karen Ann Quinlan, in which the New Jersey Supreme Court ruled that individuals could terminate treatment even if that would lead to their deaths, and if persons were incompetent, this decision could be made by an appropriate surrogate. In *Quinlan,* the judges relied on a mixture of traditional common law rules against unwanted touching, as well as the recently enunciated constitutional right of privacy.

Over the next decade, state courts and legislatures fashioned rules to govern how these cessation of treatment decisions could be made and implemented. Most states followed a fairly liberal evidentiary rule regarding how surrogates could judge what incompetent and comatose patients would want, but Missouri, Maine, and New York required a higher standard of evidence.

In *Cruzan,* the Court recognized that a liberty interest in personal autonomy existed under the Due Process Clause of the Fourteenth Amendment, giving people the right to terminate treatment. But the majority also held that a state's traditional interest in preserving life allowed it to set reasonable restrictions around that right to protect vulnerable individuals.

See Peter Filene, *In the Arms of Others: A History of the Right-to-Die in America* (1998); and Melvin I. Urofsky, *Letting Go: Death, Dying and the Law* (1993).

Chief Justice REHNQUIST delivered the opinion of the Court:

The common-law doctrine of informed consent is viewed as generally encompassing the right of a competent individual to refuse medical treatment. Beyond that, these decisions demonstrate both similarity and diversity in their approach to decision of what all agree is a perplexing question with unusually strong moral and ethical overtones. State courts have available to them for decision a number of sources—state constitutions, statutes, and common law—which are not available to us. In this Court, the question is simply and starkly whether the United States Constitution prohibits Missouri from choosing the rule of decision which it did. This is the first case in which we have been squarely presented with the issue of whether the United States Constitution grants what is in common parlance referred to as a "right to die" . . . It is the [better] part of wisdom not to attempt, by any general statement, to cover every possible phase of the subject.

The Fourteenth Amendment provides that no State shall "deprive any person of life, liberty, or property, without due process of law." The principle that a competent person has a constitutionally protected liberty interest in refusing unwanted medical treatment may be inferred from our prior decisions.

Just this Term, in the course of holding that a State's procedures for administering antipsychotic medication to prisoners were sufficient to satisfy due process concerns, we recognized that prisoners possess "a significant liberty interest in avoiding the unwanted administration of antipsychotic drugs under the Due Process Clause of the Fourteenth Amendment." Still other cases support the recognition of a general liberty interest in refusing medical treatment. But determining that a person has a "liberty interest" under the Due Process Clause does not end the inquiry; "whether respondent's constitutional rights have been violated must be determined by balancing his liberty interests against the relevant state interests."

Petitioners insist that under the general holdings of our cases, the forced administration of life-sustaining medical treatment, even of artificially delivered food and water essential to life, would implicate a competent person's liberty interest. Although we think the logic of the cases discussed above would embrace such a liberty interest, the dramatic consequences involved in refusal of such treatment would inform the inquiry as to whether the deprivation of that interest is constitutionally permissible. But for purposes of this case, we assume that the United States Constitution would grant a competent person a constitutionally protected right to refuse lifesaving hydration and nutrition.

Petitioners go on to assert that an incompetent person should possess the same right in this respect as is possessed by a competent person.

The difficulty with petitioners' claim is that in a sense it begs the question: an incompetent person is not able to make an informed and voluntary choice to exercise a hypothetical right to refuse treatment or any other rights. Such a "right" must be exercised for her, if at all, by some sort of surrogate.

Here, Missouri has in effect recognized that under certain circumstances a surrogate may act for the patient in electing to have hydration and nutrition withdrawn in such a way as to cause death, but it has established a procedural safeguard to assure that the action of the surrogate conforms as best it may to the wishes expressed by the patient when competent. Missouri requires evidence of the incompetent's wishes as to the with-

Source: 497 U.S. 261 (1990)

drawal of treatment to be proved by clear and convincing evidence. The question, then, is whether the United States Constitution forbids the establishment of this procedural requirement by the State. We hold that it does not.

Whether or not Missouri's clear and convincing evidence requirement comports with the United States Constitution depends in part on what interests the State may properly seek to protect in this situation. Missouri relies on its interest in the protection and preservation of human life, and there can be no gainsaying this interest. The choice between life and death is a deeply personal decision of obvious and overwhelming finality. We believe Missouri may legitimately seek to safeguard the personal element of this choice through the imposition of heightened evidentiary requirements. It cannot be disputed that the Due Process Clause protects an interest in life as well as an interest in refusing life-sustaining medical treatment. Not all incompetent patients will have loved ones available to serve as surrogate decisionmakers. And even where family members are present, "there will, of course, be some unfortunate situations in which family members will not act to protect a patient." A State is entitled to guard against potential abuses in such situations. Similarly, a State is entitled to consider that a judicial proceeding to make a determination regarding an incompetent's wishes may very well not be an adversarial one, with the added guarantee of accurate factfinding that the adversary process brings with it. Finally, we think a State may properly decline to make judgments about the "quality" of life that a particular individual may enjoy, and simply assert an unqualified interest in the preservation of human life to be weighed against the constitutionally protected interests of the individual.

In our view, Missouri has permissibly sought to advance these interests through the adoption of a "clear and convincing" standard of proof to govern such proceedings. The more stringent the burden of proof a party must bear, the more that party bears the risk of an erroneous decision. We believe that Missouri may permissibly place an increased risk of an erroneous decision on those seeking to terminate an incompetent individual's life-sustaining treatment. An erroneous decision not to terminate results in a maintenance of the status quo; the possibility of subsequent developments such as advancements in medical science, the discovery of new evidence regarding the patient's intent, changes in the law, or simply the unexpected death of the patient despite the administration of life-sustaining treatment, at least create the potential that a wrong decision will eventually be corrected or its impact mitigated. An erroneous decision to withdraw life-sustaining treatment, however, is not susceptible of correction.

It is also worth noting that most, if not all, States simply forbid oral testimony entirely in determining the wishes of parties in transactions which, while important, simply do not have the consequences that a decision to terminate a person's life does. At common law and by statute in most States, the parole evidence rule prevents the variations of the terms of a written contract by oral testimony. There is no doubt that statutes requiring wills to be in writing, and statutes of frauds which require that a contract to make a will be in writing, on occasion frustrate the effectuation of the intent of a particular decedent, just as Missouri's requirement of proof in this case may have frustrated the effectuation of the not-fully-expressed desires of Nancy Cruzan. But the Constitution does not require general rules to work faultlessly; no general rule can.

In sum, we conclude that a State may apply a clear and convincing evidence standard in proceedings where a guardian seeks to discontinue nutrition and hydration of a person diagnosed to be in a persistent vegetative state. We note that many courts which have adopted some sort of substituted judgment procedure in situations like this, whether they limit consideration of evidence to the prior expressed wishes of the incompetent individual, or whether they allow more general proof of what the individual's decision would have been, require a clear and convincing standard of proof for such evidence.

The Supreme Court of Missouri held that in this case the testimony adduced at trial did not amount to clear and convincing proof of the patient's desire to have hydration and nutrition withdrawn. In so doing, it reversed a decision of the Missouri trial court which had found that the evidence "suggested" Nancy Cruzan would not have desired to continue such measures, but which had not adopted the standard of "clear and convincing evidence" enunciated by the Supreme Court. The testimony adduced at trial consisted primarily of Nancy Cruzan's statements made to a housemate about a year before her accident that she would not want to live should she face life as a "vegetable" and other observations to the same effect. The observations did not deal in terms with withdrawal of medical treatment or of hydration and nutrition. We cannot say that the Supreme Court of Missouri committed constitutional error in reaching the conclusion that it did.

Petitioners alternatively contend that Missouri must accept the "substituted judgment" of close family members even in the absence of substantial proof that their views reflect the views of the patient. In *Michael H.,* we *upheld* the constitutionality of California's favored treatment of traditional family relationships; such a holding may not be turned around into a constitutional requirement that a State *must* recognize the primacy of those relationships in a situation like this. . . . Petitioners would seek to turn a decision which allowed a State to rely on family decisionmaking into a constitutional requirement that the State recognize such decisionmaking. But constitutional law does not work that way.

No doubt is engendered by anything in this record but that Nancy Cruzan's mother and father are loving and caring parents. If the State were required by the United States Constitution to repose a right of "substituted judgment" with anyone, the Cruzans would surely qualify. But we do not think the Due Process Clause requires the State to repose judgment on these matters with anyone but the patient herself. Close family members may have a strong feeling—a feeling not at all ignoble or unworthy, but not entirely disinterested, either—that they do not wish to witness the continuation of the life of a loved one which they regard as hopeless, meaningless, and even degrading. But there is no automatic assurance that the view of close family members will necessarily be the same as the patient's would have been had she been confronted with the prospect of her situation while competent. All of the reasons previously discussed for allowing Missouri to require clear and convincing evidence of the patient's wishes lead us to conclude that the State may choose to defer only to those wishes, rather than confide the decision to close family members.

The judgment of the Supreme Court of Missouri is
Affirmed.

Justice SCALIA, concurring:

The various opinions in this case portray quite clearly the difficult, indeed agonizing, questions that are presented by the constantly increasing power of science to keep the human body alive for longer than any reasonable person would want to inhabit it.

The States have begun to grapple with these problems through legislation. I am concerned, from the tenor of today's opinions, that we are poised to confuse that enterprise as successfully as we have confused the enterprise of legislating concerning abortion—requiring it to be conducted against a background of federal constitutional imperatives that are unknown because they are being newly crafted from Term to Term. That would be a great misfortune.

While I agree with the Court's analysis today, and therefore join in its opinion, I would have preferred that we announce, clearly and promptly, that the federal courts have no business in this field; that American law has always accorded the State the power to prevent, by force if necessary, suicide—including suicide by refusing to take appropriate measures necessary to preserve one's life; that the point at which life becomes "worthless," and the point at which the means necessary to preserve it become "extraordinary" or "inappropriate," are neither set forth in the Constitution nor known to the nine Justices of this Court any better than they are known to nine people picked at random from the Kansas City telephone directory; and hence, that even when it *is* demonstrated by clear and convincing evidence that a patient no longer wishes certain measures to be taken to preserve her life, it is up to the citizens of Missouri to decide, through their elected representatives, whether that wish will be honored. It is quite impossible (because the Constitution says nothing about the matter) that those citizens will decide upon a line less lawful than the one we would choose; and it is unlikely (because we know no more about "life-and-death" than they do) that they will decide upon a line less reasonable. . . .

What I have said above is not meant to suggest that I would think it desirable, if we were sure that Nancy Cruzan wanted to die, to keep her alive by the means at issue here. I assert only that the Constitution has nothing to say about the subject. To raise up a constitutional right here we would have to create out of nothing (for it exists neither in text nor tradition) some constitutional principle whereby, although the State may insist that an individual come in out of the cold and eat food, it may not insist that he take medicine; and although it may pump his stomach empty of poison he has ingested, it may not fill his stomach with food he has failed to ingest. Are there, then, no reasonable and humane limits that ought not to be exceeded in requiring an individual to preserve his own life? There obviously are, but they are not set forth in the Due Process Clause. What assures us that those limits will not be exceeded is the same constitutional guarantee that is the source of most of our protection—what protects us, for example, from being assessed a tax of 100% of our income above the subsistence level, from being forbidden to drive cars, or from being required to send our children to school for 10 hours a day, none of which horribles is categorically prohibited by the Constitution. Our salvation is the Equal Protection Clause, which requires the democratic majority to accept for themselves and their loved ones what they impose on you and me. This Court need not, and has no authority to, inject into every field of human activity where irrationality and oppression may theoretically occur, and if it tries to do so it will destroy itself.

Justice BRENNAN, with whom Justice MARSHALL and Justice BLACKMUN join, dissenting:

Today the Court, while tentatively accepting that there is some degree of constitutionally protected liberty interest in avoiding unwanted medical treatment, including life-sustaining medical treatment such as artificial nutrition and hydration, affirms the decision of the Missouri Supreme Court. The majority opinion, as I read it, would affirm that decision on the ground that a State may require "clear and convincing" evidence of Nancy Cruzan's prior decision to forgo life-sustaining treatment under circumstances such as hers in order to ensure that her actual wishes are honored. Because I believe that Nancy Cruzan has a fundamental right to be free of unwanted artificial nutrition and hydration, which right is not outweighed by any interests of the State, and because I find that the improperly biased procedural obstacles imposed by the Missouri Supreme Court impermissibly burden that right, I respectfully dissent. Nancy Cruzan is entitled to choose to die with dignity.

The question before this Court is a relatively narrow one: whether the Due Process Clause allows Missouri to require a now-incompetent patient in an irreversible persistent vegetative state to remain on life-support absent rigorously clear and convincing evidence that avoiding the treatment represents the patient's prior, express choice. If a fundamental right is at issue, Missouri's rule of decision must be scrutinized under the standards this Court has always applied in such circumstances. Fundamental rights "are protected not only against heavy-handed frontal attack, but also from being stifled by more subtle governmental interference."

The starting point for our legal analysis must be whether a competent person has a constitutional right to avoid unwanted medical care. Earlier this Term, this Court held that the Due Process Clause of the Fourteenth Amendment confers a significant liberty interest in avoiding unwanted medical treatment. Today, the Court concedes that our prior decisions "support the recognition of a general liberty interest in refusing medical treatment." The Court, however, avoids discussing either the measure of that liberty interest or its application by assuming, for purposes of this case only, that a competent person has a constitutionally protected liberty interest in being free of unwanted artificial nutrition and hydration. . . .

I cannot agree with the majority that where it is not possible to determine what choice an incompetent patient would make, a State's role as *parens patriae* permits the State automatically to make that choice itself. A State's legitimate interest in safeguarding a patient's choice cannot be furthered by simply appropriating it.

The majority justifies its position by arguing that, while close family members may have a strong feeling about the question, "there is no automatic assurance that the view of close family members will necessarily be the same as the patient's would have been had she been confronted with the prospect of her situation while competent." I cannot quarrel with this observation. But it leads only to another question: Is there any reason to suppose that a State is *more* likely to make the choice that the patient would have made than someone who knew the patient intimately? To ask this is to answer it.

A State's inability to discern an incompetent patient's choice still need not mean that a State is rendered powerless to protect that choice. But I would find that the Due Process Clause prohibits a State from doing more than that. A State may ensure that the person who makes the decision on the patient's behalf is the one whom the patient himself would have selected to make that choice for him. And a State may exclude from consideration anyone having improper motives. But a State generally must either repose the choice with the person whom the patient himself would most likely have chosen as proxy or leave the decision to the patient's family.

The new medical technology can reclaim those who would have been irretrievably lost a few decades ago and restore them to active lives. For Nancy Cruzan, it failed, and for others with wasting incurable disease it may be doomed to failure. In these unfortunate situations, the bodies and preferences and memories of the victims do not escheat to the State; nor does our Constitution permit the State or any other government to commandeer them. No singularity of feeling exists upon which such a government might confidently rely as *parens patriae*. Yet Missouri and this Court have displaced Nancy's own assessment of the processes associated with dying. They have discarded evidence of her will, ignored her values, and deprived her of the right to a decision as closely approximating her own choice as humanly possible. They have done so disingenuously in her name, and openly in Missouri's own. That Missouri and this Court may truly be motivated only by concern for incompetent patients makes no matter. As one of our most prominent jurists warned us decades ago: "Experience should teach us to be most on our guard to protect liberty when the government's purposes are beneficent. . . . The greatest dangers to liberty lurk in insidious encroachment by men of zeal, well meaning but without understanding."

I respectfully dissent.

248

Employment Division, Department of Human Resources v. Smith (1990)

Beginning with *Sherbert v. Verner* (1963), the Court had consistently held that under the protection afforded free exercise of religion by the First Amendment, states had to make reasonable accommodations to the religious practices of their citizens. In most instances the laws involved were general in their application, such as induction into military service or compulsory school attendance. These laws were also civil in nature.

Alfred Smith and Galen Black were fired from their jobs because they had participated in a peyote ceremony of the Native American Church, and were then turned down for unemployment insurance. They appealed the decision based on *Sherbert's* rule that unemployment insurance could not be conditioned on a person's religiously required conduct. The difference was that in the cases following *Sherbert,* none of the religious activity had been in conflict with criminal laws. In Oregon the ingestion of peyote, even for religious purposes, is considered criminal conduct.

The response to this case, in which the Court held religious activity could not trump general criminal laws, led to the passage of the Religious Freedom Restoration Act (Document 251).

See Michael McConnell, "Free Exercise Revisionism and the Smith Decision," 57 *University of Chicago Law Review* 1109 (1990); Philip Hamburger, "A Constitutional Right of Religious Exemption: An Historical Perspective," 60 *George Washington Law Review* 915 (1992); and Garrett Epps, *To an Unknown God: Religious Freedom on Trial* (2001).

————

Justice SCALIA delivered the opinion of the Court:

Oregon law prohibits the knowing or intentional possession of a "controlled substance" unless the substance has been prescribed by a medical practitioner. The law defines "controlled substance" as [including] the drug peyote, a hallucinogen derived from the plant *Lophophorawilliamsii Lemaire.*

Respondents Alfred Smith and Galen Black were fired from their jobs with a private drug rehabilitation organization because they ingested peyote for sacramental purposes at a ceremony of the Native American Church, of which both are members. When respondents applied to petitioner Employment Division for unemployment compensation, they were determined to be ineligible for benefits because they had been discharged for work-related "misconduct."

[Respondents' claim for relief rests on] our decisions in *Sherbert v. Verner, Thomas v. Review Board, Indiana Employment Security Div.* (1981), . . . and *Hobbie v. Unemployment Appeals Commission of Florida,* in which we held that a State could not condition the availability of unemployment insurance on an individual's willingness to forgo conduct required by his religion. . . . However, the conduct at issue in those cases was not prohibited by law.

The free exercise of religion means, first and foremost, the right to believe and profess whatever religious doctrine one desires. Thus, the First Amendment obviously excludes all "governmental regulation of religious *beliefs* as such."

But the "exercise of religion" often involves not only belief and profession but the performance of (or abstention from) physical acts: assembling with others for a worship service, participating in the sacramental use of bread and wine, proselytizing, abstaining from certain foods or certain modes of transportation. It would be true, we think (though no case of ours has involved the point), that a state would be "prohibiting the free exercise [of religion]" if it sought to ban such acts or abstentions only when they are engaged in for religious reasons, or only because of the religious belief that they display. It would doubtless be unconstitutional, for example, to ban the casting of statues that are to be used for worship purposes," or to prohibit bowing down before a golden calf.

We have never held that an individual's religious beliefs excuse him from compliance with an otherwise valid law prohibiting conduct that the State is free to regulate. On the contrary, the record of more than a century of our free exercise jurisprudence contradicts that proposition. As described succinctly by Justice Frankfurter in *Minersville School Dist. Bd. of Educ. v. Gobitis:* "Conscientious scruples have not, in the course of the long struggle for religious toleration, relieved the individual from obedience to a

Source: 494 U.S. 872 (1990)

general law not aimed at the promotion or restriction of religious beliefs. The mere possession of religious convictions which contradict the relevant concerns of a political society does not relieve the citizen from the discharge of political responsibilities." We first had occasion to assert that principle in *Reynolds v. United States,* where we rejected the claim that criminal laws against polygamy could not be constitutionally applied to those whose religion commanded the practice. "Laws," we said. "are made for the government of actions, and while they cannot interfere with mere religious belief and opinions, they may with practices. . . . Can a man excuse his practices to the contrary because of his religious belief? To permit this would be to make the professed doctrines of religious belief superior to the law of the land, and in effect to permit every citizen to become a law unto himself."

Our most recent decision involving a neutral, generally applicable regulatory law that compelled activity forbidden by an individual's religion was *United States v. Lee.* There, an Amish employer, on behalf of himself and his employees, sought exemption from collection and payment of Social Security taxes on the ground that the Amish faith prohibited participation in governmental support programs. We rejected the claim that an exemption was constitutionally required. There would be no way, we observed, to distinguish the Amish believer's objection to Social Security taxes from the religious objections that others might have to the collection or use of other taxes. . . .

Respondents argue that even though exemption from generally applicable criminal laws need not automatically be extended to religiously motivated actors, at least the claim for a religious exemption must be evaluated under the balancing test set forth in *Sherbert v. Verner.* Under the *Sherbert* test, governmental actions that substantially burden a religious practice must be justified by a compelling governmental interest. . . . In recent years we have abstained from applying the *Sherbert* test (outside the unemployment compensation field) at all.

Even if we were inclined to breathe into *Sherbert* some life beyond the unemployment compensation field, we would not apply it to require exemptions from a generally applicable criminal law.

[It is not] possible to limit the impact of respondents' proposal by requiring a "compelling state interest" only when the conduct prohibited is "central" to the individual's religion. It is no more appropriate for judges to determine the "centrality" of religious beliefs before applying a "compelling interest" test in the free exercise field, than it would be for them to determine the "importance" of ideas before applying the "compelling interest" test in the free speech field. . . . As we affirmed only last Term, "[i]t is not within the judicial ken to question the centrality of particular beliefs or practices to a faith, or the validity of particular litigants' interpretation of those creeds."

Because respondents' ingestion of peyote was prohibited under Oregon law, and because that prohibition is constitutional, Oregon may, consistent with the Free Exercise Clause, deny respondents unemployment compensation when their dismissal results from use of the drug. The decision of the Oregon Supreme Court is accordingly reversed.

Justice O'CONNOR, with whom Justice BRENNAN, Justice MARSHALL, and Justice BLACKMUN join, concurring in the judgments:

. . . Respondents invoke our traditional compelling interest test to argue that the Free Exercise Clause requires the State to grant them a limited exemption from its general criminal prohibition against the possession of peyote. The Court today, however, denies them even the opportunity to make that argument, concluding that "the sounder approach, and the approach in accord with the vast majority of our precedents, is to hold the [compelling interest] test inapplicable to" challenges to general criminal prohibitions.

In my view, however, the essence of a free exercise claim is relief from a burden imposed by government on religious practices or beliefs, whether the burden is imposed directly through laws that prohibit or compel specific religious practices, or indirectly through laws that, in effect, make abandonment of one's own religion or conformity to the religious beliefs of others the price of an equal place in the civil community. . . .

A State that makes criminal an individual's religiously motivated conduct burdens that individual's free exercise of religion in the severest manner possible, for it "results in the choice to the individual of either abandoning his religious principle or facing criminal prosecution."

Given the range of conduct that a State might legitimately make criminal, we cannot assume, merely because a law carries criminal sanctions and is generally applicable, that the First Amendment *never* requires the State to grant a limited exemption for religiously motivated conduct.

Moreover, we have not "rejected" or "declined to apply" the compelling interest test in our recent cases. Recent cases have instead affirmed that test as a fundamental part of our First Amendment doctrine. . . .

There is no dispute that Oregon's criminal prohibition of peyote places a severe burden on the ability of respondents to freely exercise their religion. Peyote is a sacrament of the Native American Church and is regarded as vital to respondents' ability to practice their religion. . . . Under Oregon law, as construed by that State's highest court, members of the Native American Church must choose between carrying out the ritual embodying their religious beliefs and avoidance of criminal prosecution. That choice is, in my view, more than sufficient to trigger First Amendment scrutiny. . . .

Thus, the critical question in this case is whether exempting respondents from the State's general criminal prohibition "will unduly interfere with fulfillment of the governmental interest." . . .

I believe that granting a selective exemption in this case would seriously impair Oregon's compelling interest in prohibiting possession of peyote by its citizens. Under such circumstances, the Free Exercise Clause does not require the State to accommodate respondents' religiously motivated conduct. . . .

Justice BLACKMUN, with whom Justice BRENNAN and Justice MARSHALL join, dissenting:

In weighing respondents' clear interest in the free exercise of their religion against Oregon's asserted interest in enforcing its drug laws, it is important to articulate in precise terms the state interest involved. It is not the State's broad interest in fighting the critical "war on drugs" that must be weighed against respondents' claim, but the State's narrow interest in refusing to make an exception for the religious, ceremonial use of peyote. . . .

The State's interest in enforcing its prohibition in order to be sufficiently compelling to outweigh a free exercise claim, cannot be merely abstract or symbolic. The State cannot plausibly assert that unbending application of a criminal prohibition is essential to fulfill any compelling interest, if it does not, in fact, attempt to enforce that prohibition. . . . Oregon has never sought to prosecute respondents, and does not claim that it has made significant enforcement efforts against other religious users of peyote. The State's asserted interest thus amounts only to the symbolic preservation of an unenforced prohibition. But a government interest in "symbolism, even symbolism for so worthy a cause as the abolition of unlawful drugs," cannot suffice to abrogate the constitutional rights of individuals.

Similarly, this Court's prior decisions have not allowed a government to rely on mere speculation about potential harms, but have demanded evidentiary support for a refusal to allow a religious exception. . . .

The State of Oregon cannot, consistently with the Free Exercise Clause, deny respondents unemployment benefits.

I dissent.

---

249 Planned Parenthood of Southeastern Pennsylvania v. Casey (1992)

In *Webster v. Reproductive Health Services* (1989), four members of the Court indicated their willingness to reverse *Roe v. Wade* (Document 223), and many people assumed that with the appointments of David Souter to replace William Brennan and Clarence Thomas to take Thurgood Marshall's seat, there would be sufficient votes to do so.

But in this case the center held. Justices O'Connor and Kennedy, both of whom had impeccable conservative credentials, found that the conservative rule of *stare decisis*—the force of precedent—required that the view of bodily autonomy enunciated in *Roe* and its progeny could not be overturned. While the state had important interests in preserving life—interests it could legally express through some restrictions on abortion—it could not deny women the right to terminate pregnancies before fetal viability.

The case marked the emergence of a new centrist bloc, O'Connor, Kennedy, and Souter, which could often count on the vote of Stevens. With the appointment of Ruth Bader Ginsburg and David Breyer, the centrists would have a solid six votes throughout the last decade of the twentieth century. Note in particular the comments of Justice Blackmun.

See David A. Strauss, "Abortion, Toleration, and Moral Uncertainty," 1993 *Supreme Court Review* 1; Kathleen Sullivan, "Foreword: The Justices of Rules and Standards,"

106 *Harvard Law Review* 24 (1992); B. H. Craig and David M. O'Brien, *Abortion and American Politics* (1993); and Martha A. Field, "Abortion Law Today," 14 *Journal of Legal Medicine* 3 (1993).

Justice O'CONNOR, Justice KENNEDY, and Justice SOUTER announced the judgment of the Court:

Liberty finds no refuge in a jurisprudence of doubt. Yet 19 years after our holding that the Constitution protects a woman's right to terminate her pregnancy in its early stages, *Roe v. Wade* (1973), that definition of liberty is still questioned. Joining the respondents as amicus curiae, the United States, as it has done in five other cases in the last decade, again asks us to overrule *Roe*.

At issue in these cases are five provisions of the Pennsylvania Abortion Control Act of 1982, as amended in 1988 and 1989. The Act requires that a woman seeking an abortion give her informed consent prior to the abortion procedure, and specifies that she be provided with certain information at least 24 hours before the abortion is performed. Section 3205. For a minor to obtain an abortion, the Act requires the informed consent of one of her parents, but provides for a judicial bypass option if the minor does not wish to or cannot obtain a parent's consent. Section 3206. Another provision of the Act requires that, unless certain exceptions apply, a married woman seeking an abortion must sign a statement indicating that she has notified her husband of her intended abortion. Section 3209. The Act exempts compliance with these three requirements in the event of a "medical emergency," which is defined in Section 3203 of the Act. In addition to the above provisions regulating the performance of abortions, the Act imposes certain reporting requirements on facilities that provide abortion services.

After considering the fundamental constitutional questions resolved by *Roe*, principles of institutional integrity, and the rule of *stare decisis*, we are led to conclude this: the essential holding of *Roe v. Wade* should be retained and once again reaffirmed.

It must be stated at the outset and with clarity that *Roe's* essential holding, the holding we reaffirm, has three parts. First is a recognition of the right of the woman to choose to have an abortion before viability and to obtain it without undue interference from the State. Before viability, the State's interests are not strong enough to support a prohibition of abortion or the imposition of a substantial obstacle to the woman's effective right to elect the procedure. Second is a confirmation of the State's power to restrict abortions after fetal viability, if the law contains exceptions for pregnancies which endanger the woman's life or health. And third is the principle that the State has legitimate interests from the outset of the pregnancy in protecting the health of the woman and the life of the fetus that may become a child. These principles do not contradict one another; and we adhere to each.

. . . . Neither the Bill of Rights nor the specific practices of States at the time of the adoption of the Fourteenth Amendment marks the outer limits of the substantive sphere of liberty which the Fourteenth Amendment protects. . . .

Source: 505 U.S. 833 (1992)

The inescapable fact is that adjudication of substantive due process claims may call upon the Court in interpreting the Constitution to exercise that same capacity which by tradition courts always have exercised: reasoned judgment. Its boundaries are not susceptible of expression as a simple rule. That does not mean we are free to invalidate state policy choices with which we disagree; yet neither does it permit us to shrink from the duties of our office. . . . Men and women of good conscience can disagree, and we suppose some always shall disagree, about the profound moral and spiritual implications of terminating a pregnancy, even in its earliest stage. Some of us as individuals find abortion offensive to our most basic principles of morality, but that cannot control our decision. Our obligation is to define the liberty of all, not to mandate our own moral code. The underlying constitutional issue is whether the State can resolve these philosophic questions in such a definitive way that a woman lacks all choice in the matter, except perhaps in those rare circumstances in which the pregnancy is itself a danger to her own life or health, or is the result of rape or incest. . . .

Our law affords constitutional protection to personal decisions relating to marriage, procreation, contraception, family relationships, child rearing, and education. Our cases recognize "the right of the individual, married or single, to be free from unwarranted governmental intrusion into matters so fundamentally affecting a person as the decision whether to bear or beget a child." Our precedents "have respected the private realm of family life which the state cannot enter." These matters, involving the most intimate and personal choices a person may make in a lifetime, choices central to personal dignity and autonomy, are central to the liberty protected by the Fourteenth Amendment. At the heart of liberty is the right to define one's own concept of existence, of meaning, of the universe, and of the mystery of human life. Beliefs about these matters could not define the attributes of personhood were they formed under compulsion of the State.

These considerations begin our analysis of the woman's interest in terminating her pregnancy but cannot end it, for this reason: though the abortion decision may originate within the zone of conscience and belief, it is more than a philosophic exercise. Abortion is a unique act. It is an act fraught with consequences for others: for the woman who must live with the implications of her decision; for the persons who perform and assist in the procedure; for the spouse, family, and society which must confront the knowledge that these procedures exist, procedures some deem nothing short of an act of violence against innocent human life; and, depending on one's beliefs, for the life or potential life that is aborted. Though abortion is conduct, it does not follow that the State is entitled to proscribe it in all instances. That is because the liberty of the woman is at stake in a sense unique to the human condition and so unique to the law. The mother who carries a child to full term is subject to anxieties, to physical constraints, to pain that only she must bear. That these sacrifices have from the beginning of the human race been endured by woman with a pride that ennobles her in the eyes of others and gives to the infant a bond of love cannot alone be grounds for the State to insist she make the sacrifice. Her suffering is too intimate and personal for the State to insist, without more, upon its own vision of the woman's role, however dominant that vision has been in the course of our history and our culture. The density of the woman must be shaped to a large extent on her own conception of her spiritual imperatives and her place in society.

It should be recognized, moreover, that in some critical respects the abortion decision is of the same character as the decision to use contraception, to which *Griswold v.*

Connecticut, Eisenstadt v. Baird, and *Carey v. Population Services International* afford constitutional protection. We have no doubt as to the correctness of those decisions. They support the reasoning in *Roe* relating to the woman's liberty because they involve personal decisions concerning not only the meaning of procreation but also human responsibility and respect for it. . . .

While we appreciate the weight of the arguments made on behalf of the State in the cases before us, arguments which in their ultimate formulation conclude that *Roe* should be overruled, the reservations any of us may have in reaffirming the central holding of *Roe* are outweighed by the explication of individual liberty we have given combined with the force of *stare decisis.* We turn now to that doctrine. . . . A decision to overrule *Roe's* essential holding under the existing circumstances would address error, if error there was, at the cost of both profound and unnecessary damage to the Court's legitimacy, and to the Nation's commitment to the rule of law. It is therefore imperative to adhere to the essence of *Roe's* original decision, and we do so today.

    . . . . Much criticism has been directed at *Roe,* a criticism that always inheres when the Court draws a specific rule from what in the Constitution is but a general standard. We conclude, however, that the urgent claims of the woman to retain the ultimate control over her destiny and her body, claims implicit in the meaning of liberty, require us to perform that function. Liberty must not be extinguished for want of a line that is clear. And it falls to us to give some real substance to the woman's liberty to determine whether to carry her pregnancy to full term.

    We conclude the line should be drawn at viability, so that before that time the woman has a right to choose to terminate her pregnancy. We adhere to this principle for two reasons.

    First . . . *stare decisis.* . . .

    The second reason is that the concept of viability is the time at which there is a realistic possibility of maintaining and nourishing a life outside the womb, so that the independent existence of the second life can in reason and all fairness be the object of state protection that now overrides the rights of the woman. . . . The viability line also has, as a practical matter, an element of fairness. In some broad sense it might be said that a woman who fails to act before viability has consented to the State's intervention on behalf of the developing child.

    The woman's right to terminate her pregnancy before viability is the most central principle of *Roe v. Wade.* It is a rule of law and a component of liberty we cannot renounce.

    On the other side of the equation is the interest of the State in the protection of potential life. . . . The weight to be given this state interest, not the strength of the woman's interest, was the difficult question faced in *Roe.* We do not need to say whether each of us, had we been Members of the Court when the valuation of the state interest came before it as an original matter, would have concluded, as the *Roe* Court did, that its weight is insufficient to justify a ban on abortions prior to viability even when it is subject to certain exceptions. The . . . immediate question is not the soundness of *Roe's* resolution of the issue, but the precedential force that must be accorded to its holding. And we have concluded that the essential holding of *Roe* should be reaffirmed.

    Yet it must be remembered that *Roe v. Wade* speaks with clarity in establishing not only the woman's liberty but also the State's "important and legitimate interest in potential life." That portion of the decision in *Roe* has been given too little acknowledgment and implementation by the Court in its subsequent cases. Those cases decided that any regulation touching upon the abortion decision must survive strict scrutiny, to be sustained only if drawn in narrow terms to further a compelling state interest. Not all of the cases decided under that formulation can be reconciled with the holding in *Roe* itself that the State has legitimate interests in the health of the woman and in protecting the potential life within her. In resolving this tension, we choose to rely upon *Roe,* as against the later cases. . . .

The trimester framework no doubt was erected to ensure that the woman's right to choose not become so subordinate to the State's interest in promoting fetal life that her choice exists in theory but not in fact. We do not agree, however, that the trimester approach is necessary to accomplish this objective. A framework of this rigidity was unnecessary and in its later interpretation sometimes contradicted the State's permissible exercise of its powers.

Though the woman has a right to choose to terminate or continue her pregnancy before viability, it does not at all follow that the State is prohibited from taking steps to ensure that this choice is thoughtful and informed. Even in the earliest stages of pregnancy, the State may enact rules and regulations designed to encourage her to know that there are philosophic and social arguments of great weight that can be brought to bear in favor of continuing the pregnancy to full term and that there are procedures and institutions to allow adoption of unwanted children as well as a certain degree of state assistance if the mother chooses to raise the child herself. . . .

We reject the trimester framework, which we do not consider to be part of the essential holding of *Roe.* . . . Measures aimed at ensuring that a woman's choice contemplates the consequences for the fetus do not necessarily interfere with the right recognized in *Roe,* although those measures have been found to be inconsistent with the rigid trimester framework announced in that case. . . . The trimester framework suffers from these basic flaws: in its formulation it misconceives the nature of the pregnant woman's interest; and in practice it undervalues the State's interest in potential life, as recognized in *Roe.*

. . . . The Court's experience applying the trimester framework has led to the striking down of some abortion regulations which in no real sense deprived women of the ultimate decision. Those decisions went too far because the right recognized by *Roe* is a right "to be free from unwarranted governmental intrusion into matters so fundamentally affecting a person as the decision whether to bear or beget a child." Not all governmental intrusion is of necessity unwarranted; and that brings us to the other basic flaw in the trimester framework: even in *Roe's* terms, in practice it undervalues the State's interest in the potential life within the woman. . . .

The very notion that the State has a substantial interest in potential life leads to the conclusion that not all regulations must be deemed unwarranted. Not all burdens on the right to decide whether to terminate a pregnancy will be undue. In our view, the undue burden standard is the appropriate means of reconciling the State's interest with the woman's constitutionally protected liberty.

The concept of an undue burden has been utilized by the Court as well as individual Members of the Court, including two of us, in ways that could be considered inconsistent. . . . A finding of an undue burden is a shorthand for the conclusion that a state regulation has the purpose or effect of placing a substantial obstacle in the path of a woman seeking an abortion of a nonviable fetus. A statute with this purpose is invalid because the means chosen by the State to further the interest in potential life must be calculated to inform the woman's free choice, not hinder it. And a statute which, while furthering the interest in potential life or some other valid state interest, has the effect of placing a substantial obstacle in the path of a woman's choice cannot be considered a permissible means of serving its legitimate ends. . . . In our considered judgment, an undue burden is an unconstitutional burden. . . . A law designed to further the State's interest in fetal life which imposes an undue burden on the woman's decision before fetal viability is unconstitutional.

Some guiding principles should emerge. What is at stake is the woman's right to make the ultimate decision, not a right to be insulated from all others in doing so. Regulations which do no more than create a structural mechanism by which the State, or the parent or guardian of a minor, may express profound respect for the life of the unborn are permitted, if they are not a substantial obstacle to the woman's exercise of the right to choose. Unless it has that effect on her right of choice, a state measure designed to persuade her to choose childbirth over abortion will be upheld if reasonably related to that goal. Regulations designed to foster the health of a woman seeking an abortion are valid if they do not constitute an undue burden.

There was a time, not so long ago, when a different understanding of the family and of the Constitution prevailed. In *Bradwell v. State* (1873),three Members of this Court reaffirmed the common-law principle that "a woman had no legal existence separate from her husband . . . " Only one generation has passed since this Court observed that "woman is still regarded as the center of home and family life," with attendant "special responsibilities" that precluded full and independent legal status under the Constitution. These views, of course, are no longer consistent with our understanding of the family, the individual, or the Constitution.

[*In her discussion of the spousal notification requirement, Justice O'Connor noted that in stable and happy marriages, women would of course discuss a question as serious as abortion with their husbands. But the fact of the matter was that one reason some women sought an abortion was because they did not enjoy a good marriage, and feared their husbands.*]

. . . . For the great many women who are victims of abuse inflicted by their husbands, or whose children are the victims of such abuse, a spousal notice requirement enables the husband to wield an effective veto over his wife's decision. Whether the prospect of notification itself deters such women from seeking abortions, or whether the husband, through physical force or psychological pressure or economic coercion, prevents his wife from obtaining an abortion until it is too late, the notice requirement will often be tantamount to the veto found unconstitutional in Danforth. The women most affected by this law—those who most reasonably fear the consequences of notifying their husbands that they are pregnant—are in the gravest danger.

The husband's interest in the life of the child his wife is carrying does not permit the State to empower him with this troubling degree of authority over his wife. . . . A State may not give to a man the kind of dominion over his wife that parents exercise over their children. Women do not lose their constitutionally protected liberty when they marry. . . .

We next consider the parental consent provision. Except in a medical emergency, an unemancipated young woman under 18 may not obtain an abortion unless she and one of her parents (or guardian) provides informed consent. If neither a parent nor a guardian provides consent, a court may authorize the performance of an abortion upon a determination that the young woman is mature and capable of giving informed consent and has in fact given her informed consent, or that an abortion would be in her best interests.

We have been over most of this ground before. Our cases establish, and we reaffirm today, that a State may require a minor seeking an abortion to obtain the consent of a parent or guardian, provided that there is an adequate judicial bypass procedure. . . .

Our Constitution is a covenant running from the first generation of Americans to us and then to future generations. It is a coherent succession. Each generation must learn anew that the Constitution's written terms embody ideas and aspirations that must survive more ages than one. We accept our responsibility not to retreat from interpreting the full meaning of the covenant in light of all of our precedents. We invoke it once again to define the freedom guaranteed by the Constitution's own promise, the promise of liberty.

[*Justice STEVENS concurred with the plurality, but like Justice BLACKMUN, would have struck down all of the law's provisions.*]

Justice BLACKMUN, concurring in part, concurring in the judgment in part, and dissenting in part:

Three years ago, in *Webster v. Reproductive Health Services* (1989), four Members of this Court appeared poised to "cast into darkness the hopes and visions of every woman in this country" who had come to believe that the Constitution guaranteed her the right to reproductive choice. All that remained between the promise of *Roe* and the darkness of the plurality was a single, flickering flame. Decisions since *Webster* gave little reason to hope that this flame would cast much light. But now, just when so many expected the darkness to fall, the flame has grown bright.

I do not underestimate the significance of today's joint opinion. Yet I remain steadfast in my belief that the right to reproductive choice is entitled to the full protection afforded by this Court before *Webster.* And I fear for the darkness as four Justices anxiously await the single vote necessary to extinguish the light.

Make no mistake, the joint opinion of Justices O'CONNOR, KENNEDY, and SOUTER is an act of personal courage and constitutional principle. . . . What has happened today should serve as a model for future Justices and a warning to all who have tried to turn this Court into yet another political branch.

In striking down the Pennsylvania Statute's spousal notification requirement, the Court has established a framework for evaluating abortion regulations that responds to the social context of women facing issues of reproductive choice. . . . And in applying its test, the Court remains sensitive to the unique role of women in the decisionmaking process. . . .

While I believe that the joint opinion errs in failing to invalidate the other regulations, I am pleased that the joint opinion has not ruled out the possibility that these regulations may be shown to impose an unconstitutional burden. The joint opinion makes clear that its specific holdings are based on the insufficiency of the record before it. I am confident that in the future evidence will be produced to show that "in a large fraction of the cases in which [these regulations are] relevant, [they] will operate as a substantial obstacle to a woman's choice to undergo an abortion." . . .

In one sense, the Court's approach is worlds apart from that of THE Chief Justice and Justice SCALIA. And yet, in another sense, the distance between the two approaches is short—the distance is but a single vote.

I am 83 years old. I cannot remain on this Court forever, and when I do step down, the confirmation process for my successor well may focus on the issue before us today. That, I regret, may be exactly where the choice between the two worlds will be made.

Chief Justice REHNQUIST, with whom Justice WHITE, Justice SCALIA, and Justice THOMAS join, concurring in the judgment in part and dissenting in part:

The joint opinion, following its newly minted variation on *stare decisis,* retains the outer shell of *Roe v. Wade,* but beats a wholesale retreat from the substance of that case. We believe that *Roe* was wrongly decided, and that it can and should be overruled consistently with our traditional approach to *stare decisis* in constitutional cases. We would adopt the approach of the plurality in *Webster v. Reproductive Health Services* (1989), and uphold the challenged provisions of the Pennsylvania statute in their entirety.

In *Roe v. Wade,* the Court recognized a "guarantee of personal privacy" which "is broad enough to encompass a woman's decision whether or not to terminate her pregnancy." We are now of the view that, in terming this right fundamental, the Court in *Roe* read the earlier opinions upon which it based its decision much too broadly. Unlike marriage, procreation, and contraception, abortion "involves the purposeful termination of a potential life." *Harris v. McRae* (1980). The abortion decision must therefore "be recognized as *sui generis,* different in kind from the others that the Court has protected under the rubric of personal or family privacy and autonomy." One cannot ignore the fact that a woman is not isolated in her pregnancy, and that the decision to abort necessarily involves the destruction of a fetus. . . .

Nor do the historical traditions of the American people support the view that the right to terminate one's pregnancy is "fundamental." The common law which we inherited from England made abortion after "quickening" an offense. At the time of the adoption of the Fourteenth Amendment, statutory prohibitions or restrictions on abortion were commonplace; in 1868, at least 28 of the then 37 States and 8 Territories had statutes banning or limiting abortion. By the turn of the century virtually every State had a law prohibiting or restricting abortion on its books. By the middle of the present century, a liberalization trend had set in. But 21 of the restrictive abortion laws in effect in 1868 were still in effect in 1973 when *Roe* was decided, and an overwhelming majority of the States prohibited abortion unless necessary to preserve the life or health of the mother. On this record, it can scarcely be said that any deeply rooted tradition of relatively unrestricted abortion in our history supported the classification of the right to abortion as "fundamental" under the Due Process Clause of the Fourteenth Amendment. . . .

In the end . . . the joint opinion's argument is based solely on generalized assertions about the national psyche, on a belief that the people of this country have grown accustomed to the *Roe* decision over the last 19 years and have "ordered their thinking and living around" it. As an initial matter, one might inquire how the joint opinion can view the "central holding" of *Roe* as so deeply rooted in our constitutional culture, when it so casually uproots and disposes of that same decision's trimester framework. Furthermore, at various points in the past, the same could have been said about this Court's erroneous decisions that the Constitution allowed "separate but equal" treatment of minorities, see *Plessy v. Ferguson* (1896), or that "liberty" under the Due Process Clause protected "freedom of contract," see *Lochner v. New York* (1905). The "separate but equal" doctrine lasted 58 years after *Plessy*, and *Lochner's* protection of contractual freedom lasted 32 years. However, the simple fact that a generation or more had grown used to these major decisions did not prevent the Court from correcting its errors in those cases, nor should it prevent us from correctly interpreting the Constitution here.

We therefore would hold that each of the challenged provisions of the Pennsylvania statute is consistent with the Constitution. It bears emphasis that our conclusion in this regard does not carry with it any necessary approval of these regulations. Our task is, as always, to decide only whether the challenged provisions of a law comport with the United States Constitution. If, as we believe, these do, their wisdom as a matter of public policy is for the people of Pennsylvania to decide.

250   *Lee v. Weisman (1992)*

As with the previous case, the appointment of conservative justices by presidents Reagan and Bush led many to hope that the liberal activist decisions of the Warren and Burger eras could be reversed. In this instance, conservatives hoped that the Court would abandon the proscription against school prayer first enunciated in *Engel v. Vitale* (Document 205).

In Providence, Rhode Island, the Weisman family had complained when at a middle school graduation of one of their children, there had been an official prayer. When another child, Deborah Weisman, was scheduled to graduate, the school invited a rabbi to deliver the prayers and furnished him with a list of guidelines in order to make the prayers as non sectarian and inoffensive as possible. Deborah raised a challenge on the grounds that prayer at any school function involving a captive audience violated the Establishment Clause.

Once again, the centrists on the Court dominated.

See Jesse H. Choper, "The Unpredictability of the Supreme Court's Doctrine in Establishment Clause Cases," 43 *Wayne Law Review* 1439 (1997); and George W. Dent, Jr., "Of God and Caesar: The Free Exercise Rights of Public School Students," 43 *Case Western Reserve Law Review* 707 (1993).

Justice KENNEDY delivered the opinion of the Court:

These dominant facts mark and control the confines of our decision: State Officials direct the performance of a formal religious exercise at promotional and graduation ceremonies for secondary schools. Even for those students who object to the religious exercise, their attendance and participation in the state-sponsored religious activity are in a fair and real sense obligatory, though the school district does not require attendance as a condition for receipt of the diploma. . . . The controlling precedents as they relate to prayer and religious exercise in primary and secondary public schools compel the holding here that the policy of the city of Providence is an unconstitutional one. We can decide the case without reconsidering the general constitutional framework by which public schools' efforts to accommodate religion are measured. Thus we do not accept the invitation of petitioners and amicus the United States to reconsider our decision in *Lemon v. Kurtzman.* The government involvement with religious activity in this case is pervasive, to the point of creating a state-sponsored and state-directed religious exercise in a public school. Conducting this formal religious observance conflicts with settled rules pertaining to prayer exercises for students, and that suffices to determine the question before us.

Petitioners argue, and we find nothing in the case to refute it, that the directions for the content of the prayers were a good-faith attempt by the school to ensure that the sectarianism which is so often the flashpoint for religious animosity be removed from the graduation ceremony. . . . The question is not the good faith of the school in attempting to make the prayer acceptable to most persons, but the legitimacy of its undertaking that enterprise at all when the object is to produce a prayer to be used in a formal religious exercise which students, for all practical purposes, are obliged to attend. We are asked to recognize the existence of a practice of nonsectarian prayer, prayer within the embrace of what is known as the Judeo-Christian tradition, prayer which is more acceptable than one which, for example, makes explicit references to the God of Israel, or to Jesus Christ, or to a patron saint. . . . But though the First Amendment does not allow the government to stifle prayers which aspire to [a civic religion], neither does it permit the government to undertake that task for itself.

The First Amendment's Religion Clauses mean that religious beliefs and religious expression are too precious to be either proscribed or prescribed by the State. The design of the Constitution is that preservation and transmission of religious beliefs and worship is a responsibility and a choice committed to the private sphere, which itself is promised freedom to pursue that mission. . . . The suggestion that government may establish an official or civic religion as a means of avoiding the establishment of a religion with more specific creeds strikes us as a contradiction that cannot be accepted.

The degree of school involvement here made it clear that the graduation prayers bore the imprint of the State and thus put school-age children who objected in an untenable position. . . . The lessons of the First Amendment are as urgent in the modern world as in the 18th century when it was written. One timeless lesson is that if citizens are subjected to state-sponsored religious exercises, the State disavows its own duty to guard

Source: 505 U.S. 577 (1992)

and respect that sphere of inviolable conscience and belief which is the mark of a free people. To compromise that principle today would be to deny our own tradition and forfeit our standing to urge others to secure the protections of that tradition for themselves. As we have observed before, there are heightened concerns with protecting freedom of conscience from subtle coercive pressure in the elementary and secondary public schools. Our decisions in *Engel* and Abington recognize, among other things, that prayer exercises in public schools carry a particular risk of indirect coercion. The concern may not be limited to the context of schools, but it is most pronounced there. What to most believers may seem nothing more than a reasonable request that the nonbeliever respect their religious practices, in a school context may appear to the nonbeliever or dissenter to be an attempt to employ the machinery of the State to enforce a religious orthodoxy.

We need not look beyond the circumstances of this case to see the phenomenon at work. The undeniable fact is that the school district's supervision and control of a high school graduation ceremony places public pressure, as well as peer pressure, on attending students to stand as a group or, at least, maintain respectful silence during the invocation and benediction. This pressure, though subtle and indirect, can be as real as any overt compulsion. Of course, in our culture standing or remaining silent can signify adherence to a view or simple respect for the views of others. And no doubt some persons who have no desire to join a prayer have little objection to standing as a sign of respect for those who do. But for the dissenter of high school age, who has a reasonable perception that she is being forced by the State to pray in a manner her conscience will not allow, the injury is no less real. There can be no doubt that for many, if not most, of the students at the graduation, the act of standing or remaining silent was an expression of participation in the rabbi's prayer. That was the very point of the religious exercise. It is of little comfort to a dissenter, then, to be told that for her the act of standing or remaining in silence signifies mere respect, rather than participation. What matters is that, given our social conventions, a reasonable dissenter in this milieu could believe that the group exercise signified her own participation or approval of it.

Finding no violation under these circumstances would place objectors in the dilemma of participating, with all that implies, or protesting. We do not address whether that choice is acceptable if the affected citizens are mature adults, but we think the State may not, consistent with the Establishment Clause, place primary and secondary school children in this position. Research in psychology supports the common assumption that adolescents are often susceptible to pressure from their peers towards conformity, and that the influence is strongest in matters of social convention. To recognize that the choice imposed by the State constitutes an unacceptable constraint only acknowledges that the government may no more use social pressure to enforce orthodoxy than it may use more direct means.

The injury caused by the government's action, and the reason why Daniel and Deborah Weisman object to it, is that the State, in a school setting, in effect required participation in a religious exercise. It is, we concede, a brief exercise during which the individual can concentrate on joining its message, meditate on her own religion, or let her mind wander. But the embarrassment and the intrusion of the religious exercise cannot be refuted by arguing that these prayers, and similar ones to be said in the future, are of a de minimis character. To do so would be an affront to the rabbi who offered them and to all those for whom the prayers were an essential and profound recognition of divine authority. And for the same reason, we think that the intrusion is greater than the two minutes or so of time consumed for prayers like these. Assuming, as we must, that the prayers were offensive to the student and the parent who now object, the intrusion was both real and, in the context of a secondary school, a violation of the objectors' rights. That the intrusion was in the course of promulgating religion that sought to be civic or nonsectarian rather than pertaining to one sect does not lessen the offense or isolation to the objectors. At best it narrows their number, at worst increases their sense of isolation and affront.

There was a stipulation in the District Court that attendance at graduation and promotional ceremonies is voluntary. Petitioners and the United States, as amicus, made this a center point of the case, arguing that the option of not attending the graduation excuses any inducement or coercion in the ceremony itself. The argument lacks all persuasion. Law reaches past formalism. And to say a teenage student has a real choice not to attend her high school graduation is formalistic in the extreme. True, Deborah could elect not to attend commencement without renouncing her diploma; but we shall not allow the case to turn on this point. Everyone knows that in our society and in our culture high school graduation is one of life's most significant occasions. A school rule which excuses attendance is beside the point. Attendance may not be required by official decree, yet it is apparent that a student is not free to absent herself from the graduation exercise in any real sense of the term "voluntary," for absence would require forfeiture of those intangible benefits which have motivated the student through youth and all her high school years. Graduation is a time for family and those closest to the student to celebrate success and express mutual wishes of gratitude and respect, all to the end of impressing upon the young person the role that it is his or her right and duty to assume in the community and all of its diverse parts.

The Government's argument gives insufficient recognition to the real conflict of conscience faced by the young student. The essence of the Government's position is that with regard to a civic, social occasion of this importance it is the objector, not the majority, who must take unilateral and private action to avoid compromising religious scruples, hereby electing to miss the graduation exercise. This turns conventional First Amendment analysis on its head. It is a tenet of the First Amendment that the State cannot require one of its citizens to forfeit his or her rights and benefits as the price of resisting conformance to state-sponsored religious practice. To say that a student must remain apart from the ceremony at the opening invocation and closing benediction is to risk compelling conformity in an environment analogous to the classroom setting, where we have said the risk of compulsion is especially high. Just as in *Engel* and Schempp, where we found that provisions within the challenged legislation permitting a student to be voluntarily excused from attendance or participation in the daily prayers did not shield those practices from invalidation, the fact that attendance at the graduation ceremonies is voluntary in a legal sense does not save the religious exercise. . . .

We do not hold that every state action implicating religion is invalid if one or a few citizens find it offensive. People may take offense at all manner of religious as well as nonreligious messages, but offense alone does not in every case show a violation. We know too that sometimes to endure social isolation or even anger may be the price of conscience or nonconformity. But, by any reading of our cases, the conformity required of the student in this case was too high an exaction to withstand the test of the Establishment Clause. The prayer exercises in this case are especially improper because the State has in every practical sense compelled attendance and participation in an explicit religious exercise at an event of singular importance to every student, one the objecting student had no real alternative to avoid. Our jurisprudence in this area is of necessity one of line-drawing, of determining at what point a dissenter's rights of religious freedom are infringed by the State. . . .

The sole question presented is whether a religious exercise may be conducted at a graduation ceremony in circumstances where, as we have found, young graduates who object are induced to conform. No holding by this Court suggests that a school can persuade or compel a student to participate in a religious exercise. That is being done here, and it is forbidden by the Establishment Clause of the First Amendment.

Justice BLACKMUN, with whom Justice STEVENS and Justice O'CONNOR join, concurring. I join the Court's opinion today because I find nothing in it inconsistent with the essential precepts of the Establishment Clause developed in our precedents. The Court holds that the graduation prayer is unconstitutional because the State "in effect required participation in a religious exercise." Although our precedents make clear that proof of government coercion is not necessary to prove an Establishment Clause violation, it is sufficient. Government pressure to participate in a religious activity is an obvious indication that the government is endorsing or promoting religion.

But it is not enough that the government restrain from compelling religious practices: It must not engage in them either. The Court repeatedly has recognized that a violation of the Establishment Clause is not predicated on coercion. The Establishment Clause proscribes public schools from "conveying or attempting to convey a message that religion or a particular religious belief is favored or preferred," even if the schools do not actually "impose pressure upon a student to participate in a religious activity." There is no doubt that attempts to aid religion through government coercion jeopardize freedom of conscience. Even subtle pressure diminishes the right of each individual to choose voluntarily what to believe. . . . Our decisions have gone beyond prohibiting coercion, however, because the Court has recognized that "the fullest possible scope of religious liberty" entails more than freedom from coercion. The Establishment Clause protects religious liberty on a grand scale; it is a social compact that guarantees for generations a democracy and a strong religious community—both essential to safeguarding religious liberty. For the reasons we have stated, the judgment of the Court of Appeals is Affirmed.

[*Justice SOUTER, with whom Justice STEVENS and Justice O'CONNOR joined, concurred separately, exploring the larger implications of coercion in the school context.*]

Justice SCALIA, with whom the CHIEF JUSTICE, Justice WHITE, and Justice THOMAS join, dissenting:

In holding that the Establishment Clause prohibits invocations and benedictions at public school graduation ceremonies, the Court—with nary a mention that it is doing so—lays waste a tradition that is as old as public school graduation ceremonies themselves, and that is a component of an even more longstanding American tradition of nonsectarian prayer to God at public celebrations generally. As its instrument of destruction, the bulldozer of its social engineering, the Court invents a boundless, and boundlessly manipulable, test of psychological coercion, which promises to do for the Establishment Clause what the Durham rule did for the insanity defense. Today's opinion shows more forcefully than volumes of argumentation why our Nation's protection, that fortress which is our Constitution, cannot possibly rest upon the changeable philosophical predilections of the Justices of this Court, but must have deep foundations in the historic practices of our people.

From our Nation's origin, prayer has been a prominent part of governmental ceremonies and proclamations. The Declaration of Independence, the document marking our birth as a separate people, "appealed to the Supreme Judge of the world for the rectitude of our intentions" and avowed "a firm reliance on the protection of divine Providence." In his first inaugural address, after swearing his oath of office on a Bible, George Washington deliberately made a prayer a part of his first official act as President. . . . Such supplications have been a characteristic feature of inaugural addresses ever since. . . .

The Court's notion that a student who simply sits in "respectful silence" during the invocation and benediction (when all others are standing) has somehow joined—or would somehow be perceived as having joined—in the prayers is nothing short of ludicrous. We indeed live in a vulgar age. But surely "our social conventions," have not coarsened to the point that anyone who does not stand on his chair and shout obscenities can reasonably be deemed to have assented to everything said in his presence. . . . But let us assume the very worst, that the nonparticipating graduate is "subtly coerced" . . . to stand! Even that does not remotely establish a "participation" (or an "appearance of participation") in a religious exercise. . . .

The deeper flaw in the Court's opinion does not lie in its wrong answer to the question whether there was state-induced "peer-pressure" coercion; it lies, rather, in the Court's making violation of the Establishment Clause hinge on such a precious question. The coercion that was a hallmark of historical establishments of religion was coercion of religious orthodoxy and of financial support by force of law and threat of penalty. Typically, attendance at the state church was required; only clergy of the official church could lawfully perform sacraments; and dissenters, if tolerated, faced an array of civil disabilities. . . . Thus, while I have no quarrel with the Court's general proposition that the Establishment Clause "guarantees that government may not coerce anyone to support or participate in religion or its exercise," I see no warrant for expanding the concept of coercion beyond acts backed by threat of penalty—a brand of coercion that, happily, is readily discernible to those of us who have made a career of reading the disciples of Blackstone rather than of Freud. The Framers were indeed opposed to coercion of religious worship by the National Government; but, as their own sponsorship of nonsectarian prayer in public events demonstrates, they understood that "speech is not coercive; the listener may do as he likes." . . .

Our Religion Clause jurisprudence has become bedeviled (so to speak) by reliance on formulaic abstractions that are not derived from, but positively conflict with, our long-accepted constitutional traditions. Foremost among these has been the so-called *Lemon* test. The Court today demonstrates the irrelevance of *Lemon* by essentially ignoring it, and the interment of that case may be the one happy byproduct of the Court's otherwise lamentable decision. Unfortunately, however, the Court has replaced *Lemon* with its psycho-coercion test, which suffers the double disability of having no roots whatever in our people's historic practice, and being as infinitely expandable as the reasons for psychotherapy itself.

Another happy aspect of the case is that it is only a jurisprudential disaster and not a practical one. Given the odd basis for the Court's decision, invocations and benedictions will be able to be given at public school graduations next June, as they have for the past century and a half, so long as school authorities make clear that anyone who abstains from screaming in protest does not necessarily participate in the prayers. All that is seemingly needed is an announcement, or perhaps a written insertion at the beginning of the graduation program, to the effect that, while all are asked to rise for the invocation and benediction, none is compelled to join in them, nor will be assumed, by rising, to have done so. That obvious fact recited, the graduates and their parents may proceed to thank God, as Americans have always done, for the blessings He has generously bestowed on them and on their country. . . .

251

Religious Freedom Restoration Act (1993)

After the Court denied a rehearing in *Smith* (Document 248), a broad coalition of religious groups began working legislation to force the Court to return to the broader view of free exercise contained in *Sherbert v. Verner* (1963) and *Wisconsin v. Yoder* (1972). The coalition attracted broad bipartisan support, but the effort almost bogged down in details as conservatives wanted provisions that liberals found crossed the line between church and state, such as restrictions on abortion. In the end, broad and in large measure vague language was adopted. A popular law, the Religious Freedom Restoration Act (RFRA) purported to bind government at all levels—federal, state, and local—as well as all branches of government—executive, legislative, and judicial.

But where did Congress get the authority to pass RFRA? While a legislature can always override a court's interpretation of a statute by repassing it with more explicit language, what provision of the Constitution allowed Congress to override the high court's interpretation of the First Amendment? Unlike the Reconstruction amendments with their Enforcement Clauses, the first eight amendments bind Congress and do not give them any enforcement authority.

A clear challenge to the Court's authority, no one doubted that a test case would soon be heard. For that case, see Document 262.

See Douglas Laycock, "The Religious Freedom Restoration Act," 1993 *Brigham Young University Law Review* 221; Scott Idleman, "The Religious Freedom Restoration Act: Pushing the Limits of Legislative Power," 73 *Texas Law Review* 247 (1994); and Christopher L. Eisgruber and Lawrence G. Sager, "Why the Religious Freedom Restoration Act Is Unconstitutional," 69 *N.Y.U. Law Review* 437 (1994).

§ 2000bb. Congressional Findings and Declaration of Purposes

(a) Findings

(1) the framers of the Constitution, recognizing free exercise of religion as an unalienable right, secured its protection in the First Amendment to the Constitution;

(2) laws "neutral" toward religion may burden religious exercise as surely as laws intended to interfere with religious exercise;

(3) governments should not substantially burden religious exercise without compelling justification;

(4) in Employment Division v. Smith, 494 U.S. 872 (1990) the Supreme Court virtually eliminated the requirement that the government justify burdens on religious exercise imposed by laws neutral toward religion; and

(5) the compelling interest test as set forth in prior Federal court rulings is a workable test for striking sensible balances between religious liberty and competing prior governmental interests.

(b) Purposes

(1) to restore the compelling interest test as set forth in *Sherbert v. Verner*, 374 U.S. 398 (1963) and *Wisconsin v. Yoder*, 406 U.S. 205 (1972) and to guarantee its application in all cases where free exercise of religion is substantially burdened; and

(2) to provide a claim or defense to persons whose religious exercise is substantially burdened by government.

§ 2000bb–1. Free Exercise of Religion Protected

(a) In General

Government shall not substantially burden a person's exercise of religion even if the burden results from a rule of general applicability, except as provided in subsection (b) of this section.

(b) Exception

Government may substantially burden a person's exercise of religion only if it demonstrates that application of the burden to the person—

1. is in furtherance of a compelling governmental interest; and
2. is the least restrictive means of furthering that compelling governmental interest

(c) Judicial relief

A person whose religious exercise has been burdened in violation of this section may assert that violation as a claim or defense in a judicial proceeding and obtain appropriate relief against a government. Standing to assert a claim or defense under this section shall be governed by the general rules of standing under Article III of the Constitution.

Source: 42 U.S.C. §§ 2000bb *et seq.*

§ 2000bb–2. Definitions

As used in this chapter—

1. the term "government" includes a branch, department, agency, instrumentality, and official (or other person acting under color of law) of the United States, a State, or a subdivision of a State;
2. the term "State" includes the District of Columbia, the Commonwealth of Puerto Rico, and each territory and possession of the United States;
3. the term "demonstrates" means meets the burdens of going forward with the evidence and of persuasion; and
4. the term "exercise of religion" means the exercise of religion under the First Amendment to the Constitution.

§ 2000bb–3. Applicability

(a) In General

This chapter applies to all Federal and State law, and the implementation of that law, whether statutory or otherwise, and whether adopted before or after November 16, 1993.

(b) Rule of construction

Federal statutory law adopted after November 16, 1993 is subject to this chapter unless such law explicitly excludes such application by reference to this chapter.

(c) Religious belief unaffected

Nothing in this chapter shall be construed to authorize any government to burden any religious belief.

§ 2000bb–4. Establishment Clause Unaffected

Nothing in this chapter shall be construed to affect, interpret, or in any way address that portion of the First Amendment prohibiting laws respecting the establishment of religion (referred to in this section as the "Establishment Clause.") Granting government funding, benefits, or exemption, to the extent permissible under the Establishment Clause, shall not constitute a violation of this chapter. As used in this section, the term "granting," used with respect to government funding, benefits, or exemptions. does not include the denial of government funding, benefits, or exemption.

252   *Shaw v. Reno (1993)*

After the census of 1990, many states had to redraw their congressional as well as state assembly district lines. The U.S. Department of Justice, acting under §§ 2 and 5 of the 1965 Voting Rights Act, strongly encouraged the creation of a number of "majority-minority districts," districts drawn such that racial groups that were a minority in the state as a whole would be a majority in the particular district. The states had little choice but to comply, but in doing so triggered a number of lawsuits objecting to what many termed racial gerrymandering.

In earlier cases, the Court had seemingly approved such districts to redress the effect of past discrimination, and it seemed to rely on the Fifteenth Amendment's Enforcement Clause for utilizing a minimal rational basis test. By the 1990s, however, conservatives argued that the time for such action had passed, and race should not be a factor in electoral districting. They argued that here as in other areas, the state's use of racial classification should be subject to strict scrutiny. With a conservative majority on the Court, they saw the time as right to challenge redistricting based on race.

In this case, the Court agreed that white citizens of North Carolina who lived in majority-minority districts had a justiciable claim under the Equal Protection Clause and that the Court would, when it heard the merits of the case, apply strict scrutiny.

The issue would come before the Court again; see *Bush v. Vera* (Document 257) and *Abrams v. Johnson* (Document 260).

See Note, "The Constitutional Imperative of Proportional Representation," 94 *Yale Law Journal* 163 (1984); Abigail Thernstrom, "Shaw v. Reno: Notes from a Political Thicket," 1994 *Public Interest Law Review* 35; Pamela S. Karlan, "Still Hazy After All These Years: Voting Rights in the Post-Shaw Era," 26 *Cumberland Law Review* 287 (1995); Samuel Issacharoff, "The Constitutional Contours of Race and Politics," 1995 *Supreme Court Review* 45; and Lani Guinier, "(E)racing Democracy: the Voting Rights Cases," 1108 *Harvard Law Review* 109 (1994).

———

Justice O'CONNOR delivered the opinion of the Court:

This case involves two of the most complex and sensitive issues this Court has faced in recent years: the meaning of the constitutional "right" to vote, and the propriety of race-based state legislation designed to benefit members of historically disadvantaged racial minority groups. As a result of the 1990 census, North Carolina became entitled to a

Source: 509 U.S. 630 (1993)

twelfth seat in the United States House of Representatives. The General Assembly enacted a reapportionment plan that included one majority-black congressional district. After the Attorney General of the United States objected to the plan pursuant to § 5 of the Voting Rights Act, the General Assembly passed new legislation creating a second majority-black district. Appellants allege that the revised plan, which contains district boundary lines of dramatically irregular shape, constitutes an unconstitutional racial gerrymander. The question before us is whether appellants have stated a cognizable claim.

The voting age population of North Carolina is approximately 78% white, 20% black, and 1% Native American; the remaining 1% is predominantly Asian. The black population is relatively dispersed; blacks constitute a majority of the general population in only 5 of the State's 100 counties. The largest concentrations of black citizens live in the Coastal Plain, primarily in the northern part. The General Assembly's first redistricting plan contained one majority-black district centered in that area of the State. This district is somewhat a hook shaped. Centered in the northeast portion of the State, it moves southward until it tapers to a narrow band; then, with finger-like extensions, it reaches far into the southern-most part of the State near the South Carolina border. District 1 has been compared to a "Rorschach ink-blot test" and a "bug splattered on a windshield."

The second majority-black district, District 12, is even more unusually shaped. It is approximately 160 miles long and, for much of its length, no wider than the I-85 corridor. It winds in snake-like fashion through tobacco country, financial centers, and manufacturing areas "until it gobbles in enough enclaves of black neighborhoods." Of the 10 counties through which District 12 passes, five are cut into three different districts; even towns are divided. One state legislator has remarked that "if you drove down the interstate with both car doors open, you'd kill most of the people in the district."

An understanding of the appellants' claim is critical to our resolution of the case. In their complaint, appellants did not claim that the General Assembly's reapportionment plan unconstitutionally "diluted" white voting strength. They did not even claim to be white. Rather, they alleged that the deliberate segregation of voters into separate districts on the basis of race violated their constitutional right to participate in a "color-blind" electoral process. This Court never has held that race-conscious state decisionmaking is impermissible in all circumstances. What appellants object to is redistricting legislation that is so extremely irregular on its face that it rationally can be viewed only as an effort to segregate the races for purposes of voting, without regard for traditional districting principles and without sufficiently compelling justification. We conclude that appellants have stated a claim upon which relief can be granted under equal protection.

Appellants contend that redistricting legislation that is so bizarre on its face that it is "unexplainable on grounds other than race," demands the same close scrutiny that we give other state laws that classify citizens by race. Our voting rights precedents support that conclusion. Redistricting differs from other kinds of state decisionmaking in that the legislature always is aware of race when it draws district lines, just as it is aware of age, economic status, religious and political persuasion, and a variety of other demographic factors. That sort of race consciousness does not lead inevitably to impermissible race discrimination. When members of a racial group live together in one community, a reapportionment plan that concentrates members of the group in one district and excludes them from others may reflect wholly legitimate purposes. The district lines may be drawn, for example, to provide for compact districts of contiguous territory, or to maintain the integrity of political subdivisions. The difficulty of proof, of course, does not mean that a racial gerrymander, once established, should receive less scrutiny than other state legislation classifying citizens by race. Moreover, it seems clear to us that proof sometimes will not be difficult at all. In some exceptional cases, a reapportionment plan may be so highly irregular that, on its face, it rationally cannot be understood as anything other than an effort to segregate voters on the basis of race. *Gomillion* was such a case. So, too, would be a case in which a State concentrated a dispersed minority population in a single district by disregarding traditional districting principles such as compactness, contiguity, and respect for political subdivisions. We emphasize that these criteria are important not because they are constitutionally required—they are not—but because they are objective factors that may serve to defeat a claim that a district has been gerry-mandered on racial lines.

Put differently, we believe that reapportionment is one area in which appearances do matter. A reapportionment plan that includes in one district individuals who belong to the same race, but who are otherwise widely separated by geographical and political boundaries, and who may have little in common with one another but the color of their skin, bears an uncomfortable resemblance to political apartheid. It reinforces the per-ception that members of the same racial group—regardless of their age, education, eco-nomic status, or the community in which the live—think alike, share the same political interests, and will prefer the same candidates at the polls. We have rejected such per-ceptions elsewhere as impermissible racial stereotypes. By perpetuating such notions, a racial gerrymander may exacerbate the very patterns of racial bloc voting that majority-minority districting is sometimes said to counteract. The message that such districting sends to elected representatives is equally pernicious. When a district obviously is cre-ated solely to effectuate the perceived common interests of one racial group, elected offi-cials are more likely to believe that their primary obligation is to represent only the mem-bers of that group, rather than their constituency as a whole. This is altogether antithetical to our system of representative democracy. For these reasons, we conclude that a plaintiff challenging a reapportionment statute under equal protection may state a claim by alleging that the legislation, though race-neutral on its face, rationally cannot be understood as anything other than an effort to separate voters into different districts on the basis of race, and that the separation lacks sufficient justification. . . .

The state appellees suggest that a covered jurisdiction may have a compelling inter-est in creating majority-minority districts in order to comply with the Voting Rights Act. The States certainly have a very strong interest in complying with federal antidiscrimi-nation laws that are constitutionally valid as interpreted and as applied. But in the con-text of a Fourteenth Amendment challenge, courts must bear in mind the difference between what the law permits, and what it requires. For example, on remand North Car-olina might claim that it adopted the revised plan in order to comply with the "nonret-rogression" principle. Under that principle, a proposed voting change cannot be pre-cleared if it will lead to "a retrogression in the position of racial minorities with respect to their effective exercise of the electoral franchise." In *Beer v. United States* (1976), we held that a reapportionment plan that created one majority-minority district where none existed before passed muster under section 5 because it improved the position of racial minorities. Although the Court concluded that the redistricting scheme at issue in *Beer* was nonretrogressive, it did not hold that the plan, for that reason, was immune from constitutional challenge. The Court expressly declined to reach that question. Thus, we do not read *Beer* or any of our other cases to give covered jurisdictions carte blanche to engage in racial gerrymandering in the name of nonretrogression. The state appellees alternatively argue that the General Assembly's plan advanced a compelling interest entirely distinct from the Voting Rights Act. We previously have recognized a significant state interest in eradicating the effects of past racial discrimination. But the State must have a "strong basis in evidence for concluding that remedial action is necessary."

Racial classifications of any sort pose the risk of lasting harm to our society. They reinforce the belief, held by too many for too much of our history, that individuals should be judged by the color of their skin. Racial classifications with respect to voting carry particular dangers. Racial gerrymandering, even for remedial purposes, may balkanize us into competing racial factions; it threatens to carry us further from the goal of a political system in which race no longer matters. It is for these reasons that race-based districting by our state legislatures demands close judicial scrutiny. We hold that appellants have stated a claim under equal protection by alleging that the North Carolina General Assembly adopted a reapportionment scheme so irrational on its face that it can be understood only as an effort to segregate voters into separate voting districts because of their race, and that the separation lacks sufficient justification.

Justice WHITE, with whom Justice BLACKMUN and Justice STEVENS join, dissenting:

The notion that North Carolina's plan, under which whites remain a voting majority in a disproportionate number of congressional districts, might have violated appellants' constitutional rights is both a fiction and a departure from settled equal protection principles. The grounds for my disagreement are simply stated: Appellants have not presented a cognizable claim, because they have not alleged a cognizable injury. To date, we have held that only two types of state voting practices could give rise to a constitutional claim. The first involves direct and outright deprivation of the right to vote, for example by means of a poll tax or literacy test. Plainly, this variety is not implicated by appellants' allegations. The second type of unconstitutional practice is that which "affects the political strength of various groups," in violation of the Equal Protection Clause. As for this latter category, we have insisted that members of the political or racial group demonstrate that the challenged action have the intent and effect of unduly diminishing their influence on the political process.

The majority imagines a heretofore unknown type of constitutional claim. The logic of its theory appears to be that race-conscious redistricting that "segregates" by drawing odd-shaped lines is qualitatively different from race-conscious redistricting that affects groups in some other way. The distinction is without foundation. . . . As I understand the majority's theory, a redistricting plan that uses race to "segregate" voters by drawing "uncouth" lines is harmful in a way that a plan that uses race to distribute voters differently is not, for the former "bears an uncomfortable resemblance to political apartheid." The distinction is untenable. The other part of the majority's explanation of its holding is related to its simultaneous discomfort and fascination with irregularly shaped districts. Lack of compactness or contiguity, like uncouth district lines, certainly is a helpful indicator that some form of gerrymandering (racial or other) might have taken place. But while district irregularities may provide strong indicia of a potential gerrymander, they do no more than that. In particular, they have no bearing on whether the plan ultimately is found to violate the Constitution. Given two districts drawn on similar, race-based grounds, the one does not become more injurious than the other simply by virtue of being snake-like. By focusing on looks rather than impact, the majority in its approach will unnecessarily hinder to some extent a State's voluntary effort to ensure a modicum of minority representation where the minority population is geographically dispersed. When the creation of a majority-minority district does not unfairly minimize the voting power of any other group, the Constitution does not justify, much less mandate, such obstruction.

Justice SOUTER also dissented.

---

253 *Dolan v. City of Tigard (1994)*

In recent years, state and local governments have become increasingly concerned about the effects of development upon the environment and the strains put upon existing municipal resources such as schools, police, and fire protection. In *Nollan v. California Coastal Commission* (1987), the Court had seemingly imposed extremely high standards to justify public control of private property and indicated that any deprivation of the use of that property amounted to a taking. Five years later, in *Lucas v. South Carolina Coastal Council* (1992), the Court again struck down an environmental zoning ordinance, although it did so in a manner that raised more questions than it answered. The record from the state courts had been clearly incomplete in terms of the valuation of the property, and the Court accepted those findings without exploring other options, leaving unanswered questions about public interest, environmental safety, and land regulation.

In this case, the Court reiterated its commitment to property rights, and held that governmental regulation of land is subject to heightened judicial scrutiny to ensure that under the guise of legitimate exactions the state does not in effect confiscate land. The Court also distinguished between land use regulations that simply imposed restrictions on use, and those that required the landowner to transfer parts of the land to government for its uses. The test would now be that the government must prove a clear nexus between the restriction and a public interest, and then show a rough proportionality between the condition and the desired outcome.

See Symposium, "Land Use Law and the 21st Century," 12 *Journal of Environmental Law & Litigation* 1 (1997); Julian R. Kossow, "Dolan v. City of Tigard, Takings Law, and the Supreme Court: Throwing the Baby out with the Floodwater," 14 *Stanford Environmental Law Journal* 215 (1995); and Jeremy Walker, "Property Rights After Dolan," 20 *William and Mary Environmental Law and Policy Review* 263 (1996).

———

Chief Justice REHNQUIST delivered the opinion of the Court:

Petitioner challenges the decision of the Oregon Supreme Court which held that the city of Tigard could condition the approval of her building permit on the dedication of a portion of her property for flood control and traffic improvements. . . . We granted *certiorari* to resolve a question left open by our decision in *Nollan v. California Coastal Commission* (1987), of what is the required degree of connection between the exactions imposed by the city and the projected impacts of the proposed development.

The State of Oregon enacted a comprehensive land use management program in 1973. . . . Pursuant to the State's requirements, the city of Tigard, a community of some 30,000 residents on the southwest edge of Portland, developed a comprehensive plan and codified it in its Community Development Code (CDC). . . .

Petitioner Florence Dolan owns a plumbing and electric supply store located on Main Street in the Central Business District of the city. The store covers approximately 9,700 square feet on the eastern side of a 1.67-acre parcel, which includes a gravel parking lot. Fanno Creek flows through the southwestern corner of the lot and along its western boundary. The year-round flow of the creek renders the area within the creek's 100-year floodplain virtually unusable for commercial development. The city's comprehensive plan includes the Fanno Creek floodplain as part of the city's greenway system.

Petitioner applied to the city for a permit to redevelop the site. Her proposed plans called for nearly doubling the size of the store to 17,600 square feet, and paving a 39-space parking lot. The existing store, located on the opposite side of the parcel, would be razed in sections as construction progressed on the new building. In the second phase of the project, petitioner proposed to build an additional structure on the northeast side of the site for complementary businesses, and to provide more parking. The proposed expansion and intensified use are consistent with the city's zoning scheme in the Central Business District. . . .

The City Planning Commission . . . granted petitioner's permit application subject to conditions . . . that petitioner dedicate the portion of her property lying within the 100-year floodplain for improvement of a storm drainage system along Fanno Creek and that she dedicate an additional 15-foot strip of land adjacent to the floodplain as a pedestrian/bicycle pathway. . . .

Without question, had the city simply required petitioner to dedicate a strip of land along Fanno Creek for public use, rather than conditioning the grant of her permit to redevelop her property on such a dedication, a taking would have occurred. . . . Such public access would deprive petitioner of the right to exclude others, "one of the most essential sticks in the bundle of rights that are commonly characterized as property."

Petitioner contends that the city has forced her to choose between the building permit and her right under the Fifth Amendment to just compensation for the public easements. Petitioner does not quarrel with the city's authority to exact some forms of dedication as a condition for the grant of a building permit, but challenges the showing made by the city to justify these exactions. She argues that the city has identified "no special benefits" conferred on her, and has not identified any "special quantifiable burdens" created by her new store that would justify the particular dedications required from her which are not required from the public at large.

In evaluating petitioner's claim, we must first determine whether the "essential nexus" exists between the "legitimate state interest" and the permit condition exacted by the city. If we find that a nexus exists, we must then decide the required degree of connection between the exactions and the projected impact of the proposed development. We were not required to reach this question in *Nollan,* because we concluded that the connection did not meet even the loosest standard. Here, however, we must decide this question. . . .

Undoubtedly, the prevention of flooding along Fanno Creek and the reduction of traffic congestion in the Central Business District qualify as the type of legitimate public purposes we have upheld. . . . It seems equally obvious that a nexus exists between preventing flooding along Fanno Creek and limiting development within the creek's 100-year floodplain. Petitioner proposes to double the size of her retail store and to pave her now-gravel parking lot, thereby expanding the impervious surface on the property and increasing the amount of stormwater run-off into Fanno Creek.

The same may be said for the city's attempt to reduce traffic congestion by providing for alternative means of transportation. In theory, a pedestrian/bicycle pathway provides a useful alternative means of transportation for workers and shoppers. . . .

The second part of our analysis requires us to determine whether the degree of the exactions demanded by the city's permit conditions bear the required relationship to the projected impact of petitioner's proposed development. . . .

The city required that petitioner dedicate "to the city as Greenway all portions of the site that fall within the existing 100-year floodplain [of Fanno Creek] . . . and all property 15 feet above [the floodplain] boundary." In addition, the city demanded that the retail store be designed so as not to intrude into the greenway area. The city relies on the Commission's rather tentative findings that increased stormwater flow from petitioner's property "can only add to the public need to manage the [floodplain] for drainage purposes" to support its conclusion that the "requirement of dedication of the floodplain area on the site is related to the applicant's plan to intensify development on the site." . . .

We think a term such as "rough proportionality" best encapsulates what we hold to be the requirement of the Fifth Amendment. No precise mathematical calculation is required, but the city must make some sort of individualized determination that the required dedication is related both in nature and extent to the impact of the proposed development. . . .

It is axiomatic that increasing the amount of impervious surface will increase the quantity and rate of storm-water flow from petitioner's property. . . . Therefore, keeping the floodplain open and free from development would likely confine the pressures on Fanno Creek created by petitioner's development. In fact, because petitioner's property lies within the Central Business District, the Community Development Code already required that petitioner leave 15% of it as open space and the undeveloped floodplain would have nearly satisfied that requirement. . . . But the city demanded more—it not only wanted petitioner not to build in the floodplain, but it also wanted petitioner's property along Fanno Creek for its Greenway system. The city has never said why a public greenway, as opposed to a private one, was required in the interest of flood control.

The difference to petitioner, of course, is the loss of her ability to exclude others. . . . It is difficult to see why recreational visitors trampling along petitioner's floodplain easement are sufficiently related to the city's legitimate interest in reducing flooding problems along Fanno Creek, and the city has not attempted to make any individualized determination to support this part of its request. . . .

If petitioner's proposed development had somehow encroached on existing greenway space in the city, it would have been reasonable to require petitioner to provide some alternative greenway space for the public either on her property or elsewhere. . . . We conclude that the findings upon which the city relies do not show the required reasonable relationship between the floodplain easement and the petitioner's proposed new building.

With respect to the pedestrian/bicycle pathway, we have no doubt that the city was correct in finding that the larger retail sales facility proposed by petitioner will increase traffic on the streets of the Central Business District. The city estimates that the proposed development would generate roughly 435 additional trips per day. Dedications for streets, sidewalks, and other public ways are generally reasonable exactions to avoid excessive congestion from a proposed property use. But on the record before us, the city has not met its burden of demonstrating that the additional number of vehicle and bicycle trips generated by the petitioner's development reasonably relate to the city's requirement for a dedication of the pedestrian/bicycle pathway easement. The city simply found that the creation of the pathway "could offset some of the traffic demand . . . and lessen the increase in traffic congestion." . . .

The judgment of the Supreme Court of Oregon is reversed, and the case is remanded for further proceedings consistent with this opinion.

Justice STEVENS, with whom Justice BLACKMUN and Justice GINSBURG join, dissenting:

. . . It is not merely state cases, but our own cases as well, that require the analysis to focus on the impact of the city's action on the entire parcel of private property. *In Penn Central Transportation Co. v. New York City* (1978), we stated that takings jurisprudence "does not divide a single parcel into discrete segments and attempt to determine whether rights in a particular segment have been entirely abrogated." . . . *Andrus v. Allard* (1979), reaffirmed the nondivisibility principle outlined in *Penn Central,* stating that "at least where an owner possesses a full 'bundle' of property rights, the destruction of one 'strand' of the bundle is not a taking, because the aggregate must be viewed in its entirety.". . . . Although limitation of the right to exclude others undoubtedly constitutes a significant infringement upon property ownership, . . . restrictions on that right do not alone constitute a taking, and do not do so in any event unless they "unreasonably impair the value or use" of the property. . . .

In our changing world one thing is certain: uncertainty will characterize predictions about the impact of new urban developments on the risks of floods, earthquakes, traffic congestion, or environmental harms. When there is doubt concerning the magnitude of those impacts, the public interest in averting them must outweigh the private interest of the commercial entrepreneur. If the government can demonstrate that the conditions it has imposed in a land-use permit are rational, impartial and conducive to fulfilling the aims of a valid land-use plan, a strong presumption of validity should attach to those conditions. The burden of demonstrating that those conditions have unreasonably impaired the economic value of the proposed improvement belongs squarely on the shoulders of the party challenging the state action's constitutionality. That allocation of burdens has served us well in the past. The Court has stumbled badly today by reversing it.

I respectfully dissent.

---

254   *United States v. Lopez (1995)*

Following the constitutional crisis of 1937, the Court for more than a half-century upheld a very broad interpretation of the Commerce Power. Since there are no explicit federal police powers, whenever Congress wanted to act in a way to protect public safety, it would usually claim that the evil being attacked impeded interstate commerce, and the courts normally agreed.

But Ronald Reagan and the men and women he appointed to the courts did believe in federalism and did not share this expansive view of federal power for some issues. Although politicians since Richard Nixon's time had been talking of a "new federalism," the Court in fact began reviving federalism with a series of decisions that made clear it would no longer accept the Commerce Clause as a blanket justification for anything Congress wanted to do.

In 1990, Congress enacted the Gun-Free School Zones Act that made it a federal offense for an individual to possess a firearm within the boundaries of a school zone. A twelfth-grade student in San Antonio came to school with a .38 caliber handgun and five bullets; he was arrested under a Texas law forbidding the possession of guns on school property, but the state charge was dismissed when federal agents charged the youth with violating the 1990 law.

In a decision not seen since the heyday of the Four Horsemen, the Court, by a narrow majority, held that Congress had exceeded its constitutional authority under the Commerce Clause. The Court has continued its efforts to resuscitate federalism, such as its decision to strike down part of the Brady Law (see Document 261). But all of these decisions have been by 5–4 votes, and it is unclear whether the trend will continue when new members join the Court.

See Nicole Huberfield, "The Commerce Clause post-Lopez: It's Not Dead Yet," 28 *Seton Hall Law Review* 182 (1997); Lisa Gillette, "Lawyers, Guns and Commerce: United States v. Lopez and the New Commerce Clause," 46 *DePaul Law Review* 823 (1997); and Stephen Gauter, "Did United States v. Lopez Turn Back the Clock on the Commerce Clause?" 21 *Thurgood Marshall Law Review* 343 (1996).

———

Chief Justice REHNQUIST delivered the opinion of the Court:
 . . . We start with first principles. The Constitution creates a Federal Government of enumerated powers. . . . As James Madison wrote, "the powers delegated by the proposed Constitution to the federal government are few and defined. Those which are to remain in the State governments are numerous and indefinite." The *Federalist No. 45*. . . . This constitutionally mandated division of authority "was adopted by the Framers to ensure protection of our fundamental liberties." . . . "Just as the separation and independence of the coordinate branches of the Federal Government serves to prevent the accumulation of excessive power in any one branch, a healthy balance of power between the States and the Federal Government will reduce the risk of tyranny and abuse from either front." . . .

The Constitution delegates to Congress the power "to regulate Commerce with foreign Nations, and among the several States, and with the Indian Tribes." . . . The Court, through Chief Justice Marshall, first defined the nature of Congress' commerce power in *Gibbons v. Ogden* (1824) . . .

The *Gibbons* Court, however, acknowledged that limitations on the commerce power are inherent in the very language of the Commerce Clause.

 "It is not intended to say that these words comprehend that commerce, which is completely internal, which is carried on between man and man in a State, or between different parts of the same State, and which does not extend to or affect other States." . . .

For nearly a century thereafter, the Court's Commerce Clause decisions dealt but rarely with the extend of Congress' power, and almost entirely with the Commerce Clause as a limit on state legislation that discriminated against interstate commerce. . . .

[In cases decided during the era of the New Deal the Court] ushered in an era of Commerce Clause jurisprudence that greatly expanded the previously defined authority of Congress under that Clause. In part, this was a recognition of the great changes that had occurred in the way business was carried on in this country. Enterprises that had once been local or at most regional in nature had become national in scope. But the doctrinal change also reflected a view that earlier Commerce Clause cases artificially had constrained the authority of Congress to regulate interstate commerce.

But even these modern-era precedents which have expanded congressional power under the Commerce Clause confirm that this power is subject to outer limits. . . .

Consistent with this structure, we have identified three broad categories of activity that Congress may regulate under its commerce power. . . . First, Congress may regulate the use of the channels of interstate commerce. . . . Second, Congress is empowered to regulate and protect the instrumentalities of interstate commerce, or persons or things in interstate commerce, even though the threat may come only from intrastate activities. . . . Finally, Congress' commerce authority includes the power to regulate those activities having a substantial relation to interstate commerce, . . . i.e., those activities that substantially affect interstate commerce. . . .

Within the final category, admittedly, our case law has not been clear whether an activity must "affect" or "substantially affect" interstate commerce in order to be within Congress' power to regulate it under the Commerce Clause. . . . We conclude, consistent with the great weight of our case law, that the proper test requires an analysis of whether the regulated activity "substantially affects" interstate commerce.

We now turn to consider the power of Congress, in the light of this framework, to enact § 922(q). The first two categories of authority may be quickly disposed of: the statute is not a regulation of the use of the channels of interstate commerce, nor is it an attempt to prohibit the interstate transportation of a commodity through the channels of commerce; nor can [the statute] be justified as a regulation by which Congress has sought to protect an instrumentality of interstate commerce or a thing in interstate commerce. Thus, if § 922(q) is to be sustained, it must be under the third category as a regulation of an activity that substantially affects interstate commerce.

First, . . . § 922(q) is a criminal statute that by its terms has nothing to do with "commerce" or any sort of economic enterprise, however broadly one might define those terms. . . .

Second, § 922(q) contains no jurisdictional element which would ensure, through case-by-case inquiry, that the firearm possession in question affects interstate commerce. . . .

. . . The Government argues that possession of a firearm in a school zone may result in violent crime and that violent crime can be expected to affect the functioning of the national economy in two ways. First, the costs of violent crime are substantial, and, through the mechanism of insurance, those costs are spread throughout the population. . . . Second, violent crime reduces the willingness of individuals to travel to areas within the country that are perceived to be unsafe. . . . The Government also argues that the presence of guns in schools poses a substantial threat to the educational process by threatening the learning environment. A handicapped educational process, in turn, will result in a less productive citizenry. That, in turn, would have an adverse effect on the Nation's economic well-being. As a result, the Government argues that Congress could rationally have concluded that § 922(q) substantially affects interstate commerce.

We pause to consider the implications of the Government's arguments. The Government admits, under its "costs of crime" reasoning, that Congress could regulate not only all violent crime, but all activities that might lead to violent crime, regardless of how tenuously they relate to interstate commerce. . . . Similarly, under the Government's "national productivity" reasoning, Congress could regulate any activity that it found was related to the economic productivity of individual citizens: family law (including marriage, divorce, and child custody), for example. Under the theories that the Government presents in support of § 922(q), it is difficult to perceive any limitation on federal power, even in areas such as criminal law enforcement or education where States historically have been sovereign. Thus, if we were to accept the Government's arguments, we are hard-pressed to posit any activity by an individual that Congress is without power to regulate.

Although Justice Breyer argues that acceptance of the Government's rationales would not authorize a general federal police power, he is unable to identify any activity that the States may regulate but Congress may not. . . .

For instance, if Congress can, pursuant to its Commerce Clause power, regulate activities that adversely affect the learning environment, then *a fortiori,* it also can regulate the educational process directly. Congress could determine that a school's curriculum has a "significant" effect on the extent of classroom learning. As a result, Congress could mandate a federal curriculum for local elementary and secondary schools because what is taught in local schools has a significant "effect on classroom learning, and that, in turn has a substantial effect on interstate commerce. . . .

Admittedly, a determination whether an intrastate activity is commercial or non-commercial may in some cases result in legal uncertainty. . . .

. . . The possession of a gun in a local school zone is in no sense an economic activity that might, through repetition elsewhere, substantially affect any sort of interstate commerce. Respondent was a local student at a local school; there is no indication that he had recently moved in interstate commerce, and there is no requirement that his possession of the firearm have any concrete tie to interstate commerce.

To uphold the Government's contentions here, we would have to pile inference upon inference in a manner that would bid fair to convert congressional authority under the Commerce clause to a general police power of the sort retained by the States. Admittedly, some of our prior cases have taken long steps down that road, giving great deference to congressional action. The broad language in these opinions has suggested the possibility of additional expansion, but we decline here to proceed any further. . . .

Affirmed.

Justice BREYER, with whom Justice STEVENS, Justice SOUTER, and Justice GINSBERG join, dissenting:
. . . In my view, the statute falls well within the scope of the commerce power as this Court has understood that power over the last half-century.

In reaching this conclusion, I apply three basic principles of Commerce Clause interpretation. First, the power to "regulate Commerce . . . among the several States" . . . encompasses the power to regulate local activities insofar as they significantly affect interstate commerce. . . .

Second, in determining whether a local activity will likely have a significant effect upon interstate commerce, a court must consider, not the effect of any individual act (a single instance of gun possession), but rather the cumulative effect of all similar instances (*i.e.,* the effect of all guns possessed in or near schools). . . .

Third, the Constitution requires us to judge the connection between a regulated activity and interstate commerce, not directly, but at one remove. Courts must give Congress a degree of leeway in determining the existence of a significant factual connection between the regulated activity and interstate commerce—both because the Constitution delegates the commerce power directly to Congress and because the determination requires an empirical judgment of a kind that a legislature is more likely than a court to make with accuracy. The traditional words "rational basis" capture this leeway. . . . Thus, the specific question before us, as the Court recognizes, is not whether the "regulated activity sufficiently affected interstate commerce," but, rather, whether Congress could have had "*a rational basis*" for so concluding. . . .

Applying these principles to the case at hand, we must ask whether Congress could have had a *rational basis* for finding a significant (or substantial) connection between gun-related school violence and interstate commerce. . . . Could Congress rationally have found that "violent crime in school zones," through its effect on the "quality of education," significantly (or substantially) affects "interstate" or "foreign commerce"? . . . The answer to this question must be yes. Numerous reports and studies—generated both inside and outside government—make clear that Congress could reasonably have found the empirical connection that its law, implicitly or explicitly, asserts. . . .

For one thing, reports, hearings, and other readily available literature make clear that the problem of guns in and around schools is widespread and extremely serious. . . . This wide-spread violence in schools throughout the Nation significantly interferes with the quality of education in those schools. . . . Congress obviously could have thought that guns and learning are mutually exclusive. . . . And, Congress could therefore have found a substantial educational problem—teachers unable to teach, students unable to learn—and concluded that guns near schools contribute substantially to the size and scope of that problem.

Having found that guns in schools significantly undermine the quality of education in our Nation's classrooms, Congress could also have found, given the effect of education upon interstate and foreign commerce, that gun-related violence in and around schools is a commercial, as well as a human, problem. Education, although far more than a matter of economics, has long been inextricably intertwined with the Nation's economy. . . .

In recent years the link between secondary education and business has strengthened, becoming both more direct and more important. Scholars on the subject report that technological changes and innovations in management techniques have altered the nature of the workplace so that more jobs now demand greater education skills. . . .

Increasing global competition also has made primary and secondary education economically more important. . . .

Finally, there is evidence that, today more than ever, many firms base their location decisions upon the presence, or absence, of a work force with a basic education. . . .

The economic links I have just sketched seem fairly obvious. Why then is it not equally obvious, in light of those links, that a widespread, serious, and substantial physical threat to teaching and learning *also* substantially threatens the commerce to which that teaching and learning is inextricably tied? . . .

. . . Upholding this legislation would no more than simply recognize that Congress had a "rational basis" for finding a significant connection between guns in or near schools and (through their effect on education) the interstate and foreign commerce they threaten. For these reasons, I would reverse the judgment of the Court of Appeals. Respectfully, I dissent.

255

U.S. Term Limits, Inc.
v. Thornton (1995)

In the 1990s, a reaction against perceived abuse of congressional power led not only to ratification of the Twenty-Seventh Amendment, but also to efforts to limit the number of terms a person could serve in Congress. A variety of grass roots organizations began circulating petitions to limit congressional tenure. Although the Constitution sets no limits, advocates of term limits claimed that the powers inherent in the states permitted imposition of limits. Proponents of term limits managed to win several referendums, secure the amendment of some state constitutions, and also won some legislative victories. Needless to say, few politicians favored these initiatives, and it was only a matter of time before a challenge reached the Supreme Court.

In November 1992, Arkansas voters approved Amendment 73 to the state constitution, limiting the number of terms their representatives could serve in the two houses of Congress. By a bare 5–4 majority the centrist bloc prevailed and struck down the measure. What is interesting is that both the majority opinion by Justice Stevens as well as the dissent by Justice Thomas rely heavily on history to support their positions.

See Christopher A. Marks, "*U.S. Term Limits v. Thornton* and *United States v. Lopez:* The Supreme Court Resuscitates the Tenth Amendment," 68 *University of Colorado Law Review* 541 (1997); Elizabeth Garrett, "Term Limits and the Myth of the Citizen-Legislator," 81 *Cornell Law Review* 623 (1996); and Ronald D. Rotunda, "The Aftermath of Thornton," 13 *Constitutional Commentary* 201 (1996).

———

Justice STEVENS delivered the opinion of the Court:

The Constitution sets forth qualifications for membership in the Congress of the United States. Article I, Section 2, cl. 2, which applies to the House of Representatives, provides:

"No Person shall be a Representative who shall not have attained to the Age of twenty five Years, and been seven Years a Citizen of the United States, and who shall not, when elected, be an Inhabitant of that State in which he shall be chosen."

Article I, Section 3, cl. 3, which applies to the Senate, similarly provides:

Source: 514 U.S. 779 (1995)

"No Person shall be a Senator who shall not have attained to the Age of thirty Years, and have been nine Years a Citizen of the United States, and who shall not, when elected, be an Inhabitant of that State for which he shall be chosen."

Today's cases present a challenge to an amendment to the Arkansas State Constitution that prohibits the name of an otherwise-eligible candidate for Congress from appearing on the general election ballot if that candidate has already served three terms in the House of Representatives or two terms in the Senate. The Arkansas Supreme Court held that the amendment violates the Federal Constitution. We agree with that holding. Such a state-imposed restriction is contrary to the "fundamental principle of our representative democracy," embodied in the Constitution, that "the people should choose whom they please to govern them." . . . Allowing individual States to adopt their own qualifications for congressional service would be inconsistent with the Framers' vision of a uniform National Legislature representing the people of the United States. If the qualifications set forth in the text of the Constitution are to be changed, that text must be amended. . . .

The constitutionality of Amendment 73 depends critically on the resolution of two distinct issues. The first is whether the Constitution forbids States from adding to or altering the qualifications specifically enumerated in the Constitution. The second is, if the Constitution does so forbid, whether the fact that Amendment 73 is formulated as a ballot access restriction rather than as an outright disqualification is of constitutional significance. Our resolution of these issues draws upon our prior resolution of a related but distinct issue: whether Congress has the power to add to or alter the qualifications of its Members.

In *Powell v. McCormack* (1969) we reviewed the history and text of the Qualifications Clauses in a case involving an attempted exclusion of a duly elected Member of Congress. The principal issue was whether the power granted to each House in Art. I, Section 5, to judge the "Qualifications of its own Members" includes the power to impose qualifications other than those set forth in the text of the Constitution. In an opinion by Chief Justice Warren for eight Members of the Court, we held that it does not. . . .

Petitioners argue that the Constitution contains no express prohibition against state-added qualifications, and that Amendment 73 is therefore an appropriate exercise of a State's reserved power to place additional restrictions on the choices that its own voters may make. We disagree for two independent reasons. First, we conclude that the power to add qualifications is not within the "original powers" of the States, and thus is not reserved to the States by the Tenth Amendment. Second, even if States possessed some original power in this area, we conclude that the Framers intended the Constitution to be the exclusive source of qualifications for members of Congress, and that the Framers thereby "divested" States of any power to add qualifications. . . .

Contrary to petitioners' assertions, the power to add qualifications is not part of the original powers of sovereignty that the Tenth Amendment reserved to the States. Petitioners' Tenth Amendment argument misconceives the nature of the right at issue because that Amendment could only "reserve" that which existed before. As Justice Story recognized, "the states can exercise no powers whatsoever, which exclusively spring out of the existence of the national government, which the constitution does not delegate to them. . . . No state can say, that it has reserved, what it never possessed." . . .

With respect to setting qualifications for service in Congress, no such right existed before the Constitution was ratified. The contrary argument overlooks the revolutionary character of the government that the Framers conceived. Prior to the adoption of the Constitution, the States had joined together under the Articles of Confederation. In that system, "the States retained most of their sovereignty, like independent nations bound together only by treaties." . . . After the Constitutional Convention convened, the Framers were presented with, and eventually adopted a variation of, "a plan not merely to amend the Articles of Confederation but to create an entirely new National Government with a National Executive, National Judiciary, and a National Legislature." . . . In adopting that plan, the Framers envisioned a uniform national system, rejecting the notion that the Nation was a collection of States, and instead creating a direct link between the National Government and the people of the United States. . . . In that National Government, representatives owe primary allegiance not to the people of a State, but to the people of the Nation. . . .

Even if we believed that States possessed as part of their original powers some control over congressional qualifications, the text and structure of the Constitution, the relevant historical materials, and, most importantly, the "basic principles of our democratic system" all demonstrate that the Qualifications Clauses were intended to preclude the States from exercising any such power and to fix as exclusive the qualifications in the Constitution. . . .

Our conclusion that States lack the power to impose qualifications vindicates the same "fundamental principle of our representative democracy" that we recognized in *Powell,* namely that "the people should choose whom they please to govern them." . . .

As we noted earlier, the *Powell* Court recognized that an egalitarian ideal—that election to the National Legislature should be open to all people of merit—provided a critical foundation for the Constitutional structure. This egalitarian theme echoes throughout the constitutional debates. . . .

Similarly, we believe that state-imposed qualifications, as much as congressionally imposed qualifications, would undermine the second critical idea recognized in *Powell:* that an aspect of sovereignty is the right of the people to vote for whom they wish. Again, the source of the qualification is of little moment in assessing the qualification's restrictive impact.

Finally, state-imposed restrictions, unlike the congressionally imposed restrictions at issue in *Powell,* violate a third idea central to this basic principle: that the right to choose representatives belongs not to the States, but to the people. . . . Thus the Framers, in perhaps their most important contribution, conceived of a Federal Government directly responsible to the people, possessed of direct power over the people, and chosen directly, not by States, but by the people. The Framers implemented this ideal most clearly in the provision, extant from the beginning of the Republic, that calls for the Members of the House of Representatives to be "chosen every second Year by the People of the several States." . . .

Consistent with these views, the constitutional structure provides for a uniform salary to be paid from the national treasury, allows the States but a limited role in federal elections, and maintains strict checks on state interference with the federal election process. The Constitution also provides that the qualifications of the representatives of each State will be judged by the representatives of the entire Nation. The Constitution thus creates a uniform national body representing the interests of a single people.

Permitting individual States to formulate diverse qualifications for their representatives would result in a patchwork of state qualifications, undermining the uniformity and the national character that the Framers envisioned and sought to ensure. . . .

Petitioners attempt to overcome this formidable array of evidence against the States' power to impose qualifications by arguing that the practice of the States immediately after the adoption of the Constitution demonstrates their understanding that they possessed such power. One may properly question the extent to which the States' own practice is a reliable indicator of the contours of restrictions that the Constitution imposed on States, especially when no court has ever upheld a state-imposed qualification of any sort. But petitioners' argument is unpersuasive even on its own terms. . . .

The contemporaneous state practice with respect to term limits is similar. At the time of the Convention, States widely supported term limits in at least some circumstances. The Articles of Confederation contained a provision for term limits. As we have noted, some members of the Convention had sought to impose term limits for Members of Congress. In addition, many States imposed term limits on state officers, four placed limits on delegates to the Continental Congress, and several States voiced support for term limits for Members of Congress. Despite this widespread support, no State sought to impose any term limits on its own federal representatives. Thus, a proper assessment of contemporaneous state practice provides further persuasive evidence of a general understanding that the qualifications in the Constitution were unalterable by the States. . . .

Petitioners argue that, even if States may not add qualifications, Amendment 73 is constitutional because it is not such a qualification, and because Amendment 73 is a permissible exercise of state power to regulate the "Times, Places and Manner of Holding Elections." We reject these contentions. . . .

In our view, Amendment 73 is an indirect attempt to accomplish what the Constitution prohibits Arkansas from accomplishing directly. . . .

Petitioners do, however, contest the Arkansas Supreme Court's conclusion that the Amendment has the same practical effect as an absolute bar. They argue that the possibility of a write-in campaign creates a real possibility for victory, especially for an entrenched incumbent. One may reasonably question the merits of that contention. . . . But even if petitioners are correct that incumbents may occasionally win reelection as write-in candidates, there is no denying that the ballot restrictions will make it significantly more difficult for the barred candidate to win the election. In our view, an amendment with the avowed purpose and obvious effect of evading the requirements of the Qualifications Clauses by handicapping a class of candidates cannot stand. . . .

Justice THOMAS, with whom The Chief Justice, Justice O'CONNOR, and Justice SCALIA join, dissenting:

It is ironic that the Court bases today's decision on the right of the people to "choose whom they please to govern them." . . . Under our Constitution, there is only one State whose people have the right to "choose whom they please" to represent Arkansas in Congress. The Court holds, however, that neither the elected legislature of that State nor the people themselves (acting by ballot initiative) may prescribe any qualifications for those representatives. The majority therefore defends the right of the people of Arkansas to "choose whom they please to govern them" by invalidating a provision that won nearly 60% of the votes cast in a direct election and that carried every congressional district in the State.

I dissent. Nothing in the Constitution deprives the people of each State of the power to prescribe eligibility requirements for the candidates who seek to represent them in Congress. The Constitution is simply silent on this question. And where the Constitution is silent, it raises no bar to action by the States or the people. . . .

Our system of government rests on one overriding principle: all power stems from the consent of the people. To phrase the principle in this way, however, is to be imprecise about something important to the notion of "reserved" powers. The ultimate source of the Constitution's authority is the consent of the people of each individual State, not the consent of the undifferentiated people of the Nation as a whole. . . .

As far as the Federal Constitution is concerned, then, the States can exercise all powers that the Constitution does not withhold from them. The Federal Government and the States thus face different default rules: where the Constitution is silent about the exercise of a particular power—that is, where the Constitution does not speak either expressly or by necessary implication—the Federal Government lacks that power and the States enjoy it.

These basic principles are enshrined in the Tenth Amendment, which declares that all powers neither delegated to the Federal Government not prohibited to the States "are reserved to the States respectively, or to the people." With this careful last phrase, the Amendment avoids taking any position on the division of power between the state governments and the people of the States: it is up to the people of each State to determine which "reserved" powers their state government may exercise. But the Amendment does make clear that powers reside at the state level except where the Constitution removes them from that level. . . .

The majority begins by announcing an enormous and untenable limitation on the principle expressed by the Tenth Amendment. According to the majority, the States possess only those powers that the Constitution affirmatively grants to them or that they enjoyed before the Constitution was adopted; the Tenth Amendment "could only 'reserve' that which existed before." . . .

The majority is therefore quite wrong to conclude that the people of the States cannot authorize their state governments to exercise any powers that were unknown to the States when the Federal Constitution was drafted. Indeed, the majority's position frustrates the apparent purpose of the Amendment's final phrase. . . .

The majority also sketches out what may be an alternative (and narrower) argument. Again citing Justice Story, the majority suggests that it would be inconsistent with the notion of "national sovereignty for the States or the people of the States to have any reserved powers over the selection of Members of Congress." . . . The majority apparently reaches this conclusion in two steps. First, it asserts that because Congress as a whole is an institution of the National Government, the individual Members of Congress "owe primary allegiance not to the people of a State, but to the people of the Nation."

Second, it concludes that because each Member of Congress has a nationwide constituency once he takes office, it would be inconsistent with the Framers' scheme to let a single State prescribe qualifications for him. . . .

But the selection of representatives in Congress is indisputably an act of the people of each State, not some abstract people of the Nation as a whole. . . .

When the people of Georgia pick their representatives in Congress, they are acting as the people of Georgia, not as the corporate agents for the undifferentiated people of the Nation as a whole. See *In re Green* (1890) . . .

The Qualifications Clauses do prevent the individual States from abolishing all eligibility requirements for Congress. . . . Because Congress wields power over all the States, the people of each State need some guarantee that the legislators elected by the people of other States will meet minimum standards of competence. The Qualifications Clauses provide that guarantee: they list the requirements that the Framers considered essential to protect the competence of the National Legislature.

If the people of a State decide that they would like their representatives to possess additional qualifications, however, they have done nothing to frustrate the policy behind the Qualifications Clauses. . . .

Although the Qualifications Clauses neither state nor imply the prohibition that it finds in them, the majority infers from the Framers' "democratic principles" that the Clauses must have been generally understood to preclude the people of the States and their state legislatures from prescribing any additional qualifications for their representatives in Congress. But the majority's evidence on this point establishes only two more modest propositions: (1) the Framers did not want the Federal Constitution itself to impose a broad set of disqualifications for congressional office, and (2) the Framers did not want the Federal Congress to be able to supplement the few disqualifications that the Constitution does set forth. . . .

In addition to its arguments about democratic principles, the majority asserts that more specific historical evidence supports its view that the Framers did not intend to permit supplementation of the Qualifications Clauses. But when one focuses on the distinction between congressional power to add qualifications for congressional office and the power of the people or their state legislatures to add such qualifications, one realizes that this assertion has little basis. . . .

Here too, state practice immediately after the ratification of the Constitution refutes the majority's suggestion that the Qualifications Clauses were commonly understood as being exclusive. Five States supplemented the constitutional disqualifications in their very first election laws, and the surviving records suggest that the legislatures of these States considered and rejected the interpretation of the Constitution that the majority adopts today.

As the majority concedes, the first Virginia election law erected a property qualification for Virginia's contingent in the Federal House of Representatives. . . . What is more, while the Constitution merely requires representatives to be inhabitants of their State, the legislatures of five of the seven States that divided themselves into districts for House elections added that representatives also had to be inhabitants of the district that elected them. Three of these States adopted durational residency requirements too, insisting that representatives have resided within their districts for at least a year (or, in one case, three years) before being elected. . . .

No matter how narrowly construed, . . . today's decision reads the Qualifications Clauses to impose substantial implicit prohibitions on the States and the people of the States. I would not draw such an expansive negative inference from the fact that the Constitution requires Members of Congress to be a certain age, to be inhabitants of the States that they represent, and to have been United States citizens for a specified period. Rather, I would read the Qualifications Clauses to do no more than what they say. I respectfully dissent.

256

Rosenberger v. Rector and Visitors of the University of Virginia (1995)

Wide Awake Publications, a student-sponsored Christian evangelical magazine, sought funding from the University of Virginia, claiming that as a student organization it should not be denied funds simply because it focused on religious rather than secular matters. The university declined, arguing that to support a seemingly proselytizing club would violate the Establishment Clause. The university's case had a number of weak spots, including the fact that it routinely funded other clearly religious groups, such as the Jewish Hillel Society and a Muslim student organization. By a 5–4 vote, the Court held that the university could not discriminate against Wide Awake. Justice Kennedy's opinion is a mixture of both speech and establishment jurisprudence, since denying funds to a student publication because of the content violated the Speech Clause. The dissenters, led by Justice Souter, denied this interpretation, and rallied once again to the notion of a wall of separation.

See Casey M. Nault, "Bridging the Separation of Church and State: How Rosenberger Threatens Religious Liberty," 70 *Southern California Law Review* 1049 (1997); Kent Greenawalt, "Viewpoints from Olympus," 96 *Columbia Law Review* 697 (1996); and A. Louise Oliver, "Tearing Down the Wall," 19 *Harvard Journal of Law and Public Policy* 587 (1996).

———

Justice KENNEDY delivered the opinion of the Court:
    The University of Virginia, an instrumentality of the Commonwealth for which it is

Source: 515 U.S. 819 (1995)

named and thus bound by the First and Fourteenth Amendments, authorizes the payment of outside contractors for the printing costs of a variety of student publications. It withheld any authorization for payments on behalf of petitioners for the sole reason that their student paper "primarily promotes or manifests a particular belief in or about a deity or an ultimate reality." That the paper did promote or manifest views within the defined exclusion seems plain enough. The challenge is to the University's regulation and its denial of authorization, the case raising issues under the Speech and Establishment Clauses of the First Amendment.

The public corporation we refer to as the "University" is denominated by state law as "the Rector and Visitors of the University of Virginia," and it is responsible for governing the school. Founded by Thomas Jefferson in 1819, and ranked by him, together with the authorship of the Declaration of Independence and of the Virginia Act for Religious Freedom, as one of his proudest achievements, the University is among the Nation's oldest and most respected seats of higher learning. It has more than 11,000 undergraduate students, and 6,000 graduate and professional students. An understanding of the case requires a somewhat detailed description of the program the University created to support extracurricular student activities on its campus.

Before a student group is eligible to submit bills from its outside contractors for payment by the fund described below, it must become a "Contracted Independent Organization" (CIO). CIO status is available to any group the majority of whose members are students, whose managing officers are full-time students, and that complies with certain procedural requirements. . . .

All CIOs may exist and operate at the University, but some are also entitled to apply for funds from the Student Activities Fund (SAF). . . . The SAF receives its money from a mandatory fee of $14 per semester assessed to each full-time student. The Student Council, elected by the students, has the initial authority to disburse the funds, but its actions are subject to review by a faculty body chaired by a designee of the Vice President for Student Affairs.

Some, but not all, CIOs may submit disbursement requests to the SAF. The Guidelines recognize 11 categories of student groups that may seek payment to third-party contractors because they "are related to the educational purpose of the University of Virginia." One of these is "student news, information, opinion, entertainment, or academic communications media groups." The Guidelines also specify, however, that the costs of certain activities of CIOs that are otherwise eligible for funding will not be reimbursed by the SAF. The student activities which are excluded from SAF support are religious activities, philanthropic contributions and activities, political activities, activities that would jeopardize the University's tax exempt status, those which involve payment of honoraria or similar fees, or social entertainment or related expenses. The prohibition on "political activities" is defined so that it is limited to electioneering and lobbying. The Guidelines provide that "these restrictions on funding political activities are not intended to preclude funding of any otherwise eligible student organization which . . . espouses particular positions or ideological viewpoints, including those that may be unpopular or are not generally accepted." A "religious activity," by contrast, is defined as any activity that "primarily promotes or manifests a particular belief in or about a deity or an ultimate reality." . . .

Petitioners' organization, Wide Awake Productions (WAP), qualified as a CIO. Formed by petitioner Ronald Rosenberger and other undergraduates in 1990, WAP was established "to publish a magazine of philosophical and religious expression," "to facilitate discussion which fosters an atmosphere of sensitivity to and tolerance of Christian viewpoints," and "to provide a unifying focus for Christians of multicultural backgrounds." WAP publishes Wide Awake: A Christian Perspective at the University of Virginia. The paper's Christian viewpoint was evident from the first issue, in which its editors wrote that the journal "offers a Christian perspective on both personal and community issues, especially those relevant to college students at the University of Virginia." The editors committed the paper to a two-fold mission: "to challenge Christians to live, in word and deed, according to the faith they proclaim and to encourage students to consider what a personal relationship with Jesus Christ means." The first issue had articles about racism, crisis pregnancy, stress, prayer, C. S. Lewis' ideas about evil and free will, and reviews of religious music. In the next two issues, Wide Awake featured stories about homosexuality, Christian missionary work, and eating disorders, as well as music reviews and interviews with University professors. Each page of Wide Awake, and the end of each article or review, is marked by a cross. The advertisements carried in Wide Awake also reveal the Christian perspective of the journal. For the most part, the advertisers are churches, centers for Christian study, or Christian bookstores. By June 1992, WAP had distributed about 5,000 copies of Wide Awake to University students, free of charge.

WAP had acquired CIO status soon after it was organized. This is an important consideration in this case, for had it been a "religious organization," WAP would not have been accorded CIO status. As defined by the Guidelines, a "religious organization" is "an organization whose purpose is to practice a devotion to an acknowledged ultimate reality or deity." At no stage in this controversy has the University contended that WAP is such an organization.

A few months after being given CIO status, WAP requested the SAF to pay its printer $5,862 for the costs of printing its newspaper. The Appropriations Committee of the Student Council denied WAP's request on the ground that Wide Awake was a "religious activity" within the meaning of the Guidelines, i.e., that the newspaper "promoted or manifested a particular belief in or about a deity or an ultimate reality." It made its determination after examining the first issue. WAP appealed the denial to the full Student Council, contending that WAP met all the applicable Guidelines and that denial of SAF support on the basis of the magazine's religious perspective violated the Constitution. The appeal was denied without further comment, and WAP appealed to the next level, the Student Activities Committee. In a letter signed by the Dean of Students, the committee sustained the denial of funding. . . .

It is axiomatic that the government may not regulate speech based on its substantive content or the message it conveys. Other principles follow from this precept. In the realm of private speech or expression, government regulation may not favor one speaker over another. Discrimination against speech because of its message is presumed to be unconstitutional. These rules informed our determination that the government offends the First Amendment when it imposes financial burdens on certain speakers based on the content of their expression. When the government targets not subject matter but particular views taken by speakers on a subject, the violation of the First Amendment is all the more blatant. Viewpoint discrimination is thus an egregious form of content discrimination. The government must abstain from regulating speech when the specific motivating ideology or the opinion or perspective of the speaker is the rationale for the restriction. . . .

The University does acknowledge (as it must in light of our precedents) that "ideologically driven attempts to suppress a particular point of view are presumptively unconstitutional in funding, as in other contexts," but insists that this case does not present that issue because the Guidelines draw lines based on content, not viewpoint. As we have noted, discrimination against one set of views or ideas is but a subset or particular instance of the more general phenomenon of content discrimination. And, it must be acknowledged, the distinction is not a precise one. It is, in a sense, something of an understatement to speak of religious thought and discussion as just a viewpoint, as distinct from a comprehensive body of thought. The nature of our origins and destiny and their dependence upon the existence of a divine being have been subjects of philosophic inquiry throughout human history. We conclude, nonetheless, that here, as in *Lamb's Chapel,* viewpoint discrimination is the proper way to interpret the University's objections to Wide Awake. By the very terms of the SAF prohibition, the University does not exclude religion as a subject matter but selects for disfavored treatment those student journalistic efforts with religious editorial viewpoints. Religion may be a vast area of inquiry, but it also provides, as it did here, a specific premise, a perspective, a standpoint from which a variety of subjects may be discussed and considered. The prohibited perspective, not the general subject matter, resulted in the refusal to make third-party payments, for the subjects discussed were otherwise within the approved category of publications. . . .

The University tries to escape the consequences of our [prior precedents] by urging that this case involves the provision of funds rather than access to facilities. The University begins with the unremarkable proposition that the State must have substantial discretion in determining how to allocate scarce resources to accomplish its educational mission. Citing our decisions, the University argues that content-based funding decisions are both inevitable and lawful. . . .

It does not follow, however, . . . that viewpoint-based restrictions are proper when the University does not itself speak or subsidize transmittal of a message it favors but instead expends funds to encourage a diversity of views from private speakers. A holding that the University may not discriminate based on the viewpoint of private persons whose speech it facilitates does not restrict the University's own speech, which is controlled by different principles . . .

Vital First Amendment speech principles are at stake here. The first danger to liberty lies in granting the State the power to examine publications to determine whether or not they are based on some ultimate idea and if so for the State to classify them. The second, and corollary, danger is to speech from the chilling of individual thought and expression. That danger is especially real in the University setting, where the State acts against a background and tradition of thought and experiment that is at the center of our intellectual and philosophic tradition. . . . For the University, by regulation, to cast disapproval on particular viewpoints of its students risks the suppression of free speech and creative inquiry in one of the vital centers for the nation's intellectual life, its college and university campuses. . . .

The prohibition on funding on behalf of publications that "primarily promote or manifest a particular belief in or about a deity or an ultimate reality," in its ordinary and commonsense meaning, has a vast potential reach. The term "promote" as used here would comprehend any writing advocating a philosophic position that rests upon a belief in a deity or ultimate reality. And the term "manifests" would bring within the scope of the prohibition any writing that is explicable as resting upon a premise which presupposes the existence of a deity or ultimate reality . . .

Based on the principles we have discussed, we hold that the regulation invoked to deny SAF support, both in its terms and in its application to these petitioners, is a denial of their right of free speech guaranteed by the First Amendment. It remains to be considered whether the violation following from the University's action is excused by the necessity of complying with the Constitution's prohibition against state establishment of religion. We turn to that question.

. . . A central lesson of our decisions is that a significant factor in upholding governmental programs in the face of Establishment Clause attack is their neutrality toward religion. We have decided a series of cases addressing the receipt of government benefits where religion or religious views are implicated in some degree . . . We have held that the guarantee of neutrality is respected, not offended, when the government, following neutral criteria and evenhanded policies, extends benefits to recipients whose ideologies and viewpoints, including religious ones, are broad and diverse. More than once have we rejected the position that the Establishment Clause even justifies, much less requires, a refusal to extend free speech rights to religious speakers who participate in broad-reaching government programs neutral in design.

The governmental program here is neutral toward religion. There is no suggestion that the University created it to advance religion or adopted some ingenious device with the purpose of aiding a religious cause. The object of the SAF is to open a forum for speech and to support various student enterprises, including the publication of newspapers, in recognition of the diversity and creativity of student life. The University's SAF Guidelines have a separate classification for, and do not make third-party payments on behalf of, "religious organizations," which are those "whose purpose is to practice a devotion to an acknowledged ultimate reality or deity." The category of support here is for "student news, information, opinion, entertainment, or academic communications media groups," of which Wide Awake was 1 of 15 in the 1990 school year. WAP did not seek a subsidy because of its Christian editorial viewpoint; it sought funding as a student journal, which it was.

The neutrality of the program distinguishes the student fees from a tax levied for the direct support of a church or group of churches. A tax of that sort, of course, would run contrary to Establishment Clause concerns dating from the earliest days of the Republic. The apprehensions of our predecessors involved the levying of taxes upon the public for the sole and exclusive purpose of establishing and supporting specific sects. The exaction here, by contrast, is a student activity fee designed to reflect the reality that student life in its many dimensions includes the necessity of wide-ranging speech and inquiry and that student expression is an integral part of the University's educational mission. The fee is mandatory, and we do not have before us the question whether an objecting student has the First Amendment right to demand a pro rata return to the extent the fee is expended for speech to which he or she does not subscribe. We must treat it, then, as an exaction upon the students. But the $14 paid each semester by the students is not a general tax designed to raise revenue for the University. The SAF cannot be used for unlimited purposes, much less the illegitimate purpose of supporting one religion.

Much like the arrangement in *Widmar,* the money goes to a special fund from which any group of students with CIO status can draw for purposes consistent with the University's educational mission; and to the extent the student is interested in speech, withdrawal is permitted to cover the whole spectrum of speech, whether it manifests a religious view, an antireligious view, or neither. Our decision, then, cannot be read as addressing an expenditure from a general tax fund. Here, the disbursements from the fund go to private contractors for the cost of printing that which is protected under the Speech Clause of the First Amendment. This is a far cry from a general public assessment designed and effected to provide financial support for a church. . . .

It does not violate the Establishment Clause for a public university to grant access to its facilities on a religion-neutral basis to a wide spectrum of student groups, including groups which use meeting rooms for sectarian activities, accompanied by some devotional exercises. This is so even where the upkeep, maintenance, and repair of the facilities attributed to those uses is paid from a student activities fund to which students are required to contribute. The government usually acts by spending money . . .

By paying outside printers, the University in fact attains a further degree of separation from the student publication, for it avoids the duties of supervision, escapes the costs of upkeep, repair, and replacement attributable to student use, and has a clear record of costs . . .

To obey the Establishment Clause, it was not necessary for the University to deny eligibility to student publications because of their viewpoint. The neutrality commanded of the State by the separate Clauses of the First Amendment was compromised by the University's course of action. The viewpoint discrimination inherent in the University's regulation required public officials to scan and interpret student publications to discern their underlying philosophic assumptions respecting religious theory and belief. That course of action was a denial of the right of free speech and would risk fostering a pervasive bias or hostility to religion, which could undermine the very neutrality the Establishment Clause requires. There is no Establishment Clause violation in the University's honoring its duties under the Free Speech Clause.

The judgment of the Court of Appeals must be, and is, reversed.

It is so ordered.

Justice SOUTER, with whom Justice STEVENS, Justice GINSBURG and Justice BREYER join, dissenting:

The Court today, for the first time, approves direct funding of core religious activities by an arm of the State. It does so, however, only after erroneous treatment of some familiar principles of law implementing the First Amendment's Establishment and Speech Clauses, and by viewing the very funds in question as beyond the reach of the Establishment Clause's funding restrictions as such. Because there is no warrant for distinguishing among public funding sources for purposes of applying the First Amendment's prohibition of religious establishment, I would hold that the University's refusal to support petitioners' religious activities is compelled by the Establishment Clause. I would therefore affirm.

The central question in this case is whether a grant from the Student Activities Fund to pay Wide Awake's printing expenses would violate the Establishment Clause. Although the Court does not dwell on the details of Wide Awake's message, it recognizes something sufficiently religious in the publication to demand Establishment Clause scrutiny. Although the Court places great stress on the eligibility of secular as well as religious activities for grants from the Student Activities Fund, it recognizes that such evenhanded availability is not by itself enough to satisfy constitutional requirements for any aid scheme that results in a benefit to religion. Something more is necessary to justify any religious aid. Some members of the Court, at least, may think the funding permissible on a view that it is indirect, since the money goes to Wide Awake's printer, not through Wide Awake's own checking account. The Court's principal reliance, however, is on an argument that providing religion with economically valuable services is permissible on the theory that services are economically indistinguishable from religious access to governmental speech forums, which sometimes is permissible. But this reasoning would commit the Court to approving direct religious aid beyond anything justifiable for the sake of access to speaking forums. The Court implicitly recognizes this in its further attempt to circumvent the clear bar to direct governmental aid to religion. Different members of the Court seek to avoid this bar in different ways. The opinion of the Court makes the novel assumption that only direct aid financed with tax revenue is barred, and draws the erroneous conclusion that the involuntary Student Activities Fee is not a tax. . . .

257

Bush v. Vera (1996)

In *Shaw v. Reno* (Document 252), the Court did not reach the merits of majority-minority districting under an equal protection claim, but merely stated that such a claim could exist. Encouraged by this, opponents to majority-minority districting launched dozens of lawsuits. On the same day, the Court handed down decisions in two cases. In *Shaw v. Hunt* (sometimes called *Shaw II*), Chief Justice Rehnquist reiterated that strict scrutiny should be the standard for review and found that North Carolina lacked the requisite compelling interest to create racially drawn districts.

Bush v. Vera grew out of a Texas districting plan, and it is clear that the Court could not agree either on a rationale or on appropriate tests once one got beyond the strict scrutiny standard. Justice O'Connor wrote a plurality opinion joined only by the chief justice and Justice Kennedy, and then went and wrote a concurrence to her own opinion so she could say things that Rehnquist and Kennedy did not agree with. Kennedy wrote his own concurrence, justices Thomas and Scalia concurred only in the result (providing the needed five votes). Justices Stevens and Souter dissented separately, and Justices Ginsburg and Breyer agreed with both dissents.

The Court was not finished with the issue; see Document 260.

See items listed at Document 252; and Scott A. Carlson, "The Gerrymandering of the Reconstruction Amendments," 23 *Thurgood Marshall Law Review* 71 (1997); and Stephen Light, "Too (Color) Blind to See: The Voting Rights Act of 1965 and the Supreme Court," 8 *George Mason University Civil Rights Law Journal* 1 (1997).

Justice O'CONNOR announced the judgment of the Court and delivered an opinion, in which The Chief Justice and Justice KENNEDY join:

This is the latest in a series of appeals involving racial gerrymandering challenges to state redistricting efforts in the wake of the 1990 census. . . . The plaintiffs, six Texas voters, challenged the state redistricting plan, alleging that 24 of Texas' 30 congressional districts constitute racial gerrymanders in violation of the Fourteenth Amendment. The three-judge United States District Court for the Southern District of Texas held Districts 18, 29, and 30 unconstitutional. Finding that, under this Court's decisions in *Shaw* I and *Miller,* the district lines at issue are subject to strict scrutiny, and that they are not narrowly tailored to serve a compelling state interest, we affirm. . . .

[*In the first part of the plurality opinion, Justice O'Connor concluded that because the case centered around racial classification, the traditional standard of strict scruinty would apply, although in earlier redistricting cases the Court had adopted a lower standard and deferred to congressional findings.*]

Having concluded that strict scrutiny applies, we must determine whether the racial classifications embodied in any of the three districts are narrowly tailored to further a compelling state interest. Appellants point to three compelling interests: the interest in avoiding liability under the "results" test of VRA [Voting Rights Act] Section (b), the interest in remedying past and present racial discrimination, and the "nonretrogression" principle of VRA Section 5 (for District 18 only). We consider them in turn. . . .

A Section 2 district that is *reasonably* compact and regular, taking into account traditional districting principles such as maintaining communities of interest and traditional boundaries, may pass strict scrutiny without having to defeat rival compact districts designed by plaintiffs' experts in endless "beauty contests." The dissenters misread us when they make the leap from our disagreement about the facts of this case to the conclusion that we are creating a "stalemate" by requiring the States to "get things just right," . . . or to draw "the precise compact district that a court would impose in a successful Section 2 challenge." Rather, we adhere to our longstanding recognition of the importance in our federal system of each State's sovereign interest in implementing its redistricting plan. . . . The constitutional problem arises only from the subordination of those principles to race.

Strict scrutiny remains, nonetheless, strict. The State must have a "strong basis in evidence" for finding that the threshold conditions for Section 2 liability are present. . . . And, as we have noted above, the district drawn in order to satisfy Section 2 must not subordinate traditional districting principles to race substantially more than is

---

Source: 517 U.S. 952 (1996)

"reasonably necessary" to avoid Section 2 liability. Districts 18, 29, and 30 fail to meet these requirements. . . .

We have, however, already found that all three districts are bizarrely shaped and far from compact, and that those characteristics are predominantly attributable to gerrymandering that was racially motivated and/or achieved by the use of race as a proxy. District 30, for example, reaches out to grab small and apparently isolated minority communities which, based on the evidence presented, could not possibly form part of a compact majority-minority district, and does so in order to make up for minority populations closer to its core that it shed in a further suspect use of race as a proxy to further neighboring incumbents' interests.

These characteristics defeat any claim that the districts are narrowly tailored to serve the State's interest in avoiding liability under Section 2, because Section 2 does not require a State to create, on predominantly racial lines, a district that is not "reasonably compact." . . . If, because of the dispersion of the minority population, a reasonably compact majority-minority district cannot be created, Section 2 does not require a majority-minority district; if a reasonably compact district can be created, nothing in [the law] requires the race-based creation of a district that is far from compact.

Appellants argue that bizarre shaping and noncompactness do not raise narrow tailoring concerns. Appellants claim that under [our precedents] "shape is relevant only as evidence of an improper motive." The United States takes a more moderate position, accepting that in the context of narrow tailoring, "consideration must be given to the extent to which the districts drawn by a State substantially depart from its customary redistricting practices," but asserting that insofar as bizarreness and noncompactness are necessary to achieve the State's compelling interest in compliance with Section 2 "while simultaneously achieving other legitimate redistricting goals," such as incumbency protection, the narrowly tailoring requirement is satisfied. . . .

These arguments cannot save the districts before us: district shape is not irrelevant to the narrow tailoring inquiry. Our [prior] discussion served only to emphasize that the ultimate constitutional values at stake involve the harms caused by the use of unjustified racial classifications, and that bizarreness is not necessary to trigger strict scrutiny. Significant deviations from traditional districting principles, such as the bizarre shape and noncompactness demonstrated by the districts here, cause constitutional harm insofar as they convey the message that political identity is, or should be, predominantly racial. For example, the bizarre shaping of Districts 18 and 29, cutting across pre-existing precinct lines and other natural or traditional divisions, is not merely evidentially significant; it is part of the constitutional problem insofar as it disrupts nonracial bases of political identity and thus intensifies the emphasis on race.

Nor is the United States' argument availing here. In determining that strict scrutiny applies here, we agreed with the District Court that in fact the bizarre shaping and noncompactness of these districts were predominantly attributable to racial, not political, manipulation. The United States' argument, and that of the dissent address the case of an otherwise compact majority-minority district that is misshapen by predominantly nonracial, political manipulation. We disagree with the factual premise of Justice STEVENS' dissent, that these districts were drawn using "racial considerations only in a way reasonably designed" to avoid a Section 2 violation. The districts before us exhibit a level of racial manipulation that exceeds what Section 2 could justify.

The United States and the State next contend that the district lines at issue are justified by the State's compelling interest in "ameliorating the effects of racially polarized voting attributable to past and present racial discrimination. In support of that contention, they cite Texas' long history of discrimination against minorities in electoral processes, stretching from the Reconstruction to modern times, including violations of the Constitution and of the VRA.

A State's interest in remedying discrimination is compelling when two conditions are satisfied. First, the discrimination that the State seeks to remedy must be specific, "identified discrimination"; second, the State "must have had a 'strong basis in evidence' to conclude that remedial action was necessary, 'before it embarks on an affirmative action program.'" Here, the only current problem that appellants cite as in need of remediation is alleged vote dilution as a consequence of racial bloc voting, the same concern that underlies their VRA Section 2 compliance defense, which we have assumed to be valid for purposes of this opinion. We have indicated that such problems will not justify race-based districting unless "the State employs sound districting principles, and . . . the affected racial group's residential patterns afford the opportunity of creating districts in which they will be in the majority." Once that standard is applied, our agreement with the District Court's finding that these districts are not narrowly tailored to comply with Section 2 forecloses this line of defense.

The final contention offered by the State and private appellants is that creation of District 18 (only) was justified by a compelling state interest in complying with VRA Section 5. We have made clear that Section 5 has a limited substantive goal: "to insure that no voting-procedure changes would be made that would lead to a retrogression in the position of racial minorities with respect to their effective exercise of the electoral franchise." Appellants contend that this "nonretrogression" principle is implicated because Harris County had, for two decades, contained a congressional district in which African-American voters had succeeded in selecting representatives of their choice, all of whom were African-Americans.

The problem with the State's argument is that it seeks to justify not maintenance, but substantial augmentation, of the African-American population percentage in District 18. At the previous redistricting, in 1980, District 18's population was 40.8% African-American. As a result of Hispanic population increases and African-American emigration from the district, its population had reached 35.1% African-American and 42.2% Hispanic at the time of the 1990 census. The State has shown no basis for concluding that the increase to a 50.9% African-American population in 1991 was necessary to insure nonretrogression. Nonretrogression is not a license for the State to do whatever it deems necessary to insure continued electoral success; it merely mandates that the minority's opportunity to elect representatives of its choice not be diminished, directly or indirectly, by the State's actions. Applying that principle, it is clear that District 18 is not narrowly tailored to the avoidance of Section 5 liability.

The judgment of the District Court is

Affirmed.

[Justice O'CONNOR concurred with the plurality opinion in order to note two points. First, compliance with Section 2 of the Voting Rights Act does constitute a compelling state interest, and second, that this test can coexist in principle with the Court's ruling. In other words, minority-majority districts could be drawn in a way to satisfy both the Court's strict scrutiny standard as well as the results test of Section 2 of the VRA. She went on to agree with the dissenters that Section 2 constitutes a critical part of the nation's commitment to racial equality. Justice KENNEDY also concurred separately, noting that even with a compelling interest, the state would still have to tailor narrowly its solution to the problem of racial discrimination. Justice THOMAS, joined by Justice SCALIA, concurred in the result, but argued that whether or not strict scrutiny was the proper test was never a close question, insofar as any racial classification automatically triggers strict scrutiny.]

Justice STEVENS, with whom Justice GINSBURG and Justice BREYER join, dissenting:

Today, the Court strikes down three of Texas' majority-minority districts, concluding, *inter alia,* that their odd shapes reveal that the State impermissibly relied on predominantly racial reasons when it drew the districts as it did. For two reasons, I believe that the Court errs in striking down those districts.

First, I believe that the Court has misapplied its own tests for racial gerrymandering, both by applying strict scrutiny to all three of these districts, and then by concluding that none can meet that scrutiny. In asking whether strict scrutiny should apply, the Court improperly ignores the "complex interplay" of political and geographical considerations that went into the creation of Texas' new congressional districts, and focuses exclusively on the role that race played in the State's decisions to adjust the shape of its districts. A quick comparison of the unconstitutional majority-minority districts with three equally bizarre majority-Anglo districts, demonstrates that race was not necessarily the predominant factor contorting the district lines. I would follow the fair implications of the District Court's findings, and conclude that Texas' entire map is a political, not a racial, gerrymander.

Even if strict scrutiny applies, I would find these districts constitutional, for each considers race only to the extent necessary to comply with the State's responsibilities under the Voting Rights Act while achieving other race-neutral political and geographical requirements. The plurality's finding to the contrary unnecessarily restricts the ability of States to conform their behavior to the Voting Rights Act while simultaneously complying with other race-neutral goals.

Second, even if I concluded that these districts failed an appropriate application of this still-developing law to appropriately read facts, I would not uphold the District Court decision. The decisions issued today serve merely to reinforce my conviction that the Court has, with its "analytically distinct" jurisprudence of racial gerrymandering, struck out into a jurisprudential wilderness that lacks a definable constitutional core and threatens to create harms more significant than any suffered by the individual plaintiffs challenging these districts. Though we travel ever farther from it with each passing decision, I would return to the well-traveled path that we left in *Shaw* I.

Justice SOUTER, with whom Justice GINSBURG and Justice BREYER join, dissenting:

When the Court devises a new cause of action to enforce a constitutional provision, it ought to identify an injury distinguishable from the consequences of concededly constitutional conduct, and it should describe the elements necessary and sufficient to make out such a claim. Nothing less can give notice to those whose conduct may give rise to liability or provide standards for courts charged with enforcing the Constitution. Those principles of justification, fair notice, and guidance, have never been satisfied in the instance of the action announced three Terms ago in *Shaw v. Reno,* (1993), when a majority of this Court decided that a State violates the Fourteenth Amendment's Equal Protection Clause by excessive consideration of race in drawing the boundaries of voting districts, even when the resulting plan does not dilute the voting strength of any voters and so would not otherwise give rise to liability under the Fourteenth or Fifteenth Amendments, or under the Voting Rights Act.

The result of this failure to provide a practical standard for distinguishing between the lawful and unlawful use of race has not only been inevitable confusion in state houses and courthouses, but a consequent shift in responsibility for setting district boundaries from the state legislatures, which are invested with front-line authority by Article I of the Constitution, to the courts, and truly to this Court, which is left to superintend the drawing of every legislative district in the land.

Today's opinions do little to solve *Shaw*'s puzzles or return districting responsibility to the States. To say this is not to denigrate the importance of Justice O'CONNOR's position in her separate opinion, that compliance with Section 2 of the Voting Rights Act is a compelling state interest; her statement takes a very significant step toward alleviating apprehension that *Shaw* is at odds with the Voting Rights Act. It is still true, however, that the combined plurality, minority, and Court opinions do not ultimately leave the law dealing with a *Shaw* claim appreciably clearer or more manageable than *Shaw I* itself did. And to the extent that some clarity follows from the knowledge that race may be considered when reasonably necessary to conform to the Voting Rights Act, today's opinions raise the specter that this ostensible progress may come with a heavy constitutional price. The price of *Shaw I,* indeed, may turn out to be the practical elimination of a State's discretion to apply traditional districting principles, widely accepted in States without racial districting issues as well as in States confronting them. As the flaws of *Shaw I* persist, and as the burdens placed on the States and the courts by *Shaw* litigation loom larger with the approach of a new census and a new round of redistricting, the Court has to recognize that *Shaw*'s problems result from a basic misconception about the relation between race and districting principles, a mistake that no amount of case-by-case tinkering can eliminate. There is, therefore, no reason for confidence that the Court will eventually bring much order out of the confusion created by *Shaw I,* and because it has not, in any case, done so yet, I respectfully dissent.

258

Romer v. Evans (1996)

Several cities and townships in Colorado passed laws banning discrimination based on sexual orientation in housing, employment, education, public accommodations, and other areas. Opponents to gay rights managed to get a referendum, known as "Amendment 2," on the ballot, forbidding all legislative, executive, or judicial action at any level in state or local governments to protect the status of persons based on their "homosexual, lesbian or bisexual orientation, conduct, practices or relationships." The referendum passed and was immediately challenged in courts by both local governments as well as individual homosexuals. The Colorado Supreme Court ruled Amendment 2 subject to strict scrutiny under the Fourteenth Amendment's Equal Protection Clause, since it infringed on the basic rights of gays to participate in the political process. At a new trial, a lower state court ruled that Amendment 2 failed to satisfy the criteria of strict scrutiny.

Colorado then appealed to the U.S. Supreme Court, where many observers thought that Amendment 2 would be sustained. After all, the Court in its only previous case involving homosexual rights had upheld sodomy laws, and beyond that, the Rehnquist Court was known to be opposed to the creation of any new rights. But by a 6–3 vote, the justices agreed with the lower court's determination, despite an impassioned and angry dissent by Justice Scalia.

See H. Jefferson Powell, "The Lawfulness of Romer v. Evans," 77 *North Carolina Law Review* 241 (1998); Robert D. Dodson, "Homosexual Discrimination and Gender: Was Romer v. Evans Really a Victory for Gay Rights?" 35 *California Western Law Review* 271 (1999); and Richard A. Posner, "Against Constitutional Theory," 73 *N.Y.U. Law Review* 1 (1998).

———

Justice KENNEDY delivered the opinion of the Court:

One century ago, the first Justice Harlan admonished this Court that the Constitution "neither knows nor tolerates classes among citizens." *Plessy v. Ferguson* (1896) (dissenting opinion) Unheeded then, those words now are understood to state a commitment to the law's neutrality where the rights of persons are at stake. The Equal Protection Clause enforces this principle and today requires us to hold invalid a provision of Colorado's Constitution.

The enactment challenged in this case is an amendment to the Constitution of the State of Colorado, adopted in a 1992 statewide referendum. The parties and the state

Source: 517 U.S. 620 (1996)

courts refer to it as "Amendment 2," its designation when submitted to the voters. The impetus for the amendment and the contentious campaign that preceded its adoption came in large part from ordinances that had been passed in various Colorado municipalities. . . . What gave rise to the statewide controversy was the protection the ordinances afforded to persons discriminated against by reason of their sexual orientation. Amendment 2 repeals these ordinances to the extent they prohibit discrimination on the basis of "homosexual, lesbian or bisexual orientation, conduct, practices or relationships." Colo. Const., Art. II, Section 30b.

Yet Amendment 2, in explicit terms, does more than repeal or rescind these provisions. It prohibits all legislative, executive or judicial action at any level of state or local government designed to protect the named class, a class we shall refer to as homosexual persons or gays and lesbians. . . . The State's principal argument in defense of Amendment 2 is that it puts gays and lesbians in the same position as all other persons. So, the State says, the measure does no more than deny homosexuals special rights. This reading of the amendment's language is implausible. We rely not upon our own interpretation of the amendment but upon the authoritative construction of Colorado's Supreme Court. The state court, deeming it unnecessary to determine the full extent of the amendment's reach, found it invalid even on a modest reading of its implications. . . .

Sweeping and comprehensive is the change in legal status effected by this law. So much is evident from the ordinances that the Colorado Supreme Court declared would be void by operation of Amendment 2. Homosexuals, by state decree, are put in a solitary class with respect to transactions and relations in both the private and governmental spheres. The amendment withdraws from homosexuals, but no others, specific legal protection from the injuries caused by discrimination, and it forbids reinstatement of these laws and policies. . . .

Amendment 2 bars homosexuals from securing protection against the injuries that these public accommodations laws address. That in itself is a severe consequence, but there is more. Amendment 2, in addition, nullifies specific legal protections for this targeted class in all transactions in housing, sale of real estate, insurance, health and welfare services, private education, and employment. . . . The repeal of these measures and the prohibition against their future reenactment demonstrates that Amendment 2 has the same force and effect in Colorado's governmental sector as it does elsewhere and that it applies to policies as well as ordinary legislation.

Amendment 2's reach may not be limited to specific laws passed for the benefit of gays and lesbians. It is a fair, if not necessary, inference from the broad language of the amendment that it deprives gays and lesbians even of the protection of general laws and policies that prohibit arbitrary discrimination in governmental and private settings. . . . If this consequence follows from Amendment 2, as its broad language suggests, it would compound the constitutional difficulties the law creates. The state court did not decide whether the amendment has this effect, however, and neither need we. . . . In any event, even if, as we doubt, homosexuals could find some safe harbor in laws of general application, we cannot accept the view that Amendment 2's prohibition on specific legal protections does no more than deprive homosexuals of special rights. To the contrary, the amendment imposes a special disability upon those persons alone. Homosexuals are forbidden the safeguards that others enjoy or may seek without constraint. They can obtain specific protection against discrimination only by enlisting the citizenry of Colorado to amend the state constitution or perhaps, on the State's view, by trying to pass helpful laws of general applicability. This is so no matter how local or discrete the harm, no matter how public and widespread the injury. We find nothing special in the protections Amendment 2 withholds. These are protections taken for granted by most people either because they already have them or do not need them; these are protections against exclusion from an almost limitless number of transactions and endeavors that constitute ordinary civic life in a free society.

The Fourteenth Amendment's promise that no person shall be denied the equal protection of the laws must coexist with the practical necessity that most legislation classifies for one purpose or another, with resulting disadvantage to various groups or persons. . . . We have attempted to reconcile the principle with the reality by stating that, if a law neither burdens a fundamental right nor targets a suspect class, we will uphold the legislative classification so long as it bears a rational relation to some legitimate end. . . .

Amendment 2 fails, indeed defies, even this conventional inquiry. First, the amendment has the peculiar property of imposing a broad and undifferentiated disability on a single named group, an exceptional and, as we shall explain, invalid form of legislation. Second, its sheer breadth is so discontinuous with the reasons offered for it that the amendment seems inexplicable by anything but animus toward the class that it affects; it lacks a rational relationship to legitimate state interests.

Taking the first point, even in the ordinary equal protection case calling for the most deferential of standards, we insist on knowing the relation between the classification adopted and the object to be attained. The search for the link between classification and objective gives substance to the Equal Protection Clause; it provides guidance and discipline for the legislature, which is entitled to know what sorts of laws it can pass; and it marks the limits of our own authority. In the ordinary case, a law will be sustained if it can be said to advance a legitimate government interest, even if the law seems unwise or works to the disadvantage of a particular group, or if the rationale for it seems tenuous. . . .

Amendment 2 confounds this normal process of judicial review. It is at once too narrow and too broad. It identifies persons by a single trait and then denies them protection across the board. The resulting disqualification of a class of persons from the right to seek specific protection from the law is unprecedented in our jurisprudence. The absence of precedent for Amendment 2 is itself instructive; "discriminations of an unusual character especially suggest careful consideration to determine whether they are obnoxious to the constitutional provision."

. . . It is not within our constitutional tradition to enact laws of this sort. Central both to the idea of the rule of law and to our own Constitution's guarantee of equal protection is the principle that government and each of its parts remain open on impartial terms to all who seek its assistance. "Equal protection of the laws is not achieved through indiscriminate imposition of inequalities." . . . Respect for this principle explains why laws singling out a certain class of citizens for disfavored legal status or general hardships are rare. A law declaring that in general it shall be more difficult for one group of citizens than for all others to seek aid from the government is itself a denial of equal protection of the laws in the most literal sense. "The guaranty of 'equal protection of the laws is a pledge of the protection of equal laws.'" . . .

A second and related point is that laws of the kind now before us raise the inevitable inference that the disadvantage imposed is born of animosity toward the class of persons affected. "[I]f the constitutional conception of 'equal protection of the laws' means anything, it must at the very least mean that a bare . . . desire to harm a politically unpopular group cannot constitute a legitimate governmental interest." . . . Even laws enacted for broad and ambitious purposes often can be explained by reference to legitimate public policies which justify the incidental disadvantages they impose on certain persons. Amendment 2, however, in making a general announcement that gays and lesbians shall not have any particular protections from the law, inflicts on them immediate, continuing, and real injuries that outrun and belie any legitimate justifications that may be claimed for it. We conclude that, in addition to the far reaching deficiencies of Amendment 2 that we have noted, the principles it offends, in another sense, are conventional and venerable; a law must bear a rational relationship to a legitimate governmental purpose, . . . and Amendment 2 does not.

The primary rationale the State offers for Amendment 2 is respect for other citizens' freedom of association, and in particular the liberties of landlords or employers who have personal or religious objections to homosexuality. Colorado also cites its interest in conserving resources to fight discrimination against other groups. The breadth of the Amendment is so far removed from these particular justifications that we find it impossible to credit them. We cannot say that Amendment 2 is directed to any identifiable legitimate purpose or discrete objective. It is a status based enactment divorced from any factual context from which we could discern a relationship to legitimate state interests; it is a classification of persons undertaken for its own sake, something the Equal Protection Clause does not permit. "Class legislation . . . is obnoxious to the prohibitions of the Fourteenth Amendment. . . ."

We must conclude that Amendment 2 classifies homosexuals not to further a proper legislative end but to make them unequal to everyone else. This Colorado cannot do. A State cannot so deem a class of persons a stranger to its laws. Amendment 2 violates the Equal Protection Clause, and the judgment of the Supreme Court of Colorado is affirmed.

Justice SCALIA, whom Chief Justice REHNQUIST and Justice THOMAS join, dissenting:

The Court has mistaken a *Kulturkampf* for a fit of spite. The constitutional amendment before us here is not the manifestation of a "bare . . . desire to harm" homosexuals, but is rather a modest attempt by seemingly tolerant Coloradans to preserve traditional sexual mores against the efforts of a politically powerful minority to revise those mores through use of the laws. . . .

In holding that homosexuality cannot be singled out for disfavorable treatment, the Court contradicts a decision, unchallenged here, pronounced only 10 years ago, see *Bowers v. Hardwick* and places the prestige of this institution behind the proposition that opposition to homosexuality is as reprehensible as racial or religious bias. Whether it is or not is precisely the cultural debate that gave rise to the Colorado constitutional amendment (and to the preferential laws against which the amendment was directed).

Since the Constitution of the United States says nothing about this subject, it is left to be resolved by normal democratic means, including the democratic adoption of provisions in state constitutions. This Court has no business imposing upon all Americans the resolution favored by the elite class from which the Members of this institution are selected, pronouncing that "animosity" toward homosexuality, is evil. I vigorously dissent. . . .

Despite all of its hand wringing about the potential effect of Amendment 2 on general antidiscrimination laws, the Court's opinion ultimately does not dispute all this, but assumes it to be true. The only denial of equal treatment it contends homosexuals have suffered is this: They may not obtain preferential treatment without amending the state constitution. That is to say, the principle underlying the Court's opinion is that one who is accorded equal treatment under the laws, but cannot as readily as others obtain preferential treatment under the laws, has been denied equal protection of the laws. If merely stating this alleged "equal protection" violation does not suffice to refute it, our constitutional jurisprudence has achieved terminal silliness.

The central thesis of the Court's reasoning is that any group is denied equal protection when, to obtain advantage (or, presumably, to avoid disadvantage), it must have recourse to a more general and hence more difficult level of political decisionmaking than others. The world has never heard of such a principle, which is why the Court's opinion is so long on emotive utterance and so short on relevant legal citation. And it seems to me most unlikely that any multilevel democracy can function under such a principle. . . .

I turn next to whether there was a legitimate rational basis for the substance of the constitutional amendment—for the prohibition of special protection for homosexuals. It is unsurprising that the Court avoids discussion of this question, since the answer is so obviously yes. The case most relevant to the issue before us today is not even mentioned in the Court's opinion: In *Bowers v. Hardwick,* we held that the Constitution does not prohibit what virtually all States had done from the founding of the Republic until very recent years—making homosexual conduct a crime. That holding is unassailable, except by those who think that the Constitution changes to suit current fashions. . . . If it is constitutionally permissible for a State to make homosexual conduct criminal, surely it is constitutionally permissible for a State to enact other laws merely disfavoring homosexual conduct. . . .

The foregoing suffices to establish what the Court's failure to cite any case remotely in point would lead one to suspect: No principle set forth in the Constitution, nor even any imagined by this Court in the past 200 years, prohibits what Colorado has done here. But the case for Colorado is much stronger than that. What it has done is not only unprohibited, but eminently reasonable, with close, congressionally approved precedent in earlier constitutional practice. . . . The Court's opinion contains grim, disapproving hints that Coloradans have been guilty of "animus" or "animosity" toward homosexuality, as though that has been established as Unamerican. Of course it is our moral heritage that one should not hate any human being or class of human beings. But I had thought that one could consider certain conduct reprehensible—murder, for example, or polygamy, or cruelty to animals—and could exhibit even "animus" toward such conduct. Surely that is the only sort of "animus" at issue here: moral disapproval of homosexual conduct, the same sort of moral disapproval that produced the centuries old criminal laws that we held constitutional in *Bowers.* . . .

That is where Amendment 2 came in. It sought to counter both the geographic concentration and the disproportionate political power of homosexuals by (1) resolving the controversy at the statewide level, and (2) making the election a single issue contest for both sides. It put directly, to all the citizens of the State, the question: Should homosexuality be given special protection? They answered no. The Court today asserts that this most democratic of procedures is unconstitutional. Lacking any cases to establish that facially absurd proposition, it simply asserts that it must be unconstitutional, because it has never happened before. . . .

. . . The Court today, announcing that Amendment 2 "defies . . . conventional [constitutional] inquiry," and "confounds the normal process of judicial review," employs a constitutional theory heretofore unknown to frustrate Colorado's reasonable effort to preserve traditional American moral values. The Court's stern disapproval of "animosity" towards homosexuality might be compared with what an earlier Court (including the revered Justices Harlan and Bradley) said in *Murphy v. Ramsey* (1885), rejecting a constitutional challenge to a United States statute that denied the franchise in federal territories to those who engaged in polygamous cohabitation. . . .

I would not myself indulge in such official praise for heterosexual monogamy, because I think it no business of the courts (as opposed to the political branches) to take sides in this culture war. . . .

When the Court takes sides in the culture wars, it tends to be with the knights rather than the villains—and more specifically with the Templars, reflecting the views and values of the lawyer class from which the Court's Members are drawn. How that class feels about homosexuality will be evident to anyone who wishes to interview job applicants at virtually any of the Nation's law schools. The interviewer may refuse to offer a job because the applicant is a Republican; because he is an adulterer; because he went to the wrong prep school or belongs to the wrong country club; because he eats snails; because he is a womanizer; because she wears real animal fur; or even because he hates the Chicago Cubs. But if the interviewer should wish not to be an associate or partner of an applicant because he disapproves of the applicant's homosexuality, then he will have violated the pledge which the Association of American Law Schools requires all its member schools to exact from job interviewers: "assurance of the employer's willingness" to hire homosexuals. . . . This law school view of what "prejudices" must be stamped out may be contrasted with the more plebeian attitudes that apparently still prevail in the United States Congress, which has been unresponsive to repeated attempts to extend to homosexuals the protections of federal civil rights laws. . . .

Today's opinion has no foundation in American constitutional law, and barely pretends to. The people of Colorado have adopted an entirely reasonable provision which does not even disfavor homosexuals in any substantive sense, but merely denies them preferential treatment. Amendment 2 is designed to prevent piecemeal deterioration of the sexual morality favored by a majority of Coloradans, and is not only an appropriate means to that legitimate end, but a means that Americans have employed before. Striking it down is an act, not of judicial judgment, but of political will. I dissent.

259   *United States v. Virginia (1996)*

For decades, single-sex schools were the norm in the United States, but by 1990, while there were still a number of women-only colleges, there were less than a handful of all-male colleges. Public colleges and universities had long since segregated, and in the 1970s and 1980s, so too had most private colleges. But two of the nation's oldest state military academies, the Citadel in Charleston, South Carolina and Virginia Military Institute (VMI) in Lexington, Virginia, clung to their traditional role of educating male officers and gentlemen.

The Citadel found itself the object of bad press when it totally mishandled the court-required admission of young women, with authorities allowing cadets to harass the women well beyond the scope of either tradition or common sense. VMI, founded in 1839, fought the battle in the courts and in the legislature. It won in the district court, but the Court of Appeals for the Fourth Circuit ruled that VMI violated the Equal Protection Clause. It gave the state three options: admit women, establish an equivalent all-women's program, or transform VMI into a private school. The Virginia Assembly founded Virginia Women's Institute for Leadership (VWIL) at nearby Mary Baldwin College. The Justice Department, arguing that a separate program for women could not be equal, appealed to the Supreme Court, where it won by a 7–1 vote (Justice Thomas recused because his son attended VMI).

After the decision, the VMI board considered turning the institution into a private college, but eventually bowed the Court's decision. Commandant Josiah Bunting made sure that, unlike the Citadel, VMI would undergo a painful transition without violence and that women would be integrated into the academy with minimal loss of tradition.

See Jennifer R. Cowan, "Distinguishing Private Women's Colleges from the VMI Decision," 30 *Columbia Journal of Law and Social Problems* 137 (1997); Karen L. Kupetz, "Equal Benefits, Equal Burdens," 30 *Loyola of Los Angeles Law Review 1333* (1997); and Richard A. Posner, "Against Constitutional Theory," 73 *N.Y.U. Law Review* 1 (1998).

———

Justice Ginsburg delivered the opinion of the Court:

Virginia's institutions of higher learning include an incomparable military college, Virginia Military Institute (VMI). The United States maintains that the Constitution's equal protection guarantee precludes Virginia from reserving exclusively to men the unique educational opportunities VMI affords. We agree.

Source: 518 U.S. 515 (1996)

Founded in 1839, VMI is today the sole single sex school among Virginia's 15 public institutions of higher learning. VMI's distinctive mission is to produce "citizen soldiers," men prepared for leadership in civilian life and in military service. VMI pursues this mission through pervasive training of a kind not available anywhere else in Virginia. Assigning prime place to character development, VMI uses an "adversative method" modeled on English public schools and once characteristic of military instruction. VMI constantly endeavors to instill physical and mental discipline in its cadets and impart to them a strong moral code. The school's graduates leave VMI with heightened comprehension of their capacity to deal with duress and stress, and a large sense of accomplishment for completing the hazardous course.

VMI has notably succeeded in its mission to produce leaders; among its alumni are military generals, Members of Congress, and business executives. The school's alumni overwhelmingly perceive that their VMI training helped them to realize their personal goals. VMI's endowment reflects the loyalty of its graduates; VMI has the largest per student endowment of all undergraduate institutions in the Nation.

Neither the goal of producing citizen soldiers nor VMI's implementing methodology is inherently unsuitable to women. And the school's impressive record in producing leaders has made admission desirable to some women. Nevertheless, Virginia has elected to preserve exclusively for men the advantages and opportunities a VMI education affords.

From its establishment in 1839 as one of the Nation's first state military colleges, . . . VMI has remained financially supported by Virginia and "subject to the control of the [Virginia] General Assembly,". . . . VMI today enrolls about 1,300 men as cadets. Its academic offerings in the liberal arts, sciences, and engineering are also available at other public colleges and universities in Virginia. But VMI's mission is special: "'to produce educated and honorable men, prepared for the varied work of civil life, imbued with love of learning, confident in the functions and attitudes of leadership, possessing a high sense of public service, advocates of the American democracy and free enterprise system, and ready as citizen soldiers to defend their country in time of national peril.'" . . .

The cross petitions in this case present two ultimate issues. First, does Virginia's exclusion of women from the educational opportunities provided by VMI—extraordinary opportunities for military training and civilian leadership development—deny to women "capable of all of the individual activities required of VMI cadets," . . . the equal protection of the laws guaranteed by the Fourteenth Amendment? Second, if VMI's "unique" situation, . . . —as Virginia's sole single sex public institution of higher education—offends the Constitution's equal protection principle, what is the remedial requirement?

We note, once again, the core instruction of this Court's pathmarking decisions in *J. E. B. v. Alabama ex rel. T. B.* . . . (1994), and *Mississippi Univ. for Women, . . .* : Parties who seek to defend gender based government action must demonstrate an "exceedingly persuasive justification" for that action. . . .

Without equating gender classifications, for all purposes, to classifications based on race or national origin, the Court, in post-*Reed* decisions, has carefully inspected official action that closes a door or denies opportunity to women (or to men). . . . To summarize the Court's current directions for cases of official classification based on gender: Focusing on the differential treatment or denial of opportunity for which relief is sought, the reviewing court must determine whether the proffered justification is "exceedingly persuasive." The burden of justification is demanding and it rests entirely on the State. The State must show "at least that the [challenged] classification serves 'important governmental objectives and that the discriminatory means employed' are 'substantially related to the achievement of those objectives.'" . . . The justification must be genuine, not hypothesized or invented post hoc in response to litigation. . . .

The heightened review standard our precedent establishes does not make sex a proscribed classification. Supposed "inherent differences" are no longer accepted as a ground for race or national origin classifications. . . . Physical differences between men and women, however, are enduring. . . . "Inherent differences" between men and women, we have come to appreciate, remain cause for celebration, but not for denigration of the members of either sex or for artificial constraints on an individual's opportunity. Sex classifications may be used to compensate women "for particular economic disabilities [they have] suffered," . . . to "promote equal employment opportunity," . . . to advance full development of the talent and capacities of our Nation's people. But such classifications may not be used, as they once were, . . . to create or perpetuate the legal, social, and economic inferiority of women.

Measuring the record in this case against the review standard just described, we conclude that Virginia has shown no "exceedingly persuasive justification" for excluding all women from the citizen soldier training afforded by VMI. We therefore affirm the Fourth Circuit's initial judgment, which held that Virginia had violated the Fourteenth Amendment's Equal Protection Clause. Because the remedy proffered by Virginia—the Mary Baldwin VWIL program—does not cure the constitutional violation, i.e., it does not provide equal opportunity, we reverse the Fourth Circuit's final judgment in this case.

The Fourth Circuit initially held that Virginia had advanced no state policy by which it could justify, under equal protection principles, its determination "to afford VMI's unique type of program to men and not to women." Virginia challenges that "liability" ruling and asserts two justifications in defense of VMI's exclusion of women. First, the Commonwealth contends, "single sex education provides important educational benefits," . . . and the option of single sex education contributes to "diversity in educational approaches." Second, the Commonwealth argues, "the unique VMI method of character development and leadership training," the school's adversative approach, would have to be modified were VMI to admit women. We consider these two justifications in turn.

Single sex education affords pedagogical benefits to at least some students, Virginia emphasizes, and that reality is uncontested in this litigation. Similarly, it is not disputed that diversity among public educational institutions can serve the public good. But Virginia has not shown that VMI was established, or has been maintained, with a view to diversifying, by its categorical exclusion of women, educational opportunities within the State. In cases of this genre, our precedent instructs that "benign" justifications proffered in defense of categorical exclusions will not be accepted automatically; a tenable justification must describe actual state purposes, not rationalizations for actions in fact differently grounded. . . .

In sum, we find no persuasive evidence in this record that VMI's male only admission policy "is in furtherance of a state policy of 'diversity.'" No such policy, the Fourth Circuit observed, can be discerned from the movement of all other public colleges and universities in Virginia away from single sex education. . . . A purpose genuinely to advance an array of educational options, as the Court of Appeals recognized, is not served by VMI's historic and constant plan—a plan to "afford a unique educational benefit only to males." However "liberally" this plan serves the State's sons, it makes no provision whatever for her daughters. That is not equal protection.

Virginia next argues that VMI's adversative method of training provides educational benefits that cannot be made available, unmodified, to women. Alterations to accommodate women would necessarily be "radical," so "drastic," Virginia asserts, as to transform, indeed "destroy," VMI's program. . . .

It is also undisputed, however, that "the VMI methodology could be used to educate women." The District Court even allowed that some women may prefer it to the methodology a women's college might pursue. "Some women, at least, would want to attend [VMI] if they had the opportunity," the District Court recognized, and "some women," the expert testimony established, "are capable of all of the individual activities required of VMI cadets." The parties, furthermore, agree that "some women can meet the physical standards [VMI] now imposes on men." In sum, as the Court of Appeals stated, "neither the goal of producing citizen soldiers," VMI's *raison d'être,* "nor VMI's implementing methodology is inherently unsuitable to women.". . . .

The United States does not challenge any expert witness estimation on average capacities or preferences of men and women. Instead, the United States emphasizes that time and again since this Court's turning point decision in *Reed v. Reed* (1971), we have cautioned reviewing courts to take a "hard look" at generalizations or "tendencies" of the kind pressed by Virginia, and relied upon by the District Court. State actors controlling gates to opportunity, we have instructed, may not exclude qualified individuals based on "fixed notions concerning the roles and abilities of males and females." *Mississippi Univ. for Women.* . . .

It may be assumed, for purposes of this decision, that most women would not choose VMI's adversative method. . . . It is also probable that"many men would not want to be educated in such an environment." . . . Education, to be sure, is not a "one size fits all" business. The issue, however, is not whether "women—or men—should be forced to attend VMI"; rather, the question is whether the State can constitutionally deny to women who have the will and capacity, the training and attendant opportunities that VMI uniquely affords. . . .

Women's successful entry into the federal military academies, and their participation in the Nation's military forces, indicate that Virginia's fears for the future of VMI may not be solidly grounded. The State's justification for excluding all women from "citizen soldier" training for which some are qualified, in any event, cannot rank as "exceedingly persuasive," as we have explained and applied that standard. . . .

In the second phase of the litigation, Virginia presented its remedial plan—maintain VMI as a male only college and create VWIL as a separate program for women. . . . A remedial decree, this Court has said, must closely fit the constitutional violation; it must be shaped to place persons unconstitutionally denied an opportunity or advantage in "the position they would have occupied in the absence of [discrimination]." . . . Virginia chose not to eliminate, but to leave untouched, VMI's exclusionary policy. For women only, however, Virginia proposed a separate program, different in kind from VMI and unequal in tangible and intangible facilities. . . .

VWIL affords women no opportunity to experience the rigorous military training for which VMI is famed. . . . Instead, the VWIL program "deemphasize[s]" military education, and uses a "cooperative method" of education "which reinforces self esteem." . . . Virginia maintains that these methodological differences are "justified pedagogically," based on "important differences between men and women in learning and developmental needs," "psychological and sociological differences" Virginia describes as "real" and "not stereotypes." . . . As earlier stated, generalizations about "the way women are," estimates of what is appropriate for most women, no longer justify denying opportunity to women whose talent and capacity place them outside the average description. Notably, Virginia never asserted that VMI's method of education suits most men. It is also revealing that Virginia accounted for its failure to make the VWIL experience "the entirely militaristic experience of VMI" on the ground that VWIL "is planned for women who do not necessarily expect to pursue military careers." By that reasoning, VMI's "entirely militaristic" program would be inappropriate for men in general or as a group, for "[o]nly about 15% of VMI cadets enter career military service." . . . In myriad respects other than military training, VWIL does not qualify as VMI's equal. VWIL's student body, faculty, course offerings, and facilities hardly match VMI's. Nor can the VWIL graduate anticipate the benefits associated with VMI's 157-year history, the school's prestige, and its influential alumni network. . . .

Virginia, in sum, while maintaining VMI for men only, has failed to provide any "comparable single gender women's institution." Instead, the Commonwealth has created a VWIL program fairly appraised as a "pale shadow" of VMI in terms of the range of curricular choices and faculty stature, funding, prestige, alumni support and influence. . . . Virginia's remedy does not match the constitutional violation; the State has shown no "exceedingly persuasive justification" for withholding from women qualified for the experience premier training of the kind VMI affords. . . .

Women seeking and fit for a VMI quality education cannot be offered anything less, under the State's obligation to afford them genuinely equal protection. . . . There is no reason to believe that the admission of women capable of all the activities required of VMI cadets would destroy the Institute rather than enhance its capacity to serve the "more perfect Union."

Justice SCALIA dissenting:

Today the Court shuts down an institution that has served the people of the Commonwealth of Virginia with pride and distinction for over a century and a half. To achieve that desired result, it rejects (contrary to our established practice) the factual findings to two courts below, sweeps aside the precedents of the Court, and ignores the history of our people. As to fact: it explicitly rejects the finding that there exist "gender-based developmental differences" supporting Virginia's restriction of the "adversative" method to only a men's institution, and the finding that the all-male composition of the Virginia Military Institute (VMI) is essential to that institution's character. As to precedent: it drastically revises our established standards for reviewing sex-based classifications. And as to history: it counts for nothing the long tradition, enduring down to the present, of men's military colleges supported by both States and the Federal Government.

Much of the Court's opinion is devoted to deprecating the closed mindedness of our forebears with regard to women's education, and even with regard to the treatment of women in areas that have nothing to do with education. Closed minded they were—as every age is, including our own, with regard to matters it cannot guess, because it simply does not consider them debatable. The virtue of a democratic system with a First Amendment is that it readily enables the people, over time, to be persuaded that what they took for granted is not so, and to change their laws accordingly. That system is destroyed if the smug assurances of each age are removed from the democratic process and written into the Constitution. So to counterbalance the Court's criticism of our ancestors, let me say a word in their praise: they left us free to change. The same cannot be said of this most illiberal Court, which has embarked on a course of inscribing one after another of the current preferences of the society (and in some cases only the counter majoritarian preferences of the society's law trained elite) into our Basic Law. Today it enshrines the notion that no substantial educational value is to be served by an all men's military academy—so that the decision by the people of Virginia to maintain such an institution denies equal protection to women who cannot attend that institution but can attend others. Since it is entirely clear that the Constitution of the United States—the old one—takes no sides in this educational debate, I dissent.

I shall devote most of my analysis to evaluating the Court's opinion on the basis of our current equal protection jurisprudence, which regards this Court as free to evaluate everything under the sun by applying one of three tests: "rational basis" scrutiny, intermediate scrutiny, or strict scrutiny. These tests are no more scientific than their names suggest, and a further element of randomness is added by the fact that it is largely up to us which test will be applied in each case. . . .

I have no problem with a system of abstract tests such as rational basis, intermediate, and strict scrutiny (though I think we can do better than applying strict scrutiny and intermediate scrutiny whenever we feel like it). Such formulas are essential to evaluating whether the new restrictions that a changing society constantly imposes upon private conduct comport with that "equal protection" our society has always accorded in the past. But in my view the function of this Court is to preserve our society's values regarding (among other things) equal protection, not to revise them; to prevent backsliding from the degree of restriction the Constitution imposed upon democratic government, not to prescribe, on our own authority, progressively higher degrees. For that reason it is my view that, whatever abstract tests we may choose to devise, they cannot supersede—and indeed ought to be crafted so as to reflect—those constant and unbroken national traditions that embody the people's understanding of ambiguous constitutional texts. More specifically, it is my view that "when a practice not expressly prohibited by the text of the Bill of Rights bears the endorsement of a long tradition of open, widespread, and unchallenged use that dates back to the beginning of the Republic, we have no proper basis for striking it down."

The all male constitution of VMI comes squarely within such a governing tradition. . . . In other words, the tradition of having government funded military schools for men is as well rooted in the traditions of this country as the tradition of sending only men into military combat. The people may decide to change the one tradition, like the other, through democratic processes; but the assertion that either tradition has been unconstitutional through the centuries is not law, but politics smuggled into law. And the same applies, more broadly, to single sex education in general, which, as I shall discuss, is threatened by today's decision with the cut off of all state and federal support. . . .

Today, however, change is forced upon Virginia, and reversion to single sex education is prohibited nationwide, not by democratic processes but by order of this Court. Even while bemoaning the sorry, bygone days of "fixed notions" concerning women's education, . . . the Court favors current notions so fixedly that it is willing to write them into the Constitution of the United States by application of custom built "tests." This is not the interpretation of a Constitution, but the creation of one. . . .

As is frequently true, the Court's decision today will have consequences that extend far beyond the parties to the case. What I take to be the Court's unease with these consequences, and its resulting unwillingness to acknowledge them, cannot alter the reality.

Under the constitutional principles announced and applied today, single sex public education is unconstitutional. By going through the motions of applying a balancing test—asking whether the State has adduced an "exceedingly persuasive justification" for its sex based classification—the Court creates the illusion that government officials in some future case will have a clear shot at justifying some sort of single sex public education. . . .

The Supreme Court of the United States does not sit to announce "unique" dispositions. Its principal function is to establish precedent—that is, to set forth principles of law that every court in America must follow. As we said only this Term, we expect both ourselves and lower courts to adhere to the "rationale upon which the Court based the results of its earlier decisions.". . . .

And the rationale of today's decision is sweeping: for sex based classifications, a redefinition of intermediate scrutiny that makes it indistinguishable from strict scrutiny. Indeed, the Court indicates that if any program restricted to one sex is "unique[e]," it must be opened to members of the opposite sex "who have the will and capacity" to participate in it. I suggest that the single sex program that will not be capable of being characterized as "unique" is not only unique but nonexistent.

In any event, regardless of whether the Court's rationale leaves some small amount of room for lawyers to argue, it ensures that single sex public education is functionally dead. The costs of litigating the constitutionality of a single sex education program, and the risks of ultimately losing that litigation, are simply too high to be embraced by public officials. . . . Should the courts happen to interpret that vacuous phrase as establishing a standard that is not utterly impossible of achievement, there is considerable risk that whether the standard has been met will not be determined on the basis of the record evidence—indeed, that will necessarily be the approach of any court that seeks to walk the path the Court has trod today. No state official in his right mind will buy such a high cost, high risk lawsuit by commencing a single sex program. The enemies of single sex education have won; by persuading only seven Justices (five would have been enough) that their view of the world is enshrined in the Constitution, they have effectively imposed that view on all 50 States.

260 *Abrams v. Johnson (1997)*

After the Georgia legislature had failed to develop a redistricting plan that met court requirements, the federal district court fashioned a plan of its own, which included one majority-minority district. The plan was attacked on the grounds that the court, while it had the power to draft a plan, had failed to follow the rules in such situations laid down by the Supreme Court in earlier decisions.

In his dissent in *Bush v. Vera* (Document 257), Justice Souter had warned that the Court's failure to provide clear guidelines on redistricting would lead to the courts arrogating unto themselves the power that properly belonged in the legislature. Despite the fact that the Rehnquist Court repeatedly avowed the principle of judicial deference to legislative policy-making, in the case of majority-minority districting a majority of the justices consistently denied the power of the Congress under the Fourteenth Amendment's Enforcement Clause to impose plans it deemed necessary to give minorities voting effectiveness. The Court also denied states their usual leeway in drawing less than compact or contiguous district lines.

Although the Court never said that majority-minority districts were per se unconstitutional, after *Abrams* it appeared unlikely that state legislatures could create such districts except in large cities, where such districts could be created in any event. Efforts to draw together minorities in rural areas into bizarrely shaped districts would in all likelihood fail the Court's strict scrutiny review.

See readings for Documents 252 and 257, and Thalia L. D. Carroll, "One Step Forward or Two Step Back? *Abrams v. Johnson* and the Voting Rights Act of 1965," 31 *Creighton Law Review* 917 (1998).

———

Justice KENNEDY delivered the opinion of the Court:

The electoral district lines for Georgia's congressional delegation are before us a second time, appeal now being taken from the trial court's rulings and determinations after our remand in *Miller v. Johnson,* (1995). The three-judge panel of the United States District Court for the Southern District of Georgia was affirmed in *Miller* after it found the Eleventh Congressional District unconstitutional as then drawn. Race, we held, must not be a predominant factor in drawing the district lines.

Given the contorted shape of the district and the undue predominance of race in drawing its lines, it was unlikely the district could be redrawn without changing most or all of Georgia's congressional districts, 11 in total number. The plan being challenged

Source: 521 U.S. 74 (1997)

contained three majority-black districts, and after our remand the complaint was amended to challenge another of these, the then Second District. The trial court found this district, too, was improperly drawn under the standards we confirmed in Miller.

For the task of drawing a new plan, the court deferred to Georgia's legislature, but the legislature could not reach agreement. The court then drew its own plan, and the 1996 general elections were held under it. The court's plan contained but one majority-black district. The absence of a second, if not a third, majority-black district has become the principal point of contention. Though the elections have been completed, the plan remains in effect until changed by a valid legislative act, and the appellants ask us to set it aside.

The private appellants are various voters, defendant-intervenors below, who contend that the interests of Georgia's black population were not adequately taken into account. The United States, also a defendant-intervenor, joins in the appeal. The state officials, defendants below, do not object to the plan and appeared before us as appellees to defend it. The other set of appellees are the private plaintiffs, who argued that racial gerrymandering under the previous plan violated their right to equal protection.

The private appellants attack the court's plan on five grounds. First, citing *Upham v. Seamon* (1982), they say the District Court erred in disregarding the State's legislative policy choices and in making more changes than necessary to cure constitutional defects in the previous plan. Second and third, they allege the plan violates Sections 2 and 5 of the Voting Rights Act of 1965. Fourth, they argue the court's plan contains significant population deviations and so violates the constitutional one person, one vote requirement. Fifth, they claim the District Court erred in not allowing private intervention on the question of the Second District's unconstitutionality. The challenges are unavailing, and we affirm the judgment of the District Court.

We first address appellants' argument that the court exceeded the remedial power authorized by our decisions, particularly *Upham v. Seamon,* by failing to follow policies of the state legislature. When faced with the necessity of drawing district lines by judicial order, a court, as a general rule, should be guided by the legislative policies underlying the existing plan, to the extent those policies do not lead to violations of the Constitution or the Voting Rights Act. Much of the argument from the parties centers around what legislative redistricting principles the District Court should have acknowledged in drawing its plan. The appellants say the relevant redistricting guideline should be the three majority-black districts of the precleared plan at issue in *Miller v. Johnson;* and, if not, the two majority-black districts in an earlier legislative effort. These contentions require us to recite some of the background against which the Georgia Legislature—and later the trial court—attempted to draw the districts.

[*The Court here summarized the history of the suit, and the inability of the Georgia legislature to reach agreement on a redistricting plan that would have passed constitutional muster, thus leading the district court to develop its own plan, with only one majority-minority district.*]

Given this background, appellants say, the District Court's plan violates our direction in *Upham v. Seamon* to take account of legislative preferences. In Upham, the district court considered a reapportionment plan passed by the Texas Legislature. The Attorney General had objected under Section 5 of the Voting Rights Act to a specific part of the plan, namely the lines drawn for two contiguous districts in south Texas. He had approved the other 25 districts. The trial court, required to draw new lines, redrew not just the two districts found objectionable and their neighbors but also some unrelated districts in Dallas County, hundreds of miles to the north. In the absence of a finding that the legislature's reapportionment plan offended either the Constitution or the Voting Rights Act, we held, the district court "was not free . . . to disregard the political program" of the state legislature.

The instant case presents a quite different situation from *Upham,* and for several reasons. In the first place, the precleared plan is not owed *Upham* deference to the extent the plan subordinated traditional districting principles to racial considerations. *Upham* called on courts to correct—not follow—constitutional defects in districting plans. In *Miller,* we found that when the Georgia Legislature yielded to the Justice Department's threats, it also adopted the Justice Department's entirely race-focused approach to redistricting— the max-black policy. Using the precleared plan as the basis for a remedy would validate the very maneuvers that were a major cause of the unconstitutional districting.

Second, the constitutional violation here affects a large geographic area of the State; any remedy of necessity must affect almost every district. Almost every major population center in Georgia was split along racial lines. Under the circumstances, the district court was justified in making substantial changes to the existing plan consistent with Georgia's traditional districting principles, and considering race as a factor but not allowing it to predominate. This approach conforms to the rule explained in Upham.

Appellants' most specific objection under *Upham* is that the court's plan does not contain two majority-black districts. In particular, they point to the State's original 1991 redistricting plan, denied preclearance, which contained two majority-black districts. As we have suggested above, however, the State was subjected to steady Justice Department pressure to create the maximum number of majority-black districts, and there is considerable evidence the State was predominantly driven by this consideration even in developing its 1991 plan. . . .

There is strong support, then, for finding the second majority-black district in Georgia's 1991 unprecleared plan resulted in substantial part from the Justice Department's policy of creating the maximum number of majority-black districts. It is not Justice Department interference *per se* that is the concern, but rather the fact that Justice Department pressure led the State to act based on an overriding concern with race. Given this background, it would have been most problematic for the trial court to insist on retaining a second majority-black district without regard to other, neutral districting factors. The trial court did not adopt this course. Instead, it gave careful consideration to creation of a second black district on grounds that a black voting population was one factor in drawing a district; and it concluded it could not draw the second majority-black district without allowing that one consideration to predominate over other traditional and neutral districting principles, principles which were a valid expression of legislative policy. There is ample basis in the record to support these conclusions. No other plan demonstrated a second majority-black district could be drawn while satisfying the constitutional requirement that race not predominate over traditional districting principles. The District Court said in its opinion that "if Georgia had a concentrated minority population large enough to create a second majority-minority district without subverting traditional districting principles, the Court would have included one since Georgia's legislature probably would have done so." The statements of several witnesses support the trial court's independent conclusion it was not possible to do so. . . .

The court-ordered plan is not violative of Section 2 of the Voting Rights Act. We reject appellants' contrary position, which is premised on impermissible vote dilution in the court's failure to create a second majority-black district. Section 2 of the Voting Rights Act applies to any "voting qualification or prerequisite to voting or standard, practice, or procedure . . . imposed or applied by any State or political subdivision."

Our decision in *Thornburg v. Gingles* (1986), set out the basic framework for establishing a vote dilution claim against at-large, multimember districts; we have since extended the framework to single-member districts. Plaintiffs must show three threshold conditions: first, the minority group "is sufficiently large and geographically compact to constitute a majority in a single-member district"; second, the minority group is "politically cohesive"; and third, the majority "votes sufficiently as a bloc to enable it . . . to defeat the minority's preferred candidate." Once plaintiffs establish these conditions, the court considers whether, "on the totality of circumstances," minorities have been denied an "equal opportunity" to "participate in the political process and to elect representatives of their choice."

The trial court found that to create a second majority-black district in Georgia would require subordinating Georgia's traditional districting policies and allowing race to predominate. We considered the determination in our discussion above and concluded it was well founded. If race is the predominant motive in creating districts, strict scrutiny applies, and the districting plan must be narrowly tailored to serve a compelling governmental interest in order to survive. We have assumed, without deciding, that compliance with Section 2 can be a compelling state interest. Here, there was no "strong basis in evidence," to conclude that vote dilution, in violation of Section 2, would occur in consequence of the court's plan. In fact, none of the three *Gingles* factors, the threshold findings for a vote dilution claim, were established here. . . .

The private appellants contend the District Court's plan also violates Section 5 of the Voting Rights Act. As we noted above, Section 5 requires covered jurisdictions to obtain either administrative preclearance by the Attorney General or approval from the United States District Court for the District of Columbia for any change in a "standard, practice, or procedure with respect to voting," and requires that the proposed change "not have the purpose and will not have the effect of denying or abridging the right to vote on account of race or color." We have explained that "the purpose of Section 5 has always been to insure that no voting-procedure changes would be made that would lead to a retrogression in the position of racial minorities with respect to their effective exercise of the electoral franchise."

The question arises whether a court decree is subject to Section 5. We have held that "a decree of the United States District Court is not within reach of Section 5 of the Voting Rights Act" such that it must be precleared. The exception applies to judicial plans, devised by the court itself, not to plans submitted to the court by the legislature of a covered jurisdiction in response to a determination of unconstitutionality. Here, the District Court made clear it had devised its own plan, a proposition not in dispute. In *McDaniel v. Sanchez* (1981), we emphasized language in a Senate Committee report saying that, although preclearance does not apply to court-devised plans, "'in fashioning the plan, the court should follow the appropriate Section 5 standards, including the body of administrative and judicial precedents developed in Section 5 cases.'" This is a reasonable standard, at the very least as an equitable factor to take into account, if not as a statutory mandate.

Appellants, however, have some difficulty fixing on a benchmark against which to measure any retrogression. Private appellants say the benchmark should be either the State's initial 1991 plan, containing two majority-black districts, or the State's "policy and goal of creating two majority black districts." The Justice Department, for its part, contends the proper benchmark is the 1992 precleared plan, altered to cure its constitutional defects.

Here, as we have noted above in our discussions of both *Upham* and Section 2, appellants have not demonstrated it was possible to create a second majority-black district within constitutional bounds. So, even were we to accept one of their proposed benchmarks, their desired remedy would be unconstitutional. As it happens, none of appellants' proposed benchmarks is appropriate. . . . The appropriate benchmark is, in fact, what the District Court concluded it would be: the 1982 plan, in effect for a decade. Appellants have not shown that black voters in any particular district suffered a retrogression in their voting strength under the court plan measured against the 1982 plan. Absent such proof, there is no violation of Section 5. We reject appellants' assertion that, even using the 1982 plan as a benchmark, the court's plan is retrogressive. They claim that under the 1982 plan one of the ten districts (10%) was majority black, while under the District Court's plan one of eleven districts (9%) is majority black, and therefore blacks do not have the same electoral opportunities under the District Court's plan. Under that logic, each time a State with a majority-minority district was allowed to add one new district because of population growth, it would have to be majority-minority. This the Voting Rights Act does not require.

Finally, appellants contend the District Court's plan violates the constitutional guarantee of one person, one vote under Article I, Section 2. [*The Court rejected the argument that a minor diminution in the percentage of black voters in majority black districts constituted a deprivation of the one person, one vote rule.*]

The task of redistricting is best left to state legislatures, elected by the people and as capable as the courts, if not more so, in balancing the myriad factors and traditions in legitimate districting policies. Here, the legislative process was first distorted and then unable to reach a solution. The District Court was left to embark on a delicate task with limited legislative guidance. The court was careful to take into account traditional state districting factors, and it remained sensitive to the constitutional requirement of equal protection of the laws. The judgment of the District Court is affirmed.

It is so ordered.

Justice BREYER, with whom Justice STEVENS, Justice SOUTER, and Justice GINSBURG join, dissenting:

The basic legal issue before us now is whether the District Court should have retained (not one but) two majority-minority districts. The majority holds that the District Court could lawfully create a new districting plan that retained only one such district. But in my view that decision departs dramatically from the Georgia Legislature's preference for two such districts—a preference embodied in the legislature's earlier congressional district plans. A two-district plan is not unconstitutional. And the District Court here, like the District Court in *Upham v. Seamon* (1982), "was not free . . . to disregard the political program of the . . . Legislature." For that reason, and others, I dissent.

The majority fully understands the relevance, and the importance, here of this Court's *Upham* decision. In *Upham* the Court said: "Just as a federal district court . . . should follow the policies and preferences of the State, as expressed . . . in the reapportionment plans proposed by the state legislature, whenever adherence to state policy does not detract from the requirements of the Federal Constitution, . . . a district court should similarly honor state policies in the context of congressional reapportionment." The majority here, referring to this language, agrees: "A court, as a general rule, should be guided by the legislative policies underlying the existing plan, to the extent those policies do not lead to violations of the Constitution or the Voting Rights Act." It is therefore common ground among us that the District Court should have drawn boundaries so as to leave two majority-minority districts rather than one—unless there was no such state policy or preference; unless the creation of two such districts would have violated the Constitution or the Voting Rights Act of 1965; or unless doing so simply would have proved impractical in light of other important districting objectives. Unlike the majority, I cannot find present here any of these three countervailing justifications.

No one denies that, if one looks at the redistricting plans proposed by the Georgia Legislature, one will find in them expressions of state "policies and preferences" for two majority-minority districts. . . . What the District Court and the majority deny is that the "preferences" expressed in these three redistricting plans reflect the Georgia Legislature's true preference. The District Court said that "Georgia's current plan was not the product of Georgia's legislative will," but rather "was tainted by unconstitutional DOJ [Department of Justice] interference" into the "process" that produced the plan. The majority repeats the District Court's comment about DOJ's "thorough 'subversion of the redistricting process' since the 1990 census," adds that the "State was predominantly driven" by "steady Justice Department pressure," and concludes: "Interference by the Justice Department . . . disturbed any sound basis to defer to the 1991 unprecleared plan."

I believe, however, that the majority's conclusion—its reason for refusing to recognize the Georgia Legislature's two-district preference—is wrong both as a matter of fact and as a matter of law. The conclusion is factually inadequate because the testimony cited to show unusual DOJ pressure in the 1991 redistricting process shows nothing unusual. It shows only that the Justice Department told Georgia that it must comply with the VRA, which statement Georgia legislators might have considered an exhortation to create more than one majority-minority district. Indeed, the record indicates that a number of Georgia legislators affirmatively wanted two majority-minority districts. It also shows that the 1991 two-district plan was the result of an "'understanding' between the leadership in the legislature and the black caucus."

The majority is legally wrong because this Court has said that a court should determine a State's redistricting preferences by looking to the "plans proposed by the state legislature," not by evaluating the various political pressures that might have led individual legislators to vote one way rather than another (or, for that matter, by reviewing after-the-fact testimony regarding legislative intent). District plans, like other legislative Acts, may reflect not only reasoned argument but also political pressures, brought to bear by many different individuals and groups using subtle or unsubtle suggestions, promises or threats, of votes, support, publicity, and even lawsuits.

How can a court say that a legislative Act is legitimate—that it reflects legislative preferences or policies—when those who reason or cajole (or threaten suit) are farmers, businessmen, or consumer groups, but that the same legislative Act becomes illegitimate—that it does not reflect "true" legislative policy or preference—simply because those who seek to persuade (or threaten suit) represent the Justice Department. One cannot say that the Department's power is any less legitimate than that exercised by the many other groups that seek to influence legislative decisions; and its employees' sworn duty to uphold the law would seem more suitably characterized as a reason for paying greater attention to its views rather than as a reason for heeding them less. Regardless, I am not aware of any legal principle that supports the kind of distinction (among legislative pressures) that the District Court made; and the District Court's necessary reliance upon such a distinction, by itself, should warrant vacating the District Court's decision.

Moreover, what reason is there to believe that Georgia's Legislature did not "really" want the two majority-minority districts that its earlier plans created? There is—as I indicated earlier—evidence that a number of legislators did want two majority-minority districts. And the legislature was aware of Georgia's long, well documented history of past discrimination in voting. . . .

I do not necessarily agree or disagree with those other aspects of the majority's opinion that I have not mentioned. But I shall stop with the main point. The Court, perhaps by focusing upon what it considered to be unreasonably pervasive positive use of race as a redistricting factor, has created a legal doctrine that will unreasonably restrict legislators' use of race, even for the most benign, or antidiscriminatory purposes. And that doctrine will draw the Court too deeply into an area of legislative responsibility. For the reasons set forth here, and in previous dissenting opinions, I do not believe that the Constitution embodies the doctrine that the majority enunciates. And I believe that *Upham* requires us to vacate the District Court's judgment and remand the suit.

---

261   *Printz v. United States (1997)*

In a unitary system, there is only one set of laws, and all government officials are required to uphold them. In a federal system, state officials normally enforce state laws, while representatives of the federal government enforce federal laws. It is not unusual for state officials to cooperate with federal officers, especially in the area of law enforcement, but while the Supremacy Clause mandates that federal law supersedes state law, it is not clear just how far the federal government can go in *requiring* state officers to enforce federal law.

The first modern effort at controlling guns, the Gun Control Act of 1968, established a federal scheme governing the sale, distribution, and possession of firearms, and established proscribed classes who could not own guns, such as convicted felons, unlawful users of controlled substances, and others. In 1993 Congress, responding to an "epidemic of gun violence," passed the Brady Act, which required the attorney general to establish a national instant background check system by 1998. In the meantime, interim provisions of the act imposed duties upon local chief law enforcement officers (CLEOs), requiring them to do background checks applicable to local firearm sales and to keep records in accordance with a national system to be established by the Justice Department.

Two sheriffs, one in Montana and the other in Arizona, challenged the Brady Act's constitutionality, and by a 5–4 vote, the justices invalidated the interim provisions of the law requiring CLEOs to enforce a federal law. That provision, according to Justice Scalia, "commandeered" state officials into the administration of a federal program and thus violated state sovereignty.

See Vicki C. Jackson, "Federalism and the Uses and Limits of Law: Printz and Principle?" 111 *Harvard Law Review* 2180 (1998); Symposium, "Reviving the Structural Constitution," 22 *Harvard Journal of Law and Public Policy* 1 (1998); and David B. Kopel, "The Brady Bill Comes Due: The Printz case and State Autonomy," 9 *George Mason University Civil Rights Law Journal* 189 (1999).

———

Justice SCALIA delivered the opinion of the Court:

The question presented in these cases is whether certain interim provisions of the Brady Handgun Violence Prevention Act, . . . commanding state and local law enforcement officers to conduct background checks on prospective handgun purchases and to perform certain related tasks, violate the Constitution. . . .

From the description set forth above, it is apparent that the Brady Act purports to direct state law enforcement officers to participate, albeit only temporarily, in the administration of a federally enacted regulatory scheme. Regulated firearms dealers are required to forward Brady Forms not to a federal officer or employee, but to the CLEOs, whose obligation to accept those forms is implicit in the duty imposed upon them to make "reasonable efforts" within five days to determine whether the sales reflected in the forms are lawful. . . .

The petitioners here object to being pressed into federal service, and contend that congressional action compelling state officers to execute federal laws is unconstitutional. Because there is no constitutional text speaking to this precise question, the answer to the CLEO's challenge must be sought in historical understanding and practice, in the structure of the Constitution, and in the jurisprudence of this Court. We treat those three sources, in that order, in this and the next two sections of this opinion.

Petitioners contend that compelled enlistment of state executive officers for the administration of federal programs is, until very recent years at least, unprecedented. The

Source: 521 U.S. 898 (1997)

Government contends, on the contrary, that "the earliest Congresses enacted statutes that required the participation of state officials in the implementation of federal laws." . . .

These early laws establish, at most, that the Constitution was originally understood to permit imposition of an obligation on state *judges* to enforce federal prescriptions, insofar as those prescriptions related to matters appropriate for the judicial power. . . .

For these reasons, we do not think the early statutes imposing obligations on state courts imply a power of Congress to impress the state executive into its service. . . .

In addition to early legislation, the Government also appeals to other sources we have usually regarded as indicative of the original understanding of the Constitution. It points to portions of The Federalist. . . . But none of these statements necessarily implies—what is the critical point here—that Congress could impose these responsibilities *without the consent of the States.* They appear to rest on the natural assumption that the States would consent to allowing their officials to assist the Federal Government, . . . an assumption proved correct by the extensive mutual assistance the States and Federal Government voluntarily provided one another in the early days of the Republic. . . .

To complete the historical record, we must note that there is not only an absence of executive-commandeering statutes in the early Congresses, but there is an absence of them in our later history as well, at least until very recent years. . . .

The Government points to a number of federal statutes enacted within the past few decades that require the participation of state or local officials in implementing federal regulatory schemes. Some of these are connected to federal funding measures, and can perhaps be more accurately described as conditions upon the grant of federal funding than as mandates to the States; others, which require only the provision of information to the Federal Government, do not involve the precise issue before us here, which is the forced participation of the States' executive in the actual administration of a federal program. We of course do not address these or other currently operative enactments that are not before us; it will be time enough to do so if and when their validity is challenged in a proper case. For deciding the issue before us here, they are of little relevance. Even assuming they represent assertion of the very same congressional power challenged here, they are of such recent vintage that they are no more probative than the statute before us of a constitutional tradition that lends meaning to the text. Their persuasive force is far outweighed by almost two centuries of apparent congressional avoidance of the practice. . . .

The constitutional practice we have examined above tends to negate the existence of the congressional power asserted here, but is not conclusive. We turn next to consideration of the structure of the Constitution, to see if we can discern among its "essential postulate[s]" . . . a principle that controls the present cases.

It is incontestable that the Constitution established a system of "dual sovereignty." . . . Although the States surrendered many of their powers to the new Federal Government, they retained "a residuary and inviolable sovereignty," *The Federalist No. 39* (J. Madison). This is reflected throughout the Constitution's text. . . . Residual state sovereignty was also implicit, of course, in the Constitution's conferral upon Congress of not all governmental powers, but only discrete, enumerated ones, Art. I, Section 8, which implication was rendered express by the Tenth Amendment's assertion that "[t]he powers not delegated to the United States by the Constitution, nor prohibited by it to the States, are reserved to the States respectively, or to the people."

The Framers' experience under the Articles of Confederation had persuaded them that using the States as the instruments of federal governance was both ineffectual and provocative of federal-state conflict. . . . Preservation of the States as independent political entities being the price of union, and "[t]he practicality of making laws, with coercive sanctions, for the States as political bodies" having been, in Madison's words, "exploded on all hands," . . . the Framers rejected the concept of a central government that would act upon and through the States, and instead designed a system in which the state and federal governments would exercise concurrent authority over the people—who were, in Hamilton's words, "the only proper objects of government." . . . "The Framers explicitly chose a Constitution that confers upon Congress the power to regulate individuals, not States." . . . The great innovation of this design was that "our Citizens would have two political capacities, one state and one federal, each protected from incursion by the other"—"a legal system unprecedented in form and design, establishing two orders of government, each with its own direct relationship, its own privity, its own set of mutual rights and obligations to the people who sustain it and are governed by it." . . . The Constitution thus contemplates that a State's government will represent and remain accountable to its own citizens. . . .

This separation of the two spheres is one of the Constitution's structural protections of liberty. "Just as the separation and independence of the coordinate branches of the Federal Government serve to prevent the accumulation of excessive power in any one branch, a healthy balance of power between the States and the Federal Government will reduce the risk of tyranny and abuse from either front." . . . To quote Madison once again:

> "In the compound republic of America, the power surrendered by the people is first divided between two distinct governments, and then the portion allotted to each subdivided among distinct and separate departments. Hence a double security arises to the rights of the people. The different governments will control each other, at the same time that each will be controlled by itself." The Federalist No. 51. . . .

The power of the Federal Government would be augmented immeasurably if it were able to impress into its service—and at no cost to itself—the police officers of the 50 States. . . .

Finally, and most conclusively in the present litigation, we turn to the prior jurisprudence of this Court. Federal commandeering of state governments is such a novel phenomenon that this Court's first experience with it did not occur until the 1970s, when the Environmental Protection Agency promulgated regulations requiring States to prescribe auto emissions testing, monitoring and retrofit programs, and to designate preferential bus and carpool lanes. . . .

Although we had no occasion to pass upon the subject in [the EPA case], later opinions of ours have made clear that the Federal Government may not compel the States to implement, by legislation or executive action, federal regulatory programs. . . .

When we were at last confronted squarely with a federal statute that unambiguously required the States to enact or administer a federal regulatory program, our decision should have come as no surprise. At issue in *New York v. United States* . . . (1992), were the so-called "take title" provisions of the Low-Level Radioactive Waste Policy Amendments Act of 1985, which required States either to enact legislation providing for the disposal of radioactive waste generated within their borders, or to take title to, and possession of the waste—effectively requiring the States either to legislate pursuant to Congress's directions, or to implement an administrative solution. . . . We concluded that Congress could constitutionally require the States to do neither. . . . "The Federal Government," we held, "may not compel the States to enact or administer a federal regulatory program.". . .

The Government contends that *New York* is distinguishable on the following ground: unlike the "take title" provisions invalidated there, the background-check provision of the Brady Act does not require state legislative or executive officials to make policy, but instead issues a final directive to state CLEOs. It is permissible, the Government asserts, for Congress to command state or local officials to assist in the implementation of federal law so long as "Congress itself devises a clear legislative solution that regulates private conduct" and requires state or local officers to provide only "limited, non-policymaking help in enforcing that law." "The constitutional line is crossed only when Congress compels the States to make law in their sovereign capacities." . . .

Executive action that has utterly no policy-making component is rare, particularly at an executive level as high as a jurisdiction's chief law-enforcement officer. . . .

Even assuming, moreover, that the Brady Act leaves no "policymaking" discretion with the States, we fail to see how that improves rather than worsens the intrusion upon state sovereignty. Preservation of the States as independent and autonomous political entities is arguably less undermined by requiring them to make policy in certain fields than (Judge Sneed aptly described it over two decades ago) by "reduc[ing] [them] to puppets of a ventriloquist Congress" . . . It is an essential attribute of the States' retained sovereignty that they remain independent and autonomous within their proper sphere of authority. . . . It is no more compatible with this independence and autonomy that their officers be "dragooned" . . . into administering federal law, than it would be compatible with the independence and autonomy of the United States that its officers be impressed into service for the execution of state laws. . . .

By forcing state governments to absorb the financial burden of implementing a federal regulatory program, Members of Congress can take credit for "solving" problems without having to ask their constituents to pay for the solutions with higher federal taxes. And even when the States are not forced to absorb the costs of implementing a federal program, they are still put in the position of taking the blame for its burdensomeness and for its defects. . . . Under the present law, for example, it will be the CLEO and not some federal official who stands between the gun purchaser and immediate possession of his gun. And it will likely be the CLEO, not some federal official, who will be blamed for any error (even one in the designated federal database) that causes a purchaser to be mistakenly rejected.

Finally, the Government puts forward a cluster of arguments that can be grouped under the heading: "The Brady Act serves very important purposes, is most efficiently administered by CLEOs during the interim period, and places a minimal and only temporary burden upon state officers." . . . But where, as here, it is the whole *object* of the law to direct the functioning of the state executive, and hence to compromise the structural framework of dual sovereignty, such a "balancing" analysis is inappropriate. It is the very *principle* of separate state sovereignty that such a law offends, and no comparative assessment of the various interests can overcome that fundamental defect. . . . We adhere to that principle today, and conclude categorically, as we concluded categorically

in *New York:* "The Federal Government may not compel the States to enact or administer a federal regulatory program." . . . The mandatory obligation imposed on CLEOs to
perform background checks on prospective handgun purchasers plainly runs afoul of
that rule. . . .

Justice STEVENS, with whom Justice SOUTER, Justice GINSBERG, and Justice
BREYER join, dissenting:

When Congress exercises the powers delegated to it by the Constitution, it may
impose affirmative obligations on executive and judicial officers of state and local governments as well as ordinary citizens. The conclusion is firmly supported by the text of
the Constitution, and early history of the Nation, decisions of this Court, and a correct
understanding of the basic structure of the Federal Government.

These cases do not implicate the more difficult questions associated with congressional coercion of state legislatures addressed in *New York v. United States* . . . (1992).
Nor need we consider the wisdom of relying on local officials rather than federal agents
to carry out aspects of a federal program, or even the question whether such officials may
be required to perform a federal function on a permanent basis. The question is whether
Congress, acting on behalf of the people of the entire Nation, may require local law
enforcement officers to perform certain duties during the interim needed for the development of a federal gun control program. . . .

Indeed, since the ultimate issue is one of power, we must consider its implications
in times of national emergency. Matters such as the enlistment of air raid wardens, the
administration of a military draft, the mass inoculation of children to forestall an epidemic, or perhaps the threat of an international terrorist, may require a national response
before federal personnel can be made available to respond. . . .

The text of the Constitution provides a sufficient basis for a correct disposition of
this case.

Article I, Section 8, grants the Congress the power to regulate commerce among the
States. Putting to one side the revisionist views expressed by Justice THOMAS in his
concurring opinion in *United States v. Lopez* . . . (1995), there can be no question that
that provision adequately supports the regulation of commerce in handguns effected by
the Brady Act. Moreover, the additional grant of authority in that section of the Constitution "to make all Laws which shall be necessary and proper for carrying into Execution the foregoing Powers" is surely adequate to support the temporary enlistment of
local police officers in the process of identifying persons who should not be entrusted
with the possession of handguns. In short, the affirmative delegation of power in Article
I provides ample authority for the congressional enactment.

Unlike the First Amendment, which prohibits the enactment of a category of laws
that would otherwise be authorized by Article I, the Tenth Amendment imposes no
restriction on the exercise of delegated powers. . . .

There is not a clause, sentence, or paragraph in the entire text of the Constitution of
the United States that supports the proposition that a local police officer can ignore a
command contained in a statute enacted by Congress pursuant to an express delegation
of power enumerated in Article I. . . .

Indeed, the historical materials strongly suggest that the Founders intended to enhance the capacity of the federal government by empowering it—as a part of the new authority to make demands directly on individual citizens—to act through local officials. Hamilton made clear that the new Constitution, "by extending the authority of the federal head to the individual citizens of the several States, will enable the government to employ the ordinary magistracy of each, in the execution of its laws." *The Federalist No. 27.* . . . Hamilton's meaning was unambiguous; the federal government was to have the power to demand that local officials implement national policy programs. . . .

This point is made especially clear in Hamilton's statement that "the legislatures, courts, and magistrates, of the respective members, will be incorporated into the operations of the national government *as far as its just and constitutional authority extends; and will be rendered auxiliary to the enforcement of its laws." Ibid.* (second emphasis added). It is hard to imagine a more unequivocal statement that state judicial and executive branch officials may be required to implement federal law where the National Government acts within the scope of its affirmative powers. . . .

Bereft of support in the history of the founding, the Court rests its conclusion on the claim that there is little evidence the National Government actually exercised such a power in the early years of the Republic. . . . This reasoning is misguided in principle and in fact. . . . We have never suggested that the failure of the early Congresses to address the scope of federal power in a particular area or to exercise a particular authority was an argument against its existence. That position, if correct, would undermine most of our post-New Deal Commerce Clause jurisprudence. . . .

More importantly, the fact that Congress did elect to rely on state judges and the clerks of state courts to perform a variety of executive functions is surely evidence of a contemporary understanding that their status as state officials did not immunize them from federal service. The majority's description of these early statutes is both incomplete and at times misleading. . . .

[As to the] Court's "structural" arguments, the . . . fact that the Framers intended to preserve the sovereignty of the several States simply does not speak to the question whether individual state employees may be required federal obligations, such as registering young adults for the draft, . . . creating state emergency response commissions designed to manage the release of hazardous substances, . . . collecting and reporting data on underground storage tanks that may pose an environmental hazard, . . . and reporting traffic fatalities, . . . and missing children . . . to a federal agency.

Given the fact that the Members of Congress are elected by the people of the States, with each State receiving an equivalent number of Senators in order to ensure that even the smallest States have a powerful voice in the legislature, it is quite unrealistic to assume that they will ignore the sovereignty concerns of their constituents. It is far more reasonable to presume that their decisions to impose modest burdens on state officials from time to time reflect a considered judgment that the people in each of the States will benefit therefrom.

Indeed, the presumption of validity that supports all congressional enactments has added force with respect to policy judgments concerning the impact of a federal statute upon the respective States. The majority points to nothing suggesting that the political safeguards of federalism identified in *Garcia* need be supplemented by a rule, grounded in neither constitutional history nor text, flatly prohibiting the National Government from enlisting state and local officials in the implementation of federal law. . . .

Perversely, the majority's rule seems more likely to damage than to preserve the safeguards against tyranny provided by the existence of vital state governments. By limiting the ability of the Federal Government to enlist state officials in the implementation of its programs, the Court creates incentives for the National Government to aggrandize itself. In the name of State's rights, the majority would have the Federal Government create vast national bureaucracies to implement its policies. This is exactly the sort of thing that the early Federalists promised would not occur, in part as a result of the National Government's ability to rely on the magistracy of the states. . . .

Our statements, taken in context, clearly did not decide the question presented here, whether state executive officials—as opposed to state legislators—may in appropriate circumstances be enlisted to implement federal policy. . . .

The provision of the Brady Act that crosses the Court's newly defined constitutional threshold is more comparable to a statute requiring local police officers to report the identity of missing children to the Crime Control Center of the Department of Justice than to an offensive federal command to a sovereign state. If Congress believes that such a statute will benefit the people of the Nation, and serve the interests of cooperative federalism better than an enlarged federal bureaucracy, we should respect both its policy judgment and its appraisal of its constitutional power.

Accordingly, I respectfully dissent.

---

262   *City of Boerne v. Flores (1997)*

The Religious Freedom Restoration Act (Document 251) did not only attempt to reverse specific decisions of the Court. Congress declared that the Court had decided wrongly in *Smith* (Document 248) and other cases, and set out a particular interpretation of the First Amendment for the Court to follow. Such a move, which trenched upon the Court's authority to interpret the Constitution, appalled both conservatives and moderates on the bench, and it would be only a matter of time before the Court took a case testing the validity of RFRA.

In *Boerne v. Flores,* the Court chose a lower court decision that not only exposed the weaknesses of RFRA, but allowed the Court to lecture Congress on separation of powers and, in effect, warn them not to commit such a silliness again.

The basic question that had existed at the time RFRA passed Congress by overwhelming majorities—what source of authority did Congress have to pass such a rule—was answered by the Court very simply: Congress had no such authority.

See Gary S. Gildin, "A Blessing in Disguise," 23 *Harvard Journal of Law and Public Policy* 411 (2000); Douglas Laycock, "Federalism as a Structural Threat to Liberty," 22 *Harvard Journal of Law and Public Policy* 67 (1998); and Ronald Rotunda, "The Powers of Congress Under Section Five of the Fourteenth Amendment After *City of Boerne v. Flores*," 32 *Indiana Law Review* 163 (1998).

───

Justice KENNEDY delivered the opinion of the Court:

A decision by local zoning authorities to deny a church a building permit was challenged under the Religious Freedom Restoration Act of 1993 (RFRA). The case calls into question the authority of Congress to enact RFRA. We conclude the statute exceeds Congress' power.

Situated on a hill in the city of Boerne, Texas, some 28 miles northwest of San Antonio, is St. Peter Catholic Church. Built in 1923, the church's structure replicates the mission style of the region's earlier history. The church seats about 230 worshippers, a number too small for its growing parish. Some 40 to 60 parishioners cannot be accommodated at some Sunday masses. In order to meet the needs of the congregation the Archbishop of San Antonio gave permission to the parish to plan alterations to enlarge the building.

A few months later, the Boerne City Council passed an ordinance authorizing the city's Historic Landmark Commission to prepare a preservation plan with proposed historic landmarks and districts. Under the ordinance, the Commission must preapprove construction affecting historic landmarks or buildings in a historic district.

Soon afterwards, the Archbishop applied for a building permit so construction to enlarge the church could proceed. City authorities, relying on the ordinance and the designation of a historic district (which, they argued, included the church), denied the application. The Archbishop brought this suit challenging the permit denial in the United States District Court for the Western District of Texas.

The complaint contained various claims, but to this point the litigation has centered on RFRA and the question of its constitutionality. The Archbishop relied upon RFRA as one basis for relief from the refusal to issue the permit. The District Court concluded that by enacting RFRA Congress exceeded the scope of its enforcement power under Section 5 of the Fourteenth Amendment. The court certified its order for interlocutory appeal and the Fifth Circuit reversed, finding RFRA to be constitutional. We granted *certiorari* and now reverse.

Congress enacted RFRA in direct response to the Court's decision in *Employment Div., Dept. of Human Resources of Oregon v. Smith.* There we considered a Free Exercise Clause claim brought by members of the Native American Church who were denied unemployment benefits when they lost their jobs because they had used peyote. Their practice was to ingest peyote for sacramental purposes, and they challenged an Oregon statute of general applicability which made use of the drug criminal. In evaluating the claim, we declined to apply the balancing test set forth in *Sherbert v. Verner,* under which we would have asked whether Oregon's prohibition substantially burdened a religious practice and, if it did, whether the burden was justified by a compelling government interest. We stated: "[G]overnment's ability to enforce generally applicable prohibitions of socially harmful conduct . . . cannot depend on measuring the effects of a governmental action on a religious objector's spiritual development. To make an individual's obligation to obey such a law contingent upon the law's coincidence with his religious beliefs, except where the State's interest is 'compelling' . . . contradicts both constitutional tradition and common sense." The application of the *Sherbert* test, the *Smith* decision explained, would have produced an anomaly in the law, a constitutional right to ignore neutral laws of general applicability. The anomaly would have been accentuated, the Court reasoned, by the difficulty of determining whether a particular practice was central to an individual's religion. We explained, moreover, that it "is not within the judicial ken to question the centrality of particular beliefs or practices to a faith, or the validity of particular litigants' interpretations of those creeds." . . .

Under our Constitution, the Federal Government is one of enumerated powers. *McCulloch v. Maryland* (1819). The judicial authority to determine the constitutionality of laws, in cases and controversies, is based on the premise that the "powers of the legislature are defined and limited; and that those limits may not be mistaken, or forgotten, the constitution is written." *Marbury v. Madison.*

Congress relied on its Fourteenth Amendment enforcement power in enacting the most far reaching and substantial of RFRA's provisions, those which impose its requirements on the States. The Fourteenth Amendment provides, in relevant part: "Section 1. . . . No State shall make or enforce any law which shall abridge the privileges or immunities of citizens of the United States; nor shall any State deprive any person of life, liberty, or property, without due process of law; nor deny to any person within its jurisdiction the equal protection of the laws. . . . Section 5. The Congress shall have power to enforce, by appropriate legislation, the provisions of this article." The parties disagree over whether RFRA is a proper exercise of Congress' Section 5 power "to enforce" by "appropriate legislation" the constitutional guarantee that no State shall deprive any person of "life, liberty, or property, without due process of law" nor deny any person "equal protection of the laws." . . .

While the line between measures that remedy or prevent unconstitutional actions and measures that make a substantive change in the governing law is not easy to discern, and Congress must have wide latitude in determining where it lies, the distinction exists and must be observed. There must be a congruence and proportionality between the injury to be prevented or remedied and the means adopted to that end. Lacking such a connection, legislation may become substantive in operation and effect. History and our case law support drawing the distinction, one apparent from the text of the Amendment.

Regardless of the state of the legislative record, RFRA cannot be considered remedial, preventive legislation, if those terms are to have any meaning. RFRA is so out of proportion to a supposed remedial or preventive object that it cannot be understood as responsive to, or designed to prevent, unconstitutional behavior. It appears, instead, to attempt a substantive change in constitutional protections. . . .

The stringent test RFRA demands of state laws reflects a lack of proportionality or congruence between the means adopted and the legitimate end to be achieved. If an objector can show a substantial burden on his free exercise, the State must demonstrate a compelling governmental interest and show that the law is the least restrictive means of furthering its interest. Claims that a law substantially burdens someone's exercise of religion will often be difficult to contest. . . . Laws valid under *Smith* would fall under RFRA without regard to whether they had the object of stifling or punishing free exercise. . . .

The substantial costs RFRA exacts, both in practical terms of imposing a heavy litigation burden on the States and in terms of curtailing their traditional general regulatory power, far exceed any pattern or practice of unconstitutional conduct under the Free Exercise Clause as interpreted in *Smith.* Simply put, RFRA is not designed to identify and counteract state laws likely to be unconstitutional because of their treatment of religion. . . .

When Congress acts within its sphere of power and responsibilities, it has not just the right but the duty to make its own informed judgment on the meaning and force of the Constitution. This has been clear from the early days of the Republic. . . .

Our national experience teaches that the Constitution is preserved best when each part of the government respects both the Constitution and the proper actions and determinations of the other branches. When the Court has interpreted the Constitution, it has acted within the province of the Judicial Branch, which embraces the duty to say what the law is. *Marbury v. Madison.* When the political branches of the Government act against the background of a judicial interpretation of the Constitution already issued, it must be understood that in later cases and controversies the Court will treat its precedents with the respect due them under settled principles, including *stare decisis,* and contrary expectations must be disappointed. RFRA was designed to control cases and controversies, such as the one before us; but as the provisions of the federal statute here invoked are beyond congressional authority, it is this Court's precedent, not RFRA, which must control. . . .

The judgment of the Court of Appeals sustaining the Act's constitutionality is reversed.
[*In a concurring opinion, Justice STEVENS argued that RFRA also violated the Establishment Clause by granting special preferences to persons who seek exemption from governmental actions on religious grounds. In a concurring opinion, Justice SCALIA attacked the arguments of Justice O'CONNOR that Smith should be reconsidered and overruled.*]

Justice O'CONNOR, with whom Justice BREYER joins except as to a portion of Part I, dissenting:

I dissent from the Court's disposition of this case. I agree with the Court that the issue before us is whether the Religious Freedom Restoration Act (RFRA) is a proper exercise of Congress' power to enforce Section 5 of the Fourteenth Amendment. But as a yardstick for measuring the constitutionality of RFRA, the Court uses its holding in *Employment Div., Dept. of Human Resources of Oregon v. Smith,* the decision that prompted Congress to enact RFRA as a means of more rigorously enforcing the Free Exercise Clause. I remain of the view that *Smith* was wrongly decided, and I would use this case to reexamine the Court's holding there. Therefore, I would direct the parties to brief the question whether *Smith* represents the correct understanding of the Free Exercise Clause and set the case for reargument. If the Court were to correct the misinterpretation of the Free Exercise Clause set forth in *Smith*, it would simultaneously put our First Amendment jurisprudence back on course and allay the legitimate concerns of a majority in Congress who believed that *Smith* improperly restricted religious liberty. We would then be in a position to review RFRA in light of a proper interpretation of the Free Exercise Clause. . . .

[In dissenting opinions, Justice SOUTER and Justice BREYER agreed with Justice O'CONNOR that Smith *should be reconsidered.]*

263   *Agostini v. Felton (1997)*

The fears of many that a Rehnquist Court would, in the name of accommodation, tear down the wall of separation between church and state, seemed groundless in the late 1980s and early 1990s. In a variety of cases, the Court stuck to the precedents it had developed, and in some ways the Religious Freedom Restoration Act (Document 251) was a response to what many perceived as a too rigid interpretation of the Establishment and Free Exercise Clauses. But most of those cases were decided by shifting majorities, often 5–4, and given a proper case, the accommodationists on the Court stood a good chance of having their way.

In *Witters v. Washington Dept. of Services to the Blind* (1986), the Court permitted a recipient of a grant from a public agency to use the money to attend a religious-sponsored college for the express purpose of becoming a minister. In *Zobrest v. Catalina Foothills School District* (1993), it allowed public funds to be used to pay a sign-language interpreter in a religious school. That message was not lost on the original plaintiffs in *Aguilar v. Felton* (1985), in which a closely divided Court had struck down a popular New York program that used Title I money to pay for public school teachers going into parochial schools and conducting remedial programs during regular school hours, as well as a community program offering courses in these schools after hours.

Following that ruling, the district court had issued an injunction against continued use of Title I monies for the programs. Using a procedural device— Rule 60(b) of the Federal Rules of Civil Procedure—to get their argument back before the high court, plaintiffs claimed that intervening decisions had effectively overruled the basis for that injunction. The slim majority of the justices who had long been unhappy with the *Lemon* test and its consequences seized upon the Rule 60(b) petition in order to overrule the earlier decision.

It is unclear just how far the Court is willing to go down this road and reverse nearly three decades of Establishment Clause jurisprudence. Commentators expected the accommodationists to win in other cases, but the centrists managed to cobble together majorities to thwart those efforts.

See Robert G. Neill, "Agostini v. Felton: The Gnat Is Swallowed, but the Camel Goes Free," 24 *Journal of Contemporary Law* 192 (1998); Daniel P. Whitehead, "Agostini v. Felton: Rectifying the Chaos of Establishment Clause Jurisprudence," 27 *Capital University Law Review* 639 (1999); and Jeremy Bunnow, "Reinventing the Lemon," 1998 *Wisconsin Law Review* 1133.

────────

Justice O'CONNOR delivered the opinion of the Court:

In *Aguilar v. Felton* (1985), this Court held that the Establishment Clause of the First Amendment barred the city of New York from sending public school teachers into parochial schools to provide remedial education to disadvantaged children pursuant to a congressionally mandated program. On remand, the [district court] entered a permanent injunction reflecting our ruling. Twelve years later, petitioners—the parties bound by that injunction—seek relief from its operation. Petitioners maintain that *Aguilar* cannot be squared with our intervening Establishment Clause jurisprudence and ask that we explicitly recognize what our more recent cases already dictate: *Aguilar* is no longer good law. We agree with petitioners that *Aguilar* is not consistent with our subsequent Establishment Clause decisions and further conclude that, on the facts presented here, petitioners are entitled under Federal Rule of Civil Procedure 60(b)(5) to relief from the operation of the District Court's prospective injunction.

Title I of the Elementary and Secondary Education Act of 1965 channels federal funds, through the States, to "local educational agencies" (LEA's) to provide remedial education, guidance, and job counseling to students who are failing, or at risk of failing, the State's student performance standards. Title I funds must be made available to all eligible children, regardless of whether they attend public schools, and the services provided to children attending private schools must be "equitable in comparison to services and other benefits for public school children." An LEA providing services to children enrolled in private schools is subject to a number of constraints that are not imposed when it provides aid to public schools. Title I services may be provided only to those private school students eligible for aid, and cannot be used to provide services on a "schoolwide" basis. In addition, the LEA must retain complete control over Title I funds; retain title to all materials used to provide Title I services; and provide those services through public employees or other persons independent of the private school and any religious institution. The Title I services themselves must be "secular, neutral, and nonideological," and must "supplement, and in no case supplant, the level of services" already provided by the private school. . . .

In 1978, six federal taxpayers—respondents here—sued the Board in the District Court. The District Court granted summary judgment for the Board, but the Court of Appeals for the Second Circuit reversed. In a 5–4 decision, this Court affirmed on the ground that the Board's Title I program necessitated "an excessive entanglement of church and state in the administration of Title I benefits." On remand the District Court permanently enjoined the Board "from using public funds for any plan or program under Title I to the extent that it requires, authorizes or permits public school teachers and guidance counselors to provide teaching and counseling services on the premises of sectarian schools within New York City."

The Board reverted to its prior practice of providing instruction at public school sites, at leased sites, and in mobile instructional units (essentially vans converted into classrooms) parked near the sectarian school. The Board also offered computer-aided instruction, which could be provided "on premises" because it did not require public employees to be physically present on the premises of a religious school. It is not disputed that the additional costs of complying with *Aguilar*'s mandate are significant. Since the 1986–1987 school year, the Board has spent over $100 million providing computer-aided instruction, leasing sites and mobile instructional units, and transporting students to those sites. These "*Aguilar* costs" reduce the amount of Title I money an LEA has available for remedial education, and LEA's have had to cut back on the number of students who receive Title I benefits.

The question we must answer is a simple one: Are petitioners entitled to relief from the District Court's permanent injunction under Rule 60(b)? Rule 60(b)(5) states: "On motion and upon such terms as are just, the court may relieve a party . . . from a final judgment or order . . . when it is no longer equitable that the judgment should have prospective application." We have held that it is appropriate to grant a Rule 60(b)(5) motion when the party seeking relief from an injunction or consent decree can show "a significant change either in factual conditions or in law." Petitioners argue that there have been two significant legal developments since *Aguilar* was decided: In *Board of Education of Kiryas Joel v. Grumet* (1994); a majority of Justices have expressed their views that *Aguilar* should be reconsidered or overruled and *Aguilar* has in any event been undermined by subsequent Establishment Clause decisions, including *Witters v. Washington Department of Services for the Blind* (1986), *Zobrest v. Catalina Foothills School District* (1993), and *Rosenberger v. Rector and Visitors of the University of Virginia* (1995). The statements made by five Justices in *Kiryas Joel* do not, in themselves, furnish a basis for concluding that our Establishment Clause jurisprudence has changed. The question of *Aguilar's* propriety was not before us there. Thus, petitioners' ability to satisfy the prerequisites of Rule 60(b)(5) hinges on whether our later Establishment Clause cases have so undermined *Aguilar* that it is no longer good law.

In order to evaluate whether *Aguilar* has been eroded by our subsequent Establishment Clause cases, it is necessary to understand the rationale upon which *Aguilar;* as well as its companion case, *School District of Grand Rapids v. Ball* (1985), rested. . . . Distilled to essentials, the Court's conclusion that the Shared Time program in *Ball* had the impermissible effect of advancing religion rested on three assumptions: (i) any public employee who works on the premises of a religious school is presumed to inculcate religion in her work; (ii) the presence of public employees on private school premises creates a symbolic union between church and state; and (iii) any and all public aid that directly aids the educational function of religious schools impermissibly finances religious indoctrination, even if the aid reaches such schools as a consequence of private decisionmaking. Additionally, in *Aguilar* there was a fourth assumption: that

New York City's Title I program necessitated an excessive government entanglement with religion because public employees who teach on the premises of religious schools must be closely monitored to ensure that they do not inculcate religion.

Our more recent cases have undermined the assumptions upon which *Ball* and *Aguilar* relied. To be sure, the general principles we use to evaluate whether government aid violates the Establishment Clause have not changed since *Aguilar* was decided. For example, we continue to ask whether the government acted with the purpose of advancing or inhibiting religion and to explore whether the aid has the "effect" of advancing or inhibiting religion. What has changed since we decided *Ball* and *Aguilar* is our understanding of the criteria used to assess whether aid to religion has an impermissible effect.

As we have repeatedly recognized, government inculcation of religious beliefs has the impermissible effect of advancing religion. Our cases subsequent to *Aguilar* have, however, modified in two significant respects the approach we use to assess indoctrination. First, we have abandoned the presumption that the placement of public employees on parochial school grounds inevitably results in the impermissible effect of state-sponsored indoctrination or constitutes a symbolic union between government and religion. *Zobrest* expressly rejected the notion—relied on in *Ball* and *Aguilar*—that, solely because of her presence on private school property, a public employee will be presumed to inculcate religion in the students. *Zobrest* also implicitly repudiated the assumption that the presence of a public employee on private school creates an impermissible "symbolic link" between government and religion. . . .

Second, we have departed from the rule relied on in *Ball* that all government aid that directly aids the educational function of religious schools is invalid. In *Witters,* we held that the Establishment Clause did not bar a State from issuing a vocational tuition grant to a blind person who wished to use the grant to attend a Christian college and become a pastor, missionary, or youth director. We observed that the tuition grants were "made available generally without regard to the sectarian-nonsectarian nature of the institution benefitted" and that the grants were disbursed directly to students and thus that any money that ultimately went to religious institutions did so "only as a result of the genuinely independent and private choices" of individuals. The same logic applied in *Zobrest.*

Zobrest and *Witters* make clear that, under current law, the Shared Time program in *Ball* and New York City's Title I program in *Aguilar* will not, as a matter of law, be deemed to have the effect of advancing religion through indoctrination. First, there is no reason to presume that, simply because she enters a parochial school classroom, a full-time public employee such as a Title I teacher will depart from her assigned duties and instructions and embark on religious indoctrination, any more than there was a reason in *Zobrest* to think an interpreter would inculcate religion by altering her translation of classroom lectures. *Zobrest* also repudiates *Ball's* assumption that the presence of Title I teachers in parochial school classrooms will . . . create the impression of a "symbolic union" between church and State. Justice Souter maintains that Title I continues to foster a "symbolic union" between the Board and sectarian schools because it mandates "the involvement of public teachers in the instruction provided within sectarian schools" and "fuses public and private faculties." Justice Souter does not disavow the notion that Title I services may be provided to sectarian school students in off-campus locations. We do not see any perceptible (let alone dispositive) difference in the degree of symbolic union between a student receiving remedial instruction in a classroom on his sectarian school's campus and one receiving instruction in a van parked just at the school's curbside. . . .

Where aid is allocated on the basis of neutral, secular criteria that neither favor nor disfavor religion, and is made available to both religious and secular beneficiaries on a nondiscriminatory basis, the aid is less likely to have the effect of advancing religion. In *Ball* and *Aguilar,* the Court gave this consideration no weight. Before and since those decisions, we have sustained programs that provided aid to all eligible children regardless of where they attended school. Applying this reasoning to New York City's Title I program, it is clear that Title I services are allocated on the basis of criteria that neither favor nor disfavor religion. The services are available to all children who meet the Act's eligibility requirements, no matter what their religious beliefs or where they go to school. The Board's program does not, therefore, give aid recipients any incentive to modify their religious beliefs or practices in order to obtain those services.

We turn now to *Aguilar's* conclusion that New York City's Title I program resulted in an excessive entanglement between church and state. . . . After *Zobrest* we no longer presume that public employees will inculcate religion simply because they happen to be in a sectarian environment. Since we have abandoned the assumption that properly instructed public employees will fail to discharge their duties faithfully, we must also discard the assumption that pervasive monitoring of Title I teachers is required.

To summarize, New York City's Title I program does not run afoul of any of three primary criteria we currently use to evaluate whether government aid has the effect of advancing religion: it does not result in governmental indoctrination; define its recipients by reference to religion; or create an excessive entanglement. We therefore hold that a federally funded program providing supplemental, remedial instruction to disadvantaged children on a neutral basis is not invalid under the Establishment Clause when such instruction is given on the premises of sectarian schools by government employees pursuant to a program containing safeguards such as those present here. The same considerations that justify this holding require us to conclude that this carefully constrained program also cannot reasonably be viewed as an endorsement of religion. Accordingly, we must acknowledge that *Aguilar,* as well as the portion of *Ball* addressing Grand Rapids' Shared Time program, are no longer good law.

Stare decisis does not prevent us from overruling a previous decision where there has been a significant change in or subsequent development of our constitutional law. Our Establishment Clause jurisprudence has changed significantly since we decided *Ball* and *Aguilar,* so our decision to overturn those cases rests on far more than "a present doctrinal disposition to come out differently from the Court of 1985." We therefore overrule *Ball* and *Aguilar* to the extent those decisions are inconsistent with our current understanding of the Establishment Clause. We are only left to decide whether this change in law entitles petitioners to relief under Rule 60(b)(5). We conclude that it does. We reverse the judgment of the Court of Appeals and remand to the District Court with instructions to vacate its 1985 order.

Justice SOUTER, with whom Justices STEVENS and GINSBURG join, and with whom Justice BREYER joins in part, dissenting:

I believe *Aguilar* was a correct and sensible decision, and my only reservation about its opinion is that the emphasis on the excessive entanglement produced by monitoring religious instructional content obscured those facts that independently called for the application of two central tenets of Establishment Clause jurisprudence. The State is forbidden to subsidize religion directly and is just as surely forbidden to act in any way that could reasonably be viewed as religious endorsement. The flat ban on subsidization antedates the Bill of Rights and has been an unwavering rule in Establishment Clause cases, qualified only by the conclusion that state exactions from college students are not the sort of public revenues subject to the ban. (*Rosenberger v. Rector.*) The rule expresses the hard lesson learned over and over again in the American past and in the experiences of the countries from which we have come, that religions supported by governments are compromised just as surely as the religious freedom of dissenters is burdened when the government supports religion. The ban against state endorsement of religion addresses the same historical lessons. Governmental approval of religion tends to reinforce the religious message (at least in the short run) and, by the same token, to carry a message of exclusion to those of less favored views. The human tendency, of course, is to forget the hard lessons, and to overlook the history of governmental partnership with religion when a cause is worthy, and bureaucrats have programs. That tendency to forget is the reason for having the Establishment Clause (along with the Constitution's other structural and libertarian guarantees), in the hope of stopping the corrosion before it starts.

These principles were violated by the programs at issue in *Aguilar* and *Ball,* as a consequence of several significant features common to both: each provided classes on the premises of the religious schools, covering a wide range of subjects including some at the core of primary and secondary education, like reading and mathematics; while their services were termed "supplemental," the programs and their instructors necessarily assumed responsibility for teaching subjects that the religious schools would otherwise have been obligated to provide; the public employees carrying out the programs had broad responsibilities involving the exercise of considerable discretion; while the programs offered aid to nonpublic school students generally (and Title I went to public school students as well), participation by religious school students in each program was extensive; and, finally, aid flowed directly to the schools in the form of classes and programs, as distinct from indirect aid that reaches schools only as a result of independent private choice. . . .

The Court's holding that *Aguilar* and the portion of *Ball* addressing the Shared Time program are "no longer good law" rests on mistaken reading. *Zobrest* is no sanction for overruling *Aguilar* or any portion of *Ball.* In *Zobrest* the Court did indeed recognize that the Establishment Clause lays down no absolute bar to placing public employees in a sectarian school, but the rejection of such a per se rule was hinged expressly on the nature of the employee's job, sign-language interpretation (or signing) and the circumscribed role of the signer. The Court explained: "The task of a sign-language interpreter seems to us quite different from that of a teacher or guidance counselor. . . . Nothing in this record suggests that a sign-language interpreter would do more than accurately interpret whatever material is presented to the class as a whole. In fact, ethical guidelines require interpreters to 'transmit everything that is said in exactly the same way it was intended.'" The signer could thus be seen as more like a hearing aid than a teacher, and the signing could not be understood as an opportunity to inject religious content in what was supposed to be secular instruction. *Zobrest* accordingly holds only that in these limited circumstances where a public employee simply translates for one student the material presented to the class for the benefit of all students, the employee's presence in the sectarian school does not violate the Establishment Clause. Nor did *Zobrest,* implicitly or otherwise, repudiate the view that the involvement of public teachers in the instruction provided within sectarian schools looks like a partnership or union and implies approval of the sectarian aim. On the subject of symbolic unions and the strength of their implications, the lesson of *Zobrest* is merely that less is less.

The Court next claims that *Ball* rested on the assumption that "any and all public aid that directly aids the educational function of religious schools impermissibly finances religious indoctrination, even if the aid reaches such schools as a consequence of private decision-making." This mischaracterizes *Ball. Ball* did not establish that "any and all" such aid to religious schools necessarily violates the Establishment Clause. It held that the Shared Time program subsidized the religious functions of the parochial schools by taking over a significant portion of their responsibility for teaching secular subjects. The Court noted that it had "never accepted the mere possibility of subsidization . . . as sufficient to invalidate an aid program," and instead enquired whether the effect of the proffered aid was "direct and substantial" (and, so, unconstitutional) or merely "indirect and incidental" (and, so, permissible) emphasizing that the question "is one of degree." *Witters* and *Zobrest* did nothing to repudiate the principle, emphasizing rather the limited nature of the aid at issue in each case as well as the fact that religious institutions did not receive it directly from the State. . . .

Finally, instead of aid that comes to the religious school indirectly in the sense that its distribution results from private decision-making, a public educational agency distributes Title I aid in the form of programs and services directly to the religious schools. In *Zobrest* and *Witters,* it was fair to say that individual students were themselves applicants for individual benefits. But under Title I, a local educational agency may receive federal funding by proposing programs approved to serve individual students who meet the criteria of need, which it then uses to provide such programs at the religious schools; students eligible for such programs may not apply directly for Title I funds. In sum, nothing since *Ball* and *Aguilar* and before this case has eroded the distinction between "direct and substantial" and "indirect and incidental." That principled line is being breached only here and now. And if a scheme of government aid results in support for religion in some substantial degree, or in endorsement of its value, the formal neutrality of the scheme does not render the Establishment Clause helpless or the holdings in *Aguilar* and *Ball* inapposite.

(*Justice GINSBURG dissented, joined by Justices STEVENS, SOUTER, and BREYER. She objected on technical grounds to the Court's use of Rule 60(b), claiming that a new majority had distorted the intent of the rule and also ignored* stare decisis *in order to reach a result it wanted, a result unsupported by cases following* Ball *and* Aguilar.)

264

Reno v. American Civil Liberties Union (1997)

New technologies have often led to efforts at censorship. The Supreme Court long upheld the rights of states to censor cinema, and even today, radio and television enjoy less freedom of expression than do print media. When cable television came along, the Court upheld congressional mandates requiring that cable systems carry all signals of local public and commercial stations. Against this backdrop, it is hardly surprising that Congress tried to impose rules on the Internet as it became a popular medium of expression in the mid-nineties.

In early 1996, Congress passed the Communications Decency Act, which made it an offense to post "indecent" or "patently offensive" material on the Internet that would be available to minors. Sponsors of the bill, as well as the Justice Department, were worried about the constitutionality of the measure, but hoped that its emphasis on protecting minors would earn it constitutional legitimacy. The law provided for a "fast track" challenge, in which it would go directly from a three-judge panel to the high court.

Even as President Clinton signed the measure, opponents of the bill were filing challenges. In the case that would reach the Supreme Court, a coalition of librarians, public interest groups, information resource providers, and nonprofit entities convinced a three-judge panel in Philadelphia that the "indecency" provision was much too vague and open to serious misinterpretation by overzealous law enforcement officials. In addition, the judges agreed that none of the defenses Congress had put into the bill would really enable providers to be certain that allegedly "indecent" material had been screened out of the reach of minors.

Both the district court and Supreme Court opinions are notable not only for the strong enunciation of free expression, but also for sophistication about the Internet and how it works.

See Douglas W. Vick, "The Internet and the First Amendment," 61 *Modern Law Review* 414 (1998); Eugene Volokh, "Freedom of Speech, Shielding Children, and Transcending Balancing," 1997 *Supreme Court Review* 141; and Gary D. Allison, "The Cyberwar of 1997: Timidity and Sophistry at the First Amendment Front," 33 *Tulsa Law Journal* 103 (1997).

———

Justice STEVENS delivered the opinion of the Court:
. . . The Internet is an international network of interconnected computers. . . . The

Source: 521 U.S. 844 (1997)

Internet has experienced "extraordinary growth." . . . Individuals can obtain access to the Internet from many different sources, generally hosts themselves or entities with a host affiliation. . . . Anyone with access to the Internet may take advantage of a wide variety of communication and information retrieval methods. These methods are constantly evolving and difficult to categorize precisely. But, as presently constituted, those most relevant to this case are electronic mail ("e-mail"), automatic mailing list services ("mail exploders," sometimes referred to as "listservs"), "newsgroups," "chat rooms," and the "World Wide Web." All of these methods can be used to transmit text; most can transmit sound, pictures, and moving video images. Taken together, these tools constitute a unique medium—known to its users as "cyberspace"—located in no particular geographical location but available to anyone, anywhere in the world, with access to the Internet. . . .

Sexually explicit material on the Internet includes text, pictures, and chat and "extends from the modestly titillating to the hardest-core." . . . Though such material is widely available, users seldom encounter such contact accidentally. "A document's title or a description of the document will usually appear before the document itself . . . and in many cases the user will receive detailed information about a site's content before he or she need take the step to access the document. Almost all sexually explicit images are preceded by warnings as to the content." For that reason, the "odds are slim" that a user would enter a sexually explicit site by accident. . . . "A child requires some sophistication and some ability to read to retrieve material and thereby to use the Internet unattended." . . . In *Ginsberg,* we upheld the constitutionality of a New York statute that prohibited selling to minors under 17 years of age material that was considered obscene as to them even if not obscene to adults. . . . In *Pacifica,* we upheld a declaratory order of the Federal Communications Commission, holding that the broadcast of a recording of 12-minute monologue entitled "Filthy Words" that had previously been delivered to a live audience "could have been the subject of administrative sanctions." . . .

As with the New York statute at issue in *Ginsberg,* there are significant differences between the order upheld in *Pacifica* and the CDA. First, the order in *Pacifica,* issued by an agency that had been regulating radio stations for decades, targeted a specific broadcast that represented a rather dramatic departure from traditional program content in order to designate when—rather than whether—it would be permissible to air such a program in that particular medium. The CDA's broad categorical prohibitions are not limited to particular times and are not dependent on any evaluation by an agency familiar with the unique characteristics of the Internet. Second, unlike the CDA, the Commission's declaratory order was not punitive; we expressly refused to decide whether the indecent broadcast "would justify a criminal prosecution. *Id.,* at 750. Finally, the Commission's order applied to a medium which as a matter of history had "received the most limited First Amendment protection," *id.,* at 748, in large part because warnings could not adequately protect the listener from unexpected program content. The Internet, however, has no comparable history. Moreover, the District Court found that the risk of encountering indecent material by accident is remote because a series of affirmative steps is required to access specific material. . . .

In *Southeastern Promotions, Ltd.* v. *Conrad,* . . . we observed that "[e]ach medium of expression . . . may present its own problems." Thus, some of our cases have recognized special justifications for regulation of the broadcast media that are not applicable to other speakers. . . . In these cases, the Court relied on the history of extensive government regulation of the broadcast medium, . . . the scarcity of available frequencies at its inception, . . . and its "invasive" nature. . . . Those factors are not present in cyberspace. Neither before nor after the enactment of the CDA have the vast democratic fora of the Internet been subject to the type of government supervision and regulation that has attended the broadcast industry. Moreover, the Internet is not as "invasive" as radio or television. The District Court specifically found that "[c]ommunications over the Internet do not 'invade' an individual's home or appear on one's computer screen unbidden. Users seldom encounter content 'by accident.'" . . . It also found that "[a]lmost all sexually explicit images are preceded by warnings as to the content," and cited testimony that "'odds are slim' that a user would come across a sexually explicit sight by accident." . . .

Finally, unlike the conditions that prevailed when Congress first authorized regulation of the broadcast spectrum, the Internet can hardly be considered a "scarce" expressive commodity. It provides relatively unlimited, low-cost capacity for communication of all kinds. . . . This dynamic, multifaceted category of communication includes not only traditional print and news services, but also audio, video, and still images, as well as interactive, real-time dialogue. Through the use of chat rooms, any person with a phone line can become a town crier with a voice that resonates farther than it could from any soapbox. Through the use of Web pages, mail exploders, and newsgroups, the same individual can become a pamphleteer. As the District Court found, "the content on the Internet is as diverse as human thought." . . . We agree with its conclusion that our cases provide no basis for qualifying the level of First Amendment scrutiny that should be applied to this medium.

Regardless of whether the CDA is so vague that it violates the Fifth Amendment, the many ambiguities concerning the scope of its coverage render it problematic for purposes of the First Amendment. For instance, each of the two parts of the CDA uses a different linguistic form. The first uses the word "indecent," . . . while the second speaks of material that "in context, depicts or describes, in terms patently offensive as measured by contemporary community standards, sexual or excretory activities or organs". . . . Given the absence of a definition of either term, this difference in language will provoke uncertainty among speakers about how the two standards relate to each other and just what they mean. Could a speaker confidently assume that a serious discussion about birth control practices, homosexuality, . . . or the consequences of prison rape would not violate the CDA? This uncertainty undermines the likelihood that the CDA has been carefully tailored to the congressional goal of protecting minors from potentially harmful materials. The vagueness of the CDA is a matter of special concern for two reasons. First, the CDA is a content-based regulation of speech. The vagueness of such a regulation raises special First Amendment concerns because of its obvious chilling effect on free speech. . . . Second, the CDA is a criminal statute. In addition to the opprobrium and stigma of a criminal conviction, the CDA threatens violators with penalties including up to two years in prison for each act of violation. The severity of criminal sanctions may well cause speakers to remain silent rather than communicate even arguably unlawful words. . . .

The Government argues that the statute is no more vague than the obscenity standard this Court established in *Miller* v. *California*. . . . In contrast to *Miller* and our other previous cases, the CDA thus presents a greater threat of censoring speech that, in fact, falls outside the statute's scope. Given the vague contours of the coverage of the statute, it unquestionably silences some speakers whose messages would be entitled to constitutional protection. That danger provides further reason for insisting that the statute not be overly broad. The CDA's burden on protected speech cannot be justified if it could be avoided by a more carefully drafted statute.

We are persuaded that the CDA lacks the precision that the First Amendment requires when a statute regulates the content of speech. In order to deny minors access to potentially harmful speech, the CDA effectively suppresses a large amount of speech that adults have a constitutional right to receive and to address to one another. That burden on adult speech is unacceptable if less restrictive alternatives would be at least as effective in achieving the legitimate purpose that the statute was enacted to serve. . . . In arguing that the CDA does not so diminish adult communication, the Government relies on the incorrect factual premise that prohibiting a transmission whenever it is known that one if its recipients is a minor would not interfere with adult-to-adult communication. . . .

The District Court found that at the time of trial existing technology did not include any effective method for a sender to prevent minors from obtaining access to its communications on the Internet without also denying access to adults. The Court found no effective way to determine the age of a user who is accessing material through e-mail, mail exploders, newsgroups, or chat rooms. . . . As a practical matter, the Court also found that it would be prohibitively expensive for noncommercial—as well as some commercial—speakers who have Web sites to verify that their users are adults. . . .

The breadth of CDA's coverage is wholly unprecedented. Unlike the regulations upheld in *Ginsberg* and *Pacifica,* the scope of the CDA is not limited to commercial speech or commercial entities. Its open-ended prohibitions embrace all non-profit entities and individuals posting indecent messages or displaying them on their own computers in the presence of minors. The general, undefined terms "indecent" and "patently offensive" cover large amounts of nonpornographic material with serious educational or other value. Moreover, the "community standards" criterion as applied to the Internet means that any communication available to a nation-wide audience will be judged by the standards of the community most likely to be offended by the message. The regulated subject matter includes any of the seven "dirty words" used in the *Pacifica* monologue, the use of which the Government's expert acknowledged could constitute a felony. . . . It may also extend to discussions about prison rape or safe sexual practices, artistic images that include nude subjects, and arguably the card catalogue of the Carnegie library. . . . The breadth of this content-based restriction of speech imposes an especially heavy burden on the Government to explain why a less restrictive provision would not be as effective as the CDA. It has not done so. . . . Particularly in the light of the absence of any detailed findings by the Congress, or even hearings addressing the special problems of the CDA, we are persuaded that the CDA is not narrowly tailored if that requirement has any meaning at all. . . .

As a matter of constitutional tradition, in the absence of evidence to the contrary, we presume that the governmental regulation of the content of speech is more likely to interfere with the free exchange of ideas than to encourage it. The interest in encouraging freedom of expression in a democratic society outweighs any theoretical but unproven benefit of censorship. . . .

Justice O'CONNOR, with whom The Chief Justice joins, concurring in the judgment in part and dissenting in part:

I write separately to explain why I view the Communications Decency Act of 1996 (CDA) as little more than an attempt by Congress to create "adult zones" on the Internet. Our precedent indicates that the creation of such zones can be constitutionally sound. Despite the soundness of its purpose, however, portions of the CDA are unconstitutional because they stray from the blueprint our prior cases have developed from constructing a "zoning law" that passes constitutional muster.

---

265   *Washington v. Glucksberg (1997)*

Following the decision in *Cruzan* (Document 247), right-to-die advocates began to push for the right of people with terminal illnesses, regardless of whether they were on life support, to end their suffering with the help of third parties, such as physicians. At almost the same time, Dr. Jack Kevorkian, a retired Detroit pathologist, began to help people commit suicide, bringing the whole issue of physician-assisted suicide into public debate.

Although suicide had once been a felony, by 1997, all states had decriminalized both suicide and attempted suicide, although a majority of states still made it a crime for one person to assist another in ending his or her life. A number of advocacy groups, in particular the Washington-based Compassion in Dying, as well as individuals such as Dr. Timothy Quill, began challenging these laws. On the West Coast, the Court of Appeals for the Ninth Circuit held that Washington's ban on assisted suicide violated the liberty interest in autonomy protected by the Due Process Clause of the Fourteenth Amendment. On the East Coast, the Second Circuit struck down a similar New York law, arguing that allowing a person on life support to terminate treatment—even if that led to death—but forbidding a person not on life support to end their life, violated the Equal Protection Clause.

When the Supreme Court granted certiorari, most commentators accurately predicted that it was to reverse the circuits and deny any constitutional right to assisted suicide. That was in fact what happened, but five justices—a majority of the Court—wrote concurrences that in effect said we are willing to go along with this result now, but if the states make end-of-life choices too narrow, we will revisit the issue. Of special note is Justice David Souter's concurrence, reprinted here, which laid out how, under the Fourteenth Amendment, the right to physician-assisted suicide could be brought within the reach of the Due Process Clause.

See Melvin I. Urofsky, *Lethal Judgments: Assisted Suicide and the Law* (2000); Daniel Callahan, *The Troubled Dream of Life* (1993); Cass Sunstein, "The Right to Die," 106 *Yale Law Journal* 1123 (1997); and numerous web sites, including www.euthanasia.com.

———

Chief Justice REHNQUIST delivered the opinion of the Court:

The question presented in this case is whether Washington's prohibition against "causing" or "aiding" a suicide offends the Fourteenth Amendment to the United States Constitution. We hold that it does not.

It has always been a crime to assist a suicide in the State of Washington. In 1854, Washington's first Territorial Legislature outlawed "assisting another in the commission of self-murder." Today, Washington law provides: "A person is guilty of promoting a suicide attempt when he knowingly causes or aids another person to attempt suicide."

Petitioners in this case are . . . doctors [who] occasionally treat terminally ill, suffering patients, and declare that they would assist these patients in ending their lives if not for Washington's assisted-suicide ban. In January 1994, respondents, along with three gravely ill, pseudonymous plaintiffs who have since died and Compassion in Dying, a nonprofit organization that counsels people considering physician-assisted suicide, sued in the United States District Court, seeking a declaration that the Washington law is, on its face, unconstitutional.

. . . The District Court agreed, and concluded that Washington's assisted-suicide ban is unconstitutional because it "places an undue burden on the exercise of [that] constitutionally protected liberty interest." [The Court of Appeals affirmed] We reverse.

We begin, as we do in all due-process cases, by examining our Nation's history, legal traditions, and practices. . . . In almost every State—indeed, in almost every western democracy—it is a crime to assist a suicide. The States' assisted-suicide bans are not innovations. Rather, they are longstanding expressions of the States' commitment to the protection and preservation of all human life. . . . Indeed, opposition to and condemnation of suicide—and, therefore, of assisting suicide—are consistent and enduring themes of our philosophical, legal, and cultural heritages.

More specifically, for over 700 years, the Anglo-American common-law tradition has punished or otherwise disapproved of both suicide and assisting suicide.

For the most part, the early American colonies adopted the common-law approach. For example, the legislators of the Providence Plantations, which would later become Rhode Island, declared, in 1647, that "self-murder is by all agreed to be the most unnatural, and it is by this present Assembly declared, to be that, wherein he that doth it, kills himself out of a premeditated hatred against his own life or other humor: . . . his goods and chattels are the king's custom, but not his debts nor lands; but in case he be an infant, a lunatic, mad or distracted man, he forfeits nothing." . . .

———

Source: 521 U.S. 702 (1997)

Over time, however, the American colonies abolished these harsh common-law penalties. . . . That suicide remained a grievous, though nonfelonious, wrong is confirmed by the fact that colonial and early state legislatures and courts did not retreat from prohibiting assisting suicide. . . . The earliest American statute explicitly to outlaw assisting suicide was enacted in New York in 1828.

Though deeply rooted, the States' assisted-suicide bans have in recent years been reexamined and, generally, reaffirmed. Because of advances in medicine and technology, Americans today are increasingly likely to die in institutions, from chronic illnesses. Public concern and democratic action are therefore sharply focused on how best to protect dignity and independence at the end of life, with the result that there have been many significant changes in state laws and in the attitudes these laws reflect. Many States, for example, now permit "living wills," surrogate health-care decisionmaking, and the withdrawal or refusal of life-sustaining medical treatment. At the same time, however, voters and legislators continue for the most part to reaffirm their States' prohibitions on assisting suicide.

The Due Process Clause guarantees more than fair process, and the "liberty" it protects includes more than the absence of physical restraint. In a long line of cases, we have held that, in addition to the specific freedoms protected by the Bill of Rights, the "liberty" specially protected by the Due Process Clause includes the rights to marry, to have children, to direct the education and upbringing of one's children, to marital privacy, to use contraception, to bodily integrity, and to abortion. We have also assumed, and strongly suggested, that the Due Process Clause protects the traditional right to refuse unwanted lifesaving medical treatment.

But we "have always been reluctant to expand the concept of substantive due process because guideposts for responsible decisionmaking in this unchartered area are scarce and open-ended." By extending constitutional protection to an asserted right or liberty interest, we, to a great extent, place the matter outside the arena of public debate and legislative action. We must therefore "exercise the utmost care whenever we are asked to break new ground in this field," lest the liberty protected by the Due Process Clause be subtly transformed into the policy preferences of the members of this Court.

The history of the law's treatment of assisted suicide in this country has been and continues to be one of the rejection of nearly all efforts to permit it. That being the case, our decisions lead us to conclude that the asserted "right" to assistance in committing suicide is not a fundamental liberty interest protected by the Due Process Clause.

The Constitution also requires, however, that Washington's assisted-suicide ban be rationally related to legitimate government interests. This requirement is unquestionably met here. As the court below recognized, Washington's assisted-suicide ban implicates a number of state interests.

First, Washington has an "unqualified interest in the preservation of human life." The State's prohibition on assisted suicide, like all homicide laws, both reflects and advances its commitment to this interest. . . .

Respondents admit that "the State has a real interest in preserving the lives of those who can still contribute to society and enjoy life." The Court of Appeals also recognized Washington's interest in protecting life, but held that the "weight" of this interest depends on the "medical condition and the wishes of the person whose life is at stake." Washington, however, has rejected this sliding-scale approach and, through its assisted-suicide ban, insists that all persons' lives, from beginning to end, regardless of physical or mental condition, are under the full protection of the law. As we have previously affirmed, the States "may properly decline to make judgments about the 'quality' of life that a particular individual may enjoy." This remains true, as Cruzan makes clear, even for those who are near death.

The State also has an interest in protecting the integrity and ethics of the medical profession. In contrast to the Court of Appeals' conclusion that "the integrity of the medical profession would not be threatened in any way by [physician-assisted suicide]," the American Medical Association, like many other medical and physicians' groups, has concluded that "physician-assisted suicide is fundamentally incompatible with the physician's role as healer."

Next, the State has an interest in protecting vulnerable groups—including the poor, the elderly, and disabled persons—from abuse, neglect, and mistakes. The Court of Appeals dismissed the State's concern that disadvantaged persons might be pressured into physician-assisted suicide as "ludicrous on its face." We have recognized, however, the real risk of subtle coercion and undue influence in end-of-life situations.

The State's interest here goes beyond protecting the vulnerable from coercion; it extends to protecting disabled and terminally ill people from prejudice, negative and inaccurate stereotypes, and "societal indifference." The State's assisted-suicide ban reflects and reinforces its policy that the lives of terminally ill, disabled, and elderly people must be no less valued than the lives of the young and healthy, and that a seriously disabled person's suicidal impulses should be interpreted and treated the same way as anyone else's.

Finally, the State may fear that permitting assisted suicide will start it down the path to voluntary and perhaps even involuntary euthanasia. The Court of Appeals struck down Washington's assisted-suicide ban only "as applied to competent, terminally ill adults who wish to hasten their deaths by obtaining medication prescribed by their doctors." Washington insists, however, that the impact of the court's decision will not and cannot be so limited. If suicide is protected as a matter of constitutional right, it is argued, "every man and woman in the United States must enjoy it."

We need not weigh exactly the relative strengths of these various interests. They are unquestionably important and legitimate, and Washington's ban on assisted suicide is at least reasonably related to their promotion and protection. We therefore hold that Wash. Rev. Code § 9A.36.060(1) (1994) does not violate the Fourteenth Amendment, either on its face or "as applied to competent, terminally ill adults who wish to hasten their deaths by obtaining medication prescribed by their doctors."

Throughout the Nation, Americans are engaged in an earnest and profound debate about the morality, legality, and practicality of physician-assisted suicide. Our holding permits this debate to continue, as it should in a democratic society. The decision of the en banc Court of Appeals is reversed, and the case is remanded for further proceedings consistent with this opinion.

It is so ordered.

[*Chief Justice Rehnquist repeated most of these arguments in the companion case of* Vacco v. Quill, *reversing the Court of Appeals for the Second Circuit, which had held that New York's law against assisted suicide violated the Equal Protection Clause, since it unduly differentiated between people on life support and others who, while suffering, were not on life support.*]

Justice SOUTER, concurring in the judgment:

The question is whether the statute sets up one of those "arbitrary impositions" or "purposeless restraints" at odds with the Due Process Clause of the Fourteenth Amendment. I conclude that the statute's application to the doctors has not been shown to be unconstitutional, but I write separately to give my reasons for analyzing the substantive due process claims as I do, and for rejecting this one. . . .

[*Justice Souter reviewed the development of substantive due process first in state courts and then in the federal judiciary in the nineteenth and early parts of the twentieth century, its rejection after the constitutional crisis of 1937, and its revival and exposition, especially in Justice Harlan's dissent in* Poe v. Ullman.]

[Justice Harlan's] approach calls for a court to assess the relative "weights" or dignities of the contending interests, and to this extent the judicial method is familiar to the common law. Common law method is subject, however, to two important constraints in the hands of a court engaged in substantive due process review. First, such a court is bound to confine the values that it recognizes to those truly deserving constitutional stature, either to those expressed in constitutional text, or those exemplified by "the traditions from which [the Nation] developed," or revealed by contrast with "the traditions from which it broke." "'We may not draw on our merely personal and private notions and disregard the limits . . . derived from considerations that are fused in the whole nature of our judicial process . . . , considerations deeply rooted in reason and in the compelling traditions of the legal profession.'"

The second constraint, again, simply reflects the fact that constitutional review, not judicial lawmaking, is a court's business here. The weighing or valuing of contending interests in this sphere is only the first step, forming the basis for determining whether the statute in question falls inside or outside the zone of what is reasonable in the way it resolves the conflict between the interests of state and individual. It is no justification for judicial intervention merely to identify a reasonable resolution of contending values that differs from the terms of the legislation under review. It is only when the legislation's justifying principle, critically valued, is so far from being commensurate with the individual interest as to be arbitrarily or pointlessly applied that the statute must give way. Only if this standard points against the statute can the individual claimant be said to have a constitutional right. . . .

The *Poe* dissent thus reminds us of the nature of review for reasonableness or arbitrariness and the limitations entailed by it. But the opinion cautions against the repetition of past error in another way as well, more by its example than by any particular statement of constitutional method: it reminds us that the process of substantive review by reasoned judgment, is one of close criticism going to the details of the opposing interests and to their relationships with the historically recognized principles that lend them weight or value.

Although the *Poe* dissent disclaims the possibility of any general formula for due process analysis (beyond the basic analytic structure just described), Justice Harlan of course assumed that adjudication under the Due Process Clauses is like any other instance of judgment dependent on common-law method, being more or less persuasive according to the usual canons of critical discourse. When identifying and assessing the competing interests of liberty and authority, for example, the breadth of expression that a litigant or a judge selects in stating the competing principles will have much to do with the outcome and may be dispositive. As in any process of rational argumentation, we recognize that when a generally accepted principle is challenged, the broader the attack the less likely it is to succeed. The principle's defenders will, indeed, often try to characterize any challenge as just such a broadside, perhaps by couching the defense as if a broadside attack had occurred. So the Court in *Dred Scott* treated prohibition of slavery in the Territories as nothing less than a general assault on the concept of property. . . .

So, in *Poe,* Justice Harlan viewed it as essential to the plaintiffs' claimed right to use contraceptives that they sought to do so within the privacy of the marital bedroom. This detail in fact served two crucial and complementary functions, and provides a lesson for today. It rescued the individuals' claim from a breadth that would have threatened all state regulation of contraception or intimate relations; extramarital intimacy, no matter how privately practiced, was outside the scope of the right Justice Harlan would have recognized in that case. It was, moreover, this same restriction that allowed the interest to be valued as an aspect of a broader liberty to be free from all unreasonable intrusions into the privacy of the home and the family life within it, a liberty exemplified in constitutional provisions such as the Third and Fourth Amendments, in prior decisions of the Court involving unreasonable intrusions into the home and family life, and in the then-prevailing status of marriage as the sole lawful locus of intimate relations. The individuals' interest was therefore at its peak in *Poe,* because it was supported by a principle that distinguished of its own force between areas in which government traditionally had regulated (sexual relations outside of marriage) and those in which it had not (private marital intimacies), and thus was broad enough to cover the claim at hand without being so broad as to be shot-through by exceptions.

On the other side of the balance, the State's interest in *Poe* was not fairly characterized simply as preserving sexual morality, or doing so by regulating contraceptive devices. Just as some of the earlier cases went astray by speaking without nuance of individual interests in property or autonomy to contract for labor, so the State's asserted interest in *Poe* was not immune to distinctions turning (at least potentially) on the precise purpose being pursued and the collateral consequences of the means chosen. It was assumed that the State might legitimately enforce limits on the use of contraceptives through laws regulating divorce and annulment, or even through its tax policy, ibid., but not necessarily be justified in criminalizing the same practice in the marital bedroom, which would entail the consequence of authorizing state enquiry into the intimate relations of a married couple who chose to close their door.

The same insistence on exactitude lies behind questions, in current terminology, about the proper level of generality at which to analyze claims and counter-claims, and the demand for fitness and proper tailoring of a restrictive statute is just another way of testing the legitimacy of the generality at which the government sets up its justification. We may therefore classify Justice Harlan's example of proper analysis in any of these ways: as applying concepts of normal critical reasoning, as pointing to the need to attend to the levels of generality at which countervailing interests are stated, or as examining the concrete application of principles for fitness with their own ostensible justifications.

But whatever the categories in which we place the dissent's example, it stands in marked contrast to earlier cases whose reasoning was marked by comparatively less discrimination, and it points to the importance of evaluating the claims of the parties now before us with comparable detail. For here we are faced with an individual claim not to a right on the part of just anyone to help anyone else commit suicide under any circumstances, but to the right of a narrow class to help others also in a narrow class under a set of limited circumstances. And the claimants are met with the State's assertion, among others, that rights of such narrow scope cannot be recognized without jeopardy to individuals whom the State may concededly protect through its regulations.

Respondents claim that a patient facing imminent death, who anticipates physical suffering and indignity, and is capable of responsible and voluntary choice, should have a right to a physician's assistance in providing counsel and drugs to be administered by the patient to end life promptly. They accordingly claim that a physician must have the corresponding right to provide such aid, contrary to the provisions of Wash. Rev. Code § 9A.36.060 (1994). I do not understand the argument to rest on any assumption that rights either to suicide or to assistance in committing it are historically based as such. Respondents, rather, acknowledge the prohibition of each historically, but rely on the fact that to a substantial extent the State has repudiated that history. The result of this, respondents say, is to open the door to claims of such a patient to be accorded one of the options open to those with different, traditionally cognizable claims to autonomy in deciding how their bodies and minds should be treated. They seek the option to obtain the services of a physician to give them the benefit of advice and medical help, which is said to enjoy a tradition so strong and so devoid of specifically countervailing state concern that denial of a physician's help in these circumstances is arbitrary when physicians are generally free to advise and aid those who exercise other rights to bodily autonomy. . . .

This liberty interest in bodily integrity was phrased in a general way by then-Judge Cardozo when he said, "every human being of adult years and sound mind has a right to determine what shall be done with his own body" in relation to his medical needs. The familiar examples of this right derive from the common law of battery and include the right to be free from medical invasions into the body, as well as a right generally to resist enforced medication. Thus "it is settled now . . . that the Constitution places limits on a State's right to interfere with a person's most basic decisions about . . . bodily integrity." Constitutional recognition of the right to bodily integrity underlies the assumed right, good against the State, to require physicians to terminate artificial life support.

It is, indeed, in the abortion cases that the most telling recognitions of the importance of bodily integrity and the concomitant tradition of medical assistance have occurred. In *Roe v. Wade,* the plaintiff contended that the Texas statute making it criminal for any person to "procure an abortion," for a pregnant woman was unconstitutional insofar as it prevented her from "terminating her pregnancy by an abortion 'performed by a competent, licensed physician, under safe, clinical conditions,'" and in striking down the statute we stressed the importance of the relationship between patient and physician.

The analogies between the abortion cases and this one are several. Even though the State has a legitimate interest in discouraging abortion, the Court recognized a woman's right to a physician's counsel and care. Like the decision to commit suicide, the decision to abort potential life can be made irresponsibly and under the influence of others, and yet the Court has held in the abortion cases that physicians are fit assistants. Without physician assistance in abortion, the woman's right would have too often amounted to nothing more than a right to self-mutilation, and without a physician to assist in the suicide of the dying, the patient's right will often be confined to crude methods of causing death, most shocking and painful to the decedent's survivors.

There is, finally, one more reason for claiming that a physician's assistance here would fall within the accepted tradition of medical care in our society, and the abortion cases are only the most obvious illustration of the further point. While the Court has held that the performance of abortion procedures can be restricted to physicians, the Court's opinion in *Roe* recognized the doctors' role in yet another way. For, in the course of holding that the decision to perform an abortion called for a physician's assistance, the Court recognized that the good physician is not just a mechanic of the human body whose services have no bearing on a person's moral choices, but one who does more than treat symptoms, one who ministers to the patient. This idea of the physician as serving the whole person is a source of the high value traditionally placed on the medical relationship. Its value is surely as apparent here as in the abortion cases, for just as the decision about abortion is not directed to correcting some pathology, so the decision in which a dying patient seeks help is not so limited. . . .

The argument supporting respondents' position thus progresses through three steps of increasing forcefulness. First, it emphasizes the decriminalization of suicide. Reliance on this fact is sanctioned under the standard that looks not only to the tradition retained, but to society's occasional choices to reject traditions of the legal past. While the common law prohibited both suicide and aiding a suicide, with the prohibition on aiding largely justified by the primary prohibition on self-inflicted death itself, State's rejection of the traditional treatment of the one leaves the criminality of the other open to questioning that previously would not have been appropriate. The second step in the argument is to emphasize that the State's own act of decriminalization gives a freedom of choice much like the individual's option in recognized instances of bodily autonomy. One of these, abortion, is a legal right to choose in spite of the interest a State may legitimately invoke in discouraging the practice, just as suicide is now subject to choice, despite a state interest in discouraging it. The third step is to emphasize that respondents claim a right to assistance not on the basis of some broad principle that would be subject to exceptions if that continuing interest of the State's in discouraging suicide were to be recognized at all. Respondents base their claim on the traditional right to medical care and counsel, subject to the limiting conditions of informed, responsible choice when death is imminent, conditions that support a strong analogy to rights of care in other situations in which medical counsel and assistance have been available as a matter of course. There can be no stronger claim to a physician's assistance than at the time when death is imminent, a moral judgment implied by the State's own recognition of the legitimacy of medical procedures necessarily hastening the moment of impending death.

In my judgment, the importance of the individual interest here, as within that class of "certain interests" demanding careful scrutiny of the State's contrary claim, cannot be gainsaid. Whether that interest might in some circumstances, or at some time, be seen as "fundamental" to the degree entitled to prevail is not, however, a conclusion that I need draw here, for I am satisfied that the State's interests described in the following section are sufficiently serious to defeat the present claim that its law is arbitrary or purposeless.

The State has put forward several interests to justify the Washington law as applied to physicians treating terminally ill patients, even those competent to make responsible choices: protecting life generally, discouraging suicide even if knowing and voluntary, and protecting terminally ill patients from involuntary suicide and euthanasia, both voluntary and nonvoluntary.

It is not necessary to discuss the exact strengths of the first two claims of justification in the present circumstances, for the third is dispositive for me. That third justification is different from the first two, for it addresses specific features of respondents' claim, and it opposes that claim not with a moral judgment contrary to respondents', but with a recognized state interest in the protection of nonresponsible individuals and those who do not stand in relation either to death or to their physicians as do the patients whom respondents describe. The State claims interests in protecting patients from mistakenly and involuntarily deciding to end their lives, and in guarding against both voluntary and involuntary euthanasia. . . .

At least at this moment there are reasons for caution in predicting the effectiveness of the [measures] proposed. Respondents' proposals, as it turns out, sound much like the guidelines now in place in the Netherlands, the only place where experience with physician-assisted suicide and euthanasia has yielded empirical evidence about how such regulations might affect actual practice. Dutch physicians must engage in consultation before proceeding, and must decide whether the patient's decision is voluntary, well considered, and stable, whether the request to die is enduring and made more than once, and whether the patient's future will involve unacceptable suffering. There is, however, a substantial dispute today about what the Dutch experience shows. Some commentators marshall evidence that the Dutch guidelines have in practice failed to protect patients from involuntary euthanasia and have been violated with impunity. The day may come when we can say with some assurance which side is right, but for now it is the substantiality of the factual disagreement, and the alternatives for resolving it, that matter. They are, for me, dispositive of the due process claim at this time.

I take it that the basic concept of judicial review with its possible displacement of legislative judgment bars any finding that a legislature has acted arbitrarily when the following conditions are met: there is a serious factual controversy over the feasibility of recognizing the claimed right without at the same time making it impossible for the State to engage in an undoubtedly legitimate exercise of power; facts necessary to resolve the controversy are not readily ascertainable through the judicial process; but they are more readily subject to discovery through legislative factfinding and experimentation. It is assumed in this case, and must be, that a State's interest in protecting those unable to make responsible decisions and those who make no decisions at all entitles the State to bar aid to any but a knowing and responsible person intending suicide, and to prohibit euthanasia. How, and how far, a State should act in that interest are judgments for the State, but the legitimacy of its action to deny a physician the option to aid any but the knowing and responsible is beyond question. . . .

Legislatures have superior opportunities to obtain the facts necessary for a judgment about the present controversy. Not only do they have more flexible mechanisms for factfinding than the Judiciary, but their mechanisms include the power to experiment, moving forward and pulling back as facts emerge within their own jurisdictions. There is, indeed, good reason to suppose that in the absence of a judgment for respondents here, just such experimentation will be attempted in some of the States.

I do not decide here what the significance might be of legislative foot-dragging in ascertaining the facts going to the State's argument that the right in question could not be confined as claimed. Sometimes a court may be bound to act regardless of the institutional preferability of the political branches as forums for addressing constitutional claims. Now, it is enough to say that our examination of legislative reasonableness should consider the fact that the Legislature of the State of Washington is no more obviously at fault than this Court is in being uncertain about what would happen if respondents prevailed today. We therefore have a clear question about which institution, a legislature or a court, is relatively more competent to deal with an emerging issue as to which facts currently unknown could be dispositive. The answer has to be, for the reasons already stated, that the legislative process is to be preferred. . . . While I do not decide for all time that respondents' claim should not be recognized, I acknowledge the legislative institutional competence as the better one to deal with that claim at this time.

266

Articles of Impeachment Against William Jefferson Clinton (1998)

There seems little debate about what President Clinton did in his affair with White House intern Monica Lewinsky, but controversy continues to swirl over the role of the independent counsel Kenneth Starr, the broad-ranging inquiry that led from the original investigation into the Clintons' investments in an Arkansas land deal—and from which Starr had to conclude that no evidence existed that the president or his wife had done anything illegal—to the president's private peccadilloes, and the methods Starr used, which gave the appearance of a right-wing vendetta against Clinton.

Far more than the investigation into Watergate, the attack on Clinton bore all the hallmarks of a partisan *putsch*. The Republicans bet everything in the 1998 mid-term election that they could exploit the Lewinsky affair to increase their control over both houses of Congress. Instead, the American people essentially said they did not believe that Clinton's private life, no matter how distasteful, had any great bearing on public policy debate. When the Republicans actually lost seats in the election, they turned in fury on Clinton and a lame duck 105th House of Representatives impeached him on a near party-line vote. In the Senate, not only did the Republicans not have the two-thirds majority needed for conviction, but many Republican senators refused to go along with their colleagues in the House.

When it was over, the question of what constitutes an impeachable offense remained unanswered, but it seems clear that no one emerged from the ordeal untainted. The House Republicans had acted in partisan bad faith, and Clinton had lowered the moral tone of the presidency to a level not seen since Warren Harding.

See Emily F. Van Tassell and Paul Finkelman, *Impeachable Offenses: A Documentary History from 1787 to the Present* (1999); and Richard A. Posner, *An Affair of State: The Investigation, Impeachment, and Trial of President Clinton* (1999).

RESOLUTION IMPEACHING WILLIAM JEFFERSON CLINTON, PRESIDENT OF THE UNITED STATES, FOR HIGH CRIMES AND MISDEMEANORS

Resolved, That William Jefferson Clinton, President of the United States, is impeached for high crimes and misdemeanors, and that the following articles of impeachment by exhibited to the United States Senate:

Articles of impeachment exhibited by the House of Representatives of the United States of America in the name of itself and of the people of the United States of America, against William Jefferson Clinton, President of the United States of America, in maintenance and support of its impeachment against him for high crimes and misdemeanors.

Article I

In his conduct while President of the United States, William Jefferson Clinton, in violation of his constitutional oath faithfully to execute the office of President of the United States and, to the best of his ability, preserve, protect, and defend the Constitution of the United States, and in violation of his constitutional duty to take care that the laws be faithfully executed, has willfully corrupted and manipulated the judicial process of the United States for his personal gain and exoneration, impeding the administration of justice, in that:

On August 17, 1998, William Jefferson Clinton swore to tell the truth, the whole truth, and nothing but the truth before a Federal grand jury of the United States. Contrary to that oath, William Jefferson Clinton willfully provided perjurious, false and misleading testimony to the grand jury concerning one or more of the following: (1) the nature and details of his relationship with a subordinate Government employee, (2) prior perjurious, false and misleading testimony he gave in a Federal civil rights action brought against him; (3) prior false and misleading statements he allowed his attorney

Source: Impeachment of President William Jefferson Clinton, Senate Document 106–2, 106th Cong., 1st Sess. (Washington, 1999), 15–18.

to make to a Federal judge in that civil rights action; and (4) his corrupt efforts to influence the testimony of witnesses and to impede the discovery of evidence in that civil rights action.

In doing this, William Jefferson Clinton has undermined the integrity of his office, has brought disrepute on the Presidency, has betrayed his trust as President, and has acted in a manner subversive of the rule of law and justice, to the manifest injury of the people of the United States.

Wherefore, William Jefferson Clinton, by such conduct, warrants impeachment and trial, and removal from office and disqualification to hold and enjoy any office of honor, trust, or profit under the United States.

Article II

In his conduct while President of the United States, William Jefferson Clinton, in violation of his constitutional oath faithfully to execute the office of President of the United States and, to the best of his ability, preserve, protect, and defend the Constitution of the United States, and in violation of his constitutional duty to take care that the laws be faithfully executed, has prevented, obstructed, and impeded the administration of justice, and has to that end engaged personally, and through his subordinates and agents, in a course of conduct or scheme designed to delay, impede, cover up, and conceal the existence of evidence and testimony related to a Federal civil rights action brought against him in a duly instituted judicial proceeding.

The means used to implement this course of conduct or scheme included one or more of the following acts:

(1) On or about December 17, 1997, William Jefferson Clinton corruptly encouraged a witness in a Federal civil rights action brought against him to execute a sworn affidavit in that proceeding that he knew to be perjurious, false and misleading.

(2) On or about December 17, 1997, William Jefferson Clinton corruptly encouraged a witness in a Federal civil rights action brought against him to give perjurious, false and misleading testimony if and when called to testify personally in that proceeding.

(3) On or about December 28, 1997, William Jefferson Clinton corruptly engaged in, encouraged, or supported a scheme to conceal evidence that had been subpoenaed in a Federal civil rights action brought against him.

(4) Beginning on or about December 7, 1997, and continuing through and including January 14, 1998, William Jefferson Clinton intensified and succeeded in an effort to secure job assistance to a witness in a Federal civil rights action brought against him in order to corruptly prevent the truthful testimony of that witness in that proceeding at a time when the truthful testimony of that witness would have been harmful to him.

(5) On January 17, 1998, at his deposition in a Federal civil rights action brought against him, William Jefferson Clinton corruptly allowed his attorney to make false and misleading statements to a Federal judge characterizing an affidavit, in order to prevent questioning deemed relevant by the judge. Such false and misleading statements were subsequently acknowledged by his attorney in a communication to that judge.

(6) On or about January 18 and January 20–21, 1998, William Jefferson Clinton related a false and misleading account of events relevant to a Federal civil rights action brought against him to a potential witness in that proceeding, in order to corruptly influence the testimony of that witness.

(7) On or about January 21, 23, and 26, 1998, William Jefferson Clinton made false and misleading statements to potential witnesses in a Federal grand jury proceeding in order to corruptly influence the testimony of those witnesses. The false and misleading statements made by William Jefferson Clinton were repeated by the witnesses to the grand jury, causing the grand jury to receive false and misleading information.

In all of this, William Jefferson Clinton has undermined the integrity of his office, has brought disrepute on the Presidency, has betrayed his trust as President, and has acted in a manner subversive of the rule of law and justice, to the manifest injury of the people of the United States.

Wherefore, William Jefferson Clinton, by such conduct, warrants impeachment and trial, and removal from office and disqualification to hold and enjoy any office of honor, trust, or profit under the United States.

Passed the House of Representatives December 19, 1998.

Newt Gingrich, speaker of the House of Representatives.
Attest: Robin H. Carle, Clerk.

---

267   *Vermont Act Relating to Civil Unions (2000)*

The drive for gay and lesbian rights picked up enormous momentum in the 1990s, and activists began to demand that some form of same-sex marriage be recognized by the state, an idea that appalled social and religious conservatives. Gays and lesbians argued that their unions were as stable and loving as those of heterosexual couples, but they were denied important benefits under existing law. For example, if one partner worked, he or she could not carry the other on health insurance or take sick leave to take care of the partner.

In Vermont, the state Supreme Court ruled that the state's existing marriage law discriminated against homosexual couples, and gave the legislature one of two options—either allow for gay marriage, or provide an alternative that gave gay couples the same economic and legal benefits as those of heterosexual unions.

Vermont legislators chose the latter option, and while protesting that they were not establishing gay marriage, the bill providing for civil unions looks a great deal like the law defining marriage.

Sec. 1. LEGISLATIVE FINDINGS

The General Assembly finds that:

(1) Civil marriage under Vermont's marriage statutes consists of a union between a man and a woman. This interpretation of the state's marriage laws was upheld by the Supreme Court in *Baker v. State.*

(2) Vermont's history as an independent republic and as a state is one of equal treatment and respect for all Vermonters. This tradition is embodied in the Common Benefits Clause of the Vermont Constitution, Chapter I, Article 7th.

(3) The state's interest in civil marriage is to encourage close and caring families, and to protect all family members from the economic and social consequences of abandonment and divorce, focusing on those who have been especially at risk.

(4) Legal recognition of civil marriage by the state is the primary and, in a number of instances, the exclusive source of numerous benefits, responsibilities and protections under the laws of the state for married persons and their children.

(5) Based on the state's tradition of equality under the law and strong families, for at least 25 years, Vermont Probate Courts have qualified gay and lesbian individuals as adoptive parents.

(6) Vermont was one of the first states to adopt comprehensive legislation prohibiting discrimination on the basis of sexual orientation (Act No. 135 of 1992).

(7) The state has a strong interest in promoting stable and lasting families, including families based upon a same-sex couple.

(8) Without the legal protections, benefits and responsibilities associated with civil marriage, same-sex couples suffer numerous obstacles and hardships.

(9) Despite longstanding social and economic discrimination, many gay and lesbian Vermonters have formed lasting, committed, caring and faithful relationships with persons of their same sex. These couples live together, participate in their communities together, and some raise children and care for family members together, just as do couples who are married under Vermont law.

(10) While a system of civil unions does not bestow the status of civil marriage, it does satisfy the requirements of the Common Benefits Clause. Changes in the way significant legal relationships are established under the constitution should be approached carefully, combining respect for the community and cultural institutions most affected with a commitment to the constitutional rights involved. Granting benefits and protections to same-sex couples through a system of civil unions will provide due respect for tradition and long-standing social institutions, and will permit adjustment as unanticipated consequences or unmet needs arise.

(11) The constitutional principle of equality embodied in the Common Benefits Clause is compatible with the freedom of religious belief and worship guaranteed in Chapter I, Article 3rd of the state constitution. Extending the benefits and protections of marriage to same-sex couples through a system of civil unions preserves the fundamental constitutional right of each of the multitude of religious faiths in Vermont to choose freely and without state interference to whom to grant the religious status, sacrament or blessing of marriage under the rules, practices or traditions of such faith.

Source: Vermont Statutes Annotated, Title 15, Ch. 23 §§ 1201–1207 (2000)

Sec. 2. PURPOSE

(a) The purpose of this act is to respond to the constitutional violation found by the Vermont Supreme Court in *Baker v. State,* and to provide eligible same-sex couples the opportunity to "obtain the same benefits and protections afforded by Vermont law to married opposite-sex couples" as required by Chapter I, Article 7th of the Vermont Constitution.

(b) This act also provides eligible blood-relatives and relatives related by adoption the opportunity to establish a reciprocal beneficiaries relationship so they may receive certain benefits and protections and be subject to certain responsibilities that are granted to spouses.

Sec. 3.–15 V.S.A. chapter 23 is added to read:

Chapter 23.   Civil Unions

§ 1201.   Definitions

As used in this chapter:

(1) "Certificate of civil union" means a document that certifies that the persons named on the certificate have established a civil union in this state in compliance with this chapter and 18 V.S.A. chapter 106.

(2) "Civil union" means that two eligible persons have established a relationship pursuant to this chapter, and may receive the benefits and protections and be subject to the responsibilities of spouses.

(3) "Commissioner" means the commissioner of health.

(4) "Marriage" means the legally recognized union of one man and one woman.

(5) "Party to a civil union" means a person who has established a civil union pursuant to this chapter and 18 V.S.A. chapter 106.

§ 1202.   Requisites of a Valid Civil Union

For a civil union to be established in Vermont, it shall be necessary that the parties to a civil union satisfy all of the following criteria:

(1) Not be a party to another civil union or a marriage.

(2) Be of the same sex and therefore excluded from the marriage laws of this state.

(3) Meet the criteria and obligations set forth in 18 V.S.A. chapter 106.

§ 1204.   Benefits, Protections and Responsibilities of Parties to a Civil Union

(a) Parties to a civil union shall have all the same benefits, protections and responsibilities under law, whether they derive from statute, administrative or court rule, policy, common law or any other source of civil law, as are granted to spouses in a marriage.

(b) A party to a civil union shall be included in any definition or use of the terms "spouse," "family," "immediate family," "dependent," "next of kin," and other terms that denote the spousal relationship, as those terms are used throughout the law.

(c) Parties to a civil union shall be responsible for the support of one another to the same degree and in the same manner as prescribed under law for married persons.

(d) The law of domestic relations, including annulment, separation and divorce, child custody and support, and property division and maintenance shall apply to parties to a civil union.

(e) The following is a nonexclusive list of legal benefits, protections and responsibilities of spouses, which shall apply in like manner to parties to a civil union:

(1) laws relating to title, tenure, descent and distribution, intestate succession, waiver of will, survivorship, or other incidents of the acquisition, ownership, or transfer, inter vivos or at death, of real or personal property, including eligibility to hold real and personal property as tenants by the entirety (parties to a civil union meet the common law unity of person qualification for purposes of a tenancy by the entirety);

(2) causes of action related to or dependent upon spousal status, including an action for wrongful death, emotional distress, loss of consortium, dramshop, or other torts or actions under contracts reciting, related to, or dependent upon spousal status;

(3) probate law and procedure, including nonprobate transfer;

(4) adoption law and procedure;

(5) group insurance for state employees under 3 V.S.A. § 631, and continuing care contracts under 8 V.S.A. § 8005;

(6) spouse abuse programs under 3 V.S.A. § 18;

(7) prohibitions against discrimination based upon marital status;

(8) victim's compensation rights under 13 V.S.A. § 5351;

(9) workers' compensation benefits;

(10) laws relating to emergency and nonemergency medical care and treatment, hospital visitation and notification, including the Patient's Bill of Rights under 18 V.S.A. chapter 42 and the Nursing Home Residents' Bill of Rights under 33 V.S.A. chapter 73;

(11) terminal care documents under 18 V.S.A. chapter 111, and durable power of attorney for health care execution and revocation under 14 V.S.A. chapter 121;

(12) family leave benefits under 21 V.S.A. chapter 5, subchapter 4A;

(13) public assistance benefits under state law;

(14) laws relating to taxes imposed by the state or a municipality other than estate taxes;

(15) laws relating to immunity from compelled testimony and the marital communication privilege;

(16) the homestead rights of a surviving spouse under 27 V.S.A. § 105 and homestead property tax allowance under 32 V.S.A. § 6062;

(17) laws relating to loans to veterans under 8 V.S.A. § 1849;

(18) the definition of family farmer under 10 V.S.A. § 272;

(19) laws relating to the making, revoking and objecting to anatomical gifts by others under 18 V.S.A. § 5240;

(20) state pay for military service under 20 V.S.A. § 1544;

(21) application for absentee ballot under 17 V.S.A. § 2532;

(22) family landowner rights to fish and hunt under 10 V.S.A. § 4253;

(23) legal requirements for assignment of wages under 8 V.S.A. § 2235; and

(24) affirmance of relationship under 15 V.S.A. § 7.

(f) The rights of parties to a civil union, with respect to a child of whom either becomes the natural parent during the term of the civil union, shall be the same as those of a married couple, with respect to a child of whom either spouse becomes the natural parent during the marriage.

§ 1205. *Modification of Civil Union Terms*

Parties to a civil union may modify the terms, conditions, or effects of their civil union in the same manner and to the same extent as married persons who execute an antenuptial agreement or other agreement recognized and enforceable under the law, setting forth particular understandings with respect to their union.

§ 1206. *Dissolution of Civil Unions*

The family court shall have jurisdiction over all proceedings relating to the dissolution of civil unions. The dissolution of civil unions shall follow the same procedures and be subject to the same substantive rights and obligations that are involved in the dissolution of marriage in accordance with chapter 11 of this title, including any residency requirements.

§ 1207. *Commissioner of Health; Duties*

(a) The commissioner shall provide civil union license and certificate forms to all town and county clerks.

(b) The commissioner shall keep a record of all civil unions.

§ 5160. *Issuance of Civil Union License; Certification; Return of Civil Union Certificate*

(a) Upon application in a form prescribed by the department, a town clerk shall issue a civil union license in the form prescribed by the department, and shall enter thereon the names of the parties to the proposed civil union, fill out the form as far as practicable and retain a copy in the clerk's office. At least one party to the proposed civil union shall sign the application attesting to the accuracy of the facts stated. The license shall be issued by the clerk of the town where either party resides or, if neither is a resident of the state, by any town clerk in the state.

(b) A civil union license shall be delivered by one of the parties to a proposed civil union, within 60 days from the date of issue, to a person authorized to certify civil unions by section 5164 of this title. If the proposed civil union is not certified within 60 days from the date of issue, the license shall become void. After a person has certified the civil union, he or she shall fill out that part of the form on the license provided for such use, sign and certify the civil union. Thereafter, the document shall be known as a civil union certificate.

(c) Within ten days of the certification, the person performing the certification shall return the civil union certificate to the office of the town clerk from which the license was issued. The town clerk shall retain and file the original according to sections 5007 and 5008 of this title.

(d) A town clerk who knowingly issues a civil union license upon application of a person residing in another town in the state, or a county clerk who knowingly issues a civil union license upon application of a person other than as provided in section 5005 of this title, or a clerk who issues such a license without first requiring the applicant to fill out, sign and make oath to the declaration contained therein as provided in section 5160 of this title, shall be fined not more than $50.00 nor less than $20.00.

(e) A person making application to a clerk for a civil union license who makes a material misrepresentation in the declaration of intention shall be deemed guilty of perjury.

(f) A town clerk shall provide a person who applies for a civil union license with information prepared by the secretary of state that advises such person of the benefits, protections and responsibilities of a civil union and that Vermont residency may be required for dissolution of a civil union in Vermont.

§ 5161.   Issuance of License

(a) A town clerk shall issue a civil union license to all applicants who have complied with the provisions of section 5160 of this title, and who are otherwise qualified under the laws of the state to apply for a civil union license.

268

Bush v. Gore (2000)

The presidential election of 2000 proved one of the closest in American history. Although the Democratic candidate, Albert Gore of Tennessee, had several hundred thousand more popular votes than his Republican opponent, George W. Bush of Texas, in the electoral college neither man had a majority without Florida. In that state Bush had a very narrow lead of a few hundred votes, while tens of thousands of ballots had been declared void because of voter failure to push the punch instruments completely through the ballots. The law suits began almost immediately, with Gore succeeding in winning judicial approval of a recount in state courts, and Bush initially being rebuffed in federal courts. But then in a surprise move, the Supreme Court accepted Bush's petition seeking to block a recount. Although seven of the nine justices believed that the voting procedures violated the Equal Protection Clause, there was widespread criticism of the Court that it had overstepped its bounds in entering the partisan political arena. Although the Court tried to indicate that its opinion had a narrow holding, it appeared inevitable that that its ruling would directly affect the way elections are carried out in nearly every state.

See the *Washington Post* political staff, *Deadlock* (2001).

Per Curiam

The petition presents the following questions: whether the Florida Supreme Court established new standards for resolving Presidential election contests, thereby violating Art. II, § 1, cl. 2, of the United States Constitution . . . and whether the use of standardless manual recounts violates the Equal Protection and Due Process Clauses. With respect to the equal protection question, we find a violation of the Equal Protection Clause.

The closeness of this election, and the multitude of legal challenges which have followed in its wake, have brought into sharp focus a common, if heretofore unnoticed, phenomenon. Nationwide statistics reveal that an estimated 2% of ballots cast do not register a vote for President for whatever reason, including deliberately choosing no candidate at all or some voter error, such as voting for two candidates or insufficiently marking a ballot. In certifying election results, the votes eligible for inclusion in the certification are the votes meeting the properly established legal requirements.

This case has shown that punch card balloting machines can produce an unfortunate number of ballots which are not punched in a clean, complete way by the voter. After the current counting, it is likely legislative bodies nationwide will examine ways to improve the mechanisms and machinery for voting. . . .

The right to vote is protected in more than the initial allocation of the franchise. Equal protection applies as well to the manner of its exercise. Having once granted the right to vote on equal terms, the State may not, by later arbitrary and disparate treatment, value one person's vote over that of another. It must be remembered that "the right of suffrage can be denied by a debasement or dilution of the weight of a citizen's vote just as effectively as by wholly prohibiting the free exercise of the franchise." *Reynolds v. Sims* (1964).

There is no difference between the two sides of the present controversy on these basic propositions. Respondents say that the very purpose of vindicating the right to vote justifies the recount procedures now at issue. The question before us, however, is whether the recount procedures the Florida Supreme Court has adopted are consistent with its obligation to avoid arbitrary and disparate treatment of the members of its electorate. . . .

Much of the controversy seems to revolve around ballot cards designed to be perforated by a stylus but which, either through error or deliberate omission, have not been perforated with sufficient precision for a machine to count them. In some cases a piece of the card—a chad—is hanging, say by two corners. In other cases there is no separation at all, just an indentation.

Source: 121 S.Ct. 525 (2000)

The Florida Supreme Court has ordered that the intent of the voter be discerned from such ballots. For purposes of resolving the equal protection challenge, it is not necessary to decide whether the Florida Supreme Court had the authority under the legislative scheme for resolving election disputes to define what a legal vote is and to mandate a manual recount implementing that definition. The recount mechanisms implemented in response to the decisions of the Florida Supreme Court do not satisfy the minimum requirement for non-arbitrary treatment of voters necessary to secure the fundamental right. Florida's basic command for the count of legally cast votes is to consider the "intent of the voter." This is unobjectionable as an abstract proposition and a starting principle. The problem inheres in the absence of specific standards to ensure its equal application. The formulation of uniform rules to determine intent based on these recurring circumstances is practicable and, we conclude, necessary. . . .

The want of those rules here has led to unequal evaluation of ballots in various respects. As seems to have been acknowledged at oral argument, the standards for accepting or rejecting contested ballots might vary not only from county to county but indeed within a single county from one recount team to another. . . .

An early case in our one person, one vote jurisprudence arose when a State accorded arbitrary and disparate treatment to voters in its different counties. *Gray v. Sanders* (1963). The Court found a constitutional violation. We relied on these principles in the context of the Presidential selection process in *Moore v. Ogilvie* (1969), where we invalidated a county-based procedure that diluted the influence of citizens in larger counties in the nominating process. There we observed that "the idea that one group can be granted greater voting strength than another is hostile to the one man, one vote basis of our representative government." . . .

The State Supreme Court ratified this uneven treatment. It mandated that the recount totals from two counties, Miami-Dade and Palm Beach, be included in the certified total. The court also appeared to hold *sub silentio* that the recount totals from Broward County, which were not completed until after the original November 14 certification by the Secretary of State, were to be considered part of the new certified vote totals even though the county certification was not contested by Vice President Gore. Yet each of the counties used varying standards to determine what was a legal vote. Broward County used a more forgiving standard than Palm Beach County, and uncovered almost three times as many new votes, a result markedly disproportionate to the difference in population between the counties.

In addition, the recounts in . . . [Miami-Dade, Palm Beach and Broward Counties] were not limited to so-called undervotes but extended to all of the ballots. The distinction has real consequences. A manual recount of all ballots identifies not only those ballots which show no vote but also those which contain more than one, the so-called overvotes. Neither category will be counted by the machine. This is not a trivial concern. At oral argument, respondents estimated there are as many as 110,000 overvotes statewide. As a result, the citizen whose ballot was not read by a machine because he failed to vote for a candidate in a way readable by a machine may still have his vote counted in a manual recount; on the other hand, the citizen who marks two candidates in a way discernable by the machine will not have the same opportunity to have his vote count, even if a manual examination of the ballot would reveal the requisite indicia of intent. Furthermore, the citizen who marks two candidates, only one of which is discernable by the machine, will have his vote counted even though it should have been read as an invalid ballot. The State Supreme Court's inclusion of vote counts based on these variant standards exemplifies concerns with the remedial processes that were under way.

That brings the analysis to yet a further equal protection problem. The votes certified by the court included a partial total from one county, Miami-Dade. The Florida Supreme Court's decision thus gives no assurance that the recounts included in a final certification must be complete. Indeed, it is respondent's submission that it would be consistent with the rules of the recount procedures to include whatever partial counts are done by the time of final certification, and we interpret the Florida Supreme Court's decision to permit this. This accommodation no doubt results from the truncated contest period established by the Florida Supreme Court. The press of time does not diminish the constitutional concern. A desire for speed is not a general excuse for ignoring equal protection guarantees.

In addition to these difficulties the actual process by which the votes were to be counted under the Florida Supreme Court's decision raises further concerns. That order did not specify who would recount the ballots. The county canvassing boards were forced to pull together *ad hoc* teams comprised of judges from various Circuits who had no previous training in handling and interpreting ballots. Furthermore, while others were permitted to observe, they were prohibited from objecting during the recount. . . .

The question before the Court is not whether local entities, in the exercise of their expertise, may develop different systems for implementing elections. Instead, we are presented with a situation where a state court with the power to assure uniformity has ordered a statewide recount with minimal procedural safeguards. When a court orders a statewide remedy, there must be at least some assurance that the rudimentary requirements of equal treatment and fundamental fairness are satisfied.

Given the Court's assessment that the recount process underway was probably being conducted in an unconstitutional manner, the Court stayed the order directing the recount so it could hear this case and render an expedited decision. The contest provision, as it was mandated by the State Supreme Court, is not well calculated to sustain the confidence that all citizens must have in the outcome of elections. The State has not shown that its procedures include the necessary safeguards. The problem, for instance, of the estimated 110,000 overvotes has not been addressed, although Chief Justice Wells called attention to the concern in his dissenting opinion.

Upon due consideration of the difficulties identified to this point, it is obvious that the recount cannot be conducted in compliance with the requirements of equal protection and due process without substantial additional work. It would require not only the adoption (after opportunity for argument) of adequate statewide standards for determining what is a legal vote, and practicable procedures to implement them, but also orderly judicial review of any disputed matters that might arise. In addition, the Secretary of State has advised that the recount of only a portion of the ballots requires that the vote tabulation equipment be used to screen out undervotes, a function for which the machines were not designed. If a recount of overvotes were also required, perhaps even a second screening would be necessary. Use of the equipment for this purpose, and any new software developed for it, would have to be evaluated for accuracy by the Secretary of State. . . .

Florida law . . . requires that any controversy or contest that is designed to lead to a conclusive selection of electors be completed by December 12. That date is upon us, and there is no recount procedure in place under the State Supreme Court's order that comports with minimal constitutional standards. Because it is evident that any recount seeking to meet the December 12 date will be unconstitutional for the reasons we have discussed, we reverse the judgment of the Supreme Court of Florida ordering a recount to proceed.

Seven Justices of the Court agree that there are constitutional problems with the recount ordered by the Florida Supreme Court that demand a remedy. (SOUTER, J., dissenting); (BREYER, J., dissenting). The only disagreement is as to the remedy. . . .

None are more conscious of the vital limits on judicial authority than are the members of this Court, and none stand more in admiration of the Constitution's design to leave the selection of the President to the people, through their legislatures, and to the political sphere. When contending parties invoke the process of the courts, however, it becomes our unsought responsibility to resolve the federal and constitutional issues the judicial system has been forced to confront.

The judgment of the Supreme Court of Florida is reversed, and the case is remanded for further proceedings not inconsistent with this opinion. . . .

It is so ordered.

CHIEF JUSTICE REHNQUIST, with whom JUSTICE SCALIA and JUSTICE THOMAS join, concurring:

In most cases, . . . respect for federalism compels us to defer to the decisions of state courts on issues of state law. That practice reflects our understanding that the decisions of state courts are definitive pronouncements of the will of the States as sovereigns. Of course, in ordinary cases, the distribution of powers among the branches of a State's government raises no questions of federal constitutional law, subject to the requirement that the government be republican in character. But there are a few exceptional cases in which the Constitution imposes a duty or confers a power on a particular branch of a State's government. This is one of them. Article II, § 1, cl. 2, provides that "each State shall appoint, in such Manner as the Legislature thereof may direct," electors for President and Vice President. Thus, the text of the election law itself, and not just its interpretation by the courts of the States, takes on independent significance. . . .

In Florida, the legislature has chosen to hold statewide elections to appoint the State's 25 electors. Importantly, the legislature has delegated the authority to run the elections and to oversee election disputes to the [Florida] Secretary of State. Isolated sections of the code may well admit of more than one interpretation, but the general coherence of the legislative scheme may not be altered by judicial interpretation so as to wholly change the statutorily provided apportionment of responsibility among these various bodies. In any election but a Presidential election, the Florida Supreme Court can give as little or as much deference to Florida's executives as it chooses, so far as Article II is concerned, and this Court will have no cause to question the court's actions. But, with respect to a Presidential election, the court must be both mindful of the legislature's role under Article II in choosing the manner of appointing electors and deferential to those bodies expressly empowered by the legislature to carry out its constitutional mandate.

JUSTICE STEVENS, with whom JUSTICE GINSBURG AND JUSTICE BREYER join, dissenting:

The Constitution assigns to the States the primary responsibility for determining the manner of selecting the Presidential electors. When questions arise about the meaning of state laws, including election laws, it is our settled practice to accept the opinions of the highest courts of the States as providing the final answers. On rare occasions, however, either federal statutes or the Federal Constitution may require federal judicial intervention in state elections. This is not such an occasion.

The federal questions that ultimately emerged in this case are not substantial. Article II provides that "each State shall appoint, in such Manner as the Legislature thereof may direct, a Number of Electors." It does not create state legislatures out of whole cloth, but rather takes them as they come—as creatures born of, and constrained by, their state constitutions. Lest there be any doubt, we stated over 100 years ago in *McPherson v. Blacker* (1892), that "what is forbidden or required to be done by a State" in the Article II context "is forbidden or required of the legislative power under state constitutions as they exist." In the same vein, we also observed that "the State's legislative power is the supreme authority except as limited by the constitution of the State." The legislative power in Florida is subject to judicial review pursuant to Article V of the Florida Constitution, and nothing in Article II of the Federal Constitution frees the state legislature from the constraints in the state constitution that created it. Moreover, the Florida Legislature's own decision to employ a unitary code for all elections indicates that it intended the Florida Supreme Court to play the same role in Presidential elections that it has historically played in resolving electoral disputes. The Florida Supreme Court's exercise of appellate jurisdiction therefore was wholly consistent with, and indeed contemplated by, the grant of authority in Article II.

It hardly needs stating that Congress, pursuant to 3 U.S.C. § 5, did not impose any affirmative duties upon the States that their governmental branches could "violate." Rather, § 5 provides a safe harbor for States to select electors in contested elections "by judicial or other methods" established by laws prior to the election day. Section 5, like Article II, assumes the involvement of the state judiciary in interpreting state election laws and resolving election disputes under those laws. Neither § 5 nor Article II grants federal judges any special authority to substitute their views for those of the state judiciary on matters of state law. . . .

Admittedly, the use of differing substandards for determining voter intent in different counties employing similar voting systems may raise serious concerns. Those concerns are alleviated—if not eliminated—by the fact that a single impartial magistrate will ultimately adjudicate all objections arising from the recount process. Of course, as a general matter, "the interpretation of constitutional principles must not be too literal. We must remember that the machinery of government would not work if it were not allowed a little play in its joints." If it were otherwise, Florida's decision to leave to each county the determination of what balloting system to employ—despite enormous differences in accuracy—might run afoul of equal protection. So, too, might the similar decisions of the vast majority of state legislatures to delegate to local authorities certain decisions with respect to voting systems and ballot design. . . .

What must underlie petitioners' entire federal assault on the Florida election procedures is an unstated lack of confidence in the impartiality and capacity of the state judges who would make the critical decisions if the vote count were to proceed. Otherwise, their position is wholly without merit. The endorsement of that position by the majority of this Court can only lend credence to the most cynical appraisal of the work of judges throughout the land. It is confidence in the men and women who administer the judicial system that is the true backbone of the rule of law. Time will one day heal the wound to that confidence that will be inflicted by today's decision. One thing, however, is certain. Although we may never know with complete certainty the identity of the winner of this year's Presidential election, the identity of the loser is perfectly clear. It is the Nation's confidence in the judge as an impartial guardian of the rule of law.

I respectfully dissent.

JUSTICE SOUTER, with whom JUSTICE BREYER joins and with whom JUSTICE STEVENS and JUSTICE GINSBURG join with regard to all but Part C, dissenting:

The Court should not have reviewed either *Bush v. Palm Beach County Canvassing Bd.* or this case, and should not have stopped Florida's attempt to recount all undervote ballots, by issuing a stay of the Florida Supreme Court's orders during the period of this review. If this Court had allowed the State to follow the course indicated by the opinions of its own Supreme Court, it is entirely possible that there would ultimately have been no issue requiring our review, and political tension could have worked itself out in the Congress following the procedure provided in 3 U. S. C. § 15. The case being before us, however, its resolution by the majority is another erroneous decision. . . .

C

In deciding what to do about this, we should take account of the fact that electoral votes are due to be cast in six days. I would therefore remand the case to the courts of Florida with instructions to establish uniform standards for evaluating the several types of ballots that have prompted differing treatments, to be applied within and among counties when passing on such identical ballots in any further recounting (or successive recounting) that the courts might order.

Unlike the majority, I see no warrant for this Court to assume that Florida could not possibly comply with this requirement before the date set for the meeting of electors, December 18. Although one of the dissenting justices of the State Supreme Court estimated that disparate standards potentially affected 170,000 votes, the number at issue is significantly smaller. The 170,000 figure apparently represents all uncounted votes, both undervotes (those for which no Presidential choice was recorded by a machine) and overvotes (those rejected because of votes for more than one candidate. But as JUSTICE BREYER has pointed out, no showing has been made of legal overvotes uncounted, and counsel for Gore made an uncontradicted representation to the Court that the statewide total of undervotes is about 60,000. To recount these manually would be a tall order, but before this Court stayed the effort to do that the courts of Florida were ready to do their best to get that job done. There is no justification for denying the State the opportunity to try to count all disputed ballots now.

I respectfully dissent.

JUSTICE BREYER, with whom JUSTICE STEVENS and JUSTICE GINSBURG join except as to Part I-A-1, and with whom JUSTICE SOUTER joins as to Part I, dissenting:

The Court was wrong to take this case. It was wrong to grant a stay. It should now vacate that stay and permit the Florida Supreme Court to decide whether the recount should resume.

I

The political implications of this case for the country are momentous. But the federal legal questions presented, with one exception, are insubstantial.

A

I

The majority raises three Equal Protection problems with the Florida Supreme Court's recount order: first, the failure to include overvotes in the manual recount; second, the fact that all ballots, rather than simply the undervotes, were recounted in some, but not all, counties; and third, the absence of a uniform, specific standard to guide the recounts. As far as the first issue is concerned, petitioners presented no evidence, to this Court or to any Florida court, that a manual recount of overvotes would identify additional legal votes. The same is true of the second, and, in addition, the majority's reasoning would seem to invalidate any state provision for a manual recount of individual counties in a statewide election.

The majority's third concern does implicate principles of fundamental fairness. The majority concludes that the Equal Protection Clause requires that a manual recount be governed not only by the uniform general standard of the "clear intent of the voter," but also by uniform subsidiary standards (for example, a uniform determination whether indented, but not perforated, "undervotes" should count). The opinion points out that the Florida Supreme Court ordered the inclusion of Broward County's undercounted "legal votes" even though those votes included ballots that were not perforated but simply "dimpled," while newly recounted ballots from other counties will likely include only votes determined to be "legal" on the basis of a stricter standard. In light of our previous remand, the Florida Supreme Court may have been reluctant to adopt a more specific standard than that provided for by the legislature for fear of exceeding its authority under Article II. However, since the use of different standards could favor one or the other of the candidates, since time was, and is, too short to permit the lower courts to iron out significant differences through ordinary judicial review, and since the relevant distinction was embodied in the order of the State's highest court, I agree that, in these very special circumstances, basic principles of fairness may well have counseled the adoption of a uniform standard to address the problem. In light of the majority's disposition, I need not decide whether, or the extent to which, as a remedial matter, the Constitution would place limits upon the content of the uniform standard. . . .

Of course, the selection of the President is of fundamental national importance. But that importance is political, not legal. And this Court should resist the temptation unnecessarily to resolve tangential legal disputes, where doing so threatens to determine the outcome of the election.

The Constitution and federal statutes themselves make clear that restraint is appropriate. They set forth a road map of how to resolve disputes about electors, even after an election as close as this one. That road map foresees resolution of electoral disputes by state courts. But it nowhere provides for involvement by the United States Supreme Court.

To the contrary, the Twelfth Amendment commits to Congress the authority and responsibility to count electoral votes. A federal statute, the Electoral Count Act, enacted after the close 1876 Hayes-Tilden Presidential election, specifies that, after States have tried to resolve disputes (through "judicial" or other means), Congress is the body primarily authorized to resolve remaining disputes. . . .

The decision by both the Constitution's Framers and the 1886 Congress to minimize this Court's role in resolving close federal presidential elections is as wise as it is clear. However awkward or difficult it may be for Congress to resolve difficult electoral disputes, Congress, being a political body, expresses the people's will far more accurately than does an unelected Court. And the people's will is what elections are about. . . .

The Court is not acting to vindicate a fundamental constitutional principle, such as the need to protect a basic human liberty. No other strong reason to act is present. Congressional statutes tend to obviate the need. And, above all, in this highly politicized matter, the appearance of a split decision runs the risk of undermining the public's confidence in the Court itself. That confidence is a public treasure. It has been built slowly over many years, some of which were marked by a Civil War and the tragedy of segregation. It is a vitally necessary ingredient of any successful effort to protect basic liberty and, indeed, the rule of law itself. We run no risk of returning to the days when a President (responding to this Court's efforts to protect the Cherokee Indians) might have said, "John Marshall has made his decision; now let him enforce it!" But we do risk a self-inflicted wound—a wound that may harm not just the Court, but the Nation.

I fear that in order to bring this agonizingly long election process to a definitive conclusion, we have not adequately attended to that necessary "check upon our own exercise of power," "our own sense of self-restraint." Justice Brandeis once said of the Court, "The most important thing we do is not doing." What it does today, the Court should have left undone. I would repair the damage done as best we now can, by permitting the Florida recount to continue under uniform standards.

I respectfully dissent.

[A dissenting opinion by Justice GINSBERG, joined by Justice STEVENS in whole, and by Justices SOUTER and BREYER in part, is omitted.]

269

The Constitution of the
United States of America (1787)

We the People of the United States, in Order to form a more perfect Union, establish Justice, insure domestic Tranquility, provide for the common defence, promote the general Welfare, and secure the Blessings of Liberty to ourselves and our Posterity, do ordain and establish this Constitution for the United States of America.

Article I

Section 1. All legislative Powers herein granted shall be vested in a Congress of the United States, which shall consist of a Senate and House of Representatives.

Section 2. The House of Representatives shall be composed of Members chosen every second Year by the People of the several States, and the Electors in each State shall have the Qualifications requisite for Electors of the most numerous Branch of the State Legislature.

No Person shall be a Representative who shall not have attained to the Age of twenty five Years, and been seven Years a Citizen of the United States, and who shall not, when elected, be an Inhabitant of that State in which he shall be chosen.

Representatives and direct Taxes shall be apportioned among the several States which may be included within this Union, according to their respective Numbers, which shall be determined by adding to the whole Number of free Persons, including those bound to Service for a Term of Years, and excluding Indians not taxed, three fifths of all other Persons. The actual Enumeration shall be made within three Years after the first Meeting of the Congress of the United States, and within every subsequent Term of ten Years, in such Manner as they shall by Law direct. The Number of Representatives shall not exceed one for every thirty Thousand, but each State shall have at Least one Representative; and until such enumeration shall be made, the State of New Hampshire shall be entitled to chuse three, Massachusetts eight, Rhode Island and Providence Plantations one, Connecticut five, New-York six, New Jersey four, Pennsylvania eight, Delaware one, Maryland six, Virginia ten, North Carolina five, South Carolina five, and Georgia three.

When vacancies happen in the Representation from any State, the Executive Authority thereof shall issue Writs of Election to fill such Vacancies.

The House of Representatives shall chuse their Speaker and other Officers; and shall have the sole Power of Impeachment.

Section 3. The Senate of the United States shall be composed of two Senators from each State, chosen by the Legislature thereof, for six Years; and each Senator shall have one Vote.

Immediately after they shall be assembled in Consequence of the first Election, they shall be divided as equally as may be into three Classes. The Seats of the Senators of the first Class shall be vacated at the Expiration of the second Year, of the second Class at the Expiration of the fourth Year, and of the third Class at the Expiration of the sixth Year, so that one third may be chosen every second Year; and if Vacancies happen by Resignation, or otherwise, during the Recess of the Legislature of any State, the Executive thereof may make temporary Appointments until the next Meeting of the Legislature, which shall then fill such Vacancies.

No Person shall be a Senator who shall not have attained to the Age of thirty Years, and been nine Years a Citizen of the United States, and who shall not, when elected, be an Inhabitant of that State for which he shall be chosen.

The Vice President of the United States shall be President of the Senate, but shall have no Vote, unless they be equally divided.

The Senate shall chuse their other Officers, and also a President pro tempore, in the Absence of the Vice President, or when he shall exercise the Office of President of the United States.

The Senate shall have the sole Power to try all Impeachments. When sitting for that Purpose, they shall be on Oath or Affirmation. When the President of the United States is tried the Chief Justice shall preside: And no Person shall be convicted without the Concurrence of two thirds of the Members present.

Judgment in Cases of Impeachment shall not extend further than to removal from Office, and disqualification to hold and enjoy any Office of honor, Trust or Profit under the United States: but the Party convicted shall nevertheless be liable and subject to Indictment, Trial, Judgment and Punishment, according to Law.

Section 4. The Times, Places and Manner of holding Elections for Senators and Representatives, shall be prescribed in each State by the Legislature thereof; but the Congress may at any time by Law make or alter such Regulations, except as to the Places of chusing Senators.

The Congress shall assemble at least once in every Year, and such Meeting shall be on the first Monday in December, unless they shall by Law appoint a different Day.

Section 5. Each House shall be the Judge of the Elections, Returns and Qualifications of its own Members, and a Majority of each shall constitute a Quorum to do Business; but a smaller Number may adjourn from day to day, and may be authorized to compel the Attendance of absent Members, in such Manner, and under such Penalties as each House may provide.

Each House may determine the Rules of its Proceedings, punish its Members for disorderly Behaviour, and, with the Concurrence of two thirds, expel a Member.

Each House shall keep a Journal of its Proceedings, and from time to time publish the same, excepting such Parts as may in their Judgment require Secrecy; and the Yeas and Nays of the Members of either House on any question shall, at the Desire of one fifth of those Present, be entered on the Journal.

Neither House, during the Session of Congress, shall, without the Consent of the other, adjourn for more than three days, nor to any other Place than that in which the two Houses shall be sitting.

Section 6. The Senators and Representatives shall receive a Compensation for their Services, to be ascertained by law, and paid out of the Treasury of the United States. They shall in all Cases, except Treason, Felony and Breach of the Peace, be privileged from

Arrest during their Attendance at the Session of their respective Houses, and in going to and returning from the same; and for any Speech or Debate in either House, they shall not be questioned in any other Place.

No Senator or Representative shall, during the Time for which he was elected, be appointed to any civil Office under the Authority of the United States, which shall have been created, or the Emoluments whereof shall have been encreased during such time; and no Person holding any Office under the United States, which shall be a Member of either House during his Continuance in Office.

Section 7. All Bills for raising Revenue shall originate in the House of Representatives; but the Senate may propose or concur with amendments as on other Bills.

Every Bill which shall have passed the House of Representatives and the Senate, shall, before it become a Law, be presented to the President of the United States; If he approve he shall sign it, but if not he shall return it with his Objections to that House in which it shall have originated, who shall enter the Objections at large on their Journal, and proceed to reconsider it. If after such Reconsiderations two thirds of that House shall agree to pass the Bill, it shall be sent, together with the Objections, to the other House, by which it shall likewise be reconsidered, and if approved by two thirds of that House, it shall become a Law. But in all such Cases the Votes of both Houses shall be determined by Yeas and Nays, and the Names of the Persons voting for and against the Bill shall be entered on the Journal of each House respectively. If any Bill shall not be returned by the President within ten Days (Sunday excepted) after it shall have been presented to him, the Same shall be a Law, in like Manner as if he had signed it, unless the Congress by their Adjournment prevent its Return, in which Case it shall not be a Law.

Every Order, Resolution, or Vote to which the Concurrence of the Senate and House of Representatives may be necessary (except on a question of Adjournment) shall be presented to the President of the United States; and before the Same shall take Effect, shall be approved by him, or being disapproved by him, shall be repassed by two thirds of the Senate and House of Representatives, according to the Rules and Limitations prescribed in the Case of a Bill.

Section 8. The Congress shall have Power To lay and collect Taxes, Duties, Imposts and Excises, to pay the Debts and provide for the common Defence and general Welfare of the United States; but all Duties, Imposts and Excises shall be uniform throughout the United States;

To borrow Money on the credit of the United States;

To regulate Commerce with foreign Nations, and among the several States, and with the Indian Tribes;

To establish an uniform Rule of Naturalization, and uniform Laws on the subject of Bankruptcies throughout the United States;

To coin Money, regulate the Value thereof, and of foreign Coin, and fix the Standard of Weights and Measures;

To provide for the Punishment of counterfeiting the Securities and current Coin of the United States;

To establish Post Offices and post Roads;

To promote the Progress of Science and useful Arts, by securing for limited Times to Authors and Inventors the exclusive Right to their respective Writings and Discoveries;

To constitute Tribunals inferior to the supreme Court;

To define and punish Piracies and Felonies committed on the high Seas, and Offences against the Law of Nations;

To declare War, grant Letters of Marque and Reprisal, and make Rules concerning Captures on Land and Water;

To raise and support Armies, but no Appropriation of Money to that Use shall be for a longer Term than two Years;

To provide and maintain a Navy;

To make Rules for the Government and Regulation of the land and naval Forces;

To provide for calling forth the Militia to execute the Laws of the Union, suppress Insurrections and repel Invasions;

To provide for organizing, arming, and disciplining, the Militia, and for governing such Part of them as may be employed in the Service of the United States, reserving to the States respectively, the Appointment of the Officers, and the Authority of training the Militia according to the discipline prescribed by Congress;

To exercise exclusive Legislation in all Cases whatsoever, over such District (not exceeding ten Miles square) as may, by Cession of particular States, and the Acceptance of Congress, become the Seat of the Government of the United States, and to exercise like Authority over all Places purchased by the Consent of the Legislature of the State in which the Same shall be, for the Erection of Forts, Magazines, Arsenals, dock-Yards, and other needful Buildings;—And

To make all Laws which shall be necessary and proper for carrying into Execution the foregoing Powers, and all other Powers vested by this Constitution in the Government of the United States, or in any Department or Officer thereof.

Section 9. The Migration or Importation of such Persons as any of the States now existing shall think proper to admit, shall not be prohibited by the Congress prior to the Year one thousand eight hundred and eight, but a Tax or duty may be imposed on such Importation, not exceeding ten dollars for each Person.

The Privilege of the Writ of Habeas Corpus shall not be suspended, unless when in Cases of Rebellion or Invasion the public Safety may require it.

No Bill of Attainder or ex post facto Law shall be passed.

No Capitation, or other direct, Tax shall be laid, unless in Proportion to the Census or Enumeration herein before directed to be taken.

No Tax or Duty shall be laid on Articles exported from any State.

No Preference shall be given by any Regulation of Commerce or Revenue to the Ports of one State over those of another; nor shall Vessels bound to, or from, one State, be obliged to enter, clear or pay Duties in another.

No Money shall be drawn from the Treasury, but in Consequence of Appropriations made by Law; and a regular Statement and Account of the Receipts and Expenditures of all public Money shall be published from time to time.

No Title of Nobility shall be granted by the United States: And no Person holding any Office of Profit or Trust under them, shall, without the Consent of the Congress, accept of any present, Emolument, Office, or Title, of any kind whatever, from any King, Prince or foreign State.

Section 10. No State shall enter into any Treaty, Alliance, or Confederation; grant

Letters of Marque and Reprisal, coin Money; emit Bills of Credit, make any Thing but gold and silver Coin a Tender in Payment of Debts; pass any Bill of Attainder, ex post facto Law, or Law impairing the Obligation of Contracts, or grant any Title of Nobility.

No State shall, without the Consent of the Congress, lay any Imposts or Duties on Imports or Exports, except what may be absolutely necessary for executing its inspection Laws: and the net Produce of all Duties and Imposts, laid by any State on Imports or Exports, shall be for the Use of the Treasury of the United States; and all such Laws shall be subject to the Revision and Controul of the Congress.

No State shall, without the Consent of Congress, lay any Duty of Tonnage, keep Troops, or Ships of War in time of Peace, enter into any Agreement or Compact with another State, or with a foreign Power, or engage in War, unless actually invaded, or in such imminent Danger as will not admit of delay.

Article II

Section 1. The executive Power shall be vested in a President of the United States of America. He shall hold his Office during the Term of four Years, and, together with the Vice President, chosen for the same Term, be elected, as follows.

Each State shall appoint, In such Manner as the Legislature thereof may direct, a Number of Electors, equal to the whole Number of Senators and Representatives to which the State may be entitled in the Congress: but no Senator or Representative, or Person holding an Office of Trust or Profit under the United States, shall be appointed an Elector.

The Electors shall meet in their respective States, and vote by Ballot for two Persons, of whom one at least shall not be an Inhabitant of the same State with themselves. And they shall make a List of all the Persons voted for, and of the number of Votes for each; which List they shall sign and certify, and transmit sealed to the Seat of the Government of the United States, directed to the President of the Senate. The President of the Senate shall, in the Presence of the Senate and House of Representatives, open all the Certificates, and the Votes shall then be counted. The Person having the greatest number of Votes shall be the President, if such Number be a Majority of the whole Number of Electors appointed; and if there be more than one who have such Majority, and have an equal Number of Votes, then the House of Representatives shall immediately chuse by Ballot one of them for President; and if no Person have a Majority, then from the five highest on the List the said House shall in like Manner chuse the President. But in chusing the President, the Votes shall be taken by States, the Representation from each State having one Vote; a quorum for this Purpose shall consist of a Member or Members from two thirds of the States, and a Majority of all the States shall be necessary to a Choice. In every Case, after the Choice of the President, the Person having the greatest Number of Votes of the Electors shall be the Vice President. But if there should remain two or more who have equal Votes, the Senate shall chuse from them by Ballot the Vice President.

The Congress may determine the Time of chusing the Electors, and the Day on which they shall give their Votes; which Day shall be the same throughout the United States.

No Person except a natural born Citizen, or a Citizen of the United States, at the time of the Adoption of this Constitution, shall be eligible to the Office of President; neither shall any Person be eligible to that Office who shall not have attained to the Age of thirty five Years, and been fourteen Years a Resident within the United States.

In Case of the Removal of the President from Office, or of his Death, Resignation, or Inability to discharge the Powers and Duties of the said Office, the Same shall devolve on the Vice President, and the Congress may by Law provide for the Case of Removal, Death, Resignation or Inability, both of the President and Vice President, declaring what Officer shall then act as President, and such Officer shall act accordingly, until the Disability be removed, or a President shall be elected.

The President shall, at stated Times, receive for his Services, a Compensation, which shall neither be encreased nor diminished during the Period for which he shall have been elected, and he shall not receive within that Period any other emolument from the United States, or any of them.

Before he enter on the Execution of his Office, he shall take the following Oath or Affirmation:—"I do solemnly swear (or affirm) that I will faithfully execute the Office of President of the United States, and will to the best of my Ability, preserve, protect and defend the Constitution of the United States."

Section 2. The President shall be Commander in Chief of the Army and Navy of the United States, and of the Militia of the several States, when called into the actual Service of the United States; he may require the Opinion, in writing, of the principal Officer in each of the executive Departments, upon any Subject relating to the Duties of their respective Offices, and he shall have Power to grant Reprieves and Pardons for Offences against the United States, except in Cases of Impeachment.

He shall have Power, by and with the Advice and Consent of the Senate, to make Treaties, provided two thirds of the Senators present concur; and he shall nominate, and by and with the Advice and Consent of the Senate, shall appoint Ambassadors, other public Ministers and Consuls, Judges of the supreme Court, and all other Officers of the United States, whose Appointments are not herein otherwise provided for, and which shall be established by Law: but the Congress may by Law vest the Appointment of such inferior Officers, as they think proper, in the President alone, in the Courts of Law, or in the Heads of Departments.

The President shall have Power to fill up all Vacancies that may happen during the Recess of the Senate, by granting Commissions which shall expire at the End of their next Session.

Section 3. He shall from time to time give to the Congress Information of the State of the Union, and recommend to their Consideration such Measures as he shall judge necessary and expedient; he may, on extraordinary Occasions, convene both Houses, or either of them, and in Case of Disagreements between them, with Respect to the Time of Adjournment, he may adjourn them to such Time as he shall think proper; he shall receive Ambassadors and other public Ministers; he shall take Care that the Laws be faithfully executed, and shall Commission all the Officers of the United States.

Section 4. The President, Vice President and all Civil Officers of the United States, shall be removed from Office on Impeachment for, and Conviction of, Treason, Bribery, or other high Crimes and Misdemeanors.

Article III

Section 1. The judicial Power of the United States, shall be vested in one supreme Court, and in such inferior Courts as the Congress may from time to time ordain and establish. The Judges, both of the supreme and inferior Courts, shall hold their Offices during good Behaviour, and shall, at stated Times, receive for their Services, a Compensation, which shall not be diminished during their Continuance in Office.

Section 2. The judicial Power shall extend to all Cases, in Law and Equity, arising under this Constitution, the Laws of the United States, and Treaties made, or which shall be made, under their Authority;—to all Cases affecting Ambassadors, other public Ministers and Consuls;—to all Cases of admiralty and maritime Jurisdiction;—to Controversies to which the United States shall be a Party;—to Controversies between two or more States;—between a State and Citizens of another State;—between Citizens of different States;—between Citizens of the same State claiming Lands under Grants of different States, and between a State, or the Citizens thereof, and foreign States, Citizens or Subjects.

In all Cases affecting Ambassadors, other public Ministers and Consuls, and those in which a State shall be Party, the Supreme Court shall have original Jurisdiction. In all the other Cases before mentioned, the supreme Court shall have appelate Jurisdiction, both as to Law and Fact, with such Exceptions, and under such Regulations as the Congress shall make.

The Trial of all Crimes, except in Cases of Impeachment, shall be by Jury; and such Trial shall be held in the State where the said Crimes shall have been committed; but when not committed within any State, the Trial shall be at such Place or Places as the Congress may by Law have directed.

Section 3. Treason against the United States, shall consist only in levying War against them, or in adhering to their Enemies, giving them Aid and Comfort. No Person shall be convicted of Treason unless on the Testimony of two Witnesses to the same overt Act, or on Confession in open Court.

The Congress shall have Power to declare the Punishment of Treason, but no Attainder of Treason shall work Corruption of Blood, or Forfeiture except during the Life of the Person attainted.

Article IV

Section 1. Full Faith and Credit shall be given in each State to the public Acts, Records, and judicial Proceedings of every other State. And the Congress may by general Laws prescribe the Manner in which such Acts, Records and Proceedings shall be proved, and the Effect thereof.

Section 2. The Citizens of each State shall be entitled to all Privileges and Immunities of Citizens in the several States.

A Person charged in any State with Treason, Felony, or other Crime, who shall flee from Justice, and be found in another State, shall on Demand of the executive Authority of the State from which he fled, be delivered up, to be removed to the State having Jurisdiction of the Crime.

No Person held to Service or Labour in one State, under the Laws thereof, escaping into another, shall, in Consequence of any Law or Regulation therein, be discharged from such Service or Labour, but shall be delivered up on Claim of the Party to whom such Service or Labour may be due.

Section 3. New States may be admitted by the Congress into this Union; but no new State shall be formed or erected within the Jurisdiction of any other State; nor any State be formed by the Junction of two or more States, or Parts of States, without the Consent of the Legislatures of the States concerned as well as of the Congress.

The Congress shall have Power to dispose of and make all needful Rules and Regulations respecting the Territory or other Property belonging to the United States; and nothing in this Constitution shall be so construed as to Prejudice any Claims of the United States, or of any particular State.

Section 4. The United States shall guarantee to every State in this Union a Republican Form of Government, and shall protect each of them against Invasion; and on Application of the Legislature, or of the Executive (when the Legislature cannot be convened) against domestic Violence.

Article V

The Congress, whenever two thirds of both Houses shall deem it necessary, shall propose Amendments to this Constitution, or, on the Application of the Legislatures of two thirds of the several States, shall call a Convention for proposing Amendments, which, in either Case, shall be valid to all Intents and Purposes, as Part of this Constitution, when ratified by the Legislatures of three fourths of the several States, or by Conventions in three fourths thereof, as the one or the other Mode of Ratification may be proposed by the Congress; provided that no Amendment which may be made prior to the Year One thousand eight hundred and eight shall in any Manner affect the first and fourth Clauses in the Ninth Section of the first Article; and that no State, without its Consent, shall be deprived of its equal Suffrage in the Senate.

Article VI

All Debts contracted and Engagements entered into, before the Adoption of this Constitution, shall be as valid against the United States under this Constitution, as under the Confederation.

This Constitution, and the Laws of the United States which shall be made in Pursuance thereof; and all Treaties made, or which shall be made, under the Authority of the United States, shall be the supreme Law of the Land; and the Judges in every State shall be bound thereby, any Thing in the Constitution or Laws of any State to the Contrary notwithstanding.

The Senators and Representatives before mentioned, and the Members of the several State Legislatures, and all executive and judicial Officers, both of the United States and of the several States, shall be bound by Oath or Affirmation, to support this Constitution; but no religious Test shall ever be required as a Qualification to any Office or public Trust under the United States.

Article VII

The Ratification of the Conventions of nine States, shall be sufficient for the Establishment of this Constitution between the States so ratifying the Same.

Done in Convention by the Unanimous Consent of the States present the Seventeenth Day of September in the Year of our Lord one thousand seven hundred and Eighty seven and of the Independence of the United States of America the Twelfth. In witness thereof We have hereunto subscribed our Names,

George Washington—President
and Deputy from Virginia

New Hampshire { John Langdon / Nicholas Gilman

Massachusetts { Nathaniel Gorham / Rufus King

Connecticut { William Samuel Johnson / Roger Sherman

New York { Alexander Hamilton

New Jersey { William Livingston / David A. Brearley / William Paterson / Jonathan Dayton

Pennsylvania { Benjamin Franklin / Thomas Mifflin / Robert Morris / George Clymer / Thomas FitzSimons / Jared Ingersoll / James Wilson / Gouverneur Morris

Delaware { George Read / Gunning Bedford, Junior / John Dickinson / Richard Bassett / Jacob Broom

Maryland { James McHenry / Daniel of St. Tho. Jenifer / Daniel Carroll

Virginia { John Blair / James Madison Jr.

North Carolina { William Blount / Richard Dobbs Spaight / Hugh Williamson

South Carolina { John Rutledge / Charles Cotesworth Pinckney / Charles Pinckney / Pierce Butler

Georgia { William Few / Abraham Baldwin

ARTICLES IN ADDITION TO, AND AMENDMENT OF, THE CONSTITUTION OF THE UNITED STATES OF AMERICA, PROPOSED BY CONGRESS, AND RATIFIED BY THE SEVERAL STATES, PURSUANT TO THE FIFTH ARTICLE OF THE ORIGINAL CONSTITUTION

Amendment I

Congress shall make no law respecting an establishment of religion, or prohibiting the free exercise thereof; or abridging the freedom of speech, or of the press; or the right of the people peaceably to assemble, and to petition the Government for a redress of grievances.

Amendment II

A well regulated Militia, being necessary to the security of a free State, the right of the people to keep and bear Arms, shall not be infringed.

Amendment III

No Soldier shall, in time of peace be quartered in any house, without the consent of the Owner, nor in time of war, but in a manner to be prescribed by law.

Amendment IV

The right of the people to be secure in their persons, houses, papers, and effects, against unreasonable searches and seizures, shall not be violated, and no Warrants shall issue, but upon probable cause, supported by Oath or affirmation, and particularly describing the place to be searched, and the persons or things to be seized.

Amendment V

No person shall be held to answer for a capital, or otherwise infamous crime, unless on a presentment or indictment of a Grand Jury, except in cases arising in the land or naval forces, or in the Militia, when in actual service in time of War or public danger; nor shall any person be subject for the same offence to be twice put in jeopardy of life or limb; nor shall be compelled in any criminal case to be a witness against himself, nor be deprived of life, liberty, or property, without due process of law; nor shall private property be taken for public use, without just compensation.

Amendment VI

In all criminal prosecutions, the accused shall enjoy the right to a speedy and public trial by an impartial jury of the State and district wherein the crime shall have been committed, which district shall have been previously ascertained by law, and to be informed of the nature and cause of the accusation; to be confronted with the witness against him; to have compulsory process for obtaining Witnesses in his favor, and to have the Assistance of Counsel for his defence.

Amendment VII

In Suits at common law, where the value in controversy shall exceed twenty dollars, the right of trial by jury shall be preserved, and no fact tried by a jury, shall be otherwise reexamined in any Court of the United States, than according to the rules of the common law.

Amendment VIII

Excessive bail shall not be required, nor excessive fines imposed, nor cruel and unusual punishments inflicted.

Amendment IX

The enumeration in the Constitution, of certain rights, shall not be construed to deny or disparage others retained by the people.

Amendment X

The powers not delegated to the United States by the Constitution, nor prohibited by it to the States, are reserved to the States respectively, or to the people. [The first ten amendments were ratified Dec. 15, 1791.]

Amendment XI

The Judicial power of the United States shall not be construed to extend to any suit in law or equity, commenced or prosecuted against one of the United States by Citizens of another State, or by Citizens or Subjects of any Foreign State. [Jan. 8, 1798]

Amendment XII

The Electors shall meet in their respective states and vote by ballot for President and Vice-President, one of whom, at least, shall not be an inhabitant of the same state with themselves; they shall name in their ballots the person voted for as President, and in distinct ballots the person voted for as Vice-President, and they shall make distinct lists of all persons voted for as President, and of all persons voted for as Vice-President, and of the number of votes for each, which lists they shall sign and certify, and transmit sealed to the seat of the government of the United States, directed to the President of the Senate;—The President of the Senate shall, in the presence of the Senate and House of Representatives, open all the certificates and the votes shall then be counted;—The person having the greatest number of votes for President, shall be the President, if such number be a majority of the whole number of Electors appointed; and if no person have such majority, then from the persons having the highest numbers not exceeding three on the list of those voted for as President, the House of Representatives shall choose immediately, by ballot, the President. But in choosing the President, the votes shall be taken by states, the representation from each state having one vote; a quorum for this purpose shall consist of a member or members from two-thirds of the states, and a majority of all the states shall be necessary to a choice. And if the House of Representatives shall not choose a President whenever the right of choice shall devolve upon them, before the fourth day of March next following, then the Vice-President shall act as President, as in the case of the death or other constitutional disability of the President—The person having the greatest number of votes as Vice-President, shall be the Vice-President, if such number be a majority of the whole number of Electors appointed, and if no person have a majority, then from the two highest numbers on the list, the Senate shall choose the Vice-President; a quorum for the purpose shall consist of two-thirds of the whole number of Senators, and a majority of the whole number shall be necessary to a choice. But no person constitutionally ineligible to the office of President shall be eligible to that of Vice-President of the United States. [Sept. 25, 1804]

Amendment XIII

Section 1. Neither slavery nor involuntary servitude, except as a punishment for crime whereof the party shall have been duly convicted, shall exist within the United States, or any place subject to their jurisdiction.

Section 2. Congress shall have power to enforce this article by appropriate legislation. [Dec. 18, 1865]

Amendment XIV

Section 1. All persons born or naturalized in the United States and subject to the jurisdiction thereof, are citizens of the United States and of the State wherein they reside. No State shall make or enforce any law which shall abridge the privileges or immunities of citizens of the United States; nor shall any State deprive any person of life, liberty, or property, without due process of law; nor deny any person within its jurisdiction the equal protection of the laws.

Section 2. Representatives shall be apportioned among the several States according to their respective numbers, counting the whole number of persons in each State, excluding Indians not taxed. But when the right to vote at any election for the choice of electors for President and Vice President of the United States, Representatives in Congress, the Executive and Judicial officers of a State, or the members of the Legislature thereof, is denied to any of the male inhabitants of such State, being twenty-one years of age, and citizens of the United States, or in any way abridged, except for participation in rebellion, or other crime, the basis of representation therein shall be reduced in the proportion which the number of such male citizens shall bear to the whole number of male citizens twenty-one years of age in such State.

Section 3. No person shall be a Senator or Representative in Congress, or elector of President and Vice President, or hold any office, civil or military, under the United States, or under any State, who, having previously taken an oath, as a member of Congress, or as an officer of the United States, or as a member of any State legislature, or as an executive or judicial officer of any State, to support the Constitution of the United States, shall have engaged in insurrection or rebellion against the same, or given aid or comfort to the enemies thereof. But Congress may by a vote of two-thirds of each House, remove such disability.

Section 4. The validity of the public debt of the United States, authorized by law, including debts incurred for payment of pensions and bounties for services in suppressing insurrection or rebellion, shall not be questioned. But neither the United States nor any State shall assume or pay any debt or obligation incurred in aid of insurrection or rebellion against the United States, or any claim for the loss or emancipation of any slave; but all such debts, obligations and claims shall be held illegal and void.

Section 5. The Congress shall have power to enforce by appropriate legislation, the provisions of this article. [July 28, 1868]

Amendment XV

Section 1. The right of citizens of the United States to vote shall not be denied or abridged by the United States or by any State on account of race, color, or previous condition of servitude.

Section 2. The Congress shall have power to enforce this article by appropriate legislation. [March 30, 1870]

Amendment XVI

The Congress shall have power to lay and collect taxes on incomes, from whatever source derived, without apportionment among the several States, and without regard to any census or enumeration. [Feb. 25, 1913]

Amendment XVII

The Senate of the United States shall be composed of two Senators from each State, elected by the people thereof, for six years; and each Senator shall have one vote. The electors in each State shall have the qualifications requisite for electors of the most numerous branch of the State legislatures.

When vacancies happen in the representation of any State in the Senate, the executive authority of such State shall issue writs of election to fill such vacancies: *Provided,* That the legislature of any State may empower the executive thereof to make temporary appointments until the people fill the vacancies by election as the legislature may direct.

This amendment shall not be so construed as to affect the election or term of any Senator chosen before it becomes valid as part of the Constitution. [May 31, 1913]

Amendment XVIII

Section 1. After one year from the ratification of this article the manufacture, sale, or transportation of intoxicating liquors within, the importation thereof into, or the exportation thereof from the United States and all territory subject to the jurisdiction thereof for beverage purposes is hereby prohibited.

Section 2. The Congress and the several States shall have concurrent power to enforce this article by appropriate legislation.

Section 3. This article shall be inoperative unless it shall have been ratified as an amendment to the Constitution by the legislatures of the several States, as provided in the Constitution, within seven years from the date of the submission hereof to the States by the Congress. [Jan. 29, 1919]

Amendment XIX

The right of citizens of the United States to vote shall not be denied or abridged by the United States or by any State on account of sex.

Congress shall have power to enforce this article by appropriate legislation. [Aug. 26, 1920]

Amendment XX

Section 1. The terms of the President and Vice President shall end at noon on the 20th day of January, and the terms of Senators and Representatives at noon on the 3d day of January, of the years in which such terms would have ended if this article had not been ratified; and the terms of their successors shall then begin.

Section 2. The Congress shall assemble at least once in every year, and such meeting shall begin at noon on the 3d day of January, unless they shall by law appoint a different day.

Section 3. If, at the time fixed for the beginning of the term of the President, the President elect shall have died, the Vice President elect shall become President. If a President shall not have been chosen before the time fixed for the beginning of his term, or if the President elect shall have failed to qualify, then the Vice President elect shall act as President until a President shall have qualified; and the Congress may by law provide for the case wherein neither a President elect nor a Vice President elect shall have qualified, declaring who shall then act as President, or the manner in which one who is to act shall be selected, and such person shall act accordingly until a President or Vice President shall have qualified.

Section 4. The Congress may by law provide for the case of the death of any of the persons for whom the House of Representatives may choose a President whenever the right of choice shall have devolved upon them, and for the case of the death of any of the persons from whom the Senate may choose a Vice President whenever the right of choice shall have devolved upon them.

Section 5. Sections 1 and 2 shall take effect on the 15th day of October following the ratification of this article.

Section 6. This article shall be inoperative unless it shall have been ratified as an amendment to the Constitution by the legislatures of three-fourths of the several States within seven years from the date of its submission. [Feb. 6, 1933]

Amendment XXI

Section 1. The eighteenth article of amendment to the Constitution of the United States is hereby repealed.

Section 2. The transportation or importation into any State, Territory, or possession of the United States for delivery or use therein of intoxicating liquors, in violation of the laws thereof, is hereby prohibited.

Section 3. This article shall be inoperative unless it shall have been ratified as an amendment to the Constitution by conventions in the several States, as provided in the Constitution, within seven years from the date of the submission hereof to the States by the Congress. [Dec. 5, 1933]

Amendment XXII

Section 1. No person shall be elected to the office of the President more than twice, and no person who has held the office of President, or acted as President, for more than two years of a term to which some other person was elected President shall be elected to the office of the President more than once. But this Article shall not apply to any person holding the office of President when this Article was proposed by the Congress, and shall not prevent any person who may be holding the office of President, or acting as President, during the term within which this Article becomes operative from holding the office of President or acting as President during the remainder of such term.

Section 2. This article shall be inoperative unless it shall have been ratified as an amendment to the Constitution by the legislatures of three-fourths of the several States within seven years from the date of its submission to the States by the Congress. [Feb. 27, 1951]

Amendment XXIII

Section 1. The District constituting the seat of Government of the United States shall appoint in such manner as the Congress may direct:

A number of electors of President and Vice President equal to the whole number of Senators and Representatives in Congress to which the District would be entitled if it were a State, but in no event more than the least populous State; they shall be in addition to those appointed by the States, but they shall be considered, for the purposes of the election of President and Vice President, to be electors appointed by a State; and they shall meet in the District and perform such duties as provided by the twelfth article of amendment.

Section 2. The Congress shall have power to enforce this article by appropriate legislation. [Mar. 29, 1961]

Amendment XXIV

Section 1. The right of citizens of the United States to vote in any primary or other election for President or Vice President, for electors for President or Vice President, or for Senator or Representative in Congress, shall not be denied or abridged by the United States or any State by reason of failure to pay any poll tax or other tax.

Section 2. The Congress shall have power to enforce this article by appropriate legislation. [Jan. 23, 1964]

Amendment XXV

Section 1. In case of the removal of the President from office or of his death or resignation, the Vice President shall become President.

Section 2. Whenever there is a vacancy in the office of the Vice President, the President shall nominate a Vice President who shall take office upon confirmation by a majority vote of both Houses of Congress.

Section 3. Whenever the President transmits to the President pro tempore of the Senate and the Speaker of the House of Representatives his written declaration that he is unable to discharge the powers and duties of his office, and until he transmits to them a written declaration to the contrary, such powers and duties shall be discharged by the Vice President as Acting President.

Section 4. Whenever the Vice President and a majority of either the principal officers of the executive departments or of such other body as Congress may by law provide, transmit to the President pro tempore of the Senate and the Speaker of the House of Representatives their written declaration that the President is unable to discharge the powers and duties of his office, the Vice President shall immediately assume the powers and duties of the office as Acting President.

Thereafter, when the President transmits to the President pro tempore of the Senate and the Speaker of the House of Representatives his written declaration that no inability exists, he shall resume the powers and duties of his office unless the Vice President and a majority of either the principal officers of the executive department or of such other body as Congress may by law provide, transmit within four days to the President pro tempore of the Senate and the Speaker of the House of Representatives their written declaration that the President is unable to discharge the powers and duties of his office. Thereupon Congress shall decide the issue, assembling within forty-eight hours for that purpose if not in session. If the Congress, within twenty-one days after receipt of the latter written declaration, or, if Congress is not in session, within twenty-one days after Congress is required to assemble, determines by two-thirds vote of both Houses that the President is unable to discharge the powers and duties of his office, the Vice President shall continue to discharge the same as Acting President; otherwise, the President shall resume the powers and duties of his office. [Feb. 10, 1967]

Amendment XXVI

Section 1. The right of citizens of the United States, who are eighteen years of age or older, to vote shall not be denied or abridged by the United States or by any State on account of age.

Section 2. The Congress shall have power to enforce this article by appropriate legislation. [June 30, 1971]

Amendment XXVII

No law varying the compensation for the services of the Senators and Representatives shall take effect until an election of Representatives shall have intervened. [May 13, 1992]

Case Index